Nation of Nations

VOLUME ONE: TO 1877

Nation of Nations

A CONCISE NARRATIVE OF THE AMERICAN REPUBLIC

VOLUME ONE: TO 1877

THIRD EDITION

James West Davidson

William E. Gienapp
Harvard University

Christine Leigh Heyrman
University of Delaware

Mark H. Lytle
Bard College

Michael B. Stoff
University of Texas, Austin

Boston   Burr Ridge, IL   Dubuque, IA   Madison, WI   New York
San Francisco   St. Louis   Bangkok   Bogotá   Caracas   Kuala Lumpur
Lisbon   London   Madrid   Mexico City   Milan   Montreal   New Delhi
Santiago   Seoul   Singapore   Sydney   Taipei   Toronto

McGraw-Hill Higher Education

A Division of The **McGraw-Hill** Companies

NATION OF NATIONS: A CONCISE NARRATIVE OF THE AMERICAN REPUBLIC
Published by McGraw-Hill, an imprint of The McGraw-Hill Companies, Inc. 1221 Avenue of the Americas, New York, NY, 10020. Copyright © 2002, 1999, 1996 by The McGraw-Hill Companies, Inc. All rights reserved. No part of this publication may be reproduced or distributed in any form or by any means, or stored in a database or retrieval system, without the prior written consent of The McGraw-Hill Companies, Inc., including, but not limited to, in any network or other electronic storage or transmission, or broadcast for distance learning. Some ancillaries, including electronic and print components, may not be available to customers outside the United States.

This book is printed on acid-free paper.

1 2 3 4 5 6 7 8 9 0 DOC/DOC 0 9 8 7 6 5 4 3 2 1

ISBN: 0-07-241772-2 (main text)
ISBN: 0-07-241774-9 (volume I)
ISBN: 0-07-241775-7 (volume II)

Publisher: *Jane Karpacz*
Editor: *Lyn Uhl*
Developmental editor: *Kristen Mellitt*
Marketing manager: *Janise Fry*
Project manager: *Diane M. Folliard*
Production supervisor: *Gina Hangos*
Designer: *Gino Cieslik*
Cover Photos (l. to r.): © *British Museum*, © *ROM*, © *Library of Congress*, © *Corbis*, © *Corbis*
Photo research coordinator: *David A. Tietz*
Photo researcher: *Mary Reeg*
Supplement coordinator: *Vicki Laird*
Producer, Media technology: *Sean Crowley*
Compositor: **TECH**BOOKS
Typeface: *10.5/13 Janson*
Printer: *R.R. Donnelley & Sons Company, Crawfordsville*

Library of Congress Cataloging-in-Publication Data

Nation of nations : a concise narrative of the American republic/James West Davidson
. . . [et al.].—3rd ed.
   p. cm.
  Includes bibliographical references (p.) and index.
  ISBN 0-07-241772-2 (main text : alk. paper)—ISBN 0-07-241774-9 (v. 1 : alk. paper)
  —ISBN 0-07-241775-7 (v. 2 : alk. paper)
    1. United States—History. I. Davidson, James West.
E178.1N345 2002
973—dc21   2001030614

www.mhhe.com

About the Authors

James West Davidson received his Ph.D. from Yale University. A historian who has pursued a full-time writing career, he is the author of numerous books, among them *After the Fact: The Art of Historical Detection* (with Mark H. Lytle), *The Logic of Millennial Thought: Eighteenth-Century New England*, and *Great Heart: The History of a Labrador Adventure* (with John Rugge).

William E. Gienapp has a Ph.D. from the University of California, Berkeley. He taught at the University of Wyoming before going to Harvard University, where he is a Harvard College Professor. In 1988 he received the Avery O. Craven Award for his book *The Origins of the Republican Party, 1852–1856*. His essay on "The Antebellum Era" appeared in the *Encyclopedia of Social History* (1992), and he edited *The Civil War and Reconstruction: A Documentary History* (2001). His biography of Abraham Lincoln will be published in 2002. Currently he is working on a history of the Civil War.

Christine Leigh Heyrman is Professor of History at the University of Delaware. She received a Ph.D. in American Studies from Yale University and is the author of *Commerce and Culture: The Maritime Communities of Colonial Massachusetts, 1690–1750*. Her book *Southern Cross: The Beginnings of the Bible Belt* was awarded the Bancroft Prize in 1998.

Mark H. Lytle, who received a Ph.D. from Yale University, is Professor of History and Environmental Studies and Chair of the American Studies Program at Bard College. He recently taught as a Fulbright Scholar at University College, Dublin, in Ireland. His publications include *The Origins of the Iranian-American Alliance, 1941–1953* and *After the Fact: The Art of Historical Detection* (with James West Davidson) and "An Environmental Approach to American Diplomatic History," in *Diplomatic History*. He is at work on *The Uncivil War: America in the Vietnam Era*.

Michael B. Stoff is Associate Professor of History at the University of Texas at Austin, where he also directs the graduate program in history. The recipient of a Ph.D. from Yale University, he wrote *Oil, War, and American Security: The Search for a National Policy on Foreign Oil, 1941–1947* and coedited (with Jonathan Fanton and R. Hal Williams) *The Manhattan Project: A Documentary Introduction to the Atomic Age*. His most recent publication, an essay on Herbert Hoover, can be found in Alan Brinkley and Dyer Davis, eds., *The Reader's Companion to the American Presidency*. He has been honored many times for his teaching, most recently with the Friars' Centennial Teaching Excellence Award.

Preface

History is both a discipline of rigor, bound by rules and scholarly methods, and something more: the unique, compelling, even strange way in which we humans define ourselves. We are all the sum of the tales of thousands of people, great and small, whose actions have etched their lines upon us. History supplies our very identity—a sense of the social groups to which we belong, whether family, ethnic group, race, class, or gender. It reveals to us the foundations of our deepest religious beliefs and traces the roots of our economic and political systems. It explores how we celebrate and grieve, sing the songs we sing, weather the illnesses to which time and chance subject us. It commands our attention for all these good reasons and for no good reason at all, other than a fascination with the way the myriad tales play out. Strange that we should come to care about a host of men and women so many centuries gone, some with names eminent and familiar, others unknown but for a chance scrap of information left behind in an obscure letter.

Yet we do care. We care about Sir Humphrey Gilbert, "devoured and swallowed up of the Sea" one black Atlantic night in 1583; about George Washington at Kips Bay, red with fury as he takes a riding crop to his retreating soldiers. We care about Octave Johnson, a slave fleeing through Louisiana swamps trying to decide whether to stand and fight the approaching hounds or take his chances with the bayou alligators; about Clara Barton, her nurse's skirts so heavy with blood from the wounded, she must wring them out before tending to the next soldier. We are drawn to the fate of Chinese laborers, chipping away at the Sierras' looming granite; a Georgian named Tom Watson seeking to forge a color-blind political alliance; and desperate immigrant mothers, kerosene in hand, storming Brooklyn butcher shops that had again raised prices. We follow, with a mix of awe and amusement, the fortunes of the quirky Henry Ford ("Everybody wants to be somewhere he ain't"), turning out identical automobiles, insisting his factory workers wear identical expressions ("Fordization of the Face"). We trace the career of young Thurgood Marshall, crisscrossing the South in his own "little old beat-up '29 Ford," typing legal briefs in the back seat, trying to get black teachers to sue for equal pay, hoping to get his people somewhere they weren't. The list could go on and on, spilling out as it did in Walt Whitman's *Leaves of Grass*: "A southerner soon as a northerner, a planter nonchalant and hospitable,/A Yankee bound my own way . . . a Hoosier, a Badger, a Buckeye, a Louisianian or Georgian." Whitman embraced and celebrated them all, inseparable strands of what made him an American and what made him human:

In all people I see myself, none more and not one a barleycorn less,
And the good or bad I say of myself I say of them.

To encompass so expansive an America Whitman turned to poetry; historians have traditionally chosen *narrative* as their means of giving life to the past. That mode of explanation permits them to interweave the strands of economic, political, and social history in a coherent chronological framework. By choosing narrative, historians affirm the multicausal nature of historical explanation—the insistence that events be portrayed in context. By choosing narrative, they are also acknowledging that, while long-term economic and social trends shape societies in significant ways, events often take on a logic (or an illogic) of their own, jostling one another, being deflected by unpredictable personal decisions, sudden deaths, natural catastrophes, and chance. There are literary reasons, too, for preferring a narrative approach, since it supplies a dramatic force usually missing from more structural analyses of the past.

In some ways, surveys like this are the natural antithesis of narrative history. They strive, by definition, to be comprehensive: to furnish a broad, orderly exposition of their chosen field. Yet to cover so much ground in so limited a space necessarily deprives readers of the context of more detailed accounts. Then, too, the resurgence of social history—with its concern for class and race, patterns of rural and urban life, the spread of market and industrial economies—lends itself to more analytic, less chronological treatments. The challenge facing historians is to incorporate these areas of research without losing the story's narrative drive or the chronological flow that orients readers to the more familiar events of the past.

But in the end, it is indefensible to separate the world of ordinary Americans from the corridors of political maneuvering or the ceremonial pomp of an inauguration. To treat political and social history as distinct spheres is counterproductive. The primary question of this narrative—how the fledgling, often tumultuous confederation of "these United States" managed to transform itself into an enduring republic—is not only political but necessarily social. In order to survive, a republic must resolve conflicts between citizens of different geographic regions and economic classes, of diverse racial and ethnic origins, of competing religions and ideologies. The resolution of these conflicts has produced tragic consequences, perhaps, as often as noble ones. But tragic or noble, the destiny of these states cannot be understood without comprehending both the social and the political dimensions of the story. To weave together those narratives has been our goal in *Nation of Nations.*

Creating a Concise Edition
This edition provides a briefer alternative to the full-length text. In the belief that the original authors could best preserve both the themes and the narrative approach of the longer work, we have done the abridgment ourselves. Indeed, the task forced us to think again about the core elements of narrative history, for the task of condensing a full-length survey presents devilish temptations. Most teachers rightly

resist sacrificing breadth of coverage; yet if an edition is to be brief, the words, the sentences, the paragraphs must go. The temptation is to excise the apparently superfluous "details" of a full-dress narrative: trimming character portraits, cutting back on narrative color, lopping off concrete examples. Yet too draconian a campaign risks producing either a bare-bones compendium of facts or a bloodless thematic outline, dispossessed of the tales that engaged the reader in the first place.

The intent, then, is to provide a text that remains a *narrative*—a history with enough contextual detail for readers to grasp the story. The fuller introductions to each chapter, a distinctive feature of the original text, have been preserved, though streamlined where possible. Within each chapter, we have attempted to maintain a balance between narrative and thematic analysis. Paradoxically, doing so has occasionally meant *adding* material to the brief edition: replacing longer stories with shorter emblematic sketches or recasting sections to ensure that students are not overwhelmed by the compression of too many details into too few paragraphs.

As with any history, the narrative keeps changing. Historians constantly revalue the past, searching for more revealing ways to connect *then and there* with *here and now*. The story shifts, sometimes in subtle ways, other times more boldly. The third edition of this text has been significantly revised.

New Global Context

Most broadly, the changes we have made arise from our conviction that the American past cannot be understood without linking its story to events worldwide. Half a millennium ago, the societies of Europe, Africa, and Asia first began a sustained interaction with the civilizations of the Americas. The interplay between newcomers and natives, between old cultures and new, continues to this day. We still introduce each of the book's six parts with Global Essays.

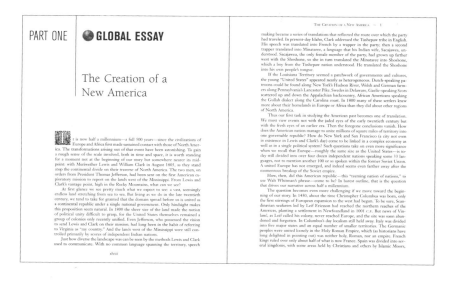

For this edition we have also woven into the text additional shorter narratives underscoring our history's global links (identified by a globe icon in the margin). These narratives are not separate special features. Sometimes only a paragraph in length, sometimes an entire section, they integrate an international perspective, whether we are discussing the trans-Atlantic culture of the early slave trade, the rise of postal networks, the influenza pandemic of 1918–1919, or international examples of the student rebellions of the 1960s.

> lion French, 1.2 million Austro-Hungarians, and nearly a million Britons. The American contribution had nonetheless been crucial, providing vital convoys at sea and fresh, confident troops on land. The United States emerged from the war stronger than ever. Europe, on the other hand, looked forward—as one newspaper put it—to "Disaster . . . Exhaustion . . . Revolution."
>
> *The Influenza Pandemic of 1918–1919*
>
> The truce brought an end to the killing but not to the dying. In the months before the armistice, a scourge more lethal than war had begun to engulf the globe. It started innocently enough. At Fort Riley, Kansas, on the morning of March 11, 1918, company cook Albert Mitchell reported to the infirmary on sick call. His head and muscles ached, his throat was sore, and he had a low-grade fever.
>
> It was the flu, dangerous for the very young and the old but ordinarily no problem for a robust young man like Mitchell. By noon, however, 107 soldiers had reported similar symptoms. Within a week, the number had jumped to over 500, and cases of the flu were being reported in virtually every state in the Union, even on the isolated island of Alcatraz in San Francisco Bay.
>
> The first wave of flu produced few deaths in the United States. But as the virus spread and mutated over the next year, its victims experienced more and more distressing symptoms: vomiting, dizziness, labored breathing, incessant sweating. Pulmonary hemorrhages brought on projectile nosebleeds and fits of coughing that

Changes in Organization

As the title of the book's new final chapter makes clear, we have become a "Nation of Nations in a Global Community." This narrative of the 1990s views events through twin engines of social change: the recent wave of immigration, whose upsurge rivals the influx at the beginning of the century; and the global culture being wrought by the communications revolution of the Internet and the World Wide Web.

In addition, a number of structural changes help the narrative flow as well as reflect recent scholarship:

- Part Four employs a new chapter order. Chapter 18, following our treatment of Reconstruction, now covers the New South and the Trans-Mississippi West. The chapter's narrative opening (on the Exodusters) provides a useful bridge between the two chapters. Chapter 19 is now "The New Industrial Order" and Chapter 20 is "The Rise of an Urban Order."
- The coverage of the 1920s and 1930s has been consolidated into two chapters, down from three. Chapter 24, "The New Era," takes the narrative through the Great Crash, while Chapter 25 has become "The Great Depression and the New Deal."
- Part Six (the post–World War II material) has been thoroughly revised to create a more coherent, thematic story—always a challenge in narrating the most recent years of the American survey.
  - Chapter 28, "The Suburban Era," extends its political and foreign policy narrative through the Kennedy administration, ending with (and incorporating new scholarship about) the Cuban missile crisis of 1962. This approach delineates more clearly the arc of the first half of the cold war, culminating in the confrontation that brought the world the closest it has yet come to a full-scale nuclear war.
  - Chapter 29—now titled "Civil Rights and the Crisis of Liberalism"—is strongly focused on the civil rights crusade as the era's defining social movement. Coverage begins with the social and economic background of the 1950s, followed by *Brown v. Board of Education*, the Montgomery bus

boycott, and the crisis at Little Rock—materials originally treated in "The Suburban Era." New material emphasizes the grassroots elements of the crusade and provides coverage of *Hernandez v. Texas*, the 1954 Supreme Court decision that proved as pivotal for Latino civil rights as was *Brown v. Board of Education* for African Americans. Lyndon Johnson's Great Society and the Counterculture remain in this chapter, as does the material on the Warren Court.

- Chapter 30, "The Vietnam Era," reorients its coverage of minority activism by focusing on the theme of identity group politics. Coverage of the feminist movement, the Equal Rights Amendment, and abortion rights has been moved to this chapter to join expanded coverage of Latino protests (Chavez and the farmworkers, Mexican American student activists) as well as the campaigns of Native Americans, Asian Americans, and gay activists.

- Chapter 32 now focuses, as its new name suggests, on the conservative challenge. It covers the years from 1980–1992.

- And, as already indicated, Chapter 33 examines the renewed immigration of the 1980s and 1990s, the rise of the Internet and its social implications, and the influence of multiculturalism on the contested nature of American identity. Of course, the chapter also recounts the turbulent events of the Clinton administration, both foreign and domestic, including the election of 2000.

Tools for the Student

Significant pedagogical changes appear in this edition. Building on the popularity of our marginal notes, which highlight key terms and concepts, we now include a succinct preview that introduces each chapter's main themes.

New bulleted summaries reinforce the chapter's main points, also making student review easier.

"Significant Events" chronologies at the end of each chapter show the temporal relationship among important events.

The "Eyewitness to History" features are designed to reinforce the centrality of narrative and to draw readers further into the story. Each Eyewitness is a primary source excerpt, some written by eminent Americans, others by everyday people who were intimately involved in the changes affecting their times.

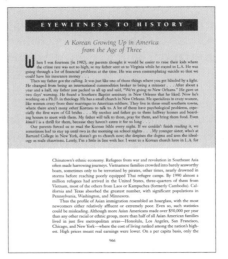

A Note on the Initial Blocks

History records change over time in countless ways. We have tried to reflect the flow of history not only in our narrative but in the decorative types used in the text's design. Our initial blocks—the large decorative initials beginning the first word of every chapter—are drawn from type styles popular during the era covered by each of the book's six parts.

Part One uses hand-engraved initials of the sort imported from England and Europe by colonial printers in the seventeenth and eighteenth centuries. Engravers created the designs on metal or wood by paring away the sections of the initial block that were not meant to be inked. In the tradition of medieval illuminated manuscripts, these initials are interwoven with ornamental decorations, such as leaves or twining ivy.

Part Two displays mortised initial blocks, sometimes referred to by printers of the day as "factotums." These ornamental blocks had holes cut in the middle of the design so printers could insert the initial of their choice. The holes provided greater flexibility, especially when the supply of ornaments was limited.

Part Three features mass-produced initial blocks cut from wood, an approach pioneered in New York City in 1827. This design is a standard Roman face, whose lines use varying thick and thin stroke weights. The typeface also uses serifs, the fine lines finishing off the main strokes of each letter top and bottom. Serifs were originally developed by the ancient Romans, who needed a way to neatly finish letters that were being chiseled in stone.

Part Four makes use of a more ornamental initial block, a style common in the late nineteenth and early twentieth century. The increased ornamentation reflected the rising industrial culture. Printed headlines were in demand not only for books, but for thousands upon thousands of new catalogs and advertising circulars being printed to sell consumer goods. This font's style is actually relatively reserved. It uses light, shadow, and finely engraved lines to create a sense of three-dimensional depth.

Part Five illustrates an initial block whose clean lines reflect the Art Deco movement of the 1920s and 1930s. Printers of the New Era turned away from the flowery Victorian styles of the nineteenth century. This font is Broadway Engraved. It creates drama by increasing the contrast between thick and thin line strokes. The elimination of all serifs contributes a clean elegance as well.

Part Six features a style associated with the 1970s and 1980s: OCR, or Optical Character Reader. The type, with its blocky and oddly weighted shapes, was developed as a way to help more primitive computers recognize type when it was scanned from a page of print. During the heydey of OCR, designers of science fiction books often displayed it to give their material a futuristic feel. But historians have had the last laugh. Because today's computers no longer need OCR to recognize print, this font now appears hopelessly antique!

Supplements

The supplements listed here may accompany *Nation of Nations: A Concise Narrative of the American Republic*. Please contact your local McGraw-Hill representative for details concerning policies, prices, and availability as some restrictions may apply.

For the Instructor

The **Instructor's Manual** offers a variety of resources, including chapter overviews, ideas for classroom discussion, lecture strategies, and lists of relevant films for each chapter. In addition, it offers suggestions for integrating the media technology materials that accompany *Nation of Nations*.

The **Test Bank** contains numerous multiple-choice, fill-in, matching, and essay questions for instructors to use in constructing exams.

A **Computerized Test Bank** for both the PC and the Mac is available on CD-ROM.

A set of 140 full-color **Overhead Transparencies** includes both maps and images that appear in the textbook as well as many supplemental images not found in the text. Organized by chapter, the transparencies are punched so that they can easily be inserted into a three-ring binder.

The **Instructor's Resource CD-ROM** offers an array of materials for use in the classroom, including PowerPoint presentations and an image gallery containing electronic versions of more than 200 maps and photographs, many in full color.

In the **Instructor Center** of the text-specific **Online Learning Center** (www.mhhe.com/davidsonconcise3), instructors can find a series of online tools to meet a range of classroom needs. The Instructor's Manual and PowerPoint presentations can be downloaded by instructors, but are password-protected to prevent tampering. A large gallery of electronic maps and images is also available as well as a guide to using films in the classroom.

PageOut (www.mhhe.com/pageout) enables instructors to create their own course Web sites. PageOut requires no prior knowledge of HTML, no long hours of coding, and no design skills on the instructor's part. Instructors simply plug the course information into a template and select one of 16 designs. The process takes no time at all and leaves instructors with a professionally designed Web site. Powerful features include an interactive course syllabus that lets instructors post content and links, an online gradebook, lecture notes, bookmarks, and even a discussion board where instructors and students can discuss course-related topics.

A wide range of **Videos** on topics in American history is available through the Films for the Humanities and Sciences collection. For instructors who wish to emphasize African American history in their survey courses, McGraw-Hill offers a series of three videos narrated by John Hope Franklin and Alfred A. Moss Jr. on the topics of slavery, Reconstruction, and the continuing struggle for equality. Contact your local McGraw-Hill sales representative for further information.

For the Student

After the Fact Interactive is packaged free with every copy of the textbook: Volume 1 includes "After the Fact Interactive: The Visible and Invisible Worlds of Salem," Volume 2 includes "After the Fact Interactive: USDA Government Inspected," and the combined volume includes both. These rich, visually appealing modules on CD-ROM allow students to be apprentice historians, examining a variety of multimedia primary source materials and constructing arguments based on their research.

The **Student Study Guide with Map Exercises** (Volume 1: 0072315040; Volume 2: 0072315059) includes a list of learning objectives, key events, quizzes, mapping exercises, primary source documents with questions, and other resources for each chapter to help students master the material covered in the text.

The **Student Center** of the text-specific **Online Learning Center** (www.mhhe.com/davidsonconcise3) provides a range of tools for students to use to test their knowledge of the textbook, including learning objectives, drag-and-drop key terms exercises, multiple-choice quizzes with feedback, and fill-in exercises. Interactive maps accompanied by critical thinking questions emphasize the important relationship between geography and history, and Internet activities and research links guide students in exploring the vast amount of material available on the Web.

Created by Magellan Geographix, a leader in quality map products, the **U.S. Map Atlas** is a full-color collection of 52 historical maps. It is a perfect accompaniment for students who need or want extra help with geography.

Web of Connections is a brief guide that explores the many ways that the World Wide Web facilitates the study of history. It also includes a history of the Internet, instructions for navigating and searching the Web, a glossary of Web jargon, and lists of significant Web sites in history.

An online supplement, **PowerWeb: American History** is a collection of readings delivered electronically, along with other tools for conducting research in history. In addition, student study tools, web research tips and exercises, and free access to the Northern Lights search engine are included. For more information, visit www.dushkin.com/powerweb.

Acknowledgments

We are grateful to the many reviewers who were generous enough to offer comments and suggestions at various stages in our development of this manuscript. Our thanks go to:

David Arnold, Columbia Basin College
Robert Becker, Louisiana State University
Robert Cummings, Truman State University
Walter Fraser, Georgia Southern University
Andrew C. Holman, Bridgewater State College
Raymond Hyser, James Madison University
Don Karvelis, Cerritos College
Gabrielle M. Lanier, James Madison University
John L. Larson, Purdue University
Bruce Leslie, SUNY–Brockport
Lynn Mappes, Grand Valley State University
Robert Meckley, Miami University
J. S. Moore, Radford University
John Moore, Tidewater Community College
Earl Mulderink, Southern Utah University
Percy E. Murray, North Carolina Central University

James H. O'Donnell, Marietta College
Matthew Oyos, Radford University
Linda Pitelka, Maryville University
Raul Ramos, University of Utah
Carl Rasmussen, University of Nevada
Steven A. Reich, James Madison University
Marc Richards, Western Washington University
David Sicilia, University of Maryland
Morgan Tanner, Mesa Community College
Gary Trogdon, University of Nebraska–Lincoln
Michael Weiss, Linn-Benton Community College
Jeffrey R. Young, Georgia Southern University

In addition, friends and colleagues contributed their advice and constructive criticism in ways both small and large. We owe a debt to Michael Bellesiles, Lawrence A. Cardoso, Dinah Chenven, Christopher Collier, James E. Crisp, R. David Edmunds, George Forgie, Erica Gienapp, Richard John, Virginia Joyner, Philip Kuhn, Stephen E. Maizlish, Drew McCoy, James McPherson, Walter Nugent, Vicki L. Ruiz, Harold Selesky, Jim Sidbury, David J. Weber, Devra Weber, and John Womack.

The division of labor for this book was determined by our respective fields of scholarship: Christine Heyrman, the colonial era, in which Europeans, Africans, and Indians participated in the making of both a new America and a new republic; William Gienapp, the 90 years in which the young nation first flourished, then foundered on the issues of section and slavery; Michael Stoff, the post–Civil War era, in which industrialization and urbanization brought the nation more centrally into an international system constantly disrupted by depression and war; and Mark Lytle, the modern era, in which Americans finally faced the reality that even the boldest dreams of national greatness are bounded by the finite nature of power and resources both natural and human. Finally, because the need to specialize inevitably imposes limits on any project as broad as this one, our fifth author, James Davidson, served as a general editor and writer, with the intent of fitting individual parts to the whole as well as providing a measure of continuity, style, and overarching purpose. In producing this collaborative effort, all of us have shared the conviction that the best history speaks to a larger audience.

James West Davidson
William E. Gienapp
Christine Leigh Heyrman
Mark H. Lytle
Michael B. Stoff

Brief Contents

Contents

CHAPTER TWO

The First Century of Settlement in the Colonial South (1600–1750) 33

CHAPTER THREE
The First Century of Settlement in the Colonial North (1600–1700)   63

CHAPTER FOUR
The Mosaic of Eighteenth-Century America   90

CHAPTER SIX

The American People and the American Revolution (1775–1783)   146

CHAPTER SEVEN

Crisis and Constitution (1776–1789) 172

CHAPTER EIGHT
The Republic Launched (1789–1801) 200

CHAPTER NINE

The Jeffersonian Republic (1801–1824)   224

PART THREE
GLOBAL ESSAY: THE REPUBLIC TRANSFORMED AND TESTED   250

CHAPTER ELEVEN
The Rise of Democracy (1824–1840)   280

CHAPTER TWELVE
The Fires of Perfection (1820–1850) 308

CHAPTER THIRTEEN
The Old South (1820–1860)   335

CHAPTER FOURTEEN
Western Expansion and the Rise of the Slavery Issue (1820–1850)   364

CHAPTER FIFTEEN

The Union Broken (1850–1861) 391

CHAPTER SIXTEEN
Total War and the Republic (1861–1865) 419

CHAPTER SEVENTEEN
Reconstructing the Union (1865–1877)   453

List of Maps and Charts

Nation of Nations

Volume One: To 1877

PART ONE |  GLOBAL ESSAY

The Creation of a
New America

It is now half a millennium—a full 500 years—since the civilizations of Europe and Africa first made sustained contact with those of North America. The transformations arising out of that event have been astonishing. To gain a rough sense of the scale involved, both in time and space, it is worth standing for a moment not at the beginning of our story but somewhere nearer its midpoint: with Meriwether Lewis and William Clark in August 1805, as they stand atop the continental divide on their traverse of North America. The two men, on orders from President Thomas Jefferson, had been sent on the first American exploratory mission to report on the lands west of the Mississippi. From Lewis and Clark's vantage point, high in the Rocky Mountains, what can we see?

At first glance we see pretty much what we expect to see: a vast, seemingly endless land stretching from sea to sea. But living as we do in the late twentieth century, we tend to take for granted that the domain spread before us is united as a continental republic under a single national government. Only hindsight makes this proposition seem natural. In 1800 the sheer size of the land made the notion of political unity difficult to grasp, for the United States themselves remained a group of colonies only recently unified. Even Jefferson, who possessed the vision to send Lewis and Clark on their mission, had long been in the habit of referring to Virginia as "my country." And the lands west of the Mississippi were still controlled primarily by scores of independent Indian nations.

Just how diverse the landscape was can be seen by the methods Lewis and Clark used to communicate. With no common language spanning the territory, speech making became a series of translations that reflected the route over which the party had traveled. In present-day Idaho, Clark addressed the Tushepaw tribe in English. His speech was translated into French by a trapper in the party; then a second trapper translated into Minataree, a language that his Indian wife, Sacajawea, understood. Sacajawea, the only female member of the party, had grown up farther west with the Shoshone, so she in turn translated the Minataree into Shoshone, which a boy from the Tushepaw nation understood. He translated the Shoshone into his own people's tongue.

If the Louisiana Territory seemed a patchwork of governments and cultures, the young "United States" appeared nearly as heterogeneous. Dutch-speaking patroons could be found along New York's Hudson River, Welsh and German farmers along Pennsylvania's Lancaster Pike, Swedes in Delaware, Gaelic-speaking Scots scattered up and down the Appalachian backcountry, African Americans speaking the Gullah dialect along the Carolina coast. In 1800 many of these settlers knew more about their homelands in Europe or Africa than they did about other regions of North America.

Thus our first task in studying the American past becomes one of translation. We must view events not with the jaded eyes of the early twentieth century but with the fresh eyes of an earlier era. Then the foregone conclusions vanish. How does the American nation manage to unite millions of square miles of territory into one governable republic? How do New York and San Francisco (a city not even in existence in Lewis and Clark's day) come to be linked in a complex economy as well as in a single political system? Such questions take on even more significance when we recall that Europe—roughly the same size as the United States—is today still divided into over four dozen independent nations speaking some 33 languages, not to mention another 100 or so spoken within the former Soviet Union. A united Europe has not emerged, and indeed seems even farther away after the momentous breakup of the Soviet empire.

How, then, did this American republic—this "teeming nation of nations," to use Walt Whitman's phrase—come to be? In barest outline, that is the question that drives our narrative across half a millennium.

The question becomes even more challenging if we move toward the beginning of our story. In 1450, about the time Christopher Columbus was born, only the first stirrings of European expansion to the west had begun. To be sure, Scandinavian seafarers led by Leif Ericsson had reached the northern reaches of the Americas, planting a settlement in Newfoundland in 1001 C.E. But news of Vinland, as Leif called his colony, never reached Europe, and the site was soon abandoned and forgotten. In Columbus's day localism still held sway. Italy was divided into five major states and an equal number of smaller territories. The Germanic peoples were united loosely in the Holy Roman Empire, which (as historians have long delighted in pointing out) was neither holy, Roman, nor an empire. French kings ruled over only about half of what is now France. Spain was divided into several kingdoms, with some areas held by Christians and others by Islamic Moors, whose forebears came from Africa. England, a contentious little nation, was beginning a series of bitter civil conflicts among the nobility, known eventually as the Wars of the Roses. The only country pushing beyond the boundaries of the known European world was Portugal, whose sailors were advancing down the coast of Africa in search of gold and slaves.

Localism was also evident in the patterns of European transportation and trade. For the most part, goods moving overland were carried by wheeled carts or pack animals over rutted paths. Rivers and canals provided another option, but lords repeatedly taxed boats that crossed their territories. On the Seine River, greedy toll-keepers lay in wait every six or seven miles. Travel across the Mediterranean Sea and along Europe's northern coastlines was possible, but storms and pirates made the going dangerous and slow. Under good conditions a ship might reach London from Venice in only 9 days; under bad it might take 50.

European peoples at this time had limited but continuous dealings with Africa, mostly along the Mediterranean Sea. There, North African culture had been shaped since the seventh century by the religion of Islam, whose influence spread as well into Spain. Below the Sahara desert the Bantu, an agricultural people, had migrated over the course of 2000 years from their West African homeland to establish societies throughout the continent. The tempo of these migrations increased as the Bantu learned to produce iron and—equally important—introduced bananas into their diet after the plants were imported to Africa from Asia around 300 to 500 C.E. As a result, the sub-Saharan African populations rose sharply from around 11 million at the beginning of the first millennium C.E. to over 22 million at the end of it.

Traditionally, Bantu agricultural societies governed themselves through family and kinship groups, clustered in villages of around a hundred people and linked with nearby villages in a district. But larger political states developed in response to the arrival of Muslim trading caravans penetrating the Sahara desert beginning around 800 C.E. The first was Ghana, a kingdom that flourished in the eleventh and twelfth centuries. It was followed in the thirteenth century by the even larger Mali empire. Mali's princes controlled almost all of the considerable trade in gold, ivory, and slaves, sending and receiving desert caravans that boasted as many as 25,000 camels. Yet Mali too was split by faction from within and military challenges from without. By the 1490s the Songhai empire had replaced Mali as the most important centralized kingdom in West Africa.

If Europe in 1450 was less unified and dynamic than we might have imagined, the civilizations of North and South America were more complex and populous than historians once thought. Earlier estimates suggested that when Europeans first arrived, about 10 million people were living in Central and South America, with another million living north of Mexico. More recently these figures have been raised tenfold, to perhaps as many as 100 million people in Central and South America and 5 to 10 million north of Mexico. In 1492, when Columbus landed on Hispaniola, that island alone may have held some 7 to 8 million people—a number roughly equal to the entire population of Spain. Tenochtitlán, capital of the Aztec empire, held an estimated 165,000 inhabitants, a population greater than the largest European cities of the day. Such dense urban populations were supported by sophisticated agricultural techniques, including canals, irrigation, and drainage systems.

North America was far from being as heavily populated, but neither was it sparsely settled. From one end of the continent to the other, native cultures actively shaped their environments, burning the forests and plains to promote the growth of vegetation as well as animal populations, which they harvested. As we shall see, Amerindian agricultural achievements were so remarkable that they eventually revolutionized eating habits across the rest of the globe.

In 1490 these three worlds—Europe, Africa, the Americas—remained largely separate from one another, Europe's fleeting encounter with North America had long been forgotten; the empires of interior Africa remained unvisited by Europeans. Only Portugal had begun to explore the West African coast by the sea. Yet currents of change would soon bring together these worlds in ways both vibrant and creative as well as violent and chaotic. What social and economic forces spurred so many Europeans—desperate and opportunistic, high-minded and idealistic—to turn west to the Americas in pursuit of their dreams? How did the civilizations of North and South America react to the European invaders? And not least, how did the mix of cultures from Africa, Europe, and North America create what was truly a new America, in which some of the most independent-minded individuals prospered in provinces that exhibited some of the harshest examples of human slavery? These are among the questions we seek to answer as our narrative unfolds.

CHAPTER 1

Old World, New Worlds

(Prehistory–1600)

preview • In the century after 1492, Europeans expanded boldly and often ruthlessly into the Americas, thanks to a combination of technological advances in sailing and firearms, the rise of new trading networks, and stronger, more centralized governments. Spain established a vast and profitable empire, but at fearful human cost. A diverse Mesoamerican population of some 20 million was reduced to only 2 million through warfare, European diseases, and exploitation.

All the world lay before them. Or so it seemed to mariners from England's seafaring coasts, pushing westward toward unknown lands in the far Atlantic. Since the time of King Arthur, the English living along the rugged southwestern coasts of Devon and Cornwall had followed the sea. From the wharves of England's West Country seaports like Bristol, ships headed west and north to Ireland, bringing back animal hides as well as timber for houses and barrels. Or they turned south, fetching wines from France and olive oil or figs and raisins from the Spanish and Portuguese coasts. In return, West Country ports offered woven woolen cloth and codfish, caught wherever the best prospects beckoned.

The search for cod had long drawn West Country sailors north and west, toward Iceland. In the 1480s and 1490s, however, a few English pushed even farther west. Old maps, after all, claimed that the bountiful *Hy-Brasil*—Gaelic for "Isle of the Blessed"—lay somewhere west of Ireland. These western ventures returned with little to show for their daring until the coming of an Italian named Giovanni Caboto, called John Cabot by the English. Cabot, who hailed from Venice, obtained the blessing of King Henry VII to hunt for unknown lands. From the port of Bristol his lone ship set out in the spring of 1497.

Cabot discovers Newfoundland

This time the return voyage brought news of a "new-found" island where the trees were tall enough to make fine masts and the codfish were plentiful. After returning to Bristol, Cabot marched off to London to inform His Majesty, received 10 pounds as his reward, and with the proceeds dressed himself in dashing silks. The multitudes of London flocked after him, wondering over "the Admiral"; then Cabot returned triumphantly to Bristol to undertake a more ambitious search for a northwest passage to Asia. He set sail with five ships in 1498 and was never heard from again.

By the 1550s Cabot's island, now known as Newfoundland, attracted 400 vessels annually, fishermen not only from England but also from France, Portugal, and Spain. The trip was not easy. Individual merchants or a few partners outfitted small ships with provisions, fishing boats, and guns to ward off sea-roving pirates. As early in the season as they dared, crews of 10 or 20 would catch the spring easterlies, watching as familiar roofs and primitive lighthouses burning smoky coal sank beneath the horizon.

The fishing season

Weeks after setting sail the sailors sighted Newfoundland's fog-shrouded beaches. Seals and walruses played along the rocks offshore, and the encircling sea teemed with cod and flounder, salmon and herring. Throughout the summer men launched little boats from each harbor and fished offshore all day and into the night. With lines and nets, and baskets weighted with stones, they scooped fish from the sea and then dried and salted the catch on the beach. In odd hours, sailors traded with the native Indians, who shared their summer fishing grounds and the skins of fox and deer.

St. John's, Newfoundland, served as the hub of the North Atlantic fishery. Portuguese, English, and French vessels all dropped anchor there, either to take on supplies in the spring or to prepare for the homeward voyage in autumn. Besides trading, there was much talking, for these seafarers knew as much as anyone about the world of wonders opening to Europeans. They were acquainted with names like Cristoforo Colombo, the Italian from Genoa whom Cabot might have known as a boy. They listened to Portuguese tales of sailing around Africa in pursuit of Asian spices and to stories of Indian empires to the south, rich in gold and silver.

Indeed, Newfoundland was one of the few places in the world where so many ordinary folk of different nations could gather and talk, crammed aboard dank ships moored in St. John's harbor, huddled before blazing fires on its beaches, or crowded into smoky makeshift taverns. When the ships sailed home in autumn, the tales went with them, repeated in the tiniest coastal villages by those pleased to have cheated death and the sea one more time. Eager to fish, talk, trade, and take profits, West Country mariners were almost giddy at the prospect of Europe's expanding horizons.

THE MEETING OF EUROPE AND AMERICA

Most seafarers who fished the waters of Newfoundland's Grand Banks remain unknown today. Yet it is well to begin with these ordinary fisherfolk, for the European discovery of the Americas cannot be looked upon simply as the voyages of a few bold explorers. Adventurers like Christopher Columbus or John Cabot were only the most visible representatives of a much larger expansion of European peoples and culture that began in the 1450s. That expansion arose out of a series of gradual but telling changes in the fabric of European society—changes that were reflected in the lives of ordinary seafarers as much as in the careers of explorers decked out in flaming silks.

Some of these changes were technological, arising out of advances in the arts of navigating and shipbuilding and the use of gunpowder. Some were economic, involving the development of trade networks like those linking Bristol with ports in Iceland and Spain. Some were demographic, bringing about a rise in Europe's population after a devastating century of plague. Other changes were religious, adding a dimension of devout belief to the political rivalries that fueled discoveries in the Americas. Yet others were political, making it possible for kingdoms to centralize and extend their influence across the ocean. Portugal, Spain, France, and England—all possessing coasts along the Atlantic—led the way in exploration, spurred on by Italian "admirals" like Caboto and Colombo, Spanish *conquistadores* like Cortés and Pizarro, and English sea dogs like Humphrey Gilbert and Walter Raleigh. Ordinary folk rode these currents too. The great and the small alike were propelled by forces that were remolding the face of Europe.

Changes in European society

The Portuguese Wave

In 1450 all of the world known to western Europeans was Asia and Africa. Most sailors traveled only along the coast of western Europe, following the shores between Norway and the southern tip of Spain, seldom daring to lose sight of land. Beginning in the fifteenth century, bolder seafarers groped down the coast of western Africa, half-expecting to be boiled alive in the Atlantic as they approached the equator. Europeans had traded with Asia through the Muslims of the eastern Mediterranean and across an overland route called the "Silk Road." But they had only vague notions about "the Indies"—China and Japan, the Spice Islands, and the lands lying between Thailand and India. What little they knew, they had learned mainly from Marco Polo, whose account of his travels in the East was not published until 1477, more than 150 years after his death.

But a revolution in European geography began in the middle decades of the fifteenth century, as widening networks of travel and trade connected Europeans to civilizations beyond western Europe. The Portuguese took the lead, encouraged by Prince Henry, known as the Navigator. The devout Henry, a member of Portugal's royal family, had heard tales of Prester John, a Catholic priest rumored to rule a Christian kingdom somewhere beyond the Muslim kingdoms of Africa and Asia. Henry dreamed of joining forces with Prester John and trapping the Muslims in a vise. To that end, he helped finance a series of expeditions down the coast of west Africa. He founded an informal school of navigation on the Portuguese coast, supplying shipmasters with information about wind and currents as well as with navigational charts.

Revolution in geography

Portuguese merchants, who may or may not have believed in Prester John, never doubted there was money to be made in Africa. They invested in Prince Henry's voyages in return for trading monopolies of ivory and slaves, grain and

This stately ivory mask made by a west African artist in the early sixteenth century is adorned with 10 bearded heads of white men, representing Portuguese explorers and traders.

gold. A few may have hoped that the voyages down the coast of west Africa would lead to a direct sea route to the Orient. By discovering such a route, Portugal would be able to cut out the Muslim merchants who funneled all the Asian trade in silks, dyes, drugs, and perfumes through Mediterranean ports.

While Portugal's merchants were establishing trading posts along the west coast of Africa, its mariners were discovering islands in the Atlantic: the Canaries, Madeira, and the Azores. Settlers planted sugarcane and imported slaves from Africa to work their fields. The Portuguese might have pressed even farther west but for the daring of Bartholomeu Dias. In 1488 Dias rounded the Cape of Good Hope on the southern tip of Africa, sailing far enough up that continent's eastern coast to claim discovery of a sea route to India. Ten years later Vasco da Gama reached India itself, and Portuguese interests ultimately extended to Indochina and China. With the trade of Africa and Asia to occupy them, they showed less interest in exploring the Atlantic.

The Portuguese focus on Africa and Asia

By 1500, all of seafaring Europe sought the services of Portuguese pilots, prizing their superior maps and skills with the quadrant. That instrument made it possible to determine latitude fairly accurately, allowing ships to plot their position after months out of the sight of land. The Portuguese had also pioneered the caravel, a lighter, more maneuverable ship that could sail better against contrary winds and in rough seas.

The Spanish and Columbus

From among the international community of seafarers and pilots, it was a sailor from Genoa, Cristoforo Colombo, who led the Spanish to the Americas. Columbus (the Latinized version of his name survives) had knocked about in a number of harbors, picking up valuable navigation skills by sailing Portugal's merchant ships to Madeira, west Africa, and the North Atlantic.

That experience instilled in Columbus the belief that the quickest route to the Indies lay west, across the Atlantic—and that his destiny was to prove it. Perhaps a mere 4500 miles, he reckoned, separated Europe from Japan. His wishful estimate raised eyebrows whenever Columbus asked European monarchs for the money to meet his destiny. Most educated Europeans agreed that the world was round, but they also believed that the Atlantic barrier between themselves and Asia was far wider than Columbus allowed. The kings of England, France, and Portugal dismissed him as a crackpot.

Almost a decade of rejection had grayed Columbus's red hair when Spain's monarchs, Ferdinand and Isabella, finally agreed to subsidize his expedition in 1492. For the past 20 years they had worked to drive the Muslims out of their last stronghold on the Iberian peninsula, the Moorish kingdom of Granada. In 1492 they completed this *reconquista*, or battle of reconquest, expelling many Jews as well. Yet the Portuguese, by breaking the Muslim stranglehold on trade with Asia, had taken the lead in the competition to smite the Islamic powers. Ferdinand and Isabella were so desperate to even the score with Portugal that jealousy overcame common sense: they agreed to take a risk on Columbus.

The reconquista

Columbus's first voyage across the Atlantic could only have confirmed his conviction that he was destiny's darling. His three ships, no bigger than fishing vessels that sailed to Newfoundland, plied their course over placid seas, south from Seville to the Canary Islands and then due west. On October 11, branches, leaves, and flowers floated by their hulls, signals that land lay near. Just after midnight, a sailor spied cliffs shining white in the moonlight. On the morning of October 12, the *Niña*, the *Pinta*, and the *Santa Maria* set anchor in a shallow sapphire bay, and their crews knelt on the white coral beach. Columbus christened the place San Salvador (Holy Savior).

Like many men of destiny, Columbus did not recognize his true destination. At first he confused his actual location, the Bahamas, with an island off the coast of Japan. He coasted along Cuba and Hispaniola (Haiti), expecting at any moment to catch sight of gold-roofed Japanese temples or to happen upon a fleet of Chinese junks. He encountered instead a gentle, generous people who knew nothing of the Great Khan, but who showed him their islands. He dubbed the Arawak people "Indians"—inhabitants of the Indies.

The four voyages of Columbus

Columbus crossed the Atlantic three more times between 1493 and 1504. On his second voyage he established a permanent colony at Hispaniola and explored

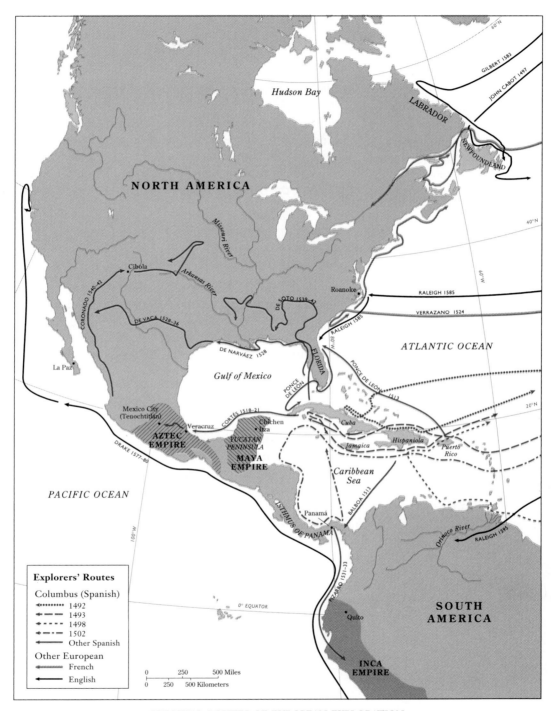

Explorers' Routes

Columbus (Spanish)

- •••••••• 1492
- ◄––•––• 1493
- ◄– – – 1498
- ◄–·–·– 1502
- ◄––––– Other Spanish

Other European

- ◄▪▪▪▪▪ French
- ◄––––– English

| 0 | 250 | 500 Miles |
| 0 | 250 | 500 Kilometers |

PRINCIPAL ROUTES OF EUROPEAN EXPLORATION

other Caribbean islands. On his third voyage he reached Venezuela on the continent of South America; and on his last sailing he made landfalls throughout Central America. Everywhere he looked for proof that these lands formed part of Asia.

Columbus died in 1506, rich in titles, treasure, and tales—everything but recognition. During the last decade of his life, most Spaniards no longer believed that Columbus had discovered the Indies or anyplace else of significance. Instead, another Italian stamped his own name on the New World. Amerigo Vespucci, a Florentine banker with a flair for self-promotion, cruised the coast of Brazil in 1501 and again in 1503. His sensational report misled a German mapmaker into crediting Vespucci with discovering the barrier between Europe and Asia, and so naming it "America."

EARLY NORTH AMERICAN CULTURES

The Americas were a new world only to European latecomers. To the Asian peoples and their native American descendants who had settled the continents tens of thousands of years earlier, Columbus's new world was their own old world. But the first nomadic hunters who crossed from Siberia over the Bering Strait to Alaska probably did not consider themselves discoverers or recognize what they had found—a truly new world wholly uninhabited by humans.

The First Inhabitants

The first passage of people from Asia to America probably took place during a prehistoric glacial period—either before 35,000 B.C.E. or about 10,000 years later—when huge amounts of the world's water froze into sheets of ice. Sea levels dropped so drastically that the Bering Strait became a broad, grassy plain. Across that land bridge between the two continents both humans and animals escaped icebound Siberia for ice-free Alaska. Whenever the first migration took place, the movement of Asians to America continued, even after 8000 B.C.E. when world temperatures rose again and the water from melting glaciers flooded back into the ocean, submerging the Bering Strait. Over a span of 25,000 years settlement spread down the Alaskan coast, then deeper into the North American mainland, and finally throughout Central and South America.

Native Americans remained nomadic hunters and gatherers for thousands of years, as did many Europeans, Africans, and Asians of those millennia. But American cultures gradually diversified, especially after about 5500 B.C.E., when the peoples of central Mexico discovered how to cultivate food crops. As this "agricultural revolution" spread slowly northward, native American societies were able to grow larger and develop distinctive forms of economic, social, and political organization. By the end of the fifteenth century, the inhabitants of North America, perhaps 5 to 10 million people, spoke as many as 1000 languages. Although later Europeans,

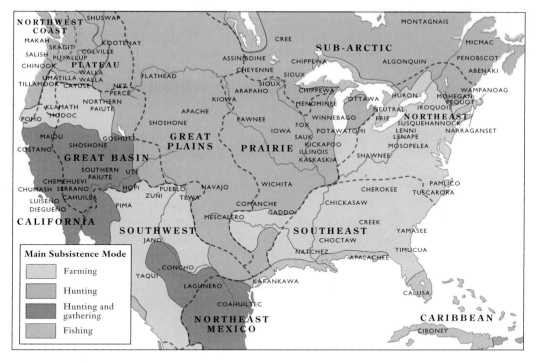

INDIANS OF NORTH AMERICA, CIRCA 1500

like Columbus, lumped these societies together by calling them Indian, any cultural unity had vanished long before 1492.

The simplest Indian societies were those that still relied on hunting and gathering, like the Eskimos of the Arctic and the Serrano, Cahuilla, Luiseño, and Diegueño of southern California, Arizona, and the Baja peninsula of Mexico. Stark deserts and frozen tundra defied cultivation and yielded food supplies that could sustain nomadic bands numbering no more than about 50 people. Families occasionally joined together for a collective hunt or wintered in common quarters, but for most of the year they scattered across the landscape, the women gathering plants and seeds, making baskets, and cooking meals while the men hunted for meat and hides. Political authority lay with either the male family head or the "headman" of a small band. "Shamans"—any tribesmen claiming spiritual powers—enlisted the supernatural to assist individuals.

Societies of Increasing Complexity

In the densely forested belt that stretched from Newfoundland to the Bering Strait, resources more generous than those of the tundra to the north made for larger populations and more closely knit societies. Northeastern bands like the Montagnais, the Micmac, and the Penobscot and northwestern tribes like the Yellowknife

Hunters and gatherers

and the Beaver traveled forests in moccasins and snowshoes, stalking deer, elk, moose, bear, and caribou; they speared fish in icy lakes and streams from birch-bark canoes. Their environment encouraged cooperative economic pursuits. Leading men assigned several families to specific territories that they hunted together, dividing the returns among the whole band. Religious beliefs strengthened the ties of kinship: each family had a "totem," a particular animal from which they claimed descent.

While men dominated Indian bands based on hunting, women assumed more influence in societies that relied for part of their food on settled agriculture. Among

Women in agricultural societies

the Pueblo peoples of Arizona and New Mexico, the Hopi and Zuñi tribes, men hunted bison and cultivated corn and beans, but women owned the fields, the crops, and even the tools. They also owned the sun-baked dwellings of adobe and stone, some of which rose to several stories, that housed the families of their daughters. By 1540 some 70 Pueblo villages flourished, as more reliable food supplies swelled the size and number of clans (families sharing a common ancestry). A council of religious elders drawn from the different clans governed each village. Pueblo religious ceremonies, in contrast to those of simpler Indian societies, involved elaborate rituals celebrating tribal unity and seeking the gods' blessing for hunts and harvests. Thousands of miles to the northeast, in a natural setting far different from the semiarid Southwest, the Iroquois created a remarkably similar culture.

More complex Indian civilizations arose in the bountiful environments of the Pacific Northwest and the coastal region reaching from Virginia to Texas. The seas and rivers from eastern Alaska to northern California teemed with fish, humpback whales, seals, and otters. In the Southeast fertile soil and temperate climate encouraged the cultivation of maize, rice, and a variety of fruits. By harvesting these resources and developing techniques to preserve food supplies, settlements could become larger and more complex. Far less egalitarian than nomadic hunting bands or even the Pueblo and Iroquois, these tribes developed elaborate systems of status. Among southeastern tribes like the Natchez, below the chief, or "Great Sun," stood a hereditary nobility of lesser "Suns," who demanded elaborate displays of respect from the lowly "Stinkards," the common people.

Mesoamerican Empires

Even more advanced were the vast agricultural empires of Mesoamerica—south and central Mexico and Guatemala. As the Roman empire was declining in Europe, the civilization of the Mayas was flourishing in the lowland jungles of Central America. They built cities filled with palaces, bridges, aqueducts, baths, astronomical observatories, and temples topped by pyramids. Their priests developed a written language, their mathematicians discovered the zero, and their astronomers devised a calendar more accurate than any then existing.

A Spanish Conquistador Visits the Aztec Marketplace in Tenochtitlán

n reaching the market-place . . . we were astounded at the great number of people and the quantities of merchandise, and at the orderliness and good arrangements that prevailed, for we had never seen such a thing before. . . . Every kind of merchandise was kept separate and had its fixed place marked for it.

Let us begin with the dealers in gold, silver, and precious stones, feathers, cloaks, and embroidered goods, and male and female slaves who are also sold there. They bring as many slaves to be sold in that market as the Portuguese bring Negroes from Guinea. Some are brought there attached to long poles by means of collars round their necks to prevent them from escaping, but others are left loose. Next there were those who sold coarser cloth, and cotton goods and fabrics made of twisted thread, and there were chocolate merchants. . . . In this way you could see every kind of merchandise to be found anywhere in New Spain, laid out in the same way as goods are laid out in my own district [in Spain] of Medina del Campo, a center for fairs, where each line of stalls has its own particular sort. So it was in this great market. There were those who sold sisal cloth and ropes and the sandals they wear on their feet . . . and in another part were skins of tigers and lions, otters, jackals, and deer, badgers, mountain cats, and other wild animals.

. . . I must also mention, with all apologies, that they sold many canoe-loads of human excrement, which they kept in the creeks near the market. This was for the manufacture of salt and the curing of skins, which they say cannot be done without it. I know that many gentlemen will laugh at this, but I assure them it is true. I may add that on all the roads they have shelters made of reeds or straw or grass so that they can retire when they wish to do so, and purge their bowels unseen by passers-by, and also in order that their excrement shall not be lost.

Source: Excerpt from *The Conquest of New Spain* by Bernal Diaz, translated by J. M. Cohen (Penguin Classics, 1963), pp. 232–233. Copyright ©1963 J. M. Cohen. Reprinted by permission of Penguin UK.

The Aztecs, who invaded central Mexico from the north in the fourteenth century, built on the Mayas' achievements. Within a century Aztec conquest had created an empire of several million people. The capital, Tenochtitlán, was a glittering island metropolis with a population in 1400 of perhaps a quarter of a million—several times the size of London. The Great

Rise of the Aztecs

Temple of the Sun dominated the center of the city, and through the canals leading to Tenochtitlán flowed gold, silver, exotic feathers, cocoa, and millions of pounds of maize—all trade goods and tribute from other Mexican city-states conquered by the Aztecs.

In many ways, the world of the Aztecs paralleled the societies of early modern Europe. Both worlds were predominantly rural, most of their inhabitants living in small villages and engaging in agriculture. In both worlds, merchants and specialized craftworkers clustered in cities, organized themselves into guilds, and clamored for protection from the government. And, as in Europe, Aztec noble and priestly classes took the lead in politics and religion, demanding tribute from the common people.

Yet there was at least one crucial difference between Aztec and European civilizations. Aztec expansion did not take the form of colonial settlements that spanned the oceans—indeed, the globe. That difference reflected a host of distinctive changes in European social, economic, and political development during the fourteenth and fifteenth centuries. It was these transformations that made it possible for bold sailors like Columbus and Cabot or anonymous fisherfolk and traders to dream of profit, glory, and empire.

THE EUROPEAN BACKGROUND OF AMERICAN COLONIZATION

Europe in the age of discovery was a world graced by the courage of explorers like Columbus and the genius of artists like Michelangelo. It was also a world riddled with war, disease, and uncertainty. In 1450 the continent was still recovering from the ravages of the Black Death. Under such vibrant, often chaotic conditions, a sense of crisis mixed with a sense of possibility. Indeed, it was this blend of desperation and ambition that made the newly discovered Americas so attractive to Europeans. Here were strange and distant lands like the island paradises spoken of in legends, like that of the fabled kingdom of Atlantis. Here were opportunities and riches for the daring to grasp. Here were salvation and security for those escaping a world full of violence and sin or oppressed by disease and poverty.

Life and Death in Early Modern Europe

During the fourteenth and the fifteenth centuries 90 percent of Europe's people, widely dispersed in small villages, made their living from the land. But warfare, poor transportation, and low grain yields all created food shortages, and undernourishment produced a population prone to disease. Under these circumstances life was nasty, brutish, and usually short. One-quarter of all children died in the first year of life. People who reached the ripe age of 40 counted themselves fortunate.

It was also a world of sharp inequalities, where nobles and aristocrats enjoyed several hundred times the income of peasants or craftworkers. It was a world with no strong, centralized political authority, where kings were weak and warrior lords held sway over small towns and tiny fiefdoms. It was a world of hierarchy and dependence, where the upper classes provided land and protection for the lower orders. It was a world of violence and sudden death, where homicide, robbery, and rape occurred with brutal frequency. It was a world where security and order of any kind seemed so fragile that most people clung to tradition and feared change.

Into that world in 1347 came the Black Death. In only four years that plague swept away one-third of Europe's population, disrupting both agriculture and commerce. Yet the sudden drop in population restored the balance between people and resources. Survivors of the Black Death found that the relative scarcity of workers and consumers made for better wages, lower prices, and more land.

Plague and recovery

But by the time Columbus reached America, nearly 150 years after the outbreak of the Black Death, Europe again confronted its old problem. Too many people were again competing for a limited supply of food and land. Throughout the sixteenth century diets became poorer, land and work less available, crime and beggary more common. Inflation compounded these problems when prices doubled at the end of the fifteenth century and then quadrupled between 1520 and 1590. To keep pace with the "Price Revolution," landlords raised rents, adding to the burden of Europe's peasantry.

To Europe's hopeful and desperate alike, this climate of disorder and uncertainty led to dreams that the New World would provide an opportunity to renew the Old. As Columbus wrote eagerly of Hispaniola: "This island and all others are very fertile to a limitless degree. . . . There are very large tracts of cultivated land. . . . In the interior there are mines and metals." Columbus and many other Europeans expected that the Americas would provide land for the landless, work for the unemployed, and wealth beyond the wildest dreams of the daring.

The Conditions of Colonization

Sixteenth-century Europeans sought to colonize the Americas, not merely to escape from scarcity and disruption at home. They were also propelled across the Atlantic by dynamic changes in their society. Revolutions in technology, economics, and politics made overseas settlement practical and attractive to seekers of profit and power.

The improvements in navigation and sailing also fostered an expansion of trade. By the late fifteenth century Europe's merchants and bankers had devised more efficient ways of transferring money and establishing credit in order to support commerce across the longer distances. And although rising prices and rents pinched Europe's peasantry, that same inflation enriched those who had goods to sell, money to lend, and land to rent.

Expansion of trade and capital

Wealth flowed into the coffers of sixteenth-century traders, financiers, and landlords, creating a pool of capital that those investors could plow into colonial development. Both the commercial networks and the private fortunes needed to sustain overseas trade and settlement were in place by the time of Columbus's discovery.

The direction of Europe's political development also paved the path for American colonization. After 1450 strong monarchs in Europe steadily enlarged the sphere of royal power at the expense of warrior lords. Henry VII, the founder of England's Tudor dynasty, Francis I of France, and Ferdinand and Isabella of Spain began the trend, forging modern nation-states by extending their political control over more territory, people, and resources. Those larger, more centrally organized states were able to marshal the resources necessary to support colonial outposts and to sustain the professional armies and navies capable of protecting empires abroad.

Political centralization

Europeans, Chinese, and Aztecs on the Eve of Contact

It was the growing power of monarchs as well as commercial and technological development that allowed early modern Europeans to establish permanent settlements—even empires—in a world an ocean away..But that conclusion raises an intriguing question: why didn't China, the most advanced civilization of the early modern world, expand and colonize the Americas? For that matter, if events had fallen out a little differently, why didn't the Aztecs discover and colonize Europe?

The Chinese undoubtedly possessed the capability to navigate the world's oceans and to establish overseas settlements. A succession of Ming dynasty emperors and their efficient bureaucrats marshaled China's resources to develop a thriving shipbuilding industry and trade with ports throughout southeast Asia and India. By the opening of the fifteenth century, the Chinese seemed poised for even greater maritime exploits. Seven times between 1405 and 1433, its "treasure fleet" of 300 ships manned by 28,000 sailors and commanded by Zheng He (pronounced *Jung Huh*) unfurled their red silk sails off the south China coast and sailed as far as the kingdoms of east Africa. The treasure fleet's largest craft were nine-masted junks measuring 400 feet long that boasted multiple decks and luxury cabins with balconies. By contrast, when Columbus's three ships set sail to find the Indies, the biggest was a mere 85 feet long, and the crew aboard all three ships totaled just 90 men.

Zheng He could have been another Columbus, given the resources available to him. But the Chinese had little incentive either to seek out the world's trade or to conquer and colonize new territories. Unlike western Europeans, they faced no shortages of land or food, and they led the world in producing luxury goods. On the other hand, China faced the threat of attack from the Mongols on its northwestern border—a threat so pressing that by 1433 the Ming emperor mobilized all the country's wealth and warriors to fend it off. Thus ended the great era of Chinese maritime expansion. Zheng He's treasure fleet, which would remain the world's most impressive navy until the beginning of the twentieth century, rotted away in the ports of southern China.

Why China did not explore farther

As for the Aztecs, despite their formidable talents, they lacked the knowledge of ocean navigation. Equally important, Aztec rulers had not established their sovereign authority over powerful nobles. The absence of a strong, centralized power made it impossible for the Aztecs to launch a more ambitious expansion. Although their armies put down disturbances in conquered territories and protected trade routes, the Aztecs had not developed the resources to impose their way of life on the other places. Instead, conquered city-states within the Aztec empire retained their distinctive languages and customs—and bitterly resented Aztec rule. The result was an empire vulnerable to division from within and to attack from abroad.

Barriers to Aztec colonization

SPAIN'S EMPIRE IN THE NEW WORLD

By the reckoning of the Aztecs it was the year 12-House, a time, they believed, when the fate of the whole world hung by a thread. According to their calendar, a 52-year cycle had come to an end. Now the gods might extinguish the sun with a flood or a great wind. The end of this particular cycle had been marked with a chilling omen. In one of the canals, fishermen caught a bird "the color of ashes" with a strange mirror in the crown of its head. They brought the creature to their ruler, Moctezuma II, who looked in the mirror and saw ranks of men mounted on animals resembling deer and moving across a plain.

Two years later, the Aztecs' worst fears were fulfilled. Dust rose in whirlwinds on the roads from the hooves of horses and the boots of men in battle array. "It was as if the earth trembled beneath them, or as if the world were spinning . . . as it spins during a fit of vertigo," one Aztec scribe recorded. This was no image in a magic mirror: Hernando Cortés and his army of Spaniards were marching on Tenochtitlán. By Cortés's calculations, it was 1519 C.E.

Spanish Conquest

To Cortés and the other Spanish explorers who had followed Columbus across the Atlantic over the previous quarter century, a new and remarkable world was opening. By 1513 the Spanish had explored and mastered the Caribbean basin. In that year too, Vasco Nuñez de Balboa crossed the Isthmus of Panama and glimpsed the Pacific Ocean. North and South America were revealed as continents of vast size, separated from Asia by another ocean. And Ferdinand Magellan finally did reach the Orient by sailing west across the vast Pacific. After his death in the Philippines in 1521, his shipmates completed the first circumnavigation of the globe.

Balboa and Magellan

From their bases in the islands of the Caribbean, the Spanish pressed outward. To the north they met mostly with disappointment. Juan Ponce de León vainly scoured the shores of the Florida peninsula for the fabled "Fountain of

The dignity and grace of this Mexican woman, drawn in the 1550s possibly by a Spanish priest, may reflect the sympathetic influence of Bartolomé de Las Casas—sentiments most Spaniards did not share.

Youth," while Hernando de Soto trekked through Florida and into the southeastern interior as far west as the Mississippi River. Between 1540 and 1542 Francisco Vásquez de Coronado moved through Arizona, New Mexico, Texas, Oklahoma, and Kansas. But reports of fantastic cities of gold proved to be merely the stuff of dreams.

During these same decades, however, the Spanish found golden opportunities elsewhere. Those who had first rushed to Hispaniola immediately started scouring the island for gold—and enslaving Indians to work the mines. As for Cortés, when

Cortés conquers the Aztecs

Moctezuma's ambassadors met him on the road to Tenochtitlán in 1519 and attempted to appease him with gold ornaments and other gifts, an Indian witness recorded that "the Spaniards . . . picked up the gold and fingered it like monkeys. . . . Their bodies swelled with greed." For nearly half a year Cortés dominated the indecisive Moctezuma by imprisoning him in his own capital. The Aztecs drove the Spanish out after Moctezuma's death, but Cortés returned with reinforcements, set siege to Tenochtitlán, and in 1521 conquered it. The Aztec empire lay in ruins.

Role of the Conquistadors

To the conquistadors—a motley lot of minor nobles, landless gentlemen, and professional soldiers—the Americas seemed more than a golden opportunity. They resented the Spanish monarchy's growing strength at home and aimed to recreate in the New World a much older world of their own dreaming. Like me-

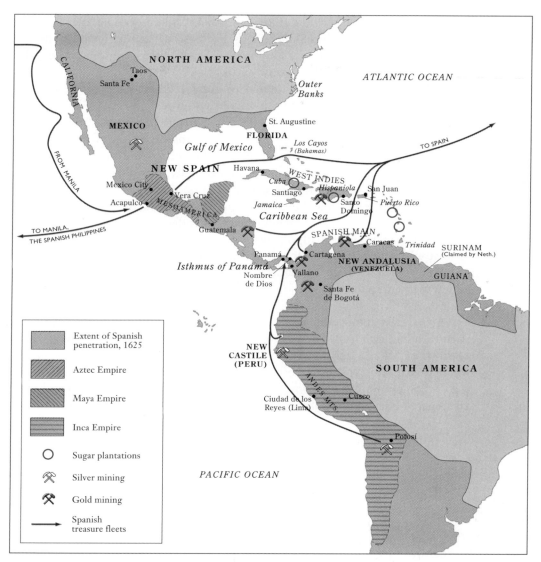

SPANISH AMERICA, CIRCA 1600   By 1600, Spain was extracting large amounts of gold and silver from Central and South America as well as profits from sugar plantations in the Caribbean.

dieval knights, Cortés and other conquistadors hoped to establish themselves as a powerful nobility that would enjoy virtual independence from the Spanish Crown an ocean away.

For a time the conquistadors succeeded. By the 1540s Cortés and just 1500 men had taken all of Mexico and the southwestern portion of North America.

During the 1550s the ruthless Pizarro brothers and an even smaller band of conquistadors sailed along South America's Pacific coast and overthrew the Incas in Peru, an Andean civilization as impressive as that of the Aztecs. They also laid claim to Ecuador, Chile, Argentina, and Bolivia.

How did a handful of gentlemen heading a rabble of soldiers, seamen, and criminals bring down sophisticated Indian empires in the span of a generation? Certainly, the Spanish enjoyed the edge of surprise and technological superiority. The sight of ships and the explosion of guns at first terrified the Indians, as did men on horseback whom they took at first to be single creatures. The only domesticated animals known to the Aztecs were small dogs; the Spanish provided them with their first glimpse of horses and, later, cattle, sheep, oxen, pigs, goats, donkeys, mules, and chickens.

Reasons for Spain's success

What delivered a more lasting shock to Indian civilizations was exposure to European infections. Smallpox, influenza, typhus, and measles, disease strains against which they had developed no biological resistance, ravaged entire villages and tribes. Tenochtitlán surrendered to Cortés after a siege of 85 days, during which many died from starvation but many more died of smallpox contracted from the Spanish.

An equally important factor in the swift conquest was the political disunity within Indian empires. The Aztecs and Incas had subdued the native Indian populations of Mexico and Peru only 100 years before the Spanish invasion. Resentment at Aztec and Inca rule brought the conquistadors eager allies among the subject Indian tribes. But by aiding the Spanish overthrow of the Aztecs and the Incas, the native Indians only substituted one set of overlords for another.

Spanish Colonization

The conquistadors did not long enjoy their mastery in the Americas. The Spanish monarchs who had just tamed an aristocracy at home were not about to allow a colonial nobility to arise across the Atlantic. The Crown bribed the conquistadors into retirement—or was saved the expense when men like the Pizarro brothers were assassinated by their own followers. The task of governing Spain's new colonies passed from the conquistadors to a small army of officials, soldiers, lawyers, and Catholic bishops, all appointed by the Crown, reporting to the Crown, and loyal to the Crown. Headquartered in urban centers like Mexico City (formerly Tenochtitlán), an elaborate, centralized bureaucracy administered the Spanish empire, regulating nearly every aspect of economic and social life.

Royal control replaces the conquistadors

Few Spaniards besides imperial officials settled in the Americas. By 1600 only about 5 percent of the colonial population was of Spanish descent, the other 95 percent being either Indian or African. Even by 1800 only 300,000 Spanish immigrants had come to Central and South America. Indians remained on the lands that they had farmed under the Aztecs and the Incas, now paying Spanish overlords their taxes and producing livestock for export. The Indians were not enslaved outright, but the Spanish compelled them to work for specified periods of time, a system of forced labor known as *encomienda*. The Spanish also established sugar plantations in the West Indies; these were worked by black slaves who were being imported from Africa in large numbers by 1520.

Spain's colonies returned even more spectacular profits after 1540, when silver deposits were discovered in both Mexico and Peru. European investors and Spanish immigrants who had profited from cattle raising and sugar planting poured their capital into silver mining. The Spanish government pressed whole villages of Indians to serve in the mines, joining black slaves and free white workers employed there. Local farmers who supplied mining centers with food and Spanish merchants in Seville who exported European goods to Potosí profited handsomely. So did the Spanish Crown, which claimed one-fifth of the silver extracted.

> Discovery of silver

The Effects of Colonial Growth

Its American riches made Spain the dominant power in Europe. But that dominance was purchased at a fearful human cost. Devastated by warfare, disease, and exploitation, the Indians of the Caribbean were virtually wiped out within a century. In Mesoamerica, a native population of 20 million was reduced to 2 million.

Only a few of the Spanish spoke out against the exploitation of the natives. Among them was Bartolomé de Las Casas, a Spanish priest who became a bishop in southern Mexico. His writings, reprinted in many translations and illustrated with gruesome drawings, circulated throughout Europe, becoming the basis of the "Black Legend" of Spanish oppression in the Americas.

> Las Casas

Most did not share Las Casas's scruples. They justified their conquest by claiming that they had "delivered" the Indians from Aztec and Inca tyranny and replaced native "barbarism" and "paganism" with European civilization and Christianity. The extent of the Spanish conquest itself fostered a heady sense of superiority. By the beginning of the seventeenth century Spain's dominions in the Americas spanned 8000 miles, stretching from Baja California to the Straits of Magellan at South America's southern tip. The prevailing mood was captured by the portrait of a Spanish soldier that adorns the frontispiece of his book about the West Indies. He stands with one hand on his sword and the other holding a pair of compasses on top of a globe. Beneath is inscribed the motto "By compasses and the sword/More and more and more and more."

THE REFORMATION IN EUROPE

Spain met with little interference in the Americas from rival European nations for most of the sixteenth century. One reason was religious upheaval in Europe. During the second decade of the sixteenth century—the same decade in which Cortés laid siege to Tenochtitlán—enormous religious changes swept Europe. That revolution in Christianity, known as the Protestant Reformation, also played a crucial role in shaping the later history of the Americas.

Backdrop to Reform

During the Middle Ages, the Roman Catholic church defined what it meant to be a Christian in western Europe. Like other institutions of medieval society, the Catholic church was a hierarchy. At the top was the pope in Rome, and under him were the descending ranks of other church officials—cardinals, archbishops, bishops. At the bottom of the Catholic hierarchy were parish priests, each serving his own village, as well as monks and nuns living in monasteries and convents. But medieval popes were weak, their power felt little in the lives of most Europeans. Like political units of the era, religious institutions of the Middle Ages were local and decentralized.

As the monarchs of Europe grew more powerful, so too did the popes. By 1500 a large bureaucracy of church officials supported the papacy. The Catholic church acquired land throughout Europe and added to its income by tithing **Rise of the papacy** (collecting taxes from church members) and by collecting fees from those appointed to church offices. In the thirteenth century, church officials also began to sell "indulgences." For ordinary believers, who expected to spend time after death purging their sins in purgatory, the purchase of an indulgence promised to shorten that punishment by supposedly drawing on a "treasury of merit" amassed by the good works of Christ and the saints.

By the fifteenth century the Catholic church and the papacy had become enormously powerful but increasingly indifferent to popular religious concerns. Church officials meddled in secular politics. Popes and bishops flaunted their wealth, while poorly educated parish priests neglected their pastoral duties. At the same time, popular demands for religious assurance grew increasingly intense. The concern for salvation swelled in response to the disorienting changes sweeping the continent during the fifteenth and sixteenth centuries—the widening gulf between rich and poor, the rise in prices, and the discovery of America.

The Teachings of Martin Luther

Into this climate of heightened spirituality stepped Martin Luther, who abandoned studying the law to enter a monastery. Like many contemporaries, Luther was consumed by fears over his eternal fate. He was convinced that he was damned, and he could not find any consolation in the Catholic church. Catholic doctrine taught that a person could be saved by faith in God and by his or her own good works—by leading a virtuous life, observing the sacraments (such as baptism, the Mass, and penance), making pilgrimages to holy places, and praying to Christ and the saints. Since Luther believed that human nature was innately evil, he despaired of being able to lead a life that "merited" salvation. If men and women were so bad, he reasoned, how could they ever win their way to heaven with good works?

Luther finally broke through his despair by reading the Bible. It convinced him that God did not require fallen humankind to earn salvation. Salvation, he concluded, came by faith alone, the "free gift" of God to undeserving sinners. The ability to live a good life could not be the *cause* of salvation but its *consequence*: once men and women believed that they had saving faith, moral behavior was possible. Luther elaborated that idea, known as "justification by faith alone," between 1513 and 1517.

Luther was ordained a priest and then assigned to teach at a university in Wittenberg, Germany. Still, he became increasingly critical of the Catholic church as an institution. In 1517 he posted on the door of a local church 95 theses attacking the Catholic hierarchy for selling salvation in the form of indulgences.

Justification by faith alone

The novelty of this attack was not Luther's open break with Catholic teaching. Challenges to the church had cropped up throughout the Middle Ages. What was new was the passion behind Luther's attacks. Using the earthy Germanic tongue he expressed the anxieties of so many devout laypeople and their outrage at the church hierarchy's neglect. The "gross, ignorant asses and knaves at Rome," he warned, should keep their distance from Germany, or else "jump into the Rhine or the nearest river, and take . . . a cold bath."

The pope and his representatives in Germany at first tried to silence Martin Luther, then excommunicated him. But opposition only pushed Luther toward more radical positions. He asserted that the church and its officials were not infallible; only the Scriptures were without error. Every person, he said, should read and interpret the Bible for himself or herself. In an even more direct assault on church authority, he advanced an idea known as "the priesthood of all believers." Catholic doctrine held that salvation came only through the church and its clergy, a privileged group that possessed special access to God. Luther asserted that every person had the power claimed by priests.

Attacks on church authority

Although Luther had not intended to start a schism within Catholicism, independent Lutheran churches were forming in Germany by the 1520s. And during the 1530s, Luther's ideas spread throughout Europe, where they were eagerly taken up by other reformers.

The Contribution of John Calvin

The most influential of Luther's successors was John Calvin, a French lawyer turned theologian. Calvin agreed with Luther that men and women could not merit their salvation. But while Luther's God was a loving deity who extended his mercy to sinful humankind, Calvin conceived of God as an awesome sovereign, all-knowing and all-powerful, the controlling force in human history who would ultimately triumph over Satan. To bring about that final victory, Calvin believed, God had selected certain people as his agents for usher-

The elect

John Calvin promoted an activist theology.

ing in his heavenly kingdom. These people—"the saints," or "the elect"—had been "predestined" by God for eternal salvation in heaven.

Calvin's emphasis on predestination led him to another distinctively Protestant notion—the doctrine of calling. How could a person learn whether he or she belonged to the elect who were saved? Calvin answered: strive to behave like a saint. God expected his elect to serve the good of society by unrelenting work in a "calling," or occupation, in the world. In place of the Catholic belief in the importance of good works, Calvin emphasized the goodness of work itself. Success in attaining self-control, in bringing order into one's own life and the entire society, revealed that a person might be among the elect.

Calvin fashioned a religion to change the world. Whereas Luther believed that Christians should accept the existing social order, Calvin called on Christians to become activists, reshaping society and government to conform with God's laws laid down in the Bible. He wanted all of Europe to become like Geneva, the Swiss city that he had converted into a holy commonwealth where the elect regulated the behavior and morals of everyone else. And unlike Luther, who wrote primarily for a German audience, Calvin addressed his most important book, *The Institutes of the Christian Religion* (1536), to Christians throughout Europe. Reformers from every country flocked to Geneva to learn more about Calvin's ideas.

An activist theology

The English Reformation

While the Reformation went forward in Europe, King Henry VIII of England was striving for a goal more modest than those of Luther and Calvin. He wanted only to produce a male heir to carry on the Tudor dynasty. When his wife, Catherine of Aragon, gave birth to a daughter, Mary, Henry decided to do something less modest. He set out to get his marriage to Catherine annulled by the pope. This angered Catherine's father, the king of Spain, who convinced the pope to refuse. Defiantly Henry went ahead with the divorce and married his mistress, Anne Boleyn.

Henry then widened this breach with Rome by making himself, and not the pope, the head of the Church of England. In 1534 Parliament formalized the relationship with the Act of Supremacy. But Henry, who fancied himself a theologian, had no fondness for Protestant doctrine. Under his leadership the Church of England remained essentially Catholic in its teachings and rituals.

Henry VIII breaks with Rome

England's Protestants gained ground during the six-year reign of Edward VI, but then found themselves persecuted when his Catholic half-sister, Mary, became queen in 1553. Five years later the situation turned again, when Elizabeth (Anne Boleyn's daughter) took the throne, proclaiming herself the defender of Protestantism.

Still, Elizabeth was no radical Calvinist. A vocal minority of her subjects were reformers of that stripe, calling for the English church to purge itself of bishops, elaborate ceremonies, and other Catholic "impurities." Because of the austerity and zeal of such Calvinist radicals, their opponents proclaimed them "Puritans."

English Puritans

The Protestant Reformation shattered the unity of Christendom in western Europe. Spain, Ireland, and Italy remained firmly Catholic. England, France, Scotland, the Netherlands, and Switzerland developed either dominant or substantial Calvinist constituencies. Much of Germany and Scandinavia opted for Lutheranism. As these religious groups competed for political power and the loyalties of believers, brutal wars racked sixteenth-century Europe. Protestants and Catholics slaughtered each other in the name of Christianity.

ENGLAND'S ENTRY INTO AMERICA

In 1562 Queen Elizabeth gave her blessing to an English army that set sail for France, to aid Calvinists there being suppressed by the government. Perhaps the most dashing of the army's captains was a red-faced and robust West Country gentleman, Sir Humphrey Gilbert.

Like so many West Country boys in search of honor and fortune, Gilbert was eager to seize the main chance. In the early 1560s, that seemed to be fighting for the Protestant cause in France. Gilbert's stepfather, the seafarer Walter Raleigh, had done a good deal of his own seizing, mostly from Spanish silver ships along the South American coast. Like the conquistadors, Raleigh wanted more. He merely decided he could get more a bit more easily if he let Spain dig and refine the silver first.

If France had not beckoned, Humphrey Gilbert would surely have been happy to harass the Spanish too, along with his stepbrother, the young Walter Raleigh (named after his plundering father). But as Gilbert and young Raleigh came of age, they began to consider more ambitious schemes than the mere plundering of treasure. They looked to

Ambitious West Country gentlemen

conquer Spain's empire—or, at least, to carve out for England a rival empire of its own. During the late 1570s and 1580s, when Queen Elizabeth felt confident enough to challenge Spain in the Americas, Gilbert and Raleigh were ready to lead the way.

The English Colonization of Ireland

During the 1560s, however, England was too deeply distracted by religious and political turmoil to pursue empire across the Atlantic. For Elizabeth, privateers like the senior Walter Raleigh stirred up more trouble than they were worth. Spain, after all, was England's ally against a common rival, France. And the Netherlands, which was then controlled by Spain, imported English cloth. Elizabeth had good reason to pursue a policy that would soothe Spain, not offend it.

Reasons for England to soothe Spain

The queen also worried about Catholic Ireland to the west. She feared that the French or the Spanish might use the island as a base for invading England. Beginning in 1565 Elizabeth encouraged a number of her subjects, mainly gentlemen and aristocrats from the West Country, to sponsor private ventures for subduing the native Irish and settling English families on Irish land. Among the gentlemen eager to win fame and fortune were Humphrey Gilbert and Walter Raleigh.

The English invaders of Ireland, almost all ardent Protestants, regarded the native Catholic inhabitants as superstitious, pagan savages. Thus did the English justify their conquest: by proclaiming it their duty to teach the Irish the discipline of hard work, the rule of law, and the truth of Christianity. And while the Irish were learning civilized ways, they would not be allowed to buy land or hold office or serve on juries or give testimony in courts or learn a trade or bear arms.

When the Irish rebelled at that program of "liberation," the English ruthlessly repressed native resistance, slaughtering combatants and civilians. Most English in Ireland, like most Spaniards in America, believed that native peoples who resisted civilization and Christianity should be subdued at any cost. No scruples stopped Humphrey Gilbert, in an insurgent county, from planting the path to his camp with the severed heads of Irish rebels.

English repression of the Irish

England's efforts to settle and subdue Ireland would serve as a rough model for later efforts at colonization. The approach was essentially military, like that of the conquistadors. More ominously, it sanctioned the savage repression of any "inferior race." Not only Gilbert but also Raleigh and many other West Country gentry soon turned their attention toward North America. "Neither reputation, or profytt is to be wonne" in Ireland, concluded Gilbert. They wanted more.

Renewed Interest in the Americas

After hard service in France and Ireland, Gilbert and Raleigh returned to England. Her cautious bureaucrats who had been enlarging royal power considered the two swaggering gentlemen insufferable if not downright dangerous, much as the Spanish officials distrusted their conquistadors. Still, England was becoming more receptive to the schemes of such hotheaded warrior lords for challenging Spain overseas. English Protestantism, English nationalism, and English economic interests all came together to increase support for English exploration and colonization.

The turning point for the English came during the 1570s when Calvinist Dutch in the Netherlands rebelled against their rule by Catholic Spain. The Spanish retaliated savagely by sacking the city of Antwerp, which was England's major European market for cloth. Forced to look elsewhere for markets and investment opportunities, merchants combined in joint stock companies to develop a trade with Africa, Russia, the East Indies, and the Mediterranean. These private corporations, in which many shareholders pooled small amounts of capital, also began to plow money into Atlantic privateering voyages.

Joint stock companies

Joining English merchants in the new interest in overseas exploration were gentry families. The high birthrate among England's upper classes throughout the sixteenth century had produced a surplus of younger sons, who stood to inherit no share of family estates. The shortage of land for their sons at home stirred up support among the gentry for England to claim territory across the Atlantic.

With the support of England's leading merchants and gentlemen, Elizabeth now needed little encouragement to adopt a more belligerent stance toward Spain. But she got more encouragement from Spain itself, which made no secret of wanting to restore England to Catholicism, by armed invasion if necessary. Elizabeth was not yet prepared to provoke open warfare with Spain, but she watched with interest the exploits of a new generation of English explorers in North America.

The Failures of Frobisher and Gilbert

The adventurer who first caught the queen's eye was Martin Frobisher, the veteran of slaving voyages to west Africa, privateering raids in the Atlantic, the fighting in Ireland, and other unsavory enterprises. In 1576 he sailed on another search for a Northwest Passage to Asia.

After sailing north of Labrador, Frobisher returned to England with an Eskimo (plucked, kayak and all, from the Atlantic) and a shiny black stone that seemed to be gold ore. With royal backing, Frobisher made two more voyages to his "New Peru" in 1577 and 1578, hauling back nearly 2000 tons of black rock. When upon closer inspection all of the rock turned out to be "fool's gold," his reputation fell under a cloud.

Because Humphrey Gilbert had refused to invest in this fiasco, Frobisher's disgrace became Gilbert's opportunity. In 1578 Elizabeth granted Gilbert a vague patent—the first English colonial charter—to explore, occupy, and govern any territory in America "not actually possessed of any Christian prince or people." That charter, ignoring the Indian possession of North America, made Gilbert lord and proprietor of all the land lying between Florida and Labrador.

Gilbert pictured himself and his heirs as manorial lords of a colony filled with loyal tenant farmers paying rents in return for protection. In a sense his dreams resembled those of Spain's conquistadors: to recreate an older, nearly

Gilbert's colonial plans

feudal world that would remain largely free of royal control. Yet Gilbert's vision also looked forward to a utopian society. He planned to encourage England's poor to emigrate by providing them free land and a government "to be chosen by consent of the people."

In the end, the dreams foundered in a stormy present. Gilbert set sail in June 1583, but a late start forced him to turn back before he could scout the North American coast. Then his two ships met with foul weather. Gilbert, with characteristic bravado, sat on the deck of the smaller *Squirrel*, reading a book. "We are as neere to Heaven by sea as by land," he shouted across the heaving swells. The men aboard the *Golden Hind* recognized the words of Thomas More, whose *Utopia*—a dialogue about an ideal society in the New World—Gilbert held in his hand. Gilbert was nearer to heaven than he hoped: around midnight, the crew of

Martin Frobisher, his face frozen in a glare, a horse pistol fixed in his fist, exemplified the ruthless ambition of England's West Country adventurers.

the *Golden Hind* saw the lights of the *Squirrel* extinguished and the ship "devoured and swallowed up by the sea."

Raleigh's Roanoke Venture

Raleigh had been eager to accompany his stepbrother's ill-fated expedition, but Elizabeth's many favors made it hard for him to leave. He was dining on food from palace kitchens, sleeping in a bed adorned with green velvet and spangled plumes of white feathers. Still, Raleigh was restless—and envious when another West Country adventurer, Sir Francis Drake, returned from circumnavigating the globe in 1580, his ships heavy with Spanish plunder.

Raleigh's ambitions led him to Richard Hakluyt, a clergyman with a passion for spreading knowledge of overseas discoveries. At Raleigh's request, Hakluyt wrote an eloquent plea to Elizabeth for the English settlement of America, titled *A Discourse Concerning Westerne Planting*. The temperate and fertile lands of North America, Hakluyt argued, would provide a perfect base from which to harry the Spanish, search for a Northwest Passage, and extend the influence of Protestantism. He also stressed the advantages of colonies as sources of new commodities, as markets for English goods, and as havens for the poor and unemployed.

Raleigh's chance to settle American lands finally came in 1584, when Elizabeth granted him a patent nearly identical with that of Gilbert. By the summer Raleigh had sent Philip Amadas and Arthur Barlowe across the Atlantic, their two small ships coasting the Outer Banks of present-day North Carolina. Amadas and Barlowe established cordial relations with the Roanoke tribe, ruled by a "werowance," or chief, named Wingina. The following summer a full-scale expedition returned to Roanoke Island.

Raleigh apparently aimed to establish on Roanoke a mining camp and a military garrison modeled on Frobisher's venture of the 1570s. In a stroke of genius, he included in the company of 108 men a scientist, Thomas Hariot, to study the country's natural resources and an artist, John White, to make drawings of the Virginia Indians. *A Briefe and True Reporte of the New Found Land of Virginia* (1588), written by Hariot and illustrated by White, served as one of the principal sources about North America and its Indian inhabitants for more than a century. Far less inspired was Raleigh's choice to lead the expedition—two veterans of the Irish campaigns, Sir Richard Grenville and Ralph Lane. Even his fellow conquistadors in Ireland considered Lane proud and greedy, and Grenville was given to breaking wineglasses between his teeth and then swallowing the shards to show that he could stand the sight of blood, even his own.

The bullying ways of both men quickly alienated the natives of Roanoke. After a year, in response to rumors of an imminent Indian attack, Lane and his men attacked Wingina's main village and killed him. All that averted an Indian counterattack was the arrival of Drake and Frobisher, fresh from freebooting up and

Hakluyt publicizes America

The first colony at Roanoke

down the Caribbean. The settlement's 102 survivors piled onto the pirate fleet and put an ocean between themselves and the avenging Roanokes.

A Second Attempt

Undaunted, Raleigh organized a second expedition to plant a colony farther north, in the Chesapeake Bay. He now projected an agricultural community modeled on Humphrey Gilbert's manorial dreams. He recruited 119 men, women, and children, members of the English middle class, granting each person an estate of 500 acres. He also appointed as governor the artist John White, who brought along a suit of armor for ceremonial occasions.

From the moment of first landfall in July 1587, everything went wrong. The expedition's pilot, Simon Ferdinando, insisted on putting off the colonists at Roanoke Island rather than the Chesapeake. Even before Ferdinando weighed anchor, the settlers were skirmishing with the local Indians. Sensing that the situation on Roanoke could quickly become desperate, White sailed back with Ferdinando, hoping to bring reinforcements.

But White returned home in 1588 when the massive Spanish navy, the Armada, was marshaling for an assault on England. Blocked by the war with Spain, Raleigh left the Roanoke colonists to shift for themselves. When White finally returned to Roanoke Island in 1590, he found only an empty fort and a few cottages in a clearing. The sole clue to the colony's fate was carved on a post: CROATOAN. It was the name of a nearby island off Cape Hatteras.

Had the Roanoke colonists fled to Croatoan for safety? Had they moved to the mainland and joined Indian tribes in the interior? Had they been killed by Wingina's people? The fate of the "lost colony" remains a mystery. White sailed back to England, leaving behind the little cluster of cottages that would soon be overgrown with vines and his suit of armor that was already "almost eaten through with rust."

All the world lay before them. Or so it had seemed to the young men from England's West Country who dreamed of gold and glory, conquest and colonization. Portugal had sent slave and gold traders to Africa as well as merchants to trade with the rich civilizations of the Indies. Spanish conquerors like Cortés had toppled Indian empires and brought home silver. But England's would-be conquistadors had met only with frustration. In 1600, over a century after Columbus's first crossing, not a single English settlement existed anywhere in the Americas. The Atlantic had swallowed up Gilbert and his hopes for a manorial utopia; Roanoke lay in ruins.

What was left of the freebooting world of West Country adventurers? Raleigh, his ambition unquenchable, sailed to South America in quest of a rich city named El Dorado. In 1603, however, Elizabeth's death brought to the English throne her cousin James I, the founder of the Stuart dynasty. The new king arrested the old queen's favorite for treason and left him to languish 15 years in the Tower of London. Set free in 1618 at the age of 64, Raleigh returned to South America, his lust for El Dorado undiminished. Along the way he plundered some Spanish silver ships, defying James's orders. It was a fatal mistake, for England had made peace with Spain. Raleigh lost his head.

James I did not want to harry the king of Spain; he wanted to imitate him. The Stuarts were even more determined than the Tudors to enlarge the sphere of royal power. There would be no room in America for a warrior nobility of conquistadors, no room for a feudal fiefdom ruled by the likes of Raleigh or Gilbert. Instead, there would be English colonies in America like the new outpost of Jamestown, planted on the Chesapeake Bay in Virginia in 1607. There would be profitable plantations and other bold enterprises, enriching English royalty and managed by loyal, efficient bureaucrats. Settling America would strengthen English monarchs, paving their path to greater power, just as the dominions of Mexico and Peru had enlarged the authority of the Spanish crown. America would be the making of kings and queens.

Or would it? For some in Europe, weary of freebooting conquistadors and sea rovers, the order and security that Crown rule and centralized states promoted in western Europe would be enough. But others, the desperate and idealistic men and women who sailed to the world that lay before them, would want more.

 **c h a p t e r   s u m m a r y**

During the late fifteenth century, Europeans made their first sustained contact with North and South America.

- A combination of technological advances, the rise of new trade networks and techniques, and increased political centralization made Europe's expansion overseas possible.

- The pressure of Europe's growing population on its limited resources of land and food made expansion overseas essential.

- At the time of contact, native cultures in the Americas ranged from the hunting and gathering societies of the Great Plains to the Aztecs in Mesoamerica, a society similar in many ways to that of sixteenth-century Europe.

- Spain took the lead in exploring and colonizing the Americas, consolidating a vast and profitable empire of its own in the place of Aztec and Inca civilizations.

- Both divisions within Indian empires and the devastating effects of European diseases made Spanish conquest possible.

- England, fearful of Spain's power, did not turn its attention to exploration and colonization until the 1570s and 1580s.

- England's merchants and gentry in search of new markets and land lent support to colonizing ventures, although early efforts, such as those at Roanoke, failed.

 For quizzes and a variety of interactive resources, visit the book's Online Learning Center at www.mhhe.com/davidsonconcise3

SIGNIFICANT EVENTS

ca. 50,000–25,000 B.P. (before the present)	First Asian penetration of the Americas
ca. 1300 C.E.	Rise of the Aztec empire
1271–1295	Marco Polo travels to China from Italy
1347	First outbreak of the Black Death
1420s	Portuguese settlements in the Atlantic islands
1488	Dias rounds the tip of Africa
1492	Columbus discovers America
1497	John Cabot discovers Newfoundland
1498	da Gama reaches India
1517	Luther posts his 95 theses
1519–1522	Magellan circumnavigates the globe
1521	Tenochtitlán surrenders to Cortés
1540	Discovery of silver in Mexico and Peru
1558	Elizabeth I becomes queen of England
1565	England begins its conquest of Ireland
1576–1578	Frobisher searches for Northwest Passage
1583	Gilbert's quest for a North American colony
1584–1590	Roanoke voyages

In the year 1617, as Europeans counted time, on a bay they called the Chesapeake, in a land they named Virginia, an old Indian chief surveyed his domain. It had all worked according to plan, and Powhatan, leader of the Pamunkeys, had laid his plans carefully. While in his prime, the tall, robust man had drawn some 30 smaller tribes along the Virginia coast into a powerful confederacy.

By 1607 Powhatan's confederacy numbered nearly 9000, a political alliance that had overcome formidable obstacles. The natives of Virginia, like the other peoples who inhabited the length of eastern North America, were seminomadic. They lived for most of the year in small villages and ranged over tribal hunting and fishing grounds, following the game from one season to the next. Rivalries over trade, territorial boundaries, and leadership had often erupted into armed conflict. Some coastal tribes had fiercely resisted Powhatan's efforts to incorporate them; other tribes to the west still threatened the security of his confederacy. After 1607 Powhatan was forced to take into account yet another tribe. The English, as this new people called themselves, came by sea, followed a river deep into his territory, and built a fort on a swampy, mosquito-infested site that they called Jamestown.

The First Century of Settlement in the Colonial South
(1600–1750)

preview • Instability and conflict wracked England's southern colonies for most of the seventeenth century. But by 1720 one-crop plantation economies dominated the region—tobacco in the Chesapeake, rice in the Carolinas, sugar in the Caribbean. In the process, the original system of labor, based on white indentured servitude, gave way to the slave labor fueled by a massive importation of Africans. Spain too extended its empire in Florida and New Mexico.

Powhatan's confederacy

Powhatan was not frightened. The English did have larger boats and louder, more deadly weapons. But the Indians quickly learned how to use guns, and they vastly outnumbered the English, an inferior race who seemed unlikely to live long and prosper in Powhatan's land. They could not even manage to feed themselves from the rich resources of the Chesapeake. With bows and arrows, spears and nets, Indian men brought in an abundance of meat and fish. The fields tended by Indian women yielded crops of corn, beans, squash, and melon, and edible nuts and fruits grew wild. Still the English starved, and not just during the first months of their settlement but for several years after.

Powhatan could understand why the English refused to grow food. Cultivating crops, like building houses, or making clothing, pottery, and baskets, or caring for children, was women's work, and the English settlement included no women until two arrived in the fall of 1608. Yet even after more women came, the English still starved, and they expected—no, they demanded—that the Indians supply them with food.

Most incredible to Powhatan was that the inferior English considered themselves a superior people. They boasted constantly about the power of their god—they had only one—and denounced the Indians' "devil-worship" of "false gods." The English also boasted without end about the power of their king, James I, who expected Powhatan to become his vassal. The English had even planned a "coronation" to crown Powhatan as a "subject king."

It was inconceivable to Powhatan that he should bow before this King James, the ruler of so savage a race. When the Indians made war, they killed the male warriors of rival tribes but adopted their women and children. But when Powhatan's people withheld food or defended their land from these invaders, the English retaliated by murdering Indian women and children. Worse, the English could not

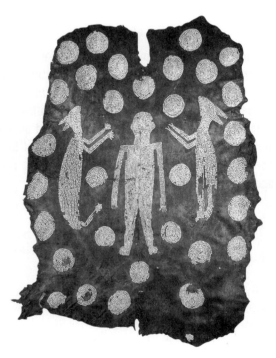

When the English attempted to crown Powhatan as a subject king, he may have sent King James I this cloak as a reciprocal present. Made from four tanned deerskins, the mantle is decorated with many small marine shells sewn into designs. In addition to human and animal figures, the cloak has 34 roundlets that may represent the Indian districts under Powhatan's control.

even keep order within their own tribe. Too many of them wanted to be chiefs, and they squabbled constantly.

Only one man, a brash fellow called Captain John Smith, had briefly been able to bring order to the English settlement. Powhatan granted him a grudging respect, though Smith would have enslaved the Indians if it had been in his power. But Smith returned to England in 1609 after being injured when some of the white people's gunpowder blew up by mistake. Thereafter the English returned to squabbling and starving. Small wonder that some English had deserted their settlement to live among Powhatan's people. Anyone could see the superiority of Indian culture to English ways.

The temptation to wipe out the helpless, troublesome, arrogant tribe of English—or simply to let them starve—had been almost overwhelming. But Powhatan allowed the English to survive because he had decided that even these barbaric people had their uses. English labor, English trading goods, and, **Powhatan's strategy** most important, English guns would help him quell resistance within his confederacy and subdue his Indian rivals in the west. In 1614 Powhatan cemented his claim on the English and their weapons with the marriage between his favorite child, Pocahontas, and a white settler, John Rolfe.

By 1617 events had vindicated Powhatan's strategy of tolerating the English. His empire flourished, ready to be passed on to his brother, Opechancanough. Powhatan's people still outnumbered the English, who seldom starved outright now but continued to fight among themselves and sicken and die. Only one thing had changed in the Chesapeake by 1617: the English were clearing woodland along the rivers and planting tobacco.

That was the doing of Powhatan's son-in-law, Rolfe, a man as strange as any of his tribe, all of them eager to store up wealth and worldly goods. Rolfe had been obsessed with finding a crop that could be grown in Virginia and then sold for gain across the sea. When he succeeded by growing tobacco, other English followed his lead. Odder still, not women but men tended the tobacco fields. Here was more evidence of English inferiority. Men wasted long hours laboring when they might supply their needs with far less effort.

In 1617 Powhatan, ruler of the Pamunkeys, surveyed his empire, and sometime in that year, he looked no longer. He had lived long enough to see the tobacco fields lining the riverbanks, straddling the charred stumps of felled trees. But he died believing that he had bent the English to his purposes—died before those stinking tobacco weeds spread over the length of his land and sent his hard-won empire up in smoke.

ENGLISH SOCIETY ON THE CHESAPEAKE

While the chief of the Chesapeake was expanding his dominions and consolidating his power, the king of England was doing the same. Just as Spain had begun to profit from the riches of silver mines and sugar plantations, James I of England hoped that the wealth and power of his kingdom would grow as English colonists settled the American coasts north of Spain's empire. The first newcomers clustered along the many bays of the Chesapeake as well as in a few island outposts of the Caribbean. A generation later, during the 1670s and 1680s, colonists from the Caribbean hopscotched to the mainland to found colonies along the Carolina coast. As the English struggled to put down roots, the ambitions of merchants and planters and kings clashed with the conflicting goals of Indian leaders like Powhatan.

The result was a chaotic and deadly landscape. During much of the seventeenth century, ambitious colonists scrambled to control the land and the labor needed to secure profits from tobacco, sugar, and rice. Only after decades of uncertainty, violence, and high mortality did the colonies along the southern Atlantic crescent begin to prosper. Even then, stability was bought at a high price. In order to supply the workers so desperately sought by plantation owners, English colonists introduced the institution of slavery.

Instability of the southern colonies

The Mercantilist Impulse

When European powers established permanent colonies in America, they were putting into practice a theory about how best to attain national wealth and influence.

Mercantilism

That idea, which guided Europe's commercial expansion for 200 years, was named "mercantilism" by the eighteenth-century economist Adam Smith. Mercantilists called for the state to regulate and protect industry and commerce. Their objective was to enrich the nation by fostering a favorable balance of trade. Once the value of exports exceeded the cost of imports, they theorized, gold and silver would flow into home ports.

If a nation could dispense entirely with imports from other countries, so much the better, and it was here that the idea of colonies entered the mercantilist scheme. Colonial producers would supply raw materials that the mother country could not produce, while colonial consumers swelled demand for the finished goods and financial services that the mother country could provide.

Mercantilist notions appealed to Europe's monarchs. A thriving trade meant that more taxes and customs duties would fill royal coffers, increasing royal power. That logic led James I to lend his approval to the private venture that brought the first white settlers to the Chesapeake.

The Virginia Company

In 1606 the king granted a charter to a number of English merchants, gentlemen, and aristocrats, incorporating them as the Virginia Company of London. The members of the new joint stock company sold stock in their venture to English investors as well as awarding a share to those willing to settle in Virginia at their own expense. With the proceeds from the sale of stock, the company planned to send to

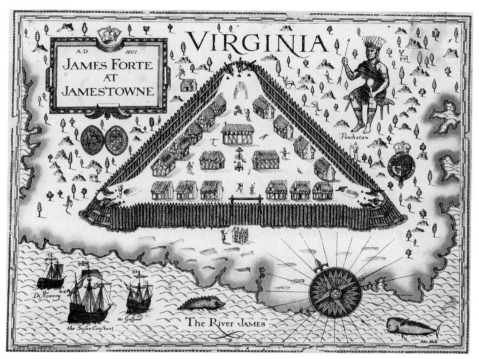

The Jamestown fort's heavy palisades and its strategic location upriver and some distance inland underscore the colonists' concern for defense—as does the imposing figure of Powhatan seated at the right.

Virginia hundreds of poor and unemployed people as well as scores of skilled craft-workers. These laborers were to serve the company for seven years in return for their passage, pooling their efforts to produce any commodities that would return a profit to stockholders. In the spring of 1607 the first expedition dispatched by the Virginia Company, 104 men and boys, founded Jamestown.

Making the first of many mistakes, Jamestown's settlers pitched their fort on an inland peninsula in order to prevent a surprise attack from the Spanish. Unfortunately, the marshy, thickly wooded site served as an ideal breeding ground for malaria. The Virginia Company settlers, weakened by bouts of malaria and then beset by dysentery, typhoid, and yellow fever, died by the scores.

Jamestown's problems

Even before sickness took its toll, many of Jamestown's first settlers had little taste for labor. The gentlemen of the expedition expected to lead rather than to work, while most other members of the early colonizing parties were gentlemen's servants and craftworkers who knew nothing about growing crops. The settlers resorted to bullying Powhatan's people for food. Many colonists suffered from malnutrition, which heightened their susceptibility to disease. Only 60 of Jamestown's 500 inhabitants lived through the winter of 1609–1610, known as the "starving time." Some desperate colonists unearthed and ate corpses; one settler even butchered his wife.

Reports of starvation and staggering death rates stiffened the Virginia Company's resolve: in 1611 it imposed on the colonists what amounted to martial law. Company officials in Virginia organized the settlers into work gangs and severely punished the lazy and the disorderly. Still the company failed to turn a profit. And after 1617, skirmishes with the Indians became more brutal and frequent, as rows of tobacco plants steadily invaded tribal lands.

Reform and a Boom in Tobacco

Desperate to salvage their investment, Virginia Company managers in 1618 set in place sweeping reforms. To attract more capital and colonists, the company established a "headright" system for granting land to individuals. Those already settled in the colony received 100 acres apiece. New settlers each received 50 acres, and anyone who paid the passage of other immigrants to Virginia—either family members or servants—received 50 acres per "head." The company also abolished martial law, allowing the planters to elect a representative assembly. Along with a governor and an advisory council appointed by the company, the House of Burgesses had the authority to make laws for the colony. It met for the first time in 1619, beginning what would become a strong tradition of representative government in the English colonies.

Headrights

The new measures met with immediate success. The free and unfree laborers who poured into Virginia during the 1620s made up the first wave of an English migration to the Chesapeake that numbered between 130,000 and 150,000 over the seventeenth century. Drawn from the ranks of ordinary English working people, the immigrants were largely men, outnumbering women by six to one. Most were young, ranging in age from 15 to 24. Because of their youth, most lacked skills or wealth. Some of those who came to the Chesapeake as free immigrants prospered, because during the 1620s the demand for tobacco soared and prices spiked in Europe. But for the vast majority of settlers—and, specifically, the three-quarters of all immigrants who arrived in the Chesapeake as indentured servants—the future was far grimmer.

For most new servants, the crossing to Virginia was simply the last of many moves made in the hope of finding work. Although England's population had been rising since the middle of the fifteenth century, the demand for farm laborers was falling because many landowners were converting croplands into pastures for sheep. The search for work pushed young men and women out of their villages, sending them through the countryside and then into the cities. Down and out in London, Bristol, or Liverpool, some chanced a move to America by signing indentures. Pamphlets promoting immigration promised abundant land and quick riches once servants had finished their terms of four to seven years.

Indentured servants

Even the most skeptical immigrants were shocked at what they found. The death rate in Virginia during the 1620s was higher than that of England during times of epidemic disease. The life expectancy for Chesapeake men who reached the age of 20 was a mere 48 years; for women it was lower still. Servants fared worst of all, since malnutrition, overwork, and abuse made them vulnerable to disease. As masters scrambled to make quick profits, they extracted the maximum amount of work before death carried off their laborers. An estimated 40 percent of servants did not survive to the end of their indentured terms.

The expanding cultivation of tobacco also claimed many lives by putting unbearable pressure on Indian land. After Powhatan's death in 1617, leadership of the confederacy passed to Opechancanough, who watched, year after year, as the tobacco mania grew. In March 1622 he coordinated a sweeping attack on white settlements that killed about one-fifth of Virginia's white population. Swift English retaliation wiped out whole tribes and cut down an entire generation of young Indian men.

War with the confederacy

News of the Indian war jolted English investors into determining the true state of their Virginia venture. It came to light that, despite the tobacco boom, the Virginia Company was plunging toward bankruptcy. Nor was that the worst news. Stockholders discovered that over 3000 immigrants had not survived the brutal conditions of Chesapeake life. An investigation by James I brought out the grisly truth, causing the king to dissolve the Virginia Company and take control of the colony himself in 1624. Henceforth Virginia would be governed as a royal colony.

Settling Down in the Chesapeake

During the 1630s and 1640s the fever of the tobacco boom broke, and a more settled social and political life emerged in Virginia. The settlers who had become wealthy by exploiting servant labor now began to acquire political power. They established local bases of influence in Virginia's counties, serving as justices of the peace and sheriffs, maintaining roads and bridges, collecting taxes, and supervising local elections. They organized all able-bodied adult males into militias for local defense and sat on vestries, the governing bodies of local Anglican parishes, hiring the handful of clergy who came to Virginia and providing for the neighborhood poor.

The biggest tobacco planters of each county also dominated colony politics. Even though King James had replaced the Virginia Company's government with his own royal administration, the colony's elected assembly continued making laws for the colony. Along with the council (the upper house of the legislature), the assembly resisted interference in Virginia's affairs from the royal governor, the king's representative.

The colony's growing stability was reflected in improved conditions for less powerful Virginians. Although servants still streamed into the colony, the price of

A Virginia Settler Describes the Indian War of 1622 to Officials in England

Such was the treacherous dissumulation of that people who then had contrived our destruction, that even two dayes before the Massacre, some of our men were guided thorow [through] the woods by them in safety . . . as well on the Friday morning (the fatal day) of the 22 of March . . . they came unarmed into our houses, without Bowes or arrowes, or other weapons, with Deere, Turkies, Fish, Furres, and other provisions, to sell and trucke with us, for glasse, beades, and other trifles: yea in some places sate downe at Breakfast with our people at their tables, whom immediately with their owne tooles and weapons, eyther laid downe, or standing in their houses, they basely and barbarously murthered [murdered], not sparing eyther age or sexe, man, woman, or childe. . . . In which manner they also slew many of our people then at their severall workes and husbandries in the fields . . . some in planting Corne and Tobacco, some in gardening, some in making Bricke, building, sawing, and other kindes of husbandry, they well knowing in what places and quarters each of our men were, in regard of their daily familiarity, and resort to us for trading and other negotiations, which the more willingly was by us continued and cherished for the desire we had of effecting that great masterpeece of workes, their conversion. And by this meanes that fatall Friday morning, there fell under the bloudy and barbarous hands of that perfidious and inhumane people, contrary to all lawes of God and men, of Nature and Nations, three hundred forty seven men, women and children, most by their owne weapons; and not being content with taking away life alone, they fell after again upon the dead, making as well as they could, a fresh murder, defacing, dragging and mangling the dead carkasses into many pieces, and carrying some parts away in derision, with base and brutish triumph.

Sources: Edward Waterhouse, *A Declaration of the State of the Colonie and Affaires in Virginia* (1622). Susan Myra Kingsbury, ed., *The Records of the Virginia Company of London*, (Washington, D.C., 1906–1935) III, pp. 459–556.

Decline in mortality rates

tobacco leveled off. That meant planters were less likely to drive their servants to death in search of overnight fortunes. As tobacco became less profitable, planters raised more corn and cattle, and mortality rates declined as food supplies rose. Freed servants who survived their indentures usually worked a few more years as hired hands or tenant farmers. In doing so, most managed to save enough money to buy their own land and become independent planters. For women who survived servitude, prospects were even better. With wives at a premium, single women stood a good chance of improving their status by marriage. By 1650 Virginia could boast about 15,000 inhabitants, with more servants and free immigrants coming to the colony every year.

The Founding of Maryland and the Renewal of Indian Wars

Unlike Virginia, which was first settled by a private corporation and later converted into a royal colony, Maryland was founded by a single aristocratic family, the Calverts. Indeed, it was the first of several such "proprietary" colonies given by English monarchs to loyal followers. Thus in 1632, Maryland became the private preserve of the Calverts. They held absolute authority to dispose of 10 million acres of land, administer justice, and establish a civil government. All of these powers they exercised, granting estates, or "manors," to their friends and dividing other holdings into smaller farms for ordinary immigrants. From all of these "tenants"—that is, every settler in the colony—the Calverts collected "quitrents" every year, fees for use of the land. The Calverts appointed a governor and a council to oversee their own interests, while allowing the largest landowners to dispense local justice in manorial courts and make laws for the entire colony in a representative assembly.

`Proprietary colonies`

Virginians liked nothing at all about their neighbors in the northerly bays of the Chesapeake. To begin with, the Calvert family was Catholic and had extended complete religious freedom to all Christians, making Maryland a haven for Catholics. Worse, the Marylanders were a source of economic competition. Two thousand inhabitants had settled on Calvert holdings by 1640, virtually all of them planting tobacco on land coveted by the Virginians.

Another obstacle to Virginia's expansion was the remnant of the Powhatan confederacy, still determined to repel white invaders. Opechancanough led a new generation of Indians into battle in 1644 against the encroaching Virginia planters. The hostilities inflicted as many casualties on both sides as the fighting in 1622.

Changes in English Policy in the Chesapeake

Throughout the 1630s and 1640s colonial affairs drew little concern from royal officials. England itself had become engulfed by first a political crisis and then a civil war.

The conflict grew out of efforts by both James I and Charles I (who succeeded his father in 1625) to expand their royal power and rule the nation without the nuisance of having to consult Parliament. When Parliament condemned Charles for usurping its power to raise money, he simply dissolved that body in 1629. But when the Scots invaded England in 1639, Charles found he could raise funds to pay for an army only by calling Parliament back into session. By then, many of the merchants and landed gentlemen who were members had decided that the Stuart kings themselves might be dispensable. In 1642 Parliament and its Puritan allies squared off against Charles I and his royalist supporters, defeated them in battle, and, in 1649, beheaded the king. England became a republic ruled by Oliver Cromwell, the man who had led Parliament's army.

`The English Civil War`

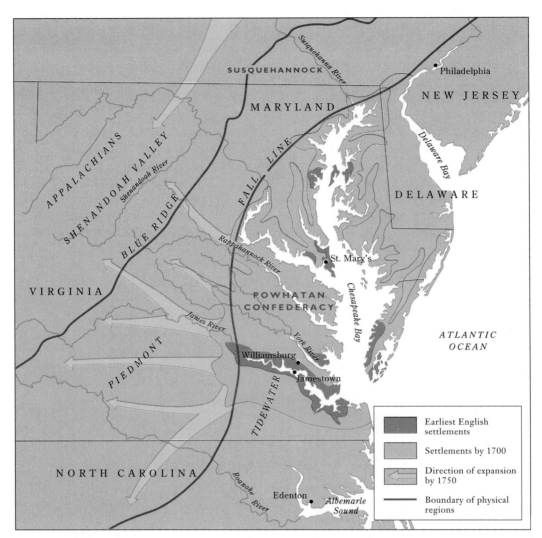

COLONIES OF THE CHESAPEAKE   Settlements in Virginia and Maryland spread out along the many bays of the Chesapeake, where tobacco could easily be loaded from plantation wharves. The fall line on rivers, dividing the Tidewater and Piedmont regions, determined the extent of commercial agriculture, since ships could not pick up exports beyond that point.

In truth, Cromwell's "republic" more accurately resembled a military dictatorship. After his death, most English were happy to see their throne restored in 1660 to Charles II, the son of the beheaded king. And the new king was determined to ensure that not only his subjects at home but his American colonies abroad contributed to England's prosperity. His colonial policy was reflected in a series of regulations known as the Navigation Acts.

The first, passed by Parliament in 1660, gave England and English colonial merchants a monopoly on the shipping and marketing of all colonial goods. It also ordered that the colonies could export certain "enumerated commodities" only to England or other British ports. These goods included sugar, tobacco, cotton, ginger, and indigo (a blue dye). In 1663 Parliament added another regulation, giving British merchants a virtual monopoly on the sale of European manufactured goods to Americans by requiring that most imports going to the colonies had to pass through England. In 1673 a third Navigation Act placed duties on the coastal trade of the American colonies and provided for customs officials to collect tariffs and enforce commercial regulations.

The Navigation Acts

CHESAPEAKE SOCIETY IN CRISIS

The regulations of trade put in place by Restoration kings Charles II and James II and their Parliaments had a decisive impact on colonials. Accustomed to conducting their affairs as they pleased—and they were often pleased to trade with the Dutch—Chesapeake planters chafed under the Navigation Acts. What was worse, the new restrictions came at the same time as a downturn in tobacco prices. In the effort to consolidate its empire, England unintentionally worsened the economic and social difficulties of Chesapeake society.

The Conditions of Unrest

The Chesapeake colonies were heading for trouble partly because of their success. As inhabitants had started to live longer, more servants survived their terms of service and set up as independent tobacco planters. More planters meant more production, and overproduction sent the price of tobacco plummeting, especially between 1660 and 1680. To maintain their advantage, the biggest planters bought up all the prime property along the coast, forcing newly freed servants to become tenants or to settle on unclaimed land in the interior. Either way, poorer men lost. Depending on bigger planters for land and credit made the small farmers vulnerable to debt. Moving to the frontier made them vulnerable to Indian attack.

Diminishing opportunities

The slim resources of small planters were stretched even thinner, not only from county taxes but also from export duties on tobacco paid under the Navigation Acts. During the hard times after 1660, many small planters fell deeply into debt, and some were forced back into servitude. By 1676 one-quarter of Virginia's free white men were landless. Many former servants were unable to gain a foothold even as tenants.

Diminishing opportunity in the 1660s and 1670s provided the tinder for unrest in Virginia. As the discontent of poor men mounted, so did the worries of big planters. The assembly of the colony lengthened terms of servitude, hoping to limit the number of servants entering the free population. It curbed the political rights of landless men, hoping to stifle opposition by depriving them of the vote. But these measures only set off a spate of mutinies among servants and protests over rising taxes among small planters.

Bacon's Rebellion and Coode's Rebellion

Those tensions came to a head in 1676 when civil war erupted. The immediate catalyst of the rebellion was renewed skirmishing between whites expanding westward and Indians. Virginia's royal governor, William Berkeley, favored building forts to contain the Indian threat, but frontier farmers opposed his plan as an expensive and ineffective way to defend their scattered plantations. As they clamored for an expedition to punish the Indians, Nathaniel Bacon stepped forward to lead it.

Wealthy and well connected, Bacon had arrived recently from England, expecting to receive every favor from the governor—including permission to trade with the Indians from his frontier plantation. But Berkeley and a few select friends already held a monopoly on the Indian trade. When they declined to include Bacon, he took up the cause of his poorer frontier neighbors against their common enemy, the governor. Other recent, well-to-do immigrants who resented being excluded from Berkeley's circle of power and patronage also joined Bacon.

`Nathaniel Bacon`

In the summer of 1676 Bacon marched into Jamestown with a body of armed men and bullied the assembly into approving his expedition to kill Indians. While Bacon carried out that grisly business, slaughtering friendly as well as hostile tribes, Berkeley rallied his supporters and declared Bacon a rebel. Bacon retaliated by turning his forces against those led by the governor. Both sides sought allies by offering freedom to servants and slaves willing to join their ranks. Many were willing: for months the followers of Bacon and Berkeley plundered one another's plantations. In September 1676 Bacon reduced Jamestown itself to a mound of ashes. It was only his death from dysentery a month later that snuffed out the rebellion.

Political upheaval also shook Maryland, where colonists had long resented the Calverts' rule. As proprietors, the Calverts and their favorites monopolized political offices, just as Berkeley's circle had in Virginia. Well-to-do planters wanted a share of the power. Smaller farmers, like those in Virginia, wanted a less expensive and more representative government. Compounding the tensions were religious differences: the Calverts and their friends were Catholic, but other colonists, including its most successful planters, were Protestant.

`Coode's Rebellion`

The unrest among Maryland's discontented planters peaked in July 1689. A former member of the assembly, John Coode, gathered an army, captured the proprietary governor, and then took his grievances to authorities in England. There Coode received a sympathetic hearing.

The Calverts' charter was revoked and not restored until 1715, by which time the family had become Protestant.

After 1690 rich planters in both Chesapeake colonies fought among themselves less and cooperated more. In Virginia older leaders and newer arrivals divided the spoils of political office. In Maryland Protestants and Catholics shared power and privilege. Those arrangements ensured that no future Bacon or Coode would mobilize restless gentlemen against the government. By acting together in legislative assemblies, they managed to curb the power of royal and proprietary governors for decades.

Growing stability

But the greater unity among the Chesapeake's leading families did little to ease that region's most fundamental problem, which was the sharp inequality of white society. The gulf between rich and poor planters, which had been etched ever more deeply by the troubled tobacco economy, persisted long after the rebellions of Bacon and Coode. All that saved white society in the Chesapeake from renewed crisis and conflict was the growth of black slavery.

From Servitude to Slavery

Like the tobacco plants that spread across Powhatan's land, a labor system based on slavery had not figured in the first plans for the Chesapeake. Both early promoters and planters preferred buying English servants to importing alien African slaves. Black slaves, because they served for life, were more expensive than white workers, who served only for several years. Since neither white nor black emigrants lived long, cheaper servant labor was the logical choice. The black population of the Chesapeake remained small for most of the seventeenth century, comprising just 5 percent of all inhabitants in 1675.

The earliest record of Africans in Virginia dates from 1619, probably brought by the Dutch, who dominated the slave trade until the middle of the eighteenth century. The lives of those newcomers resembled the lot of white servants, with whom they shared harsh work routines and living conditions. White and black bound laborers socialized with each other and formed sexual liaisons. They conspired to steal from their masters and

The lives of servants and slaves

ran away together, and if caught, they endured similar punishments. There was more common ground: many of the first black settlers did not arrive directly from Africa but came from the Caribbean, where some had learned English and adopted Christian beliefs. And not all were slaves: some were indentured servants, and a handful were free.

A number of changes after 1680 caused planters to invest more heavily in slaves than in servants. First, declining mortality rates in the Chesapeake made slaves the more profitable investment. Although slaves were more expensive than servants, planters could now expect to get many years of work from their bondspeople. Equally important, masters would have title to the children that slaves would now live long enough to have. At the same time, the influx of white servants was falling off just as the pool of available black labor was expanding. When the Royal Africa Company lost its monopoly on the English slave trade in 1698, other merchants entered the market. The number of Africans sold by British dealers swelled to 20,000 annually.

Africa and the Atlantic Slave Trade

The rising demand for slaves from the Chesapeake—and later, from all the colonies of mainland North America—played only a small part in spurring the growth of the Atlantic slave trade. Rather, it was the spread of plantation economies in the Caribbean and South America that created and sustained the traffic in human beings. Between the mid-fifteenth and late nineteenth centuries, perhaps as many as 13 million men, women, and children crossed the Atlantic as slaves—a number not equaled by voluntary European migrants to the Americas until as late as the 1880s. For a century after Columbus's arrival, the traffic in slaves to the Americas had numbered a few thousand annually. But as sugar cultivation steadily prospered after 1600, slave imports rose to 19,000 a year during the seventeenth century and mushroomed to 60,000 a year during the eighteenth century. All told, as many as 21 million people were captured in West Africa between 1700 and 1850: some 9 million among them entered the Americas as slaves, but millions died before or during the Atlantic crossing, and as many as 7 million remained slaves in Africa.

The rapid growth of the Atlantic slave trade transformed not only the Americas but also Africa. Slavery became more widespread within West African society, and slave trading more central to its domestic and international commerce. Most important, the African merchants and political leaders who were most deeply invested in the slave trade used their profits for political advantage—to build new chiefdoms and states. Their ambitions and the greed of European slave dealers drew an increasingly large number of Africans, particularly people living in the interior, into slavery's web. By the late seventeenth century, Africans being sold into slavery were no longer only those who had put themselves at risk by committing crimes, running into debt, or voicing unpopular political and religious views. The larger number were instead captives taken by soldiers or kidnappers in raids launched specifically to acquire prisoners for the slave trade. During the decades after 1680, captives coming directly from Africa made up more than 80 percent of all new slaves entering the Chesapeake and the rest of mainland North America. Many were shipped from the coast of Africa that Portuguese explorers had first probed, between the Senegal and Niger rivers, and most of the rest from Angola, farther south.

> Growth of slave trade within Africa

Seized by other Africans, captives were yoked together at the neck and marched hundreds of miles through the interiors to coastal forts or other outposts along the Atlantic. There, they were penned in hundreds of prisons, in lots of anywhere from twenty or thirty to more than a thousand.

Worse than the imprisonment was the voyage itself: the so-called Middle Passage, a journey of 500 miles across the Atlantic to America. As many as 200 black

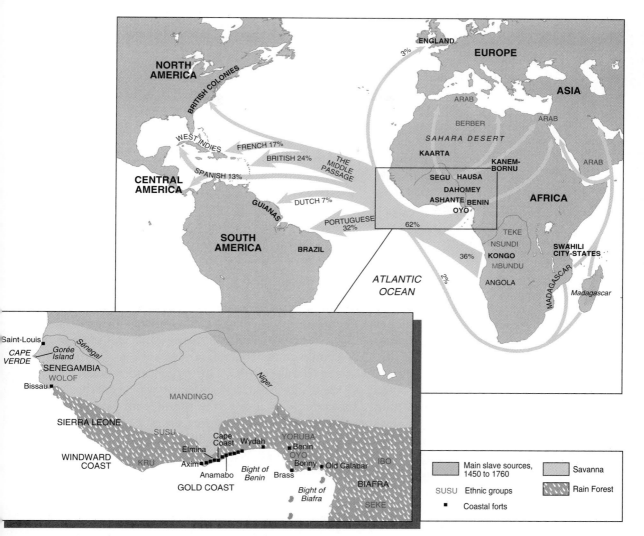

THE AFRICAN TRANSATLANTIC SLAVE TRADE, 1450–1760   Toward the end of the seventeenth century, Chesapeake and Carolina planters began importing increasing numbers of slaves. In Africa, the center of that trade lay along a mountainous region known as the Gold Coast, where over a hundred European trading posts and forts funneled the trade. Unlike most of the rest of West Africa's shoreline, the Gold Coast had very little dense rain forest. Despite the heavy trade, only about 4 percent of the total transatlantic slave trade went to North America.

men, women, and children were packed below decks, squeezed onto platforms built in tiers spaced so close that sitting upright was impossible. Slaves were taken out and forced to exercise for their health for a few hours each day; the rest of the day, the sun beat down and the heat below decks was "so excessive," one voyager recalled, that the doctors who went below to examine slaves "would faint away, and the candles would not burn." At night, the

Middle Passage

slaves "were often heard making a howling melancholy kind of noise, something expressive of extreme anguish," noted a doctor aboard another ship. When he made inquiries, he discovered that the slaves, while asleep, had dreamed "that they were back in their own country again, amongst their families and friends; when they woke up to find themselves in reality on a slave ship they began to bay and shriek."

After the numb, exhausted survivors of the Middle Passage reached American ports, they faced more challenges to staying alive. The first year in the colonies was the most deadly for new, unseasoned slaves. The sickle cell genetic trait gave black Africans a greater immunity than white Europeans had to malaria, but slaves were highly susceptible to respiratory infections. One-quarter of all Africans died during their first year in the Chesapeake, and among Carolina and Caribbean slaves, mortality rates were even higher. In addition to the new disease environment, Africans were forced to adapt to lives without freedom in a wholly unfamiliar country and culture.

A Changing Chesapeake Society

Exchanging a labor system based on servitude for one based on slavery transformed the character of Chesapeake society. Most obviously, the number of black Virginians rose sharply. By 1740, 40 percent of all Virginians were black, and most were African-born. Unlike black men and women who had arrived earlier, they had little familiarity with English language and culture. This larger, more distinctively African community was also locked into a slave system that was becoming ever more rigid and demeaning. By the late decades of the seventeenth century, laws were in place making it more difficult for masters to free slaves. Other legislation systematically separated the races by prohibiting free black settlers from owning white servants and by outlawing interracial marriages and sexual relationships. The legal code encouraged white contempt for black Virginians in a variety of other ways. While masters were prohibited from whipping their white servants on the bare back, slaves had no such protection. And "any Negro that shall presume to strike any white" was to receive 30 lashes for that rash act.

The new laws both reflected and encouraged racism among white colonists of all classes. Deepening racial hatred, in turn, made it unlikely that poor white planters, tenants, and servants would ever join with poor black slaves to challenge the privilege of great planters. Instead of identifying with the plight of the slaves, the Chesapeake's poorer white residents considered black Virginians their natural inferiors. They could pride themselves on sharing with wealthy white gentlemen the same skin color and on being their equals in the eyes of the law.

Racism

The leaders of the Chesapeake colonies cultivated unity among white inhabitants by improving economic prospects for freed servants and lesser planters. The Virginia assembly lowered taxes, allowing small planters to keep more of their earnings. New laws also gave most

Opportunities for white settlers

white male Virginians a vote in elections, allowing them an outlet to express their grievances. Economic trends toward the end of the seventeenth century contributed to the greater prosperity of small planters, as tobacco prices rose slightly and then stabilized. As a result of Bacon's savage campaign against the Virginia Indians, new land on the frontier became available. Even the domestic lives of ordinary men improved as the numbers of men and women in the white population evened out around the turn of the century.

After 1700 the Chesapeake evolved into a more stable society. Virginia and Maryland became colonies of farming families, most of them headed by small planters who owned between 50 and 200 acres. These families held no slaves, or at most two or three. And they accepted, usually without question, the social and political leadership of their acknowledged "superiors," great planters who styled themselves the "gentry."

The Chesapeake Gentry

The new Chesapeake gentry were the sons of well-to-do London merchant families, many of whom had intermarried with England's landed gentry. For both classes Virginia offered new prospects for land and commercial wealth. Enterprising fathers sent their sons to the Chesapeake between 1640 and 1670 to establish family interests in America by creating vast plantations.

George Booth, the son of a wealthy planter family in Gloucester County, Virginia, was being raised for mastery. The young man's self-assured stance, the bow and arrows, the dog at his feet clutching the kill, the classical busts of women flanking his figure, and his family estate in the distance all suggest the gentry's concern for controlling the natural and social worlds.

The gentry's fortunes rested in part on the cultivation of tobacco on thousands of acres by hundreds of slaves. But the leading planters made even more money by marketing the tobacco of their humbler neighbors, selling them manufactured goods, supplying them with medical and legal services, lending money, and hiring out slaves. Unlike the rough-hewn barons of the early tobacco boom, the gentry's profit did not depend on wringing work from poor whites. It hinged instead on wringing work from black slaves while converting their white "inferiors" into modestly prosperous small planters and paying clients.

The basis of gentry power

But the gentry wanted more than money: they wanted the respect of lesser whites. On election days, when voters in the county assembled, each approached in his turn the gentleman candidate he preferred, publicly announced his vote, and sometimes made a brief, flattering speech about his choice. At militia musters, when every able-bodied man in the county gathered, gentlemen officers led the military drills. On court days, defendants and plaintiffs testified before gentlemen justices of the peace, bedecked in wigs and robes and seated on raised benches. And every Sunday, when many in the county came to worship at the Anglican chapel, families filed into the church in order of their social rank, with the gentlemen vestry heading the procession. The courthouse and church, the tavern and training field—all served as theaters in which the new Chesapeake gentry dramatized their superiority and lesser men deferred.

If anything, the evolving plantation societies of Virginia and Maryland were becoming even more unequal, because the rise of slavery sharpened economic distinctions within the white population. Those who owned slaves enjoyed a decided economic edge over those who did not. But while extreme economic inequality persisted, social tension between richer and poorer white settlers lessened. As racism unified all classes within white society and as economic and political gains eased discontent among small planters, the changing character of the Chesapeake's leaders also reduced social friction. The unscrupulous scoundrels who once dominated society had been replaced by gentlemen planters who fancied themselves the "fathers" of their plantations and neighborhoods.

Stability in the Chesapeake

FROM THE CARIBBEAN TO THE CAROLINAS

During the same decade that the English invaded Powhatan's land, they began to colonize the Caribbean. A century earlier, Columbus had charted the route: ships picked up the trade winds off Madeira and the Canary Islands and headed west across the Atlantic to paradise. At journey's end the surf broke over shores rimmed with white sand beaches that rose sharply to coral terraces, then to broad plateaus or mountain peaks shrouded in rain forests.

Paradise was lost to the Indians of the Caribbean, or at least to those few remaining alive. European diseases, combined with Spanish exploitation, had eliminated virtually all the natives of Hispaniola by the 1520s. Over the next century those living in Cuba, Puerto Rico, the Bahamas, the Lesser Antilles, and Jamaica would follow. And the "paradise" that remained was filled with plants and animals that would have been strange to natives only a century earlier. Hogs and cattle, now wild, had been imported by Europeans, as had figs, oranges, pomegranates, and African yams. That ecological migration of flora and fauna would continue to transform the Americas in the century to come.

Transformation of the Caribbean

Paradise was lost to the English as well. At first they came to the Caribbean intending not to colonize but to steal from the Spanish. Even after 1604 when some English settled on the islands, few intended to stay. Yet not only did the English establish permanent plantation colonies in the West Indies, their Caribbean settlements became the jumping-off points for a new colony on the North American mainland, South Carolina. Because of the strong West Indian influence, South Carolina developed a social order in some ways distinct from that of the Chesapeake. Yet in other ways, the development of the Carolinas paralleled Virginia and Maryland's path from violence, high mortality, and uncertainty toward relative stability.

Paradise Lost

The English had traded and battled with the Spanish in the Caribbean since the 1560s. From those island bases English buccaneers conducted an illegal trade with Spanish settlements, sacked the coastal towns, and plundered silver ships bound for Seville. Weakened by decades of warfare, Spain could not hold the West Indies. The Dutch drove a wedge into Caribbean trade routes, and the French and the English began to colonize the islands.

In the 40 years after 1604, some 30,000 immigrants from the British Isles planted crude frontier outposts on St. Kitts, Barbados, Nevis, Montserrat, and Antigua. The settlers—some free, many others indentured servants, and almost all young men—devoted themselves to working as little as possible, drinking as much as possible, and returning to England as soon as possible. They cultivated for export a poor quality of tobacco, which returned just enough to maintain straggling settlements of small farms.

Then, nearly overnight, sugar cultivation transformed the Caribbean. In the 1640s Barbados planters learned from the Dutch how to process sugarcane. The Dutch also supplied African slaves to work the cane fields and marketed the sugar for high prices in the Netherlands. Sugar plantations and slave labor rapidly spread to other English and French islands as Europeans developed an insatiable sweet tooth for the once scarce commodity. Caribbean sugar made more money for England than the total volume of commodities exported by all of the mainland American colonies.

Caribbean sugar

Even though its great planters became the richest people in English America, they could not have confused the West Indies with paradise. Throughout the seventeenth century, disease took a fearful toll, and island populations grew only because of immigration. In the scramble for land, small farmers were pushed onto tiny plots that barely allowed them to survive.

The desperation of bound laborers posed another threat. After the conversion to sugar, black slaves gradually replaced white indentured servants in the cane fields.

Slavery in the Caribbean

By the beginning of the eighteenth century, black inhabitants outnumbered white residents by four to one. Fear of servant mutinies and slave rebellions frayed the nerves of island masters. They tried to contain the danger by imposing harsh slave codes and inflicting brutal punishments on white and black laborers alike. But planters lived under a constant state of siege. One visitor to Barbados observed that whites fortified their homes with parapets from which they could pour scalding water on attacking servants and slaves. During the first century of settlement, seven major slave uprisings shook the English islands.

As more people, both white and black, squeezed onto the islands, some settlers looked for a way out. With all of the land in use, the Caribbean no longer offered opportunity to freed servants or even planters' sons. It was then that the West Indies started to shape the history of the American South.

The Founding of the Carolinas

The colonization of the Carolinas began with the schemes of Virginia's royal governor, William Berkeley, and Sir John Colleton, a supporter of Charles I who had been exiled to the Caribbean at the end of England's civil war. Colleton saw that the Caribbean had a surplus of white settlers, and Berkeley knew that Virginians needed room to expand as well. Together the two men set their sights on the area south of Virginia. Along with a number of other aristocrats, they convinced Charles II to make them joint proprietors in 1663 of a place they called the Carolinas, in honor of the king.

A few hardy souls from Virginia had already squatted around Albemarle Sound in the northern part of the Carolina grant. The proprietors provided them with a

North Carolina

governor and a representative assembly. About 40 years later, in 1701, they set off North Carolina as a separate colony. The desolate region quickly proved a disappointment. Lacking good harbors and navigable rivers, the colony had no convenient way of marketing its produce. North Carolina remained a poor colony, its sparse population engaged in general farming and the production of masts, pitch, tar, and turpentine.

The southern portion of the Carolina grant held far more promise, especially in the eyes of one of its proprietors, Sir Anthony Ashley Cooper, earl of

South Carolina

Shaftesbury. In 1669 he sponsored an expedition of a few hundred English and Barbadian immigrants, who planted the first permanent settlement in South Carolina. By 1680 the colonists established the center of economic, social, and political life at the confluence of the Ashley and the Cooper rivers, naming the site Charles Town (later Charleston) after the king.

Most of the Carolina proprietors regarded their venture simply as land speculation. But Cooper, like others before him, hoped to create an ideal society in America. Cooper's utopia was one in which a few landed aristocrats and gentlemen would rule with the consent of many smaller propertyholders. With his personal secretary, John Locke, Cooper drew up an intricate scheme of government, the Fundamental Constitutions. The design provided Carolina with a proprietary governor and a hereditary nobility who, as a Council of Lords, would recommend all laws to a Parliament elected by lesser landowners.

The Fundamental Constitutions

The Fundamental Constitutions met the same fate as other lordly dreams for America. Instead of peacefully observing its provisions, Carolinians plunged into the political wrangling that had plagued Maryland's proprietary rule. Assemblies resisted the sweeping powers granted to the proprietary governors. Ordinary settlers protested against paying quitrents claimed by the proprietors. Political unrest in North Carolina triggered three rebellions between 1677 and 1711. In South Carolina opposition to the proprietors gathered strength more slowly, but finally exploded with equal force.

Early Instability

Immigrants from Barbados, the most numerous among the early settlers, came quickly to dominate South Carolina politics. Just as quickly, they objected to proprietary power. To offset the influence of the Barbadians, most of whom were Anglican, the proprietors encouraged the migration of French Huguenots and English Presbyterians and Baptists. The stream of newcomers only heightened tensions, splitting South Carolinians into two camps with competing political and religious loyalties.

Meanwhile, settlers spread out along the coastal plain. Searching for a profitable export, the first colonists raised grains and cattle, foodstuffs that they exported to the West Indies. South Carolinians also developed a large trade in deerskins with coastal tribes like the Yamasee and the Creeks and Catawbas of the interior. More numerous than the Indians of the Chesapeake and even more deeply divided, the Carolina tribes competed to become the favored clients of white traders. Southeastern Indian economies quickly became dependent on English guns, rum, and clothing. To repay their debts to white traders, Indians enslaved and sold to white buyers large numbers of men, women, and children taken in wars waged against rival tribes.

Indian slavery

Provisions, deerskins, and Indian slaves proved less profitable for South Carolinians than rice, which became the colony's cash crop by the opening of the eighteenth century. Constant demand for rice in Europe made South Carolina the richest colony and South Carolina planters the richest people on the mainland of North America.

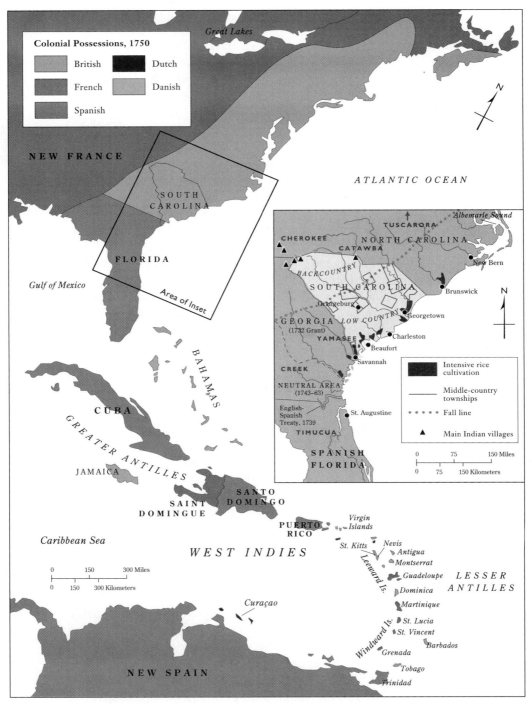

Colonial Possessions, 1750
- British
- French
- Spanish
- Dutch
- Danish

Great Lakes

NEW FRANCE

ATLANTIC OCEAN

SOUTH CAROLINA

FLORIDA

Gulf of Mexico

Area of Inset

BAHAMAS

CUBA

GREATER ANTILLES

JAMAICA

Caribbean Sea

WEST INDIES

SANTO DOMINGO

SAINT DOMINGUE

PUERTO RICO

Virgin Islands

St. Kitts

Nevis

Antigua

Montserrat

Guadeloupe

Dominica

Martinique

St. Lucia

St. Vincent

Barbados

Grenada

Tobago

Trinidad

Leeward Is.

Windward Is.

LESSER ANTILLES

Curaçao

NEW SPAIN

0   150   300 Miles
0   150   300 Kilometers

Inset:

TUSCARORA

Albemarle Sound

CHEROKEE

CATAWBA

NORTH CAROLINA

New Bern

BACKCOUNTRY

SOUTH CAROLINA

Brunswick

Orangeburg

Georgetown

GEORGIA (1732 Grant)

LOW COUNTRY

YAMASEE

Charleston

Beaufort

CREEK

Savannah

NEUTRAL AREA (1743–63)

English-Spanish Treaty, 1739

TIMUCUA

St. Augustine

SPANISH FLORIDA

Intensive rice cultivation

Middle-country townships

Fall line

Main Indian villages

0   75   150 Miles
0   75   150 Kilometers

THE CAROLINAS AND THE CARIBBEAN   The map underscores the link between West Indian and Carolina settlements. Emigrants from Barbados dominated politics in early South Carolina, while Carolinians provided foodstuffs, grain, and cattle to the West Indies.

Unfortunately, South Carolina's swampy coast, so perfectly suited to growing rice, was less suited for human habitation. Weakened by chronic malaria, settlers died in epic numbers from yellow fever, smallpox, and respiratory infections. The white population grew slowly, through immigration rather than natural increase, and numbered a mere 10,000 by 1730.

Early South Carolinians had little in common but the harsh conditions of frontier existence. Most colonists lived on isolated plantations; early deaths fragmented families and neighborhoods. Immigration after 1700 only intensified the colony's ethnic and religious diversity, adding Swiss and German Lutherans, Scots-Irish Presbyterians, Welsh Baptists, and Spanish Jews. The colony's only courts were in Charleston; churches and clergy of any denomination were scarce. On those rare occasions when early Carolinians came together, they gathered at Charleston to escape the pestilent air of their plantations, to sue each other for debt and to haggle over prices, or to fight over religious differences and proprietary politics.

White, Red, and Black: The Search for Order

By the opening decades of the eighteenth century, South Carolina seemed as strife-torn and unstable as the early Chesapeake colonies. In addition to internal tensions, external dangers threatened the very life of the Carolina settlements. The Spanish were rattling their sabers in Florida, the French filtering into the Gulf region, and pirates lurking along the North Carolina coast.

Most menacing were the Indians, and in 1715 they struck. The Yamasee of the coast allied themselves with the Creeks farther inland, launching a series of assaults that nearly pushed white Carolinians into the sea. All that saved the colony was an alliance with the Cherokee, another interior tribe who, in return for trading privileges, mounted a counterattack against their Indian rivals.

Yamasee War

As colonists reeled from the Yamasee War, opposition mounted against the proprietors, who had done nothing to protect their vulnerable colony. Military expenses had also forced Carolinians to fall into greater debt, to pay higher taxes, and to struggle with an inflated currency that month by month became worth less. Even Presbyterians, Baptists, and Huguenots, who had once defended the proprietors, shifted their sympathies because they disapproved of more recent attempts to establish the Church of England as South Carolina's official religion. During the 1720s, mass meetings and riots so disrupted government that it all but ground to a halt. Finally, in 1729, the Crown formally established royal government; by 1730 economic recovery had done much to ease the strife. Even more important in bringing greater political stability, the white colonists of South Carolina came to realize that they must unite if they were to counter the Spanish in Florida and the French and their Indian allies to the southwest.

The end of proprietary rule

The growing black population gave white Carolinians another reason to maintain a united front. During the first decades of settlement, frontier conditions and the scarcity of labor had forced masters to allow enslaved Africans greater freedom within bondage. White and black laborers shared chores on small farms. On stockraising plantations, called "cowpens," black cowboys ranged freely over the countryside. Black contributions to the defense of the colony also reinforced racial interdependence and muted white domination. Whenever the Spanish, the French, or the Indians threatened, black Carolinians were enlisted in the militia.

Slavery in South Carolina

White Carolinians depended on black labor even more after turning to rice as their cash crop. Indeed, the skills of west Africans in cultivating rice led to a greater demand for them. But whites harbored deepening fears of the workers whose labor built planter fortunes. As early as 1708 black men and women had become a majority in the colony, and by 1730 they outnumbered white settlers by two to one. Like Caribbean planters, white Carolinians put into effect strict slave codes that converted their colony into an armed camp and snuffed out the freedoms that black settlers had enjoyed earlier.

The ever-present threat of revolt on the part of the black majority gave all white South Carolinians an incentive to cooperate, whatever their religion, politics, or ethnic background. To be sure, the colony's high death rates and cultural differences persisted, while local government and churches remained weak. Yet against all these odds, white South Carolinians prospered and political peace prevailed after 1730. Any course except harmony would have exacted too high a price.

The Founding of Georgia

After 1730 South Carolinians could also take comfort from the founding of a new colony on their southern border. South Carolinians liked Georgia a great deal more than the Virginians had liked Maryland, for the colony formed a defensive buffer between British North America and Spanish Florida.

Enhancing the military security of South Carolina was only one reason for the founding of Georgia. More important to General James Oglethorpe and other idealistic English gentlemen was the aim of aiding the "worthy poor" by providing them with land, employment, and a new start. They envisioned a colony of hardworking small farmers who would produce silk and wine, sparing England the need to import those commodities. That dream seemed within reach when George II made Oglethorpe and his friends the trustees of the new colony in 1732, granting them a charter for 21 years. At the end of that time Georgia would revert to royal control.

James Oglethorpe

The trustees did not, as legend has it, empty England's debtors' prisons to populate Georgia. They freed few debtors but recruited from every country in Europe paupers who seemed willing to work hard—and who professed Protestantism. They paid their passage and provided each with 50 acres of land, tools, and a year's worth of supplies. The trustees encouraged settlers who could pay their own way to come by granting them larger tracts of land. Much to the trustees' dismay, that generous offer was taken up not only by many hoped-for Protestants but also by several hundred Ashkenazim (German Jews) and Sephardim (Spanish and Portuguese Jews), who established a thriving community in early Savannah.

The trustees were determined to ensure that Georgia became a small farmers' utopia. Rather than selling land the trustees gave it away, but none of the colony's settlers could own more than 500 acres. The trustees also outlawed slavery and hard liquor, in order to cultivate habits of industry and sustain equality among whites. This design for a virtuous and egalitarian utopia was greeted with little enthusiasm by Georgians. They pressed for a free market in land and argued that the colony could never prosper until the trustees revoked their ban on slavery. Since the trustees had provided for no elective assembly, settlers could express their discontent only by moving to South Carolina— which many did during the early decades.

`Utopian designs`

In the end, the trustees caved in to the opposition. They revoked their restrictions on land, slavery, and liquor a few years before the king assumed control of the colony in 1752. Under royal control, Georgia continued to develop an ethnically and religiously diverse society like that of South Carolina. In addition, its economy was similarly based on rice cultivation and the Indian trade.

Although South Carolina and the English West Indies were both more opulent and more embattled societies than were Virginia and Maryland, the plantation colonies stretching from the Chesapeake to the Caribbean had much in common. Everywhere planters depended on a single staple crop, which brought both wealth and political power to those commanding the most land and the most labor. Everywhere the biggest planters relied for their success on the very people whom they deeply feared: enslaved African Americans. Everywhere that fear was reflected in the development of repressive slave codes and the spread of racism throughout all classes of white society.

`Similarities among the plantation colonies`

THE SPANISH BORDERLANDS

When the English founded Jamestown, Spanish settlement in the present-day United States consisted of one feeble fort in southeastern Florida and a single outpost in New Mexico. Hoping both to intimidate privateers who preyed on silver ships and to assert their sovereign claim to the Americas, Spain had established St. Augustine on the Florida coast in 1565. But for decades the place remained a squalid garrison town of a few hundred soldiers and settlers beleaguered by hurricanes, pirates, and Indians. Meanwhile, the Spanish planted a straggling settlement under azure skies and spectacular mesas near present-day Santa Fe in 1598. Their desire was to create colonies in the

`St. Augustine and Santa Fe`

This Native American drawing on a canyon wall in present-day Arizona represents the progress of the Spanish into the Southwest. The prominence of horses underscores their novelty to the Indians, an initial advantage enjoyed by the invaders. "The most essential thing in new lands is horses," one of Coronado's men emphasized. "They instill greatest fear in the enemy and make the Indians respect the leaders of the army." Many Indian peoples soon put the horse to their own uses, however, and even outshone the Spanish in their riding skills.

Southwest that would prove more richly profitable than even those in Central and South America.

Defending both outposts proved so great a drain on royal resources that the Spanish government considered abandoning its footholds in North America. Only the pleas of Catholic missionaries, who hoped to convert the native peoples, persuaded the Crown to sustain its support. But even by 1700, St. Augustine could boast only about 1500 souls, a motley assortment of Spaniards, black slaves, and Hispanicized Indians. New Mexico's colonial population amounted to fewer than 3000 Spanish ranchers, soldiers, and clergy, scattered among the haciendas (cattle and sheep ranches), presidios (military garrisons), and Catholic missions along the Rio Grande river. There, the native Pueblo Indians numbered some 30,000.

Still, during these years the Catholic clergy remained active, creating mission communities designed to incorporate native tribes into colonial society. In New Mexico, Franciscan friars supervised Pueblo women (who traditionally built their people's adobe homes) in the construction of over 30 missions. By 1675 in Florida, perhaps 10,000 Indians were living in 35 Indian villages where the friars came to stay.

Mission communities

Unlike the English, the Spanish projected a place in their colonies for the Indians. Homes, workshops, granaries, and stables clustered around the church. The missionaries taught Indians European agricultural techniques and crafts. At mission schools, adults as well as children learned to say prayers, sing Christian hymns, and speak Spanish. In 1675, when the Bishop of Cuba toured Florida's missions, he spoke enthusiastically of converts who embraced "with devotion the mysteries of our holy faith."

The Indians were selective, however, in the European "mysteries" they chose to adopt. Some natives regarded the friars' presence simply as a means of protecting themselves against the harsher treatment of Spanish soldiers and ranchers. Other Indians used the Spanish presence to give them the upper hand in dealing with rival tribes, just as Powhatan had used white Virginians to further his own designs. And in their religious ceremonies, many natives simply placed Jesus, Mary, and Christian saints beside the other deities they honored.

Indian and Spanish cultures bumped up against each other in material ways as well. When the Spanish at St. Augustine found the climate unsuitable for growing wheat, olives, and grapes, they turned to Indian maize, beans, and squash. Indians

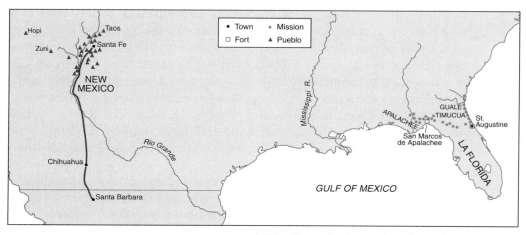

SPANISH MISSIONS IN NORTH AMERICA, CIRCA 1675 From St. Augustine, Spanish missionaries spread north into Guale Indian villages in present-day Georgia and westward among the Indians of Timucua, Apalachee, and Apalachicola. In New Mexico, missions radiated outward from the Rio Grande, as distant as Hopi Pueblo in the west.

adopted domesticated animals from Europe—horses, cattle, sheep, mules, and donkeys. Watermelons and peach trees, brought to the Atlantic coast by the Spanish, spread quickly along Indian trade routes, often ahead of Europeans themselves.

To their dismay, Indians discovered that in the long run, becoming "civilized" usually meant learning to work for Spanish masters as docile servants. The labor was harsh enough to send many to an early death. European diseases, too, took a gruesome toll among mission Indians. As the population dropped sharply, the demand by Spanish colonists rose for increasingly scarce Indian labor.

As the abuses increased, so did the resentment. Indians regularly fled the mission settlements; others made life miserable for their "benefactors." One padre at Taos Pueblo was served corn tortillas laced with urine and mouse meat. On occasion discontent and anger ignited major insurrections. The most successful was the Pueblo Revolt of 1680, which would drive the Spanish out of New Mexico for more than a decade. Popé, an Indian spiritual leader in Taos, coordinated an uprising of several Pueblo tribes that vented the full force of their hatred of Spanish rule. They killed 400 people in outlying haciendas, burned their Spanish-style houses and churches to the ground, and even exterminated the livestock introduced by the Spanish. The attack wiped out one-fifth of the Spanish population of 2500 and sent survivors scurrying for refuge down Dead Man's Road to El Paso, Texas.

Indian resistance

Despite native opposition, the Spanish persisted, especially as they saw their European rivals making headway in North America. By the end of the seventeenth century, English settlements in South Carolina were well entrenched, which prompted the Spanish in Florida to offer freedom to any escaped slaves willing to defend the colony and convert to Catholicism. The black fugitives established a fortified settlement north of St. Augustine, Gracia Real de Santa Teresa de Mose, which served as a barrier against English attacks and as a base for raiding Carolina's plantations. Meanwhile the French were building forts at Biloxi and Mobile near the mouth of the Mississippi River, signaling their designs on the Gulf of Mexico. As a counterweight the Spanish added a second military outpost in Florida at Pensacola and founded several missions in present-day Texas. After 1769, to secure their claims to the Pacific coast from England and Russia, Spanish soldiers and missionaries began colonizing California. Led by the Franciscan friar Junípero Serra, they established 20 communities along the Pacific coastal plain.

Empire . . . utopia . . . independence. For more than a century after the founding of Jamestown in 1607, those dreams inspired the inhabitants of the Chesapeake, the Carolinas and Georgia, the Caribbean, and the American Southwest. The regions served as staging grounds where kings and commoners, free and unfree, men and women, red, white, and black played out their hopes. Most met only disappointment and many met disaster in the painful decades before the new colonies achieved a measure of stability.

The dream of an expanding empire faltered for the Spanish, who found no new El Dorado in the Southwest. The dream of empire failed, too, when James I and Charles I, England's early Stuart kings, found their power checked by Parliament. And the dream foundered fatally for Powhatan's successors, who were unable to resist both white diseases and land-hungry tobacco planters.

English lords had dreamed of establishing feudal utopias in America. But proprietors like the Calvert family in Maryland and Cooper in the Carolinas found themselves hounded by frontier planters and farmers who sought economic and political power. Georgia's trustees struggled in vain to nurture their dream of a utopia for the poor. The dream of a Spanish Catholic utopia brought by missionaries to the American Southwest dimmed with Indian resistance.

The dream of independence proved the most deceptive of all, especially for the inhabitants of England's colonies. Just a bare majority of the white servant immigrants to the Chesapeake survived to enjoy freedom. The rest were struck down by disease or worn down at the hands of tobacco barons eager for profit. Not only in the Chesapeake but also in the Caribbean and the Carolinas, real independence eluded the English planters. Poorer people were dependent on richer people for land and leadership; they deferred to them at church and on election days and depended on them to buy crops or to extend credit. Even the richest planters depended on the English and Scottish merchants who supplied them with credit and marketed their crops as well as on the English officials who made colonial policy.

And everywhere in the American South and Southwest, white people's lingering dreams were realized only through the labor of the least free members of colonial America. In the Southwest the Spanish made servants of the Indians. Along the southern Atlantic coast and in the Caribbean, English plantation owners (like the Spanish before them) turned for labor to the African slave trade. Only after slavery became firmly established as a social and legal institution did England's southern colonies begin to settle down and grow: during the late seventeenth century for the Chesapeake region and the early eighteenth for the Carolinas. That stubborn reality would haunt Americans of all colors who continued to dream of freedom and independence.

c h a p t e r   s u m m a r y

During the seventeenth century, plantation economies based on slavery gradually developed throughout the American South.

- Native peoples everywhere in the American South resisted white settlement, but their populations were drastically reduced by warfare, disease, and enslavement.

- Thriving monocultures were established throughout the region—tobacco in the Chesapeake, rice in the Carolinas, and sugar in the Caribbean.

- African slavery emerged as the dominant labor system in all the southern colonies.

- Instability and conflict characterized the southern colonies for most of the first century of their existence.

- As the English colonies took shape, the Spanish extended their empire in Florida and New Mexico, establishing military garrisons, missions, and cattle ranches.

 For quizzes and a variety of interactive resources, visit the book's Online Learning Center at www.mhhe.com/davidsonconcise3

SIGNIFICANT EVENTS

late 1500s	Formation of Powhatan's confederacy
1603	James I becomes king of England; beginning of Stuart dynasty
1604	First English settlements in the Caribbean
1607	English settle Jamestown
1610	Founding of Santa Fe
1619	First record of Africans in Virginia
1620s	Tobacco boom in Virginia
1622	White-Indian warfare in Virginia
1624	Virginia becomes a royal colony
1625	Charles I becomes king of England
1632	Calvert founds Maryland
1640s	Sugar boom begins in the Caribbean
1660	Parliament passes the first of the Navigation Acts
1669	First permanent settlement in South Carolina
1676	Bacon's Rebellion in Virginia
1680	Pueblo Revolt in New Mexico
1689	Coode's Rebellion in Maryland
ca. 1700	Rice boom begins in South Carolina
1708	Africans make up a majority of South Carolina population
1715	Yamasee uprising in South Carolina
1732	Chartering of Georgia

They came to her one night while she slept. Into her dreams drifted a small island, and on the island were tall trees and living creatures, one of them wearing the fur of a white rabbit. When she told of her vision, no one took her seriously, not even the wise men among her people, shamans and conjurers whose business it was to interpret dreams. No one, that is, until two days later, when the island appeared to all, floating toward shore. On the island, as she had seen, were tall trees, and on their branches— bears. Or creatures that looked so much like bears that the men grabbed their weapons and raced to the beach, eager for the good hunt sent by the gods. They were disappointed. The island was not an island at all, but a strange wooden ship planted with the trunks of trees. And the bears were not bears at all but a strange sort of men whose bodies were covered with hair. Strangest among them, as she had somehow known, was a man dressed all in white. He commanded great respect among the bearlike men as their shaman, or "priest."

The First Century of Settlement in the Colonial North
(1600–1700)

preview • Europe's religious rivalries shaped seventeenth-century colonies along America's northern rim: the Protestant Reformation stamping English Puritan settlements from Maine to Long Island and the Catholic Counter Reformation encouraging the less numerous settlers of French Canada. New England's stable societies, with their strong family bonds and growing tradition of self-government, contrasted with the more prosperous and ethnically diverse Middle Colonies.

In that way, foretold by the dreams of a young woman, the Micmac Indians in 1869 recounted their tribe's first meeting with whites more than two centuries earlier. Uncannily, the traditions of other northern tribes record similar dreams predicting the European arrival: "large canoes with great white wings like those of a giant bird," filled with pale bearded men bearing "long black tubes." Perhaps the dreamers gave shape in their sleep to stories heard from other tribes who had actually seen white strangers and ships. Or perhaps, long before they ever encountered Europeans, these Indians imagined them, just as Europeans fantasized about a new world. The first whites seen by those tribes might have been English or Dutch. But probably, like the party met by the Micmacs, they were French, the most avid early adventurers in the northern reaches of the Americas.

For the time being, few French had dreams of their own about settling in the Americas. Jacques Cartier looked for a Northwest Passage to Asia in 1535, and instead discovered the St. Lawrence River. But not until 1605 did the French plant a permanent colony, at Port Royal in Acadia (Nova Scotia). Three years later, Samuel de Champlain shifted French interests to the St. Lawrence valley, where he founded Quebec. His plan was to follow the network of rivers and lakes leading from Quebec into the interior, exploring the continent for furs and a passage to the Pacific.

Cartier and Champlain

Over the next several decades the handful of soldiers, traders, and missionaries who came to New France established friendly relations with tribes of expert fishers and hunters. There were the Algonquin and Montagnais of the St. Lawrence valley; and in the fertile meadows and rich forests around Georgian Bay there was Huronia, a nation 25,000 strong. In return for French goods, these peoples traded beaver, otter, and raccoon they had trapped. The furs went to make fashionable European hats, while mink and marten were sent to adorn the robes of high-ranking European officials and churchmen. The French had a name for what New France had become by 1630—a *comptoir*, a storehouse for the skins of dead animals, not a proper colony.

That began to change when other French with their own dreams took responsibility for Canada. Louis XIII and his chief minister, Cardinal Richelieu, hoped that American wealth might be the making of France and its monarchs. In the 1630s they granted large tracts of land and a trading monopoly to a group of private investors, the Company of the Hundred Associates. The Associates brought a few thousand French farmers across the Atlantic and scattered them over 200 miles of company lands along the St. Lawrence.

Religious zeal, as much as the hope of profit, spurred France's renewed interest in colonization. Throughout Europe the Catholic church was enjoying a revival of religious piety as a result of the Counter Reformation, an effort to correct those abuses that had prompted the Protestant Reformation. To reclaim members lost to Protestantism, the Counter Reformation also launched an aggressive campaign of repression in Europe and missionary work abroad.

The shock troops of these missions, not only in the Americas but also in India and Japan, were the Jesuits, members of the Society of Jesus. With Richelieu's encouragement Jesuit missionaries streamed into Canada to assist other French settlers in bringing the Indians the "right" kind of Christianity. At first, it seemed unlikely that the Jesuits would shake the Indians' strong belief in the superiority of their own cultures. In Indian eyes these spiritual soldiers were a joke—men with effeminate robes and "very ugly" beards, who were forbidden physical pleasure by their vow of celibacy. The Jesuits were also a nuisance. Not content to preach at French settlements and Indian villages, they

The Jesuits

undertook "flying" missions to the nomadic tribes, tagging along with Indian trappers. Once in the wilderness the Jesuits were a disaster—tangling in their snowshoes as they marched through wintry drifts, trying for a first and last time to stand in canoes, refusing to carry any weapons, and sponging off the Indians for food and shelter.

Some Indians gradually formed a better opinion of the French and their priests. French traders, known as *coureurs du bois*, and their soldiers often adopted the native way of life and married Indian women. More to the point, the French were still relatively few. Interested primarily in trade, they had no designs on Indian land. The Jesuits, too, won acceptance among some tribes. Their lack of interest in Indian land, furs, and women made them a novelty among white men, while their greater immunity to the diseases that killed many Indians confirmed their claims to superior power. And once the Jesuits got the hang of native tongues, they showed a talent for smooth talk that the Indians, who prized oratory, greatly admired.

Throughout the seventeenth century, the French in North America remained relatively few. Instead, it was English Protestants who established the most populous settlements along the north Atlantic coast, challenging Indian dreams with religious visions of their own. Just as Jesuit crusaders of the Counter Reformation

Converts of the French Jesuits, these women of the Caughnawaga tribe (right) are kneeling before a statue of the Virgin Mary, taking vows of celibacy. One cuts her hair, a symbol of banishing pride, in imitation of the practice of Catholic nuns like Marguerite Bourgeoys (left), who founded a religious community dedicated to the education of young girls.

shaped the culture of New France, so the zealous followers of John Calvin left their unmistakable imprint on New England.

THE FOUNDING OF NEW ENGLAND

The English regarded the northern part of North America as a place in which only the mad French could see possibility. English fisherfolk who strayed from Newfoundland to the coast of Acadia and New England carried home descriptions of the long, lonely coast, rockbound and rugged. Long winters of numbing cold melted into short summers of steamy heat. There were no minerals to mine, no crops suitable for export, no large native population available for enslaving. The Chesapeake, with its temperate climate and long growing season, seemed a much likelier spot.

But by 1620, worsening conditions at home instilled in some English men and women the mixture of desperation and idealism needed to settle an uninviting, unknown world. Religious differences among English Protestants became a matter of sharper controversy during the seventeenth century. Along with the religious crisis came mounting political tensions and continuing problems of unemployment and recession. The anticipation of even worse times to come swept men and women to the shores of New England.

The Puritan Movement

The settlement of New England started with a king who chose his enemies unwisely. James I, shortly after succeeding Elizabeth I in 1603, vowed to purge England of all radical Protestant reformers. The radicals James had in mind were the Puritans, most of whom were either Presbyterians or Congregationalists. Although both groups of Puritan reformers embraced Calvin's ideas, they differed on the best form of church organization. Individual Presbyterian churches (or congregations) were guided by higher governing bodies of ministers and laypersons. Congregationalists, on the other hand, believed that each congregation should conduct its own affairs independently, answering to no other authority.

King James angered not only the Puritans but also members of Parliament, who objected to his attempts to levy taxes without their consent. The enmity of both Parliament and the Puritans did not bode well for James's reign. In Parliament he faced influential landowners and merchants, who were convinced that law was on their side. And in the Puritans he faced determined zealots who were convinced that God was on their side.

Like all Christians, Protestant and Catholic, the Puritans believed that God was all-knowing and all-powerful. And like all Calvinists, the Puritans emphasized that idea of divine sovereignty known as predestination. At the center of their thinking was the belief that God had ordained

Predestination

the outcome of history, including the eternal fate of every human being. The Puritans found comfort in their belief in predestination because it provided their lives with meaning and purpose. They felt assured that a sovereign God was directing the fate of individuals, nations, and all of creation. The Puritans strove to play their parts in that divine drama of history and to discover in their performances some signs of personal salvation.

The divine plan, as the Puritans understood it, called for reforming both church and society along the lines laid down by John Calvin. It seemed to the Puritans that England's government hampered rather than promoted religious purity and social order. It tolerated drunkenness, theatergoing, gambling, extravagance, public swearing, and Sabbath breaking.

What was worse, the state had not done enough to purify the English church of the "corruptions" of Roman Catholicism. The Church of England counted as its members everyone in the nation, saint and sinner alike. To the Puritans, belonging to a church was no birthright. They wished to limit membership and the privileges of baptism and communion to godly men and women. The Puritans also deplored the hierarchy of bishops and archbishops in the Church of England, as well as its elaborate ceremonies in which priests wore ornate vestments. Too many Anglican clergy were "dumb dogges" in Puritan eyes, too poorly educated to instruct churchgoers in the truths of Scripture or to deliver a decent sermon.

Puritan calls for reform

Because English monarchs had refused to take stronger measures to reform church and society, the Puritans became their outspoken critics. Elizabeth I had tolerated this opposition, but James I would not endure it and intended to rid England of these radicals. With some of the Puritans, known as the Separatists, he seemed to succeed.

The Pilgrim Settlement at Plymouth Colony

The Separatists were Congregationalists who concluded that the Church of England was too corrupt to be reformed. They abandoned Anglican worship and met secretly in small congregations. From their first appearance in England during the 1570s, the Separatists suffered persecution from the government—fines, imprisonment, and in a few cases, execution. Always a tiny minority within the Puritan movement, the Separatists were people from humble backgrounds, craftworkers and farmers without the influence to challenge the state. By 1608 some had become so discouraged that they migrated to Holland, where the Dutch government permitted complete freedom of religion. But when their children began to adopt Dutch customs and other religions, some Separatists decided to move again, this time to Virginia.

It can only be imagined what fate would have befallen the unworldly Separatists if they had actually settled in the Chesapeake during the tobacco boom. But a series of mistakes—including an error in

Early difficulties

charting the course of their ship, the *Mayflower*—landed the little band in New England instead. In November 1620, some 88 Separatist "Pilgrims" set anchor at a place they called Plymouth on the coast of present-day southeastern Massachusetts. They were sick with scurvy, weak from malnutrition, and shaken by a shipboard mutiny; and neither the site nor the season invited settlement. As one of their leaders, William Bradford, later remembered:

> For summer being done, all things stand upon them with a weatherbeaten face, and the whole country, full of woods and thickets represented a savage hue. If they looked behind them, there was the mighty ocean which they had passed and was now as a main bar and gulf to separate them from all the civil parts of the world.

Few Pilgrims could have foreseen founding the first permanent white settlement in New England, and many did not live long enough to enjoy the distinction. They had arrived too late to plant crops, and the colonists had failed to bring an adequate supply of food. By the spring of 1621, half of the immigrants had died. English merchants who had financed the *Mayflower* voyage failed to send supplies to the struggling colony.

Plymouth might have become another doomed colony if the Pilgrims had not received better treatment from native inhabitants than they did from their English backers. Samoset and Squanto, two Indians who had learned to speak English from visiting fishermen, introduced the settlers to native strains of corn. They also arranged a treaty between the Pilgrims and the region's main tribe, the Wampanoags.

The Pilgrims also set up a government for their colony, the framework of which was the Mayflower Compact. That agreement provided for a governor and several assistants to advise him, all to be elected annually by Plymouth's adult

The Mayflower Compact

males. The Plymouth settlers had no clear legal basis for their land claims or their government, for they had neither a royal charter nor approval from the Crown. But English authorities, distracted by problems closer to home, left the tiny colony of farmers alone.

The Puritan Settlement at Massachusetts Bay

Among the Crown's distractions were two groups of Puritans more numerous and influential than the gentle Pilgrims. They included both the Presbyterians and the majority of Congregationalists who, unlike the Pilgrim Separatists, still considered the Church of England capable of being reformed. But the 1620s brought these Puritans only fresh discouragements. In 1625 Charles I inherited his father's throne and all his enemies. When Parliament attempted to limit the king's power, Charles simply dissolved it in 1629 and proceeded to rule without it. When Puritans pressed for reform, he supported a host of measures proposed by his archbishop, William Laud, for purging England's parishes of ministers with Puritan leanings.

This persecution swelled a second wave of Puritan migration that also drew from the ranks of Congregationalists. Unlike the humble Separatists, these emigrants included merchants, landed gentlemen, and lawyers who organized the

Massachusetts Bay Company in 1629. Those able Puritan leaders aimed to build a better society in America, an example to the rest of the world. Unlike the Separatists, they had a strong sense of mission and destiny. They were not abandoning the English church, they insisted, but merely regrouping for another assault on corruption from across the Atlantic.

Despite the company's Puritan leanings, it somehow obtained a royal charter confirming its title to most of present-day Massachusetts and New Hampshire. Advance parties in 1629 established the town of Salem on the coast well north of Plymouth. In 1630 the company's first governor, John Winthrop, sailed from England with a dozen other company stockholders and a fleet of men and women committed to the Puritan cause. Winthrop, a landed gentleman, was both a tough-minded lawyer and a visionary determined to set an example for the world. "We shall be as a city on a hill," he told his fellow passengers during the crossing on the ship *Arabella*.

Once established in the Bay Colony, Winthrop and the other stockholders transformed the charter for their trading company into the framework of government for a colony. The company's governor became the colony's chief executive; the company's other officers, the governor's assistants. The charter provided for annual elections of the governor and his assistants by company stockholders, known as the freemen. But to create a broad base of support for the new government, Winthrop and his assistants expanded the freemanship in 1631 to include every adult male church member.

Establishing the colony's government

The governor, his assistants, and the freemen together made up the General Court of the colony, which passed all laws, levied taxes, established courts, and made war and peace. In 1634 the whole body of the freemen stopped meeting and instead each town elected representatives, or deputies, to the General Court. Ten years later, the deputies formed themselves into the lower house of the Bay Colony legislature, and the assistants formed the upper house. By refashioning a company charter into a civil constitution, Massachusetts Bay Puritans gained full control of their future, fulfilling their dream of shaping society, church, and state to their liking.

NEW ENGLAND COMMUNITIES

Contrary to expectations, New England proved more hospitable to the English than the Chesapeake did. The character of the migration itself gave New England settlers an advantage, for most arrived in family groups—not as young, single, indentured servants of the sort whose discontents unsettled Virginia society. The heads of New England's first households were typically free men—farmers, artisans, and merchants. Most were skilled and literate. Since husbands usually migrated with their wives and children, the ratio of men to women within the population was fairly evenly balanced.

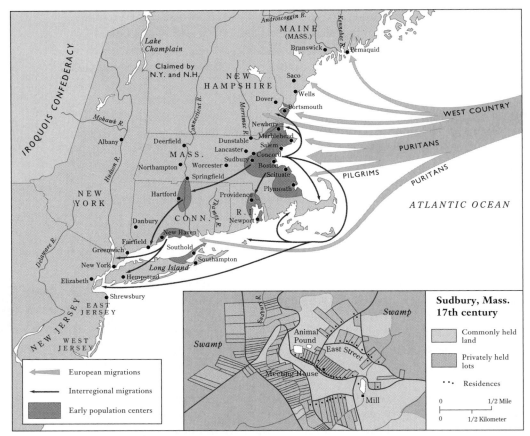

EARLY NEW ENGLAND   New England remained a relatively homogeneous and stable region, with everyday life centered in small towns like Sudbury (located to the west of Boston). Most families lived close to one another in houses clustered around the meetinghouse.

The "Great Migration"

Most immigrants, some 21,000, came in a cluster between 1630 and 1642. Thereafter new arrivals tapered off because of the outbreak of the English Civil War. This relatively rapid settlement fostered solidarity because immigrants shared a common past of persecution and a strong desire to create an ordered society modeled on Scripture.

Stability and Order in Early New England

Puritan emigrants and their descendants thrived in New England. The first generation of colonists lived to an average age of 70, nearly twice as long as Virginians and 10 years longer than English men and women. With 90 percent of all children reaching adulthood, the typical family consisted of seven or eight children who came to maturity. Because of low death rates and high birthrates, the number of New Englanders doubled about every 27 years—while the populations of Europe and the Chesapeake barely reproduced themselves. By 1700, New England and the Chesapeake each had populations of approximately 100,000. But whereas the southern population grew because of continuing immigration, New England's expanded through natural increase.

Long-lived New Englanders

As immigrants arrived in the Bay Colony after 1630, they carved out an arc of small villages around Massachusetts Bay. Within a decade settlers pressed into Connecticut, Rhode Island, and New Hampshire. Connecticut and Rhode Island received separate charters from Charles II in the 1660s, guaranteeing their residents the rights to land and government. New Hampshire, to which Massachusetts laid claim in the 1640s, did not become a separate colony until 1679. The handful of hardy souls settled along the coast of present-day Maine had also accepted the Massachusetts Bay Colony's authority.

Early New Englanders planted most of their settlements with an eye to stability and order. Unlike the Virginians, who scattered across the Chesapeake to isolated plantations, most New Englanders established tightly knit communities like those they had left behind in England. In fact, migrating families from the same village or congregation back in England often petitioned the colony government for a tract of land to found their own new town.

Patterns of settlement

All prospective adult townsmen initially owned in common this free grant of land, along with the right to set up a local government. Townsmen gradually parceled out among themselves the land granted by the colony. Each family received a lot for a house along with about 150 acres of land in nearby fields. Farmers left many of their acres uncultivated, as a legacy for future generations, for most had only the labor of their own families to work their land. While the Chesapeake abounded with servants and tenant farmers, almost every adult male in rural New England owned property.

The economy that supported most of New England's families and towns offered few chances for anyone to get rich. Farmers could coax a yield of food crops sufficient to feed their families, but the stony soil and long winters could not support cash crops like tobacco, rice, or sugar. With no resources for commercial agriculture, New England farmers also had no incentive to import large numbers of servants and slaves or to create large plantations.

Strong family institutions contributed to New England's order and stability. While the early deaths of parents regularly splintered Chesapeake families, two adult generations were often on hand to encourage order within New England households. Husbands and fathers exacted submission from wives and strict obedience from children, even after young people had come of age.

Congregational Church Order

Equally important in preserving local order was the church. Most settlers formed churches as quickly as they founded towns, and each congregation ran its own affairs, hiring and dismissing ministers, admitting and disciplining members.

A Puritan New Englander Wrestles with Her Faith

Many times hath Satan troubled me concerning the verity of the scriptures, many times by Atheisme how I could know whether there was a God; I never saw any miracles to confirm me, and those which I read of how did I know but they were feigned. That there is a God my Reason would soon tell me by the wondrous workes that I see, the vast frame of the Heaven and the Earth, the order of all things, night and day, Summer and Winter, Spring and Autumne, the dayly providing for this great houshold upon the Earth, the preserving and directing of All to its proper end. The consideration of these things would with amazement certainly resolve me that there is an Eternall Being.

But how should I know he is such a God as I worship in Trinity, and such a Saviour as I rely upon? though: this hath thousands of Times been suggested to mee, yet God hath helped me over. I have argued thus with myself. That there is a God I see. If ever this God hath revealed himself, it must bee in his word, and this must bee it or none. Have I not found that operation by it no humane Invention can work upon the Soul? hath not Judgments befallen Diverse who have scorned and contemd it? hath it not been preserved through: All Ages maugre [in spite of] all the heathen Tyrants and all of the enemyes who have opposed it? Is there any story but that which showes the beginnings of Times, and how the world came to bee as wee see? Doe wee not know the prophecyes in it fulfilled which could not have been so long foretold by any but God himself?

Source: John Harvard Ellis, Ed., *The Works of Anne Bradstreet in Prose and Verse.* Charlestown, MA A.E. Cutter, 1867, pp. 3–10.

Membership in New England's Congregational churches was voluntary, but it was not available for the asking. Those wishing to join had to satisfy the church that they had experienced "conversion." Puritans understood conversion to mean a turning of the heart and soul toward God, a spiritual rebirth that was reflected by a pious and disciplined life. In New England, believers who could credibly relate their conversions to the minister and other church members gained admission to membership. Most early New Englanders sought and received church membership, a status that entitled them to receive communion and to have their children baptized. Widespread membership also enabled the churches to oversee public morality and to expel wayward members for misbehavior.

Church membership

Everywhere in New England except Rhode Island, civil laws obliged everyone to attend worship services on the Sabbath and to pay taxes to support Congregationalist ministers. Although the separation between church and state was incomplete, it had progressed further in New England than in most nations of

Europe. New England ministers did not serve as officers in the civil government, and the Congregational churches owned no property. By contrast, Catholic and Anglican church officials wielded real temporal power in European states, and the churches held extensive tracts of land.

Separation of church and state

Colonial Governments

The final institution fostering order in daily life was the town meeting, the basis of local self-government. In every New England village, all white adult male inhabitants met regularly at the meetinghouse to decide matters of local importance. Nearly all of them could vote for town officials. The town fathers generally set the meeting's agenda and offered advice, but the unanimous consent of townsmen determined all decisions. Reaching consensus was a practical necessity because the town fathers had no means of enforcing unpopular decisions.

Colony governments in early New England also evolved into representative and responsive institutions. Typically the central government of each colony, like the General Court of Massachusetts Bay, consisted of a governor and a bicameral legislature, including an upper house, or council, and a lower house, or assembly. All officials were elected annually by the freemen—white adult men entitled to vote in colony elections. Voting qualifications varied, but the number of men enfranchised made up a much broader segment of society than in seventeenth-century England.

Communities in Conflict

Not every community in early New England was a small, self-sufficient farming village in which strong families, town fathers, and watchful churches pursued the ideals of Puritanism. Along the edges of settlement, several towns departed dramatically from the usual patterns.

One such outpost was Marblehead, a fishing port on the Massachusetts coast settled by immigrant fisherfolk from every port in the British Isles. Most eked out a bare existence as suppliers and employees of Boston merchants, who managed Marblehead's fishery. Single men dominated the population, and their brawls and drunken cavorting often spilled out of the town's many taverns into the streets. Local government remained weak for most of the seventeenth century, and inhabitants managed to avoid founding a local church for 50 years.

Commerce and "company towns"

The rest of Massachusetts tolerated chaotic "company towns" like Marblehead because their inhabitants produced what few commodities New England could trade to the rest of the world. Marblehead's fish found a ready market in Catholic Spain and Portugal. In exchange, New Englanders acquired wine, sugar, molasses, textiles, and iron goods—commodities that they needed but could not produce.

More commonly, conflicts in New England towns were likely to arise over religious differences. Although most New Englanders called themselves Puritans and Congregationalists, the very fervency of their convictions often led them to disagree about how best to carry out the teachings of the Bible and the ideas of John Calvin. The Puritans of Plymouth Colony, for example, believed that religious purity required renouncing the Church of England, while those of the Bay Colony clung to the hope of reforming the Anglican church from within.

Conflict over religious differences

Even within Massachusetts Bay, Puritans differed among themselves about how to organize their churches. During the first decades of settlement, those differences led to the founding of new colonies in New England. In 1636 Thomas Hooker, the minister of Cambridge, Massachusetts, led part of his congregation to Connecticut, where they established the first English settlement. Somewhat more liberal than other Bay Puritans, Hooker favored more lenient standards for church membership. He also opposed the Bay's policy of limiting voting in colony elections to church members. By contrast, New Haven (a separate colony until it became part of Connecticut in 1662) was begun in 1638 by strict Congregationalists who found Massachusetts too liberal. Massachusetts recognized its southern neighbors, including Separatist Plymouth, as colonies within the Puritan fold, respectable suburbs of Winthrop's city on a hill.

Heretics

The same could not be said of Rhode Island, for that little colony on Narragansett Bay began as a ghetto for heretics. While voluntary migration formed Connecticut and New Haven, enforced exile filled Rhode Island with men and women whose radical ideas unsettled the rest of Massachusetts.

Roger Williams, Rhode Island's founder, had come to New England in 1631, serving as a respected minister of Salem. But soon Williams announced that he was a Separatist, like the Pilgrims of Plymouth. He encouraged the Bay Colony to break all ties to the corrupt Church of England. He also urged a more complete separation of church and state than most New Englanders were prepared to accept, and later in his career he endorsed full religious toleration. Finally, Williams denounced the Bay's charter—the legal document that justified Massachusetts' existence—on the grounds that the king had no right to grant land that he had not purchased from the Indians. When Williams boldy suggested that Massachusetts actually inform the king of his mistake, angry authorities prepared to deport him. Instead Williams fled the colony in the dead of winter to live with the Indians. In 1636, he became the founder of Providence, later to be part of Rhode Island.

Roger Williams

Another charismatic heretic from Massachusetts arrived soon after. Anne Hutchinson, a skilled midwife and the spouse of a wealthy merchant, came to Boston in 1634. Enthusiasm for her minister, John Cotton, started her on a course of explaining his sermons to gatherings of her neighbors—and then to elaborating ideas of her own in which many of the Bay's leaders detected the dangerous heresy of "Antinomianism."

Anne Hutchinson

The Bay Puritans, like all Calvinists, denied that men and women could "earn" salvation simply by obeying God's laws. They held that salvation came through divine grace, not human actions. But many Puritans believed that the ability to lead an upright life was a natural consequence of being saved. A minority in the Puritan movement, including Anne Hutchinson, rejected that notion. Hutchinson contended that outward obedience to God's laws indicated nothing whatsoever about the soul's inward state. Those predestined for salvation knew it intuitively, she said, and could recognize the same grace in others.

When most of the Bay Colony's ministers rejected her views, Anne Hutchinson denounced them. Her attack on the clergy, along with the popularity of her preaching among many important merchant families, prompted the Bay Colony government to expel Hutchinson and her followers for sedition in 1638. She settled briefly in Rhode Island before moving on to Long Island, where she died in an Indian attack.

Colony leaders were especially critical of Hutchinson because she was a woman, who by their lights should have remained less assertive of her beliefs. In later religious controversies, the devil of dissent assumed the shape of a woman as well. The Quakers, one of the most radical religious groups produced by the Protestant Reformation in England, sent Ann Austin and Mary Fisher as their first missionaries to the Bay. Women were among the most active early converts, and one of them, Mary Dyer, was hanged for her persistence, along with three Quaker men, in 1656. Like the Antinomians, the Quakers attached great significance to an inward state of grace, called the "Light Within." Through that inner light, the Quakers claimed, God revealed his will directly to believers, enabling men and women to attain spiritual perfection. Because they held that everyone had immediate access to God, the Quakers also dispensed with a clergy and the sacraments.

Quakers

Goodwives and Witches

If Anne Hutchinson and Mary Dyer had been men, their ideas would still have been deemed heretical. On the other hand, if these women had been men, they might have found other ways to express their intelligence and magnetism. But life in colonial New England offered women, especially married women, little scope for their talents.

Most adult women were hardworking farmwives who cared for large households of children. Between marriage and middle age, most New England wives were pregnant except when breast-feeding. When they were not nursing or minding children, mothers were producing and preparing much of what was consumed and worn by their families. They planted vegetable gardens and pruned fruit trees,

By placing a woman at the center of his composition, the artist who sketched this Quaker meeting called attention to one of that sect's most controversial practices. Women were allowed to speak in Quaker worship services and to preach at public gatherings of non-Quakers.

salted beef and pork and pressed cider, milked cows and churned butter, kept bees and tended poultry, cooked and baked, washed and ironed, spun, wove, and sewed. While husbands and sons engaged in farmwork that changed with the seasons, took trips to taverns and mills, and went off to hunt or fish, housebound wives and daughters were locked into a humdrum routine with little time for themselves.

Women suffered legal disadvantages as well. English common law and colonial legal codes accorded married women no control over property. Wives could not sue or be sued, they could not make contracts, and they surrendered to their husbands any property that they possessed before marriage. Divorce was almost impossible to obtain until the late eighteenth century. Only widows and a few single women had the same property rights as men, but they could not vote in colony elections.

Legal barriers for women

The one arena in which women could attain something approaching equal standing with men was the churches. Women wielded the greatest influence among the Quakers. They could speak in Quaker meetings, preach as missionaries, and oversee the behavior of other female members in "women's meetings." Puritan women could not become ministers, but after the 1660s they made up the majority of church members. In some churches membership enabled them to vote for ministerial candidates and to voice opinions about admitting and disciplining members. Puritan doctrine itself rejected the medieval Catholic suspicion of women as "a necessary evil," seeing them instead as "a necessary good." Even so, the Puritan ideal of the virtuous woman was a chaste, submissive "helpmeet," a wife and mother who served God by serving men.

Communities sometimes responded to assertive women with accusations of witchcraft. Like most early modern Europeans, New Englanders believed in wizards and witches, men and women who were said to acquire supernatural powers by signing a compact with Satan. A total of 344 New Englanders were charged with witchcraft during the first century of settlement, with the notorious Salem Village episode of 1692 producing the largest outpouring of accusations and 20 executions. More than three-quarters of all accused witches were women, usually middle-aged and older, and most of those accused were regarded as unduly independent. Before they were charged with witchcraft, many had been suspected of heretical religious beliefs, others of sexual impropriety. Still others had inherited or stood to inherit property.

Witchcraft

Whites and Indians in Early New England

Most white settlers in New England, like those in the Chesapeake, condemned the "savagery" and "superstition" of the Indians around them. Unlike the French, however, the Puritans made only a few efforts to spread their faith to the Indians.

In truth, the "godly" New Englanders had more in common with the natives in the region than they might have cared to admit. Perhaps 100,000 Algonkian-speaking men and women lived in the area reaching from the Kennebec River in Maine to Cape Cod. Like the Puritans, they relied for food on fishing in spring and summer, hunting in winter, cultivating and harvesting food crops in spring and fall. And, to an even greater degree than among white settlers, Indian political authority was local. Within each village, a single leader known as the "sachem" or "sagamore" directed economic life, administered justice, and negotiated with other tribes and English settlers. Like New England's town fathers, a sachem's power depended on keeping the trust and consent of his people.

Puritans and Indians

The Indians of New England shared one other characteristic with all Europeans: they quarreled frequently with neighboring nations. The antagonism among the English, Spanish, Dutch, and French was matched by the hostilities among the Abenaki, Pawtucket, Massachusett, Narragansett, and Wampanoag tribes of the north Atlantic coast. Rivalries kept different tribes from forging an effective defense against white colonials. New England settlers, like those in the Chesapeake, exploited Indian disunity.

The first New England natives to put up a strong resistance to Europeans were the Pequots, whom white settlers encountered when they began to push into Connecticut. Had the Pequots allied with their

War

neighbors, the Narragansetts, they could have retarded English expansion. But the Narragansetts, bitter enemies of the Pequots, allied with the English instead. Together they virtually destroyed the Pequots in 1637. This playing of one tribe off against another finally left the Wampanoags of Plymouth as the only coastal tribe capable of resisting Puritan expansion. In 1675, their sachem Metacomet, whom the English called King Philip, organized an uprising that devastated white frontier settlements.

Faced with shortages of food and ammunition, Metacomet called for assistance from the Abenaki, a powerful Maine tribe, and from the Iroquois of New York. But those tribes withheld their support, not wishing to jeopardize their trade with the English. In the summer of 1676 Metacomet met his death in battle, and the Indian offensive collapsed. In seventeenth-century New England, as in the Chesapeake, the clash between Indians and white settlers threatened the very survival of both groups. Perhaps 20,000 whites and Indians lost their lives in Metacomet's War.

Even if the natives of New England had been able to unify against whites, they still would have had no defense against another deadly enemy—disease. Like all the Indians of the precolonial Americas, those in New England had been singularly free of the illnesses such as chicken pox and measles that most Europeans experienced in childhood and of the deadly epidemics that beset the Old World—smallpox, influenza, plague, malaria, yellow fever, and tuberculosis. But the absence of those pathogens in the pre-Columbian environment also meant that native Americans had built up no acquired immunity. For that reason, European microbes devastated Indian populations throughout the Americas. In New England, the total number of native Americans plummeted from 70,000 to fewer than 12,000 during the first 75 years of the seventeenth century.

Effect of Old World diseases

THE MIDDLE COLONIES

The inhabitants of the Middle Colonies—New York and New Jersey, Pennsylvania and Delaware—enjoyed more secure lives than most southern colonials. But they lacked the common bonds that lent stability to early New England. Instead, in each of the Middle Colonies a variety of ethnic and religious groups vied for wealth from farming and the fur trade and contended bitterly against governments that commanded little popular support.

The Founding of New Netherlands

New York was settled in 1624 as New Netherlands, an outpost of the Dutch West India Company. Far more impressed with the commercial potential of Africa and South America, the company limited its investment in North America to a few fur trading posts along the Hudson, Connecticut, and Delaware rivers.

Intent only on trade, the Dutch had little desire to plant permanent colonies abroad because they enjoyed prosperity and religious freedom at home. Most of New Netherlands' few settlers clustered in the village of New Amsterdam on Manhattan Island at the mouth of the Hudson. One hundred and fifty miles upriver lay a fur trading outpost, Fort Orange (Albany), and by the 1660s a few other farming villages dotted the west end of Long Island, upper Manhattan Island, Staten Island, and the lower Hudson valley. In all, there were fewer than 9000 New Netherlanders—a mixture of Dutch, Belgians, French, English, Portuguese, Swedes, Finns, and Africans. The first blacks had arrived in 1626, imported as slaves; some later became free, married whites, and even owned white indentured servants.

Ethnic and religious diversity

This ethnic diversity ensured a variety of religions. Although the Dutch Reformed Church predominated, other early New Netherlanders included Lutherans, Quakers, and Catholics. There were Jews as well, refugees from Portuguese Brazil, who were required by law to live in a ghetto in New Amsterdam. Yet another religious group kept to themselves by choice: New England Congregationalists. Drawn by promises of cheap land and self-government, they planted farming communities on eastern Long Island during the 1640s.

New Netherlanders knew that their cultural differences hampered the prospects for a stable social and political life. The Dutch West India Company made matters worse by appointing corrupt, dictatorial governors who ruled without an elective assembly. The company also provided little protection for its outlying settlers; when it did attack neighboring Indian nations, it did so savagely, triggering terrible retaliations. By the time the company went bankrupt in 1654, it had virtually abandoned its American colony.

New Englanders on Long Island, who had insisted on a free hand in governing their own villages, now began to demand a voice in running the colony as well. By the 1660s they were openly challenging Dutch rule and calling for English conquest of the colony.

English Rule in New York

Taking advantage of the disarray in New Netherlands, Charles II ignored Dutch claims in North America and granted his brother James, the duke of York, a proprietary charter there. It granted James all of New Netherlands to Delaware Bay, as well as Maine, Martha's Vineyard, and Nantucket Island. In 1664 James sent an invading fleet, whose mere arrival caused the Dutch to surrender.

English management of the new colony, renamed New York, did little to ease ethnic tensions or promote political harmony. The Dutch resented English rule, and only after a generation of intermarriage and acculturation did that resentment fade. James also failed to win friends among Long Island's New Englanders. He grudgingly gave in to their demand for an elective assembly in 1683, but rejected its first act, the Charter of Liberties, which would have guaranteed basic political

Many French colonials showed an abiding interest in and respect for native American culture. Among them was George Heriot, who produced a series of watercolor sketches of Iroquois ceremonies, including this portrayal of a calumet (or peace-pipe) dance.

rights. The chronic political strife discouraged prospective settlers. By 1698 the colony numbered only 18,000 inhabitants, and New York City, the former New Amsterdam, was an overgrown village of a few thousand.

The League of the Iroquois

While New York's colonists wrangled, many of its native Indians succumbed to the same pressures that shattered the natives of New England and the Chesapeake. Only one tribe of Indians in New York's interior, the Iroquois nation, actually gained greater strength from contacts with whites.

Like the tribes of South Carolina, the Indians of northern New York became important suppliers of furs to white traders. As in the Carolinas, powerful tribes dominated the interior, far outnumbering white settlers. The handful of Dutch and, later, English traders had every reason to keep peace with the Indians. But the fur trade heightened tensions among interior tribes. At first the Mahicans had supplied furs to the Dutch, but by 1625 the game in their territory had been exhausted and the Dutch had taken their business to the Iroquois. When the Iroquois faced the same extinction of fur-bearing animals in the 1640s, they found a solution. With Dutch encouragement and Dutch

The Indian trade

guns, the Iroquois virtually wiped out the neighboring Huron nation and seized their hunting grounds.

The destruction of the Huron made the Iroquois the undisputed power on the northern frontier. More successfully than Powhatan's confederacy in the Chesapeake, the League of the Iroquois welded different tribes into a coherent political unit. This union of the Five Nations (to become six after the Tuscaroras joined them in 1712) included the Mohawk, Oneida, Onondaga, Cayuga, and Seneca tribes and stretched from the lands around the upper Hudson in the east to the Genesee River in the west. Political strength enabled the Iroquois to deal effectively with their Algonquin rivals in New England as well as European newcomers. As the favored clients of the Dutch and, later, the English, they became opponents of the French.

The League's strength rested on an even more remarkable form of political and social organization, one in which men and women shared authority. The most powerful women anywhere in colonial North America were the matriarchs of the Iroquois. Matrilineal kinship formed the basis of Iroquois society, as it did among the Pueblos of the Southwest. When

Iroquois women

men married, they joined their wives' families, households over which the eldest female member presided. But unlike Pueblo women, Iroquois matriarchs also wielded political influence. The most senior Iroquois women selected the confederation's council of chiefs, advised them, and "dehorned"—removed from office—those deemed unfit. Throughout the eighteenth century, the League of the Iroquois continued to figure as a major force in North America.

The Founding of New Jersey

New Jersey took shape in the shadow of its stronger neighbors to the north. Its inhabitants were less united and powerful than the Iroquois, less wealthy and influential than New Yorkers, and less like-minded and self-governing than New Englanders.

Confusion attended New Jersey's beginnings. The lands lying west of the Hudson and east of the Delaware River had been part of the Duke of York's proprietary grant. But in 1664 he gave about 5 million of these acres to Lord Berkeley and Sir George Carteret, two of his favorites who were already involved in the proprietary colonies of the Carolinas. New Jersey's new owners guaranteed settlers land, religious freedom, and a representative assembly in exchange for a small quitrent, an annual fee for the use of the land. The proprietors' terms promptly drew Puritan settlers from New Haven, Connecticut. At the same time, unaware that James had already given New Jersey to Berkeley and Carteret, New York's Governor Richard Nicolls granted Long Island Puritans land there.

More complications ensued when Berkeley and Carteret decided to divide New Jersey into east and west and sell both halves to Quaker investors—a prospect that outraged New Jersey's Puritans. Although some English Friends migrated to West

Jersey, the Quakers quickly decided that two Jerseys were less desirable than one Pennsylvania and resold both East and West Jersey to speculators. In the end the Jerseys became a patchwork of religious and ethnic groups. Settlers who shared a common religion or national origin formed communities and established small family farms. When the Crown finally reunited east and west as a single royal colony in 1702, New Jersey was overshadowed by settlements not only to the north but now, also, to the south.

Quaker Odysseys

Religious and political idealism similar to that of the Puritans inspired the settlement of Pennsylvania, making it an oddity among the Middle Colonies. The oddity began with an improbable founder, William Penn. Young Penn devoted his early years to disappointing his distinguished father, Sir William Penn, an admiral in the royal navy. Several years after being expelled from college, he finally chose a career that may have made the admiral yearn for mere disappointment: young Penn undertook a lifelong commitment to put into practice Quaker teachings. By the 1670s he had emerged as one of the Society of Friends' acknowledged leaders.

The Quakers behaved in ways and believed in ideas that most people regarded as odd. They dressed in a deliberately plain and severe manner. They withheld from their social superiors the customary marks of respect, such as bowing, kneeling, and removing their hats. They refused to swear oaths or to make war. They allowed women public roles of religious leadership. That pattern of behavior reflected their egalitarian ideals, the belief that all men and women shared equally in the "Light Within." Some 40,000 English merchants, artisans, and farmers embraced Quakerism by 1660, and many suffered fines, imprisonment, and corporal punishment.

Quaker beliefs

Young William Penn (1666) at about the time he became a Quaker.

Since the English upper class has always prized eccentricity among its members, it is not surprising that Penn, despite his Quakerism, remained a favorite of Charles II. More surprising is that the king's favor took the extravagant form of presenting Penn in 1681 with all the land between New Jersey and Maryland. Perhaps the king was repaying Penn for the large sum that his father had lent the Stuarts. Or perhaps the king was hoping to export England's Quakers to an American colony governed by his trusted personal friend.

Pennsylvania established

Penn envisioned that his proprietary colony would provide a refuge for Quakers while producing quitrents for himself. To publicize his settlement, he distributed pamphlets praising its attractions throughout the British Isles and Europe. The response was overwhelming: by 1700 its population stood at 21,000. The only early migration of equal magnitude was the Puritan colonization of New England.

Patterns of Settlement

Perhaps half of Pennsylvania's settlers arrived as indentured servants, while the families of free farmers and artisans made up the rest. The majority were Quakers from Britain, Holland, and Germany, but the colonists also included Catholics, Lutherans, Baptists, Anglicans, and Presbyterians. In 1682 when Penn purchased and annexed the Three Lower Counties (later the colony of Delaware), his settlement included the Dutch, Swedes, and Finns living there, about 1000 people.

Quakers from other colonies—West Jersey, Maryland, and New England—also flocked to the new homeland. Those experienced settlers brought skills and connections that contributed to Pennsylvania's rapid economic growth. Farmers sowed their rich lands into a sea of wheat, which merchants exported to the Caribbean. The center of the colony's trade was Philadelphia, a superb natural harbor situated at the confluence of the Delaware and Schuylkill rivers.

In contrast to New England's landscape of villages, the Pennsylvania countryside beyond Philadelphia was dotted with dispersed farmsteads. Commercial agriculture required larger farms, which kept settlers at greater distances from one another. As a result, the county rather than the town became the basic unit of local government in Pennsylvania.

Another reason that farmers did not need to cluster their homes within a central village was that the coastal Indians, the Lenni Lenapes (also called Delawares by the English), posed no threat. Thanks to two of the odder Quaker beliefs—their commitment to pacifism and their conviction that the Indians rightfully owned their land—peace prevailed between native inhabitants and newcomers. Before Penn sold any land to white settlers, he purchased it from the Indians.

Quakers and Indians

"Our Wildernesse flourishes as a Garden," Penn declared late in 1683, and in fact, his colony lived up to its promises. New arrivals readily acquired good land on liberal terms, while Penn's Frame of Government instituted a representative assembly and guaranteed all inhabitants the basic English civil liberties and complete freedom of worship.

Quakers and Politics

Even so, Penn's colony suffered constant political strife. Rich investors whom he had rewarded with large tracts of land and trade monopolies dominated the council, which held the sole power to initiate legislation. That power and Penn's own claims as proprietor set the stage for controversy. Members of the representative assembly battled for the right to initiate legislation. Farmers opposed Penn's efforts to collect quitrents. The Three Lower Counties agitated for separation, their inhabitants feeling no loyalty to Penn or Quakerism.

Penn finally bought peace at the price of approving a complete revision of his original Frame of Government. In 1701 the Charter of Privileges, Pennsylvania's new constitution, stripped the council of its legislative power, leaving it only the role of advising the governor. The charter also limited Penn's privileges as proprietor to the ownership of ungranted land and the power to veto legislation. Thereafter an elective unicameral assembly, the only single-house legislature in the colonies, dominated Pennsylvania's government.

Penn's compromises

As Pennsylvania prospered, Philadelphia became the commercial and cultural center of England's North American empire. Gradually the interior of Pennsylvania filled with immigrants who harbored no "odd" ideas about Indian rights—mainly Germans and Scots-Irish—and the Lenni Lenapes and other tribes were bullied into moving farther west. As for William Penn, he returned to England and spent time in a debtors' prison after being defrauded by his unscrupulous colonial agents. He died in 1718, an ocean away from his American utopia.

ADJUSTMENT TO EMPIRE

In the year 1685, from the city of London, a new English king surveyed his American domains. The former duke of York, now James II, had hoped that America might contribute to the making of kings and queens. Like earlier Stuart monarchs, James hoped to ride to absolute power on a wave of colonial wealth, just as Spain's monarchs had during the previous century. To encourage colonial settlement, Stuart kings had chartered the private trading companies of Virginia, Plymouth, and Massachusetts Bay. They had rewarded their aristocratic favorites with huge tracts of land: Maryland, the Carolinas, New York, New Jersey, and Pennsylvania.

Yet to what end? Although North America now abounded in places named in honor of English monarchs, the colonies themselves lacked any strong ties to the English state. In only three colonies—New Hampshire, New York, and Virginia—did England exercise direct control through royally appointed governors and councils. Until Parliament passed the first Navigation Acts in 1660, England had not even set in place a coherent policy for regulating colonial trade. What was more disheartening, ungrateful colonists were resisting their duty to enrich the English state and the Stuarts. New Englanders seemed the worst of the lot: they ignored the Navigation Acts altogether and traded openly with the Dutch.

What was needed, in James's view, was an assertion of royal authority over America, starting with Massachusetts. His brother, Charles II, had laid the groundwork in 1673 by persuading Parliament to authorize the placement of customs agents in colonial ports to suppress illegal trade. When reports of defiance continued to surface, the king delivered the decisive blow: an English court in 1684 revoked Massachusetts' original charter, leaving the Bay Colony without a legal basis for its claim to self-government.

Control over the colonies tightened

The Dominion of New England

Charles died the following year, leaving James II to finish the job of reorganization. In 1686, at the king's urging, the Lords of Trade consolidated the colonies of Connecticut, Plymouth, Massachusetts Bay, Rhode Island, and New Hampshire into a single entity to be ruled by a royal governor and a royally appointed council. By 1688 he had added New York and New Jersey to that domain, now called the Dominion of New England. Showing the typical Stuart distaste for representative government, James also abolished all northern colonial assemblies. The king's aim to centralize authority over such a large territory made the Dominion not only a royal dream but a radical experiment in English colonial administration.

Sir Edmund Andros, a tough professional soldier sent to Boston as the Dominion's royal governor, quickly came to rival his king for the title of most unpopular man north of Pennsylvania. Andros set in force policies that outraged every segment of New England society. He strictly enforced the Navigation Acts, which slowed down commerce and infuriated merchants and workers in the maritime trades. He commandeered a Boston meetinghouse for Anglican worship and immediately angered devout Congregationalists. He abolished all titles to land granted under the old charter, alarming farmers and speculators. He imposed arbitrary taxes, censored the press, and forbade all town meetings, thereby alienating almost everyone.

Edmund Andros

The Aftershocks of the Glorious Revolution

About the same time northern colonials were reaching the end of their patience with Andros, the English decided they had taken enough from his royal master. James II had revealed himself to be the wrong sort of Stuart—one who tried to dispense with Parliament and embraced Catholicism besides. As they had before with Charles I, Parliament dispensed with the king. In a quick, bloodless coup d'état known as the Glorious Revolution, Parliament forced James into exile in 1688 and placed on the throne of England his daughter, Mary, and her Dutch husband, William of Orange. Mary was the right sort of Stuart. A staunch Protestant, she agreed to rule with Parliament.

The deposing of James II proved so popular among New Englanders that even before Parliament had officially proclaimed William and Mary king and queen, Boston's militia seized Governor Andros and sent him home in April 1689. William and Mary officially dismembered the Dominion and reinstated representative assemblies everywhere in the northern colonies.

The Dominion overthrown

Connecticut and Rhode Island were restored their old charters, but Massachusetts received a new charter in 1691. Under its terms Massachusetts, Plymouth, and present-day Maine were combined into a single royal colony headed by a governor appointed by the Crown rather than elected by the people. The charter also made property ownership rather than church membership the basis of voting rights and imposed religious toleration.

Leisler's Rebellion

The new charter did not satisfy all New Englanders, but they soon adjusted to the political realities of royal rule. By contrast, the violent political infighting that plagued New York mirrored that colony's instability.

Word of revolution in England and rebellion in Massachusetts roused New Yorkers into armed opposition in May 1689. Declaring their loyalty to William and Mary, the New York City militia forced from office Andros's second-in-command, the Dominion's lieutenant governor. In his place they installed one of their own leaders, Jacob Leisler, a German merchant.

Since James II had won few friends in New York, the rebellion met no opposition. But Leisler could not win commanding support for his authority. While Protestant Dutch farmers, artisans, and small shopkeepers stood by him, the leaders of the colony—an intermarried elite of English and Dutch merchants—considered Leisler an upstart who threatened their own influence. After royal rule was restored to New York in 1691, a jury comprised of Englishmen convicted Leisler and his son-in-law, Jacob Milburne, of treason. Their executions guaranteed a long life to the bitter political rivalries that Leisler's rebellion had fueled in New York.

Royal Authority in America in 1700

In the wake of upheaval at home and in North America, England focused its imperial policy on reaping maximum profit from the colonial trade. In 1696 Parliament enlarged the number of customs officials stationed in each colony to enforce the Navigation Acts. To help prosecute smugglers, Parliament established colonial vice-admiralty courts, tribunals without juries presided over by royally appointed justices. To keep current on all colonial

Closer regulation of trade

matters, the king appointed a new Board of Trade to replace the old Lords of Trade. The new enforcement procedures generally succeeded in discouraging smuggling and in channeling colonial trade through England.

That was enough for England and its monarchs for half a century thereafter. English kings and queens gave up any dreams of imposing the kind of centralized administration of colonial life that James II had attempted in his Dominion of New England. To be sure, royal control had increased over the previous half century. By 1700 royal governments had been established in Virginia, New York, Massachusetts, and New Hampshire. New Jersey, the Carolinas, and Georgia would shortly be added to the list. Royal rule meant that the monarch appointed governors and (everywhere except Massachusetts) also appointed their councils. Royally appointed councils could veto any law passed by a colony's representative assembly, royally appointed governors could veto any law passed by both houses, and the Crown could veto any law passed by both houses and approved by the governor.

Despite the ability to veto, the sway of royal power remained more apparent than real after 1700. The Glorious Revolution asserted once and for all that Parliament's authority—rule by the legislative branch of government— would be supreme in the governing of England. In the colonies members of representative assemblies grew more adept at dealing with royal governors and more protective of their rights. They guarded most jealously their strongest lever of power—the right of the lower houses to levy taxes.

The limits of royal power

The political reality of the assemblies' power reflected a social reality as well. No longer mere outposts along the Atlantic, the colonies of 1700 were becoming more firmly rooted societies. Their laws and traditions were based not only on what they had brought from England but on the conditions of life in America. That social reality had already ensured that Stuart ambitions to shape the future of North America would prove no more practical than the designs of lordly proprietors or the dreams of religious reformers.

Still, the dream of empire would revive among England's rulers in the middle of the eighteenth century—in part because the same dream had never died among the rulers of France. By 1663, Louis XIV had decided that kings could succeed where the enterprise of private French traders had failed: he placed New France under royal rule. Thereafter France's fortunes in America steadily improved. Soldiers strengthened Canada's defenses, colonists and traders expanded the scope of French influence, and the Jesuits made more converts among the interior tribes. Under the Sun King, as Louis was known to admiring courtiers, royal rule became absolute, and the hopes for empire grew absolutely. Louis and his heirs would continue their plans for the making of France by contending for empire with the English, both in the Old World and in the New.

chapter summary

While the Catholic Counter Reformation encouraged the French colonization of Canada, the Protestant Reformation in England spurred the settlement of New England and Pennsylvania.

- During the seventeenth century, the French slowly established a fur trade, agricultural communities, and religious institutions in Canada.

- Over the same period, English Puritans planted more populous settlements between Maine and Long Island.

- The migration of family groups and a rough equality of wealth lent stability to early New England society, reinforced by the settlers' shared commitment to Puritanism and a strong tradition of self-government.

- The mid-Atlantic colonies also enjoyed a rapid growth of people and wealth, but political wrangling as well as ethnic and religious diversity made for a higher level of social conflict.

- Whereas New Englanders attempted to subdue native people, white settlers in the mid-Atlantic colonies enjoyed more harmonious relations with local Indian tribes.

- The efforts of the later Stuart kings to centralize England's empire ended with the Glorious Revolution in 1688, which greatly reduced tensions between the colonies and the parent country.

For quizzes and a variety of interactive resources, visit the book's Online Learning Center at www.mhhe.com/davidsonconcise3

SIGNIFICANT EVENTS

late 1500s	Formation of the League of the Iroquois
1535	Cartier discovers the St. Lawrence
1608	Champlain founds Quebec on the St. Lawrence; Separatists flee to Holland
1620	Pilgrims land at Plymouth
1624	Dutch found New Netherlands
1630	Winthrop fleet arrives at Massachusetts Bay
1637	Pequot War
1642–1648	English Civil War
1649	Charles I executed
1660	English monarchy restored: Charles II becomes king
1664	New Netherlands becomes English New York; founding of New Jersey
1675–1676	Metacomet's War
1681	Founding of Pennsylvania
1685	James II becomes king of England
1686	Dominion of New England established
1688	Glorious Revolution; William and Mary become monarchs of England
1689	Massachusetts Bay overthrows Andros; Leisler's rebellion in New York
1692	Witchcraft trials in Salem
1696	Creation of the Board of Trade and Plantations

CHAPTER 4

The Mosaic of Eighteenth-Century America

preview • **British colonials were such a diverse, contentious lot that any hope of political union seemed utterly impractical. The most bitter conflicts sprang from sectional disputes between the established East and the backcountry West. The South became more embattled too, as resistance increased among enslaved African Americans. Yet despite such disagreements, a majority of white colonials took pride in their English traditions and membership in a powerful empire.**

O n the morning of June 29, 1754, about 150 Iroquois sat facing the colonial commissioners in Albany, New York. In front of the governor's house, servants had set up rows of long wooden planks, upon which the delegates from the Six Nations of the Iroquois now sat. The commissioners themselves, 25 in all, were not about to make do with planks; each had his own chair. They represented seven colonies, from Massachusetts Bay on the north to Maryland on the south.

Governor James DeLancey of New York stood and read a proclamation of welcome, pledging to "brighten the Chain of Friendship" between the Iroquois and the English. As each paragraph of the governor's speech was translated, the Iroquois were presented with a decorative belt, to which they responded with a ceremonial "*Yo-heigh-eigh*," shouted in unison. The noise unsettled those colonials attuned to the subtleties of Iroquois diplomacy. Normally, each nation voiced its agreement individually: six *Yo-heigh-eighs* coming one after another. By mixing them together, noted one observer, the delegates "had a mind to disguise that all the Nations did not universally give their hearty assent" to uniting with the English.

Unity—and not merely the unity of the Iroquois—was much on the mind of one commissioner from Philadelphia. Several chairs to the left of Governor DeLancey sat the most influential member of the Pennsylvania delegation, Benjamin Franklin. He knew that the question of whether the Iroquois would unite in an alliance with British America was only half the issue for this gathering at Albany. Equally important was whether the British colonies themselves could unite, to deal effectively with France's threat throughout North America. Franklin had a plan for bringing the colonies together, but whether they would pay any notice remained an open question.

Albany, where Benjamin Franklin proposed a plan for colonial union, is pictured on this powder horn, showing its strategic location in the fur trade.

In a sense that plan grew out of a lifetime of experience, for the imperial rivalry between England and France had begun well before Franklin's birth and had flared, on and off, throughout his adult years. In 1689 England had joined the Netherlands and the League of Augsburg (several German-speaking states) in a war against France. While the main struggle raged on the continent of Europe, French and English colonials, joined by their Indian allies, skirmished in what was known as King William's War. Peace returned in 1697, but only until 1702, when the Anglo-French struggle resumed again, four years before Franklin was born. It continued throughout his boyhood, until 1713.

Rivalry between France and England

For a quarter of a century thereafter, the two nations waged a kind of cold war, competing for position and influence. At stake was not so much control over people or even territory but control over trade. In North America, France and England vied for access to the sugar islands of the Caribbean, a monopoly on supplying manufactured goods to New Spain, and title to the fur trade. The British had the advantage of numbers: nearly 400,000 subjects in the colonies in 1720, compared with only about 25,000 French spread along a thin line of fishing stations and fur trading posts. Yet the French steadily strengthened their chain of forts, stretching from the mouth of the Mississippi north through the Illinois country and into Canada. The forts helped channel the flow of furs from the Great Lakes and the Mississippi River valley into Canada, thus keeping them out of the clutches of English traders. And the forts neatly encircled England's colonies, confining their settlement to the eastern seaboard.

Fighting again engulfed Europe and the colonies in 1744. King George's War, as the colonials dubbed it, ended four years later, but peace did nothing to diminish the old rivalry. As English traders and settlers filtered steadily into the Ohio

River valley, the French built a new line of forts in 1752, from south of Lake Erie to the Ohio River. Two years later they erected Fort Duquesne at the strategic forks of the Ohio, flush against the border of Franklin's Pennsylvania. That startled Pennsylvania and other colonies into sending commissioners to Albany in 1754 to coordinate efforts to deal with the worsening crisis. Franklin put the message plainly in his newspaper, the *Pennsylvania Gazette*, in a cartoon of a snake cut into segments. It was inscribed "Join, or Die."

As France and England maneuvered for the empire, the Iroquois League maintained a cool neutrality. They were uneasy at the prospect of a North America without the French. Without French competition for Indian furs, what would spur British colonials to offer fair prices and trade goods of high quality? Without the arc of French forts encircling the British colonies, what would halt the westward spread of white settlement? Increasingly, too, the Iroquois were impressed by the show of French military might.

For the time being, the commissioners at Albany could do little to satisfy Iroquois doubts, except lavish as much hospitality as their budgets would allow. In the end the Iroquois made vague promises of loyalty, and then hauled away 30 wagons full of presents.

But would the colonies themselves unite? On the way to the Albany Congress Franklin had sketched out a framework for colonial cooperation. He proposed establishing "one general government" for British North America: a federal council composed of representatives from each colony, presided over by a president-general appointed by the Crown. The council would assume all responsibility for colonial defense and Indian policy, building forts and patrolling harbors with taxes levied on all Americans. The commissioners were bold enough to accept the plan, alarmed by the wavering Iroquois and the looming French threat.

The Albany Plan of Union

But the union born at Albany was smothered by the jealous colonies, who were unwilling to sing *yo-heigh-eigh* either in unison or separately. Not a single assembly approved the Albany Plan of Union. And no American legislature was ready to surrender its cherished right to tax inhabitants of its own colony—not to a federal council or to any other body. "Everyone cries, a union is necessary," Franklin wrote Governor Shirley of Massachusetts in disgust; "but when they come to the manner and form of the union, their weak noodles are perfectly distracted." If the Albany Congress proved one thing, it was that American colonials were hopelessly divided.

FORCES OF DIVISION

Franklin, of course, should have known better than to hope for an intercolonial union. A practical man not given to idle dreams, he recognized the many forces of division at work in America. He knew that the colonies were divided by ethnic and regional differences as well as racial and religious prejudices. Year after year small wooden ships brought to American seaports a bewildering variety of immigrants—especially in Philadelphia, where Franklin had lived since 1723. From his efforts to reorganize the post office Franklin knew, too, that Americans were separated by vast distances, poor transportation, and slow communications. He knew how suspicious frontier districts remained of seaboard communities and how the eastern seaboard disdained the backcountry. Taken all in all, the British settlements in America were, in the eighteenth century, a diverse and divided lot.

Immigration and Natural Increase

One of the largest immigrant groups—250,000 black men, women, and children—had come to the colonies from Africa not by choice but in chains. White arrivals included many English immigrants but also a quarter of a million Scots-Irish, the descendants of seventeenth-century Scots who had regretted settling in northern Ireland; perhaps 135,000 Germans; and a sprinkling of Swiss, Swedes, Highland Scots, and Spanish Jews. Most non-English white immigrants were fleeing lives torn by famine, warfare, and religious persecution. Many had paid for passage by signing indentures to work as servants in America.

The immigrants and slaves who arrived in the colonies between 1700 and 1775 swelled population that was already growing dramatically from natural increase. The birthrate in eighteenth-century America was triple what it is today. Most women bore between five and eight children, and most children survived to maturity. Indeed, the consequences of this population **High birthrate** explosion so intrigued Franklin that he wrote an essay on the subject in 1751. He recognized that ethnic and religious diversity, coupled with the hectic pace of westward expansion, made it hard for colonials to share any common identity. Far from fostering political union, almost every aspect of social development set Americans at odds with one another.

The Settlement of the Backcountry

To white immigrants from Europe, weary of war or worn by want, the seaboard's established communities must have seemed havens of order and stability. But by the beginning of the eighteenth century, even the children of long-time settlers could not acquire land along the coast. In older New England towns, three and four generations were putting pressure on a limited supply of land, while wasteful farming practices had depleted the soil of its fertility. Farther south, earlier settlers had already snatched up the farmland of Philadelphia's outlying counties, the prime Chesapeake tobacco property, and lowcountry rice swamps.

With older rural communities offering few opportunities to either native-born or newly arrived white families, both groups were forced to create new communities on the frontier. The peopling of New England's frontier—Maine, New

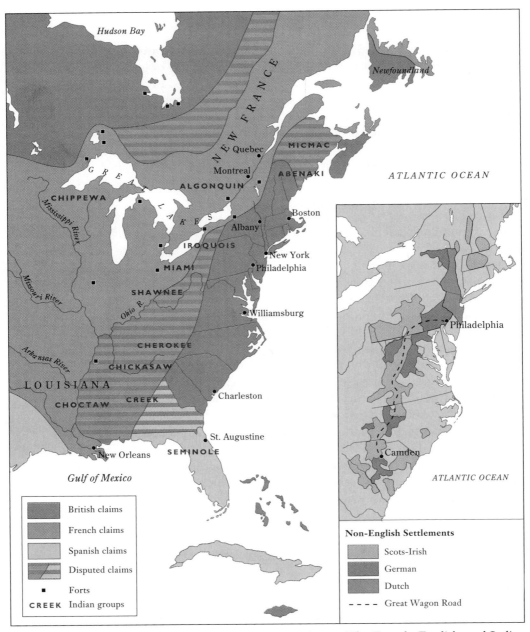

PATTERNS OF SETTLEMENT IN THE EIGHTEENTH CENTURY The French, English, and Indian nations all jockeyed for power and position across North America. The French expanded their fur trade through the interior, while English settlement at midcentury began to press the barrier of the Appalachians. Many non-English settlers spilled into the backcountry: the Scots-Irish and Germans followed the Great Wagon Road through the western parts of the middle and southern colonies, while the Dutch and Germans moved up the Hudson River valley.

Hampshire, and Vermont—was left mainly to the descendants of old Yankee families. Better opportunities for new immigrants to acquire land at cheaper prices lay south of New York. By the 1720s German and Scots-Irish immigrants as well as native-born settlers were pouring into western Pennsylvania. Some settled permanently, but others streamed southward into the backcountry of Virginia and the Carolinas, where they encountered native-born southerners pressing westward.

Backcountry settlers endured greater isolation than other colonials did. From many farms it was a day's ride to the nearest courthouse; taverns and churches were often as distant. Isolation hindered the formation of strong social bonds, as did the mobility of backcountry settlers. Many families pulled up stakes three or four times before settling permanently. Houses reflected that transience: most families crowded into one-room shacks walled with mud, turf, or crude logs.

Isolation of the backcountry

The backcountry meant economic isolation as well. Large portions of the interior were cut off from water transport because they were located above the fall line, where rivers flowing to the Atlantic became unnavigable. By 1755 several crude wagon roads linked western Pennsylvania and Virginia to towns farther east, including Philadelphia, but transporting crops and driving livestock overland proved prohibitively expensive. Cut off from outside markets, farmers grew only enough to feed their households. Most backcountry inhabitants could not afford to invest in a slave or even a servant. Those conditions made the frontier, more than anywhere else in America, a society of equals.

Hard work dominated the lives of backcountry settlers. Besides doing the usual chores of farm women, western wives and daughters joined male family members in the fields. Men found some release from their harsh lives in coarse, aggressive behavior—epic bouts of drinking, fighting, and slaughtering game. But frontier women had few consolations and longed to live closer to neighbors and churches. The reactions of women to being resettled on the frontier can be imagined from the promise that one Scottish husband offered his wife: "We would get all these trees cut down . . . [so] that we would see from house to house."

Frontier women

Social Conflict on the Frontier

Despite the discomforts of frontier life, cheap land lured many families to the West. Benjamin Franklin had observed the hordes of Scots-Irish and German immigrants lingering in Philadelphia just long enough to scrape together the purchase price of a frontier farm. From Franklin's point of view, the backcountry performed a valuable service by siphoning off surplus people from congested eastern settlements. But he knew, too, that the frontier was an American Pandora's box. Once opened, the West unleashed discord, especially between the eastern seaboard and the backcountry.

In Pennsylvania, Franklin himself mediated one such contest between east and west. In 1763 a band of Scots-Irish farmers known as "the Paxton Boys" protested

The Paxton Boys

the government's inadequate protection of frontier settlers by killing a number of Indians. Then the Paxton Boys took their protests and their guns to Philadelphia, marching as far as Lancaster before Franklin intervened and promised redress of their grievances.

Strife between east and west was even deadlier and more enduring in North and South Carolina. In both colonies legislatures dominated by coastal planters re-

Regulation movements

fused to grant inland settlers equitable political representation or even basic legal institutions. In response to those injustices, two protest movements emerged in the Carolina interior, each known as the Regulation.

Farmers in the South Carolina backcountry organized their Regulation in the 1760s, after that colony's assembly refused to set up courts in the backcountry. Westerners were desperate for protection from outlaws who stole livestock, kidnapped and raped women, and tortured and murdered men. In the absence of courts the Regulators acted as vigilantes, meting out their own brand of grisly frontier justice against these criminals. Regulator threats to march on Charleston itself finally panicked eastern political leaders into extending the court system, but bitter memories lingered among westerners.

Western North Carolinians organized their Regulation to protest not the absence of a legal system but the corruption of local government. Lawyers and merchants, backed by wealthy eastern planters, moved into the western parts of that colony and seized control of politics. Then they used local office to exploit frontier settlers, charging exorbitant fees for legal services, imposing high taxes, and manipulating debt laws. Western farmers responded to these abuses with the Regulation: they seized county courts and finally squared off against an eastern militia led by the governor. Easterners crushed the Regulators at the Battle of Alamance in 1771 but left frontier North Carolinians with an enduring hostility to the seaboard.

Ethnic differences heightened sectional tensions between east and west. While people of English descent predominated along the Atlantic coast, Germans, Scots-

Ethnic conflicts

Irish, and other white minorities were concentrated in the interior. Many English colonials regarded these new immigrants as culturally inferior. Charles Woodmason, an Anglican missionary in the Carolina backcountry, lamented the arrival of "5 or 6000 Ignorant, mean, worthless, beggarly Irish Presbyterians, the Scum of the Earth, the Refuse of Mankind," who "delighted in a low, lazy, sluttish, heathenish, hellish life."

German immigrants were generally credited with having steadier work habits as well as higher standards of sexual morality and personal hygiene. But like the clannish Scots-Irish, the Germans preferred to live, trade, and worship among themselves. By 1751 Franklin was warning that the Germans would retain their separate language and customs: the Pennsylvania English would be overrun by "the Palatine Boors."

Boundary Disputes and Tenant Wars

The settlement of the frontier also triggered disputes between colonies over their boundaries. The most serious of these border wars pitted New York against farmers from New England who had settled in present-day Vermont: Ethan Allen and the Green Mountain Boys. In the 1760s New York, backed by the Crown, claimed land that Allen and his friends had already purchased from New Hampshire. When New York tried to extend its rule over Vermont, Allen led a successful guerrilla resistance, harassing Yorker settlers and officials, occupying Yorker courthouses, and setting up a competing judicial system in the Green Mountains.

Green Mountain Boys

The spread of settlement also set the stage for mass revolts by tenants in those areas where proprietors controlled vast amounts of land. In eastern New Jersey, proprietors insisted that squatters pay quitrents on land that had become increasingly valuable. When the squatters, many of them migrants from New England, refused to pay rents, buy the land, or move, the proprietors began evictions, touching off riots in the 1740s. Tenant unrest also raged in New York's Hudson River valley. In the 1680s the royal governor had granted several prominent merchant families large estates in that region. By the middle of the eighteenth century, there were about 30 manors around New York City and Albany, totaling some 2 million acres and worked by several thousand tenants. Newcomers from New England, however, demanded to own land and preached their ideas to Dutch and German tenants. Armed insurrection exploded in 1757 and again, more violently, in 1766. Tenants refused to pay rents, formed mobs, and stormed the homes of landlords.

Eighteenth-Century Seaports

While most Americans on the move settled on the frontier, others swelled the populations of colonial cities. By present-day standards such cities were small, harboring from 8000 to 22,000 citizens by 1750. The scale of seaports remained intimate, too: all of New York City was clustered at the southern tip of Manhattan Island, and the length of Boston or Charleston could be walked in less than half an hour.

All major colonial cities were seaports, their waterfronts fringed with wharves and shipyards. A jumble of shops, taverns, and homes crowded their streets; the spires of churches studded their skylines. By the 1750s, the grandest and most populous was Philadelphia, which boasted straight, neatly paved streets, flagstone sidewalks, and three-story brick buildings. Older cities like Boston and New York had a more medieval aspect: most of their dwellings and shops were wooden structures with tiny windows and low ceilings, rising no higher than two stories to steeply pitched roofs. The narrow cobblestone streets of Boston and New York also challenged pedestrians, who competed for space with livestock being driven to the butcher, roaming herds of swine and packs of dogs, clattering carts, carriages, and horses.

Commerce, the lifeblood of seaport economies, was managed by merchants who tapped the wealth of surrounding regions. Traders in New York and Philadelphia shipped the Hudson and Delaware valleys' surplus of grain and livestock to the West Indies. Boston's merchants sent fish to the Caribbean and Catholic Europe, masts to England, and rum to west Africa. Charlestonians exported indigo to English dyemakers and rice to southern Europe. Other merchants specialized in the import trade, selling luxuries and manufactured goods produced in England—fine fabrics, ceramics, tea, and farming implements. Wealth brought many merchants political power: they dominated city governments and shared power in colonial assemblies with lawyers and the largest farmers and planters.

The commercial classes

Skilled craftworkers or artisans made up the middling classes of colonial cities. The households of master craftworkers usually included a few younger and less skilled journeymen working in other artisans' shops. Unskilled boy apprentices not only worked but also lived under the watchful eye of their masters. Some artisans specialized in the maritime trades as shipbuilders, blacksmiths, and sailmakers. Others, like butchers, millers, and distillers, processed and packed raw materials for export. Still others served the basic needs of city dwellers—the men and, occasionally, women who baked bread, mended shoes, combed and powdered wigs, and tended shops and taverns.

On the lowest rung of a seaport's social hierarchy were free and bound workers. Free laborers were mainly young white men and women—journeymen artisans, sailors, fishermen, domestic workers, seamstresses, and prostitutes. The ranks of unfree workers included apprentices and indentured servants doing menial labor in shops and on the docks. Black men and women also made up a substantial part of the bound labor force of colonial seaports. While the vast majority of African slaves were sold to southern plantations, a smaller number were bought by urban merchants and craftworkers. Laboring as porters at the docks, as assistants in craft shops, or as servants in wealthy households, black residents made up almost 20 percent of the population in New York City and 10 percent in Boston and Philadelphia.

Free and bound workers

The character of slavery in northern seaports changed decisively during the mid-eighteenth century. When wars raging in Europe reduced the supply of white indentured servants, colonial cities imported a larger number of Africans. Those newcomers brought to urban black culture a new awareness of a common west African past. The influence of African traditions appeared most vividly in an annual event known as "Negro election day," celebrated in northern seaports. During the festival, similar to ones held in west Africa, some black men and women paraded in their masters' clothes or mounted on their horses. An election followed, to choose black "kings," "governors," and "judges," who then "held court" and settled minor disputes among white and black members of the community. "Negro election day" did not challenge the established racial order with its temporary reversal of roles, but it did allow the black community of seaports to honor their own leaders.

The availability of domestic workers, both black and white, made for leisured lives among women from wealthy white families. Even those city women who could not afford household help spent less time on domestic work than did farming wives and daughters. Although some housewives grew vegetables in backyard gardens or kept a few chickens, large markets stocked by outlying farmers supplied most of the food for urban families.

Women in cities

For women who had to support themselves, seaports offered a number of employments. Young single women from poorer families worked in wealthier households as maids, cooks, laundresses, seamstresses, or nurses. The highest-paying occupations for women, midwifery and dressmaking, both required long apprenticeships and expert skills. The wives of artisans and traders sometimes assisted their husbands and, as widows, often continued to manage groceries, taverns, and printshops. But most women were confined to caring for households, husbands, and children; fewer than 1 out of every 10 women in seaports worked outside their own homes.

All seaport dwellers—perhaps 1 out of every 20 Americans—enjoyed a more stimulating environment than did other colonials. The wealthiest could attend an occasional ball or concert; those living in New York or Charleston might even see a play performed by touring English actors. The middling classes could converse with other tradespeople at private social clubs and fraternal societies. Men of every class found diversion in drink and cockfighting. Crowds of men, women, and children swarmed to tavern exhibitions of trained dogs and horses or the spectacular waxworks of one John Dyer, featuring "a lively Representation of Margaret, Countess of Herrinburg, who had 365 Children at one Birth."

Urban diversions and hazards

But city dwellers, then as now, paid a price for their pleasures. Commerce was riddled with risk: ships sank and wars disrupted trade. When such disasters struck, the lower classes suffered most. The ups and downs of seaport economies, combined with the influx of immigrants, swelled the ranks of the poor in all cities by the mid-eighteenth century. Furthermore, epidemics and catastrophic fires occurred with greater frequency and produced higher mortality rates in congested seaports than in the countryside.

Social Conflict in Seaports

The swelling of seaport populations, like the movement of whites to the West, often churned up trouble. English, Scots-Irish, Germans, Swiss, Dutch, French, and Spanish jostled uneasily against one another in the close quarters of Philadelphia and New York. To make matters worse, religious differences heightened ethnic divisions. Jewish funerals in New York, for example, drew crowds of hostile and curious Protestants, who heckled the mourners.

Class resentment also stirred unrest. Some merchant families flaunted their wealth, building imposing town mansions and dressing in the finest imported fashions. During hard times, expensive coaches and full warehouses became targets of mob vandalism. Crowds also gathered to intimidate and punish other groups who provoked popular hostility—unresponsive politicians, prostitutes, and "press gangs." Impressment, attempts to force colonials to serve in the British navy, triggered some of the most violent urban riots.

SLAVE SOCIETIES IN THE EIGHTEENTH-CENTURY SOUTH

Far starker than the inequalities and divisions among seaport dwellers were those between white and black in the South. By 1775 one out of every five Americans was of African ancestry, and over 90 percent of all black Americans lived in the South, most along the seaboard. Here, on tobacco and rice plantations, slaves fashioned a distinctive African American society and culture. But they were able to build stable families and communities only late in the eighteenth century, and against enormous odds.

Whether a slave was auctioned off to the Chesapeake or to the Lower South shaped his or her future in important ways. Slaves in the lowcountry of South Carolina and Georgia lived on large plantations with as many as 50 other black workers, about half of whom were African-born. They had infrequent contact with either their masters or the rest of the sparse white population. "They are as 'twere, a Nation within a Nation," observed Francis LeJau, an Anglican priest in the lowcountry. And their work was arduous, for rice required constant cultivation. Black laborers tended young plants and hoed fields in the sweltering summer heat of the mosquito-infested lowlands. During the winter and early spring, they built dams and canals to regulate the flow of water into the rice fields. But the use of the "task system" rather than gang labor widened the window of freedom within slavery. When a slave had completed his assigned task for the day, one planter explained, "his master feels no right to call upon him."

The Chesapeake versus the Lower South

Many Chesapeake slaves, like those in the Lower South, were African-born, but most lived on smaller plantations with fewer than 20 fellow slaves. Less densely concentrated than in the lowcountry, Chesapeake slaves also had more contact with whites. Unlike Carolina's absentee owners, who left white overseers and black drivers to run their plantations, Chesapeake masters actively managed their estates and subjected their slaves to closer scrutiny.

The Slave Family and Community

After the middle of the eighteenth century, a number of changes fostered the growth of black families and the vitality of slave communities. As slave importations began to taper off, the rate of natural reproduction among blacks started to climb. As the proportion of new Africans dropped and the number of native-born black

Americans grew, the ratio of men to women in the slave community became more equal. Those changes and the appearance of more large plantations, even in the Chesapeake, created more opportunities for black men and women to find partners and form families. Elaborate kinship networks gradually developed, often extending over several plantations in a single neighborhood.

Even so, black families remained vulnerable. If a planter fell on hard times, members of black families might be sold off to different buyers to meet his debts. When a master died, black families might be divided among surviving heirs. Even under the best circumstances, fathers might be hired out to other planters for long periods or sent to work in distant quarters.

Black families struggling with terrible uncertainties were sustained by the distinctive African American culture evolving in the slave community. The high percentage of native Africans among the eighteenth-century American black population made it easier for slaves to retain the ways of their lost homeland. Christianity won few converts, in part because white masters feared that baptizing slaves might make them more rebellious, but also because African Americans preferred their traditional religions. African influence appeared as well in the slaves' agricultural skills and practices, folktales, music, and dances.

Influence of African culture

The Old Plantation affords a rare glimpse of life in the slave quarters. At this festive gathering, both men and women dance to the music of a molo (a stringed instrument similar to a banjo) and drums.

Slavery and Colonial Society in French Louisiana

The experience of Africans unfolded differently in the lower Mississippi Valley, France's southernmost outpost in eighteenth-century North America. Louisiana's earliest colonial settlements were begun by a few thousand French soldiers, joined by indentured servants, free settlers straggling down from Canada, and immigrants from France and Germany. When they founded New Orleans in 1718, the colonists, hoping to create prosperous plantations in the surrounding Mississippi delta, immediately clamored for bound laborers. A year later, French authorities bent to their demands, and the Company of the Indies, which managed France's slave trade, brought nearly 6000 slaves, overwhelmingly men, directly from Africa to Louisiana. Yet even with this influx of new laborers, the search for a cash crop eluded white planters, whose tobacco and, later, indigo proved inferior to the varieties exported from Britain's colonies.

Instead of proving the formula for economic success, the sudden influx of Africans challenged French control. In 1729, with blacks already comprising a majority of the population, some newly arrived slaves joined forces with the Natchez Indians who feared the expansion of white settlement. Their rebellion, the Natchez Revolt, left 200 French planters dead—more than 10 percent of the European population of Louisiana. The French retaliated in a devastating counterattack, enlisting both the Choctaw Indians, who were rivals of the Natchez, and other enslaved blacks, who were promised freedom in return for their support.

Natchez revolt

The planters' costly victory persuaded French authorities to stop importing slaves into Louisiana, which helped ensure that the colony did not develop a plantation economy until the end of the eighteenth century, when the cotton boom transformed its culture. In the meantime, blacks continued to make up a majority of all Louisianans, and by the middle of the eighteenth century, nearly all were native born. The vast majority were slaves, but their work routines—tending cattle, cutting timber, producing naval stores, working on boats—afforded them greater freedom of movement than most slaves enjoyed elsewhere in the American South. Louisianan blacks were also encouraged to market the produce of their gardens, hunts, and handicrafts, which became the basis of a thriving trade with both white settlers and the dwindling numbers of native Americans. But the greatest prize—freedom—was awarded those black men who served in the French militia, defending the colony from the English and Indians as well as capturing slave runaways. The descendants of these black militiamen would become the core of Louisiana's free black population.

Greater freedom for blacks in Louisiana

Slave Resistance in Eighteenth-Century British North America

British North America had no comparable group of black soldiers, but it also had no shortage of African Americans who both resisted captivity and developed strategies for survival. Among newly arrived Africans, collective attempts at escape were most common. Groups of slaves, often made up of newcomers from the same tribe, fled inland and formed "Maroon" communities of runaways. These efforts were usually unsuccessful because the Maroon settlements were large enough to be easily detected.

More acculturated blacks adopted subtler ways of subverting slavery. Domestics and field hands alike faked illness, feigned stupidity and laziness, broke tools, pilfered from storehouses, hid in the woods for weeks at a time, or simply took off to visit other plantations. Other slaves, usually escaping bondage as solitary individuals, found a new life as craftworkers, dock laborers, or sailors in the relative anonymity of colonial seaports.

Less frequently, black rebellion took direct and violent form. Whites in communities with large numbers of blacks lived in dread of arson, poisoning, and insurrection. Four slave conspiracies were reported in Virginia before 1750. In South

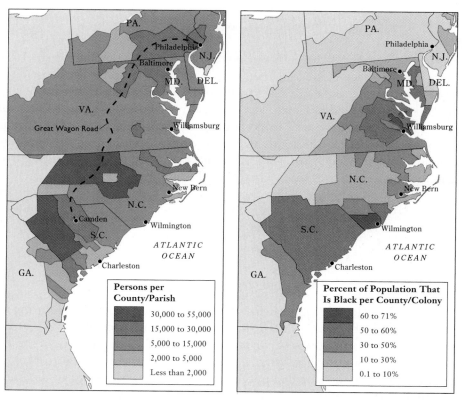

THE DISTRIBUTION OF THE AMERICAN POPULATION, 1775   The African American population expanded dramatically during the eighteenth century, especially in the southern colonies. While the high volume of slave imports accounts for most of the growth in the first half of the century, natural increase was responsible for the rising black population during later decades.

The Stono Rebellion

Carolina, more than two decades of abortive uprisings and insurrection scares culminated in the Stono Rebellion of 1739, the largest slave revolt of the colonial period. Nearly 100 African Americans, led by a slave named Jemmy, seized arms from a store in the coastal district of Stono and killed several white neighbors before they were caught and killed by the white militia.

Despite the growing rebelliousness of black slaves, southern planters continued to import Africans throughout the eighteenth century. The practice mystified Franklin, revealing at least one gap in his knowledge: the crucial importance of slavery in the southern economy. But unlike some of his Quaker neighbors in Pennsylvania, who were beginning to object to slavery on moral and humanitarian grounds, Franklin's reservations—like his opposition to German immigration—were overtly racist. "Why increase the sons of Africa by planting them in America," he asked, "where we have so fair an opportunity, by excluding all blacks and tawnys, of increasing the lovely white and red?"

ENLIGHTENMENT AND AWAKENING IN AMERICA

The differences among eighteenth-century colonials resulted in more than clashes between regions, races, classes, and ethnic groups. Those differences also made for diversity in the ways that Americans thought and believed. City dwellers were more attuned to European culture than were people living in small villages or on the frontier. White males from well-to-do families of English ancestry were far more likely to receive college educations than were those from poorer or immigrant households. White women of every class and background were excluded from higher education, and slaves received no formal education at all. Where they lived, how well they lived, whether they were male or female, native born or immigrant, slave or free—all these variables fostered among colonials distinctive worldviews, differing attitudes and assumptions about the individual's relationship to nature, society, and God.

The Enlightenment in America

The diversity of colonials' inner lives became even more pronounced during the eighteenth century because of the Enlightenment, an intellectual movement that started in Europe during the seventeenth century. The leading figures of the Enlightenment, the "philosophes," stressed the power of human reason to promote progress by revealing the laws that governed both nature and society. In the American colonies the Enlightenment influenced some curious artisans in major seaports as well as wealthy merchants, lawyers, and landowners with the leisure and education to read the latest books from Europe.

Like many devotees of the Enlightenment, Franklin was most impressed by its emphasis on useful knowledge and experimentation. He pondered air currents and then invented a stove that heated houses more efficiently. He toyed with electricity and then invented lightning rods to protect buildings in thunderstorms. Other amateur colonial scientists constructed simple telescopes, classified animal species native to North America, or sought to explain epidemics in terms of natural causes.

Some clergy educated at American colleges (six had been established by 1763) were touched by the Enlightenment, adopting a more liberal theology that stressed the reasonableness of Christian beliefs. By the middle of the eighteenth century this "rational Christianity" commanded a small following among colonials, usually Anglicans or liberal Congregationalists. Their God was not the Calvinists' awesome deity, but a benevolent creator who offered salvation to all, not just to a small, predestined elite. They believed that God's greatest gift to humanity was reason, which enabled all human beings to follow the moral teachings of Jesus. They muted the Calvinist emphasis on human sinfulness and the need for a soul-shattering conversion.

Rational versus traditional Christianity

Enlightenment philosophy and rational Christianity did not affect the outlook of most colonials. By the middle of the eighteenth century, over half of all white men (and a smaller percentage of white women) were literate. But most colonial readers were not equipped to tackle the learned writings of Enlightenment philosophes. As a result, the outlook of most colonials contrasted sharply with that of the cosmopolitan few. The great majority of Americans still looked for ultimate truth in biblical revelation rather than human reason and explained the workings of the world in terms of divine providence rather than natural law.

Widespread attachment to traditional Christian beliefs was strengthened by the hundreds of new churches built during the first half of the eighteenth century. Church attendance ran highest in the northern colonies, where some 80 percent of the population turned out for public worship on the Sabbath. In the South, because of the greater distances involved and the shortage of clergy, about half of all colonials regularly attended Sunday services.

Despite the prevalence of traditional religious beliefs, many ministers expressed concern about the dangerous influence of rational Christianity. They also worried that the lack of churches might tempt many frontier families to abandon Christianity altogether. Exaggerated as these fears may have been, the consequence was a major religious revival that swept the colonies during the middle decades of the eighteenth century.

The First Great Awakening

The Great Awakening, as the revival came to be called, deepened the influence of older forms of Protestant Christianity and, specifically, Calvinism throughout British America. Participation in the revival was the only experience that a large number of people everywhere in the colonies had in common. But the Great Awakening also heightened religious divisions among Americans.

The first stirrings of revival appeared in the 1730s among Presbyterians and Congregationalists in the Middle Colonies and New England. Many ministers in these churches preached an "evangelical" message, emphasizing the need for individuals to experience "a new birth" through religious conversion. Among them was the Reverend Jonathan Edwards of Northampton, Massachusetts. Edwards's preaching combined moving descriptions of God's grace with terrifying portrayals of eternal damnation. "The God that holds you over the pit of hell, much as one holds a spider or some loathsome insect over the fire, abhors you and is dreadfully provoked," he declaimed to one congregation; ". . . there is no other reason to be given, why you have not dropped into hell since you arise in the morning, but that God's hand has held you up."

These local revivals of the 1730s were mere tremors compared to the earthquake of religious enthusiasm that shook the colonies with the arrival in the fall of 1739 of George Whitefield. This handsome, cross-eyed "boy preacher" from England electrified crowds from Georgia to New Hampshire during his two-year tour of the colonies. He and his many imitators among colonial ministers turned the church into a theater, enlivening sermons with dramatic gestures, flowing tears, and gruesome depictions of hell's torments. The drama of such performances appealed to people of all classes, ethnic groups, and races. By the time Whitefield sailed back to England in 1741, thousands of awakened souls were joining older churches or forming new ones.

The appeal of George Whitefield

The Aftermath of the Great Awakening

Whitefield also left behind a raging storm of controversy. Many "awakened" church members now openly criticized their ministers as cold, unconverted, and uninspiring. To supply the missing fire, some laymen—"and even Women and Common Negroes"—took to "exhorting" any audience willing to listen. The most popular ministers became "itinerants," traveling like Whitefield from one town to another. Throughout the colonies conservative and moderate clergy questioned the unrestrained emotionalism and the disorder that attended the gatherings of lay exhorters and itinerants.

Religious controversies

Although Americans had been fighting over religion well before the Great Awakening, the new revivals left colonials even more divided along religious lines. The largest single group of churchgoers in the northern colonies remained within the Congregational and Presbyterian denominations. But both these groups split into factions that either supported or condemned the revivals. Some conservative Presbyterians and Congregationalists, disgusted with the disorder, defected to the Quakers and the Anglicans, who had shunned the revival. On the other hand the most radical converts joined forces with the warmest champions of the Awakening, the Baptists.

Benjamin Franklin Attends the Preaching
of George Whitefield

I happened . . . to attend one of his Sermons, in the Course of which I perceived he intended to finish with a Collection, and I silently resolved he should get nothing from me. I had in my Pocket a Handful of Copper Money, three or four silver Dollars, and five Pistoles in Gold. As he proceeded I began to soften, and concluded to give the Coppers. Another Stroke of his Oratory made me asham'd of that, and determin'd me to give the Silver; and he finish'd so admirably, that I emptied my Pocket wholly into the Collectors' Dish, Gold and all. . . .

Some of Mr. Whitefield's Enemies affected to suppose that he would apply these Collections to his own private Emolument; but I, who was intimately acquainted with him, (being employ'd in printing his Sermons and Journals, etc.) never had the least Suspicion of his Integrity, but am to this day decidedly of Opinion that he was in all his Conduct a perfectly *honest Man.* And methinks my Testimony in his Favor ought to have the more Weight, as we had no religious Connection. He us'd indeed sometimes to pray for my Conversion, but never had the Satisfaction of believing that his Prayers were heard. Ours was a mere civil Friendship, sincere on both Sides, and lasted to his Death.

He had a loud and clear Voice, and articulated his Words and Sentences so perfectly that he might be heard and understood at a great distance, especially as his Auditors, however numerous, observ'd the most exact Silence. He preach'd one Evening from the Top of the Court House Steps, which are in the Middle of Market Street. . . . I had the Curiosity to learn how far he could be heard by retiring backwards down the Street towards the River. . . . I computed that he might well be heard by more than Thirty Thousand.

Source: Excerpt from *The Autobiography of Benjamin Franklin* (New York: Washington Square Press, 1960), pp.131–133.

While northern churches splintered and bickered, the fires of revivalism spread to the South and its backcountry. From the mid-1740s until the 1770s, scores of new Presbyterian and Baptist churches were formed, but conflict often accompanied religious zeal. Ardent Presbyterians in the Carolina backcountry disrupted Anglican worship by loosing packs of dogs in local chapels. In northern Virginia, Anglicans took the offensive against the Baptists, whose strict moral code sounded a silent reproach to the hard-drinking, high-stepping, horse-racing, slaveholding gentry. County officials, prodded by resentful Anglican parsons, harassed, fined, and imprisoned Baptist ministers.

Evangelicalism on the frontier

And so a diverse lot of Americans found themselves continually at odds with one another. Because of differences in religion and education, colonials quarreled over whether rational Christianity enlightened the world or emotional revivalists

George Whitefield drew critics as well as admirers in both England and America. In this satirical English cartoon, he is depicted as a money-grubbing evangelist, while his audience, which consists mainly of women, is taken in by his pose of sanctity and youthful good looks.

destroyed its order. Because of ethnic and racial tensions, Spanish Jews found themselves persecuted, and African Americans searched for ways to resist their white masters. Because of westward expansion, Carolina Regulators waged war against coastal planters, while colonial legislatures from Massachusetts to Virginia quarreled over western boundaries.

Benjamin Franklin surely understood the depth of those divisions as he made his way toward the Albany Congress in the spring of 1754. He himself had brooded over the boatloads of non-English newcomers. He had lived in two booming seaports and felt the explosive force of the frontier. He personified the Enlightenment—and he had heard George Whitefield himself preach from the steps of the Philadelphia courthouse.

How, then, could Franklin, who knew how little held the colonials together, sustain his hopes for political unity? The answer may be that even in 1754, the majority of colonials were of English descent. And these free, white Americans liked being English. That much they had in common.

ANGLO-AMERICAN WORLDS OF THE EIGHTEENTH CENTURY

Most Americans prided themselves in being English. When colonials named their towns and counties, they named them after places in their parent country. When colonials established governments, they turned to England for their political models. They frequently claimed "the liberties of freeborn Englishmen" as their birthright. Even in diet, dress, furniture, architecture, and literature, colonists adopted English standards of taste.

Yet American society had developed in ways significantly different from that of Great Britain.* Some differences made colonials feel inferior, ashamed of their simplicity when compared with London's sophistication. But they also came to appreciate the greater equality of colonial society and the more representative character of colonial governments. If it was good to be English, it was better still to be English in America.

English Economic and Social Development

The differences between England and America began with their economies. Large financial institutions like the Bank of England and influential corporations like the East India Company were driving England's commercial development. New textile factories and mines were deepening its industrial development. Although most English men and women worked at agriculture, it, too, had become a business. Members of the gentry rented their estates to tenants, members of the rural middle class. In turn, these tenants hired workers from the swollen ranks of England's landless to perform the actual farm labor. By contrast, most colonial farmers owned their land, and most family farms were a few hundred acres. The scale of commerce and manufacturing was equally modest.

England's more developed economy fostered the growth of cities, especially London, a teeming colossus of 675,000 inhabitants in 1750. By contrast, 90 percent of all eighteenth-century colonials lived in towns with populations of less than 2000.

The Consumer Revolution

In another respect, England's more advanced economy drew the colonies and the parent country together as a consumer revolution transformed the everyday lives of people on both sides of the Atlantic. By the beginning of the eighteenth century, small manufacturers throughout England were producing a newly large and enticing array of consumer goods—fine textiles and hats, ceramics and glassware, carpets and furniture. Americans proved as eager as Britons to acquire these commodities—so eager that the per capita consumption of imported manufactures among colonials rose 120 percent between 1750 and 1773. Only the wealthy could afford goods of the highest quality, but people of all classes demanded and indulged in small luxuries like a tin of tea, a pair of gloves, or a bar of Irish soap. In both

---

*When England and Scotland were unified in 1707, the nation as a whole became known officially as Great Britain; its citizens, as British.

England and its colonies, the spare and simple material life of earlier centuries was giving way to a new order in which even ordinary people owned a wider variety of things.

Inequality in England and America

The opportunities for great wealth provided by England's more developed economy created deep class distinctions, as did the inherited privileges of its aristocracy. The members of the upper class, the landed aristocracy and gentry, made up less than 2 percent of England's population but owned 70 percent of its land. By right of birth, English aristocrats claimed membership in the House of Lords; by custom, certain powerful gentry families dominated the other branch of Parliament, the House of Commons. England's titled gentlemen shared power and wealth and often family ties with the rich men of the city—major merchants, successful lawyers, and lucky financiers. They too exerted political influence through the House of Commons. The colonies had their own prominent families but no titled ruling class holding political privilege by hereditary right. And even the wealthiest colonial families lived in far less magnificence than their English counterparts.

Class distinctions

Coffeehouses like this establishment in London were favorite gathering places for Americans visiting Britain. Here merchants and mariners, ministers and students, lobbyists and tourists warmed themselves, read newspapers, and exchanged gossip.

If England's upper classes lived more splendidly, its lower classes were larger and worse off than those in the colonies. Less than a third of England's inhabitants belonged to the "middling sort" of traders, professionals, artisans, and tenant farmers. More than two-thirds struggled for survival at the bottom of society. By contrast, the colonial middle class counted for nearly three-quarters of the white population. With land cheap, labor scarce, and wages for both urban and rural workers 100 percent higher in America than in England, it was much easier for colonials to accumulate savings and then buy farms of their own.

Colonials were both fascinated and repelled by English society. They gushed over the grandeur of aristocratic estates and imported suits of livery for their servants and tea services for their wives. They exported their sons to Britain for college educations at Oxford and Cambridge, medical school at Edinburgh, and legal training at London's Inns of Court.

Ambivalent Americans

But colonials recognized that England's ruling classes purchased their luxury and leisure at the cost of the rest of the nation. In his *Autobiography*, Benjamin Franklin painted a devastating portrait of the degraded lives of his fellow workers in a London printshop, who drowned their disappointments by drinking throughout the workday, even more excessively on the Sabbath, and then faithfully observing the holiday of "St. Monday's" to nurse their hangovers. Like Franklin, many colonials believed that gross inequalities of wealth would endanger liberty. They regarded the idle among England's rich and poor alike as ominous signs of a degenerate nation.

Politics in England and America

Colonials were also of two minds about England's government. While they praised the English constitution as the basis of all liberties, they were alarmed by the actual workings of English politics. In theory, England's "balanced constitution" was designed to give every order of English society some voice in the workings of government. While the Crown represented the monarchy and the House of Lords the aristocracy, the House of Commons represented the democracy, the people of England. In fact, the monarch's executive ministers had become dominant by creating support for their policies in Parliament through patronage—or, put more bluntly, bribery.

England's balanced constitution

Over the course of the eighteenth century, a large executive bureaucracy had evolved in order to enforce laws, collect taxes, and wage the nearly constant wars in Europe and America. The power to appoint all military and treasury officials, customs and tax collectors, judges and justices of the peace lay with the monarch and his or her ministers. By the middle of the eighteenth century, almost half of all members of Parliament held such Crown offices or government contracts. Royal patronage was also used to manipulate parliamentary elections. The executive branch used money or liquor to bribe local voters into selecting their candidates. The small size of England's electorate

Tools for "managing" Parliament

fostered executive influence. Perhaps one-fourth of all adult males could vote, and many electoral districts were not adjusted to keep pace with population growth and resettlement. The notorious "rotten boroughs" each elected a member of Parliament to represent fewer than 500 easily bribable voters, while some large cities like Manchester and Leeds, newly populous because of industrial growth, had no representation in Parliament at all.

Americans liked to think that their colonial governments mirrored the ideal English constitution. In terms of formal structure, there were similarities. Most

Colonial governments

colonies had a royal governor who represented the monarch in America and a bicameral (two-house) legislature made up of a lower house (the assembly) and an upper house (or council). The democratically elected assembly, like the House of Commons, stood for popular interests, while the council, some of which were elected and others appointed, more roughly approximated the House of Lords.

But these formal similarities masked real differences between English and colonial governments. On the face of it, royal governors had much more power than the English Crown. Unlike kings and queens, royal governors could veto laws passed by assemblies; they could dissolve those bodies at will; they could create courts and dismiss judges. However, governors who asserted such powers found that their assemblies protested that popular liberty was being endangered. In any showdown most royal governors had to give way, for they lacked the government offices and contracts that bought loyalty. The colonial legislatures possessed additional leverage, since all of them retained the sole authority to levy taxes.

Even if the governors had enjoyed greater patronage powers, their efforts to influence colonial legislatures would have been frustrated by the sheer size of the American electorate. There were too many voters in America to bribe. Over half and possibly as many as 70 percent of all white adult colonial men were enfranchised. Property requirements were the same in America as in England, but widespread ownership of land in the colonies allowed most men to meet the qualifications easily.

The colonial electorate was also more watchful. Representatives were required to reside in the districts that they served, and a few even received binding instructions from their constituents about how to vote. Representation was also apportioned according to population far more equitably than in England. Since they were so closely tied to their constituents' wishes, colonial legislators were far less likely than members of Parliament to be swayed by executive pressure.

Most Americans were as pleased with their inexpensive and representative colonial governments as they were horrified by the conduct of politics in England. John Dickinson, a young Pennsylvanian training as a lawyer in London, was scandalized by a Parliamentary election he witnessed in 1754. The king and his ministers had spent over 100,000 pounds sterling to buy support for their candidates, he wrote his father, and "if a man cannot be brought to vote as he is desired, he is made dead drunk and kept in that state, never heard of by his family and friends, till all is over and he can do no harm."

The Imperial System before 1760

Colonials like Dickinson thought long and hard about the condition of England's society and politics. Meanwhile, the English thought about their colonies little, understood them less, and wished neither to think about them more nor to understand them better.

That indifference contributed to England's haphazard administration of its colonies. The Board of Trade and Plantations, created in 1696, gathered information about Atlantic trading and fishing, reviewed laws and petitions drawn up by colonial assemblies, and exchanged letters and instructions with royal governors. But the Board of Trade was only an advisory body.

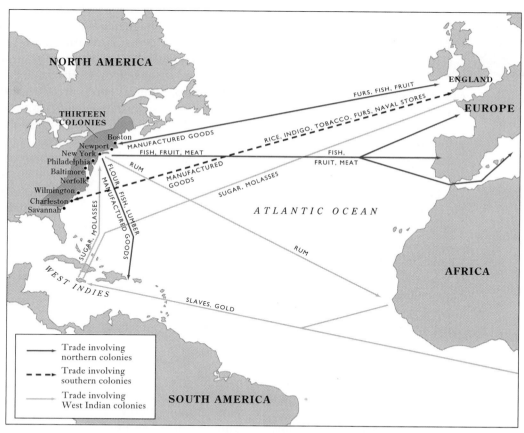

OVERSEAS TRADE NETWORKS   Commercial ties to Spain and Portugal, Africa, and the Caribbean sustained the growth of both seaports and commercial farming regions on the British North American mainland and enabled colonials to purchase an increasing volume of finished goods from England.

Real authority over the colonies was divided among an array of other agencies. The Treasury oversaw customs and gathered other royal revenues; the Admiralty Board enforced regulations of trade; the War Office orchestrated colonial defense. But these departments spent most of their hours handling more pressing responsibilities. Colonial affairs stood at the bottom of their agendas. Most British officials in America seemed equally indifferent. Often enough, they had been awarded their jobs in return for political support, not in recognition of administrative ability.

But the branch of England's government most indifferent to America was Parliament. Aside from passing an occasional law to regulate trade, restrict manufacturing, or direct monetary policy, Parliament made no effort to assert its authority in America. Its members assumed that Parliament's sovereignty extended over the entire empire, and nothing had occurred to make them think otherwise.

For the colonies, this chaotic and inefficient system of colonial administration worked well enough. The very weakness of imperial oversight left Americans with a great deal of freedom. Even England's regulation of trade rested lightly on the shoulders of most Americans. Southern planters were obliged to send their rice, indigo, and tobacco to Britain only, but they enjoyed favorable credit terms and knowledgeable marketing from English merchants. Colonials were prohibited from finishing iron products and exporting hats and textiles, but they had scant interest in developing domestic industries. Americans were required to import all manufactured goods through England, but by doing so, they acquired high-quality goods at low prices. At little sacrifice, most Americans obeyed imperial regulations. Only sugar, molasses, and tea were routinely smuggled.

The benefits of benign neglect

Following this policy of benign neglect the British empire muddled on to the satisfaction of most people on both sides of the Atlantic. Economic growth and political autonomy allowed most Americans to like being English despite their misgivings about their parent nation. The beauty of it was that Americans could be English in America, enjoying greater economic opportunity and political equality. If imperial arrangements had remained as they were in 1754, the empire might have muddled on indefinitely. But because of the French and the Indians on the American frontier, the British empire began to change. And those changes made it increasingly hard for Americans to be English in America.

TOWARD THE SEVEN YEARS' WAR

In the late spring of 1754, while Benjamin Franklin dreamed of unifying Americans, a young Virginian dreamed of military glory. As Franklin rode toward Albany, the young man, an inexperienced officer, led his company of Virginia militia toward Fort Duquesne, the French stronghold on the forks of the Ohio.

Less than a year earlier, the king's ministers had advised royal governors in America to halt the French advance into the Ohio country. The Virginia government organized an expedition against Fort Duquesne, placing at its head the young man who combined an imposing physique with the self-possession of an English gentleman. He wanted, more than anything, to become an officer in the regular British army.

But events in the Ohio country during that spring and summer did not go George Washington's way. French soldiers easily captured Fort Necessity, his crude outpost near Fort Duquesne. In early July, as the Albany Congress was debating, Washington was surrendering to a French force in the Penn-sylvania backcountry and beating a retreat back to Virginia. By the end of 1754, he had resigned his militia command and retired to his plantation at Mount Vernon. The disaster at Fort Necessity had dashed his dreams of martial glory and a regular army commission. He had no future as a soldier.

Washington at Fort Necessity

With the rout of Washington and his troops, the French grew bolder and the Indians more restless. The renewal of war between England and France was certain by the beginning of 1755. This time the contest between the two powers would decide the question of sovereignty over North America. That, at least, was the dream of William Pitt, who was about to become the most powerful man in England.

Even by the standards of English politicians, William Pitt was an odd character. Subject to bouts of illness and depression and loathed for his opportunism and egotism, Pitt surmounted every challenge, buoyed by a strong sense of destiny—his own and that of England. He believed that England must seize the world's trade, for trade meant wealth and wealth meant power. As early as the 1730s, Pitt recognized that the only obstacle between England and its destiny was France—and that the contest between the two for world supremacy would be decided in America. During King George's War, Pitt had mesmerized the House of Commons and the nation with his spellbinding oratory about England's imperial destiny. But the mounting cost of fighting prompted the government to accept peace with France in 1748. In frustration Pitt retired from public life.

The ambitions of William Pitt

But while Pitt sulked in his library, the rivalry for the American frontier moved toward a showdown. The French pressed their front lines eastward; the English pushed for land westward; the Indians maneuvered for position. Heartened by the news from America, Pitt clung to his dream of English commercial dominion and French defeat. By the late spring of 1754, as Benjamin Franklin and George Washington rode toward their defeats, William Pitt knew that he would have his war with France and his way with the world.

Other dreams would wait longer for fulfillment. The Albany Congress had demonstrated that a few Americans like Franklin had seen beyond the diversity of a divided colonial world to the possibility of union, however unaccustomed and untried. But it would take another war, one that restructured an empire, before some Americans saw in themselves a likeness that was not English.

chapter summary

Over the course of the eighteenth century, British North Americans grew increasingly diverse, which made the prospect of any future colonial political union apear remote.

- Differences became more pronounced among whites because of the immigration of larger numbers of non-English settlers, the spread of settlement to the backcountry, and the growth of major seaports.

- Although disorder was not uncommon either on the frontier or in cities, the most serious social and political conflict drew its strength from sectional controversies between east and west.

- The South became more embattled, too, as a result of the massive importation of slaves directly from Africa during the first half of the eighteenth century and a rising tide of black resistance to slavery.

- After about 1750 the growth of a native-born population strengthened black communal and family life.

- Religious conflict among colonials was intensified by the spread of Enlightenment ideas and the influence of the first Great Awakening.

- Despite their many differences, a majority of white colonials took pride in their common English ancestry and in belonging to a powerful empire.

 For quizzes and a variety of interactive resources, visit the book's Online Learning Center at www.mhhe.com/davidsonconcise3

SIGNIFICANT EVENTS

1689–1697	King William's War (War of the League of Augsburg)
1702	Anne becomes queen of England
1702–1713	Queen Anne's War (War of the Spanish Succession)
1714	George I becomes king of England, beginning Hanover dynasty
1727	George II becomes king of England
1730s–1740s	Rise in importation of black slaves in northern colonies
1739	George Whitefield's first preaching tour in America; Stono Rebellion in South Carolina
1744–1748	King George's War (War of the Austrian Succession)
1751	Franklin's essay on population
1754	The Albany Congress; Washington surrenders at Fort Necessity
1760–1769	South Carolina Regulation
1763	Paxton Boys march in Pennsylvania
1766	Tenant rebellion in New York
1766–1771	North Carolina Regulation (Battle of Alamance, 1771)

PART TWO

The Creation of a
New Republic

A s Benjamin Franklin had observed in 1751, the population of British North America was doubling approximately every 25 years. This astonishing rate was quite possibly the fastest in the world at the time. Even so, the surge was merely one part of a more general global rise in population during the second half of the eighteenth century. In sheer numbers China led the way. Its population of 150 million in 1700 had doubled to more than 313 million by the end of the century. Europe's total rose from about 118 million in 1700 to about 187 million a century later, the greatest growth coming on its eastern and western flanks, in Great Britain and Russia. African and Indian populations seem to have increased as well.

Climate may have been one reason for the worldwide rise. In Europe, warmer and drier seasons produced generally better harvests. Furthermore, health and nutrition improved globally with the spread of native American crops. Irish farmers discovered that a single acre planted with the lowly American potato could support an entire family. The tomato added crucial vitamins to the Mediterranean diet, while maize provided more calories per acre than any European or African grain. In China the American sweet potato thrived in hilly regions where rice would not grow.

Not only plants but diseases were carried back and forth by European ships. As we have seen, contact between previously isolated peoples produced extreme mortality from epidemics. But after more than two centuries of sustained contact, Indians developed increased biological resistance to European and African illnesses.

The frequent circulation of diseases worldwide led to a more stable environment in which populations began to swell.

During the years in which Europeans explored the Atlantic frontiers of North and South America, Slavic and Romanian pioneers were moving eastward into the Eurasian steppes. There they turned sparsely settled pastoral lands into feudal manors and farms. In northern forests unsuitable for farming, Russian fur traders advanced eastward across Siberia until they reached the Pacific in the 1630s. By the 1780s Russian pioneers had pushed into Alaska and down the Pacific American coast, bumping up against western Europeans who were harvesting furs from Canada's forests and streams.

Both flanks of this European thrust often depended on forced labor, especially in agricultural settings. As we have seen, the institution of slavery in North America became increasingly restrictive over the course of the seventeenth century. Similarly, the plight of serfs worsened from 1500 to 1650 as the demand for labor increased in eastern Europe. In 1574 Polish nobles received the right to punish their serfs entirely as they pleased—including execution, if they chose. By 1603, Russian peasants were routinely sold along with the land they worked.

The eighteenth-century Enlightenment penetrated eastern Europe, too, as it had the urban centers of North America. Russia's Peter the Great absorbed many ideas when he traveled to England and western Europe. As czar (1689–1725), he attempted to put them to use in westernizing Russia. During the years Catherine the Great ruled (1762–1796), she imported Western architects, sculptors, and musicians to grace her court. But Catherine's limits to toleration were made brutally clear in 1773. The same year that a group of rowdy Americans were dumping tea into Boston harbor, a Cossack soldier named Emelian Pugachev launched a peasant rebellion, seeking to abolish serfdom and taxes. Catherine ruthlessly imprisoned and executed Pugachev. In 1775 she granted Russian nobles even more absolute control over their serfs.

The Americans who rebelled more successfully in 1775 did so not out of a serf's desperation—quite the opposite. With the significant exception of enslaved African Americans, the distance between the poorest and richest colonials was smaller than anywhere in Europe. And the British tradition of representative government ensured a broader involvement of citizens in governing themselves. Thus an American Revolution was hardly inevitable in 1776.

As we shall see, the timing of the colonists' break with Great Britain was the result of specific decisions made on both sides of the Atlantic. Given the failure of the Albany Plan of Union in 1754, it is perhaps surprising that the war for independence ended in the creation of a new and remarkably stable American republic. But that is exactly what happened. American colonials, who in 1763 liked being English and gloried in the British empire, gradually came to think of themselves as independent Americans, subject neither to a British monarch nor to Parliament.

CHAPTER 5

Toward the War for American Independence (1754–1776)

preview • **Parliament passed the Sugar Act, Stamp Act, and other measures of the early 1760s in hopes of binding the American colonies more closely to the empire. Instead, once-loyal Americans became convinced that their constitutional rights were being violated: the right to consent to taxes, the right to a trial by jury, and the freedom from standing armies. With the passage of the harsh Coercive Acts of 1774, a break with Britain was not long in coming.**

Americans liked being English. They had liked being English from the beginning of colonial settlement, but they liked it more than ever for a few years after 1759. One wonderful day during those years—September 16, 1762—Bostonians turned out to celebrate belonging to the British empire. Soldiers mustered on the Common; bells pealed from the steeples of local churches; the charge of guns fired from the battery resounded through towns; strains of orchestra music from an outdoor concert floated through the city's crowded streets and narrow alleys. When darkness fell and bonfires illuminated the city, Bostonians consumed "a vast quantity of liquor," drinking "loyal healths" to their young king, George III, and in celebration of Britain's victory in the Seven Years' War.

When the great news of that triumph reached the North American mainland in the fall of 1762, similar celebrations broke out all over the colonies. But the party in America had begun long before, with a string of British victories in French Canada in the glorious year of 1759. It continued through 1760 when all of Canada fell to Anglo-American forces and George III became England's new king. In February of 1763, when the Treaty of Paris formally ended the war, Britain had become the largest and most powerful empire in the Western world. Americans were among His Majesty's proudest subjects.

Thirteen years after the celebration of 1762, Boston was a different place. Pride in belonging to the empire had shriveled to shrill charges that England conspired to enslave its colonies. Massachusetts led the way, drawing other colonies deep into resistance. Bostonians initiated many of the petitions and resolves against British authority. When words did not work, they ignited riots, harassed British officials, baited British troops, and destroyed British property. In 1775, they were laying plans for rebellion against the British empire.

An ironic fate overtook that generation of Americans who loved being English, boasted of their rights as Britons, and celebrated their membership in the all-conquering empire. That very pride drove colonials into rebellion, for the men who ran the British empire after 1763 would not allow Americans to be English. Even before the Seven Years' War, some colonials saw that diverging paths of social and political development made them different from the English. After the Seven Years' War, events demonstrated to even more colonials that they were not considered the political equals of the English who lived in England. As their disillusionment with the empire deepened, British North Americans from Massachusetts to Georgia slowly discovered a new identity as Americans and declared their independence from being English.

A process of disillusionment

THE SEVEN YEARS' WAR

The Seven Years' War, which actually lasted nine years, pitted Britain and its ally, Prussia, against France, in league with Austria and Spain. The battle raged from 1754 until 1763, ranging over the continent of Europe, the coast of west Africa, India, the Philippines, the Caribbean, and North America.

The Years of Defeat

The war started when the contest over the Ohio River valley among the English, the French, and the Indians led to George Washington's surrender at Fort Necessity in 1754 (page 115). That episode stiffened Britain's resolve to assert its own claims to the Ohio country. In the summer of 1755, as two British regiments led by Major General Edward Braddock approached the French outpost at Fort Duquesne on the forks of the Ohio, they were ambushed and cut to pieces by a party of French and Indians. Washington led the mortally wounded Braddock and the remnants of his army in a retreat. During the summer of Braddock's defeat, New Englanders fared somewhat better against French forces in Nova Scotia and deported 6000 farmers from that region. The Acadians, as they were known, had their land confiscated, and they were dispersed throughout the colonies.

Braddock's defeat

There followed two disastrous years for Britain and its allies. When England and France formally declared war in May 1756, John Campbell, the earl of Loudoun, took command of the North American theater. American soldiers and colonial assemblies alike hated Lord Loudoun. They balked at his efforts to take command over colonial troops and dragged their heels at his demands for men and supplies. Meanwhile, the French strengthened their position in Canada by

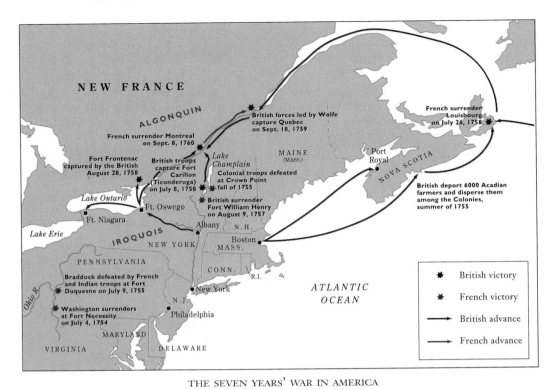

THE SEVEN YEARS' WAR IN AMERICA

appointing a new commanding general, Louis Joseph, the marquis de Montcalm. Montcalm drove southward, capturing key British forts and threatening the security of both New York and New England. While he prospered in America, the British were also taking a beating from the French in Europe and in India.

During the years when the French seemed unstoppable, the British looked for help from the strongest tribes of the interior—the Iroquois in the North, the Creek, Choctaw, and Cherokee in the South. Instead, Benjamin Franklin's worst fears were realized: most tribes adopted neutrality or joined the French. As France seemed certain to carry the continent, Indian attacks on English frontier settlements increased.

The Years of Victory

As British fortunes worsened throughout 1756 and 1757, William Pitt resumed his political career and took personal control over the war. "I know that I can save this country and that no one else can," he announced. Leaving the fighting in Europe to the Prussians, Pitt focused the full strength of the British military on beating the French in America. Pitt also renewed

William Pitt turns the tide

colonial support for the war effort by replacing Lord Loudoun and giving his successor far more limited authority over colonial troops. And Pitt sent requests for men and money directly to each colonial assembly—accompanied by promises of reimbursement in gold and silver.

With Pitt now in control, the tide of battle turned. In July of 1758, the British gained control of the St. Lawrence River when the French fortress at Louisbourg fell before the combined force of the Royal Navy and British and colonial troops. In August, a force of New Englanders strangled France's frontier defenses by capturing Fort Frontenac, thereby isolating French forts lining the Great Lakes and the Ohio valley. The Indians, seeing the French routed from the interior, switched their allegiance to the English.

The British succeeded even more brilliantly in 1759. In Canada, Brigadier General James Wolfe gambled on a daring stratagem and won Quebec from Montcalm. Under the cover of darkness, naval squadrons landed Wolfe's men beneath the city's steep bluffs, where they scaled the heights to a plateau known as the Plains of Abraham. Montcalm matched Wolfe's recklessness and offered battle. Five days later both Wolfe and Montcalm lay dead, along with 1400 French soldiers and 600 British and American troops. Quebec had fallen to the British. A year later the French surrender of Montreal ended the fighting in North America.

Wolfe and Montcalm battle for Quebec

The Treaty of Paris, signed in February 1763, ended the French presence on the continent of North America. The terms confirmed British title to all French territory east of the Mississippi as well as to Spanish Florida. (Spain had made the mistake of entering the war, against Britain, in 1762.) France ceded to its ally Spain all of its land lying west of the Mississippi and the port of New Orleans.

Postwar Expectations

Britain's victory gave rise to great expectations among Americans. The end of the war, they were sure, meant the end of high taxes. The terms of the peace, they were confident, meant the opening of the Ohio valley's fertile land. The prosperity of the war years alone made for a mood of optimism. British military spending and William Pitt's subsidies had made money for farmers, merchants, artisans, and anyone else who had anything to do with supplying the army or navy. Colonials also took pride in their contributions of troops and money to the winning of the war. In view of that support, Americans expected to be accorded more consideration within the British empire. Now, as one anonymous pamphleteer put it, Americans would "not be thought presumptuous, if they consider[ed] themselves upon an equal footing" with English in the parent country.

Colonial pride and optimism

But if Americans took pride in being English, most imperial officials in America thought that they had done a poor job of showing it. British statesmen complained that colony assemblies had been tightfisted when it came to supplying the

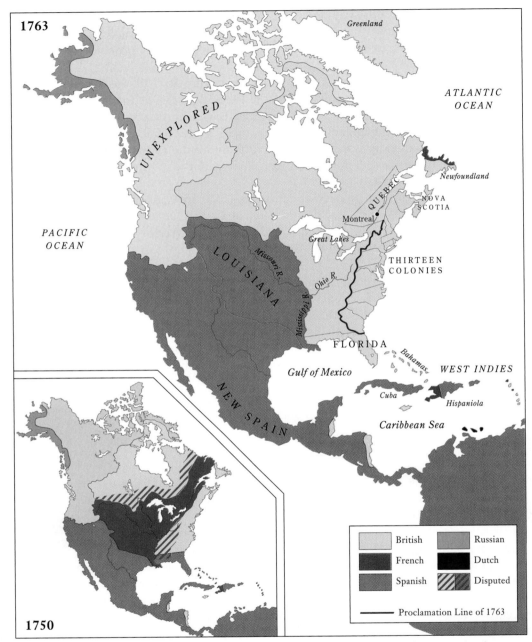

EUROPEAN CLAIMS IN NORTH AMERICA, 1750 AND 1763   The British victory in the
Seven Years' War secured their title to a large portion of the present-day
United States and Canada.

army. British commanders charged that colonial troops had been lily-livered when it came to fighting the French. Such charges were unjust, but they stuck in the minds of many Britons, who concluded that the Americans were selfish and self-interested, unconcerned with the welfare of the empire as a whole. Britain had accumulated a huge national debt that would saddle the nation with high taxes for years to come. To make matters worse, some Britons suspected that, with the French removed from North America, the colonies would move toward independence.

English resentments

Americans in 1763 were not, in truth, revolutionaries in the making. They were loyal British subjects in the flush of postwar patriotism. Americans in 1763, deeply divided among themselves, were not even "Americans." But most postwar English colonials did expect to enjoy a more equal status in the empire. And most Britons had no inclination to accord them that equality. The differing expectations of the colonies' place in the empire poised the postwar generation for crisis.

THE IMPERIAL CRISIS

It was common sense. Great Britain had waged a costly war to secure its empire in America; now it needed to consolidate those gains. The empire's North American territory needed to be protected, its administration tightened, and its colonies made as profitable as possible to the parent nation. In other words, the empire needed to be centralized. That conclusion dictated Britain's decision to leave several thousand troops in America after the Seven Years' War. The British army would prevent France from trying to regain its lost territory.

New Troubles on the Frontier

Keeping troops in North America made sense because of the Indians, too. With the French gone, English traders, speculators, and settlers would swarm into the West. Without the French as trading partners, Indian tribes were in a weaker position to deal with the British. No longer could they count on a steady supply of arms and ammunition from European rivals competing for their furs. The Indians were edgy, expecting the worst, and the British were worried.

Events bore out British fears. In the early 1760s a Lenni Lenape prophet, Neolin, began advising the tribes to return to their native ways and resist the spread of white settlement. Pontiac, an Ottawa chief, embraced Neolin's message of renaissance and rebellion. Other interior tribes joined Pontiac's offensive, and during the summer of 1763 they captured all the British outposts west of Pittsburgh. British troops and American militia finally smothered Pontiac's Rebellion.

Pontiac's Rebellion

Thereafter British administrators discovered another use for troops in America—to enforce the newly issued Proclamation of 1763. That order, issued by

Proclamation of 1763

England's Board of Trade, prohibited white settlement past the crest of the Appalachian Mountains. Restricting westward movement might ease Indian fears, the British hoped, and so stave off future conflicts. It might also keep the colonials confined to the seaboard, where they were more easily subject to the control of the empire.

George Grenville's New Measures

A final reason for keeping troops in the colonies occurred to the British by 1764: an armed presence could enforce American acceptance of other new and sensible measures for tightening the empire. Those measures were the solutions of George Grenville, the First Lord of the Treasury, to the financial problems facing England after the Seven Years' War.

Britain's national debt had doubled in the decade after 1754. Adding to that burden was the drain of supporting troops in the colonies. Grenville recognized that English taxpayers alone could not shoulder the costs of winning and maintaining an empire. As matters stood, heavy taxes were already triggering protests among hard-pressed Britons. Americans, by contrast, paid comparatively low taxes to their colonial governments and little in trade duties to the empire. Indeed, Grenville discovered that the colonial customs service paid out four times more in salaries to its collectors than it gathered in duties, operating at a net loss.

The income from customs duties was slim because colonial merchants evaded the Molasses Act of 1733. That tariff imposed a hefty duty of six pence on every gallon of molasses imported from the French and Dutch sugar islands.

Molasses Act of 1733

Parliament had designed the duty to encourage colonists to consume more British molasses, which carried a higher price but came duty-free. New England merchants, who distilled molasses into rum and then traded it to the southern colonies and to west Africa, claimed that the British sugar islands could not satisfy the demands of their distilleries. Regrettably, the merchants were forced to import more molasses from the French and Dutch. More regrettably, to keep their costs low and the price of their rum competitive, they had to bribe British customs officials. With the going rate for bribes ranging from a halfpenny to a penny and a half per gallon, the whole regrettable arrangement made handsome profits for both merchants and customs inspectors.

George Grenville reasoned that if Americans could pay out a little under the table to protect an illegal trade, they would willingly pay a little more to go legit-

Sugar Act

imate. Parliament agreed. In April 1764 it passed the Revenue Act, commonly called the Sugar Act, which actually lowered the duty on foreign molasses from six to three pence a gallon. But Grenville intended to enforce the new duty and to crack down on smugglers. Those caught on the wrong side of the law were to be tried in admiralty courts, where verdicts were handed down by royally appointed judges rather than colonial juries more likely to sympathize with their fellow citizens.

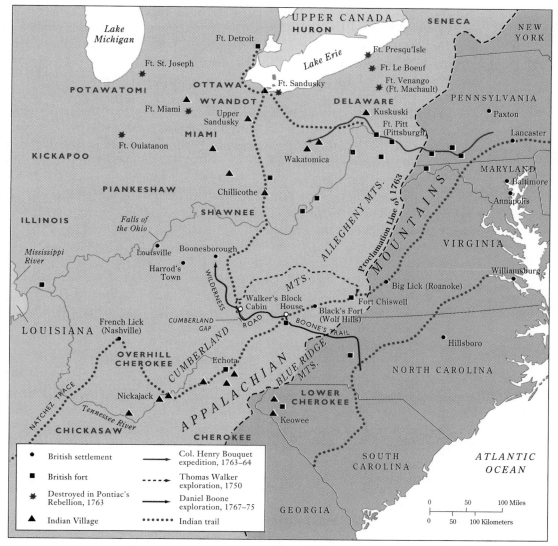

THE APPALACHIAN FRONTIER, 1750–1775 Increasingly, land-hungry colonials spilled into the west through the Cumberland Gap, a notch in the chain of mountains stretching the length of the North American interior. A route through the gap was scouted in 1750 by Dr. Thomas Walker and a party of Virginians on behalf of a company of land speculators. In 1763, Indians led by Pontiac seized eight British forts before troops under Colonel Henry Bouquet stopped the offensive. In 1775 Daniel Boone led the first large party of pioneers through the gap to Boonesborough, in present-day Kentucky.

By tightening customs enforcement, Grenville hoped to raise more revenue from the American trade. Unlike the earlier Navigation Acts, which imposed duties mainly to regulate trade, the Sugar Act's duties were intended mainly to yield revenue. Even so, Grenville regarded his demands as modest: he did not expect colonials to help reduce England's national debt or even to cover the entire cost of their defense.

Grenville made other modest proposals, all approved by Parliament. There was the Currency Act of 1764, which prohibited the colonies from making their paper money legal tender. That prevented Americans from paying their debts to British traders in currency that had fallen to less than its face value.

Currency and Quartering Acts

There was the Quartering Act of 1765, which obliged any colony in which troops were stationed to provide them with suitable accommodations. That contributed to the cost of keeping British forces in America. Finally, in March of 1765, Parliament passed the Stamp Act.

The Stamp Act placed taxes on legal documents, customs papers, newspapers, almanacs, college diplomas, playing cards, and dice. After November 1, 1765, all these items had to bear a stamp signifying that their possessor had paid the tax. Violators of the Stamp Act, like those disobeying the Sugar Act, were to be tried without juries in admiralty courts. The English

Stamp Act

had been paying a similar tax for nearly a century, so it seemed to Grenville and Parliament that colonials could have no objections.

Every packet boat from London that brought news of Parliament passing another one of Grenville's measures dampened postwar optimism. For all of the differences between the colonies and England, Americans still held much in common with the English. Those shared ideas included firm beliefs about why the British constitution, British customs, and British history all served to protect liberty and the rights of the empire's free-born citizens. For that reason the new measures, which seemed like common sense to Grenville and Parliament, did not make sense at all to Americans.

The Beginning of Colonial Resistance

Like other Britons, colonials in America accepted a maxim laid down by the English philosopher John Locke: property guaranteed liberty. Property, in this view, was not merely real estate, or wealth, or material possessions. It was

Locke on property and liberty

the source of strength for every individual, providing the freedom to think and act independently. Protecting the individual's right or property was the main responsibility of government, for if personal property was not sacred, then neither was personal liberty.

It followed from this close connection between property, power, and liberty that no people should be taxed without their consent or that of their elected representatives. The power to tax was the power to destroy by depriving a person of property. Yet both the Sugar Act and the Stamp Act were taxes passed by members of Parliament, none of whom had been elected by colonials.

Like the English, colonials also prized the right of trial by jury as one of their basic constitutional liberties. Yet both the Sugar Act and the Stamp Act would prosecute offenders in the admiralty courts, not through local courts, thus depriving colonials of the freedom claimed by all other English men and women.

The concern for protecting individual liberties was only one of the convictions shaping the colonies' response to Britain's new policies. Equally important was their deep suspicion of power itself, a preoccupation that colonials shared with a minority of radical English thinkers. These radicals were known by a variety of names—the "Country Party," the "Commonwealthmen," and "the Opposition." They drew their inspiration from the ancient tradition of classical republicanism, which held that representative government safeguarded liberty more reliably than either monarchy or oligarchy. Underlying that judgment was the belief that human beings were driven by passion and insatiable ambition. One person, or even a few people, could not be entrusted with governing, because they would inevitably become corrupted by power and turn into tyrants. Even in representative governments, the people were obliged to watch those in power at all times: the price of liberty was eternal vigilance.

Influence of the English Opposition

The Opposition believed that the people of England were not watching their rulers closely enough. During the first half of the eighteenth century, they argued, the entire executive branch of England's government—monarchs and their ministers—had been corrupted by their appetite for power. Proof of their ambition was the executive bureaucracy of military and civil officials that steadily grew larger, interfered more with citizens' lives, and drained increasing amounts of money from taxpayers. Even more alarming, in the Opposition's view, the executive branch's bribery of members of Parliament was corrupting the representative branch of England's government. They warned that a sinister conspiracy originating in the executive branch of government threatened English liberty.

Opposition thinkers commanded little attention in England, where they were dismissed as a discontented radical fringe. But they were revered by political leaders in the American colonies. The Opposition's view of politics confirmed colonial anxieties about England, doubts that ran deeper after 1763. Parliament's attempt to tax the colonies and the quartering of a standing army on the frontier confirmed all too well the Opposition's portrayal of how powerful rulers turned themselves into tyrants and reduced the people whom they ruled to slaves.

In sum, Grenville's new measures led some colonials to suspect that ambitious men ruling England might be conspiring against American liberties. At the very least, the new measures implied that colonials were not the political equals of the English living in England. They were not entitled to taxation by consent or to trial by jury. To be treated like second-class citizens wounded colonials' pride and mocked their postwar expectations. The heady dreams of the role that the colonies would play in the British empire evaporated, leaving behind the bitter dregs of disappointment. And after the passage of the Stamp Act, dismay mushroomed into militant protest.

Britain's determination to centralize its empire after 1763 was a disaster of timing, not just psychologically but also economically. By then, the colonies were in the throes of a recession. The boom produced in America by government spending during the war had collapsed once subsidies were withdrawn. Colonial merchants were left with full stocks of imported goods gathering dust on their shelves. Farmers lost the brisk and profitable market of the army.

Impact of postwar recession

Colonial response to the Sugar Act reflected the painful postwar readjustments. New England merchants led the opposition, objecting to the Sugar Act principally on economic grounds. But with the passage of the Stamp Act, the terms of the imperial debate widened, and resistance intensified within all the colonies. The Stamp Act hit all colonials, not just New England merchants. It took money from the pockets of anyone who made a will, filed a deed, traded out of a colonial port, bought a newspaper, consulted an almanac, graduated from college, took a chance at dice, or played cards. More important, the Stamp Act served notice that Parliament possessed the rightful authority to tax the colonies directly and for the sole purpose of raising revenue.

Riots and Resolves

That unprecedented assertion provoked an unprecedented development: the first display of colonial unity. A nearly unanimous chorus of outrage greeted Parliament's claim that it could tax the colonies. During the spring and summer of 1765, American assemblies passed resolves denying Parliament that authority. The right to tax Americans belonged to colonial assemblies alone, they argued, by the law of nature and by the liberties guaranteed in colonial charters and in the British constitution.

Virginia's assembly, the House of Burgesses, took the lead in protesting the Stamp Act, prodded by Patrick Henry, a young lawyer from western Virginia. The Burgesses passed Henry's resolutions upholding their exclusive right to tax Virginians. They stopped short of adopting those resolves that called for outright resistance to the Stamp Act. When news of Virginia's stand spread to the rest of the colonies, other assemblies followed suit, affirming that the sole right to tax Americans resided in their elected representatives. But some colonial newspapers deliberately printed a different story—that the Burgesses had approved all of Henry's resolves, including one that sanctioned disobedience to any Parliamentary tax. That prompted a few assemblies to endorse resistance. In October 1765 delegates from nine colonies convened in New York, where they prepared a joint statement of the American position and petitioned the king and Parliament to repeal both the Sugar Act and the Stamp Act.

Patrick Henry's resolves

Meanwhile, colonial leaders turned to the press to arouse popular opposition to the Stamp Act. Disposed by the writings of the English Opposition to think of politics in conspiratorial terms, they warned that Grenville and the king's other ministers schemed to deprive the colonies of their liberties by unlawfully taxing their property. The Stamp Act was only the first step in a sinister plan to enslave Americans. Whether or not dark fears of a ministerial conspiracy haunted most colonials in 1765, many resisted the Stamp Act. The merchants of Boston, New York, and Philadelphia agreed to stop importing English goods in order to pressure British traders to lobby for repeal. In every colony, organizations emerged to ensure that the Stamp Act, if not repealed, would never be enforced.

The new resistance groups, which styled themselves the "Sons of Liberty," consisted of traders, lawyers, and prosperous artisans. With great success, they organized the lower classes of seaports in opposition to the Stamp Act. The sailors, dockworkers, poor artisans, apprentices, and servants who poured into the streets resembled mobs that had been organized from time to time earlier in the century. Previous riots against houses of prostitution, merchants who hoarded goods, or supporters of smallpox inoculation had not been spontaneous, uncontrolled outbursts. Crowds chose their targets and their tactics carefully and then carried out the communal will with little violence.

Sons of Liberty

In every colonial city, the mobs of 1765 burnt the stamp distributors in effigy, insulted them on the streets, demolished their offices, and attacked their homes. By the first of November, the day that the Stamp Act took effect, most of the stamp distributors had resigned.

Repeal of the Stamp Act

Meanwhile, the repeal of the Stamp Act was already in the works back in England. The man who came—unintentionally—to America's relief was George III. The young king was a good man, industrious, and devoted to the empire, but he was also immature and not overendowed with intellect. Insecurity made the young king an irksome master, and he ran through ministers rapidly. By the end of 1765, George had dismissed Grenville for reasons unrelated to the uproar in America and appointed a new first minister, the marquis of Rockingham. Rockingham had opposed the Stamp Act from the outset, and he had no desire to enforce it. He received support from London merchants, who were beginning to feel the pinch of the American nonimportation campaign, and secured repeal of the Stamp Act in March 1766.

The Stamp Act controversy demonstrated to colonials how similar in political outlook they were to one another and how different they were from the British. Americans had found that they shared the same assumptions about the meaning of representation. To counter colonial objections to the Stamp Act, Grenville and his supporters had claimed that Americans *were* represented in Parliament, even though they had elected none of its members. Americans were virtually represented, Grenville insisted, for each member of Parliament stood for the interests of the whole empire, not just those of the particular constituency that had elected him.

Virtual versus actual representation

Thomas Hutchinson Recounts the Destruction of His Boston Home during the Stamp Act Riots

n the evening whilst I was at supper and my children round me somebody ran in and said the mob were coming. I directed my children to fly to a secure Place and shut up my house as I had done before intending not to quit it but my eldest daughter repented her leaving me and hastened back and protested she would not quit the house unless I did. I could not stand against this and withdrew with her to a neighbouring house where I had been but a few minutes before the hellish crew fell upon my house with the Rage of devils and in a moment with axes split down the doors and entered my son being in the great entry heard them cry damn him he is upstairs we'll have him. Some ran immediately as high as the top of the house others filled the rooms below and cellars. . . . Messages soon came one after another to the house where I was to inform me the mob were coming in Pursuit of me and I was obliged to retire thro yards and gardens to a house more remote where I remained until 4 o'clock by which time one of the best finished houses in the Province had nothing remaining but bare walls and floors. Not contented with tearing off all the wainscot and hangings and splitting the doors to pieces . . . they began to take the slate and boards from the roof and were prevented only by the approaching daylight from a total demolition of the building. The garden fence was laid flat and all my trees, etc. broke down to the ground. Such ruins were never seen in America. Besides my Plate and family Pictures houshold furniture of every kind my own children and servants apparel they carried off about 900 pounds sterling in money and emptied the house of every thing . . . not leaving a single book or paper in it and have scattered or destroyed all the manuscripts and other papers I had been collecting for 30 years.

Source: Thomas Hutchinson to Richard Jackson, August 30, 1765, Massachusetts Archives, IIVI, pp. 146–147.

Colonials could see no virtue in the theory of virtual representation. After all, the circumstances and interests of colonials, living an ocean apart, were so different from those of Britons. The newly recognized consensus among Americans was that colonials could be truly represented only by those whom they had elected. Their view, known as actual representation, emphasized that elected officials were directly accountable to their constituents.

Americans also had discovered that they agreed about the extent of Parliament's authority over the colonies: it stopped at the right to tax. Colonials conceded Parliament's right to legislate and to regulate trade for the good of the whole empire. But taxation, in their view, was the free gift of the people through their representatives—who were not sitting in Parliament.

Members of Parliament had brushed aside colonial petitions and resolves, all but ignoring their constitutional argument. To make its authority perfectly clear, Parliament accompanied the repeal of the Stamp Act with a Declaratory Act, asserting that it had the power to make laws for the colonies "in all cases whatsoever." In fact, the Declaratory Act clarified nothing: did Parliament understand the power of legislation to include the power of taxation?

Declaratory Act

The Townshend Acts

In the summer of 1766 George III—again inadvertently—gave the colonies what should have been an advantage by changing ministers again. The king replaced Rockingham with William Pitt, who enjoyed great favor among colonials for his leadership during the Seven Years' War and for his opposition to the Stamp Act. Almost alone among British politicians, Pitt had grasped and approved the colonists' constitutional objections to taxation.

If the man who believed that Americans were "the sons not the bastards of England" had been well enough to govern, matters between Great Britain and the colonies might have turned out differently. But almost immediately after Pitt took office, his health collapsed, and power passed into the hands of Charles Townshend, the chancellor of the exchequer. Townshend's two main concerns were to strengthen the authority of Parliament and royal officials in the colonies at the expense of American assemblies and to raise more revenue at the expense of American taxpayers. In 1767 he persuaded Parliament to tax the lead, paint, paper, glass, and tea that Americans imported from Britain.

This 1766 porcelain of *Lord Chatham and America* attests to the popularity of William Pitt, Earl of Chatham, among Americans who resisted the Stamp Act. The artist's representation of "America" as a black woman kneeling in gratitude echoes the colonists' association of taxation with slavery.

Townshend used several strategies to limit the power of colonial assemblies. First, he instructed the royal governors to take a firmer hand. To set the example, he singled out for punishment the New York legislature, which was refusing to comply with provisions of the Quartering Act of 1765. The New York assembly held that the cost of quartering the troops constituted a form of indirect taxation. But Parliament backed Townshend, suspending the New York assembly in 1767 until it agreed to obey the Quartering Act.

Townshend also dipped into the revenue from his new tariffs in order to support royal officials. That freed them from the influence of colonial assemblies, which had previously funded the salaries of governors, customs collectors, and judges. Townshend's policies enlarged the number of those bureaucrats. To ensure more effective enforcement of all the duties on imports, he created an American Board of Customs Commissioners, who appointed a small army of new customs collectors. He also established three new vice-admiralty courts in Boston, New York, and Charleston to bring smugglers to justice.

The Resistance Organizes

In Townshend's efforts to centralize the administration of the British empire, Americans saw new evidence that they were not being treated like the English. In newspapers and pamphlets colonial leaders repeated their earlier arguments against taxation. The most widely read publication, "A Letter from a Farmer in Pennsylvania," was the work of John Dickinson, who urged Americans to protest the Townshend duties with a show of superior virtue—hard work, thrift, simplicity, and home manufacturing. By consuming fewer imported English luxuries, Dickinson argued, Americans would advance the cause of repeal. The Townshend Acts also shaped the destiny of Samuel Adams, a leader in the Massachusetts assembly and a consummate political organizer and agitator. First his enemies and later his friends claimed that Adams had decided on independence for America as early as 1768. In that year he persuaded the assembly to send to other colonial legislatures a circular letter condemning the acts and calling for a united American resistance.

John Dickinson and Samuel Adams

As John Dickinson and Samuel Adams whipped up public outrage against the Townshend Acts, the Sons of Liberty again organized the opposition in the streets. Customs officials, like the stamp distributors before them, became targets of popular hatred. But the customs collectors gave as good as they got, using the flimsiest excuses to seize American vessels for violating royal regulations and shaking down American merchants for what amounted to protection money. The racketeering in the customs service brought tensions in Boston to a flashpoint in June 1768 after officials seized and condemned the *Liberty*, a sloop belonging to one of the city's biggest merchants, John Hancock. Several thousand Bostonians vented their anger in a night of rioting, searching out and roughing up customs officials.

The *Liberty* seized

The new secretary of state for the colonies, Lord Hillsborough, responded by sending two regiments of troops to Boston. In the fall of 1768 the redcoats, like a conquering army, paraded into town under the cover of warships lying off the harbor. In the months that followed, citizens bristled when challenged on the streets by armed soldiers.

The *Liberty* riot and the arrival of British troops in Boston pushed colonial assemblies to coordinate their resistance more closely. Most legislatures endorsed the Massachusetts circular letter and adopted agreements not to import or to consume British goods. The reluctance among some merchants to revive nonimportation in 1767 gave way to greater enthusiasm by 1768, and by early 1769, such agreements were in effect throughout the colonies.

Protests against the Townshend Acts raised the stakes by creating new institutions to carry forward the resistance. Subscribers to the nonimportation agreements established "committees of inspection" to enforce the ban on trade with Britain. The committees publicly denounced merchants who continued to import, vandalized their warehouses, forced them to stand under the gallows, and sometimes resorted to tar and feathers.

Committees of inspection

After 1768 the resistance also brought a broader range of colonials into the politics of protest. Artisans, who recognized that nonimportation would spur domestic manufacturing, began to organize as independent political groups. In many towns, women took an active part in opposing the Townshend duties. The "Daughters of Liberty" took to heart John Dickinson's advice: they wore homespun clothing instead of English finery, served coffee instead of tea, and boycotted shops selling British goods.

The Boston Massacre

The situation in Boston deteriorated steadily. British troops found themselves regularly cursed by citizens and occasionally pelted with stones, dirt, and human excrement. The British regulars were particularly unpopular among Boston's laboring classes because they competed with them for jobs. Off-duty soldiers moonlighted as maritime laborers, and they sold their services at cheaper rates than the wages paid to locals. By 1769, brawls between British regulars and waterfront workers broke out with unsettling frequency.

With some 4000 redcoats enduring daily contact with some 15,000 Bostonians under the sway of Samuel Adams, what happened on the night of March 5, 1770, was nearly inevitable. A crowd gathered around the customshouse for the sport of heckling its guard of 10 soldiers. The redcoats panicked and fended off insults and snowballs with live fire, hitting 11 rioters and killing 5. Labeling the bloodshed "the Boston Massacre," Adams and other propagandists publicized that "atrocity" throughout the colonies.

While Townshend's policies spurred the resistance in America, Parliament recognized that Townshend's duties only discouraged sales to colonials and encouraged them to manufacture at home. The way to repeal had been cleared by the unexpected death of Townshend shortly after Parliament adopted his proposals. In 1770 his successor, Lord North, convinced Parliament to repeal all the Townshend duties except the one on tea, allowing that tax to stand as a source of revenue and as a symbol of their authority.

The International Sons of Liberty

The resistance after 1768 grew broader in another sense as well. Many of its supporters in the American colonies felt a new sense of kinship with freedom fighters throughout Europe and increasingly regarded themselves as part of a trans-Atlantic network of the friends of liberty. They eagerly read about the doings of men like Charles Lucas, an Irish newspaper editor and member of the Irish Parliament, and John Wilkes, a London journalist and a leading politician of the Opposition. Both Lucas and Wilkes charged the king's ministers with corrupting the political life of the British Isles. The triumphs and setbacks of rebels combating tyrannical regimes even in distant Poland and Turkey engaged colonial sympathies. But perhaps the cause abroad dearest to the hearts of liberty's friends in America during the late 1760s was the fate of Corsica.

For years, the state of Genoa had been trying to impose its rule on this tiny island off the coast of Italy. Led by Pascal Paoli, the Corsicans had for decades waged what one New York newpaper touted as a "glorious struggle" against Genoese rule, an insurgency "interesting to every friend of liberty." In 1768, Genoa sold its title to the island to France, prompting many in the British Empire to hope that England would rally to defend Corsica's freedom. But British statesmen had no intention of going to war with France over tiny Corsica, and when French troops routed his rebel army, Paoli fled to England in 1769. To add insult to injury, Paoli, once lionized by the colonial resistance as "the greatest man of earth," snubbed Opposition leaders like John Wilkes, hobnobbed with the likes of the Duke of Grafton, the minister of the treasury, and even accepted a pension of 1000 pounds a year from George III.

> **Colonials follow Paoli's struggle**

The moral of this sad story, one closely followed by the readers of colonial newspapers, was that the British ministry's corruption pervaded not only the empire but all of Europe. Merely by doing nothing, the king's ministers had snuffed out the Corsican resistance. And by doling out a mere thousand pounds annually, they had bought the loyalty of its leader, the great Paoli himself. In the fate of Corsica and its sons of liberty, many colonials saw the threat that ambitious men posed to popular liberty—and a disturbing portent for America's future.

Resistance Revived

Repeal of the Townshend duties took the wind from the sails of American resistance for more than two years. But the controversy between England and the colonies had not been resolved. Beneath the banked fires of protest smoldered the live embers of Americans' political inequality. Any shift in the wind could fan those embers into flames.

The wind did shift, quite literally, on Narragansett Bay in 1772, running aground the *Gaspee*, a British naval schooner in hot pursuit of Rhode Island smugglers. Providence residents celebrated its misfortune with a bonfire built on the ship's deck. Outraged British officials sent a special commission to look into the matter, intending once again to bypass the established colonial court system. The arrival of the Gaspee Commission reignited the imperial crisis, and American resistance flared again.

It did so through an ingenious mechanism, the committees of correspondence. Established in all the colonies by their assemblies, the committees drew up statements of American rights and grievances, distributed those documents within and among the colonies, and solicited responses from towns and counties. The brainchild of Samuel Adams, the committee structure formed a new communications network, one that fostered an intercolonial agreement on resistance to British measures. The committees also spread the scope of the resistance from colonial seaports into rural areas, engaging farmers and other country folk in the opposition to Britain.

Committees of correspondence

The committees had much to talk about when Parliament passed the Tea Act in 1773. The law was an effort to bail out the bankrupt East India Company by granting that corporation a monopoly on the tea trade to Americans. Since the company could use agents to sell its product directly, cutting out the middlemen, it could offer a lower price than that charged by colonial merchants. Still, many colonials saw the act as Parliament's attempt to trick them into accepting its authority to tax the colonies.

In early winter of 1773 the tempest over the Tea Act peaked in Boston, with popular leaders calling for the cargoes to be returned immediately to England. On the evening of December 16, thousands of Bostonians, as well as farmers from the surrounding countryside, packed into the Old South Meetinghouse. Some members of the audience knew what Samuel Adams had on the evening's agenda, and they awaited their cue. It came when Adams told the meeting that they could do nothing more to save their country. War whoops rang through the meetinghouse, the crowd spilled onto the streets and out to the waterfront, and the Boston Tea Party commenced. From the throng emerged 50 men dressed as Indians to disguise their identities. The party boarded three vessels docked off Griffin's Wharf, broke open casks containing 90,000 pounds of tea, and brewed a beverage worth 10,000 pounds sterling in Boston harbor.

Boston Tea Party

The Empire Strikes Back

The Boston Tea Party proved to British satisfaction that the colonies aimed at independence. To reassert its authority, Parliament passed the Coercive Acts, dubbed in the colonies the "Intolerable Acts." In March 1774, two months after hearing

Coercive Acts

of the Tea Party, Parliament passed the Boston Port Bill, closing that harbor to all oceangoing traffic until such time as the king saw fit to reopen it. He would not see fit until colonials paid the East India Company for its losses. During the next three months, Parliament approved three other "intolerable" laws designed to punish Massachusetts. The Massachusetts Government Act handed over the colony government to royal officials. Even convening town meetings would require royal permission. The Impartial Administration of Justice Act permitted any royal official accused of a crime in Massachusetts to be tried in England or in another colony. The Quartering Act allowed the housing of British troops in private homes—not only in Massachusetts but in all the colonies.

Many colonials saw the Coercive Acts as proof of a plot to enslave the colonies. In truth, the taxes and duties, laws and regulations of the last decade *were* part of a deliberate design—a commonsensical plan to centralize the administration of the

While the new political activism of some American women often amused male leaders of the resistance, it inspired the scorn of some partisans of British authority. When the women of Edenton, North Carolina, renounced imported tea, this British cartoon mocked them.

British empire. But those efforts by the king's ministers and Parliament to run the colonies more efficiently and profitably were viewed by more and more Americans as a sinister conspiracy against their liberties.

Week after week in the spring of 1774, reports of legislative outrages came across the waters. Shortly after approving the Coercive Acts, Parliament passed the Quebec Act, which established a permanent government in what had been French Canada. Ominously, it included no representative assembly; it also officially recognized the Roman Catholic church and extended the bounds of the province to include all land between the Mississippi and Ohio rivers. Suddenly New York, Pennsylvania, and Virginia found themselves bordering a British colony whose subjects had no voice in their own government.

Quebec Act

As alarm deepened in the wake of the Coercive Acts, one colony after another called for an intercolonial congress—like the one that had met during the Stamp Act crisis—to determine the best way to defend their freedom. But many also remained unsettled about where the logic of their actions seemed to be taking them: toward a denial that they were any longer English.

TOWARD THE REVOLUTION

By the beginning of September 1774, when 55 delegates to the First Continental Congress gathered in Philadelphia, the news from Massachusetts was bad. The colony verged on anarchy, it was reported, as its inhabitants resisted the enforcement of the Massachusetts Government Act.

First Continental Congress called

In the midst of this atmosphere of crisis, the members of Congress also had to take one another's measure. Many of the delegates had not traveled outside their own colonies. (All but Georgia sent representatives.) Although the delegates encountered a great deal of diversity, they quickly discovered that they esteemed the same traits of character, attributes that they called "civic virtue." These traits included simplicity and self-reliance, industry and thrift, and, above all, an unselfish commitment to the public good. Most members of the Congress also shared a common mistrust of England, associating the mother country with vice, extravagance, and corruption.

Still, the delegates had some misgivings about those from other colonies. Massachusetts in particular brought with it a reputation—well deserved, considering that Samuel Adams was along—for radical action and a willingness to use force to accomplish its ends.

The First Continental Congress

As the delegates settled down to business, their aim was to reach agreement on the basis of American rights, the limits of Parliament's power, and the proper tactics for resisting the Coercive Acts. Congress quickly agreed on the first point. The delegates affirmed that the law of nature, the colonial charters, and the British constitution provided the foundations of American liberties. This position was what most colonials had argued since 1765. On the two other issues, Congress charted a middle course between the demands of radicals and the reservations of conservatives.

Since the time of the Stamp Act, most colonials had insisted that Parliament had no authority to tax the colonies. But later events had demonstrated that Parliament could undermine colonial liberties by legislation as well as by taxation. The suspension of the New York legislature, the Gaspee Commission, and the Coercive Acts all fell into this category. Given those experiences, the delegates adopted a Declaration of Rights and Grievances on October 14, 1774, asserting the right of the colonies to tax and legislate for themselves. The Declaration of Rights thus limited Parliament's power over Americans more strictly than colonials had a decade earlier.

By denying Parliament's power to make laws for the colonies, the Continental Congress blocked efforts of the most conservative delegates to reach an accommodation with England. Their leading advocate, Joseph Galloway of Pennsylvania, proposed a plan of union with Britain similar to the one set forth by the Albany Congress in 1754. Under it, a grand council of the colonies would handle all common concerns, with any laws it passed subject to review and veto by Parliament. For its part, Parliament would have to submit for the grand council's approval any acts it passed affecting America. A majority of delegates judged that Galloway's proposal left Parliament too much leeway in legislating for colonials, and they rejected his plan.

Joseph Galloway's plan

Although the Congress denied Parliament the right to impose taxes or to make laws, delegates stopped short of declaring that it had no authority at all in the colonies. They approved Parliament's regulation of trade, but only because of the interdependent economy of the empire. And although some radical pamphleteers were attacking the king for plotting against American liberties, Congress acknowledged the continuing allegiance of the colonies to George III. In other words, the delegates called for a return to the situation that had existed in the empire before 1763, with Parliament regulating trade and the colonies exercising all powers of taxation and legislation.

On the question of resistance, Congress satisfied the desires of its most radical delegates by drawing up the Continental Association, an agreement to cease all trade with Britain until the Coercive Acts were repealed. They agreed that their fellow citizens would immediately stop drinking East India Company tea, and that by December 1, 1774, merchants would no longer import goods of any sort from Britain. A ban on the export of American produce to Britain and the West Indies would go into effect a year later, during September 1775—the lag being a concession to southern rice and tobacco planters, who wanted to market their crops.

The Association

Although the Association provided for the total cessation of trade, Congress did not approve another part of the radicals' agenda: making preparations for war.

Congress approved a defensive strategy of civil disobedience but drew the line at authorizing proposals to strengthen and arm colonial militias.

Thus the First Continental Congress steered a middle course. Although determined to bring about repeal of the Coercive Acts, it held firm in resisting any revolutionary course of action. If British officials had responded to its recommendations and restored the status quo of 1763, the war for independence might have been postponed—perhaps indefinitely. On the other hand, even though the Congress did not go to the extremes urged by the radicals, its decisions drew colonials further down the road to independence.

The Last Days of the British Empire in America

Most colonials applauded the achievements of the First Continental Congress. They expected that the Association would bring about a speedy repeal of the Coercive Acts. But fear that the colonies were moving toward a break with Britain led others to denounce the doings of the Congress. Conservatives were convinced that if independence was declared, chaos would ensue. Colonials, they argued, would quarrel over land claims and sectional tensions and religious differences, as they had so often in the recent past. But without Britain to referee such disputes, the result would be civil war, followed by anarchy.

A British grenadier

The man in America with the least liking for the Continental Congress sat in the hottest seat in the colonies, that of the governor of Massachusetts. General Thomas Gage now watched as royal authority crumbled in Massachusetts and the rebellion spread to other colonies. In October 1774 a desperate Gage dissolved the Massachusetts legislature, which then formed itself into a Provincial Congress, assumed the government of the colony, and began arming the militia. Gage then started to fortify Boston and pleaded for more troops—only to find his fortifications damaged by saboteurs and his requests for reinforcements ignored by Britain.

Thomas Gage in Boston

Outside Boston, royal authority fared no better. Farmers in western Massachusetts forcibly closed the county courts, turning out royally appointed justices and establishing their own tribunals. Popularly elected committees of inspection charged with enforcing the Association took over towns everywhere in Massachusetts, not only restricting trade but also regulating many aspects of local life. The committees called upon townspeople to display civic virtue by renouncing "effeminate" English luxuries like tea and fine clothing and "corrupt" leisure activities like dancing, gambling, and racing. The committees also assigned spies to report on any citizen unfriendly to the resistance. "Enemies of American liberty" risked being roundly condemned in public or beaten and pelted with mud and dung by hooting, raucous mobs.

Collapse of royal authority

Throughout the colonies a similar process was under way. During the winter and early spring of 1775, provincial congresses, county conventions, and local committees of inspection were emerging as revolutionary governments, replacing royal authority at every level. As the spectacle unfolded before General Gage, he concluded that only force could subdue the colonies. It would take more than he had at his command, but reinforcements might be on the way. In February of 1775, Parliament had approved an address to the king declaring that the colonies were in rebellion.

The Fighting Begins

As spring came to Boston, the city waited. A band of artisans, organized as spies and express riders by Paul Revere, watched General Gage and waited for him to act. Gage waited for reinforcements from Lord North and watched the hostile town. On April 14 word from North finally arrived: Gage was to seize the leaders of the Provincial Congress. That would behead the rebellion, North said. Gage knew better than to believe North—but he also knew that he had to do something.

On the night of April 18 the sexton of Boston's Christ Church hung two lamps from its steeple. It was a signal that British troops had moved out of Boston and were now marching toward the arms and ammunition stored by the Provincial Congress in Concord. As the lamps flashed the signal, Revere and a comrade, William Dawes, rode out to arouse the countryside.

When the news of a British march reached Lexington, its militia of about 70 farmers, chilled and sleepy, mustered on the Green at the center of the small rural town. Lexington Green lay directly on the road to Concord. At about four in the morning 700 British troops massed on the Green, and their commander, Major John Pitcairn, ordered the Lexington militia to disperse. The townsmen, outnumbered and overawed, began to obey. Then a shot rang out—whether the British or the Americans fired first is unknown—and then two volleys burst from the ranks of the redcoats. With a cheer the British set off for Concord, five miles distant, leaving eight Americans dead on Lexington Green.

Lexington and Concord

By dawn, hundreds of militiamen from nearby towns were surging into Concord. The British entered Concord at about seven in the morning and moved, unopposed, toward their target, a house lying across the bridge that spanned the Concord River. While three companies of British soldiers searched for American guns and ammunition, three others, posted on the bridge itself, had the misfortune to find those American arms—borne by the rebels and being fired with deadly accuracy. By noon, the British were retreating to Boston.

The narrow road from Concord to Boston's outskirts became a corridor of carnage. Pursuing Americans fired on the column of fleeing redcoats from the cover of fences and forests. By the end of April 19, the British had sustained 273 casualties; the Americans, 95. It was only the beginning. By evening of the next day, some 20,000 New England militia had converged on Boston for a long siege.

Common Sense

The bloodshed at Lexington Green and Concord's North Bridge committed colonials to a course of rebellion—and independence. That was the conclusion drawn by Thomas Paine, who urged other Americans to do the same.

Paine himself was hardly an American at all. He was born in England, apprenticed first as a corsetmaker, appointed later a tax collector, and fated finally to become midwife to the age of republican revolutions. Paine came to Philadelphia late in 1774, set up as a journalist, and made the American cause his own. "Where liberty is, there is my country," he declared. In January 1776 he wrote a pamphlet to inform colonials of their identity as a distinct people and their destiny as a nation. *Common Sense* enjoyed tremendous popularity and wide circulation, selling 120,000 copies within three months of its publication.

After Lexington and Concord, Paine wrote, as the imperial crisis passed "from argument to arms, a new era for politics is struck—a new method of thinking has arisen." That new era for Paine was the age of republicanism. He denounced monarchy as a foolish, dangerous form of government, one that violated the dictates of reason as well as the word of the Bible. By ridicule and remorseless argument, he severed the ties of colonial allegiance to the king. *Common Sense* scorned George III as "the Royal

Thomas Paine argues for independence

Thomas Paine, author of *Common Sense*

Brute of Britain," who had enslaved the chosen people of the new age—the Americans.

Nor did Paine stop there. He rejected the idea that colonials were or should want to be English. Britain, he told his readers, far from being a tender parent, had bled colonials of their wealth and preyed on their liberties. Why suffer such enslavement? The colonies occupied a huge continent an ocean away from the tiny British Isles—clear proof that nature itself had fashioned America for independence. England lay locked in Europe, doomed to the corruption of an Old World. America had been discovered anew to become an "asylum of liberty."

Many Americans had liked being English, but being English hadn't worked. Perhaps that is another way of saying that over the course of nearly two centuries colonial society and politics had evolved in such a way that the identity between the Americans and the English no longer fit. By the end of the Seven Years' War, the colonies had established political institutions that made the rights of "freeborn Britons" more available to ordinary citizens in America than in the nation that had created those liberties. Perhaps, then, most Americans had succeeded *too* well at becoming English, regarding themselves as political equals entitled to basic constitutional freedoms. In the space of less than a generation, the logic of events made clear that despite all that the English and Americans shared, in the distribution of political power they were fundamentally at odds. And the call to arms at Lexington and Concord made retreat impossible.

On that point Paine was clear. It was the destiny of Americans to be republicans, not monarchists. It was the destiny of Americans to be independent, not subject to British dominion. It was the destiny of Americans to be American, not English. That, according to Thomas Paine, was common sense.

chapter summary

Resistance to British authority grew slowly but steadily in the American colonies during the period following the Seven Years' War.

- The new measures passed by Parliament in the early 1760s—the Proclamation of 1763, the Sugar Act, the Stamp Act, the Currency Act, and the Quartering Act—were all designed to bind the colonies more closely to the empire.

- These new measures deflated American expectations of a more equal status in the empire and also violated what Americans understood to be their constitutional and political liberties—the right to consent to taxation, the right to trial by jury, and the freedom from standing armies.

- Although Parliament repealed the Stamp Act, it reasserted its authority to tax Americans by passing the Townshend Act in 1767.

- With the passage of the Coercive Act in 1774, many Americans concluded that all British ac-

tions in the last decade were part of a deliberate plot to enslave Americans by depriving them of property and liberty.

- When the First Continental Congress convened in September 1774, delegates resisted both radical demands to mobilize for war and conservative appeals to reach an accommodation.

- The first Continental Congress denied Parliament any authority in the colonies except the right to regulate trade; it also drew up the Continental Association, an agreement to cease all trade with Britain until the Coercive Acts were repealed.

- When General Thomas Gage sent troops from Boston in April 1775 to seize arms being stored at Concord, the first battle of the Revolution took place.

SIGNIFICANT EVENTS

1755	Braddock defeated by French and Indians
1756	England and France declare war
1759	Decisive English victory at Quebec
1760	George III becomes king of England
1763	Treaty of Paris ends the Seven Years' War; Pontiac's Rebellion; royal proclamation prohibits settlement west of the Appalachians
1764	Sugar Act; Currency Act
1765	Stamp Act; Quartering Act
1766	Repeal of the Stamp Act; Declaratory Act
1767	Townshend duties; Parliament suspends New York assembly
1770	Boston Massacre; repeal of most Townshend duties
1772	Gaspee Commission
1773	Boston Tea Party
1774	Coercive Acts; First Continental Congress meets at Philadelphia
1775	Battles of Lexington and Concord
1776	Thomas Paine's *Common Sense* published

CHAPTER 6

The American People and the American Revolution

(1775–1783)

preview • Would Americans actually fight for independence? Even after the Battle of Bunker Hill, the answer was not clear. But British victories in the North were countered by an American triumph at Saratoga, convincing the French to commit to a crucial alliance with the United States. Then, when the British attempted to conquer the South, they were foiled by the Continental Army under Nathanael Greene. Their surrender to Washington at Yorktown astonished most of Europe.

From a high place somewhere in the city—Beacon Hill, perhaps, or Copse Hill—General Thomas Gage looked down on Boston. Through a spyglass his gaze traveled over the church belfries and steeples, the roofs of brick and white frame houses. Finally he fixed his sights on a figure far in the distance across the Charles River. The man was perched atop a crude fortification on Breed's Hill, an elevation lying just below Bunker Hill on the Charlestown peninsula. Gage took the measure of his enemy: an older man, past middle age, a sword swinging beneath his homespun coat, a broad-brimmed hat shading his eyes. As he passed the spyglass to his ally, an American loyalist, Gage asked Abijah Willard if he knew the man on the fort. Willard peered across the Charles and identified his own brother-in-law, Colonel William Prescott. A veteran of the Seven Years' War, Prescott was now a leader in the rebel army laying siege to Boston.

"Will he fight?" Gage wondered aloud.

"I cannot answer for his men," Willard replied, "but Prescott will fight you to the gates of hell."

Fight they did on June 17, 1775, both William Prescott and his men. The evening before, three regiments had followed the colonel from Cambridge to Breed's Hill—soldiers drawn from the thousands of militia who had surrounded British-occupied Boston after the bloodshed at Lexington and Concord. Through the night, they dug trenches and built up high earthen walls atop the hill. At the first light of day, a British warship spotted the new rebel outpost and opened fire. By noon barges were ferrying British

Battle of Bunker Hill

Will they fight? This Pennsylvania regimental flag gives one reason why some did.

troops under Major General William Howe across the half-mile of river that separated Boston from Charlestown. The 1600 raw rebel troops tensed at the sight of scarlet-coated soldiers streaming ashore, glittering bayonets grasped at the ready. The rebels were farmers and artisans, not professional soldiers, and they were frightened out of their wits.

But Prescott and his men held their ground. The British charged Breed's Hill twice, and Howe watched in horror as streams of fire felled his troops. Finally, during the third British frontal assault, the rebels ran out of ammunition and were forced to withdraw. Redcoats poured into the rebel fort, bayoneting its handful of remaining defenders. By nightfall the British had taken Breed's Hill and the rest of the Charlestown peninsula. They had bought a dark triumph at the cost of 228 dead and 800 wounded.

The cost came high in loyalties as well. The fighting on Breed's Hill fed the hatred of Britain that had been building since April. Throughout America, preparations for war intensified: militia in every colony mustered; communities stockpiled arms and ammunition. Around Charlestown civilian refugees fled the countryside, abandoning homes and shops set afire by the British shelling of Breed's Hill. "The roads filled with frightened women and children, some in carts with their tattered furniture, others on foot fleeing into the woods," recalled Hannah Winthrop, one of their number.

The bloody, indecisive fight on the Charlestown peninsula known as the Battle of Bunker Hill actually took place on Breed's Hill. And the exchange between Thomas Gage and Abijah Willard that is said to have preceded the battle may not have taken place at all. But the story has persisted in the folklore of the American Revolution. Whether it really happened or not, the conversation between Gage and Willard raised the question that both sides wanted answered: were Americans willing to fight for independence from British rule? It was one thing, after all, to oppose the British ministry's policy of taxation. It was another to support a rebellion for which the ultimate price of failure was hanging for treason. And it was another matter entirely for men to wait nervously atop a hill as the seasoned troops of one's own "mother country" marched toward them with the intent to kill.

Indeed, the question "will they fight?" was revolutionary shorthand for a host of other questions concerning how ordinary Americans would react to the tug of loyalties between long-established colonial governments and a long-revered parent nation and monarch. For slaves, the question revolved around their allegiance to masters who spoke of liberty or to their masters' enemies who promised liberation. For those who led the rebels, it was a question of strengthening the resolve of the undecided, coordinating resistance, instilling discipline—translating the *will* to fight into the ability to do so. And for those who believed the rebellion was a madness whipped up by artful politicians, it was a question of whether to remain silent or risk speaking out, whether to take up arms for the king or flee. All these questions were raised, of necessity, by the act of revolution. But the barrel of a rifle shortened them to a single, pointed question: will you fight?

Americans react to the Revolution

THE DECISION FOR INDEPENDENCE

The delegates to the Second Continental Congress gathered at Philadelphia on May 10, 1775, just one month after the battles at Lexington and Concord. They had to determine whether independence or reconciliation offered the best way to protect the liberties of their colonies.

For a brash, ambitious lawyer from Braintree, Massachusetts, British abuses dictated only one course. "The Cancer [of official corruption] is too deeply rooted," wrote John Adams, "and too far spread to be cured by anything short of cutting it out entire." Yet during the spring and summer of 1775, even strong advocates of independence did not openly seek a separation from Britain. If independence was to be achieved, radicals needed to forge greater agreement among Americans. Moderates and conservatives harbored deep misgivings about independence: they had to be brought along slowly.

The Second Continental Congress

To bring them along, Congress adopted the "Olive Branch Petition" in July 1775. Drawn up by Pennsylvania's John Dickinson, the document affirmed American loyalty to George III and asked the king to disavow the policies of his principal ministers. At the same time Congress issued a declaration denying that the colonies aimed at independence. Yet, less than a month earlier, Congress had authorized the creation of a rebel military force, the Continental Army, and had issued paper money to pay for the troops.

A Congress that sued for peace while preparing for war was a puzzle that British politicians did not even try to understand, least of all Lord George Germain. A tough-minded statesman now charged with overseeing colonial affairs, Germain was determined to subdue the rebellion by

Aggressive British response

force. George III proved just as stubborn: he refused to receive the Olive Branch Petition. By the end of that year Parliament had shut down all trade with the colonies and had ordered the Royal Navy to seize colonial merchant ships on the high seas. In November 1775 Virginia's royal governor, Lord Dunmore, offered freedom to any slaves who would join the British. During January of the next year, he ordered the shelling of Norfolk, Virginia, reducing that town to smoldering rubble.

British belligerence withered the cause of reconciliation within Congress and the colonies. Support for independence gained more momentum from the overwhelming reception of *Common Sense* in January 1776. Radicals in Congress realized that the future was theirs and were ready to act. In April 1776 the delegates opened American trade to every nation in the world except Great Britain; a month later Congress advised the colonies to establish new state governments. And on June 7 Virginia's Richard Henry Lee offered the motion "that these United Colonies are, and of right ought to be, free and independent States . . . and that all political connection between them and the State of Great Britain is, and ought to be, totally dissolved."

The Declaration

Congress postponed a final vote on Lee's motion until July. Some opposition still lingered among delegates from the Middle Colonies, and a committee appointed to write a declaration of independence needed time to complete its work. That committee included some of the leading delegates in Congress: John Adams, Benjamin Franklin, Connecticut's Roger Sherman, and New York's Robert Livingston. But the man who did most of the drafting was a young planter and lawyer from western Virginia.

Thomas Jefferson was just 33 years old in the summer of 1776 when he withdrew to his lodgings on the outskirts of Philadelphia, pulled a portable writing desk onto his lap, and wrote the statement that would explain American independence to a "candid world." In the document's brief opening section, Jefferson set forth a general justification of revolution that invoked the "self-evident truths" of human equality and "unalienable rights" to "life, liberty, and the pursuit of happiness." These natural rights had been "endowed" to all persons "by their Creator," the Declaration pointed out; thus there was no need to appeal to the narrower claim of the "rights of Englishmen."

`Thomas Jefferson`

While the first part of the Declaration served notice that Americans no longer considered themselves English, its second and longer section denied England any authority in the colonies. In its detailed history of American grievances against the British empire, the Declaration referred only once to Parliament. Instead, it blamed George III for a "long train of abuses and usurpations" designed to achieve "absolute despotism." Unlike *Common Sense*, the Declaration denounced only the reigning king of England; it did not attack the

`Blaming George III`

In John Trumbull's painting, the Committee of Five—including Adams (left), Jefferson (second from the right), and Franklin (right)—submit the Declaration of Independence to the Continental Congress.

institution of monarchy itself. But like *Common Sense*, the Declaration affirmed that government originated in the consent of the governed and it upheld the right of the people to overthrow oppressive rule. Congress adopted the Declaration of Independence on July 4, 1776.

American Loyalists

Colonial political leaders embraced independence because they believed that a majority of Americans would support a revolution. But the sentiment for independence was not universal. Those who would not back the rebellion, supporters of the king and Parliament, numbered perhaps one-fifth of the population in 1775. While they proclaimed themselves "loyalists," their rebel opponents dubbed them "tories." That division made the Revolution a conflict pitting Americans against one another as well as the British. In truth, the war for independence was the first American civil war.

Predictably, the king and Parliament commanded the strongest support in colonies that had been wracked by internal strife earlier in the eighteenth century. In New York, New Jersey, Pennsylvania, and the Carolinas, not only did memories of old struggles sharpen worries of future upheaval, but old enemies often took different sides in the Revolution. The Carolina backcountry emerged as a stronghold of loyalist sentiment because of influential local men who cast their lot with Britain. To win support against Carolina's rebels, whose ranks included most wealthy coastal planters, western loyalist leaders played on ordinary settlers' resentments of privileged easterners. Grievances dating back to the 1760s also influenced the revolutionary allegiances of former land rioters of New York and New Jersey. If their old landlord opponents opted for the rebel cause, the tenants took up loyalism.

Other influences also fostered allegiance to Britain. Government officials who owed their jobs to the empire, major city merchants who depended on British trade, and Anglicans living outside the South retained strong ties to the parent country. Loyalists were also disproportionately represented among recent emigrants from the British Isles. The inhabitants of Georgia, the newest colony, inclined toward the king, as did the Highland Scots, many of whom had arrived in the colonies as soldiers during the Seven Years' War or had worked for a short time in the southern backcountry as tobacco merchants and Indian traders.

Many who took up the king's cause had not lacked sympathy for the resistance. Loyalist leaders like Joseph Galloway and Daniel Leonard had opposed the Stamp Act in 1765 and disapproved of imperial policy thereafter. It was not until the crisis reached a fever pitch in 1774 that more colonials cast their lot with the king. Worse than British taxation, in their view, was the radicalism of American resistance—the dumping of tea into Boston harbor, the forming of the Association, and the defying of royal authority.

Such acts of defiance touched what was for loyalists the rawest nerve: a deepseated fear of the divisions and instability of colonial society. Without the British around to maintain order, they warned, differences among Americans would result in civil war. On the eve of the Revolution, Jonathan Boucher, a New York loyalist, warned with uncanny foresight that "we should as soon expect to see . . . the wolf and the lamb feed together, as Virginians form a cordial union with the saints of New England." It would take the passage of less than a century for such fears to be borne out by events—the Union divided and the North and South locked in a fratricidal war.

Although a substantial minority, loyalists never became numerous enough anywhere to pose a serious threat to the Revolution. A more formidable threat was posed by the British army. And the greatest threat of all was posed by those very Americans who claimed that they wanted independence. For the question remained: would they fight?

THE FIGHTING IN THE NORTH

In the summer of 1775 Americans who wished to remain neutral probably outnumbered either loyalists or rebels. From the standpoint of mere survival, staying neutral made more sense than fighting for independence. Even the most ardent advocates of American rights had reason to harbor doubts, given the odds against the rebel colonists defeating the armed forces of the British empire.

Perhaps no friend of American liberty saw more clearly how slim the chances of a rebel victory were than George Washington. But Washington's principles, and his sense of honor, prevailed. June of 1775 found him, then 43 years old, attending the deliberations of the Second Continental Congress and dressed—a bit conspicuously—in his officer's uniform. The other delegates listened closely to his opinions on military matters, for Washington was the most celebrated American veteran of the Seven Years' War who remained young enough to lead a campaign. Better still, as a southerner he could bring his region into what thus far had remained mostly New England's fight. Congress readily appointed him commander in chief of a newly created Continental Army.

George Washington, general

The Two Armies at Bay

Thus did Washington find himself, only a month later, looking to bring order to the rebel forces around Boston. He knew he faced a formidable foe.

Highly trained, ably led, and efficiently equipped, the king's troops were seasoned professionals. Rigorous drills and often savage discipline by an aristocratic officer corps welded rank-and-file soldiers, men drawn mainly from the bottom of

Hunting shirts, like the one worn by this rifleman (second from the right), captured the imagination of the French army officer in America who made these watercolor sketches of the uniforms of revolutionary soldiers. The enlistment of blacks (infantryman at the far left) drew the artist's attention as well.

British society, into a sleek fighting machine. At the height of the campaign in America, reinforcements brought the number of British troops to 50,000, strengthened by some 30,000 Hessian mercenaries from Germany and the support of half the ships in the British navy, the largest in the world.

Washington was more modest about the army under his command, and he had much to be modest about. At first Congress recruited his fighting force of 16,600 rebel "regulars," the Continental Army, from the ranks of local New England militia bands. Although enlistments swelled briefly during the patriotic enthusiasm of 1775, for the rest of the war Washington's Continentals suffered chronic shortages of men and supplies. Even strong supporters of the Revolution hesitated to join the regular army, with its low pay, strict discipline, and constant threat of disease and danger. Most men preferred to fight instead as members of local militia units, the "irregular" troops who turned out to support the regular army whenever British forces came close to their neighborhoods.

"Regulars" versus the militia

The general reluctance to join the Continental Army created a host of difficulties for its commander and for Congress. Washington wanted and needed an army whose size and military capability could be counted on in long campaigns. He could not create an effective fighting force out of civilians who mustered out occasionally with the militia or enlisted for short stints in the Continental Army. Washington's desire for a professional military establishment clashed with the preferences of most republican leaders. They feared standing armies and idealized "citizen-soldiers"—men of selfless civic virtue who volunteered whenever needed—as the backbone of the common defense. "Oh, that I was a soldier," chubby John Adams fantasized in 1775. "Everyone must and will and shall be a soldier."

But everyone did not become a soldier, and the dwindling number of volunteers gradually overcame republican fears of standing armies. In September 1776 Congress set terms in the Continental Army at a minimum of three years or for the duration of the war and assigned each state to raise a certain number of troops. They offered every man who enlisted in the army a cash bounty and a yearly clothing issue; enlistees for the duration were offered 100 acres of land as well. Still the problem of recruitment persisted. Less than a year later, Congress recommended that the states adopt a draft, but Congress had no authority to compel the states to meet their troop quotas.

Even in the summer of 1775, before enlistments fell off, Washington was worried. As his Continentals laid siege to British-occupied Boston, he measured them against the adversary and found them wanting. Inexperienced officers provided no real leadership, and the men under their command shirked the most basic responsibilities of soldiers. They slipped away from camp at night; they left sentry duty before being relieved; they took potshots at the British; they tolerated filthy conditions in their camps.

While Washington strove to impose discipline on his Continentals, he also attempted, without success, to rid himself of "the Women of the Army." When

Women of the army

American men went off to fight, their wives usually stayed at home. To women then fell the sole responsibility for running farms and businesses, raising children, and keeping households together. They helped to supply the troops by sewing clothing, making blankets, and saving rags and lead weights for bandages and bullets. Other women on the home front organized relief for the widows and orphans of soldiers and protests against merchants who hoarded scarce commodities.

But the wives of poor men who joined the army were often left with no means to support their families. Thousands of such women—1 for every 15 soldiers—drifted after the troops. In return for half-rations, they cooked and washed for the soldiers; and after battles, they nursed the wounded, buried the dead, and scavenged the field for clothing and equipment. An even larger number of women accompanied the redcoats: their presence was the only thing that Washington did not admire about the British army and could barely tolerate in his own. But the services that they performed were indispensable, and women followed the troops throughout the war.

Laying Strategies

At the same time that he tried to discipline the Continentals, Washington designed a defensive strategy to compensate for their weakness. To avoid exposing raw rebel troops on "open ground against their Superiors in number and Discipline," he planned to fight the British from strong fortifications. With that aim in mind, in March 1776, Washington barricaded his army on Dorchester Heights, an elevation commanding Boston harbor from the south. That maneuver, which allowed American artillery to fire on enemy warships, confirmed a decision already made by the British to evacuate their entire army from Boston and sail for Halifax, Nova Scotia.

Britain had hoped to reclaim its colonies with a strategy of strangling the resistance in Massachusetts. But by the spring of 1776 they saw clearly that more was required than a show of force against New England. Instead the situation called for Britain to wage a conventional war in America, capturing major cities and crushing the Continental forces in a decisive battle. Military victory, the British believed, would enable them to restore political control and reestablish imperial authority.

British assumptions

The first target was New York City. General William Howe and Lord George Germain, the British officials now charged with overseeing the war, chose that seaport for its central location and—they hoped—its large loyalist population. They planned for Howe's army to move from New York City up the Hudson River, meeting ultimately with British troops under General Sir Guy Carleton coming south from Canada. Either the British drive would lure Washington into a major engagement, crushing the Continentals, or if unopposed, the British offensive would cut America in two, smothering resistance to the south by isolating New England.

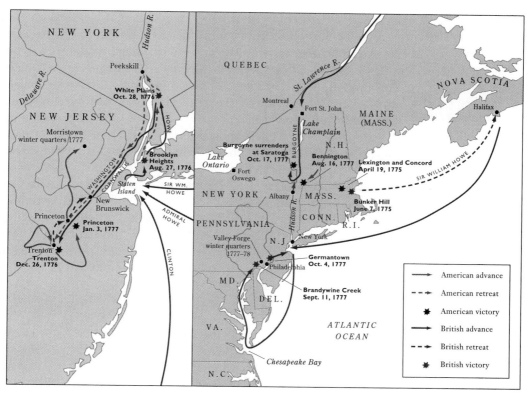

THE FIGHTING IN THE NORTH, 1775–1777

Unfortunately for the British, the strategy was sounder than the men placed in charge of executing it. General Howe took to extremes the conventional wisdom of eighteenth-century European warfare, which aimed as much at avoiding heavy casualties as at winning victories against the enemy. Concern for preserving manpower addicted Howe to caution, when daring more would have carried the day. Howe's brother, Admiral Lord Richard Howe, the head of naval operations in America, also stopped short of pressing the British advantage, owing to his personal desire for reconciliation. The reluctance of the Howe brothers to fight became the formula for British frustration in the two years that followed.

Howe brothers

The Campaigns in New York and New Jersey

However cautiously, British forces landed on Staten Island in New York harbor during July 1776. The Continentals marched from Boston and fortified Brooklyn Heights on Long Island, the key to the defenses of New York City on Manhattan

Island. By mid-August, 32,000 British troops, including 8000 Hessians, the largest expeditionary force of the eighteenth century, faced Washington's army of 23,000.

At dawn on August 22 the Howe brothers moved on Long Island and easily pushed the rebel army back across the East River to Manhattan. After lingering on Long Island for a month, the Howes again lurched into action, ferrying their forces to Kip's Bay, just a few miles south of Harlem. When the British landed, the handful of rebel defenders at Kip's Bay fled—straight into the towering wrath of Washington, who happened on the scene during the rout. For once the general lost his habitual self-restraint, flogged both officers and men with his riding crop, and came close to being captured himself. But the Howes remained reluctant to hit hard, letting Washington's army escape from Manhattan to Westchester County.

British capture New York City

Throughout the fall of 1776 General Howe's forces followed as Washington's fled southward into New Jersey. By mid-November, as the British advance picked up speed, the rebels stepped up their retreat and crossed the Delaware River into Pennsylvania on December 7. There Howe stopped, pulling back most of his army to winter in New York City and leaving the Hessians to hold the British line of advance along the New Jersey side of the Delaware River.

Although the retreat through New York and New Jersey had shriveled rebel strength to only 3000 men, Washington decided that the campaign of 1776 was not over. On a snowy Christmas night, the Continentals floated back across the Delaware, picked their way across roads sleeted with ice, and finally slid into Hessian-held Trenton at eight in the morning. One thousand German soldiers, still recovering from their spirited Christmas celebration and caught completely by surprise, quickly surrendered. Washington's luck held on January 3, 1777, when the Continentals defeated British troops on the outskirts of Princeton, New Jersey.

Rebel victories at Trenton and Princeton

During the winter of 1776–1777 the British lost more than battles: they alienated the very civilians whose loyalties they had hoped to ensure. In New York City the presence of the main body of the British army brought shortages of food and housing and caused constant friction between soldiers and city dwellers. In the New Jersey countryside still held by the Hessians, the situation was more desperate. Forced to live off the land, the Germans aroused resentment among local farmers by seizing "hay, oats, Indian corn, cattle, and horses, which were never or but very seldom paid for," as one loyalist admitted. The Hessians ransacked and destroyed homes and churches; they kidnapped and raped young women.

Many neutrals and loyalists who had had enough of the king's soldiers now took their allegiance elsewhere. Bands of militia on Long Island, along the Hudson River, and all over New Jersey rallied to support the Continentals.

Capturing Philadelphia

In the summer of 1777 General Howe still hoped to entice the Continentals into a decisive engagement or to seize a major seaport and its surrounding countryside. But he had now decided to goad the Americans into battle by capturing Philadelphia. Rather than risk his army on a march through hostile New Jersey, he approached the rebel capital by sea. In early August the redcoats disembarked on the Maryland shore and headed for Philadelphia, 50 miles away. Washington's army hurried south from New Jersey to protect the new nation's capital. Washington engaged Howe twice: in September at Brandywine Creek and in October in an early dawn attack at Germantown, but both times the rebels were beaten back. He had been unable to prevent the British occupation of Philadelphia.

Brandywine and Germantown

Still, the rebels could take satisfaction from the troubles that beset the British even in victory. In Philadelphia, as in New York, British occupation jacked up demand and prices for food, fuel, and housing. Philadelphians complained of redcoats looting their shops, trampling their gardens, and harassing them on the streets. Elizabeth Drinker, the wife of a Quaker merchant, confided in her diary that "I often feel afraid to go to bed."

Even worse, the British march through Maryland and Pennsylvania had outraged civilians, who fled before the army and then returned to find their homes and barns bare, their crops and livestock gone. Everywhere Howe's men went in the middle states, they left in their wake Americans with compelling reasons to support the rebels. Worst of all, just days after Howe marched his occupying army into Philadelphia in the fall of 1777, another British commander in North America was surrendering his entire army to rebel forces at Saratoga, New York.

Disaster for the British at Saratoga

The calamity that befell the British at Saratoga was the doing of a glory-mongering general, John "Gentleman Johnny" Burgoyne. After his superior officer, Sir Guy Carleton, bungled a drive into New York during the summer of 1776, Burgoyne won approval to command another attack from Canada. At the end of June 1777 he set out from Quebec with a force of 9500 redcoats, 2000 women and children, and an elaborate baggage train that included the commander's silver dining service, his dress uniforms, and numerous cases of champagne. As Burgoyne's huge entourage lumbered southward, a handful of Continentals and a horde of New England militia assembled several miles below Saratoga at Bemis Heights under the command of General Horatio Gates.

On September 19 Gates's rebel scouts, nested high in the trees on Bemis Heights, spied the glittering bayonets of Burgoyne's approaching force. Benedict Arnold, a brave young officer, led several thousand rebels into the surrounding woods, meeting Burgoyne's men in a clearing at Freeman's Farm. At the end of the day British reinforcements finally pushed the rebels back from a battlefield piled high with the bodies of soldiers from both sides. Burgoyne tried to flee back to Canada, but got no farther than Saratoga, where he surrendered his army to Gates on October 17.

Burgoyne surrenders at Saratoga

Saratoga changed everything. With Burgoyne's surrender, the rebels succeeded in convincing France that, with a little help, the Americans might well reap the fruits of victory.

THE TURNING POINT

France had been waiting for revenge against Britain ever since its humiliating defeat in the Seven Years' War. Since the mid-1760s, as France's agents in America sent home reports of a rebellion brewing, a scheme for evening the score had been taking shape in the mind of the French foreign minister, Charles Gravier de Vergennes. He reckoned that France might turn discontented colonials into willing allies against Britain.

The American Revolution as a Global War

Vergennes approached the Americans cautiously. He wanted to make certain that the rift between Britain and its colonies would not be reconciled and that the rebels in America stood a fighting chance. Although France had been secretly supplying the Continental Army with guns and ammunition since the spring of 1776, Vergennes would go no further than covert assistance.

Congress approached their former French enemies with equal caution. Would France, the leading Catholic monarchy in Europe, make common cause with the republican rebels? A few years earlier American colonials had fought against the French in Canada; only recently they had renounced a king, and for centuries they had overwhelmingly adhered to Protestantism.

The string of defeats dealt the Continental Army during 1776 convinced Congress that they needed the French enough to accept both the contradictions and the costs of such an alliance. In November Congress appointed a three-member commission to negotiate not only aid from France but also a formal alliance. Its senior member was Benjamin Franklin, who enchanted all of Paris when he arrived in town sporting a simple fur cap and a pair of spectacles (something no fashionable Frenchman wore in public). Hailed as a homespun sage, Franklin played the role of American innocent to the hilt and watched as admiring Parisians stamped his face on everything from the top of commemorative snuffboxes to the bottom of porcelain chamber pots.

Franklin in Paris

Still, Franklin understood that mere popularity could not produce the alliance sought by Congress. It was only news that Britain had surrendered an entire army at Saratoga that finally convinced Vergennes that the rebels could actually win. In February 1778 France signed a treaty of commerce and friendship and a treaty of alliance, which Congress approved in May. Under the terms of the treaties, both parties agreed to accept nothing short of independence for America. France pledged to renounce all future claims in continental North America and to relinquish any territory captured in the war. The alliance left the British no choice other than to declare war on France. Less than a year later Spain joined France, hoping to recover territory lost to England in earlier wars.

Winding Down the War in the North

The Revolution widened into a global war after 1778. Preparing to fight France and Spain dictated a new British strategy in America. No longer could the British concentrate on crushing the Continental Army; instead they would disperse their forces to fend off challenges all over the world. In May Sir Henry Clinton replaced William Howe as commander-in-chief and received orders to withdraw from Philadelphia to New York City. There, and in Newport, Rhode Island, Clinton was to maintain defensive bases for harrying northern coastal towns.

Only 18 miles outside of Philadelphia, at Valley Forge, Washington and his Continentals were assessing their own situation. Some 11,000 rebel soldiers had passed a harrowing winter in that isolated spot, starving for want of food, freezing for lack of clothing, huddling in miserable huts, and hating the British who lay 18 miles away in Philadelphia. The army also **Valley Forge** cursed their fellow citizens, for the misery of the soldiers resulted from congressional weakness and disorganization and civilian corruption and indifference. Congress lacked both money to pay and maintain the army and an efficient system for dispensing provisions to the troops. Most farmers and merchants preferred to supply the British, who could pay handsomely, than to do business with financially strapped Congress and the Continentals. What little did reach the army often was food too rancid to eat or clothing too rotten to wear. Perhaps 2500 perished at Valley Forge, the victims of cold, hunger, and disease.

Why did civilians who supported the rebel cause allow the army to suffer? Probably because by the winter of 1777, the Continentals came mainly from social classes that received little consideration at any time. The respectable, propertied farmers and artisans who had laid siege to Boston **Social composition of the** in 1775 had stopped enlisting. Serving in their stead were single men **Continental Army** in their teens and early twenties, some who joined the army out of desperation, others who were drafted, still others who were hired as substitutes for the more affluent. The landless sons of farmers, unemployed laborers, drifters, petty criminals, vagrants, indentured servants, slaves, even captured British and Hessian soldiers—all men with no other means and no other choice—were swept into the Continental Army. The social composition of the rebel rank and file had come to resemble that of the British army. It is the great irony of the Revolution: a war to protect liberty and property was waged by those Americans who were poorest and least free.

The beginning of spring in 1778 brought a reprieve. Supplies arrived at Valley Forge, and so did a fellow calling himself Baron von Steuben, a penniless Prussian soldier of fortune. Although Washington's men had shown spirit and resilience

The soldiers depicted in this 1777 illustration ("pinched with cold") condemn civilian neglect and the profiteering of private contractors ("damned Extortioners") who supplied the Continental Army. Such grievances provoked mutinies within the army.

ever since Trenton, they still lacked discipline and training. Those defects and more von Steuben began to remedy. Barking orders and spewing curses in German and French, the baron (and his translators) drilled the rebel regiments to march in formation and to handle their bayonets like proper Prussian soldiers. By the summer of 1778, morale had rebounded as professional pride fused solidarity among Continental ranks in the crucible of Valley Forge.

Spoiling for action after their long winter, Washington's army, now numbering nearly 13,500, set out to harass Clinton's army as it marched overland from Philadelphia to New York. The Continentals caught up with the British force on June 28 at Monmouth Courthouse, where a long, confused battle ended in a draw. After both armies retired for the night, Clinton's forces slipped away to safety in New York City. Washington pursued, longing to launch an all-out assault on New York City, but he lacked the necessary numbers.

While Washington waited outside New York City, his army started to come apart. During the two hard winters that followed, resentments mounted among the rank and file over spoiled food, inadequate clothing, and arrears in pay. The army retaliated with mutinies. Between 1779 and

Army uprisings

1780 officers managed to quell uprisings in three New England regiments. But in January 1781 both the Pennsylvania and the New Jersey lines mutinied outright and marched on Philadelphia, where Congress had reconvened. Order returned only after Congress promised back pay and provisions and Washington put two ringleaders in front of a firing squad.

War in the West

Trouble also loomed on the western frontier. There both the British and the rebels sought support from the Indians because the most powerful tribes determined the balance of power. Most of the tribes remained neutral, but those who took sides usually joined the British, who had tried to stem the tide of colonials taking Indian lands.

While George Rogers Clark and his few hundred rebel troops helped to contain British and Indian raids in the Old Northwest, General John Sullivan led an expedition against the Iroquois in upstate New York. Loyalists under Major John Butler and Iroquois fighters under a Mohawk chief, Thayendanegea (called Joseph Brant by the English), had conducted a series of raids along the New York and Pennsylvania frontiers. Sullivan and his expedition routed the marauders and burned over 40 Indian villages.

The Home Front in the North

While fighting flared on the frontier and British troops attacked a few Connecticut coastal towns in 1779, most northern civilians enjoyed a respite from the war. Since the outbreak of the fighting at Lexington and Concord, every rumor of approaching enemy troops had pitched any imperiled neighborhoods into a panic. Refugees on foot and in hastily packed carts filled the roads, fleeing the advancing armies. Those who remained to protect their homes and property might be caught in the crossfire of contending forces or cut off from supplies of food and firewood. Loyalists who remained in areas occupied by rebel troops faced harassment, imprisonment, or the confiscation of their property. Rebel sympathizers met similar fates in regions held by the British. Disease, however, disregarded political allegiances: military camps and occupied towns spawned epidemics of dysentery and smallpox that devastated civilians as well as soldiers, rebels and loyalists alike.

While plundering armies destroyed civilian property wherever they marched, military demands disrupted family economies throughout the northern countryside. The seasons of intense fighting drew men off into military service just when their labor was most needed on family farms. Wives and daughters were left to assume the work of husbands and sons while coping with loneliness, anxiety, and grief. Often enough, the disruptions, flight, and loss of family members left lasting scars. Two years after she fled before Burgoyne's advance into upstate New York, Ann Eliza Bleecker confessed to a friend,

Women and the war

"Alas! the wilderness is within: I muse so long on the dead until I am unfit for the company of the living."

Despite these hardships, many women vigorously supported the revolutionary cause in a variety of ways. The Daughters of Liberty joined in harassing those who opposed the rebel cause. One outspoken loyalist found himself surrounded by angry women who stripped off his shirt, covered him with molasses, and plastered him with flower petals. In more genteel fashion, groups of well-to-do women collected not only money but medicines, food, and pewter to melt for bullets.

THE STRUGGLE IN THE SOUTH

Between the autumn of 1778 and the summer of 1781, while Washington and his restless army waited outside New York City, the British opened another theater in the American war. Despite their armed presence in the North, the British had come to believe that their most vital aim was to regain their colonies in the mainland South. The Chesapeake and the Carolinas were more profitable to the empire and more strategically important, being so much closer to rich British sugar islands in the West Indies. That new "southern strategy" prompted Clinton to dispatch forces to the Caribbean and Florida. In addition, the British laid plans for a new offensive drive into the Carolinas and Virginia.

Britain's southern strategy

English politicians and generals believed that the war could be won in the South. Loyalists were numerous, they believed, especially in the backcountry. Resentment of the seaboard, a rebel stronghold, would breed readiness among frontier folk to take up arms for the king at the first show of British force. And southern rebels—especially the vulnerable planters along the coast—could not afford to turn their guns away from their slaves. So, at least, the British theorized. All that was needed, they concluded, was for the British army to establish a beachhead in the South and then, in league with loyalists, drive northward, pacifying the population while pressing up the coast.

The Siege of Charleston

The southern strategy worked well for a short time in a small place. In November 1778 Clinton sent 3500 troops to Savannah, Georgia. The resistance in the tiny colony quickly collapsed, and a large number of loyalists turned out to help the British. Encouraged by that success, the British moved on to South Carolina.

During the last days of 1779, an expedition under Clinton himself set sail from New York City. Landing off the Georgia coast, his troops mucked through malarial swamps to the peninsula lying between the Ashley and the Cooper rivers. At the tip of that neck of land stood Charleston, and the British began to lay siege. By then, an unseasonably warm spring had set in, making the area a heaven for mosquitoes and a hell for human beings. Sweltering and swatting, redcoats weighted down in their woolen uniforms inched their siegeworks toward the city. By early May Clinton's army closed in, and British shelling was setting fire to houses within the city. On May 12 Charleston surrendered.

Clinton sailed back to New York at the end of June 1780, leaving behind 8300 redcoats to carry the British offensive northward to Virginia. The man charged with leading that campaign was his ambitious and able subordinate, Charles, Lord Cornwallis.

The Partisan Struggle in the South

Cornwallis's task in the Carolinas was complicated by the bitter animosity between rebels and loyalists there. Many Carolinians had taken sides years before Clinton's conquest of Charleston. In the summer and fall of 1775 the supporters of Congress and the new South Carolina revolutionary government mobbed, tortured, and imprisoned supporters of the king in the backcountry. These attacks only hardened loyalist resolve: roving bands seized ammunition, broke their leaders out of jail, and besieged rebel outposts. But within a matter of months, a combined force of rebel militias from the coast and the frontier managed to defeat loyalist forces in the backcountry.

With the fall of Charleston in 1780, the loyalist movement on the frontier returned to life. Out of loyalist vengefulness and rebel desperation issued the brutal civil war that seared the southern backcountry after 1780. Neighbors and even families fought and killed each other as members of roaming rebel and tory militias. The intensity of partisan warfare in the backcountry produced unprecedented destruction. All of society, observed one minister, "seems to be at an end. Every person keeps close on his own plantation. Robberies and murders are often committed on the public roads. . . . Poverty, want, and hardship appear in almost every countenance."

Rebels and loyalists battle for the backcountry

Cornwallis, when confronted with the chaos, erred fatally. He did nothing to stop his loyalist allies or his own troops from mistreating civilians. A Carolina loyalist admitted that "the lower sort of People, who were in many parts originally attached to the British Government, have suffered so severely . . . that Great Britain has now a hundred enemies, where it had one before." Although rebels and loyalists alike plundered and terrorized the backcountry, Cornwallis's forces bore more of the blame and suffered the consequences.

A growing number of civilians outraged by the king's men cast their lot with the rebels. That upsurge of popular support enabled Francis Marion, the "Swamp Fox," and his band of white and black raiders to cut British lines of communication between Charleston and the interior. It swelled another rebel militia led by the "Gamecock," Thomas Sumter, who bloodied loyalist forces throughout the central part of South Carolina. It mobilized the "over-the-mountain men," a rebel militia in western Carolina, who claimed victory at the Battle of King's Mountain in October 1780. By the end of 1780, these successes had persuaded most civilians that only the rebels could restore order.

A North Carolina Soldier Witnesses the Partisan War in the Southern Backcountry

he evening after our battle with the Tories, we having a considerable number of prisoners, I recollect a scene which made a lasting impression on my mind. I was invited by some of my comrades to go and see some of the prisoners. We went to where six were standing together. Some discussion taking place, I heard some of our men cry out, "Remember Buford," [a rebel soldier killed by loyalists] and the prisoners were immediately hewed to pieces with broadswords. At first I bore the scene without any emotion, but upon a moment's reflection, I felt such horror as I never did before nor have since, and, returning to my quarters and throwing myself upon my blanket, I contemplated the cruelties of war until overcome and unmanned by a distressing gloom from which I was not relieved until commencing our march next morning before day by moonlight. I came to Tarleton's camp [a British officer], which he had just abandoned leaving lively rail fires. Being on the left of the road as we marched along, I discovered lying upon the ground something with the appearance of a man. Upon approaching him, he proved to be a youth about sixteen who, having come to view the British through curiosity, for fear he might give information to our troops, they had run him through with a bayonet and left him for dead. Though able to speak, he was mortally wounded. The sight of this unoffending boy, butchered . . . relieved me of my distressful feelings for the slaughter of the Tories, and I desired nothing so much as the opportunity of participating in their destruction.

Source: Moses Hall in John C. Dann, ed., *The Revolution Remembered: Eyewitness Accounts of the War for Independence* (Chicago: University of Chicago Press, 1980), pp. 202–203.

If rebel fortunes prospered in the partisan struggle, they faltered in the conventional warfare being waged at the same time in the South. In August of 1780 the Continentals commanded by Horatio Gates lost a major engagement to the British force at Camden, South Carolina. In the fall of 1780 Congress replaced Gates with Washington's candidate for the southern command, Nathanael Greene, an energetic, 38-year-old Rhode Islander and a veteran of the northern campaigns.

British victory at Camden

Greene Takes Command

Greene bore out Washington's confidence by grasping the military situation in the South. He understood the needs of his 1400 hungry, ragged, and demoralized troops and instructed von Steuben to lobby Virginia for food and clothing. He understood the importance of the rebel militias and sent Lieutenant Colonel Henry

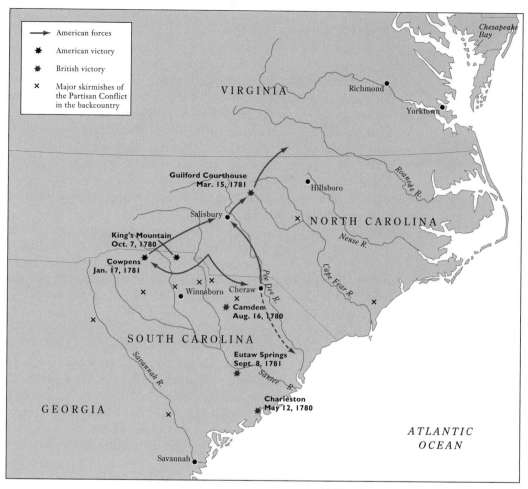

THE FIGHTING IN THE SOUTH, 1780–1781

In December 1780 Nathanael Greene made the crucial decision to split his army, sending Daniel Morgan west, where he defeated the pursuing Banastre Tarleton at Cowpens. Meanwhile Greene regrouped and replenished at Cheraw, keeping Cornwallis off balance with a raid (dotted line) toward Charleston and the coast. Then, with Cornwallis in hot pursuit, Greene and Morgan rejoined at Salisbury, retreating into Virginia. Cornwallis was worn down in this vain pursuit and lost three-quarters of the troops he began with before finally abandoning the Carolina campaign.

"Lighthorse Harry" Lee to assist Marion's raids. He understood the weariness of southern civilians and prevented his men from plundering the countryside.

Above all, Greene understood that his forces could never hold the field against the whole British army. That led him to break the first rule of conventional warfare: he divided his army. In December 1780 he dispatched to western South

Carolina a detachment of 600 men under the command of Brigadier General Daniel Morgan of Virginia.

Back at the British camp, Cornwallis worried that Morgan and his rebels, if left unchecked, might rally the entire backcountry against the British. On the other hand, Cornwallis reckoned that he could not commit his entire army to the pursuit of Morgan's men, for then Greene and his troops might retake Charleston. The only solution, unconventional to be sure, was for Cornwallis to divide *his* army.

Cowpens

That he did, sending Lieutenant Colonel Banastre Tarleton and 1100 men west after Morgan. Cornwallis had played right into Greene's hands: the rebel troops might be able to defeat a British army split into two pieces. For two weeks Morgan led Tarleton's troops on a breakneck chase across the Carolina countryside. In January 1781 at an open meadow called Cowpens, Morgan routed Tarleton's force.

Now Cornwallis took up the chase. Morgan and Greene joined forces and agreed to keep going north until the British army wore out. Cornwallis finally stopped at Hillsboro, North Carolina, but few local loyalists responded to his call for reinforcements. To ensure that loyalist ranks remained thin, Greene decided to make a show of force near the tiny village of Guilford Courthouse. On a brisk March day the two sides joined battle, each sustaining severe casualties before Greene was forced to retreat. But the high cost of victory convinced Cornwallis that he could not put down the rebellion in the Carolinas.

Although Nathanael Greene's command provided the Continentals with effective leadership in the South, it was the resilience of rebel militias that thwarted the British offensive in the Carolinas. Many Continental Army officers complained about the militia's lack of discipline, its habit of melting away when homesickness set in or harvest approached, and its record of cowardice under fire in conventional engagements. But when set the task of ambushing supply trains and dispatch riders, harrying bands of local loyalists, or making forays against isolated British outposts, the militia came through. Many southern civilians refused to join the British or to provide the redcoats with food and information because they knew that once the British army left their neighborhoods, the rebel militia would always be back. The Continental Army in the South lost many conventional battles, but the militia kept the British from restoring political control over the backcountry.

Value of the militia

African Americans in the Age of Revolution

The British also lost in the Carolinas because they did not seek greater support from those southerners who would have fought for liberty *with* the British: African American slaves.

Black Americans, virtually all in bondage, made up one-third of the population between Delaware and Georgia. Since the beginning of the resistance to Britain, white southerners had worried that the watchwords of liberty and equality would spread to the slave quarters. Gripped by the fear of slave rebellion, southern revolutionaries began to take precautions. Marylanders disarmed black inhabitants and issued extra guns to the white militia. Charlestonians hanged and then burned the body of Thomas Jeremiah, a free black who was convicted of spreading the word to others that the British "were come to help the poor Negroes."

Southern whites fully expected the British to turn slave rebelliousness to their strategic advantage. As early as 1775, Virginia's royal governor, Lord Dunmore, confirmed white fears by offering to free any slave who joined the British. When Clinton invaded the South in 1779, he renewed that offer. Janet Schaw, an English woman visiting her brother's North Carolina plantation, reported that his neighbors had heard that loyalists were "promising every Negro that would murder his master and family he should have his Master's plantation. . . . The Negroes have got it amongst them and believe it to be true."

White fears of rebellion

But in Britain there was overwhelming opposition to organizing support among African Americans. British leaders dismissed Dunmore's ambitious scheme to raise a black army of 10,000 and another plan to create a sanctuary for black loyalists on the southeastern coast. Turning slaves against masters, they recognized, was not the way to conciliate southern whites.

Even so, southern fears of insurrection made the rebels reluctant to enlist black Americans as soldiers. At first, Congress barred African Americans from the Continental Army. But as the rebels became more desperate for manpower, policy changed. Northern states actively encouraged black enlistments, and in the Upper South, some states allowed free men of color to join the army or permitted slaves to substitute for their masters.

Slaves themselves sought freedom from whichever side seemed most likely to grant it. In 1775 more than 800 took up Dunmore's offer and deserted their masters, and thousands more flocked to Clinton's forces after the fall of Charleston. For many runaways the hope of liberation proved an illusion. Although some served the British army as laborers, spies, and soldiers, many died of disease in army camps or were sold back into slavery in the West Indies. An estimated 5000 black soldiers served in the revolutionary army in the hope of gaining freedom. In addition, the number of runaways to the North soared during the Revolution. All told, some 55,000 slaves took advantage of the war's turmoil to seize their own freedom, some escaping behind British lines, others into the North.

African American quests for liberty

The slave revolts so dreaded by southern whites never materialized. Possibly the boldest slaves were drawn off into the armies; possibly greater white precautions discouraged schemes for black rebellions. In South Carolina, where the potential for revolt was greatest, most slaves chose to remain on plantations rather than risking a collective resistance and escape in the midst of the fierce partisan warfare.

THE WORLD TURNED UPSIDE DOWN

Despite his losses in the Carolinas, Cornwallis still believed that he could score a decisive victory against the Continental Army. The theater he chose for that showdown was the Chesapeake. During the spring of 1781, he and his army joined

RUN away from *Hampton*, on *Sunday* laſt, a luſty Mulatto Fellow named ARGYLE, well known about the Country, has a Scar on one of his Wriſts, and has loſt one or more of his fore Teeth; he is a very handy Fellow by Water, or about the Houſe, &c. loves Drink, and is very bold in his Cups, but daſtardly when ſober. Whether he will go for a Man of War's Man, or not, I cannot ſay; but I will give 40 s. to have him brought to me. He can read and write.
NOVEMBER 2, 1775. JACOB WRAY.

RUN away from the Subſcriber, in *New* Kent, in the Year 1772, a ſmall new New Negro Man named GEORGE, about 40 Years of Age, mith a Nick in one Ear, and ſome Marks with the Whip. He was about *Williamſburg* till laſt Winter, but either went or was ſent to Lord *Dunmore*'s Quarter in *Frederick* County, and there paſſes for his Property. Whoever conveys him to me ſhall have 5 l. Reward.
1 ‖ JAMES MOSS.

These advertisements from an issue of *The Virginia Gazette* in November 1775 indicate that some slaveowners were convinced that their male slaves might have gone to offer service to Lord Dunmore or to the British navy ("a Man of War's Man").

forces along the Virginia coast with the hero of Saratoga and newly turned loyalist, Benedict Arnold. Embarrassed by debt and disgusted by Congress's shabby treatment of the Continental Army, Arnold had started exchanging rebel secrets for British money in 1779 before defecting outright in 1780. By June of 1781 Arnold and Cornwallis were fortifying a site on the tip of the peninsula formed by the York and the James rivers, a place called Yorktown.

Meanwhile, Washington and his French ally, the Comte de Rochambeau, met in Connecticut to plan a major attack. Rochambeau urged a coordinated land-sea assault on the Virginia coast. Washington insisted instead on a full-scale offensive against New York City. Just when the rebel commander was about to have his way, word arrived that a French fleet under the Comte de Grasse was sailing for the Chesapeake to blockade Cornwallis by sea. Washington's Continentals headed south.

Surrender at Yorktown

By the end of September, 7800 Frenchmen, 5700 Continentals, and 3200 militia had sandwiched Yorktown between the devil of an allied army and the deep blue sea of French warships. "If you cannot relieve me very soon," Cornwallis wrote to

Clinton, "you must expect to hear the worst." The British navy did arrive—but seven days after Cornwallis surrendered to the rebels on October 19, 1781.

It need not have ended at Yorktown, but timing made all the difference. At the end of 1781 and early in 1782, the British army received setbacks in the other theaters of the war: India, the West Indies, and Florida. The French and the Spanish were everywhere in Europe as well, gathering in the English Channel, planning a major offensive against Gibraltar. The cost of the fighting was already enormous. British leaders recognized that the rest of the empire was at stake and set about cutting their losses in America.

The Treaty of Paris, signed on September 3, 1783, was a diplomatic triumph for the American negotiators: Benjamin Franklin, John Adams, and John Jay. They dangled before Britain the possibility that a generous settlement might weaken American ties to France. The British jumped at the bait. They recognized the independence of the United States and agreed to ample boundaries for the new nation: the Mississippi River on the west, the 31st parallel on the south, and the present border of Canada on the north. American negotiators then persuaded a skeptical France to approve the treaty by arguing that, as allies, they were bound to present a united front to the British. When the French finally persuaded Spain, the third member of the alliance, to reduce its demands on Britain for territorial concessions, the treaty became an accomplished fact. The Spanish settled for Florida and Minorca, an island in the Mediterranean.

Treaty of Paris

The Significance of a Revolution

If the Treaty of Paris marked both the end of a war and the recognition of a new nation, the surrender at Yorktown captured the significance of a revolution. Those present at Yorktown on that clear autumn afternoon in 1781 watched as the British second-in-command to Cornwallis (who had sent word that he was "indisposed") surrendered his superior's sword. He offered the sword first, in a face-saving gesture, to the French commander Rochambeau, who politely refused and pointed to Washington. But the American commander in chief, out of a mixture of military protocol, nationalistic pride, and perhaps even wit, pointed to *his* second-in-command, Benjamin Lincoln.

Some witnesses recalled that British musicians arrayed on the Yorktown green played "The World Turned Upside Down." Their recollections may have been faulty, but the story has persisted as part of the folklore of the American Revolution—and for good reasons. The world had, it seemed, turned upside down with the coming of American independence. The colonial rebels shocked the British with their answer to the question: would they fight?

The answer had been yes—but on their own terms. By 1777 most propertied Americans avoided fighting in the Continental Army. Yet whenever the war reached their homes, farms, and businesses, many Americans gave their allegiance to the new nation by turning out with rifles or supplying homespun clothing, food, or ammunition. They rallied around Washington in New Jersey, Gates in upstate New

York, Greene in the Carolinas. Middle-class American men fought, some from idealism, others out of self-interest, but always on their own terms, as members of the militia. These citizen-soldiers turned the world upside down by defeating professional armies.

Of course, the militia did not bear the brunt of the fighting. That responsibility fell to the Continental Army, which by 1777 drew its strength from the poorest ranks of American society. Yet even the Continentals, for all their desperation, managed to fight on their own terms. Some asserted their rights by raising mutinies, until Congress redressed their grievances. All of them, as the Baron von Steuben observed, behaved differently from European soldiers. Americans followed orders only if the logic of commands was explained to them. The Continentals, held in contempt by most Americans, turned the world upside down by sensing their power and asserting their measure of personal independence.

Thus did a revolutionary generation turn the world upside down. Descended from desperate, idealistic, and self-interested men and women who settled colonies named for kings and queens—ruled by kings and queens who aimed to increase the wealth and power of their dynasties and their nations—these Americans rebelled against a king. They wanted more than a monarch. But what more did they want? What awaited in a world turned upside down by republican revolutionaries?

 **c h a p t e r   s u m m a r y**

The American Revolution brought independence to Britain's former colonies after an armed struggle that began in 1775 and concluded with the Treaty of Paris in 1783.

- When the Second Continental Congress convened in the spring of 1775, many of the delegates still hoped for reconciliation—even as they approved the creation of the Continental Army.

- The Second Continental Congress adopted the Declaration of Independence on July 4, 1776, hoping that they could count on a majority of Americans to support the Revolution.

- The British scored a string of victories in the North throughout 1776 and 1777, capturing both New York and Philadelphia.

- The British suffered a disastrous defeat at the Battle of Saratoga in early 1778, which prompted France to openly ally with the American rebels soon thereafter.

- By 1780 Britain aimed to win the war by claiming the South and captured both Savannah, Georgia, and Charleston, South Carolina.

- The Continental Army in the South, led by Nathanael Greene, foiled the British strategy, and Cornwallis surrendered to Washington after the Battle of Yorktown in 1781.

- Except for the first year of fighting, the rank and file of the Continental Army was drawn from the poorest Americans, whose needs for food, clothing, and shelter were neglected by the Continental Congress.

For quizzes and a variety of interactive resources, visit the book's Online Learning Center at www.mhhe.com/davidsonconcise3

SIGNIFICANT EVENTS

1775 — Second Continental Congress convenes at Philadelphia; Congress creates the Continental Army; Battle of Bunker Hill

1776 — Publication of *Common Sense*; British troops evacuate Boston; Declaration of Independence; British occupy New York City, forcing Washington to retreat through New Jersey into Pennsylvania; Washington counterattacks at Battle of Trenton

1777 — British summer drive to occupy Philadelphia: battles of Brandywine Creek, Germantown; Burgoyne surrenders at Saratoga; Continental Army encamps for winter at Valley Forge

1778 — France allies with rebel Americans; France and Britain declare war; British shift focus to the South; Savannah falls

1780 — British occupy Charleston; partisan warfare of Marion, Sumter; rebel victory at King's Mountain, South Carolina; Nathanael Greene takes southern command

1781 — Engagements at Cowpens, Guilford Courthouse; Cornwallis surrenders at Yorktown

1783 — Treaty of Paris

CHAPTER 7

Crisis and Constitution

(1776–1789)

preview • For a decade after independence, American revolutionaries were less committed to creating a single national republic than to organizing 13 separate state republics, united only loosely under the Articles of Confederation. By the mid-1780s, however, the weakness of the Confederation seemed evident to many Americans. The Constitutional Convention of 1787 produced a new frame of government that was truly national in scope.

"I am not a Virginian, but an American," Patrick Henry declared in the Virginia House of Burgesses. Most likely he was lying. Certainly no one listening took him seriously, for the newly independent colonists did not identify themselves as members of a nation. They would have said, as did Thomas Jefferson, "Virginia, Sir, is my country." Or as John Adams wrote to another native son, "Massachusetts is our country." Jefferson and Adams were men of wide political vision and experience: both were leaders in the Continental Congress and more inclined than most to think nationally. But like other members of the revolutionary generation, they identified deeply with their home states and even more deeply with their home counties and towns.

It followed that allegiance to the states, not the Union, determined the shape of the first republican political experiments. For a decade after independence, the revolutionaries were less committed to creating an American nation than to organizing 13 separate state republics. The Declaration of Independence referred explicitly not to *the* United States but to *these* United States. It envisioned not one republic so much as a federation of 13.

Only when peace was restored during the decade of the 1780s were Americans forced to face some unanswered questions raised by their revolution. The Declaration proclaimed that these "free and independent states" had "full power to levy war, conclude peace, contract alliances, establish commerce." Did that mean that New Jersey, as a free and independent state, could sign a trade agreement with France, excluding the other states? If the United States was to be more than a loose federation, how could it assert power on a national scale? Similarly, American borderlands to the west presented problems. If these territories were settled by Americans, would they eventually join the United

How close a union?

States? Go their own ways as independent nations? Become new colonies of Spain or England?

Such problems were more than political; they were rooted in social realities. For a political union to succeed, the inhabitants of 13 separate states had to start thinking of themselves as Americans. When it came right down to it, what united a Vermont farmer working his rocky fields and a South Carolina gentleman presiding over a vast rice plantation? What bonds existed between a Kentuckian rafting the Ohio River and a Salem merchant sailing to China for porcelain?

And in a society where all citizens were said to be "created equal," the inevitable social inequalities had to be confronted. How could women participate in the Revolution's bid for freedom if they were not free to vote or to hold property? How could black Americans feel a bond with white Americans when so often the only existing bonds had been forged with chains? To these questions there were no final answers in 1781. And as the decade progressed, the sense of crisis deepened. Americans worried that factions and selfish interest groups would pull "these" United States apart. The new republican union, which spread out over so many miles, constituted a truly unprecedented venture. A good deal of experimenting would be needed if it was to succeed.

REPUBLICAN EXPERIMENTS

After independence was declared in July 1776, many of America's best political minds turned to draw up constitutions for their individual states. In truth, the state constitutions were crucial republican experiments, the first efforts at establishing a government of and by the people. All the revolutionaries agreed that the people—not a king or a few privileged aristocrats—should rule. Yet they were equally certain that republican governments were best suited to small territories. They believed that the new United States was too sprawling and its people too diverse to be safely consolidated into a single national republic. They feared, too, that the government of a large

> Belief in the need for small republics

republic would inevitably grow indifferent to popular concerns, being distant from many of its citizens. Without being under the watchful eye of the people, representatives would become less accountable to the electorate and turn tyrannical. A federation of small state republics, they reasoned, would stand a far better chance of enduring.

The State Constitutions

The new state constitutions retained the basic form of their old colonial governments, most providing for a governor and a bicameral legislature. But while most states did not alter the basic structure of their governments, they changed dramatically the balance of power among the different branches of government.

From the republican perspective in 1776, the greatest problem of any government lay in curbing executive power. What had driven Americans into rebellion was the abuse of authority by the king and his appointed officials. To ensure that the executive could never again threaten popular liberty, the new states either accorded almost no power to their governors or abolished that office entirely. The governors had no authority to convene or dissolve the legislature. They could not veto the legislatures' laws, grant land, or erect courts. Most important from the republican point of view, governors had few powers to appoint other state officials. All these limits were designed to deprive the executive of any patronage or other form of influence over the legislature.

Curbing executive power

What the state governors lost, the legislatures gained. To ensure that those powerful legislatures truly represented the will of the people, the new state constitutions called for annual elections and required candidates for the legislature to live in the district they represented. Many states even asserted the right of voters to instruct the men elected to office how to vote on specific issues. Although no state granted universal manhood suffrage, most reduced the amount of property required of qualified voters. Finally, state supreme courts were also either elected by the legislatures or appointed by an elected governor.

Strengthening legislative powers

Americans responded to independence with rituals of "killing the king," like this New York crowd in 1776, which is pulling down a statue of George III. Americans also expressed their mistrust of monarchs by establishing state governments with weak executive branches.

By investing all power in popular assemblies, Americans abandoned the British system of mixed government. In one sense, that change was fairly democratic. A majority of voters within a state could do whatever they wanted, unchecked by governors or courts. On the other hand, the arrangement opened the door for legislatures to turn as tyrannical as governors. The revolutionaries brushed that prospect aside: republican theory assured them that the people possessed a generous share of civic virtue, the capacity for selfless pursuit of the general welfare.

In an equally momentous change, the revolutionaries insisted on written state constitutions. Whenever government appeared to exceed the limits of its authority, Americans wanted to have at hand the written contract between rulers and ruled. When eighteenth-century Englishmen used the word "constitution," they meant the existing arrangement of government—not an actual document but a collection of parliamentary laws, customs, and precedents. But Americans believed that a constitution should be a written code that stood apart from and above government, a yardstick against which the people measured the performance of their rulers. After all, they reasoned, if Britain's constitution had been written down, available for all to consult, would American rights have been violated?

Written constitutions

From Congress to Confederation

While Americans lavished attention on their state constitutions, the national government nearly languished during the decade after 1776. With the coming of independence, the Second Continental Congress conducted the common business of the federated states. It created and maintained the Continental Army, issued currency, and negotiated with foreign powers.

But while Congress acted as a central government by common consent, it lacked any legal basis for its authority. To redress that need, in July 1776 Congress appointed a committee to draft a constitution for a national government. The more urgent business of waging and paying for the war made for delay, as did the consuming interest in framing state constitutions. Congress finally approved the first national constitution in November 1777, but it took four more years for all of the states to ratify these Articles of Confederation.

The Articles of Confederation provided for a government by a national legislature—essentially a continuation of the Second Continental Congress. That body had the authority to declare war and make peace, conduct diplomacy, regulate Indian affairs, appoint military and naval officers, and requisition men from the states. In affairs of finance it could coin money and issue paper currency. Extensive as these responsibilities were, Congress could not levy taxes or even regulate trade. The crucial power of the purse rested entirely with the states, as did the final power to make and execute laws. Even worse, the national government had no distinct executive branch. Congressional committees, constantly changing in their membership, not only had to make laws but had to administer and enforce them as well.

Articles of Confederation

Those weaknesses of the federal government appear more evident in hindsight. Most American leaders of the 1770s had given little thought to federalism, the organization of a United States. Political leaders had not yet recognized the need for dividing power between the states and the national government. With the new nation in the midst of a military crisis, Congress assumed—correctly in most cases—that the states did not have to be forced to contribute men and money to the common defense. Creating a strong national government would have antagonized many Americans, who after all had just rebelled against the distant, centralized authority of Britain's king and Parliament.

Guided by republican political theory and by their colonial experience, American revolutionaries created a loose confederation of 13 independent state republics under a nearly powerless national government. They succeeded so well that the United States almost failed to survive its first decade of independence. The problem was that lessons from the colonial past were not always useful guides to postwar realities. Only when events forced Americans to think nationally did they begin to consider the possibility of reinventing "these United States"—this time under the yoke of a truly federal republic.

THE TEMPTATIONS OF PEACE

The surrender of Cornwallis at Yorktown in 1781 marked the end of military crisis in America. But as the threat from Britain receded, so did the source of American unity. The many differences among Americans, most of which lay submerged during the struggle for independence, surfaced in full force. Those domestic divisions, combined with challenges to the new nation from Britain and Spain, created conflicts that neither the states nor the national government proved equal to handling.

The Temptations of the West

The greatest opportunities and the greatest problems for postwar Americans awaited in the rapidly expanding West. With the boundary of the new United States now set at the Mississippi River, more settlers spilled across the Appalachians, planting farmsteads and towns throughout Ohio, Kentucky, and Tennessee. By 1790 places that had been almost uninhabited by whites in 1760 held more than 2.25 million people, one-third of the nation's population.

After the Revolution, as before, western settlement fostered intense conflict. American claims that its territory stretched all the way to the Mississippi were by no means taken for granted by European and Indian powers. The West also confronted Americans with questions about their own national identity. Would the newly settled territories enter the nation as states on an equal footing with the original 13 states? Would they be ruled as dependent colonies? The fate of the

As the stumps dotting the landscape indicate, western farmers first sought to "improve" their acreage by felling trees. But their dwellings were far less substantial than those depicted in this idealized sketch of an "American New Cleared Farm." And while some Indians guided parties of whites into the West, as shown in the foreground, more often they resisted white encroachment. For that reason, dogs, here perched placidly in canoes, were trained to alert their white masters to the approach of Indians.

West, in other words, constituted a crucial test of whether "these" United States could grow and still remain united.

Foreign Intrigues

Both the British from their base in Canada and the Spanish in Florida and Louisiana hoped to chisel away at American borders. Their considerable success in the 1780s exposed the weakness of Confederation diplomacy.

Before the ink was dry on the Treaty of Paris, Britain's ministers were secretly instructing Canadians to maintain their forts and trading posts inside the United States's northwestern frontier. They reckoned—correctly—that with the Continental Army disbanded, the Confederation could not force the British to withdraw.

The British also made mischief along the Confederation's northern borders, mainly with Vermont. For decades, Ethan Allen and his Green Mountain Boys had waged a war of nerves with neighboring New York, which claimed Vermont as part of its territory. After the Revolution the Vermonters petitioned Congress for statehood, demanding independence of both New York and New Hampshire. When Congress dragged its feet, the British tried to woo Vermont into their empire as a province of Canada. That flirtation with the British pressured Congress into granting Vermont statehood in 1791.

The loyalty of the southwestern frontier was even less certain. By 1790 more than 100,000 settlers had poured through the Cumberland Gap to reach Kentucky and Tennessee. But the commercial possibilities of the region depended entirely on access to the Mississippi and the port of New Orleans, since it was far too costly to ship southwestern produce over the rough trails east across the Appalachians. And the Mississippi route was still dominated by the Spanish, who controlled Louisiana as well as forts along western Mississippi shores as far north as St. Louis. The Spanish, seeing their opportunity, closed the Mississippi to American navigation in 1784. That action prompted serious talk among southwesterners about seceding from the United States and joining Spain's empire.

Spanish designs on the Southwest

The Spanish also tried to strengthen their hold on North America by making common cause with the Indians. Of particular concern to both groups was protecting Florida, which had reverted to Spain's possession, from the encroachment of American settlers filtering south from Georgia. Florida's governor alerted his superiors back in Spain to the threat posed by those backwoodsmen who were "nomadic like Arabs and . . . distinguished from savages only in their color, language, and the superiority of their depraved cunning and untrustworthiness." So Spanish colonial officals responded eagerly to the overtures of Alexander McGillivray, a young Indian leader whose mother was of French-Creek descent and whose father was a Scots trader. His efforts brought about a treaty of alliance between the Creeks and the Spanish in 1784, quickly followed by similar alliances with the Choctaws and the Chickasaws. What cemented such treaties were the trade goods that the Spanish agreed to supply to the tribes. Securing European gunpower and guns had become essentail to southeastern Indians, because their entire economies now revolved around hunting and selling deerskins to white traders.

Disputes among the States

As if foreign intrigues were not divisive enough, the states continued to argue among themselves over western land claims. The old royal charters for some colonies had extended their boundaries all the way to the Mississippi and beyond. (See the map, page 179.) But the charters were often vague, granting both Massachusetts and Virginia, for example, undisputed possession of present-day Wisconsin. In contrast, other charters limited state boundaries to within a few hundred miles of the Atlantic coast. "Landed" states like Virginia wanted to secure control over the large territory granted by their charters. "Landless" states (which included Maryland, Delaware, Pennsylvania, Rhode Island, and New Jersey) called on Congress to restrict the boundaries of landed states and to convert western lands into a domain administered by the Confederation.

Landed versus landless states

WESTERN LAND CLAIMS, 1782–1802   The Confederation's settlement of conflicting western land claims was an achievement essential to the consolidation of political union. Some states asserted that their original charters extended their western borders to the Mississippi River. A few states, like Virginia, claimed western borders on the Pacific Ocean.

The landless states lost the opening round of the contest over ownership of the West. The Articles of Confederation acknowledged the old charter claims of the landed states. Then Maryland, one of the smallest landless states, retaliated by refusing to ratify the Articles. Since every state had to approve the Articles before they were formally accepted, the fate of the United States hung in the balance.

One by one the landed states relented. The last holdout, Virginia, in January 1781 ceded its charter rights to land north of the Ohio River. Once Virginia ceded, Maryland ratified the Articles in February 1781, four long years after Congress had first approved them.

The More Democratic West

More bitterly disputed than land claims in the West was the issue concerning the sort of men westerners elected to political office. The state legislatures of the 1780s were both larger and more democratic in their membership than the old colonial assemblies were. Before the Revolution no more than a fifth of the men serving in the assemblies were middle-class farmers or artisans; government was almost exclusively the domain of the wealthiest merchants, lawyers, and planters. After the Revolution twice as many state legislators were men of moderate wealth. The shift was more marked in the North, where middle-class men predominated among representatives. But in every state, some men of modest means, humble background, and little formal education attained political power.

State legislatures became more democratic in membership mainly because as backcountry districts grew, so did the number of their representatives. Since western districts tended to be less developed economically and culturally, their leading men were less rich and cultivated than the seaboard elite. Wealthy, well-educated gentlemen thus became a much smaller and less powerful group within the legislatures because of greater western representation and influence.

Changing composition of state legislatures

But many republican gentlemen, while endorsing government by popular consent, doubted whether ordinary people were fit to rule. The problem, they contended, was that the new western legislators concerned themselves only with the narrow interests of their constituents, not with the good of the whole state. As Ezra Stiles, the president of Yale College, observed, the new breed of politicians were those with "the all-prevailing popular talent of coaxing and flattering," who "whenever a bill is read in the legislature . . . instantly thinks how it will affect his constituents." And if state legislatures could not rise above petty bickering and narrow self-interest, how long would it be before civic virtue and a concern for the general welfare simply withered away?

The Northwest Territory

Such fears of "democratic excess" also influenced policy when Congress debated what to do with the Northwest Territory. Carved out of the land ceded by the states to the national government, the Northwest Territory comprised the present-day states of Ohio, Indiana, Illinois, Michigan, and Wisconsin. With so many white settlers moving into these lands, Congress was faced with a crucial test of its federal system. If the Confederation could not expand in an orderly way beyond the original 13 colonies, the new territories might well become independent countries

A Traveler from Virginia Considers the Ruins of an Ancient Indian Civilization in the Ohio Valley

have often observed while travelling thro' this country, a number of round hillocks, raised from 15 feet high and under and from 50 to 100 yards around them. It seems evident that those places are not natural, but are the work of man. The only question seems to be, "What were they made for?" Some have supposed they were once places of defence. But the most probable opinion is, that they are burying places of the former inhabitants of this country. On digging into these, I am informed, great quantities of bones are found, lying in a confus'd promiscuous manner. Some authors inform us that once in ten years the Indians collect the bones of their dead, and bring them all to one place and bury them. Thus they proceed, putting one layer over another till they get them to the height above mentioned.

An object, however, of a different kind now presents itself to our view . . . a neck of land about 4 or 500 yards wide. Across this neck of land lies an old wall, joining the river at each end and enclosing, I suppose, about 100 acres of land. This wall is composed of earth dug from the outside, where a ditch of some depth is still discernible. The wall at present is so mouldered down that a man could easily ride over it. It is however about 10 feet, as near as I can judge, in perpendicular height, and gives growth to a number of large trees. In one place I observe a breach in the wall about 60 feet wide, where I suppose the gate formerly stood through which the people passed in and out of this stronghold. Compared with this, what feeble and insignificant works are those of Fort Hamilton or Fort Washington! They are no more in comparison to it than a rail fence is to a brick wall.

Source: 18 November 1795, Journal of the Reverend James Smith. Richard H. Collins Papers, Durrett Collection, University of Chicago.

or even colonies of Spain or Britain. Congress dealt with the issue of expansion by adopting three ordinances.

The first, drafted by Thomas Jefferson in 1784, divided the Northwest Territory into 10 states, each to be admitted to the Union on equal terms as soon as its population equaled that in any of the existing states. In the meantime, Jefferson provided for democratic self-government of the territory by all free adult males. A second ordinance of 1785 set up an efficient mechanism for dividing and selling public lands. The Northwest Territory was surveyed into townships of six miles square. Each township then was divided into 36 lots of one square mile, or 640 acres.

Jefferson's plan for the Northwest

Congress waited in vain for buyers to flock to the land offices it established. The cost of even a single lot—$640—was too steep for most farmers. Disappointed by the shortage of buyers and desperate for money, Congress finally accepted a

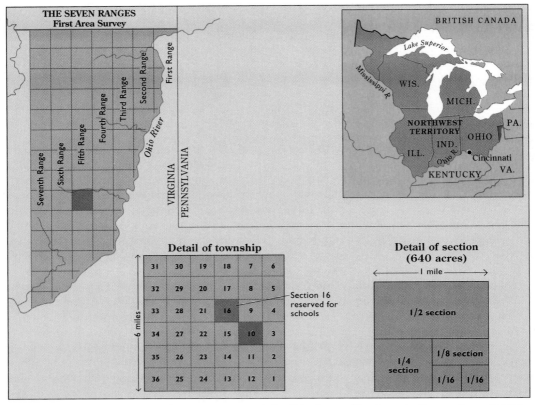

THE SEVEN RANGES
First Area Survey

First Range

Second Range

Third Range

Fourth Range

Fifth Range

Sixth Range

Seventh Range

Ohio River

VIRGINIA
PENNSYLVANIA

BRITISH CANADA

Lake Superior

Mississippi R.

WIS.

MICH.

NORTHWEST
TERRITORY

PA.

OHIO

IND.

ILL.

Ohio R.

Cincinnati

KENTUCKY

VA.

Detail of township

6 miles

31	30	19	18	7	6
32	29	20	17	8	5
33	28	21	16	9	4
34	27	22	15	10	3
35	26	23	14	11	2
36	25	24	13	12	1

Section 16
reserved for
schools

**Detail of section
(640 acres)**

1 mile

1/2 section

1/4
section

1/8 section

1/16 | 1/16

THE ORDINANCE OF 1785   Surveyors entered the Northwest Territory in September of 1785, imposing on the land regular grids of six square miles to define new townships, as shown on this range map of a portion of Ohio. Farmers purchased blocks of land within townships, each one mile square, from the federal government or from land speculators.

proposition submitted by a private company of land speculators that offered to buy some 6 million acres in present-day southeastern Ohio. That several members of Congress numbered among the company's stockholders no doubt added to enthusiasm for the deal.

The transaction concluded, Congress calmed the speculators' worries that incoming settlers might enjoy too much self-government by scrapping Jefferson's democratic design and substituting the Northwest Ordinance of 1787. That ordinance provided for a period in which Congress held sway in the territory through its appointees—a governor, a secretary, and three judges. When the population reached 5000 free adult males, a legislature was to be established, although its laws required the governor's approval. A representative could sit in Congress but had no vote. When the population reached 60,000, the inhabitants might apply for statehood, and the whole Northwest Territory was

Northwest Ordinance

to be divided into not less than three or more than five states. The ordinance also guaranteed basic rights—freedom of religion and trial by jury—and provided for the support of public education.

Congress's plan completely ignored the rights of the Shawnee, Chippewa, and other Indian peoples who lived in the region. To them, it made no difference that the British had ceded their lands to the Americans. And in terms of Jefferson's democratic ideals for white inhabitants, the ordinance of 1787 also fell short. Still, Congress had succeeded in extending republican government to the West and incorporating the frontier into the new nation. Congress also outlawed slavery throughout the territory.

That decision had an unexpected, almost ironic consequence. The Northwest Ordinance went a long way toward establishing a federal system that would minimize tensions between the East and the West, a major source of postwar conflict. The Republic now had a peaceful, orderly way to expand its federation of states. Yet by limiting the spread of slavery in the northern states, Congress deepened the critical social and economic differences between North and South, evident already in the 1780s.

Slavery and Sectionalism

When white Americans declared their independence, they owned nearly half a million black Americans. African Americans of the revolutionary generation, most of them enslaved, constituted 20 percent of the total population of the colonies in 1775, and nearly 90 percent of them lived in the South. Yet few political leaders directly confronted the issue of whether slavery should be permitted to exist in a truly republican society.

When political discussion did stray toward the subject of slavery, southerners—especially ardent republicans—bristled defensively. Theirs was a difficult position, riddled with contradictions. On the one hand, they had condemned parliamentary taxation as tantamount to political "slavery" and had rebelled, declaring that all men were "created equal." On the other hand, enslaved African Americans formed the basis of the South's plantation economy. To surrender slavery, southerners believed, would be to usher in economic ruin.

Republicanism and slavery

Some planters in the Upper South resolved the dilemma by freeing their slaves. Such decisions were made easier by changing economic conditions in the Chesapeake. As planters shifted from tobacco toward wheat, a crop demanding a good deal less labor, Virginia and Maryland liberalized their manumission statutes, laws providing for freeing slaves. Between 1776 and 1789, most southern states also joined the North in prohibiting the importation of slaves, and a few antislavery societies appeared in the Upper South. But no southern state legally abolished slavery. Masters defended their right to hold human property in the name of republicanism.

Negro Methodists Holding a Meeting in a Philadelphia Alley evokes the vibrancy of black religious life in the city that became a haven for free African Americans.
(The Metropolitan Museum of Art, New York)

Eighteenth-century republicans regarded property as crucial, for it provided a man and his family with security, status, and wealth. More important, it provided a measure of independence: to be able to act freely, without fear or favor of others. People without property were dangerous, republicans believed, because the poor could never be politically independent. Southern defenders of slavery thus argued that free, propertyless black people would pose a political threat to the liberty of propertied white citizens. Subordinating the human rights of blacks to the property rights of whites, southern republicans reached the paradoxical conclusion that their freedom depended on keeping African Americans in bondage.

The North followed a different course. Because its economy depended far less on slave labor, black emancipation did not run counter to powerful economic interests. Antislavery societies, the first founded by the Quakers in 1775, spread throughout the northern states during the next quarter century. Over the same period the legislatures of most northern states provided for the immediate or gradual abolition of slavery. Freedom for most northern African Americans came slowly, but by 1830 there were fewer than 3000 slaves out of a total northern black population of 125,000.

The Revolution, which had been fought for liberty and equality, did little to change the status of most black Americans. By 1800 more enslaved African Americans lived in the United States than had lived there in 1776. Slavery continued to grow in the Lower South as the rice culture of the Carolinas and Georgia expanded and as the new cotton culture spread westward.

Still, a larger number of slaves than ever before became free during the war and in the decades following, whether through military service, successful escape, manumission, or gradual emancipation. All these developments fostered the growth of free black communities, especially in the Upper South and in northern cities. By 1810 free African Americans made up 10 percent of the total population of Maryland and Virginia. The composition of the postwar free community changed as well. Before independence most free blacks had been either mulattoes—the offspring of interracial unions—or former slaves too sick or aged to have value as laborers. By contrast, the free population of the 1780s became darker skinned, younger, and healthier. This group injected new vitality into black communal life, organizing independent schools, churches, and mutual benefit societies for the growing number of "free people of color."

Growth of the free black community

After the Revolution slavery ceased to be a national institution. It became the "peculiar institution" of a single region, the American South. The isolation of slavery in one section set North and South on radically different courses of social development, sharpening economic and political divisions.

Wartime Economic Disruption

With the outbreak of the Revolution, Americans had suffered an immediate loss of the manufactured goods, markets, and credit that Britain had formerly supplied. Matters did not improve with the coming of peace. France and Britain flooded the new states with their manufactures, and postwar Americans, eager for luxuries, indulged in a most unrepublican spending spree. The flurry of buying left some American merchants and consumers as deeply in debt as their governments. When loans from private citizens and foreign creditors like France had proved insufficient to finance the fighting, both Congress and the states printed paper money—a whopping total of $400 million. The paper currency was backed only by the government's promise to redeem the bills with money from future taxes, since legislatures balked at the unpopular alternative of levying taxes during the war. For the bills to be redeemed, the United States had to survive, so by the end of 1776, when Continental forces sustained a series of defeats, paper money started to depreciate dramatically. By 1781 it was virtually without value, and Americans coined the expression "not worth a Continental."

Public and private debt

The printing of paper money, combined with a wartime shortage of goods, triggered an inflationary spiral of scarcer and scarcer goods costing more and more worthless dollars. In this spiral, creditors were gouged by debtors, who paid them back with depreciated currency. At the same time soaring prices for food and manufactured goods eroded the buying power of

Postwar inflation

wage earners and small farmers. And the end of the war brought on demands for prompt repayment from the new nation's foreign creditors as well as from soldiers seeking back pay and pensions.

Congress could do nothing. With no power to regulate trade, it could neither dam the stream of imported goods rushing into the states nor stanch the flow of gold and silver to Europe to pay for these items. With no power to prohibit the states from issuing paper money, it could not halt depreciation. With no power to regulate wages or prices, it could not curb inflation. With no power to tax, it could not reduce the public debt. Efforts to grant Congress greater powers met with determined resistance from the states.

Within states, too, economic problems aroused discord. Some major merchants, creditors, and large commercial farmers had profited handsomely during the war by selling supplies to the American, British, and French armies at high prices or by preying on enemy vessels as privateers. Eager to protect their windfall, they lobbied state legislatures for an end to inflationary monetary policies. That meant passing high taxes to pay wartime debts, a paper currency that was backed up with gold and silver, and an active policy to encourage foreign trade.

Political divisions over economic policy

Less affluent men fought back, pressing legislatures for programs that met their needs. Western farmers, often in debt, urged the states to print more paper money and to pass laws lowering taxes and postponing the foreclosure of mortgages. Artisans opposed merchants by calling for protection from low-priced foreign imports that competed with the goods they produced. They set themselves against farmers as well by demanding price regulation of the farm products they consumed. In the continuing struggle, the state legislatures became the battleground of competing economic factions.

As the 1780s wore on, conflicts mounted. So long as the individual states remained sovereign, the Confederation was crippled—unable to conduct foreign affairs effectively, unable to set coherent economic policy, unable to deal with discontent in the West. Equally dismaying was the discovery that many Americans, instead of being selflessly concerned for the public good, selfishly pursued their private interests.

REPUBLICAN SOCIETY

The war for independence transformed not only America's government and economy but also its society and culture. Inspired by the Declaration's ideal of equality, some Americans rejected the subordinate position assigned to them under the old colonial order. Westerners, newly wealthy entrepreneurs, urban artisans, and women all claimed greater freedom, power, and recognition. The authority of the traditional leaders of government, society, and the family came under a new scrutiny; the impulse to defer to social superiors became less automatic. The new assertiveness demonstrated how deeply egalitarian assumptions were taking root in American culture.

The New Men of the Revolution

The Revolution gave rise to a new sense of social identity and a new set of ambitions among several groups of men who had once accepted a humbler status. The war also offered opportunities to aspiring entrepreneurs everywhere, and often they were not the same men who had prospered before the war. At a stroke, independence swept away the prominence of loyalists, whose ranks included an especially high number of government officials, large landowners, and major merchants. And while loyalists found their properties confiscated by revolutionary governments, other Americans grew rich. Many northern merchants gained newfound wealth from privateering or military contracts. Commercial farmers in the mid-Atlantic states prospered from the high food prices caused by wartime scarcity and army demand.

Winners and losers

The Revolution effected no dramatic redistribution of wealth. Indeed, the gap between rich and poor increased during the 1780s. But those families newly enriched by the Revolution came to demand and receive greater social recognition and political influence. The republican ideal of "an aristocracy of merit" justified their ambitions.

City craftworkers pushed for recognition too. Their experience in organizing boycotts against British goods during the imperial crisis gave artisans a greater taste of politics. With the Revolution accomplished, they clamored for men of their own kind to represent them in government. Their assertiveness came as a rude shock to gentlemen like South Carolina's William Henry Drayton, who balked at sharing power with men "who never were in a way to study" anything except "how to cut up a beast in the market to the best advantage, to cobble an old shoe in the neatest manner, or to build a necessary house."

Urban artisans

While master craftworkers competed for political office, the laborers who worked for them also exhibited a new sense of independence. Recognizing that their interests were often distinct from those of masters, journeymen formed new organizations to secure higher wages. Between 1786 and 1816 skilled urban laborers organized the first major strikes in American history.

The New Women of the Revolution

Not long after the fighting with Britain had broken out, Margaret Livingston of New York wrote to her sister Catherine, "You know that our Sex are doomed to be obedient in every stage of life so that we shant be great gainers by this contest." By war's end, however, Eliza Wilkinson from rural South Carolina was complaining boldly to a woman friend: "The men say we have no business with political matters . . . it's not our sphere. . . . [But] I won't have it thought that because we are the weaker Sex (as to bodily strength my dear) we are Capable of nothing more, than minding the Dairy . . . surely we may have enough sense to give our Opinions."

What separated Margaret Livingston's resignation from Eliza Wilkinson's assertion of personal worth and independence was the Revolution. Eliza Wilkinson had managed her parents' plantation during the war and defended it from British marauders. Other women discovered similar reserves of skill and resourcefulness. When soldiers returned home, some were surprised to find their wives and daughters, who had been running family farms and businesses, less submissive and more self-confident.

But American men had not fought a revolution for the equality of American women. In fact, male revolutionaries gave no thought to the role of women in the new nation, assuming that those of the "weaker sex" were incapable of making informed and independent political decisions. Most women of the revolutionary generation agreed that the proper female domain was the home, not the public arena of politics. Still, the currents of the Revolution occasionally left gaps that allowed women to display their political interests. When a loosely worded provision in the New Jersey state constitution gave the vote to "all free inhabitants" owning a specified amount of property, white widows and single women went to the polls. Only in 1807 did the state legislature close the loophole.

Exclusion of women from politics

Mary Woolstonecraft's Vindication

In the wake of the Revolution there also appeared in England a book that would become a classic text of modern feminism, Mary Woolstonecraft's *A Vindication of the Rights of Women* (1792). Attracting a wide, if not widely approving, readership in America as well, it called not only for laws to guarantee women civil and political equality, but also for educational reforms to ensure their social and economic equality.

Woolstonecraft dashed off *Vindication* in six short months. She charged that men deliberately conspired to keep women in "a state of perpetual childhood" by giving them inferior, frivolous educations. That encouraged young girls to fixate

Mrs. John McAllister of Philadelphia typified the newly confident women of the Revolution.

on fashion and flirtation and made them "only anxious to inspire love, when they ought to cherish a nobler ambition, and by their abilities and virtues exact respect." Girls, she proposed, should receive the same education as boys, including training that would prepare them for careers in medicine, politics, and business. No woman should have to pin her hopes for financial security on making a good marriage, Woolstonecraft argued. On the contrary, well-educated and resourceful women capable of supporting themselves would make the best wives and mothers, assets to the family and the nation.

Vindication might have been written in gunpowder rather than ink, given the hostile reaction it aroused on both sides of the Atlantic. Both male and female critics branded Woolstonecraft eccentric at best, immoral at worst. Her reputation plummeted further after her death in childbirth in 1797, when a memoir written by her husband revealed that she had lived out of wedlock with him—and before him, with another lover. Even so, Woolstonecraft's views found some admirers in America. Among them were Aaron Burr, the future vice president, who dubbed *Vindication* "a work of genius" and promised to read it aloud to his wife, and the Philadelphia Quaker Elizabeth Drinker, who confided to her diary that "In very many of her sentiments, she . . . *speaks my mind.*"

Republican Motherhood and Education

Woolstonecraft's ideas also lent support to the leading educational reformers in the revolutionary generation. Her sentiments echo in the writings of Judith Sargent Murray, a New Englander who urged the cultivation of women's minds to encourage self-respect and celebrated "excellency in our sex." Her fellow reformer, the Philadelphian Benjamin Rush, agreed that only educated and independent-minded women could raise the informed and self-reliant citizens that a republican government required. Their view, known as "republican motherhood," contributed to the most dramatic change in the lives of women after the war—the spread of female literacy.

Between 1780 and 1830 the number of American colleges and secondary academies rose dramatically, and some of these new institutions were devoted to educating women. Not only did the number of schools for women increase, but these schools also offered a solid academic curriculum. By 1850— for the first time in American history—there were as many literate women as there were men. To counter popular prejudices, the defenders of female education contended that schooling for women would produce the ideal republican mother. An educated woman, as one graduate of a female academy claimed, would "inspire her brothers, her husband, or her sons with such a love of virtue, such just ideas of the true value of civil liberty . . . that future heroes and statesmen shall exaltingly declare, it is to my mother that I owe this elevation."

> Improved schooling and literacy rates

The Revolution also prompted some states to reform their marriage laws, making divorce somewhat easier, although it remained extremely rare. But while women

Women's legal status

won greater freedom to divorce, courts became less concerned to enforce a widow's traditional legal claim to one-third of her spouse's real estate. And married women still could not sue or be sued, make wills or contracts, or buy and sell property. Any wages that they earned went to their husbands; so did all personal property that wives brought into a marriage; so did the rents and profits of any real estate they owned. Despite the high ideals of "republican motherhood," most women remained confined to the "domestic sphere" of the home and deprived of the most basic legal and political rights.

The Attack on Aristocracy

Why wasn't the American Revolution more revolutionary? Independence secured the full political equality of white men who owned property, but women were still deprived of political rights, African Americans of human rights. Why did the revolutionaries stop short of extending equality to the most unequal groups in American society—and with so little sense that they were being inconsistent?

In part, the lack of concern was rooted in republican ideas themselves. Republican ideology viewed property as the key to independence and power. Lacking property, women and black Americans were easily consigned to the custody of husbands and masters. Then, too, prejudice played its part: the perception of women and blacks as naturally inferior beings.

Republican view of equality

But revolutionary leaders also failed to press for greater equality because they conceived their crusade in terms of eliminating the evils of a European past dominated by kings and aristocrats. They believed that the great obstacle to equality was monarchy—kings and queens who bestowed hereditary honors and political office on favored individuals and granted legal privileges and monopolies to favored churches and businesses. These artificial inequalities posed the real threat to liberty, most republicans concluded. In other words, the men of the Revolution were intent on attaining equality by leveling off the top of society. It did not occur to most republicans that the cause of equality could also be served by raising up the bottom—by attacking the laws and prejudices that kept African Americans enslaved and women dependent.

The most significant reform of the republican campaign against artificial privilege was the dismantling of state-supported churches. Most states had a religious establishment. In New York and the South, it was the Anglican church; in New England, the Congregational church. Since the 1740s, dissenters who did not worship at state churches had protested laws that taxed all citizens to support the clergy of established denominations. After the Revolution, as more dissenters became voters, state legislators gradually abolished state support for Anglican and Congregational churches.

Disestablishment

Not only in religious life but in all aspects of their culture, Americans rejected inequalities associated with a monarchical past. In that spirit reformers at-

tacked the Society of Cincinnati, a group organized by former officers of the Continental Army in 1783. The society, which was merely
a social club for veterans, was forced to disband for its policy of passing on its membership rights to eldest sons. In this way, critics charged, the
Cincinnati was creating artificial distinctions and perpetuating a hereditary warrior nobility.

Today many of the republican efforts at reform seem misdirected. While only
a handful of revolutionaries worked for the education of women and the emancipation of slaves, enormous zeal went into fighting threats from a monarchical past
that had never existed in America. Yet the threat from kings and aristocrats was
real to the revolutionaries—and indeed remained real in many parts of Europe.
Their determination to sweep away every shred of formal privilege ensured that
these forms of inequality never took root in America.

FROM CONFEDERATION TO CONSTITUTION

While Americans in many walks of life sought to realize the republican commitment to equality, leaders in Congress wrestled with the problem of preserving the
nation itself. With the new republic slowly rending itself to pieces, some political
leaders concluded that neither the Confederation nor the state legislatures were
able to remedy the basic difficulties facing the nation. But how could the states be
convinced to surrender their sovereign powers? The answer came in the wake of
two events—one foreign, one domestic—that lent momentum to the cause of
strengthening the central government.

The Jay-Gardoqui Treaty

The international episode that threatened to leave the Confederation in shambles
was a debate over a proposed treaty with Spain. In 1785 southwesterners still could
not legally navigate the Mississippi and were still threatening to secede from the
union and annex their territory to Spain's American empire. To shore up southwestern loyalties, Congress instructed its secretary of foreign affairs, John Jay, to
negotiate an agreement with Spain preserving American rights to navigate on the
Mississippi River. But the Spanish emissary, Don Diego de Gardoqui, sweet-talked
Jay into accepting a treaty by which the United States would give up all rights to
the Mississippi for 25 years. In return, Spain agreed to grant trading privileges to
American merchants.

Jay, a New Yorker, knew more than a few northern merchants who were eager to open new markets. But when the proposed treaty became public knowledge,
southwesterners denounced it as nothing short of betrayal. The treaty was never
ratified, but the hostility stirred up during the debate revealed the strength of sectional feelings.

Shays' Rebellion

On the heels of this humiliation by Spain came an internal conflict that challenged the notion that individual states could maintain order in their own territories. The trouble erupted in western Massachusetts, where many small farmers were close to ruin. Yet they still had to pay mortgages on their farms, still had other debts, and were perpetually short of money. In 1786 the lower house of the Massachusetts legislature obliged the farmers with a package of relief measures. But creditors in eastern Massachusetts, determined to safeguard their own investments, persuaded the upper house to defeat the measures.

In the summer of 1786 western farmers responded, demanding that the upper house of the legislature be abolished and that the relief measures go into effect. That autumn 2000 farmers rose in armed rebellion, led by Captain Daniel Shays, a veteran of the Revolution. They closed the county courts to halt creditors from foreclosing on their farms and marched on the federal arsenal at Springfield. The state militia quelled the uprising by February 1787, but the insurrection left many in Massachusetts and the rest of the country thoroughly shaken.

Alarmed conservatives saw Shays' Rebellion as the consequence of radical democracy. "The natural effects of pure democracy are already produced among us," lamented one republican gentleman. "It is a war against virtue, talents, and property carried on by the dregs and scum of mankind." He was wrong. Daniel Shays' rebels were no impoverished rabble. They were reputable members of western communities who wanted their property protected and believed that government existed to provide that protection. The Massachusetts state legislature had been unable to safeguard the property of farmers from the inroads of recession or to protect the property of creditors from the armed debtors who closed the courts. It had failed, in other words, to fulfill the most basic aim of republican government.

Response to agrarian unrest

Other states with discontented debtors feared what the example of western Massachusetts might mean for the future of the Confederation itself. But by 1786 Shays' Rebellion supplied only the sharpest jolt to a movement for reform that was already under way. Even before the rebellion, a group of Virginians had proposed a meeting of the states to adopt a uniform system of commercial regulations. Once assembled at Annapolis in September 1786, the delegates from five states agreed to a more ambitious undertaking. They called for a second, broader meeting in Philadelphia, which Congress approved, for the "express purpose of revising the Articles of Confederation."

Framing a Federal Constitution

It was the wettest spring anyone could remember. The 55 men who traveled over muddy roads to Philadelphia in May 1787 arrived drenched and bespattered. Fortunately, most of the travelers were men in their thirties and forties, young enough to survive a good soaking. Since most were gentlemen of some means—planters,

James Madison, the scholar and statesman whose ideas and political skill shaped the Constitution.

merchants, and lawyers with powdered wigs and prosperous paunches—they could recover from the rigors of their journey in the best accommodations offered by America's largest city.

The delegates came from all the states except Rhode Island. The rest of New England supplied shrewd backroom politicians—Roger Sherman and Oliver Ellsworth from Connecticut and Rufus King and Elbridge Gerry, Massachusetts men who had learned a trick or two from Sam Adams. The middle states marshaled much of the intellectual might: two Philadelphia lawyers, John Dickinson and James Wilson; one Philadelphia financier, Robert Morris; and the aristocratic Gouverneur Morris. From New York there was Alexander Hamilton, the mercurial and ambitious young protégé of Washington. South Carolina provided fiery orators, Charles Pinckney and John Rutledge.

It was "an assembly of the demi-gods," gushed Thomas Jefferson, who, along with John Adams, was serving as a diplomat in Europe when the convention met. In fact, the only delegate who looked even remotely divine was the convention's presiding deity. Towering a full half foot taller than most of his colleagues, George Washington displayed his usual self-possession from a chair elevated on the speaker's platform where the delegates met, in the Pennsylvania State House. At first glance, the delegate of least commanding presence was Washington's fellow Virginian, James Madison. Short and slightly built, the 36-year-old Madison had no profession except hypochondria. But he was an astute politician and a brilliant political thinker who, more than anyone else, shaped the framing of the federal Constitution.

James Madison

The delegates from 12 different states had two things in common. They were all men of considerable political experience, and they all recognized the need for a stronger national union. So when the Virginia delegation introduced Madison's outline for a new central government, the convention was ready to listen.

The Virginia and New Jersey Plans

What Madison had in mind was a truly national republic, not a confederation of independent states. His "Virginia Plan" proposed a central government with three branches: legislative, executive, and judicial. Furthermore, the legislative branch, Congress, would possess the power to veto all state legislation. In place of the Confederation's single assembly, Madison substituted a bicameral legislature, with a lower house elected directly by the people and an upper house chosen by the lower from nominations made by state legislatures. Representatives to both houses would be apportioned according to population—a change from practice under the Articles, in which each state had a single vote in Congress. Madison also revised the structure of government that had existed under the Articles by adding an executive, who would be elected by Congress, and an independent federal judiciary.

Madison's Virginia Plan

After two weeks of debate over the Virginia Plan, William Paterson, a lawyer from New Jersey, presented a less radical counterproposal. While his "New Jersey Plan" increased Congress's power to tax and to regulate trade, it kept the national government as a unicameral assembly, with each state receiving one vote in Congress under the policy of equal representation. The delegates took just four days to reject Paterson's plan. Most endorsed Madison's design for a stronger central government.

Paterson's New Jersey Plan

Even so, the issue of apportioning representation continued to divide the delegates. While smaller states pressed for each state having an equal vote in Congress, larger states backed Madison's provision for basing representation on population. Underlying the dispute over representation was an even deeper rivalry between southern and northern states. While northern and southern populations were nearly equal in the 1780s, and the South's population was growing more rapidly, the northern states were more numerous. Giving the states equal votes would put the South at a disadvantage. Southerners feared being outvoted in Congress by the northern states and felt that only proportional representation would protect the interests of their section.

That division turned into a deadlock as the wet spring burned off into a blazing summer. Delegates suffered the daily torture of staring at a large sun painted on the speaker's chair occupied by Washington. The stifling heat was made even worse because the windows remained shut, to keep any news of the proceedings from drifting out onto the Philadelphia streets.

The Deadlock Broken

Finally, as the heat wave broke, so did the political stalemate. On July 2 a committee headed by Benjamin Franklin suggested a compromise. States would be equally represented in the upper house of Congress, each state legislature appointing two senators to six-year terms. That satisfied the smaller states. In the lower house of Congress, which alone could initiate money bills, representation was to be apportioned according to population. Every 30,000 inhabitants would entitle a state to send one representative for a two-year term. A slave was to count as three-fifths of a free person in the calculation of population, and the slave trade was to continue until 1808. That satisfied the larger states and the South.

Compromise over representation

By the end of August the convention was prepared to approve the final draft of the Constitution. The delegates agreed that the executive, now called the president, would be chosen every four years. Direct election seemed out of the question—after all, how could citizens in South Carolina know anything about a presidential candidate who happened to live in distant Massachusetts, or vice versa? But if each state chose presidential electors, either by popular election or by having the state legislature name them, those eminent men would likely have been involved in national politics, have known the candidates personally, and be prepared to vote wisely. Thus the Electoral College was established, with each state's total number of senators and representatives determining its share of electoral votes.

Electoral College

An array of other powers ensured that the executive would remain independent and strong: the president would have command over the armed forces, authority to conduct diplomatic relations, responsibility to nominate judges and officials in the executive branch, and the power to veto congressional legislation. Just as the executive branch was made independent, so too the federal judiciary was separated from the other two branches of government. Madison believed that this clear separation of powers was essential to a balanced republican government.

Separation of powers

Madison's only real defeat came when the convention refused to give Congress veto power over state legislation. Still, the new bicameral national legislature enjoyed much broader authority than Congress had under the Confederation, including the power to tax and to regulate commerce. The Constitution also limited the powers of state legislatures, prohibiting them from levying duties on trade, coining money or issuing paper currency, and conducting foreign relations. The Constitution and the acts passed by Congress were declared the supreme law of the land, taking precedence over any legislation passed by the states. And changing the Constitution would not be easy. Amendments could be proposed only by a two-thirds vote of both houses of Congress or in a convention requested by two-thirds of the state legislatures. Ratification of amendments required approval by three-quarters of the states.

Amending the Constitution

On September 17, 1787, thirty-nine of the forty-two delegates remaining in Philadelphia signed the Constitution. Charged only to revise the Articles, the delegates had instead written a completely new frame of government. And to speed up ratification, the convention decided that the Constitution would go into effect after only nine states had approved it. They further declared that the people themselves—not the state legislatures—would pass judgment on the Constitution in special ratifying conventions. To serve final notice that the new central government was a republic of the people and not merely another confederation of states, Gouverneur Morris of Pennsylvania hit on a happy turn of phrase to introduce the Constitution. "We the People," the document begins, "in order to form a more perfect union . . ."

Ratification

With grave misgivings on the part of many, the states called for conventions to decide whether to ratify the new Constitution. Those with the gravest misgivings—the Anti-Federalists as they came to be called—voiced familiar republican fears.

The Anti-Federalists Older and less cosmopolitan than their Federalist opponents, the Anti-Federalists drew upon their memories of the struggle with England to frame their criticisms of the Constitution. Expanding the power of the central government at the expense of the states, they warned, would lead to corrupt and arbitrary rule by new aristocrats. Extending a republic over a large territory, they cautioned, would separate national legislators from the interests and close oversight of their constituents.

Madison responded to these objections in *The Federalist Papers*, a series of 85 essays written with Alexander Hamilton and John Jay during the winter of 1787–1788. **The Federalist Papers** He countered Anti-Federalist concerns over the centralization of power by pointing out that each separate branch of the national government would keep the others within the limits of their legal authority. That mechanism of checks and balances would prevent the executive from oppressing the people while preventing the people from oppressing themselves.

To answer Anti-Federalist objections to a national republic, Madison drew on the ideas of an English philosopher, David Hume. In his famous 10th essay in *The Federalist Papers*, Madison argued that in a great republic, "the Society becomes broken into a greater variety of interests, of pursuits, of passions, which check each other." The larger the territory, the more likely it was to contain multiple political interests and parties, so that no single faction could dominate. Instead, each would cancel out the others.

The one Anti-Federalist criticism Madison could not get around was the absence of a national bill of rights. Opponents insisted on an explicit statement of rights to secure the freedoms of individuals and minorities from being **Bill of Rights** violated by the federal government. Madison finally promised to place a bill of rights before Congress immediately after the Constitution was ratified.

Throughout the early months of 1788, Anti-Federalists continued their opposition. But they lacked the articulate and influential leadership that rallied behind the Constitution and commanded greater access to the public press. In the end, too, Anti-Federalist fears of centralized power proved less compelling than Federalist prophecies of the chaos that would follow if the Constitution were not adopted.

By June 1788 all but three states had voted in favor of ratification. The last holdout—to no one's surprise Rhode Island—finally came aboard in May 1790, after Madison had carried through on his pledge to submit a bill of rights to the new Congress. Indeed, these 10 amendments proved to be the Anti-Federalists' most impressive legacy.

Changing Revolutionary Ideals

Within the life span of a single generation, Americans had declared their independence twice. In many ways the political freedom claimed from Britain in 1776 was less remarkable than the intellectual freedom that Americans achieved by agreeing to the Constitution. The Constitution represented both a triumph of imagination and common sense and a rejection of some older, long-cherished republican beliefs.

Americans thought long and hard before changing their minds, but many did. Committed at first to limiting executive power by making legislatures supreme, they at last ratified a constitution that provided for an independent executive and a balanced government. Committed at first to preserving the sovereignty of the states, they at last established a national government with authority independent of the states. Committed at first to the proposition that a national republic was impossible, they at last created an impossibility that still endures.

What, then, became of the last tenet of the old republican creed—the belief that civic virtue would sustain popular liberty? The hard lessons of the war and the crises of the 1780s withered confidence in the capacity of Americans to sacrifice their private interests for the public welfare. Many came to share Washington's sober view that "the few . . . who act upon Principles of disinterestedness are, comparatively speaking, no more than a drop in the Ocean." The Constitution reflected the new recognition that interest rather than virtue shaped the behavior of most people most of the time and that the clash of diverse interest groups would remain a constant of public life.

Interest rather than virtue

Yet Madison and many other Federalists did not believe that the competition between private interests would somehow result in policies fostering public welfare. That goal would be met instead by the new national government acting as "a disinterested and dispassionate umpire in disputes between different passions and interests in the State." The Federalists looked to the national government to fulfill that role because they trusted that a large republic, with its millions of citizens, would yield more of that scarce resource—disinterested gentlemen dedicated to serving the public good. Such gentlemen, in Madison's words, "whose enlightened views and virtuous sentiments render them superior to local prejudices," would fill the small number of national offices.

Not all the old revolutionaries agreed. Anti-Federalists drawn from the ranks of ordinary Americans still believed that common people were more virtuous and gentlemen more interested than the Federalists allowed. "These lawyers and men of learning, and moneyed men, that talk so finely," complained one Anti-Federalist, would "get all the power and all of the money into their own hands, and then they will swallow up all us little folks." Instead of being dominated by enlightened gentlemen, the national government should be composed of representatives from every social class and occupational group.

The narrow majorities by which the Constitution was ratified reflected the continuing influence of such sentiments as well as fear that the states were surrendering too much power. That fear made Patrick Henry so ardent an Anti-Federalist that he refused to attend the Constitutional Convention in 1787, saying that he "smelt a rat." "I am not a Virginian, but an American," Henry had once declared. Most likely he was lying. Or perhaps Patrick Henry, a southerner and a slaveholder, could see his way clear to being an "American" only so long as sovereignty remained firmly in the hands of the individual states. Henry's convictions, 70 years hence, would rise again to haunt the Union.

 **c h a p t e r   s u m m a r y**

Leading Americans would give more thought to federalism, the organization of a United States, as the events of the postrevoluionary period revealed the weaknesses of the state and national governments.

- For a decade after independence, the revolutionaries were less committed to creating a single national republic than to organizing 13 separate state republics, each dominated by popularly elected legislatures.

- The Articles of Confederation provided for a government by a national legislature, but left the crucial power of the purse, as well as all final power to make and execute laws, entirely to the states.

- Many conflicts in the new republic were occasioned by westward expansion, which created both international difficulties with Britain and Spain and internal tensions over the democratization of state legislatures.

- In the wake of the Revolution, ordinary Americans struggled to define republican society: workers began to organize; some women claimed a right to greater political, legal, and educational opportunities; and religious dissenters called for disestablishment.

- In the mid-1780s the political crisis of the Confederation came to a head, prompted by the controversy over the Jay-Gardoqui Treaty and Shays' Rebellion.

- The Constitutional Convention of 1787 produced an entirely new frame of government that established a truly national republic and privided for a separation of powers among a judiciary, a bicameral legislature, and a strong executive.

- The Anti-Federalists, opponents of the Constitution, softened their objections when promised a bill of rights after ratification, which was accomplished by 1789.

 For quizzes and a variety of interactive resources, visit the book's Online Learning Center at www.mhhe.com/davidsonconcise3

SIGNIFICANT EVENTS

1777		Continental Congress approves the Articles of Confederation
1781		Articles of Confederation ratified
1784		Spain closes the Mississippi River to American navigation
1785		Jay-Gardoqui Treaty negotiated but not ratified
1786		Shays' Rebellion; Annapolis convention calls for revising the Articles
1787		Congress adopts the Northwest Ordinance; Constitutional Convention
1787–1788		Publication of *The Federalist Papers*
1788		New Hampshire becomes ninth state to ratify Constitution
1791		Bill of Rights adopted

CHAPTER 8

The Republic Launched (1789–1801)

preview • In 1789 Americans were divided into those who were rural, largely semisubsistent farmers and those tied more closely to the world of commerce. Politics in the early republic was rooted in this fundamental social division. Hamilton's Federalists, participants in the commercial markets, believed in order, hierarchy, and an active central government. Jefferson's Republicans, champions of the self-sufficient farmer, feared aristocracy and wealth and wanted a less active government.

ne spring evening in 1794 General John Neville was riding home from Pittsburgh with his wife and granddaughter. Coming up a hill his wife's saddle started to slip, so Neville dismounted to tighten the girth. As he adjusted the strap, he heard the clip-clop of horses' hooves, followed by a gruff voice asking, "Are you Neville the excise officer?"

"Yes," Neville replied, without turning around.

"Then I must give you a whipping!" announced the rider, leaping from his horse. He grabbed the startled Neville by the hair and lunged at his throat, and the two began tussling. Breaking free, Neville finally managed to knock the man down and subdue him. He recognized his assailant as Jacob Long, a local farmer. After Long fled, the badly shaken Neville resumed his journey.

John Neville was not accustomed to such treatment. As one of the wealthiest men in the area, he expected respect from those of lower social rank. And he had received it—at least he had until becoming embroiled in a controversy over the new "whiskey tax" on distilled spirits. In a frontier district like western Pennsylvania, farmers regularly distilled their grain into whiskey for barter and sale. Not surprisingly, the excise tax,* passed by Congress in 1791, was notoriously unpopular. Even so, Neville had accepted an appointment as one of the tax's regional inspectors. For three years he had endured threats as he tried to enforce the law, but this roadside assault indicated that popular hostility was rising.

---

*An excise tax is an internal tax laid upon the production, sale, or consumption of a commodity—in this case, whiskey.

Frontier farmers in Pennsylvania tar and feather a federal tax collector during the Whiskey Rebellion. The political violence of the 1790s led Americans to wonder whether the new government would succeed in uniting a socially diverse nation.

As spring turned to summer, the grain ripened, and so did the people's anger. In mid-July, a federal marshall arrived to serve summonses to a number of farmer-distillers who had not paid taxes. One, William Miller, squinted at the paper and was amazed to find the government ordering him to set aside "all manner of business and excuses" and appear in court—hundreds of miles away in Philadelphia—in little more than a month. Even worse, the papers claimed he owed $250.

And there, next to this unknown federal marshall, stood the stiff-backed, unyielding John Neville.

"I felt myself mad with passion," recalled Miller. "I thought $250 would ruin me; and . . . I felt my blood boil at seeing General Neville along to pilot the sheriff to my very door." Meanwhile word of the marshall's presence brought 30 or 40 laborers swarming from a nearby field. Armed with muskets and pitchforks, they appeared both angry and well-liquored. When a shot rang out, Neville and the marshall beat a hasty retreat.

Within hours, news of Neville's doings spread to a nearby militia company. Enraged by what they considered this latest trampling on individual liberty, the militia marched to Neville's fortified house the next morning. A battle ensued, and the general, aided by his slaves, beat back the attackers. A larger group, numbering 500 to 700, returned the following day to find Neville fled and his home garrisoned by a group of soldiers from nearby Fort Pitt. The mob burned down most of the outbuildings and, after the soldiers surrendered, torched Neville's home.

Throughout the region that summer, anonymous broadsides threatened those who "opposed the virtuous principles of republican liberty," liberty poles appeared with flags proclaiming "liberty and no excise," and marauding bands in disguise roamed the countryside, burning homes, banishing individuals, and attacking tax collectors and other enemies. To many citizens who learned of the disturbances, such echoes of the revolutionary 1760s and 1770s were deeply distressing. In the space of only 15 years, Americans had already overturned two governments: England's colonial administration and the Articles of Confederation. As the aged Benjamin Franklin remarked in 1788, although Americans were quite proficient at overthrowing governments, it remained to be seen whether they were any good at sustaining them. Six years later, Franklin's warning seemed prophetic.

Yet Federalists—supporters of the Constitution—had recognized from the beginning how risky it was to unite a territory as large as the United States's 890,000 square miles. Yankee merchants living along Boston wharves had economic interests and cultural traditions quite different from those of backcountry farmers who raised hogs, tended a few acres of corn, and distilled whiskey. Even among farmers, there was a world of difference between a South Carolina planter who shipped tons of rice to European markets and a Vermont family whose stony fields yielded barely enough to survive. Could the new government established by the Constitution provide a framework strong enough to unite such a socially diverse nation?

1789: A SOCIAL PORTRAIT

When the Constitution went into effect, the United States stretched from the Atlantic Ocean to the Mississippi River. The first federal census, compiled in 1790, put the population at approximately 4 million people, divided about evenly between the northern and southern states. The Republic's population was overwhelmingly concentrated along the eastern seaboard. Only about 100,000 settlers lived beyond the Appalachians in the Tennessee and Kentucky territories, which were soon to become states. The area north of the Ohio River was virtually unsettled by whites.

Within the Republic's boundaries were two major racial groups that lacked effective political influence: African Americans and Indians. In 1790 black Americans numbered 750,000, almost one-fifth of the total population. Over 90 percent lived in the southern states from Maryland to Georgia; most were slaves who worked on tobacco and rice plantations. The census did not count the number of Indians living east of the Mississippi. North of the Ohio, the powerful Miami Confederacy discouraged settlement, while to the south, five strong, well-organized tribes—the Creeks, Cherokees, Chickasaws, Choctaws, and Seminoles—dominated the region from the Appalachians to the Mississippi River.

That situation would change, however, as the white population continued to double approximately every 22 years. The primary cause was natural increase, for in 1790 the average American white woman gave birth to nearly eight children.* The age at first marriage was about 25 for men, 24 for women; but it was significantly lower in newly settled areas (on average perhaps 21 for males and younger for females), which contributed to the high birthrate.

Population growth

This youthful, growing population remained overwhelmingly rural. Only 24 towns or cities boasted a population of 2500 or more, and 19 out of 20 Americans lived outside them. In fact, in 1800 over 80 percent of American families were engaged in agriculture. In such a rural environment the movement of people, goods, and information was slow. Few individuals used the expensive postal system, and most roads were still little more than dirt paths. In 1790 the country had 92 newspapers, published weekly or semiweekly, mostly in towns and cities along major avenues of transportation. Americans off the beaten path only occasionally heard news of the outside world.

Poor transportation

What would divide Americans most broadly over the coming decades was whether they were primarily semisubsistence farmers, living largely on the produce of their own land and labor, or were tied more closely to the larger commercial markets. As the United States began its life under the new federal union, the distinction between a semisubsistence economy and a commercial economy was a crucial one.

The Semisubsistence Economy of Crèvecoeur's America

Most rural white Americans lived off the produce of their own land in a barter economy. It was this world that a French writer, Hector St. John de Crèvecoeur, described so well.

Arriving in 1759, Crèvecoeur traveled widely in the British colonies before settling for a number of years as a farmer in the Hudson River valley. He

---

*Because the 1790 census did not include significant data on the black population, many of the statistical figures quoted for this era apply only to white Americans.

published in 1783 his *Letters from an American Farmer,* asking in them the question that had so often recurred to him: "What then is the American, this new man?"

For Crèvecoeur what distinguished American society was the widespread equality of its people, especially the rural farmers. Americans were hostile to anything that smacked of aristocratic privilege. Furthermore, the conditions of the country promoted equality. Land was abundant and widely distributed, citizens lived decently, and the population was not divided into the wealthy few and the desperate many. (Like most of his contemporaries, Crèvecoeur glided rather quickly over the plight of black slaves.) "We are the most perfect society now existing in the world," he boasted.

Equality

Although Crèvecoeur waxed romantic about the conditions of American life, he painted a reasonably accurate portrait of most of the interior of the northern states and the backcountry of the South. Wealth in those areas, while not distributed equally, was spread fairly broadly. And subsistence remained the goal of most white families. "The great effort was for every farmer to produce anything he required within his own family," one European visitor noted. In such an economy women played a key role. Wives and daughters had to be skilled in making articles such as candles, soap, clothing, and hats, since the cost of buying such items was steep.

With labor scarce and expensive, farmers also depended on their neighbors to help clear fields, build homes, and harvest crops. If a farm family produced a small surplus, they usually exchanged it locally rather than selling it for cash in a distant market. In this barter economy money was seldom seen. Instead, residents in the countryside "supply their needs . . . by direct reciprocal exchanges," a French traveler recorded. "They write down what they give and receive on both sides and at the end of the year they settle a large variety of exchanges with a very small quantity of coin."

Barter economy

Indian economies were also based primarily on subsistence. In the division of labor women raised crops, while men fished or hunted—not only for meat but also for skins to make clothing. Because Indians followed game more seasonally than white settlers did, their villages were moved to several different locations over the course of a year. But both whites and Indians in a semisubsistence economy moved periodically to new fields after the old ones were exhausted.

Despite the popular image of both the independent "noble savage" and the self-reliant yeoman farmer, virtually no one in the backcountry operated within a truly subsistence economy. While farmers tried to grow most of the food their families ate, they normally bought salt, sugar, and coffee. In addition, necessities such as iron, glass, lead, and powder had to be purchased, usually at a country store, and many farmers hired artisans to make items such as shoes and to weave cloth. Similarly, Indians quickly became enmeshed in the wider world of European commerce, exchanging furs for iron tools or clothing and ornamental materials.

The Commercial Economy of Franklin's America

Outside the backcountry, Americans were tied much more closely to a commercial economy. Here, merchants, artisans, and even farmers did not subsist on what they produced but instead sold goods or services in a wider market and lived on their earnings. Cities and towns, of course, played a key part in the commercial economy. But so did the agricultural regions near the seaboard and along navigable rivers.

For commerce to flourish, goods had to move from producers to market cheaply enough to reap profits. Water offered the only cost-effective transportation over any distance; indeed, it cost as much to ship goods a mere 30 miles over primitive roads as to ship by boat 3000 miles across the Atlantic to London. Where transportation was prohibitively expensive, farmers had no incentive to increase production, and an economy of barter and semisubsistence persisted.

Commercial society differed from Crèvecoeur's world in another important way: its wealth was less equally distributed. By 1790, the richest 10 percent of those living in cities and in the plantation districts of the Tidewater South owned about 50 percent of the wealth. In the backcountry the top 10 percent was likely to own 25 to 35 percent.

> Inequality of wealth

Crèvecoeur argued that the American belief in equality sustained this society of small, relatively equal farm families. But he failed to see how much that equality rested on isolation. In areas with access to markets, Americans were more acquisitive and materialistic. Although semisubsistence farm families were eager to rise in life and acquire material goods, only those in the commercial economy could realistically pursue these dreams.

The man who gained international renown as a self-made citizen of commercial America was Benjamin Franklin. In his writings and in the example of his own life, Franklin offered a vision of the new nation that contrasted with Crèvecoeur's ideal of a subsistence America. He had arrived in Philadelphia as a runaway apprentice but by hard work and talent rose to be one of the leading citizens of his adopted city. The preface to Franklin's

> Benjamin Franklin and commercial values

popular *Poor Richard's Almanack*, as well as his countless essays, spelled out simple maxims for Americans seeking the upward path. "The way to wealth is as plain as the way to market," he noted. "It depends chiefly on two words, industry and frugality." Those anxious to succeed should "remember that time is money." The kind of success he preached depended on taking advantage of commerce and a wider market. As a printer, Franklin was able to lead a life of acquisition and social mobility because he could distribute his almanacs and newspapers to ever-greater audiences.

The ethics of Franklin's marketplace threatened to destroy Crèvecoeur's egalitarian America. At the time of Franklin's death in 1790, the ideal that Crèvecoeur had so eloquently described still held sway across much of America. But the political debates of the 1790s showed clearly that Franklin's world of commerce and markets was slowly transforming the nation.

The Constitution and Commerce

In many ways the fight over ratification of the Constitution represented a struggle between the commercial and the subsistence-oriented elements of American society. Urban merchants and workers as well as commercial farmers and planters generally rallied behind the Constitution. They took a broader, more cosmopolitan view of the nation's future, and they had a more favorable view of government power.

Americans who remained a part of the semisubsistence barter economy tended to oppose the Constitution. More provincial in outlook, they feared concentrated power, were suspicious of cities and commercial institutions, opposed aristocracy and special privilege, and in general just wanted to be left alone. In defeat they remained suspicious that a powerful government would tax them to benefit the commercial sectors of the economy.

And so in 1789 the United States embarked on its new national course, with two rival visions of the direction that the fledgling Republic should take. Which vision would prevail—a question that was as much social as it was political—increasingly divided the generation of revolutionary leaders during the 1790s.

THE NEW GOVERNMENT

Whatever the Republic was to become, Americans agreed that George Washington personified it. When the first Electoral College cast its votes, Washington was unanimously elected, the only president in history so honored. John Adams became vice president. Loyalty to the new Republic rested to a great degree on the trust and respect Americans gave Washington.

Time has transformed Washington from a man into a monument: remote and unknowable, stiff, unbowing, impenetrable. Even during his own lifetime, he had

Washington's character

no close friends in public life and discouraged familiarity. Critics complained about his formal public receptions, the large number of servants, and the coach emblazoned with his coat of arms—all aristocratic habits. Still, as much as Washington craved honor and military fame, he did not hunger for power and accepted the office of the presidency only reluctantly.

Organizing the Government

Washington realized that as the first occupant of the executive office, everything he did was fraught with significance. "I walk on untrodden ground," he commented. "There is scarcely any part of my conduct which may not hereafter be drawn into precedent." Cautious and deliberate, the president usually asked for written advice and made his decision only after weighing the options carefully.

Congress authorized the creation of four departments—War, Treasury, State, and Attorney General—whose heads were to be appointed with the consent of the

Senate. Washington's most important choices were Alexander Hamilton as secretary of the treasury and Thomas Jefferson to head the State Department. At first the president did not meet regularly with his advisers as a group, but gradually the idea of a cabinet that met to discuss policy matters evolved.

The cabinet

The Constitution created a federal Supreme Court but beyond that was silent about the court system. The Judiciary Act of 1789 set the size of the Supreme Court at 6 members; it also established 13 federal district courts and 3 circuit courts of appeal. The Judiciary Act made it clear that federal courts had the right to review decisions of the state courts and specified cases over which the Supreme Court would have original jurisdiction. Washington appointed John Jay of New York, a staunch Federalist, as the first chief justice.

Federal judiciary

The Bill of Rights

Congress also confronted the demand for a bill of rights, which had become an issue during the debate over ratification. At that time, nearly 200 amendments had been put forward in one form or another. Supporters of the Constitution were particularly alarmed over proposals to restrict the federal power to tax. As leader of

Washington's trip from Virginia to New York City to assume the presidency was a triumphant procession as Americans greeted him with unbridled enthusiasm bordering on adulation. Here women strew flowers before him as he passes through Trenton.

the Federalist forces in the House of Representatives, James Madison moved to head off any large-scale changes that would weaken federal power. Instead, Madison submitted a bill of rights that focused on civil liberties.

Ultimately Congress sent 12 amendments to the states. By December 1791, 10 had been ratified and incorporated into the Constitution. The advocates of strong federal power, like Hamilton, were relieved that "the structure of the government, and the mass and distribution of its powers," remained unchanged.

These first 10 amendments, known as the Bill of Rights, were destined to be of crucial importance in defining personal liberty in the United States. Among the rights guaranteed were freedom of religion, the press, and speech, as well as the right to assemble and petition and the right to bear arms.

Protected rights

The amendments also established clear procedural safeguards, including the right to a trial by jury and protection against illegal searches and seizures. They prohibited excessive bail, cruel and unusual punishment, and the quartering of troops in private homes. At the same time, an attempt in Congress to apply these same guarantees to state governments failed.

Hamilton's Financial Program

Before adjourning, Congress called on Alexander Hamilton, as secretary of the treasury, to report on the nation's finances. Hamilton undertook the assignment eagerly, for he did not intend to be a minor figure in the new administration.

Hamilton grew up on the islands of the West Indies, scarred by the stigmas of poverty and illegitimacy. To compensate, he was driven constantly to seek respectability and money. He served as a military aide to Washington during the Revolution, and marriage to the daughter of a wealthy New York politician gave him influential connections he could draw on in his political career. Hamilton's haughty manner, jealousy, and penchant for intrigue made him many enemies. He was a brilliant thinker, yet he felt out of place in the increasingly democratic society emerging around him. "All communities divide themselves into the few and the many," he declared. "The people are turbulent and changing; they seldom judge or determine right."

Hamilton's character

Convinced that human nature was at bottom selfish, Hamilton believed that the government needed to appeal to the self-interest of the rich and wellborn in order to succeed. "Men," he observed succinctly, "will naturally go to those who pay them best." He took as his model Great Britain, whose greatness he attributed to its system of public finance and its preeminence in commerce and manufacturing. Thus Hamilton set out to achieve two goals. He intended to use federal power to encourage manufacturing and commerce, in order to make the United States economically strong and independent of Europe. And he was determined to link the interests of the wealthy with those of the new government.

Neither goal could be achieved until the federal government solved its two most pressing financial problems: revenue and credit. Without revenue it could not be ef-

Hamilton, though short of stature, cut a dashing figure with his erect bearing, strutting manner, meticulous dress, and carefully powdered hair. Declared the wife of the British ambassador: "I have scarcely ever been more charmed with the vivacity and conversation of any man."

fective, and without credit—the faith that the government would repay its debts—it would lack the ability to borrow. Hamilton proposed that all $52 million of the federal debt be paid in full (or funded). He also

Funding and assumption

recommended that the federal government assume responsibility for the remaining $25 million in Revolutionary War debts that individual states owed. He intended with these policies to enhance the new federal government's power and strengthen its creditworthiness. Hamilton also proposed a series of excise taxes, including a controversial 25 percent levy on whiskey, to help meet government expenses.

After heated debate, Congress deadlocked over funding and assumption. Finally, over dinner with Hamilton, Jefferson and Madison of Virginia agreed to support his proposal if, after 10 years in Philadelphia, the permanent seat of government was located in the South, on the Potomac River between Virginia and Maryland. Aided by this understanding, funding and assumption passed

Location of the capital

Congress. In 1791 Congress also approved a 20-year charter for the first Bank of the United States. The bank would hold government deposits and issue bank notes that would be received in payment of all debts owed the federal government. Congress proved less receptive to the rest of Hamilton's program, although a limited tariff to encourage manufacturing and several excise taxes, including the one on whiskey, won approval.

Opposition to Hamilton's Program

The passage of Hamilton's program caused a permanent rupture among supporters of the Constitution. Eventually the two warring factions organized themselves into political parties: the Republicans, led by Jefferson and Madison, and the

Federalists, led by Hamilton and Adams.* But this division emerged slowly over several years.

Hamilton's program promoted the commercial sector at the expense of semi-subsistence agrarian groups. Thus it rekindled many of the concerns that had surfaced during the struggle over ratification of the Constitution. The ideology of the Revolution had stressed that republics inevitably contained groups who sought power in order to destroy popular liberties and overthrow the republic. To some Americans, Hamilton's program seemed a clear threat to establish a privileged and powerful financial aristocracy—perhaps even a monarchy.

Fears over Hamilton's program

Who, after all, would benefit from the funding proposal? During and after the Revolution, the value of notes issued by the Continental Congress dropped sharply. Speculators had bought up most of these notes for a fraction of their face value from small farmers and workers. Equally disturbing, members of Congress had been purchasing the notes before the adoption of Hamilton's program. Madison urged that only the original holders of the debt be reimbursed in full, but Hamilton rejected this idea, since commercial speculators were precisely the class of people he hoped to bind to the new government.

Similarly, when stock in the Bank of the United States went on sale, speculators snapped up all the shares in an hour. The price of a share skyrocketed from $25 to $300 in two months. Jefferson was appalled by the mania Hamilton's program encouraged. "The spirit of gambling, once it has seized a subject, is incurable," he asserted. "The taylor who has made thousands in one day, tho he has lost them the next, can never again be content with the slow and moderate earnings of his needle."

The national bank struck its critics as a dangerous mimicking of English corruption. Indeed, in Great Britain the Bank of England played a powerful role not only in fueling the economy but in controlling Parliament by making loans to members, and Jefferson warned that the same thing would happen in the United States. These fears were heightened because Americans had little experience with banks: only three existed in the country when the Bank of the United States was chartered. Then, too, banks and commerce were a part of the urban environment that rural Americans so distrusted. Moreover, the tariff favored one group in society—manufacturers—at the expense of other groups.

Opposition to a national bank

After Congress approved the bank bill, Washington hesitated to sign it. When he consulted his cabinet, Jefferson stressed that the Constitution did not specifically authorize Congress to charter a bank. Both he and Madison upheld the idea of strict construction—that the Constitution should be interpreted narrowly and

---

*The Republican party of the 1790s, sometimes referred to as the Jeffersonian Republicans, is not to be confused with the modern-day Republican party, which originated in the 1850s.

the federal government restricted to powers expressly delegated to it. Otherwise, the federal government would be the judge of its own powers, and there would be no safeguard against the abuse of power.

Hamilton countered that the Constitution contained implied as well as enumerated powers. He particularly emphasized the clause that permitted Congress to make all laws "necessary and proper" to carry out its duties. A bank would be useful in carrying out the enumerated powers of regulating commerce and maintaining the public credit; therefore Congress had a right to decide whether to establish one. In the end Washington accepted Hamilton's forceful arguments and signed the bill.

> Strict construction versus implied powers

The Specter of Aristocracy

Hamilton's opponents feared the development of an aristocracy in the United States. Because Hamilton's program deliberately aided the rich and created a class of citizens whose wealth derived from the federal government, it strengthened these traditional fears. "Money will be put under the direction of government," charged Philip Freneau, a leading Republican editor, "and the government will be put under the direction of money."

Many who opposed Hamilton's financial program had also been against the Constitution, but leadership of the opposition fell to Jefferson and Madison, who had staunchly worked for ratification. Although Jefferson and Madison were planters, well accustomed to the workings of the marketplace, they still distrusted cities and commerce and Hamilton's aristocratic ways.

Economically Hamilton's program was a success. The government's credit was restored, and the national bank ended the inflation of the previous two decades and created a sound currency. In addition, Hamilton's theory of implied powers and broad construction gave the nation the flexibility necessary to respond to unanticipated crises.

> Hamilton's success

EXPANSION AND TURMOIL IN THE WEST

In the peace treaty of 1783, Britain ceded to the United States the territory between the Appalachian Mountains and the Mississippi River. Even so, British troops continued to hold the forts in the Northwest, and Indian tribes controlled most of this region. To demonstrate the government's effectiveness, Washington moved to extend control over the West.

The Resistance of the Miamis

In principle, the United States recognized the rights of Indians to their lands. Furthermore, it had promised that any purchase of Indian land would be made only by treaty and not through private agreements. Nevertheless, the government was determined to buy out Indian titles in order to promote white settlement.

By 1790 the United States had acquired the Indian lands in most of Kentucky and about one-quarter of Tennessee. North of the Ohio, however, the Miami Confederacy (composed of eight western tribes headed by the Miami) stoutly refused to sell territory. Eventually Washington dispatched an army of 2000, commanded by "Mad Anthony" Wayne, to compel a resolution. At the Battle of Fallen Timbers in August 1794 Wayne won a decisive victory. In the Treaty of Greenville (1795), he forced the tribes to cede the southern two-thirds of the area between Lake Erie and the Ohio River, thus opening up the Northwest to white settlement.

Indian defeat at Fallen Timbers

The Whiskey Rebellion

Westerners approved of the administration's military policy against the Indians. They were far less pleased that in 1791 Congress had passed a new excise tax on distilled liquors. Most property owners along the frontier found it hard to make ends meet, and for many settlers the sale of whiskey provided essential income.

As the law began to be put into effect, farmers in the western districts of several states defied federal officials and refused to pay, launching a "whiskey rebellion." The greatest unrest flared in western Pennsylvania in 1794, where General Neville was burned out of his home (page 202). That summer an even larger gathering of angry, impoverished farmers threatened to march on Pittsburgh. For rural residents, the city had become a symbol of the corrupt cosmopolitan influences that threatened their liberty. Many in the crowd relished the idea of looting the property of wealthy residents. "I have a bad hat now, but I expect to have a better one soon," shouted one of the mob.

To distant easterners, the Whiskey Rebellion at first appeared serious. Hamilton, who had pushed the whiskey tax in order to demonstrate the power of the new government, saw the matter as a question of authority. "Shall there be government, or no government?" he asked. An alarmed Washington led an army of 13,000 men into the Pennsylvania countryside to overawe the populace and subdue the rebels. Hamilton soon took charge, but to his disappointment the troops met no organized resistance. "An insurrection was announced and proclaimed and armed against, but could never be found," Jefferson scoffed. Even some of Hamilton's allies conceded that he had overreacted.

Collapse of resistance

Western unhappiness was also eased somewhat when Washington sent Thomas Pinckney to negotiate a treaty with Spain, which controlled Florida and the mouth of the Mississippi. Pinckney's Treaty, which the Senate unanimously ratified in 1796, set the 31st parallel as the southern boundary of the United States and granted Americans free navigation of the Mississippi, with the right to deposit goods at New Orleans for reshipment to ports in the East and abroad. No longer could Spain try to detach the western settlements from American control by promising to open the Mississippi to their trade.

Pinckney's Treaty

Suppressing the Whiskey Rebellion

Men were dragged out of their beds, at two o'clock in the morning; not suffered to dress themselves, but in an unfinished manner obliged to march, some of them without putting on their shoes . . . ; dragged out of their beds, amidst the cries of children, and the tears of mothers; treated with language of the most insulting opprobrium, by those apprehending them; driven before a troop of horse, at a trot, through muddy roads, seven miles from Pittsburgh; impounded in a pen, on the wet soil. The guard baying them, and asking them how they would like to be hanged; some offering a dollar to have the privilege of shooting at them; . . . obliged to live all night upon the wet earth, without covering; under a season of sleet, rain, and snow; driven from the fire with bayonets. . . ; next day impounded in a waste house, and detained there five days; then removed to a newly built and damp room, without fire, in the garrison at Pittsburgh; at the end of ten days brought before the judiciary, and the information against them found not to be regarded. Was this the way to quell the insurrection? Was this the way to make good citizens? . . .

I do not mean to question the necessity . . . of making the arrest[s] in the night, and by squadrons of horse; but I only take notice, that, this being necessary, it was the greater hardship for a man to be arrested, who was a good citizen; for instead of being treated . . . with all the delicacy of that a still existing presumption of innocence demands, . . . he is subjected to the insults . . . from those who, having just before thought of fighting and killing, are disposed now to have, at least the satisfaction of cursing, or starving, or otherwise abusing the people.

Source: Hugh Henry Brackenridge, *Incidents of the Insurrection in the Western Parts of Pennsylvania in the Year 1794* (Philadelphia: M'Culloch, 1795), v. 2, pp. 70–71, 79.

THE EMERGENCE OF POLITICAL PARTIES

Members of the revolutionary generation fervently hoped that political parties would not take root in the United States. "If I could not go to heaven but with a party, I would not go at all," remarked Jefferson. Critics condemned parties because they divided society, were dominated by narrow special interests, and placed selfishness and party loyalty above a concern for the public good. Yet the United States was the first nation to establish truly popular parties.

Social conditions encouraged the rise of parties. Because property ownership was widespread, the nation had a broad suffrage. When parties acted as representatives of economic and social interest groups, they became one means by which a large electorate could make its feelings known. In addition, the United States had the highest literacy rate in the world and the

Social conditions and parties

largest number of newspapers, further encouraging political interest and participation. Finally, the fact that well-known patriots of the Revolution headed both the Federalists and the Republicans helped defuse the charge that either party was hostile to the Revolution or the Constitution.

Americans and the French Revolution

While domestic issues at first split the supporters of the Constitution, it was a crisis in Europe that served to push Americans toward political parties. Americans had hoped that their revolution would spark similar movements for liberty on the European continent, and in fact the American Revolution was only one of a series of revolutions in the late eighteenth century that shook the western world, the most important of which occurred in France. There a rising population, the growth of a popular press, the failure of reform, the collapse of government finances, and widespread discontent with France's constitutional system sparked a challenge to royal authority that became a mass revolution. Eventually the French revolutionary ideals of "liberty, equality, and fraternity" would spill across the continent, carried by the French army.

When news of the French Revolution arrived in the United States in 1789, Americans hailed it as the first stirring of liberty on the European continent. By 1793, however, American enthusiasm for the French Revolution cooled when radical elements instituted a reign of terror, executing the king and queen and many of the nobility. The French republic even outlawed Christianity and substituted the worship of Reason. Finally in 1793 republican France and monarchical England went to war. Americans were deeply divided over whether the United States should continue its old alliance with France or support Great Britain.

Hamilton and his allies viewed the French Revolution as sheer anarchy. Its leaders seemed to be destroying the very institutions that held civilization together: the church, social classes, property, law and order. The United States, Hamilton argued, should renounce the 1778 treaty of alliance with France and side with Britain. For Jefferson and his followers, the issue was republicanism versus monarchy. France was a sister republic, and despite deplorable excesses, its revolution was spreading the doctrine of liberty. Jefferson argued that the United States should maintain its treaty of alliance with France and insist that as neutrals, Americans had every bit as much right to trade with France as with England.

Differing views of the Revolution

As tempers flared, each faction suspected the worst of the other. To the Jeffersonians, Hamilton and his friends seemed part of a monarchist conspiracy. "The ultimate object of all this," Jefferson said of Hamilton's policies, "is to prepare the way for a change, from the present republican forms of Government, to that of a monarchy." As for the Hamiltonians, they viewed Jefferson and his faction as disciples of French radicals, conspiring to establish mob rule in the United States.

Washington's Neutral Course

Washington was convinced that in order to prosper, the United States must remain independent of Europe and its unending quarrels and wars. Thus he issued a proclamation of American neutrality.

Under international law, neutrals could trade with belligerents—nations at war—so long as the trade had existed before the outbreak of hostilities and did not involve war supplies. But both France and Great Britain began intercepting American ships and confiscating cargoes. At the same time, Britain impressed into service American sailors it suspected of being British subjects. Despite these abuses, Hamilton continued to support a friendly policy toward Britain. He realistically recognized, as did Washington, that the United States was not strong enough to challenge Britain militarily. Moreover, Hamilton's financial program depended on trade with Britain, which purchased 75 percent of America's exports and provided 90 percent of its imports.

> Neutral rights

In addition to violating neutral rights and practicing impressment, Great Britain continued to occupy the western forts it had promised to evacuate in 1783, and it closed the West Indies, a traditional source of trade, to American ships. Washington sent John Jay to Britain as a special minister to resolve these differences, but Jay persuaded the British only to withdraw their troops from the Northwest. With the West Indies still closed to American shipping, Jay's Treaty in essence reinforced the United States's position as an economic satellite of Britain.

> Jay's Treaty

To Republicans, Jay had been all too willing to bend to British demands. Their opposition in the Senate meant that the treaty was ratified in June 1795 by the narrowest possible margin.

The Federalists and Republicans Organize

Thus events in Europe contributed directly to the rise of parties in America. The war, Jefferson commented, "kindled and brought forward the two parties with an ardour which our own interests merely, could never excite." By the mid-1790s both sides were organizing on a national basis. Hamilton took the lead in coordinating the Federalist party, which grew out of the voting bloc in Congress that enacted his economic program. Increasingly, Washington drew closer to Federalist advisers and policies and became the symbol of the party.

The guiding genius of the opposition was Hamilton's one-time colleague James Madison. Jefferson, who resigned as secretary of state at the end of 1793, became the symbolic head of the party. The disputes over Jay's Treaty and the whiskey tax gave the Republicans popular issues, and they began organizing on the state and local levels. Unlike the Federalists, who cloaked themselves in Washington's mantle and claimed to uphold the

> Organization of an opposition party

government and the Constitution, the Republicans had to overcome the ingrained idea that an opposition party was seditious and therefore illegitimate.

As more and more members of Congress allied themselves with one faction or the other, voting became increasingly partisan. By 1796 even minor matters were decided by party votes. Gradually, party organization filtered downward to local communities.

The 1796 Election

Weary of the abuse heaped on him by the opposition press, Washington announced in 1796 that he would not accept a third term, thereby setting a two-term precedent followed by all presidents until Franklin Roosevelt. In his farewell address Washington urged that the United States stay out of European affairs and make no permanent alliances, a principle that would be a hallmark of American foreign policy for a century and a half. He also warned against the dangers of parties and urged a return to the earlier nonpartisan system. But when the Republicans chose Thomas Jefferson to oppose John Adams, the possibility of a nonparty constitutional system ended.

The framers of the Constitution did not anticipate that political parties would run competing candidates for both the presidency and the vice presidency. They provided that the candidate with the most electoral votes would be president and the second highest would become vice president. Ever the intriguer, Hamilton tried

Typifying the rising party spirit of the 1790s, this anti-Republican cartoon portrays Washington with American troops repulsing an invasion of bloodthirsty French radicals while Jefferson attempts to hold his chariot back. This cartoon appealed to American nationalism by linking the opposition with foreign influence and disloyalty.

to manipulate the electoral vote to defeat Adams, whom he disliked. But in the ensuing confusion, Adams won with 71 electoral votes, while his rival, Jefferson, gained the vice presidency with 68 votes.

The fault line between the two parties reflected basic divisions in American life. Geographically, the Federalists were strongest in New England, with its strong commercial ties to Great Britain and its powerful tradition of hierarchy and order. Of the southernmost states, the Federalists enjoyed significant strength only in aristocratic South Carolina. The Republicans won solid support in semisubsistence areas like the West, where Crèvecoeur's farmers were only weakly linked to the market. The middle states were closely contested, although the most cosmopolitan and commercially oriented elements remained the core of Federalist strength.

Support for the two parties

The Republicans won the backing of most of the old Anti-Federalist opponents of the Constitution as well as a number of Americans who had firmly backed the new union. These supporters included some commercial farmers in the North and planters in the South and, increasingly, urban workers and small shopkeepers who were repelled by the aristocratic tone of the Federalists. The Republicans were often led by ambitious men of new wealth who felt excluded by the entrenched Federalist elite. Jefferson also attracted the support of immigrants and members of dissenting religious sects who lacked cultural acceptance.

Federalist and Republican Ideologies

In different ways, each party looked both forward and backward: toward certain traditions of the past as well as toward newer social currents that would shape America in the nineteenth century.

Most Federalists viewed themselves as a kind of natural aristocracy making a last desperate stand against the excesses of democracy. They clung to the notion that the upper class should rule over their social and economic inferiors. Pessimistic in their view of human nature, Federalists opposed unbridled individualism and were obsessed by fear of the "mob." In a republic, they argued, government had to restrain popular power.

Federalist ideas

Although the Federalists resolutely opposed the rising tide of democracy and individualism, they were remarkably forward-looking in their economic ideas. They believed that the government ought to use its power to actively encourage growth of commerce and manufacturing.

The Republicans, in contrast, looked backward to the traditional Revolutionary fear that government power threatened liberty. The Treasury, they cried, was corrupting Congress, the army would enslave the people, and broad construction of the Constitution would make the federal government all-powerful. To them, Federalist attitudes and policies illustrated the corruption eating away at American morals, just as England had become corrupt before 1776.

Republican ideas

Nor did their economic ideals anticipate future American development. For Republicans, agriculture and not commerce stood as the centerpiece of American liberty and virtue. To be sure, some commercial activity was necessary, especially to sell America's agricultural surplus abroad. But Jefferson and his followers believed that republican values would be preserved only by limiting commerce and promoting household manufacturing instead of industry. They also failed to appreciate the role of financial institutions in fostering economic development.

On the other hand, the Jeffersonians were more farsighted in matters of equality and personal liberty. Their faith in the people put them in tune with the emerging egalitarian temper of society, and they eagerly embraced the virtues of individualism, hoping to limit government in order to free individuals to develop to their full potential without interference.

THE PRESIDENCY OF JOHN ADAMS

As president, John Adams became the nominal head of the Federalists, but in many ways he was out of step with his party. He felt no pressing need to aid the wealthy, nor was he fully committed to Hamilton's commercial-industrial vision. He also opposed any alliance with Britain.

Increasingly Adams and Hamilton clashed over policies and party leadership. Although Hamilton had resigned from the Treasury Department in 1795, key members of Adams's cabinet regularly turned to him for advice. Indeed, they opposed Adams so often that the frustrated president sometimes dealt with them, according to Jefferson, "by dashing and trampling his wig on the floor." The feud between the two rivals did not bode well for the Federalist party.

The Quasi-War with France

Adams began his term trying to stave off war with France, whose navy and privateers continued to raid American ships. In 1797 he dispatched three envoys to France, but the French foreign minister demanded a bribe even to open negotiations. The American representatives refused, and when news of these

XYZ Affair

discussions became public, it was known as the XYZ Affair (because in the official documents the letters X, Y, and Z were substituted for the names of the French officials involved). A tremendous outcry ensued.

Federalist leaders saw a chance to retain power by exploiting the crisis and going to war with France. With war fever running high, Congress in 1798 enlarged the army and navy. An unofficial naval war—the so-called Quasi-

The Quasi-War

War—broke out with France as ships in each navy openly and freely raided the fleets of the other.

Eager for war, Hamilton dreamed of using the army to seize Louisiana and Florida from Spain, France's ally. He even toyed with provoking resistance in Virginia in order to justify suppression of the Republican party. Hamilton's hotheaded behavior, however, helped cool Adams's willingness to go to war.

Suppression at Home

Meanwhile, Federalist leaders attempted to suppress disloyalty at home. In the summer of 1798 Congress passed several measures known together as the Alien and Sedition Acts. The Alien Act, which was never used, authorized the president to arrest and deport aliens suspected of "treasonable" leanings. To limit the number of immigrant voters—most of them Republicans—the Naturalization Act increased the period of residence from 5 to 14 years to become a naturalized citizen. But most controversial was the Sedition Act, which established heavy fines and even imprisonment for writing, speaking, or publishing anything of "a false, scandalous and malicious" nature against the government or any officer of the government. To cries that such censorship violated the First Amendment's guarantees of freedom of speech and the press, Federalists replied that sedition and libel were not protected by the Constitution. The government used the law to convict and imprison a number of prominent Republican editors.

`Alien and Sedition Acts`

Because of the partisan way it was enforced, the Sedition Act quickly became a symbol of tyranny. At the same time, the crisis over the Sedition Act forced Republicans to develop a broader conception of freedom of the press. Previously most Americans had agreed that newspapers should not be restrained before publication but that they could be punished afterward for sedition. Jefferson and others now argued that only overtly seditious acts, not opinions, should be subject to prosecution, a view the courts eventually endorsed.

`Freedom of the press`

The Republican-controlled legislatures of Virginia and Kentucky responded to the crisis of 1798 by each passing a set of resolutions. Madison secretly wrote those for Virginia and Jefferson, those for Kentucky. These resolutions proclaimed that the Constitution was a compact between sovereign states, that the federal government had been delegated strictly limited powers, and that states had the right to interpose their authority when the government exceeded those powers and threatened the liberties of citizens.

`Virginia and Kentucky resolutions`

But Jefferson and Madison were not ready to rend a union that had so recently been forged. Jefferson and Madison intended for the Virginia and Kentucky resolutions to rally public opinion to the Republican cause and opposed any effort to resist federal authority by force. During the last year of the Adams administration, the Alien and Sedition Acts quietly expired. Once in power, the Republicans repealed the Naturalization Act.

The Election of 1800

With a naval war raging on the high seas and the Alien and Sedition Acts sparking debate at home, Adams suddenly shocked his party by negotiating a peace treaty with France. It was a courageous act, for Adams not only split his party in two but also ruined his own chances for reelection by driving Hamilton's pro-British wing of the party into open opposition.

`Federalist split`

Again the Republican party chose Jefferson to run against Adams, along with Aaron Burr for vice president. Their efficient party organization mobilized supporters, whereas the Federalists' highhanded policies and disdain for the "mob" alienated countless ordinary citizens. Noah Webster put his finger on his fellow Federalists' problem when he observed: "They have attempted to resist the force of public opinion, instead of falling into the current with a view to direct it."

Sweeping to victory, the Republicans won control of both houses of Congress for the first time. Adams ran ahead of his party, but Jefferson outdistanced him,

Jefferson's election

73 electoral votes to 65. Once again, the election demonstrated the fragility of the fledgling political system. Jefferson and Burr received an equal number of votes, but the Constitution, with no provision for political parties, did not distinguish between the votes for president and vice president. With the election tied, the decision lay with the House of Representatives, which deadlocked for almost a week. Jefferson was finally elected on the thirty-sixth ballot. In 1804 the Twelfth Amendment corrected the problem, specifying that electors were to vote separately for president and vice president.

Political Violence in the Early Republic

The deadlocked election provided a tense end to the decade, with some Federalists even swearing they would "go without a constitution and take the risk of civil war." Indeed, it is easy for Americans today to forget how violent and unpredictable the politics of the 1790s had been.

Some of the violence was physical. The leading Republican newspaper editor in Philadelphia plunged into a street brawl with his Federalist rival; Representatives Matthew Lyon and Roger Griswold slugged it out on the floor of Congress. The political rhetoric of the era was equally extreme. Republicans accused patriots like Washington and Hamilton of being British agents and monarchists; Federalists portrayed Jefferson as an irreligious radical and the Republicans as "blood-drinking cannibals." Washington complained that he was abused "in such exaggerated and indecent terms as could scarcely be applied . . . to a common pickpocket."

What accounts for this torrent of violence—both real and rhetorical—in the first decade of the Republic? For one, Federalists and Republicans alike recognized

Ideology of republicanism

how fragile a form of government republicanism had proved over the long course of history. Its repeated failure left political leaders uneasy and uncertain about the American experiment. Then, too, the ideology of the American Revolution stressed the need to guard constantly against conspiracies to subvert liberty. All too quickly, turbulent foreign events heightened domestic suspicions.

In such overheated circumstances, both Republicans and Federalists readily assumed the worst of one another. Neither side grasped that political parties were essential in a democracy to express and resolve peacefully differences among com-

Generating strong popular emotions, elections in the early Republic involved many more voters than ever before. In this detail of an early-nineteenth-century painting by John Lewis Krimmel, party workers bring electors to the Philadelphia polls in carriages, while voters heatedly argue about candidates and celebrate.

peting social, geographic, and economic interests. Instead, each party considered the other a faction, and therefore illegitimate. Each longed to reestablish a one-party system.

The Federalists' Legacy

As John Adams prepared to leave office, he looked back on the 12 years that the Federalist party had held power with mixed feelings. Under Washington's firm leadership and his own, the Federalists had made the Constitution a workable instrument of government. They had proved that republicanism was compatible with stability and order, and they had established economic policies and principles of foreign affairs that even their opponents would continue.

Federalists' achievements

But most Federalists took no solace in such reflections, for the tide of history seemed to be running against them. As the champions of government by the well-born, they had waged one last desperate battle to save their disintegrating world—and had lost. Power had fallen into the hands of the ignorant and unwashed rabble, led by that demagogue Thomas Jefferson. Federalists shared fully the view of the British minister, who concluded in 1800 that the entire American political system was "tottering to its foundations."

The great American experiment in republicanism had failed. Of this most Federalists were certain. And surely, if history was any judge, the destruction of liberty and order would soon follow.

c h a p t e r   s u m m a r y

Politics in the early Republic was rooted in a fundamental social division between the commercial and semisubsistence areas of the country. Commercially oriented Americans were tied to international trade and depended on the widespread exchange of goods and services, whereas families in the semisubsistence economy produced most of what they consumed and did not buy and sell in an extensive market.

- The first party to organize in the 1790s was the Federalists, led by Alexander Hamilton and George Washington. They were opposed by the Republicans, led by James Madison and Thomas Jefferson.
  - Divisions over Hamilton's policies as secretary of the treasury stimulated the formation of rival political parties.
  - The commercially minded Federalists believed in order and hierarchy, supported loose construction of the Constitution, and wanted a powerful central government to promote economic growth.

- The Republican party, with its sympathy for agrarian ideals, endorsed strict construction of the Constitution, wanted a less active federal government, and harbored a strong fear of aristocracy.
- The French Revolution and foreign policy also stimulated the formation of parties in the 1790s.
  - The Federalists supported England, and the Jeffersonians supported France.
  - The major events of John Adams's presidency—the XYZ Affair, the Quasi-War, and the Alien and Sedition Acts—were all linked to the debate over foreign policy.
- In the presidential election of 1800, Thomas Jefferson became the first leader of an opposition party to be elected president.
- The Federalists demonstrated that the new government could be a more active force in American society, but their controversial domestic and foreign policies, internal divisions, and open hostility to the masses eventually led to their downfall.

For quizzes and a variety of interactive resources, visit the book's Online Learning Center at www.mhhe.com/davidsonconcise3

SIGNIFICANT EVENTS

1789	+	First session of Congress; Washington inaugurated president; French Revolution begins; Judiciary Act passed
1790	+	Funding and assumption approved
1791	+	Bank of the United States chartered; first 10 amendments (Bill of Rights) ratified
1792	+	Washington reelected
1793	+	Execution of French king and queen; war breaks out between France and England; Washington issues Neutrality Proclamation
1794	+	Battle of Fallen Timbers; Whiskey Rebellion
1795	+	Jay's Treaty ratified; Treaty of Greenville signed
1796	+	Pinckney's Treaty ratified; first contested presidential election—Adams defeats Jefferson
1798	+	XYZ Affair; Alien and Sedition Acts passed; Virginia and Kentucky resolutions approved
1798–1799	+	Quasi-War with France
1800	+	Adams sends new mission to France; Jefferson defeats Adams
1801	+	The House elects Jefferson president

CHAPTER 9

O n September 29, 1800, following a rather rocky courtship, Margaret Bayard married Samuel H. Smith. Even though Samuel was well educated and from a socially prominent family, Margaret's father consented to the marriage reluctantly, for the Bayards were staunch Federalists and Smith was an ardent Republican. Indeed, Thomas Jefferson had asked Smith, a Philadelphia editor, to follow the government to Washington, D.C., and establish a Republican newspaper in the new capital. After the wedding ceremony, the couple traveled to the new seat of government along the Potomac River.

The Jeffersonian Republic (1801–1824)

preview • Jefferson sustained his agrarian principles by acquiring the Louisiana territory. But increasingly he abandoned his earlier ideals of limited government in favor of a more active nationalism. Nationalism was also promoted by the stronger federal courts led by Chief Justice John Marshall and by the expansion of white Americans westward. The growth in national power and pride was not halted, either by a Pan-Indian alliance under Tecumseh or by Great Britain in the War of 1812.

When the Smiths arrived in Washington, they found a raw village of 3200 people. Samuel began publishing the *National Intelligencer* newspaper, while Margaret's social charm and keen intelligence made their home a center of Washington society. When she met Jefferson about a month after her arrival, she found herself captivated by his gracious manners, sparkling conversation, and gentlemanly bearing. Whatever remained of her Federalist sympathies vanished, and she became (perhaps as her father feared) a devoted supporter of the Republican leader.

In eager anticipation she went to the Senate chamber on March 4, 1801, to witness Jefferson's inauguration. To emphasize the change in attitude of the new administration, the president-elect walked to the capitol with only a small escort. Absent were the elaborate ceremonies of the years of Federalist rule. When the swearing-in was completed, the new president returned to his lodgings at Conrad and McMunn's boardinghouse, where he declined a place of honor and instead took his accustomed seat at the foot of the table. Only several weeks later did he finally move to his official residence.

As Margaret Smith proudly watched the proceedings, she could not help thinking of the most striking feature of this transfer of power: it was peaceful. "The

Jefferson's inauguration

changes of administration," she commented, "which in every government and in every age have most generally been epochs of confusion, villainy and bloodshed, in our happy country take place without any species of distraction, or disorder." After the fierce controversies of the previous decade and the harsh rhetoric of the election of 1800, to see the opposition party take power peacefully—the first such occurrence in the nation's history—was indeed remarkable.

Once in power, Jefferson set out to reshape the government and society into closer harmony with Republican principles. He later referred to his election as "the Revolution of 1800," asserting that it "was as real a revolution in the principles of our government as that of 1776 was in its form." That statement is an exaggeration, perhaps. But the rule of the Republican party during the following two decades set the nation on a distinctly more democratic tack. And in working out its relationship with Britain and France, as well as with the Indian nations of the West, America achieved a sense of its own nationhood that came only with time and the passing of the Revolutionary generation.

JEFFERSON IN POWER

Thomas Jefferson was the first president to be inaugurated in the new capital of Washington, D.C. Because the Federalists believed that government was the paramount power in a nation, they had intended that the city would be a new Rome—a cultural, intellectual, and commercial center of the Republic.

The new city, however, fell far short of this grandiose dream. Its streets were filled with tree stumps and became impenetrable seas of mud after a rain. Much of the District was wooded, and virtually all of it remained unoccupied. A British diplomat grumbled over leaving Philadelphia, the previous capital, with its bustling commerce, regular communication with the outside world, and lively society, to conduct business in "a mere swamp."

The new capital city

Yet the isolated and unimpressive capital reflected the new president's attitude toward government. Distrustful of centralized power of any kind, Jefferson deliberately set out to remake the national government into one of limited scope that touched few people's daily lives.

Jefferson's Character and Philosophy

Jefferson himself personified that vision of modesty. Even standing nearly 6 feet, 3 inches, the 57-year-old president lacked an impressive presence. Despite his wealth and genteel birth into Virginia society, Jefferson disliked pomp and with his informal manners and careless dress projected an image of republican simplicity.

Jefferson was a product of the Enlightenment, with its faith in the power of human reason to improve society and decipher the universe. "I steer my bark with Hope in the head," he once declared, "leaving fear astern."

Jefferson considered "the will of the majority" to be "the only sure guardian of the rights of man," which he defined as "life, liberty, and the pursuit of happiness." Although he conceded that the masses might err, he was confident they would soon return to correct principles. Yet in good republican fashion, he feared those in power, even if they had been elected by the people. Government seemed at best a necessary evil.

To Jefferson, agriculture was a morally superior way of life. "Those who labour in the earth are the chosen people of God, if ever he had a chosen people," he wrote

Agrarianism

in *Notes on the State of Virginia* (1787). Like Crèvecoeur, Jefferson praised rural life for nourishing the honesty, independence, and virtue so essential in a republic. Government would "remain virtuous . . . as long as [the American people] are chiefly agricultural," he assured his associate James Madison. Rather than encouraging large-scale factories, Jefferson wanted to preserve small household manufacturing, which was an essential part of the rural economy. Commerce should exist primarily to sell America's agricultural surplus.

Although Jefferson asserted that "the tree of liberty must be refreshed from time to time by the blood of patriots and tyrants," his reputation as a radical was

Jefferson's radicalism exaggerated

undeserved. While he wanted to extend the suffrage to a greater number of Americans, he clung to the traditional republican idea that voters should own property and thus be economically independent and so free to cast their votes as they wished. One of the largest slaveholders in the country, he increasingly muffled his once-bold condemnation of slavery, and despite his belief in free speech he did not have any qualms about state governments punishing political criticism.

Despite his aristocratic upbringing, Jefferson was awkward, reserved, and ill-at-ease in public. But in private conversation he sparkled.

Jefferson was an exceedingly complex, at times contradictory personality. But like most politicians, he was flexible in his approach to problems and tried to balance means and ends. And like most leaders, he quickly discovered that he confronted very different problems in power than he had in opposition.

Republican Principles

Once Jefferson settled into the executive mansion, he took steps to return the government to the republican ideals of simplicity and frugality. The states rather than the federal government, he asserted, were "the most competent administrators for our domestic concerns and the surest bulwarks against antirepublican tendencies." Ever the individualist, he recommended a government that left people "free to regulate their own pursuits of industry and improvement."

Limited government

In his inaugural address, Jefferson also went out of his way to soothe the feelings of defeated Federalists. He promised to uphold the government's credit and protect commerce as the "handmaiden" of agriculture—both Federalist concerns. Agreeing with Washington, he proposed friendship with all nations and "entangling alliances" with none. Finally, he called on Americans to unite for the common good: "We have called by different names brethren of the same principles. We are all republicans—we are all federalists."

The election of 1800 had made clear that opposition parties could be a legitimate part of American politics, and Jefferson, in this statement, seemed to endorse the validity of a party system. In reality, however, he hoped to restore one-party rule to the country by winning over moderate and honest Federalists and isolating the party's extremists, whom he still attacked as monarchists.

Jefferson's Economic Policies

But what would Jefferson do about Hamilton's economic program? As he promised in his inaugural address, the new president proceeded to cut spending, reduce the size of the government, and begin paying off the national debt. He abolished the internal taxes enacted by the Federalists, including the controversial levy on whiskey, and thus was able to get rid of all tax collectors and inspectors. "What farmer, what mechanic, what laborer, ever sees a tax gatherer in the United States?" boasted Jefferson in 1805. Land sales and the tariff duties would supply the funds needed to run the scaled-down government.

The most serious spending cuts were made in the military branches. Jefferson slashed the army budget in half, decreasing the army to 3000 men. In a national emergency, he reasoned, the militia could defend the country. Jefferson reduced the navy even more, halting work on powerful frigates authorized during the Quasi-War with France and replacing them with inexpensive gunboats.

By such steps, Jefferson made significant progress toward paying off Hamilton's hated national debt. He lowered it from $83 million to only $57 million by the end of his two terms in office, despite the added financial burden of the Louisiana Purchase (page 230). Still, Jefferson did not entirely dismantle the Federalists' economic program. Funding and assumption could not be reversed—the nation's honor was pledged to paying these debts, and Jefferson fully understood the importance of maintaining the nation's credit. The tariff had to be retained as a source of revenue to meet government expenses. More surprising, Jefferson expanded the operations of the national bank and, in words reminiscent of Hamilton, advocated tying banks and members of the business class to the government by rewarding those who supported the Republican party.

Failure to abolish Hamilton's program

Throughout his presidency, Jefferson often put pragmatic considerations above unyielding principles. As he himself expressed it, "What is practicable must often control what is pure theory."

John Marshall and Judicial Review

Having lost both the presidency and control of Congress in 1800, the Federalists took steps to shore up their power before Jefferson assumed office. They did so by expanding the size of the federal court system. The Judiciary Act of 1801 created 6 circuit courts and 16 new judgeships, along with a number of marshals, attorneys, and clerks. Adams quickly filled these with Federalists, but in 1802, by a strict party vote, Congress repealed the 1801 law and eliminated the new courts.

Marbury v. Madison

Among Adams's last-minute appointments was that of William Marbury as justice of the peace for the District of Columbia. When James Madison assumed the office of secretary of state in the new administration, he found a batch of undelivered commissions, including Marbury's. Wishing to appoint loyal Republicans to these posts, Jefferson instructed Madison not to hand over the commissions, whereupon Marbury sued under the Judiciary Act of 1789. Since that act gave the Supreme Court original jurisdiction in cases against federal officials, the case of *Marbury v. Madison* went directly to the Court in 1803.

Judicial review

Chief Justice John Marshall, a Federalist and one of Adams's outgoing appointments, seized on this case to affirm the Court's greatest power, the right to review statutes and interpret the meaning of the Constitution. "It is emphatically the province of and duty of the judicial department to say what the law is," he wrote in upholding the doctrine of judicial review. This idea meant that the Court "must of necessity expound and interpret" the Constitution and the laws when one statute conflicted with another or when a law violated the framework of the Constitution. Marshall found that the section of the Judiciary Act of 1789 that granted the Supreme Court original jurisdiction in the case was unconstitutional. Since the Constitution specified those cases in which the Court had such jurisdiction, they could not be enlarged by statute. *Marbury v. Madison* was so critical to the development of the American constitutional system that it has been called the keystone of the constitutional arch.

Marshall and his colleagues later asserted the power of the Court to review the constitutionality of state laws in *Fletcher v. Peck* (1810) when it struck down a Georgia law. In subsequent decisions, it also brought state courts under the final authority of the Supreme Court. In fact, during his tenure on the bench, Marshall extended judicial review to all acts of government. Since Marshall's time the Supreme Court has successfully defended its position as the final judge of the meaning of the Constitution.

JEFFERSON AND WESTERN EXPANSION

The Federalists feared the West as a threat to social order and stability. Frontiersmen, sneered New Englander Timothy Dwight, were "too idle; too talkative; too passionate; . . . and too shiftless to acquire either property or character." Farther south, another observer referred to squatters on western lands as "ragged, dirty, brawling, browbeating monsters, six feet high, whose vocation is robbing, drinking, fighting, and terrifying every peaceable man in the community."

Jefferson, on the other hand, viewed the West as the means to preserve the values of an agrarian republic. He anticipated that as settled regions of the country became crowded, many rural residents would migrate to the cities in search of work unless cheap land beckoned farther west. America's vast spaces provided land that would last for a thousand generations, he predicted in his inaugural address, enough to transform the United States into "an empire of liberty."

Empire of liberty

To encourage rapid settlement of the West, the Republican Congress in 1801 reduced the minimum purchase of federal lands from 640 to 320 acres. (Even so, speculators accounted for most sales under the new law.) Nevertheless, the West was overwhelmingly Republican. Thus the admission of new western states would strengthen Jefferson's party and hasten the demise of the Federalists. From the Jeffersonian perspective, western expansion was a blessing economically, socially, and politically.

The Louisiana Purchase

Because Spain's colonial empire was disintegrating, Americans were confident that before long they would gain control of Florida and of the rest of the Mississippi, either through purchase or military occupation. This comforting prospect was shattered, however, when Spain secretly ceded Louisiana—the territory lying between the Mississippi River and the Rocky Mountains—to France. Under the leadership of Napoleon Bonaparte, France had become the most powerful nation on the European continent, with the military might to protect its new colony and block American expansion. American anxiety intensified when Spain, while still in control of Louisiana, abruptly revoked Americans' right to navigate the lower

Mississippi guaranteed by Pinckney's Treaty (page 212). Western farmers, who were suddenly denied access to the sea, angrily protested Spain's highhanded action.

Jefferson dispatched James Monroe to Paris to join Robert Livingston, the American minister, to negotiate the purchase of New Orleans and West Florida from the French and thus secure control of the Mississippi. With war looming again in Europe, Napoleon needed money and thus, in April 1803, offered to sell not just New Orleans but all of Louisiana to the United States. This proposal flabbergasted Livingston and Monroe. Their instructions said nothing about acquiring all of Louisiana, and they had not been authorized to spend what the French demanded. With no time to consult Jefferson, Livingston and Monroe agreed to buy Louisiana for approximately $15 million. In one fell swoop, the American negotiators had doubled the country's size by adding some 830,000 square miles.

Sale of Louisiana

Jefferson, naturally, was immensely pleased at the prospect of acquiring so much territory, which seemed to guarantee the survival of his agrarian republic. At the same time, as someone who favored the doctrine of strict construction, he found the legality of the act deeply troubling. The Constitution, after all, did not specifically authorize the acquisition of territory by treaty. Livingston and Monroe urged haste, however, and in the end, Jefferson sent the treaty to the Senate for ratification, noting privately, "The less we say about constitutional difficulties the better." Once again pragmatism had triumphed over theory.

Jefferson's pragmatism

West Florida, which bordered part of the lower Mississippi, remained in Spanish hands, and Jefferson's efforts to acquire this region were unsuccessful. Nevertheless, western commerce could flow down the Mississippi unhindered to the sea. The Louisiana Purchase would rank as the greatest achievement of Jefferson's presidency.

Lewis and Clark

Early in 1803, even before the Louisiana Purchase was completed, Congress secretly appropriated $2500 to send an exploring party up the Missouri River to the Pacific. This expedition was led by Meriwether Lewis, Jefferson's secretary, and William Clark. They were also to look for a practical overland route to the Pacific and engage in diplomacy with the Indians along the way. Equally important, by pushing onward to the Pacific, Lewis and Clark would strengthen the American title to Oregon, which several nations claimed but none effectively controlled.

In the spring of 1804 Lewis and Clark, accompanied by 48 men, set off up the Missouri. After wintering in present-day North Dakota, they crossed the Rockies and made it to the Oregon coast, where they spent the winter before returning overland the following year. Having traveled across half the continent in both directions, navigated countless rapids, and conducted negotiations with numerous tribes, the party arrived in St. Louis in September 1806, two and a half years after they had departed. Lewis and Clark had col-

Exploration of the West

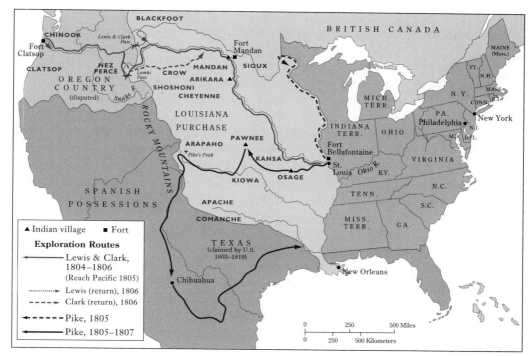

EXPLORATION AND EXPANSION: THE LOUISIANA PURCHASE The vast, largely uncharted Louisiana Purchase lay well beyond the most densely populated areas of the United States. The Lewis and Clark expedition along with Lieutenant Zebulon Pike's exploration of the upper Mississippi River and the Southwest opened the way for westward expansion.

lected thousands of useful plant and animal specimens, discovered several passes through the Rockies, and produced a remarkably accurate map, their most valuable contribution to western exploration.

WHITES AND INDIANS ON THE FRONTIER

In February 1803, as American diplomats prepared to leave for France in hopes of gaining title to western lands, another delegation was visiting Washington with a similar purpose. Black Hoof, a Shawnee chief from the Ohio River valley, asked Secretary of War Henry Dearborn to issue a deed to the tribe's lands in western Ohio. The deed, said Black Hoof, would ensure that his people could "raise good Grain and cut Hay for our Cattle" and guarantee "that nobody would take advantage" of them. The astonished Dearborn was not about to give the Shawnee any document that would strengthen their title to land in Ohio. But he did promise to provide some plows and cattle.

Unlike many Shawnees, Black Hoof had decided that the best way to get along with white Americans was to adopt their ways. For a number of years he and his

tribe settled along the Auglaize River, built log cabins, cleared land to raise corn, potatoes, cabbage, and turnips, and even planted an apple orchard. But before long Black Hoof's followers became dependent on government payments. Even Black Hoof admitted, "The white people . . . have been our ruin."

The Shawnee along the Auglaize were only one of many Indian tribes forced to make hard choices as white Americans streamed into the fertile lands of the Ohio River valley. In 1790 only about 100,000 whites lived in the West. By 1800 that number had jumped to almost 400,000 and, a decade later, to more than a million. By 1820 more than 2 million whites lived in a region they had first entered only 50 years earlier.

In this backcountry, where white and Indian cultures mixed and often clashed, both peoples experienced the breakdown of traditional cultural systems. White immigrants pushing into Indian territory often lacked structures of community such as churches, schools, and legal institutions. But Indian cultures were also severely stressed by the availability of white trade goods and by the more settled agricultural ways of white farmers, with their domesticated animals and fenced-in fields. Above all, Indians had to deal with the unceasing hunger of whites for Indian lands.

The Course of White Settlement

Following the Treaty of Greenville (page 212), white settlers poured into the Ohio Territory by wagon and flatboat. Time after time the pattern of settlement remained the same: in the first wave came backwoods families who laboriously cleared a few acres of forest by girdling the trees, removing the brush, and planting corn between the dead trunks. Their isolated one-room log cabins were crude, dark, and windowless, with mud stuffed between the chinks; their furniture and utensils were sparse and homemade. Such settlers were mostly squatters without legal title to their land. As a region began to fill up, these restless pioneers usually sold their improvements and headed west again.

The waves of settlement that followed were more permanent. Many of the newcomers were young unmarried men who left crowded regions in the East seek-

ing new opportunities. Once established, they quickly married and started families. Like the pioneers before them, most engaged in semi-subsistence agriculture. As their numbers increased and a local market developed, they switched to surplus agriculture, growing and making much of what the family needed while selling or exchanging the surplus to obtain essential items. "The woman told me that they spun and wove all the cotton and woolen garments of the family, and knit all the stockings," a visitor to an Ohio farm wrote. "Her husband, though not a shoemaker by trade, made all the shoes. She manufactured all the soap and candles they used." The wife sold butter and chickens in order to buy coffee, tea, and whiskey.

A Changing Environment

The inrush of new settlers significantly reduced the amount of original forest west of the Appalachian Mountains. Because Americans equated clearing the forest with progress, they had "an unconquerable aversion to trees," one observer noted, and "whenever a settlement is made they cut away all before them without mercy; not one is spared." By 1850 they had cleared at least 100 million acres. The resulting landscape was often bleak looking, with stumps left to slowly rot and the ground, "rugged and ill-dressed . . . as if nothing could ever be made to spring from it."

The rapid cutting of the forest led to the sharp decline of large animals, such as deer and bears, while the bison soon disappeared east of the Mississippi River. The loss of forest cover, combined with the new plowing of the land, increased runoff after rains, which lowered the water table and made destructive floods more frequent. The climate changed as well: it was hotter in the summer and the winds blew more fiercely, causing erosion in the summer and chilling gusts in the winter. Finally, deforestation also made the Ohio valley more unhealthy by creating wasteland with pools of stagnant water, which became breeding places for mosquitoes that spread diseases like malaria.

Effects of deforestation

The Second Great Awakening

It was the sparsely settled regions that became most famous for a series of revivals, known collectively as the Second Great Awakening. Like the first national outpouring of religious enthusiasm 50 years earlier, these revivals were fanned by ministers who traveled the countryside preaching to groups anywhere they could. Beginning in the late 1790s Congregationalists, Presbyterians, and Baptists all participated in these revivals, but the Methodists were the most enthusiastic and most organized in their support.

News of several revivals in Kentucky in the summer of 1800 quickly spread, and people came from 50 and 100 miles around, camping in makeshift tents and holding services out of doors. This new form of worship, the camp meeting, reached its climax at Cane Ridge, Kentucky, in August 1801, when over 10,000 gathered for a week to hear dozens of ministers. "The vast sea of human beings seemed to be agitated as if by storm," recalled one skeptic, who himself was converted at Cane Ridge. "Some of the people were singing, others praying, some crying for mercy in the most piteous accents" while "shrieks and shouts . . . rent the very heavens." In the overwhelming emotion of the moment, converts might dance, laugh hysterically, fall down, or jerk uncontrollably as they sought assurance of their salvation.

Cane Ridge

In the South, African Americans, including slaves, attended camp meetings and enthusiastically participated in the tumultuous services. Indeed, revivals were a major force in spreading Christianity to African Americans and producing slave conversions. Revivalists' clear and vivid

African Americans and revivals

Although the clergy at camp meetings were male, women played prominent roles, often pressing husbands to convert. Worshipers, especially those on the "anxious bench" below the preacher, were often overcome with emotion.

speech, their acceptance of the moral worth of every individual regardless of race, and their emphasis on the conversion experience rather than abstract theology had the same appeal to black listeners, who had little formal schooling, that they had to poorly educated white churchgoers. Blacks worshiped separately from and sometimes together with whites. As was the case with white worshipers, the Baptist and Methodist churches received the bulk of African American converts.

The revivals quickly found critics, who decried the emotionalism and hysteria they produced. For a time Presbyterians and Baptists withdrew from camp meetings, leaving the field to the Methodists. Eventually even the Methodists sought to dampen excessive emotion by restricting admittance and patrolling the meeting grounds.

Revivals like Cane Ridge provided an emotional release from the hard, isolated life on the frontier. For families with few neighbors, camp meetings offered a chance to participate in a wider social gathering. And for those at the bottom of the social hierarchy, the revivalists' message emphasized an individual's ability to gain personal triumph and salvation, regardless of his or her station in life. In the swiftly changing borderlands north and south of the Ohio River, where society seemed constantly in flux, revivals brought a sense of uplift and comfort.

Attraction of revivals

Pressure on Indian Lands and Culture

As white settlers continued to flood into the backcountry, the pressure to acquire Indian lands increased. Jefferson endorsed the policy that tribes either would have to assimilate into American culture by becoming farmers and abandoning their seminomadic hunting, or they would have to move west of the Mississippi River. Jefferson argued that otherwise the Indians faced extermination, but he also recognized that by becoming farmers they would need less land.

The hard truth about white policies toward Indians was that however enlightened individuals might be, the demographic pressure of high birthrates and aggressive expansion ensured conflict between the two cultures. Anglo-Americans never doubted the superiority of their ways. Even a disciple of the Enlightenment like Jefferson could become cynical. He encouraged the policy of selling goods on credit in order to lure Indians into debt, observing, "When these debts get beyond what the individuals can pay, they become willing to lop them off by a cession of lands." Between 1800 and 1810 whites pressed Indians into ceding more than 100 million acres in the Ohio River valley.

The loss of so much land to white settlement devastated traditional Indian cultures by reducing hunting grounds and making game and food scarce. "Stop your people from killing our game," the Shawnees complained in 1802 to federal Indian agents. "They would be angry if we were to kill a cow or hog of theirs, the little game that remains is very dear to us." Tribes

> Destruction of Indian cultures

also became dependent on white trade to obtain blankets, guns, metal utensils, alcohol, and decorative beads. To pay for these goods with furs, Indians often overtrapped, which caused them to invade the lands of neighboring tribes, provoking wars. The debilitating effects of alcohol, which Indians turned to as a means of coping with cultural stress, were especially marked during these years.

Among the Shawnees in the Ohio River valley, the strain produced by white expansion led to alcoholism, growing violence among tribal members, family disintegration, and the collapse of the clan system designed to regulate relations among different villages. These problems might have been lessened by separation from white culture, but the Shawnees had become dependent on trade for articles they could not produce themselves. The question of how to deal with white culture became a matter of anguished debate. Black Hoof, as we have seen, attempted to accommodate to white ways. But for most Indians, the course of assimilation was unappealing and fraught with risk.

The Prophet, Tecumseh, and the Pan-Indian Movement

Other Shawnees looked to revitalize their culture by severing all ties with the white world. Among the Shawnees, Lalawethika, also known as the Prophet, sparked a religious revival that began in 1805. Inspired by a series of visions, he took a new name, Tenskwatawa (the Open Door), to express his mission to "reclaim the Indians from bad habits and to cause them to live in peace with all mankind."

Tenskwatawa urged the Shawnee to renounce whiskey and white goods and return to their old ways of hunting with bows and arrows, eating customary foods like corn and beans, and wearing traditional garb. Seeking to revitalize Shawnee culture, the Prophet condemned intertribal violence and denounced the idea of private instead of communal property. Except for guns, which could be used in self-defense, his followers were to cease all contact with whites and discard all white trading goods.

Prophet's message

Setting up headquarters at a newly built village of Prophetstown in Indiana in 1808, Tenskwatawa led a religious revival among the tribes of the Northwest, who were increasingly concerned about the loss of their lands. Just as thousands of white settlers traveled to Methodist or Baptist camp meetings where preachers denounced the evils of liquor and called for a return to a purer life, so thousands from northern tribes traveled to the Prophet's village for inspiration.

While Tenskwatawa's strategy of revitalization was primarily religious, his older brother Tecumseh turned to political and military solutions. Territorial governor William Henry Harrison described Tecumseh as "one of those uncommon geniuses which spring up occasionally to produce revolutions and overturn the established order of things." In 1809 when the Lenni Lenape and Miami tribes ceded yet another 3 million acres in Indiana and Illinois under the Treaty of Fort Wayne, Tecumseh repudiated the treaty. Traveling throughout the Northwest, he urged tribes to forget their old rivalries and unite under his leadership to protect their lands from the flood of white settlers. As Tecumseh began to overshadow the Prophet, Harrison aptly termed him "really the efficient man—the Moses of the family."

Tecumseh's movement

After recruiting a number of northwestern tribes for his confederacy, Tecumseh in 1811 traveled through the South, where he encountered greater resistance.

Tecumseh advocated political unity to preserve Indian lands and cultures. He was the dominant figure among the western tribes until he died fighting alongside the British in the War of 1812.

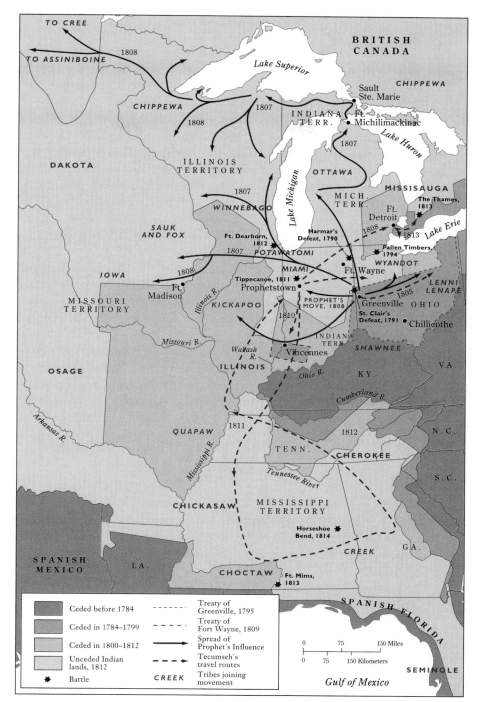

THE INDIAN RESPONSE TO WHITE ENCROACHMENT   With land cessions and white western migration placing increased pressure on Indian cultures after 1790, the Prophet's revivals quickly spread throughout the Great Lakes region. Tecumseh eventually eclipsed the Prophet as the major leader of Indian resistance, but his trips South to forge political alliances met with less success.

Tecumseh's failure in the South

In general, the southern tribes were more prosperous, were more used to white ways, and felt less immediate pressure on their land than did northern tribes. So Tecumseh's southern mission ended largely in failure.

To compound his problems, while he was away a force of Americans under Governor Harrison defeated the Prophet's forces at the Battle of Tippecanoe in November and then destroyed Prophetstown. Tecumseh became convinced that the best way to contain white expansion was to play off the Americans against the British in the Great Lakes region. Indeed, by 1811 the two nations were on the brink of war.

THE SECOND WAR FOR AMERICAN INDEPENDENCE

As Tecumseh pushed for a Pan-Indian alliance, Jefferson was looking to restore American political unity by wooing all but the most extreme Federalists into the Republican camp. The president easily won reelection in 1804 over Federalist Charles Cotesworth Pinckney, carrying 15 of 17 states. Jefferson's goal of one-party rule seemed at hand.

That unity was threatened, however, by renewed fighting in Europe. Only two weeks after Napoleon agreed to sell Louisiana to the United States, war broke out between France and Great Britain. As in the 1790s, the United States found itself caught between the world's two greatest powers. In his struggle to maintain American neutrality, Jefferson's controversial policies momentarily revived the two-party system.

Neutral Rights

At first the war benefited American trade because of the disruption in European agriculture. That stimulated demand for American foodstuffs and other raw materials. As the fighting drove most nonneutral ships from the seas, American shipping dominated the carrying trade, and the nation's foreign trade doubled between 1803 and 1805.

Nevertheless, Americans were angered when the British navy resumed its impressment of sailors and even passengers from American ships. Anywhere from

Impressment

4000 to 10,000 sailors were impressed by British naval officers, who did not always bother to distinguish naturalized from native-born Americans. Voicing American indignation, John Quincy Adams characterized impressment as an "authorized system of kidnapping upon the ocean."

Adopting a strategy of attrition, the two European powers began to raid America's ocean commerce with the other side. Between 1803 and

Seizure of American ships

1807, Britain seized over 500 American ships; France, over 300. When Britain issued new regulations in 1807, known as the Orders in Council, tightly controlling neutral trade with France, Napoleon authorized the seizure

Isaac Clark Is Impressed by the British Navy

, Isaac Clark, of Salem . . . Massachusetts, on solemn oath declare, that I was born in the Town of Randolph; . . . that on the 14th day of June, 1809, I was impressed and forcibly taken from the ship *Jane* of Norfolk, by the sailing master . . . of his majesty's ship *Porcupine*, Robert Elliot, commander. I had a protection [i.e., passport] from the Customhouse in Salem, which I showed to captain Elliot: he swore that I was an Englishman, tore my protection to pieces before my eyes, and threw it overboard, and ordered me to go to work—I told him I did not belong to his flag, and I would do no work under it. He then ordered my legs to be put in irons, and the next morning ordered the master at arms to . . . give me two dozen lashes; after receiving them, he ordered him to keep me in irons, and give me one biscuit and one pint of water for 24 hours. After keeping me in this situation for one week, I was . . . asked by captain Elliot if I would go to my duty—on my refusing, he . . . gave me two dozen more [lashes] and kept me on the same allowance another week—then . . . asked if I would go to work; I still persisted . . . [and he] gave me the third two dozen lashes, ordered a very heavy chain put round my neck . . . and that no person . . . give me any thing to eat or drink, but my one biscuit and pint of water for 24 hours, until I would go to work. I was kept in this situation for nine weeks, when being exhausted by hunger and thirst, I was obliged to yield. After being on board the ship more than two years and a half, and being wounded in an action with a French frigate, I was sent to the hospital—when partially recovered I was sent on board the *Impregnable*, a 98 gun ship. . . . The American consul received a copy of my protection from Salem, and procured my discharge on the 29th of April [1812].

Source: Clement Cleveland Sawtell, "Impressment of American Seamen by the British," *Essex Institute Historical Collections*, v. 76 (October 1940), pp. 318–319. Reprinted by permission by Peabody Essex Museum, Salem, MA.

of any neutral ship that obeyed these regulations. An irate Jefferson complained of France and England, "The one is a den of robbers, the other of pirates."

The Embargo

Yet Jefferson shrank from declaring war. He announced instead a program of "peaceable coercion," designed to protect neutral rights without war. The plan not only prohibited American ships from trading with foreign ports, it stopped the export of all American goods. Jefferson was confident that American exports were so essential to the two belligerents, they would quickly agree to respect American neutral rights. In December 1807 Congress passed the Embargo Act.

The president had seriously miscalculated. Under the embargo, American exports plunged from $108 million in 1807 to a mere $22 million a year later. At the same time, imports fell from almost $145 million to about $58 million.

Economic impact

As the center of American shipping, New England port cities were hurt the most and protested the loudest. In the face of widespread smuggling, Jefferson simply gave up trying to enforce the act during his last months in office.

Madison and the Young Republicans

Following Washington's example, Jefferson did not seek a third term. A caucus of Republican members of Congress selected James Madison to run against Federalist Charles Cotesworth Pinckney. Madison won an easy triumph.

Few men have assumed the presidency with more experience than James Madison. A leading nationalist in the 1780s, the father of the Constitution, a key floor leader in Congress, the founder of the Republican party, Jefferson's secretary of state and closest adviser, Madison had spent over a quarter of a century in public life. Yet as president he lacked the force of leadership and the inner strength to impose his will on less capable individuals.

With a president reluctant to fight for what he wanted, leadership passed to a new generation of Republicans in Congress. Much more nationalistic, they advocated an ambitious program of economic development and were aggressive expansionists, especially those from frontier districts. Their

War Hawks

feisty willingness to go to war earned them the name of War Hawks, and they quickly became the driving force in the Republican party.

The Decision for War

During Jefferson's final week in office in early 1809, Congress repealed the Embargo Act and reopened trade except with Britain and France. The following year it authorized trade with France and England but decreed that if one of the two belligerents agreed to stop interfering with American shipping, trade with the other would be prohibited.

In this situation, Napoleon outmaneuvered the British by announcing that he would set aside the French trade regulations. Madison eagerly took the French emperor at his word and reimposed a ban on trade with England. It soon became clear that Napoleon had no intention of lifting restrictions, but Madison

Growing conflict with Great Britain

refused to rescind his order unless the British revoked the Orders in Council. In the ensuing disputes, American anger focused on the British, who seized many more ships than the French and continued to impress American sailors. Westerners also accused the British of stirring up hostility among the Indian tribes.

When the British ministry finally suspended the Orders in Council on June 16, 1812, it was too late. Two days earlier, unaware of the change in policy, the United States had declared war on Britain.

Angered by the continued violations of American neutrality and pressed by the War Hawks to defend American honor, Madison on June 1 asked for a declaration of war. The vote of 79 to 49 in the House and 19 to 13 in the Senate mostly followed party lines, with every Federalist voting against war. As the representatives of commercial interests, particularly in New England, Federalists were convinced that war would ruin American commerce. They also still identified with Britain as the champion of order and conservatism. The handful of Republicans who joined the Federalists represented coastal districts, which were most vulnerable to the Royal Navy.

> Debate over going to war

Clearly, the vote for war could not be explained as a matter of outraged Americans protecting neutral rights. The coastal areas, which were most affected, preferred trade over high principle. On the other hand, members of Congress from the South and the West, regions that had a less direct interest in the issue, clamored most strongly for war. Their constituents were eager to seize territory in Canada or in Florida (owned by Britain's ally Spain) and were incensed by British intrigues with Indians along the frontier.

Perhaps most important, the War Hawks were convinced that Britain had never truly accepted the verdict of the American Revolution. To them, American independence—and with it republicanism—hung in the balance. For Americans hungering for acceptance in the community of nations, nothing rankled more than being treated by the British as colonials. John Quincy Adams expressed this point of view when he declared: "In this question something besides dollars and cents is concerned and no alternative [is] left but war or the abandonment of our rights as an independent nation."

National Unpreparedness

With Britain preoccupied with Napoleon, the War Hawks expected that the United States would win an easy victory. In truth, the United States was totally unprepared for war. Crippled by Jefferson's cutbacks, the navy was unable to lift the British blockade of the American coast. The army was small and poorly led, and volunteering lagged, even in states where sentiment for war was highest. Congress was also reluctant to levy taxes to finance the war.

A three-pronged American invasion of Canada failed dismally in 1812. The Americans fared better in 1813, when Commander Oliver Hazard Perry won a decisive victory on Lake Erie. Perry's triumph gave the United States control of Lake Erie and greatly strengthened the American position in the Northwest.

> Battle of Lake Erie

"A Chance Such as Will Never Occur Again"

As the United States struggled to organize its forces, Tecumseh discerned his long-awaited opportunity to drive Americans out of the western territories. "Here is a chance . . . such as will never occur again," he told a war council, "for us Indians of North America to form ourselves into one great combination." Joining up with the British, Tecumseh traveled south in the fall to coordinate a concerted offensive with his Creek allies for the following summer. He left a bundle of red sticks with eager Creek soldiers, who were to remove one stick each day from the bundle and attack when the sticks had run out.

A number of the older Creeks were more acculturated and preferred an American alliance. But about 2000 younger "Red Stick" Creeks launched a series of attacks. Once again, the Indians' lack of unity was a serious handicap, as warriors from the Cherokee, Choctaw, and Chickasaw tribes, traditional Creek enemies, allied with the Americans. At the Battle of Horseshoe Bend in March 1814, General Andrew Jackson soundly defeated the Creeks. Jackson promptly dictated a peace treaty under which the Creeks ceded 22 million acres of land in the Mississippi Territory. They and the other southern tribes still retained significant landholdings, but Indian military power had been broken in the Old Southwest.

Defeat of the Creeks

Farther north, in October 1813 American forces under General William Henry Harrison defeated the British and their Indian allies at the Battle of the Thames. In the midst of heavy fighting Tecumseh was slain—and with him died any hope of a Pan-Indian movement.

Tecumseh's death

The British Invasion

As long as the war against Napoleon continued, the British were unwilling to divert army units to North America. But in 1814 Napoleon was at last defeated. Free to concentrate on America, the British devised a coordinated strategy to invade the United States in the northern, central, and southern parts of the country. The main army headed south from Montreal but was checked when Captain Thomas Macdonough destroyed the British fleet on Lake Champlain.

Meanwhile, a smaller British force captured Washington and burned several public buildings, including the capitol and the president's home. The British withdrew, however, after they failed to capture Baltimore, their principal objective. Witnessing the unsuccessful British attack on Fort McHenry in the city's harbor, Francis Scott Key penned the verses of "The Star Spangled Banner," which was eventually adopted as the national anthem.

The third British target was New Orleans, where a formidable army of 7500 British troops was opposed by a hastily assembled American force commanded by Major General Andrew Jackson. Jackson's outnumbered and ill-equipped forces won a stunning victory, which made him an overnight hero. The Battle of New Orleans enabled Americans to forget the war's many failures and to boast that once again the United States had humbled the world's greatest military power.

Jackson's victory at New Orleans

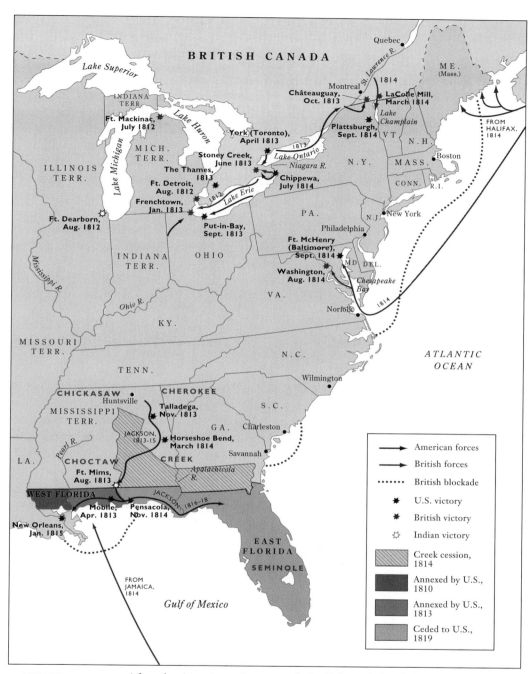

THE WAR OF 1812   After the American victory on Lake Erie and the defeat of the western Indians at the Battle of the Thames, the British adopted a three-pronged strategy to invade the United States, culminating with an attack on New Orleans. But they met their match in Andrew Jackson, whose troops marched to New Orleans after fighting a series of battles against the Creeks and forcing them to cede a massive tract of land.

The Hartford Convention

In December 1814, while Jackson was organizing the defense of New Orleans, New England Federalists met in Hartford to voice their grievances. Rejecting calls for secession, the delegates proposed a series of amendments to the Constitution that demonstrated their displeasure with the government's economic policies and their resentment of the South's national political power. The burst of national pride following Jackson's victory, however, badly undercut the Hartford Convention's position, as did news that American negotiators in Ghent, Belgium, had signed a treaty ending the war.

Like the war itself, the Treaty of Ghent accomplished little. All the major issues between the two countries were either ignored or referred to future commissions for settlement. As John Quincy Adams commented, "Nothing was adjusted, nothing was settled—nothing in substance but an indefinite suspension of hostilities was agreed to." Both sides were simply relieved to end the conflict.

Treaty of Ghent

AMERICA TURNS INWARD

Adams was right in concluding that in international relations the war had settled nothing. Psychologically, however, the nation's mood had perceptibly changed. "Let any man look at the degraded condition of this country before the war," declaimed young Henry Clay, a leading War Hawk. "The scorn of the universe, the contempt of ourselves. . . . What is our present situation? Respectability and character abroad—security and confidence at home." Indeed, the return of peace brought with it an outburst of American nationalism. Jackson's drubbing of the British at New Orleans strengthened Americans' confidence in their country's destiny. "We have stood the contest, single-handed, against the conqueror of Europe," wrote Supreme Court Justice Joseph Story to a friend, "and we are at peace, with all our blushing victories thick crowding on us."

The upsurge in nationalism sounded the death knell of the Federalist party, whose members had opposed the embargo and flirted with secession at the Hartford Convention. Although the party had made its best showing in years in 1812, when Madison narrowly won reelection, its support collapsed in the 1816 election. Madison's secretary of state, James Monroe, resoundingly defeated Federalist Rufus King of New York. Four years later Monroe ran for reelection unopposed.

Death of the Federalist party

The spirit of postwar harmony produced the so-called Era of Good Feelings, presided over by James Monroe, the last president of the Revolutionary generation. Monroe, like Jefferson before him, hoped to eliminate political parties, which he considered unnecessary in a free government. Like Washington, he thought of himself as the head of the nation rather than of a party.

The Missouri Crisis

The optimism of the era, however, was suddenly undercut by sectional rivalries that flared up in 1819 when the Missouri Territory applied for admission as a slave state.

Congress had prohibited the African slave trade in 1808, the earliest year this could be done under the Constitution, but before now, slavery had not been a major issue in American politics. In the absence of any federal legislation, slavery had crossed the Mississippi River into the Louisiana Purchase. Louisiana entered the Union in 1812 as a slave state, and in 1818 Missouri, which had about 10,000 slaves in its population, asked permission to come in, too.

At this time, there were 11 free and 11 slave states. The North's greater population gave it a majority in the House of Representatives, 105 to 81. The Senate was evenly balanced, since each state had two senators regardless of population. But Maine, which previously had been part of Massachusetts, requested admission as a free state. That would upset the balance unless Missouri came in as a slave state.

Representative James Tallmadge of New York disturbed this delicate state of affairs when in 1819 he introduced an amendment designed to establish a program of gradual emancipation in Missouri. The debate that followed was bitter, as for the first time Congress directly debated the morality of slavery. The House approved the Tallmadge amendment, but the Senate refused to accept it, and the two houses deadlocked.

When Congress reconvened in 1820, Henry Clay of Kentucky promoted what came to be known as the Missouri Compromise. Under its terms Missouri was admitted as a slave state and Maine as a free state. In addition, slavery was forever prohibited in the remainder of the Louisiana Purchase north of 36°30′ (the southern boundary of Missouri). Clay's proposal, the first of several sectional compromises he would engineer in his long career, passed Congress and was signed by Monroe, ending the crisis. But southern fears for the security of slavery and northern fears about its spread remained.

Missouri Compromise

The Transcontinental Treaty

Monroe's greatest achievements were diplomatic, accomplished largely by his talented secretary of state, John Quincy Adams, the son of President John Adams. An experienced diplomat, Adams thought of the Republic in continental terms and sought to promote expansion to the Pacific. Such a vision required dealing with Spain, which had never recognized the legality of the Louisiana Purchase. In addition, between 1810 and 1813 the United States had occupied and unilaterally annexed Spanish West Florida.

Spain was distracted by the rebellion of its Latin American colonies and feared that the United States might invade Texas or other Spanish territory. As a result,

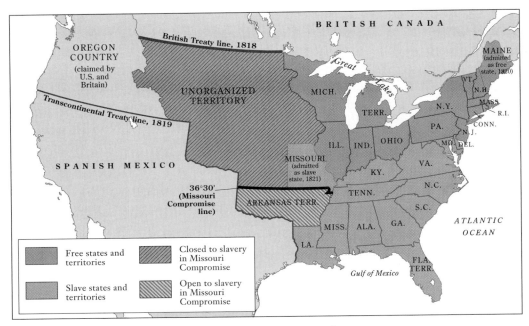

THE MISSOURI COMPROMISE AND THE UNION'S BOUNDARIES IN 1820

Spain agreed to the Transcontinental or Adams-Onís Treaty in February 1819. Its terms set the boundary between American and Spanish territory all the way to the Pacific. Spain not only gave up its claims to the Pacific Northwest, it ceded Florida in exchange for the U.S. government's assuming $5 million in claims against Spain by American citizens. Understanding the strategic commitment to expanding across the continent, Adams wrote in his diary, "The acknowledgement of a definite line of boundary to the South Sea [the Pacific] forms a great epoch in our history."

The Monroe Doctrine

The United States came to terms not only with Spain but, even more important, with Great Britain as well. Following the War of 1812, the British abandoned their connections with the western Indian tribes and no longer attempted to block American expansion to the Rocky Mountains. In a growing spirit of cooperation, the Rush-Bagot Agreement in 1817 limited naval forces on the Great Lakes and on Lake Champlain. In 1818 the countries agreed to the 49th parallel as the northern boundary of the Louisiana Purchase and also to joint control of the Oregon country for 10 years, subject to renewal.

Improved relations with Great Britain

In this atmosphere of goodwill, George Canning, the British foreign secretary, proposed in August 1823 that the United States and Britain issue a joint statement that would keep European powers from meddling in Latin America. Canning proposed that the United States and Britain declare that neither nation sought to expand in Latin America and that they opposed the transfer of Spain's colonies to any foreign power.

Monroe was inclined to accept the British offer, and both Jefferson and Madison urged him to do so. But John Quincy Adams forcefully argued that the United States should not make any pledge against acquiring territory in the future, particularly in Texas, Mexico, and the Caribbean. Monroe finally agreed to make an independent statement.

He included it in his annual message to Congress on December 2, 1823. Monroe reaffirmed that the United States would not intervene in European affairs, a principle of American foreign policy since Washington's farewell address. He also announced that the United States would not interfere with already established European colonies in the Western Hemisphere. But any intervention, he warned, in the new republics of Latin America would be considered a hostile act: "The American continents . . . are henceforth not to be considered as subjects for future colonization by any European powers." The essence of this policy was the concept of two worlds, one old and one new, each refraining from interfering in the other's affairs.

American public opinion hailed Monroe's statement and then promptly forgot it. Only years later would it be referred to as the Monroe Doctrine. Still, it represented the culmination of the American quest since 1776 for independence and sovereignty. Monroe's declaration underlined the United States's determination not to act in world affairs as a satellite of Britain. Ever since the adoption of the Constitution, the issue of independence had been at the center of American politics. It had surfaced during the 1790s, in Hamilton's quarrel with Jefferson over whether to favor Britain or France and in the differing responses of Americans to the French Revolution. It colored the debates over the embargo and finally once again came to a head in 1812 with the second war for American independence.

American independence reaffirmed

The End of an Era

The growing reconciliation with Great Britain ended the external threat to the Republic. Isolated from Europe and protected by the British fleet, the United States was free to turn its attention inward, to concentrate on expanding across the vast continent and on developing its resources. Yet how would the nation be developed? Jefferson had dreamed of an "empire of liberty," delighting in western expansion as the means to preserve a nation of small farmers, like those Crèvecoeur had celebrated.

Contrasting visions of independence

Younger, more nationalistic Republicans had a different vision. They spoke of protective tariffs to help foster American industries, and better roads and canals to link farmers with towns, cities, and wider markets. The tone of these new Republicans was not aristocratic, like that of the Federalists of old. Still, their dream of a national, commercial republic resembled Franklin's and Hamilton's more than

Jefferson's. They looked to profit from speculation in land, from the increasing market for cotton, from the new methods of industrial manufacturing. If these people represented the rising generation, what would be the fate of Crèvecoeur's semi-subsistence farm communities? The answer was not yet clear.

In one of those remarkable coincidences that Americans hailed as a sign of Providence's favor, Thomas Jefferson and John Adams died within hours of each other on July 4, 1826, the fiftieth anniversary of the adoption of the Declaration of Independence. Partners in the struggle to secure American independence, these revolutionary giants had become bitter foes in the heated party battles of the 1790s and resumed a warm friendship only after they had retired from public life. Their reconciliation was in tune with the surge of American nationalism, but their time was past. Leadership belonged now to a new generation of Americans who confronted different problems and challenges. Revolutionary America had passed from the scene. The dawn of a new nation was at hand.

chapter summary

As president, Thomas Jefferson increasingly abandoned his earlier ideals in favor of nationalism, a trend that continued under his successors, James Madison and James Monroe.

- Before becoming president, Jefferson advocated the principles of agrarianism, limited government, and strict construction of the Constitution.

- Once in power, however, he failed to dismantle Hamilton's economic program and promoted westward expansion by acquiring Louisiana from France despite his constitutional principles.

- The growth of nationalism was also reflected in the emergence of the judiciary as an equal branch of government.
  - Chief Justice John Marshall proclaimed that the courts were to interpret the meaning of the Constitution (judicial review).

- Many northern Indian tribes rallied to a religious movement led by the Shawnee prophet Tenskwatawa, which aimed to revive traditional Indian cultures.

- The Prophet's brother Tecumseh advocated a political and military confederacy to protect Indians' lands, but a number of important tribes refused to support him.
- Tecumseh's movement collapsed with his death during the War of 1812.

- France and Britain both interfered with neutral rights, and the United States went to war against Britain in 1812.

- In the years after 1815 there was a surge in American nationalism.
  - The Transcontinental Treaty with Spain (1819) foreshadowed American expansion by drawing a boundary line to the Pacific.
  - The Monroe Doctrine (1823) barred European intervention in the Western Hemisphere.
  - Britain's recognition of American sovereignty after 1815 ended the threat of foreign interference in America's internal affairs.

- The Missouri crisis, arising in the wake of the Panic of 1819, was an early manifestation of growing sectional rivalries.

For quizzes and a variety of interactive resources, visit the book's Online Learning Center at www.mhhe.com/davidsonconcise3

SIGNIFICANT EVENTS

1790s	Second Great Awakening begins
1801	Adams's last-minute appointments; Marshall becomes chief justice; Jefferson inaugurated in Washington; Cane Ridge revival
1803	*Marbury v. Madison;* Louisiana Purchase; war resumes between Great Britain and France
1804–1806	Lewis and Clark expedition
1805	Prophet's revivals begin
1807	Embargo Act passed
1808	Madison elected president
1809	Embargo repealed; Tecumseh's confederacy organized
1810	*Fletcher v. Peck*
1810–1813	West Florida annexed
1811	Battle of Tippecanoe
1812	War declared against Great Britain
1813–1814	Creek War
1813	Tecumseh killed
1814	Washington burned; Hartford Convention; Treaty of Ghent signed
1815	Battle of New Orleans
1816	Monroe elected president
1818	United States–Canada boundary fixed to the Rockies; joint occupation of Oregon established
1819	Transcontinental Treaty; United States acquires Florida
1820	Missouri Compromise enacted
1823	Monroe Doctrine proclaimed

PART THREE

The Republic Transformed and Tested

Two remarkable transformations began sweeping the world in the late eighteenth century. Both of them were so wrenching and far-reaching that they have been called revolutions. The first was a cascade of political revolts that led to increased democratic participation in the governing of many nation-states. The second was the application of machine labor and technological innovation to agricultural and commercial economies—known as the industrial revolution.

Proclaiming the values of liberty and equality, Americans in 1776 led the way with their own democratic revolution. In 1789, however, the center of revolutionary attention shifted to France. There, as in America, the ideals of the Enlightenment helped justify the rejection of rule by monarchy. Increasingly, however, the crowds marching through the streets of Paris adopted a more radical and violent stance, reflecting the burdens of the harsh feudal system as well as other social pressures. The worldwide rise in population of the previous half-century had left the French capital overcrowded, underfed, and thoroughly unruly. Paradoxically, the population pressure that had pushed matters to a crisis was relieved as the Revolution gave way to the emperor Napoleon, in whose wars of conquest the number of French soldiers killed almost offset the natural increase of the nation's population.

In Latin America, democratic and nationalist movements also spread. Just as Great Britain had attempted to pay for its colonial defenses with new revenue from its colonies, so the Spanish Crown raised taxes in the Americas, with similar results. From 1808 to 1821 Spain's American provinces declared their independence one by one. During the uprisings the writings of Jefferson and Thomas Paine circulated, as did translations of the French *Declaration of the Rights of Man*. Democracy did not always root itself in the aftermath of these revolutions, but democratic ideology remained a powerful social catalyst.

The industrial revolution was less violent but no less dramatic in its effects. It began in Great Britain, where canals built toward the end of the eighteenth century improved the transportation network, just as they would in the United States during the 1820s and 1830s. In Britain, too, James Watt in 1769 invented an engine that harnessed the power of steam, used eventually to drive mechanical textile looms. As steam power was applied to ships and rail locomotives, the reach of commercial markets widened. More dependable shipping made it possible to bring cotton from the Egyptian port of Alexandria to factories in British Manchester and American cotton from the Arkansas Red River country to New England.

In many ways the narrative of the young American republic is the story of how one nation worked out the implications of these twin revolutions, industrial and democratic. After the War of 1812 a market economy began rapidly to transform the agricultural practices of Crèvecoeur's semisubsistence America. Urban areas of the North became more diversified and industrial, as young women took jobs in textile mills and young men labored at flour mills processing grain to be shipped east. In a different way, the industrial revolution also transformed the rural South. Cotton would never have become king there without the demand for it created by textile factories.

The industrial revolution thus transformed both the North and the South—but in conflicting ways. Although the economies of the two regions depended on each other, slavery came increasingly to be the focus of disputes between them. The industrial revolution's demand for cotton increased both southern profits and a demand for slave labor. Yet the spread of democratic ideology worldwide created increased pressure to abolish slavery. In France the revolutionary government struck it down in 1794. The British empire outlawed it in 1833, about the time that American abolitionists, influenced by their British friends, became more active in opposing it. In eastern Europe the near-slavery of feudal serfdom was being eliminated as well: in 1848 within the Hapsburg empire, in 1861 in Russia, in 1864 in Romania.

If the purpose of a democratic republic is to resolve conflicts among its members in a nonviolent manner, then in 1861 the American republic failed. It took four years of bitter fighting to reconcile the twin paths of democracy and industrial development. Given the massive size of the territory involved and the depth of sectional divisions, it is perhaps not surprising that a union so diverse did not hold without the force of arms. That the separation was not final—that in the end, reunion emerged out of conflict—is perhaps one reason why the tale is so gripping.

CHAPTER 10

I n the years before the Civil War, the name of Chauncey Jerome could be found traced in neat, sharp letters in a thousand different places across the globe: everywhere from the fireplace mantels of southern planters to the log cabins of Illinois prairie farmers, and even in Chinese trading houses in Canton. For Chauncey Jerome was a New England clockmaker whose clever, inexpensive, and addictive machines had conquered the markets of the world.

The Opening of America
(1815–1850)

preview • In the quarter-century after 1815 a market revolution transformed the United States into a boom-and-bust, geographically mobile society defined above all by materialism and wealth. New transportation networks encouraged entrepreneurs to sell to wider markets. Factories appeared, first in the textile industry, employing young women from rural families. As factory discipline structured time in more precise and demanding ways, workers protested by forming labor unions.

Jerome, a Connecticut Yankee, had apprenticed himself to a carpenter during his boyhood, but after serving in the War of 1812 he decided to try his luck as a clockmaker. For years he eked out a living peddling his products from farmhouse to farmhouse, until 1824, when his career took off thanks to a "very showy" bronze looking-glass clock. The new model he had designed sold as fast as the clocks could be manufactured. Between 1827 and 1837 Jerome's factory produced more clocks than any other in the country. But when the Panic of 1837 struck, Jerome had to scramble to avoid financial ruin.

Looking for a new opportunity, he set out to produce an inexpensive brass "one-day" clock—so called because its winding mechanism kept it running that long. Traditionally, the works of these clocks were made of wood, and the wheels and teeth had to be painstakingly cut by hand. Jerome's brass version proved more accurate than earlier types and cheaper to boot. Costs came down further when he began to use interchangeable parts and combined his operations for making cases and movements within a single factory in New Haven, Connecticut. By systematically organizing the production process, Jerome brought the price of a good clock within the reach of ordinary people. So popular were the new models that desperate competitors began attaching Jerome labels to their own inferior imitations.

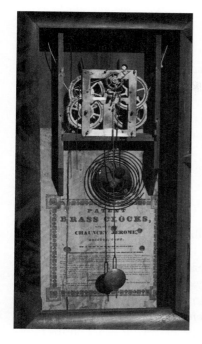

Chauncey Jerome's brass clock revolutionized clock-making and made him wealthy. The label displaying Jerome's name, the equivalent of a modern trade-mark, is visible inside the case.

Disaster struck again in 1855, when Jerome took on several unreliable partners. Within a few years his business faltered, then failed. At the age of 62, the once-prominent business leader found himself working again in a clock factory as an ordinary mechanic. He lived his last years in poverty.

Chauncey Jerome's life spanned the transition from the master-apprentice system of production to the beginnings of mechanization and the rise of the factory system. By 1850 the notion of independent American farmers living mainly on what they themselves produced (Crèvecoeur's vision of the 1780s) had become a dream of the past. In its place stood a commercial republic in which a full-blown national market encompassed most settled areas of the country.

The concept of the market is crucial here. Americans tied themselves to one another eagerly, even aggressively, through the mechanism of the free market. They sold cotton or wheat and bought manufactured cloth or brass one-day clocks. They borrowed money not merely to buy a house or farm but also to speculate and profit. They relied, even in many rural villages, on cash and paper money instead of bartering for goods and services. American life moved from less to more specialized forms of labor. It moved from subsistence-oriented to more commercially oriented outlooks and from face-to-face local dealings to impersonal, distant transactions. It shifted from the mechanically simple to the technologically complex and from less dense patterns of settlement on farms to more complex arrangements in cities and towns. Such were the changes Chauncey Jerome witnessed—indeed, changes he helped to bring about himself,

Market economy

with his clocks that divided the working days of Americans into more disciplined, orderly segments.

As these changes took place, Jerome sensed that society had taken on a different tone—that the marketplace and its ethos had become dominant. "It is all money and business, business and money which make the man now-a-days," he complained. "Success is every thing, and it makes very little difference how, or what means he uses to obtain it." The United States, according to one foreign traveler, had become "one gigantic workshop, over the entrance of which there is the blazing inscription '*No admission here except on business.*'"

THE MARKET REVOLUTION

In 1844 John Burrows heard that potatoes were selling for $2.00 a bushel in New Orleans. Potatoes fetched less than 50 cents a bushel in Davenport in the Iowa territory where Burrows was a small merchant, so he loaded 2500 bushels on a flatboat and started down the Mississippi River. Along the way, he learned that other merchants, acting on the same information, had done the same and that the market in New Orleans was now glutted with potatoes. When he reached his destination 6 weeks later, he could not sell his load at all. Desperate, he finally swapped his potatoes at 8 cents a bushel, taking a load of coffee in return. He made nothing on the transaction, since it had cost him that much to ship the load to New Orleans.

Burrows' experience demonstrated that a national market economy required not just the efficient movement of goods but also rapid communications. Looking back many years later on the amazing transformation that had occurred in his lifetime, Burrows commented, "No one can realize the difficulties of doing a produce business in those days."

Growth of a Domestic Market

This national system of markets began to develop following the War of 1812. As the United States entered a period of unprecedented economic expansion, the economy became varied enough to sustain and even accelerate its growth. Before the war it had been tied largely to international trade. If European nations suddenly stopped purchasing American commodities like tobacco and timber, the domestic economy faltered, as happened during the European wars of the 1790s and again after 1803. Since so many Americans remained rural and primarily self-sufficient, they could not absorb any increase in goods produced by American manufacturers.

But the War of 1812 marked an important turning point in the creation and expansion of a domestic market. First the embargo and then the war itself stimulated the growth of manufacturing, particularly in textiles. In addition, war had also bottled up capital in Europe. When peace was restored, this capital flowed into the United States to take advantage of burgeoning investment opportunities. Finally, the war experience led the federal government to adopt policies designed to spur economic expansion.

The New Nationalism

After the war with Britain, leadership passed to a new generation of the Republic—younger men like Henry Clay, John C. Calhoun, and John Quincy Adams. Each was an ardent nationalist eager to use federal power to promote rapid development of the nation. Increasingly dominant within the Republican party, they advocated the "New Nationalism," a set of economic policies designed to foster the prosperity of all regions of the country and bind the nation more tightly together.

Even James Madison saw the need for increased federal activity, given the problems the government experienced during the war. The national bank had closed its doors in 1811 when its charter expired, and the result had been financial chaos. With Madison's approval, Congress in 1816 chartered the Second Bank of the United States for a period of 20 years. Madison also agreed to a mildly protective tariff to aid fledgling American industries by raising the price of competing foreign goods. Passed in 1816, it set an average duty of 20 percent on selected imports. The measure enjoyed wide support in the North and West, but a number of southern representatives voted against it.

A new national bank and a protective tariff

Madison also recommended that the government provide aid for internal improvements such as roads, canals, and bridges. The war had demonstrated how cumbersome it was to move troops or supplies overland. Madison, however, believed that federal funds could not be used for merely local projects, so he vetoed the Bonus Bill, by which money was to be distributed to the states for internal improvements. This veto represented only a temporary setback for the nationalists, however, for even Madison was willing to support projects broader in scope, and his successor, James Monroe, approved additional ones.

Bonus Bill veto

The Cotton Trade

The most important spur to American economic development after 1815 was the growing cotton trade. Cotton production was limited, however, until in 1793 Eli Whitney invented the cotton gin, a mechanical device that removed sticky seeds from the lint. With a slave now able to clean 50 pounds of cotton a day (compared with only one by hand), and with prices high on the world market, cotton production in the Lower South soared. By 1840 the South produced more than 60 percent of the world supply, and cotton accounted for almost two-thirds of all American exports.

Cotton gin

The cotton trade was the major expansive force in the economy until 1839. Northern factories increasingly made money by turning raw cotton into cloth, while northern merchants reaped profits from shipping the cotton and then re-shipping the textiles. Planters used the income they earned to purchase foodstuffs from the West and goods and services from the Northeast.

The Transportation Revolution

For a market economy to become truly national, a transportation network linking various parts of the nation was essential. The economy had not become self-sustaining earlier partly because the only means of transporting goods cheaply was by water. Thus trade was limited largely to coastal and international markets, for even on rivers, bulky goods moved easily in only one direction: downstream.

All that changed, however, after 1815. From 1825 to 1855—the span of a single generation—the cost of transportation on land fell 95 percent, while its speed increased fivefold. As a result, new regions were drawn quickly into the market.

Canals attracted considerable investment capital, especially after the success of the wondrous Erie Canal. Built between 1818 and 1825, the canal stretched 364 miles from Albany on the Hudson River to Buffalo on Lake Erie. Its construction by the state was an act of faith, for in 1816 the United States had only 100 miles of canals, none longer than 28 miles. Then, too, the proposed route ran through forests, disease-ridden swamps, and unsettled wilderness.

The canal age

The project paid for itself within a few years. The Erie Canal reduced the cost of shipping a ton of goods from Buffalo to New York City from more than 19 cents a mile to less than 3 cents; by 1860 the cost had fallen to less than a penny. Where the canal's busy traffic passed, settlers flocked, and towns like Rochester and Lockport sprang up and thrived by moving goods and serving markets. The steady flow of goods eastward gave New York City the dominant position in the scramble for control of western trade.

New York's commercial rivals, like Philadelphia and Baltimore, were soon frantically trying to build their own canals to the West. Western states like Ohio and Indiana, convinced that their prosperity depended on cheap transportation, constructed canals to link interior regions with the Great Lakes. By 1840 the nation had completed more than 3300 miles of canals—a length greater than the distance from New York City to Seattle—at a cost of about $125 million. Almost half of that amount came from state governments.

Because of its vast expanse, the United States was particularly dependent on river transportation. But shipping goods downstream from Pittsburgh to New Orleans took 6 weeks, and the return journey required 17 weeks or more. Steamboats reduced the time of a trip from New Orleans to Louisville from 90 to 8 days, while cutting upstream costs by 90 percent.

Steamboats

Robert Fulton in 1807 demonstrated the commercial possibilities of propelling a boat with steam when his ship, the *Clermont*, traveled from New York City to Albany on the Hudson River. But steamboats had the greatest effect on transportation on western rivers, where the flat-bottomed boats could haul heavy loads even in low water. The number of steamboats operating in those waters jumped from 17 in 1817 to 727 in 1855. Since steamboats could make many more voyages annually, the carrying capacity on the western rivers increased 100-fold between 1820 and 1860.

Governments did not invest heavily in steamboats as they had in canals, except for removing obstacles to navigation. Although railroads would end the steamboat's dominance by 1860, it was the major form of western transportation during the establishment of a national market economy and was the most important factor in the rise of manufacturing in the Ohio and upper Mississippi valleys.

The first significant railroads appeared in the 1830s, largely as feeder lines to canals. Soon enough, cities and towns saw that their future depended on having good rail links. The country had only 13 miles of track in 1830, but 10 years later railroad and canal mileage were almost exactly equal **Railroads** (3325 miles). By 1850, the nation had a total of 8879 miles. Railroad rates were usually higher, but railroads were twice as fast as steamboats, offered more direct routes, and could operate year-round. Although railroads increasingly dominated the transportation system after 1850, canals and steamboats were initially the key to creating a national market.

Revolution in Communications

What rail and steam engines did for transportation, Samuel F. B. Morse's telegraph did for communications. Morse in 1837 patented a device that sent electrical pulses over a wire, and before long, telegraph lines fanned out in all directions, linking various parts of the country in instantaneous communication. By 1852 there were 23,000 miles of lines, and by 1860, more than 50,000. The new form of communication sped business information, helped link the transportation network, and enabled newspapers to provide readers with up-to-date news.

Indeed, the invention of the telegraph and the perfection of a power press in 1847 by Robert Hoe and his son Richard revolutionized journalism. The mechanical press sharply increased the speed with which sheets could be printed over the old hand method and brought newspapers within economic reach of ordinary families. Hoe's press had a similar impact on book publishing, as thousands of copies could be printed at affordable prices.

The Postal System

A national market economy depended on mass communications to transmit commercial information and bring into contact producers and sellers separated by great distances. Although postage was relatively expensive, the American postal system subsidized the distribution of newspapers and helped spread other forms of commercial information widely. Indeed, in the years before the Civil War, the postal system employed more laborers than any other enterprise in the country. While the postal system's primary purpose was to promote commerce, it had a profound social impact by accustoming people to long-range and even impersonal communication. By 1840, the post office handled almost 41 million letters and 39 newspapers.

When traveling in the United States in 1831, the French commentator Alexis de Tocqueville was amazed at the scope of the postal system. "There is an astonishing circulation of letters and newspapers among these savage woods," he reported from the Michigan frontier. Hardly a village or town in the country, no matter how remote, lay beyond the reach of the postal system. Nothing in Europe, he noted, could match it. While the British and French post offices throughout these years handled a greater volume of mail, the American system was much more extensive. In 1828, the United States boasted almost twice as many post offices as Great Britain, and over five times as many as France.

In the new world, the Canadian postal system was so limited that merchants and even government officials routinely used the U.S. system to get mail to other provinces, and by mid-century Mexico had only 49 post offices and no regular service for the whole country. In China, the government maintained a very efficient military-courier system for official communications, but foreigners developed the first private postal system, mainly for business correspondence; it was not until the twentieth century that a mass-based postal system was established. Most countries had no true postal system in these years, since literacy was so limited.

Agriculture in the Market Economy

The new forms of transportation had a remarkable effect on Crèvecoeur's yeoman farm families: they became linked ever more tightly to a national market system. Before the canal era, wheat could be shipped at a profit no farther than 50 miles. But given cheap transportation, farmers eagerly increased their output in order to sell the surplus at distant markets. In this shift toward commercial agriculture, farmers began cultivating more acres, working longer hours, and adopting scientific farming methods, including crop rotation and the use of manures as fertilizer. Instead of bartering goods with friends and neighbors, they more often paid cash or depended on banks to extend them credit. Instead of marketing crops themselves, they began to rely on regional merchants. Like southern planters, western wheat farmers increasingly sold in a world market.

Commercial agriculture

As transportation and market networks connected more areas of the nation, they encouraged regional specialization. The South increasingly concentrated on staple crops for export, and the West grew foodstuffs, particularly grain. By 1850, Wisconsin and Illinois were major wheat-producing states. Eastern farmers,

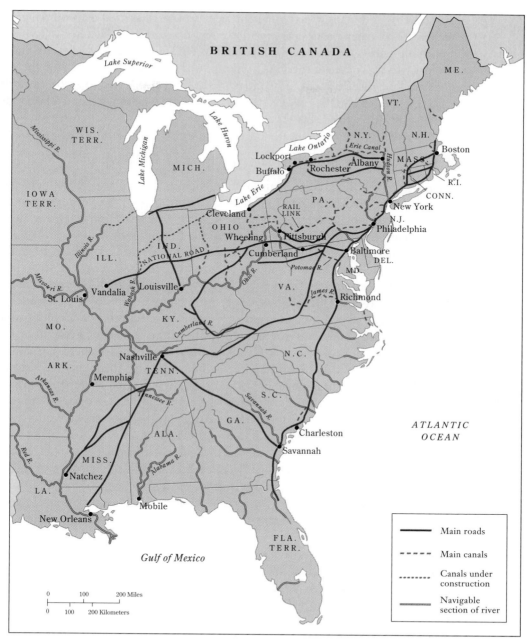

THE TRANSPORTATION NETWORK OF A MARKET ECONOMY, 1840 Canals played
their most important role in the Northeast, where they linked eastern cities to
western rivers and the Great Lakes. Steamboats were most crucial in the extensive
river systems of the South and the West.

unable to compete with wheat yields of western farms, shifted to producing fruits, vegetables, and dairy products for rapidly growing urban areas.

Although foreign commerce expanded too, it was overshadowed by the dramatic growth in domestic markets, which absorbed more and more of the goods and services being produced. The cities of the East no longer looked primarily to the sea for their trade; they looked to southern and western markets. That, indeed, was a revolution in markets.

John Marshall and the Promotion of Enterprise

For a national market system to flourish, a climate favorable to investment had to exist. Under the leadership of Chief Justice John Marshall, the Supreme Court became the branch of the federal government most aggressive in protecting the new forms of business central to the growing market economy.

Marshall, who presided over the Court from 1801 to 1835, at first glance seemed an unlikely leader. Informal in manners and almost sloppy in dress, he was nonetheless a commanding figure: tall and slender, with twinkling eyes and a contagious laugh. His forceful intellect was reinforced by his ability to persuade. Time after time he convinced his colleagues to uphold the sanctity of private property and the power of the federal government to promote economic growth.

In the case of *McCulloch v. Maryland* (1819) the Court upheld the constitutionality of the Second Bank of the United States. Just as Alexander Hamilton had

Constitutionality of the national bank

argued in the debate over the first national bank, Marshall emphasized that the Constitution gave Congress the power to make all "necessary and proper" laws to carry out its delegated powers. If Congress believed that a bank would help it meet its responsibilities, such as maintaining the public credit and regulating the currency, then it was constitutional. "Let the end be legitimate," Marshall wrote, "let it be within the scope of the Constitution, and all means which are appropriate, which are plainly adapted to that end, which are not prohibited . . . are constitutional." By upholding Hamilton's doctrine of implied powers, Marshall enlarged federal power to an extraordinary degree.

He also encouraged a more freewheeling commerce in *Gibbons v. Ogden* (1824), which gave Marshall a chance to define the greatest power of the federal government in peacetime, the right to regulate interstate commerce. In strik-

Interstate commerce

ing down a steamboat monopoly granted by the state of New York, the chief justice gave the term "commerce" the broadest possible definition, declaring that it covered all commercial dealings, and that Congress's power over interstate commerce could be "exercised to its utmost extent." The result was increased business competition throughout society.

At the heart of most commercial agreements were private contracts, made between individuals or companies. Marshall took an active role in defining contract law, which was then in its infancy. The case of *Fletcher v. Peck* (1810) showed how far he was willing to go to protect private property. The justices unanimously struck down a Georgia law rescinding a land grant to a group of speculators that had been obtained by bribing the legislature. A grant was a contract, Marshall declared, and since the Constitution forbade states from impairing "the obligation of contracts," the legislature could not interfere with the grant once it had been made. Although the framers of the Constitution probably meant contracts to refer only to agreements between private parties, Marshall made no distinction between public and private agreements, thereby greatly expanding the meaning of the contract clause.

Contracts

The most celebrated decision Marshall wrote on the contract clause was in *Dartmouth College v. Woodward*, decided in 1819. This case arose out of the attempt by New Hampshire to alter the college's charter of 1769. The Court overturned the state law on the grounds that state charters were also contracts and could not be altered by later legislatures. By this ruling Marshall intended to protect corporations, which conducted business under charters granted by individual states.

Thus the Marshall Court sought to encourage economic risk-taking by protecting property and contracts, by limiting state interference, and by creating a climate of business confidence.

General Incorporation Laws

Corporations were not new in American business, but as the economy expanded, they grew in number. By pooling investors' resources, they also provided a way to raise capital for large-scale undertakings. Then, too, corporations offered the advantage of limited liability: that is, an investor was liable only for the amount he or she had invested, which limited a person's financial risk. Ventures such as banks, insurance companies, railroads, and manufacturing firms—which all required a large amount of capital—increasingly were incorporated.

Advantages of corporations

Originally, state legislatures were required to approve a special charter for each new corporation. Beginning in the 1830s, states adopted general incorporation laws that automatically granted a corporation charter to any applicant who met certain minimum qualifications. This reform made it much easier and faster to secure a charter and stimulated organization of the national market.

A RESTLESS TEMPER

May first was "moving day" in New York City, when all the leases in the city expired, and nearly everyone, it seemed, moved to a new residence or place of business. Bedlam prevailed as furniture and personal belongings cluttered the sidewalks and people, carts, and horses crowded the streets. To Frances Trollope, it looked as if the whole population was "flying from the plague." Whereas in Europe millions of ordinary folk had never ventured beyond their local village, a Boston paper commented in 1828, "here, the whole population is in motion."

A People in Motion

Between 1815 and 1850, the nation reverberated with almost explosive energy. Tocqueville was astonished, like most Europeans, at the restless mobility of the average American. "Born often under another sky, placed in the middle of an always moving scene, . . . the American . . . grows accustomed only to change, and ends by regarding it as the natural state of man."

An emphasis on speed affected nearly every aspect of American life. Steamboat captains risked boiler explosions for the honor of having the fastest boat on the

High-speed society

river, prompting the visiting English novelist Charles Dickens to comment that traveling under these conditions seemed like taking up "lodgings on the first floor of a powder mill." American technology emphasized speed over longevity. Unlike European railroads, American railroads were lightweight, were hastily constructed, and paid little heed to the safety or comfort of passengers. Americans ate so quickly that one disgruntled European insisted food was "pitch-forked down."

Horatio Greenough, a sculptor who returned to the United States in 1836 after an extended stay abroad, was amazed and a bit frightened by the pace he witnessed. "Go ahead! is the order of the day," he observed. "The whole continent presents a scene of scrambling and roars with greedy hurry." If the economic hall-

Europeans were shocked that Americans bolted their food or gorged themselves on anything within reach, as this English drawing indicates.

mark of this new order was the growth of a national market, there were social factors that also contributed to American restlessness.

Population Growth

The American population continued to double about every 22 years—more than twice the rate of Great Britain. The census, which stood at fewer than 4 million in 1790, surpassed 23 million in 1850. Although the birthrate peaked in 1800, it declined only slowly before 1840. In the 1840s, it dropped about 10 percent, the first significant decrease in American history.

At the same time, many basic population characteristics changed little throughout the first half of the nineteenth century. The population remained quite young, and early marriage remained the norm, especially in rural areas. Life expectancy did not improve significantly. A person who survived the hazards of childhood diseases was likely to live to the age of 50 or 60.

From 1790 to 1820 natural increase accounted for virtually all of the country's population growth. But immigration, which had been disrupted by the Napoleonic Wars in Europe, revived after 1815. In the 1830s some 600,000 immigrants arrived, more than double the number in the quarter-century after 1790.

The Restless Movement West

The vast areas of land available for settlement absorbed much of the burgeoning population. As settlers streamed west, speculation in western lands reached frenzied proportions. Whereas only 68,000 acres of the public domain had been sold during the year 1800, sales peaked in 1818, at a staggering 3.5 million acres.

The Panic of 1819 sent sales and prices crashing, and in the depression that followed many farmers lost their farms. Congress reacted by abolishing credit sales and demanding payment in cash, but it tempered this policy by lowering the price of the cheapest lands to $1.25 an acre and reducing the minimum tract to 80 acres.

Even so, speculators purchased most of the public lands sold, since there was no limit on the amount of acreage an individual or a land company could buy. These land speculators played a leading role in settlement of the West. To hasten sales, they usually sold land partially on credit—a vital aid to poorer farmers. They also provided loans to purchase needed tools **Land speculation** and supplies. Many farmers became speculators themselves, buying up property in the neighborhood and selling it to latecomers at a tidy profit. "Speculation in real estate has been the ruling idea and occupation of the Western mind," one Englishman reported in the 1840s. "Clerks, labourers, farmers, storekeepers merely followed their callings for a living while they were speculating for their fortunes."

Given such rapid settlement, geographic mobility became one of the most striking characteristics of the American people. The 1850 census revealed that nearly half of all native-born free Americans lived outside the state where they had been

Geographic mobility

born. The typical American "has no root in the soil," visiting Frenchman Michel Chevalier observed, but "is always in the mood to move on, always ready to start in the first steamer that comes along from the place where he had just now landed."

It was the search for opportunity, more than anything else, that accounted for such restlessness. An American moved, noted one British observer, "if by so doing he can make $10 where before he made $8." Often, the influence of the market uprooted Americans too. In 1851, a new railroad line bypassed the village of Auburn, Illinois. Despite its pretty location, residents quickly abandoned it and moved to the new town that sprang up around the depot. A neighboring farmer purchased the old village, plowed up the streets, and Auburn reverted to a cornfield.

Urbanization

Even with the growth of a national market, the United States remained a rural nation. Nevertheless, the four decades after 1820 witnessed the fastest rate of urbanization in American history. As a result, the ratio of farmers to city dwellers steadily dropped from 15 to 1 in 1800 to 5.5 to 1 in 1850.

Reasons for urban growth

Improved transportation, the declining productivity of many eastern farms, the beginnings of industrialization, and the influx of immigrants all stimulated the growth of cities.

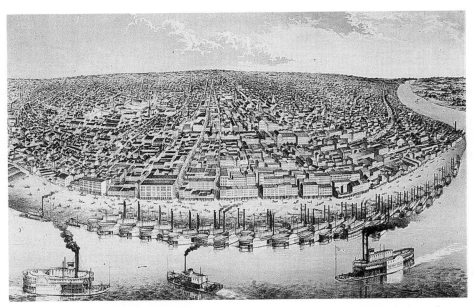

St. Louis, a major urban center that developed in the West, depended on the steamboat to sustain its commerce, as this 1859 illustration makes clear.

The Mere Love of Moving

In the course of the next morning, while we were sitting in the public parlour, at the hotel, a party came in . . . A gentleman came forward who claimed the chief of the party for his brother . . . [and] broke out thus—"Well! this is the strangest resolution for a man of your years to take into his head! Why, where are you going?"

"I am going to Florida, to be sure. . . . It is the finest country in the world—a delightful climate—rich soil—plenty of room."

"Have you been there?" asked his brother.

"No, not yet," said the wanderer; "but I know all about it. . . ."

"Pray tell me, what have you done with your estate in Maryland, on which you were fixed when I last got tidings of you? . . ."

"I've sold that property."

"What, all?"

"Yes, all, every inch of it, and I have brought away every movable thing with me. Here we are, . . . my wife, my son there, and my daughter—all my slaves, too, my furniture, horses, and so forth."

"And now, pray, answer me this question—were you not well off where you were located before—had you not plenty of good land?"

"Oh yes, plenty. . . ."

"What, then, possesses you to go seeking for a fresh place in such a country as Florida, where you must be content to take up your quarters amongst tadpoles and mosquitoes?"

While the hardy rover was puzzling himself in search of a reasonable answer, his wife took up the discourse, and . . . said, "It is all for the mere love of moving. We have been doing so all our lives—just moving from place to place—never resting—as soon as ever we get comfortably settled, then it is time to be off to something new."

Source: Basil Hall, *Travels in the United States* (Edinburgh: 3 vols., Cadell and Co., 1829), v. 3, pp. 129–132.

The most heavily urbanized area of the country was the Northeast, where in 1860 more than a third of the population lived in cities.* Important urban centers such as St. Louis and Cincinnati arose in the West. The South, with only 10 percent of its population living in cities, was the least urbanized region.

All these changes—the amazing growth of the population, the quickening movement westward, and the rising migration to the cities—pointed to a

---

*The Northeast included New England and the mid-Atlantic states (New York, Pennsylvania, and New Jersey). The South comprised the slave states plus the Distrct of Columbia.

fundamental reorientation of American development. Expansion was the keynote of the new America, and the prospects it offered both excited and unsettled Americans.

THE RISE OF FACTORIES

It was an isolated life, growing up in a rural, hilly Vermont. But stories of the textile factories that had sprung up in Lowell and other towns in Massachusetts reached even small villages like Barnard. Mary Paul was working there as a domestic servant when she asked her father for permission to move to Lowell. "I am in need of clothes which I cannot get about here," she explained. In 1845 two other friends from Barnard helped her find her first job at the Lowell mills, from which she earned $128 in 11 months. After four years she returned home, but now found "countryfied" life too confining, and before long she left her rural hometown—this time for good.

Mary Paul was one of thousands of rural Americans whose lives were fundamentally altered by the economic transformations of the young republic. The changes in her lifestyle and her working habits demonstrated that the new factories and industries needed more than technological innovation to run smoothly. Equally crucial, labor needed to be reorganized.

Technological Advances

Before 1815 manufacturing had been done in homes or shops by skilled artisans. As master craftworkers, they imparted the knowledge of their trades to apprentices and journeymen. In addition, women often worked in their homes part-time under the putting-out system, making finished articles from raw material supplied by merchant capitalists. After 1815 this older form of manufacturing began to give way to factories with machinery tended by unskilled or semiskilled laborers.

From England came many of the earliest technological innovations. But Americans often improved on the British machines or adapted them to more extensive uses. In contrast to the more tradition-oriented societies of Europe, "everything new is quickly introduced here," one visitor commented in 1820. "There is no clinging to old ways; the moment an American hears the word 'invention' he pricks up his ears." From 1790 to 1860 the United States Patent Office granted more patents than England and France combined.

To protect their economic advantage, the British forbade the export of any textile machinery or emigration of any craftworker trained in its construction. But in 1790 a mill worker named Samuel Slater eluded English authorities and built the first textile mill in America. Two decades later, the Boston merchant Francis Cabot Lowell imitated British designs for a power loom and then improved on them.

The first machines required highly skilled workers both to build and to repair them. Eli Whitney had a better idea. Having won a contract to produce 10,000 rifles for the government, he developed machinery that would mass-produce parts that were interchangeable from rifle to ri-

Interchangeable parts

fle. Such parts had to be manufactured to rigid specifications, but once the process was perfected, these parts allowed a worker to assemble a rifle quickly with only a few tools. Simeon North applied the same principle to the production of clocks, and Chauncey Jerome followed North's example and soon surpassed him.

Textile Factories

The factory system originated in the Northeast, where capital, water power, and transportation facilities were available. As in England, the production of cloth was the first manufacturing process to use the new technology on a large scale. Eventually all the processes of manufacturing fabrics were brought together in a single location, and machines did virtually all the work.

In 1820 a group of wealthy Boston merchants known as the Boston Associates set up operations at Lowell, Massachusetts, which soon became the nation's most famous center of textile manufacturing. Its founders intended to avoid the misery that surrounded English factories by combining paternalism | Textile city of Lowell with high profits. Instead of relying primarily on child labor or a permanent working class, the Lowell mills employed daughters of New England farm families. Female workers lived in company boardinghouses under the watchful eye of a matron. To its many visitors, Lowell presented an impressive sight, with huge factories and well-kept houses. Female workers were encouraged to attend lectures and use the library; they even published their own magazine, the *Lowell Offering*.

The reality of factory life, however, involved strict work rules and long hours of tedious, repetitive work. At Lowell, for example, workers could be fined for lateness or misconduct, such as talking on the job, and the women's morals in the boardinghouses were strictly guarded. Work typically began at 7 A.M. (earlier in the summer) and continued until 7 at night, six days a week. With only 30 minutes for the noon meal, many workers had to run to the boardinghouse and back to avoid being late. Winter was the "lighting up" season, when work began before daylight and ended after dark. The only light after sunset came from whale oil lamps that filled the long rooms with smoke.

Although the labor was hard, the female operators earned from $2.40 to $3.20 a week, wages that were considered good by the standards of the time. (Domestic servants and seamstresses were paid less than a dollar a week.) The average "mill girl" was between 16 and 30 years old. Most were not work- | Female workers ing to support their families back home on the farm; instead they wanted to accumulate some money for perhaps the first time in their lives and sample some of life's pleasures. "I must . . . have something of my own before many more years have passed," Sally Rice wrote in rejecting her parents' request that she return home to Somerset, Vermont. "And where is that something coming from if I go home and earn nothing?"

Like Rice, few women in the mills intended to work permanently. The majority stayed no more than five years before getting married. The sense of sisterhood that united women in the boardinghouses made it easier for farm daughters

"There are very many young ladies at work in the factories that have given up milinary dressmaking and school-keeping for to work in the mill," wrote Malenda Edwards in 1839. This young woman was one of them.

to adjust to the stress and regimen the factory imposed on them. So did their view of the situation as temporary rather than permanent.

As competition in the textile industry intensified, factory managers undertook to raise productivity. In the mid-1830s the mills began to increase the workloads and speed up the machinery. Even these changes failed to maintain previous profits, and on several occasions factories cut wages. The ever-quickening pace of work finally provoked resistance among the women in the mills. Several times in the 1830s wage cuts sparked strikes in which a minority of workers walked out. In the 1840s workers' protests focused on the demand for a 10-hour day.

Lowell mills become less paternal

As the mills expanded, a smaller proportion of the workers lived in company boardinghouses, and moral regulations were relaxed. But the greatest change was a shift in the workforce from native-born females to Irish immigrants, including men and children. The Irish, who made up only 8 percent of the Lowell workforce in 1845, amounted to almost half by 1860. Desperately poor and eager for any work, they did not view their situation as temporary. Wages continued to decline, and a permanent working class took shape.

Lowell and the Environment

Lowell was a city built on water power. Early settlers had used the power of the Merrimack River to run mills, but never on the scale of the textile factories. As the market spread, Americans came to link progress with the fullest use of the environment's natural resources.

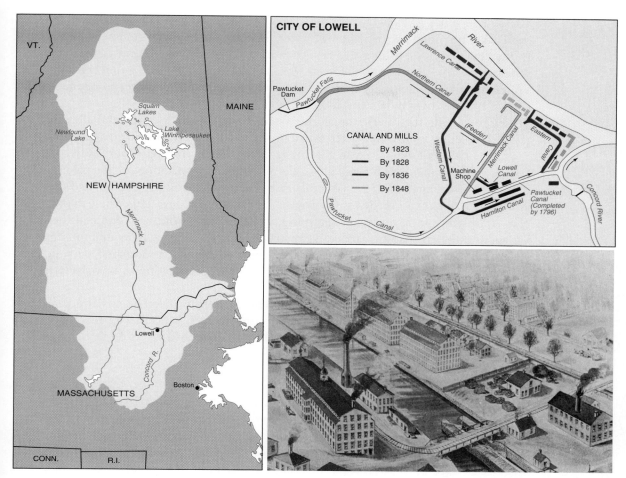

DEVELOPMENT OF THE LOWELL MILLS   As more mills were built at Lowell, the demand increased for water to power them. By 1859 the mills drew water from lakes 80 to 100 miles upstream, including Winnipesaukee, Squam, and Newfound. The map at left shows the watersheds affected. In the city of Lowell (right), a system of canals was enlarged over several decades. In the painting (done in 1845), the machine shop can be seen at left, with a row of mills alongside a canal. Rail links tied Lowell and Boston together.

By 1836, Lowell had seven canals, with a supporting network of locks and dams, to govern the Merrimack's flow and distribute water to the city's 26 mills. As more and more mills were built, both at Lowell and other sites, the Boston Associates erected dams at several points along the river to store water and divert it into power canals for factories. At Lawrence, they constructed the largest dam in the world at the time, a 32-foot-high granite structure that spanned 1600 feet across the river. But even dammed, the Merrimack's waters proved insufficient. So the Associates gained control of over

Reshaping the area's waterscape

100 square miles of New Hampshire lakes that fed the river system. Damming these lakes provided a regular flow of water, especially in the drier summer months. In the course of establishing this elaborate water control system, they came to see water as a form of property, divorced from the ownership of land along the river. Water became a commodity that was measured in terms of its power to operate a certain number of spindles and looms.

By regulating the river's waters, the Associates made the Merrimack Valley the nation's greatest industrial center in the first half of the nineteenth century. But not all who lived in the valley benefited. By raising water levels, the

Damaging effects

dams flooded farmlands, blocked the transportation of logs downstream, and damaged mills upstream by reducing the current and creating backwater that impeded waterwheels. The dams also devastated the fish population by preventing upstream spawning, while factories routinely dumped their wastes into the river to be carried downstream, thereby eventually contaminating water supplies. Epidemics of typhoid, cholera, and dysentery occurred with increasing frequency, so that by midcentury Lowell had a reputation as a particularly unhealthy city.

In the end, the factory system fundamentally transformed the environment. Far from existing in harmony with its rural surroundings, Lowell, with its clattering machines and dammed rivers, presented a glaring constrast to rural life. The founding vision of Lowell had disappeared.

Industrial Work

The creation of an industrial labor force that was accustomed to working in factories did not occur easily. Before the rise of the factory, artisans had worked within

Artisan system

the home. Apprentices were considered part of the family, and masters were responsible not only for teaching their apprentices a trade but also for providing them some education and for supervising their moral behavior. Journeymen knew that if they perfected their skill, they could become respected master artisans with their own shops. Nor did skilled artisans work by the clock, at a steady pace, but rather in bursts of intense labor alternating with greater leisure.

The factory changed that. Factory goods were not so finished or elegant as those done by hand, and pride in artisanship gave way to rates of productivity. At

Transformation of work

the same time, workers were required to discard old habits, for industrialism demanded a worker who was sober, dependable, and self-disciplined. Absenteeism, lateness, and drunkenness hurt productivity and disrupted the regular factory routine. Thus industrialization not only produced a fundamental change in the way work was organized, it transformed the very nature of work.

The first generation to experience these changes did not adopt the new attitudes easily. The factory clock became the symbol of the new work rules. One mill worker who finally quit complained revealingly about "obedience to the ding-dong of the bell—just as though we are so many living machines." With the loss of personal freedom also came the loss of standing in the community. The master-apprentice relationship gave way to factories' sharp separation of workers from management. Few workers rose through the ranks to supervisory positions, and even fewer could achieve the artisan's dream of setting up their own businesses. Even well-paid workers sensed their decline in status.

The Shoe Industry

Shoemaking illustrates one way the artisan tradition was undermined. Traditionally, a skilled cobbler possessed a good knowledge of leather, had the ability to cut out the various parts of a shoe, and could stitch and glue those parts together. He then sold the shoes in the same shop where he and his apprentices made them. Unlike the textile industry, shoemaking was not rapidly transformed in this period by a shift to heavy machinery. Even so, expanding transportation networks and national markets fundamentally altered this business.

Micajah Pratt, a cobbler from Lynn, Massachusetts, realized that there were ready markets for cheap shoes in the South and West. So he hired workers to produce shoes in larger and larger central shops. Pratt cut costs further by using new production techniques, such as standardized patterns and sole-cutting machines. Pratt eventually employed as many as 500 men and women.

Lynn, center of shoe manufacturing

Unable to keep up with demand, he and other manufacturers hired farmers, fishermen, and their families in surrounding towns to do part-time work at home. Women and girls sewed the upper parts of a shoe, men and boys attached the bottoms. While slow, this mode of production allowed wages to be reduced still further. A few highly paid workers performed critical tasks like cutting the leather, but most work was done either in large central shops or in homes. With workers no longer able to make an entire shoe, in little more than a generation shoemaking ceased to be a craft. Though not organized in a factory setting, it had become essentially an assembly-line process.

The Labor Movement

In this newly emerging economic order, workers sometimes organized to protect their rights and traditional ways of life. Craftworkers such as carpenters, printers, and tailors formed unions, and in 1834 individual unions came together in the National Trades' Union.

Union leaders argued that labor was degraded in America: workers endured long hours, low pay, and low status. Unlike most American social thinkers of the day, they accepted the idea of conflict between different classes. They did not believe that the interests of workers and employers could be reconciled, and they blamed the plight of labor on monopolies, especially banking and paper money, and on machines and the factory system.

If the unions' rhetoric sounded radical, the solutions they proposed were moderate. Reformers agitated for public education, abolition of imprisonment for debt, political action by workers, and effective unions as the means to guarantee social equality and restore labor to its former honored position. Proclaiming the republican virtues of freedom and equality, they attacked special privilege, denounced the lack of equal opportunity, and decried workers' loss of independence.

The labor movement gathered some momentum in the decade before the Panic of 1837, but in the depression that followed, labor's strength collapsed. During hard times, few workers were willing to strike or engage in collective action. Nor did skilled craftworkers, who spearheaded the union movement, feel a particularly strong bond with semiskilled factory workers and unskilled laborers. More than a decade of agitation did finally win the 10-hour day for some workers by the 1850s, and the courts also recognized workers' right to strike, but these gains had little immediate impact.

Difficulties of the union movement

Workers were united in resenting the industrial system and their loss of status, but they were divided by ethnic and racial antagonisms, gender, conflicting religious perspectives, occupational differences, party loyalties, and disagreements over tactics. For them, the factory and industrialism were not agents of opportunity but reminders of their loss of independence and a measure of control over their lives.

SOCIAL STRUCTURES OF THE MARKET SOCIETY

Thousands of miles beyond Lowell's factory gates a different sort of American roamed, who at first appeared unconnected to the bustle of urban markets. These were the legendary mountain men, who flourished from the mid-1820s through the mid-1840s. Traveling across the Great Plains, along upland streams, and over the passes of the Rockies, outdoorsmen like Jim Bridger, Jedediah Smith, and James Walker wore buckskin hunting shirts, let their hair grow to their shoulders, and stuck pistols and tomahawks in their belts. Wild and exotic, the mountain men became romantic symbols of the American quest for individual freedom.

Yet these wanderers, too, were tied to the emerging market society. The mountain men hunted beaver pelts and shipped them east, to be turned into fancy hats for gentlemen. The fur trade was not a sporting event but a business, dominated by organizations like John Jacob Astor's American Fur Company, and the trapper was the agent of an economic structure that stretched from the mountains to eastern cities and even to Europe. Most of these men went into the wilderness not to flee civilization but to make money—to accumulate capital in order to set themselves up in society. Of those who survived the fur trade, almost none remained permanently outside civilization

The mountain men tied to market society

but returned and took up new careers as shopkeepers, traders, ranchers, politicians, and even bankers. Far from rejecting society's values, the mountain men sought respectability. They, like farmers, were expectant capitalists for whom the West was a land of opportunity.

The revolution in markets, in other words, affected Americans from all walks of life: mountain men as well as merchants, laborers as well as farmers. Equally critical, it restructured American society as a whole.

Economic Specialization

To begin with, the spread of the market produced greater specialization. As we have seen, transportation networks made it possible for farmers to concentrate on producing certain crops, while factories could focus on making a single item such as cloth or shoes. Within factories, the division of labor meant that the process of manufacturing an item became more specialized. No longer did cobblers produce a pair of shoes from start to finish; the operation was broken down into more specialized (and less skilled) tasks.

This process evolved at different rates. Textiles and milling were completely mechanized, while other sectors of the economy, such as shoes and men's clothing, depended little on machinery. Moreover, large factories were the exception rather than the rule. A great deal of manufacturing was still done in smaller shops with few employees. Still, the tendency was toward more technology, greater efficiency, and increasing specialization.

Specialization had consequences at home as well as in the workplace. The average eighteenth-century American woman produced items like thread, cloth, clothing, and candles in the home for family use. As factories spread, however, household manufacturing all but disappeared, and women lost many of the economic functions they had previously performed in the family unit. Again, textiles are a striking example. Between 1815 and 1860, the price of cotton cloth fell from 18 to 2 cents a yard, and because it was also smoother and more brightly colored than homespun, most women purchased cloth rather than made it themselves. Similarly, the development of ready-made men's clothing reduced the amount of sewing women did, especially in urban centers. As Chapter 12 will make clearer, the growth of industry led to an economic reorganization of the family and a new definition of women's role in society.

Decline of women's traditional work

Materialism

European visitors were struck during these years by how much Americans were preoccupied with material goods. The new generation did not invent materialism, but the spread of the market after 1815 made it much more evident. "I know of no country, indeed," Tocqueville commented, "where the love of money has taken stronger hold on the affections of men."

In a nation that had no legally recognized aristocracy, no established church, and class lines that were only informally drawn, wealth became the most obvious symbol of status. Dismissing birth as "a mere idea," one magazine explained, "Wealth is something substantial. Everybody knows that and feels it." Materialism reflected more than a desire for goods and physical comfort. It represented a quest for respect and recognition. "Americans boast of their skill in money making," one contemporary observed, "and as it is the only standard of dignity and nobility and worth, they endeavor to obtain it by every possible means."

Wealth and status

The emphasis on money and material goods left its mark on the American character. Often enough, it encouraged sharp business practices and promoted a greater tolerance of wealth acquired by questionable means. Americans also emphasized practicality over theory. The esteem of the founding generation for intellectual achievement was mostly lost in the scramble for wealth that seemed to consume the new generation.

The Emerging Middle Class

In the years after 1815, a new middle class took shape in American society. A small class of shopkeepers, professionals, and master artisans had existed earlier, but the creation of a national market economy greatly expanded its size and influence. As specialization increased, office work and selling were more often physically separated from the production and handling of merchandise. Businesspeople, professionals, storekeepers, clerks, office workers, and supervisors began to think of themselves as a distinct social group. Members of the growing middle class had access to more education and enjoyed greater social mobility. They were paid not only more but differently. A manual worker might earn $300 a year, paid as wages computed on an hourly basis. Professionals received a yearly salary and might make $1000 a year or more.

Separation of middle class from manual laborers

Middle-class neighborhoods, segregated along income and occupational lines, also began to develop in towns and cities. In larger cities improved transportation enabled middle-class residents to move to surrounding suburbs and commute to work. Leisure also became segregated, as separate working-class and middle-class social organizations and institutions emerged.

As middle-class Americans accumulated greater wealth, they were able to consume more. Thus material goods became emblems of success and status—as clockmaker Chauncey Jerome sadly discovered when his business failed and his wealth vanished. Indeed, this materialistic ethos was most apparent in the middle class, as they strove to set themselves apart from other groups in society.

Material goods as emblems of success

The middle class also came to embrace a new concept of marriage, the family, and the home, as we will see in Chapter 12. Along with occupation and income, moral outlook also marked class boundaries during this period.

The Distribution of Wealth

As American society became more specialized, greater extremes of wealth appeared. As the new markets created fortunes for the few, the factory system lowered the wages of workers by dividing labor into smaller, less skilled tasks.

Indeed, local tax records reveal a growing concentration of wealth at the top of the social pyramid after 1815. Wealth was most highly concentrated in large eastern cities and in the cotton kingdom of the South, but everywhere the tendency was for the rich to get richer and own a larger share of the community's total wealth. By 1860, 5 percent of American families owned more than 50 percent of the nation's wealth. In villages where the market revolution had not penetrated, wealth tended to be less concentrated.

Growing inequality of wealth

In a market society, the rich were able to build up their assets because those with capital were in a position to increase it dramatically by taking advantage of new investment opportunities. Although a few men, such as Cornelius Vanderbilt and John Jacob Astor, vaulted from the bottom ranks of society to the top, most of the nation's richest individuals came from wealthy families.

Social Mobility

The existence of great fortunes is not necessarily inconsistent with the idea of social mobility or property accumulation. Although the gap between the rich and the poor widened after 1820, even the incomes of most poor Americans rose, because the total amount of wealth produced in America had become much larger. From about 1825 to 1860 the average per capita income almost doubled to $300. Voicing the popular belief, a New York judge proclaimed, "In this favored land of liberty, the road to advancement is open to all."

Social mobility existed in these years, but not as much as contemporaries boasted. Most laborers—or more often their sons—did manage to move up the social ladder, but only a rung or two. Few unskilled workers rose higher than to a semiskilled occupation. Even the children of skilled workers normally did not escape the laboring classes to enter the middle-class ranks of clerks, managers, or lawyers. For most workers improved status came in the form of a savings account or home ownership, which gave them some security during economic downswings and in old age.

Limits to social mobility

A New Sensitivity to Time

It was no accident that Chauncey Jerome's clocks spread throughout the nation along with the market economy. The new methods of doing business involved a new and stricter sense of time. Factory life necessitated a more regimented schedule, where work began at the sound of a bell, workers kept machines going at a constant pace, and the day was divided into hours and even minutes.

Clocks began to invade private as well as public space. With mass production ordinary families could now afford clocks, and even farmers became more sensitive to time as they were integrated into the market. As one frontier traveler reported in 1844, "In Kentucky, in Indiana, in Illinois, in Missouri, and here in every dale in Arkansas, and in cabins where there was not a chair to sit on, there was sure to be a Connecticut clock."

PROSPERITY AND ANXIETY

As Americans watched their nation's frontiers expand and its economy grow, many began to view history in terms of an inevitable and continuous improvement. The path of commerce, however, was not steadily upward. Rather it advanced in a series of wrenching boom-bust cycles: accelerating growth, followed by a crash, and then depression.

The country remained extraordinarily prosperous from 1815 until 1819, only to sink into a depression that lasted from 1819 to 1823. During the next cycle, the economy expanded slowly during the 1820s, followed by almost frenzied speculation in the 1830s. Then came the inevitable contraction in 1837, and the country suffered an even more severe depression from 1839 to 1843. The third cycle followed the familiar pattern: gradual economic growth during the 1840s, frantic expansion in the 1850s, and a third depression that began in 1857 and lasted until the Civil War. In each of these depressions, thousands of workers were thrown out of work, overextended farmers lost their farms, and many businesses closed their doors.

Boom-bust cycle

The impact of the boom-bust cycle can be seen in the contrasting fates of two Americans who moved west in search of opportunity. In 1820, 17-year-old Benjamin Remington left Hancock, Massachusetts, for western New York, which was just being opened to white settlement. After working at several jobs, he managed to purchase on credit a 150-acre farm near the growing city of Rochester. Remington's timing was ideal. In 1823, two years after his arrival, the new Erie Canal was completed as far as Rochester. Wheat prices rose, flour shipments from the region shot up, and Remington prospered supplying food for eastern markets. Over the years, he added to his acreage, built a comfortable house for his family, and was elected town supervisor. For Remington, the West was indeed a land of opportunity.

Somewhat younger, Addison Ward moved west when he came of age in 1831, leaving Virginia for Indiana. Unfortunately, by the time Ward arrived in Greene County, the best land had already been claimed. All he could afford was 80 acres of rough government land, which he bought in 1837 largely on credit. The region lacked adequate transportation to outside markets, but the economy was booming, and the state had begun an ambitious internal improvements program. Ward's timing, however, could not have been worse. Almost immediately the country entered a depression, driving farm prices and land values downward. Overwhelmed by debts, Ward sold his farm and fell into the ranks of tenant farmers. He continued to struggle until his death around 1850. Catching the wrong end of the boom-bust cycle, Ward never achieved economic success and social respectability.

In such an environment, prosperity, like personal success, seemed all too fleeting. Because Americans believed the good times would not last—that the bubble would burst and another "panic" set in—their optimism was often tinged by insecurity and anxiety. They knew too many individuals like Chauncey Jerome, who had been rich and then lost all their wealth in a downturn.

`Popular anxiety`

The Panic of 1819

The initial shock of this boom-and-bust psychology came with the Panic of 1819, the first major depression in the nation's history. From 1815 to 1818 cotton had commanded truly fabulous prices on the Liverpool market, reaching 32.5 cents a pound in 1818. In this heady prosperity, the federal government extended liberal credit for land purchases, and the new national bank encouraged merchants and farmers to borrow in order to catch the rising tide.

But in 1819 the price of cotton collapsed and took the rest of the economy with it. As the inflationary bubble burst, land values, which had been driven to new heights by the speculative fever, plummeted 50 to 75 percent almost overnight. As the economy went slack, so did the demand for western foodstuffs and eastern manufactured goods and services, sending the nation reeling into a severe depression.

`National depression`

Because the market economy had spread to new areas, this downturn affected not only urban Americans but those living in the countryside as well. Many farmers, especially in newly settled regions, had bought their land on credit, and others in established areas had expanded their operations in anticipation of future returns. When prices fell, both groups were hard-pressed to pay their debts. New cotton planters in the Southwest, who were especially vulnerable to fluctuations in the world market, were particularly hard hit.

In the wake of the Panic of 1819, the New Nationalism's spirit of cooperation gave way to jealousy and conflict between competing interests and social groups. One consequence was an increase in sectional tensions, but the Panic affected political life in even more direct ways. As the depression deepened and hardship spread, Americans viewed government policies as at least partly to blame. The postwar nationalism, after all, had been based on the belief that government should stimulate economic development through a national bank and protective tariff, by improving transportation, and by opening up new lands. As Americans struggled to make sense of their new economic order, they looked to take more direct control of the government that was so actively shaping their lives. During the 1820s, the popular response to the market and the Panic of 1819 produced a strikingly new kind of politics in the Republic.

chapter summary

By uniting the country in a single market, the market revolution transformed the United States during the quarter-century after 1815.

- The federal government promoted the creation of a market through a protective tariff, a national bank, and internal improvements.

- The development of new forms of transportation, including canals, steamboats, and eventually railroads, allowed goods to be transported cheaply on land.

- The Supreme Court adopted a pro-business stance that encouraged investment and risk taking.

- Economic expansion generated greater national wealth, but it also brought social and intellectual change.
  - Americans pursued opportunity, embraced a new concept of progress, viewed change as normal, developed a strong materialist ethic, and considered wealth the primary means to determine status.

- Entrepreneurs reorganized their operations to increase production and sell in a wider market.

- The earliest factories were built to serve the textile industry, and the first laborers in them were young women from rural families.
  - Factory work imposed on workers a new discipline based on time and strict routine.
  - Workers' declining status led them to form unions and resort to strikes, but the depression that began in 1837 destroyed these organizations.

- The market revolution distributed wealth much more unevenly and left Americans feeling alternatively buoyant and anxious about their social and economic status.
  - Social mobility existed, but it was more limited than popular belief claimed.
  - The economy lurched up and down in a boom-bust cycle.
  - In hard times, Americans looked to the government to relieve economic distress.

 For quizzes and a variety of interactive resources, visit the book's Online Learning Center at www.mhhe.com/davidsonconcise3

SIGNIFICANT EVENTS

1790	+	Slater's textile mill opens
1793	+	Eli Whitney invents the cotton gin
1798	+	Whitney begins work on a system of interchangeable parts
1810	+	*Fletcher v. Peck*
1810–1820	+	Cotton boom begins in the South
1811	+	First steamboat trip from Pittsburgh to New Orleans
1816	+	Second Bank of the United States chartered; protective tariff enacted
1817	+	Bonus Bill veto
1818–1825	+	Erie Canal constructed
1819	+	*Dartmouth College v. Woodward; McCulloch v. Maryland*
1819–1823	+	Panic and depression
1820	+	Lowell mills established
1824	+	*Gibbons v. Ogden*
1825–1850	+	Canal era
1834	+	National Trades' Union founded
1837	+	Panic
1839–1843	+	Depression
1844	+	Samuel F. B. Morse sends first intercity telegraphic message
1847	+	Rotary printing press invented

CHAPTER 11

The Rise of Democracy
(1824–1840)

The notice, printed in a local newspaper, made the rounds in the rural Pearl River district of Mississippi. A traveler, the advertisement announced, had lost a suitcase while fording the Tallahala River. The contents included "6 ruffled shirts, 6 cambric handkerchiefs, 1 hair-brush, 1 toothbrush, 1 nail-brush . . ."

As the list went on, the popular reaction would inevitably shift from amusement to disdain: "1 pair curling tongs, 2 sticks pomatum . . . 1 box pearl-powder, 1 bottle Cologne, 1 [bottle] rose-water, 4 pairs silk stockings, and 2 pairs kid gloves." The howls of derision that filled the air could only have increased upon learning that anyone finding said trunk was requested to contact the owner—Mr. Powhatan Ellis of Natchez.

Powhatan Ellis was no ordinary backcountry traveler. Born into a genteel Virginia family, Ellis had moved in 1816 to the raw Southwest to enlarge his fortune. With his cultivated tastes, careful dress, and stately dignity, he upheld the tradition of the gentleman politician. In Virginia he would have commanded respect: indeed, in Mississippi he had been appointed district judge and U.S. senator. But for the voters along the Pearl River, the advertisement for his trunk of ruffled shirts, hair oils, and fancy "skunkwater" proved to be the political kiss of death. His opponents branded him an aristocrat and a dandy, and his support among the piney woods farmers evaporated faster than a morning mist along Old Muddy on a sweltering summer's day.

No one was more satisfied with this outcome than the resourceful Franklin E. Plummer, one of Ellis's political enemies. For in truth, while the unfortunate Powhatan Ellis had lost a trunk fording a stream, he had not placed the advertisement trying to locate it. That was the handiwork of Plummer, who well understood the new playing field of American politics in the 1820s. Born in

preview • In the 1820s and 1830s a new democratic political culture championed the wisdom of the people and the need for political parties. Andrew Jackson personified the new spirit when he expanded the power of the presidency by rejecting South Carolina's doctrine of nullification and by destroying the national bank. Paradoxically, democratic policies intensified racism, as Indians east of the Mississippi were forced from their lands and free African Americans met increased discrimination.

New England, Plummer had made his way as a young man to the new state of Mississippi, where he set himself up as an attorney, complete with a law library of three books. Plummer's shrewdness and oratorical talent made up for his lack of legal training, however, and he was quickly elected to the legislature.

Plummer's ambition soon flowed beyond the state capital, and in 1830 he announced his candidacy for Congress. At first few observers took his candidacy seriously. In his campaign, however, he boldly portrayed himself as the champion of the people battling the aristocrats of Natchez. Contrasting his humble background with that of his wealthy opponent, Plummer proclaimed: "We are taught that the highway to office, distinction and honor, is as free to the *meritorious poor* man, as to the *rich*; to the man who has risen from obscurity by his own individual exertions, as to him who has inherited a high and elevated standing in society, founded on the patrimony of his ancestors." Taking as his slogan "Plummer for the People, and the People for Plummer," he was easily elected.

Champion of the people

Plummer was a campaigner who knew how to effect the common touch. Once, as he canvassed the district with his opponent, the pair stopped at a farmhouse. When his opponent, seeking the farmer's vote, kissed the daughter, Plummer lifted up a toddling boy and began picking red bugs off him, telling the enchanted mother, "They are powerful bad, and mighty hard on babies." On another occasion, while his opponent slept, Plummer rose at dawn to help milk the family's cow—and won another vote.

As long as Plummer maintained his image as one of the people, he remained invincible. But in 1835 when he ran for the U.S. Senate, his touch deserted him. Borrowing money from a Natchez bank, he purchased a stylish coach, put his servant in a uniform, and campaigned across the state. Aghast at such aristocratic pretensions, his followers promptly abandoned him, and he was soundly defeated. He died in 1852 in obscurity and poverty.

In fact, Franklin Plummer was being pulled two ways by the forces transforming American society. As the previous chapter explained, the growth of commerce and new markets opened up opportunities for more and more Americans during these years. "Opportunity" was one of the bywords of the age. Through his connections with bankers and the well-to-do, Plummer saw the opportunity to accumulate wealth and to gain status and respect.

Yet at the same time that new markets were producing a more stratified, unequal society, the nation's politics were becoming more democratic. The new political system that developed after 1820 differed strikingly from that of the early Republic. Just as national markets linked the regions of America economically, the new system of national politics with its mass electioneering techniques involved more voters than ever before. Plummer's world reflected that new political culture. And its central feature—another byword on everyone's lips—was "equality." In reality, the relation between the new equalities of politics and the new opportunities of the market was an uneasy one.

EQUALITY AND OPPORTUNITY

Middle- and upper-class Europeans who visited the United States during these decades were especially sensitive to the egalitarian quality of American life. Coming from the more stratified society of Europe, they were immediately struck—often unfavorably—by the "democratic spirit" that had become "infused into all the national habits and all the customs of society."

To begin with, they discovered that only one class of seats was available on stagecoaches and railcars. These were filled according to the rough-and-ready rule of first come, first served. In steamboat dining rooms or at country taverns, everyone ate at a common table, sharing food from the same serving plates. As one upper-class gentleman complained, "The rich and the poor, the educated and the ignorant, the polite and the vulgar, all herd on the cabin floor, feed at the same table, sit in each others laps, as it were."

Indeed, the democratic "manners" of Americans seemed not just shocking but downright rude. Europeans were used to social inferiors speaking only if spoken to. But Americans felt free to strike up a conversation with anyone, including total strangers. Frances Trollope was offended by the "coarse familiarity of address" between classes, while another visitor complained that in a nation where every citizen felt free to shake the hand of another, it was impossible to know anyone's social station.

Americans were self-consciously proud of such democratic behavior, which they viewed as a valued heritage of the Revolution. The keelboaters who carried the

As this nattily dressed butcher suggests, clothes were not much help in sorting out social status in America. Although the clothing of the upper class was often made of finer material and was more skillfully tailored, by the 1820s less prosperous Americans wore similar styles. "The washerwoman's Sunday attire is now as nearly like that of the merchant's wife as it can be," commented one astonished observer.

future King Louis-Philippe of France on a trip down the Mississippi made their republican feelings plain when the keelboat ran aground. "You kings down there!" bellowed the captain. "Show yourselves and do a man's work, and help us three-spots pull off this bar!" The ideology of the Revolution made it clear that, in the American deck of cards at least, "three-spots" counted as much as jacks, kings, and queens. Kings were not allowed to forget that—and neither was Franklin Plummer.

The Tension between Equality and Opportunity

While Americans praised opportunity and equality, a fundamental tension existed between these values. Inevitably, widespread opportunity would produce inequality of wealth. In Crèvecoeur's America, a rough equality of wealth and status had prevailed because of the lack of access to a market. But by the 1820s and 1830s, as the opportunities of the market expanded, wealth became much more unevenly distributed. Thus the new generation had to confront contradictions in the American creed that their parents had been able to conveniently ignore.

By equality, Americans did not mean equality of wealth or property. "I know of no country where profounder contempt is expressed for the theory of permanent equality of property," Alexis de Tocqueville wrote. Nor did equality mean that all citizens had equal talent or capacity. "Distinctions in society will always exist under every just government," Andrew Jackson declared. "Equality of talents, or education, or of wealth cannot be produced by human institutions."

Meaning of equality

In the end, what Americans upheld was equality of opportunity, not equality of condition. "True republicanism requires that every man shall have an equal chance—that every man shall be free to become as unequal as he can," one American commented. In an economy that could go bust as well as boom, Americans agreed that one primary objective of government was to safeguard opportunity. Thus the new politics of democracy walked hand in hand with the new opportunities of the market.

THE NEW POLITICAL CULTURE OF DEMOCRACY

The stately James Monroe, with his powdered hair and buckled shoes and breeches, was not part of the new politics. But in 1824 as he neared the end of his second term, a host of new leaders in the Republican party looked to succeed him. The Republican congressional caucus finally settled on William H. Crawford of Georgia as the party's presidential nominee. Condemning "King Caucus" as undemocratic, three other Republicans, all ardent nationalists, refused to withdraw from the race: Secretary of State John Quincy Adams; John C. Calhoun, Monroe's secretary of war; and Henry Clay, the Speaker of the House.

Death of the caucus system

None of these men bargained on the sudden emergence of another Republican candidate, Andrew Jackson, the hero of the Battle of New Orleans. Because of his limited experience, no one took Jackson's candidacy seriously at first, including Jackson himself. But soon the general's supporters and rivals began receiving reports of his popularity. A typical account from Cincinnati read, "Strange! Wild! Infatuated! All for Jackson!" Savvy politicians soon flocked to his standard, but it was the people who first made Jackson a serious candidate.

The Election of 1824

Calhoun eventually dropped out of the race, but none of the four remaining candidates received a majority of the popular vote. Still, Jackson led the field and also finished first in the Electoral College. Under the terms of the Twelfth Amendment, the House was to select a president from the top three candidates. Henry Clay, who finished fourth and therefore was eliminated, met privately with Adams and then rallied the votes in the House needed to put Adams over the top.

Two days later, Adams announced that Clay would be his secretary of state, the usual stepping-stone to the presidency. Jackson and his supporters promptly charged that there had been a "corrupt bargain" between Adams and Clay. Before Adams had even assumed office, the 1828 race was under way.

More significant, the election of 1824 shattered the old party system. Henry Clay and John Quincy Adams began to organize a new party, known as the National Republicans to distinguish it from Jefferson's old party. Jackson's disappointed supporters eventually called themselves Democrats. By the mid-1830s, when the National Republicans gave way to the Whigs, the second American party system was in place. Once established, it dominated the nation's politics until the 1850s.

Second party system

Social Sources of the New Politics

Why was it that a new style and new system of politics emerged in the 1820s? We have already seen that a revolution in markets, stimulated by new transportation networks, was under way. We have seen, too, that the scramble to bring western lands into the market generated a speculative land boom that collapsed in the Panic of 1819. The rise of the new political culture was rooted in these social conditions. During the sharp depression that followed, many Americans became convinced that government policy had aggravated, if not actually produced, hard times. Consequently, they decided that the government had a responsibility to relieve distress and promote prosperity.

New attitudes toward government

The connection made between government policy and economic well-being stimulated rising popular interest in politics during the 1820s. Agitation mounted, especially at the state level, for government to enact debtor relief and provide other forms of assistance. Elections became the means through which the majority expressed its policy preferences, by voting for candidates pledged to specific programs. The older idea that representatives should be independent, voting their best judgment, gave way to the notion that representatives were to carry out the will of the people, as expressed in the results of elections.

With more citizens championing the "will of the people," pressure mounted to open up the political process. Most states eliminated property qualifications for voting in favor of white manhood suffrage, under which all adult white males were allowed to vote. Similarly, property requirements for officeholders were reduced or dropped.

Democratic reforms

Presidential elections became more democratic as well. By 1832 South Carolina was the only state where the legislature rather than the voters still chose presidential electors. Parties began to hold conventions as a more democratic method of nominating candidates and approving a platform. And because a presidential candidate had to carry a number of states in different sections of the country, the backing of a national party, with effective state and local organizations, became essential.

Male Suffrage in Europe and Latin America

The democratic winds of change affected European societies and eventually other areas of the world as well. In no other major country, however, were these reforms achieved as early and with as little resistance as in the United States. Suffrage provides a good example. In Britain, in response to growing demonstrations and the cautionary example of the French monarchy's overthrow in 1830, Parliament approved the Reform Bill of 1832, which enfranchised a number of property holders and gave Britain the broadest electorate in Europe. Yet in fact, only about 15 percent of the adult males in Britain enjoyed the right of suffrage after the bill's passage. In France the figure was less than 1 percent.

The democratic revolutions of 1848 raised the standard of universal male suffrage in France and Prussia. Yet this ideal soon suffered setbacks. By 1852 the French republic had been replaced by a monarchy under Emperor Louis Napoleon. And in Prussia, the new constitution essentially negated universal male suffrage by dividing the electorate into three classes according to wealth, a formula that enabled 5 percent of the voters to elect one-third of parliament. Belgium, which had the most liberal constitution in Europe, did not approximate manhood suffrage until 1848. Even Britain's second Reform Act (1867) enfranchised only about one-third of the adult males.

Likewise, virtually all the Latin American republics established in the 1820s and 1830s imposed property requirements on voting or, like Uruguay, forbade certain occupational groups from voting, such as servants and peasants. One exception was Mexico, where under the 1824 constitution a number of states adopted an extremely broad suffrage. The 1836 constitution, however, sharply limited voting rights. The most restricted suffrage existed in the republic of Haiti, where only army officers and a few other privileged individuals enjoyed the franchise. When the revolution of 1843 led to adoption of a new constitution with mass-based suffrage, the constitution met widespread resistance among elites and the government quickly failed.

As the new reforms went into effect in the United States, voter turnout soared. Whereas in the 1824 presidential election, only 27 percent of eligible voters had bothered to go to the polls, in 1840, 78 percent of eligible voters cast ballots, probably the highest turnout in American history.

The Acceptance of Political Parties

All these developments favored the emergence of a new type of politician: one whose life was devoted to party service and whose living often depended on public office. As the number of state internal improvement projects increased during the 1820s, so did the number of government jobs that could support party workers. No longer was politics primarily the province of the wealthy, who spent only part of their time on public affairs. Instead, political leaders were more likely to come from the middle ranks of society, especially outside the South. Indeed, as Franklin Plummer demonstrated, a successful politician now had to mingle with the masses and voice their feelings—requirements that put the wealthy elite at a disadvantage.

Professional politicians

In many ways, Martin Van Buren, whose career took him to the Senate and eventually the White House, epitomized the new breed of politician. The son of a New York tavernkeeper, Van Buren lacked a magnetic personality, but he was a master organizer and tactician, highly adept at using the new party system. Unlike the older Revolutionary generation, who regarded political parties as dangerous and destructive, Van Buren argued that they were not only "inseparable from free governments" but "in many and material respects . . . highly useful to the country." While conceding they were subject to abuse, he stressed that competing parties would scrutinize each other and check abuses at the same time that they kept the masses informed.

Andrew Jackson was one of the first political leaders to grasp the new politics, in which the ordinary citizen reigned supreme. "Never for a moment believe that the great body of the citizens . . . can deliberately intend to do wrong," he asserted, endorsing an often-expressed refrain of American politics.

The new style of politics

Party leaders everywhere avoided aristocratic airs when on the stump and often dressed in plain clothing and used informal language. Politics became mass entertainment, with campaign hoopla frequently overshadowing issues. Parades, massive rallies, and barbecues were used to rouse voters, and treating to drinks became an almost universal campaign tactic. ("The way to men's hearts is down their throats," quipped one Kentucky vote-getter.) Although politicians talked often about principles, political parties were pragmatic organizations, intent on gaining and holding power.

"The Will of the People the Supreme Law" reads the banner at this county election. Election Day remained an all-male event as well as a time of excitement, heated debate, and boisterous celebration. As citizens give their oath to an election judge, diligent party workers dispense free drinks, solicit support, offer party tickets, and keep a careful tally of who has voted.

The Jacksonian era has been called the Age of the Common Man, but such democratic tendencies had distinct limits. Women and slaves were not allowed to vote, nor could free African Americans (except in a few states) or Indians. Nor did the parties always deal effectively with (or even address) basic problems in society. Still, the importance of Van Buren's insight was fundamental. Popular political parties provided an essential mechanism for peacefully resolving differences among competing interest groups, regions, and social classes.

Limitations of the democratic political system

JACKSON'S RISE TO POWER

When he assumed the presidency in 1825, John Quincy Adams might have worked to create a mass-based party. On the state level, the new democratic style of politics was already making headway. But Adams, a talented diplomat and a great secretary of state, possessed hardly a

John Quincy Adams's presidency

political bone in his body. Cold and tactless, he could build no popular support for the ambitious and often farsighted programs he proposed. His proposals that government promote not only manufacturing and agriculture but also the arts, literature, and science left his opponents aghast.

Nor would Adams take any steps to gain reelection. Henry Clay finally undertook to organize the National Republicans, but with a reluctant candidate he labored under serious handicaps. The new style of politics came into its own nationally only when Andrew Jackson swept to power at the head of a new party, the Democrats.

President of the People

Building a new coalition was a tricky business. Because Jackson's new party was made up of conflicting interests, "Old Hickory" remained vague about his own position on many issues. Thus the campaign of 1828 soon degenerated into a series of personal attacks, splattering mud on all involved. When the votes were counted, Jackson won handily.

The election marked the beginning of politics as Americans have practiced it ever since, with two disciplined national parties actively competing for votes, emphasizing personalities over issues, and resorting to mass electioneering techniques. Yet in terms of public policy, the meaning of the election was anything but clear. The people had voted for Jackson as a national hero without any real sense of what he would do with his newly won power.

Significance of the 1828 election

Certainly the people looked for change. Ordinary citizens came from miles around to see Jackson sworn in. At the White House reception pandemonium reigned. The crowd trampled on the furniture, smashed mirrors, and ruined carpets and draperies. "It was a proud day for the people," boasted Amos Kendall, one of the new president's advisers. Supreme Court Justice Joseph Story was less enraptured: "I never saw such a mixture. The reign of King Mob seemed triumphant."

Whether loved as a man of the people or hated as a demagogue leading the mob, Jackson was the representative of the new democracy. The first president from west of the Appalachians, he was a man of action, and though he had a quick mind, he had little use for learning. His troops had nicknamed him Old Hickory out of respect for his toughness, but that strength sometimes became arrogance, and he could be vindictive and a bully. He was not a man to provoke, as his reputation for dueling demonstrated.

Jackson's character

For all these flaws, Jackson was a shrewd politician. He knew how to manipulate men and could be affable or abusive as the occasion demanded. He also displayed a keen sense of public opinion, reading the shifting national mood better than any of his contemporaries.

As the nation's chief executive, he defended the spoils system, under which public offices were awarded to political supporters, as a democratic reform. Rota-

Andrew Jackson's Tumultuous Inauguration

When the speech was over, and the President made his parting bow, the barrier that had separated the people from him was broken down and they rushed up the steps all eager to shake hands with him. It was with difficulty he made his way through the Capitol and down the hill to . . . his horse. . . . Such a cortege as followed him! Country men, farmers, gentlemen, mounted and dismounted, boys, women and children, black and white. Carriages, wagons and carts all pursuing him to the President's house. . . . What a scene did we witness [at the White House]! The *Majesty of the People* had disappeared, and a rabble, a mob, of boys, negros, women, children, scrambling fighting, romping . . . the whole house had been inundated by the rabble mob. . . . The President, after having been *literally* nearly pressed to death and almost suffocated and torn to pieces by the people in their eagerness to shake hands with Old Hickory, had retreated through the back way . . . and had escaped to his lodgings at Gadsby's. Cut glass and china to the amount of several thousand dollars had been broken in the struggle to get the refreshments; punch and other articles had been carried out in tubs and buckets, but had it been in hogsheads it would have been insufficient, ice-creams, and cake and lemonade, for 20,000 people, for it is said that number were there, tho' I think the estimate exaggerated. Ladies fainted, men were seen with bloody noses, and such a scene of confusion took place as it is impossible to describe,—those who got in could not get out by the door again, but had to scramble out of windows. . . .

This concourse had not been anticipated and therefore not provided against. Ladies and gentlemen, only had been expected at this Levee, not the people en masse. But it was the People's day, and the People's President and the People would rule.

Source: Margaret Bayard Smith, *The First Forty Years of Washington Society* (New York: Charles Scribner's Sons, 1906), pp. 294–296.

tion in office, he declared, would guard against insensitive bureaucrats who presumed that they held their positions by right. The cabinet, he believed, existed more to carry out his will than to offer counsel, and throughout his term he insisted on his way—and usually got it.

Spoils system

The Political Agenda in the Market Economy

Jackson took office at a time when the market economy was expanding through-out America and the nation's population was spreading geographically. The three major problems his administration faced were directly caused by the resulting growing pains.

Jackson's stubborn determination shines through in this portrait by Asher Durand, painted in 1835. "His passions are terrible," Jefferson noted. "When I was President of the Senate, he was Senator, and he could never speak on account of the rashness of his feelings. I have seen him attempt it repeatedly, and as often choke with rage. His passions are, no doubt, cooler now; he has been much tried since I knew him, but he is a dangerous man." (Collection of the New York Historical Society.)

First, the demand for new lands put continuing pressure on Indians, whose valuable cornfields and hunting grounds could produce marketable commodities like cotton and wheat. Second, as the economies of the North, South, and West became more specialized, their rival interests forced a confrontation over the tariff. And finally, the booming economy focused attention on the role of credit and banking in society and on the new commercial attitudes that were a central part of the developing market economy. The president attacked all three issues in his characteristically combative style.

DEMOCRACY AND RACE

As a planter, Jackson benefited from the international demand for cotton that was drawing new lands into the market. He had gone off to the Tennessee frontier in 1788, a rowdy, ambitious young man who could afford to purchase only one slave. Caught up in the speculative mania of the frontier, he became a prominent land speculator, established himself as a planter, and by the time he became president, owned nearly 100 slaves. His popularity derived not only from defeating the British but also from opening extensive tracts of valuable Indian lands to white settlement.

Even so, in 1820 an estimated 125,000 Indians remained east of the Mississippi River. In the Southwest the Choctaws, Creeks, Cherokees, Chickasaws, and Seminoles retained millions of acres of prime agricultural land in the heart of the cotton kingdom. Led by Georgia, southern states demanded that the federal government clear these titles.

As white pressure for removal intensified, a shift in the attitude toward Indians and race increasingly occurred. Previously whites had generally attributed cultural differences among whites, blacks, and Indians to environment. After 1815 the dominant white culture stressed "innate" racial differences that could never be erased. A growing number of Americans began to argue that the Indian was a permanently inferior savage who blocked progress.

New attitudes toward race

Accommodate or Resist?

The clamor among southern whites for removal placed the southwestern tribes in a difficult situation. Understandably, they fiercely rejected the idea of abandoning their lands. They diverged, however, over how to respond. Among the Cherokees, mixed-bloods led by John Ross advocated a program of accommodation by adopting white ways to prevent removal. After a bitter struggle Ross prevailed, and in 1827 the Cherokees adopted a written constitution modeled after that of the United States. They also enacted the death penalty for any member who sold tribal lands to whites without consent of the governing general council. Developing their own alphabet, they published a bilingual newspaper, the *Cherokee Phoenix.*

The division between traditionalists and those favoring accommodation reflected the fact that Indians too had been drawn into a web of market relationships. As more Cherokee families began to sell their surplus crops, they ceased to share property communally as in the past. Cherokee society became more stratified and unequal, just as white society had, and economic elites dominated the tribal government. Nor were the Cherokees untouched by the cotton boom. Some tribal leaders, particularly half-bloods who could deal easily with white culture, became wealthy planters who owned many black slaves and thousands of acres of cotton land. Largely of mixed ancestry, slaveholders were the driving force behind acculturation.

Changing nature of Cherokee society

As cotton cultivation expanded among the Cherokees, slavery became harsher and a primary means of determining status, just as in southern white society. The general council passed several laws forbidding intermarriage with blacks and excluding blacks and mulattoes from voting or holding office. Ironically, at the same time that white racial attitudes toward Indians were deteriorating, the Cherokees' view of African Americans drew closer to that of white society.

Trail of Tears

As western land fever increased and racial attitudes hardened, Jackson prodded Congress to provide funds for Indian removal. At the same time, the Georgia legislature declared Cherokee laws null and void and decreed that tribal members would be tried in state courts. In 1830 Congress finally passed a removal bill.

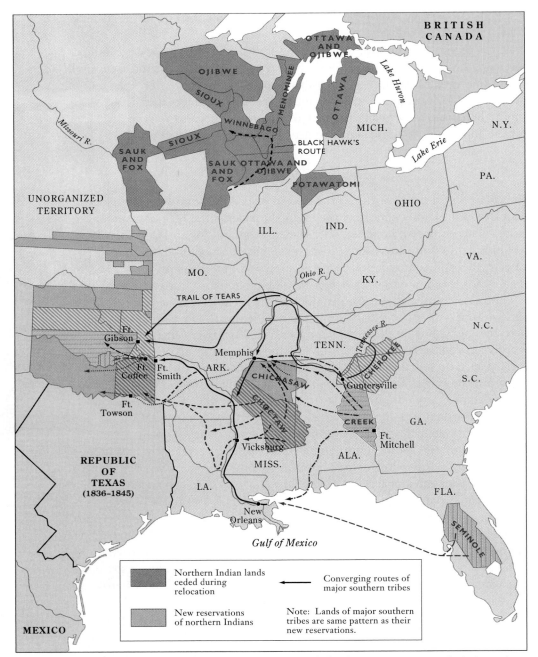

INDIAN REMOVAL   During Jackson's presidency, the federal government concluded nearly 70 treaties with Indians tribes in the Old Northwest as well as in the South. Under their terms, the United States acquired approximately 100 million acres of Indian land.

But the Cherokees brought suit in federal court against Georgia's actions. In 1832 in the case of *Worcester v. Georgia*, the Supreme Court, in an opinion written by Chief Justice John Marshall, ruled that Georgia had no right to extend its laws over Cherokee territory. Pronouncing Marshall's decision "stillborn," Jackson ignored the Court's edict and went ahead with plans for removal.

Cherokees fight removal

Although Jackson assured Indians that they could be removed only voluntarily, he paid no heed when state governments harassed tribes into surrendering lands. Under the threat of coercion, the Choctaws, Chickasaws, and Creeks reluctantly agreed to move to tracts in present-day Oklahoma. In the process, land-hungry schemers cheated tribal members out of as much as 90 percent of their land allotments.

The Cherokees held out longest, but to no avail. In order to deal with more pliant leaders of the tribe, Georgia authorities kidnapped Chief John Ross, who had led the resistance to relocation, and threw him into jail. Ross was finally released but not allowed to negotiate the treaty, which stipulated that the Cherokees leave their lands no later than 1838. When that time came, most refused to go. In response, President Martin Van Buren had the U.S. Army round up resistant members and force them, at bayonet point, to join the westward march. Of the 15,000 who traveled this Trail of Tears, approximately one-quarter died along the way of exposure, disease, and exhaustion.

Removal of the Cherokees

Some Indians chose resistance. In the Old Northwest a group of the Sauk and Fox led by Black Hawk recrossed the Mississippi into Illinois in 1832 and were crushed by federal troops and the militia. More successful was the resistance of a minority of Seminoles under the leadership of Osceola. Despite his death, they held out until 1842 in the Everglades of Florida before being subdued and removed. In the end, only a small number of southern tribe members were able to escape removal.

In his farewell address in 1837, Jackson defended his policy by piously asserting that the eastern tribes had been finally "placed beyond the reach of injury or oppression, and that [the] paternal care of the General Government will hereafter watch over them and protect them." Indians, however, knew the bitter truth of the matter. Without effective political power, they found themselves at the mercy of the pressures of the marketplace and the hardening racial attitudes of white Americans.

Free Blacks in the North

Unlike Indian removal, the rising discrimination against free African Americans did not depend directly on presidential action. Still, it was Jackson's Democratic party, which was in the vanguard of promoting white equality, that was also the most strongly proslavery and the most hostile to black rights. The intensifying racism that accompanied the emergence of democracy in American life bore down with particular force on free African Americans. "The policy and power of the national and state governments are against them," commented one northerner. "The popular feeling is against them—the interests of our citizens are against them. Their prospects . . . are dreary, and comfortless."

In the years before the Civil War, the free states never had a large free black population. Only about 171,000 lived in the North in 1840, about a quarter of whom were mulattoes. Although free African Americans made up less than 2 percent of the North's population, most states enacted laws to keep them in an inferior position. (For a discussion of free African Americans in the South, see Chapter 13.)

Most black northerners lacked any meaningful political rights. Black men could vote on equal terms with whites in only five New England states. New York imposed a property requirement only on black voters, which disfranchised the vast majority of African American males. Moreover, in New Jersey, Pennsylvania, and Connecticut, African American men lost the right to vote after having previously enjoyed that privilege.

Discrimination against free blacks

Blacks in the North were also denied basic civil rights that whites enjoyed. Five states forbade them to testify against whites, and either law or custom kept African Americans from juries everywhere except in Massachusetts. In addition, several western states passed black exclusion laws prohibiting free African Americans from immigrating into the state. These laws were seldom enforced, but they were available to harass the free black population.

Segregation, or the physical separation of the races, was widely practiced in the free states. African Americans were excluded from public transportation or assigned to special, separate sections. Throughout the North they could not go into most hotels and restaurants, and if permitted to enter theaters and lecture halls, they sat in the corners and balconies. In white churches, they sat in separate pews and took communion after white members. In virtually every community, black children were excluded from the public schools or forced to attend overcrowded and poorly funded separate schools. Commented one English visitor: "We see, in effect, two nations—one white and another black—growing up together . . . but never mingling on a principle of equality."

Discrimination pushed African American males into the lowest paying and most unskilled jobs: servants, sailors, waiters, and common laborers. African American women normally continued working after marriage, mostly as servants, cooks, laundresses, and seamstresses, since their wages were critical to the family's survival. Blacks were willing strikebreakers, because white workers, fearing economic competition and loss of status, were overtly hostile and excluded them from trade unions. A number of antiblack riots erupted in northern cities during these years. Driven into abject poverty, free blacks in the North suffered from inadequate diet, were more susceptible to disease, and in 1850 had a life expectancy 8 to 10 years less than that of whites.

Black poverty

"None but those who experience it can know what it is—this constant, galling sense of cruel injustice and wrong," grieved Charlotte Forten, a free African American from Philadelphia.

The African American Community

African Americans responded to this oppression by founding self-help societies, and the black community centered on institutions such as black churches, schools, and mutual aid societies. They also agitated against slavery in the South and for equal rights in the North. After 1840 black frustration generated a nationalist movement that emphasized racial unity, self-help, and for some, renewal of ties with Africa.

Because of limited economic opportunity, the African American community was not as diversified as white society in terms of occupation and wealth. There were distinctions, nevertheless, that rested on wealth and skin color. In general, mulattoes (lighter-skinned blacks) had greater opportunity to become more literate and skilled, were better off economically, and were more likely to be community leaders. Mulattoes' feelings of superiority were reflected in marriage choices, as they usually shunned darker-skinned blacks.

The Minstrel Show

Originating in the 1830s and 1840s and playing to packed houses in cities and towns throughout the nation, the minstrel show became the most popular form of entertainment in Jacksonian America. Featuring white actors performing in blackface, these shows revealed the deep racism embedded in American society. They dealt in the broadest of racial stereotypes, ridiculing blacks as physically different and portraying them as buffoons.

Although popular across the country, minstrelsy found its primary audience in northern cities. Its basic message was that African Americans could not cope with freedom and therefore did not belong in the

Appeal of minstrelsy

This sawyer working in New York City evidences the dignity free blacks maintained in the face of unrelenting hostility and discrimination.

North. Slaves were portrayed as happy and contented, whereas free blacks were caricatured either as strutting dandies or as helpless ignoramuses. Drawing its patrons from workers, Irish immigrants, and the poorer elements in society, minstrelsy assured these white champions of democracy that they remained superior.

The unsettling economic, social, and political changes of the Jacksonian era heightened white Americans' fear of failure, which stimulated racism. The popular yet unrealistic expectation was that any white man might become rich. Yet in fact, 20 percent or more of white adult males of this era never accumulated any property. Their lack of success prompted them to relieve personal tensions through increased hostility to their black neighbors. The power of racism in Jacksonian America stemmed at least in part from the fact that equality remained part of the nation's creed while it steadily receded as a social reality.

Deepening racism

THE NULLIFICATION CRISIS

Indian removal and antiblack discrimination provided one answer to the question of who would be given equality of opportunity in America's new democratic society: Indians and African Americans would not. The issue of nullification raised a different, equally pressing question. As the North, South, and West increasingly specialized economically in response to the market revolution, how would various regions or interest groups accommodate their differences?

The Growing Crisis in South Carolina

South Carolina had been particularly hard hit by the depression of 1819. When prosperity returned to the rest of the nation, many of the state's cotton planters remained economically depressed. With lands exhausted from years of cultivation, they could not compete with the fabulous yields of frontier planters in Alabama and Mississippi.

Under these difficult conditions, South Carolinians increasingly blamed federal tariffs for their miseries. When Congress raised the duty rates in 1824, they assailed the tariff as an unfair tax that raised the prices of goods they imported while it benefited other regions of the nation. Other southern states opposed the 1824 tariff as well, though none so vehemently as South Carolina.

The one southern state in which black inhabitants outnumbered whites, South Carolina had also been growing more sensitive about the institution of slavery. In 1822 Denmark Vesey, a daring and resourceful free black carpenter in Charleston, secretly organized a plan to seize control of the city and raise the standard of black liberty. At the last moment, white officials thwarted the conspiracy and executed Vesey and his chief lieutenants; nevertheless, white South Carolinians were convinced that other conspirators still lurked

Denmark Vesey's conspiracy

in their midst. As an additional measure of security, they began to push for stronger constitutional protection of slavery. After all, the constitutional doctrine of broad construction and implied powers had already been employed to justify higher protective tariffs. What was to prevent it from being used to end slavery? "In contending against the tariff, I have always felt that we were combatting against the symptom instead of the disease," argued Chancellor William Harper of South Carolina. "Tomorrow may witness [an attempt] to relieve . . . your slaves."

When Congress, over the protests of the state's representatives, raised the duty rates still higher in 1828 with the so-called Tariff of Abominations, South Carolina's legislature published the *South Carolina Exposition and Protest*, which outlined for the first time the theory of nullification. Only later was it revealed that its author was Jackson's own vice president, John C. Calhoun.

Calhoun's Theory of Nullification

Educated at Yale and a distinguished law school, Calhoun was the most impressive intellect of his political generation. During the 1820s the South Carolina leader made a slow but steady journey away from nationalism toward an extreme states' rights position. When he was elected Jackson's vice president, South Carolinians assumed that tariff reform would be quickly forthcoming. But Jackson and Calhoun soon quarreled, and Calhoun lost all influence in the administration.

In his theory of nullification, Calhoun argued that the Union was a compact between sovereign states. Thus the people of each state, acting in special conventions, had the right to nullify any federal law that exceeded the powers granted to Congress under the Constitution. The law would then become null and void in that state. In response, Congress could either repeal the law or propose a constitutional amendment expressly giving it the power in question. If the amendment was ratified, the nullifying state could either accept the decision or exercise its ultimate right as a sovereign state and secede from the Union.

> The Union as a compact between sovereign states

In 1831, after Senator Robert Hayne of South Carolina outlined Calhoun's theory, Senator Daniel Webster of Massachusetts replied sharply that the Union was not a compact of sovereign states. The people, and not the states, he argued, had created the Constitution. Webster also insisted that the federal government did not merely act as the agent of the states but had sovereign powers in those areas where it had been delegated responsibility. Finally, Webster endorsed the doctrine of judicial review, which gave the Supreme Court authority to determine the meaning of the Constitution.

The Nullifiers Nullified

When Congress passed another tariff in 1832 that failed to give the state any relief, South Carolina's legislature called for the election of delegates to a popular convention, which overwhelmingly adopted an ordinance in November that

This northern cartoon of 1833 portrays South Carolina's Senator John Calhoun, seeking a crown of despotism, as headed on a course that ascends from nullification toward civil war and disunion. Jackson (right) warns Calhoun and his supporters that hanging awaits them if they persist, while the figure representing the Constitution lies mortally wounded at the base of the pyramid.

declared the tariffs of 1828 and 1832 "null, void, and no law, nor binding upon this state, its officers or citizens" after February 1, 1833.

Jackson, who had spent much of his life defending the nation, was not about to tolerate any defiance of his authority or the federal government's. In his Proclamation on Nullification, issued in December 1832, he insisted that the Union was perpetual and that under the Constitution, no state had the right to secede. To reinforce his announced determination to enforce the tariff laws, Congress passed the Force Bill, reaffirming the president's military powers.

Idea of a perpetual Union

Yet Jackson was also a skillful politician. At the same time that he threatened South Carolina, he urged Congress to reduce the tariff rates. With no other state willing to follow South Carolina's lead, Calhoun reluctantly joined forces with Henry Clay to work out a compromise tariff in 1833. South Carolina's convention repealed the nullifying ordinance, and the crisis came to an end.

`Compromise of 1833`

Whatever its virtues as a theory, Calhoun's doctrine had proved too radical for the rest of the South. Even so, the controversy convinced many southerners that they were becoming a permanent minority. "We are divided into slave-holding and non-slaveholding states," concluded nullifier William Harper, "and this is the broad and marked distinction that must separate us at last." As that feeling of isolation grew, it was not nullification but the threat of secession that ultimately became the South's primary weapon.

THE BANK WAR

Jackson understood well the political ties that bound the nation. He grasped much less firmly the economic and financial connections that linked regions of the country through banks and national markets. His clash with the Second Bank of the United States led to the greatest crisis of his presidency.

The National Bank and the Panic of 1819

Chartered by Congress in 1816 for a 20-year period, the Second Bank of the United States initially suffered from woeful mismanagement. At first it helped fuel the speculative pressures in the economy. Then it turned about-face and sharply contracted credit by calling in loans when the depression hit in 1819. Critics viewed the Bank's policies not as a consequence but as the cause of the financial downswing. To many Americans, the Bank had already become a monster.

`Monster Bank`

The psychological effects of the Panic of 1819 were almost as momentous as the economic. The shock of the depression made the 1820s a time of soul-searching, during which many uneasy farmers and workers came to view the hard times as punishment for having lost sight of the old virtues of simplicity, frugality, and hard work. For these Americans, banks were a symbol of the commercialization of American society and the rapid passing of a simpler way of life.

Biddle's Bank

In 1823 Nicholas Biddle, a rich 37-year-old Philadelphia businessman, became president of the national bank. Biddle was intelligent and thoroughly familiar with the banking system, but he was also impossibly arrogant and politically unastute.

He set out to use the bank to regulate the amount of credit available in the economy, and thereby provide the nation with a sound currency.

The government regularly deposited its revenues in the national bank. These revenues were paid largely in bank notes (paper money) issued by state-chartered banks. If Biddle believed that a state bank had issued more notes than was safe, he presented them to that bank and demanded they be redeemed in specie (gold or silver). Because banks did not have enough specie reserves to back all the paper money they issued, the only way a state bank could continue to redeem its notes was to call in its loans and reduce the amount of its notes in circulation. This action had the effect of lessening the amount of credit in the economy. On the other hand, if Biddle felt that a bank's credit policies were reasonable, he simply returned the state bank notes to circulation without presenting them for redemption.

Central bank's regulation of the economy

Under Biddle's direction the Bank became a financial colossus with enormous power over state banks and over the economy. Yet Biddle used this power responsibly to provide the United States a sound paper currency, which the expanding economy needed.

Although the Bank had strong support in the business community, workers complained that they were often paid in depreciated state bank notes that could be redeemed only for a portion of their face value, a practice that cheated them of their full wages. They called for a "hard money" currency of only gold and silver. Hard money advocates viewed bankers and financiers as profiteers who manipulated the paper money system to enrich themselves at the expense of honest, hard-working farmers and laborers.

Hostility to the Second Bank

The Bank Destroyed

Jackson's own experiences left him with a deep distrust of banks and paper money. In 1804 his Tennessee land speculations had brought him to the brink of bankruptcy, from which it took years of painful struggle to free himself. Reflecting on his personal situation, he became convinced that banks and paper money threatened to corrupt the Republic.

As president, Jackson periodically called for reform of the banking system, but Biddle refused even to consider curbing the Bank's powers. Already distracted by the nullification controversy, Jackson warned Biddle not to inject the bank issue into the 1832 campaign. When Biddle went ahead and applied for a renewal of the Bank's charter in 1832, four years early, Jackson was furious. "The Bank is trying to kill me," he stormed to Van Buren, "*but I will kill it.*"

Despite the president's opposition, Congress passed a recharter bill in the summer of 1832. Immediately Jackson vetoed it as unconstitutional (rejecting Marshall's earlier ruling in *McCulloch v. Maryland*). Condemning the Bank as an agent of special privilege, the president pledged to protect "the humble members of society—the farmer, mechanics, and laborers" against "the advancement of the few at the expense of the many."

Jackson's veto

When Congress failed to override Jackson's veto, the Bank became a central issue of the 1832 campaign. Jackson's opponent was Henry Clay, a National Republican who eagerly accepted the financial support of Biddle and his bank. Clay went down to defeat, and once reelected, Jackson was determined to destroy the Bank. He believed that as a private corporation the Bank wielded a dangerous influence over government policy and the economy, and he was justly incensed over its interference in the election.

To cripple the Bank, the president simply ordered all the government's federal deposits withdrawn. Since such an act clearly violated federal law, Jackson was forced to transfer one secretary of the treasury and fire another before he finally found an ally, Roger Taney, willing to take the job and carry out the edict. Taney (pronounced "Taw-ney") gradually withdrew the government's funds while depositing new revenues in selected state banks.

Removal of the deposits

Biddle fought back by deliberately precipitating a brief financial panic in 1833, but Jackson refused to budge. "Go to Biddle," the president raged to a group of businesspeople who came seeking relief. "I will never restore the deposits." Eventually Biddle had to relent, and Jackson's victory was complete. When the Bank's charter expired in 1836, no national banking system replaced it.

Jackson's Impact on the Presidency

Jackson approached the end of his administration in triumph. Indian removal was well on its way to completion, the nullifiers had been confounded, and the "Monster Bank" had been destroyed. In the process, Jackson immeasurably enlarged the power of the presidency. "The President is the direct representative of the American people," he lectured the Senate when it opposed him. "He was elected by the people, and is responsible to them." With this declaration, Jackson redefined the character of the presidential office and its relationship to the people.

Presidential power strengthened

Jackson also converted the veto into an effective presidential power. During his two terms in office, he vetoed 12 bills, compared with only 9 for all previous presidents combined. Moreover, where his predecessors had vetoed bills only on strict constitutional grounds, Jackson felt free to block laws simply because he thought them bad policy. The threat of such action became an effective way to shape pending legislation to his liking, which fundamentally strengthened the power of the president over Congress. The development of the modern presidency began with Andrew Jackson.

VAN BUREN AND DEPRESSION

With the controls of the national bank removed, state banks rapidly expanded their activities, including the printing of more money. As the currency expanded, so did the number of banks: from 329 in 1829 to 788 in 1837. A spiraling inflation set in, as prices rose 50 percent after 1830 and interest rates by half as much.

As prices soared, so did speculative fever. By 1836 land sales, which had been only $2.6 million four years earlier, approached $25 million. Almost all these lands were bought entirely on credit with bank notes. In July 1836 Jackson issued the Specie Circular, which decreed that the government would accept only specie for the purchase of public land. Land sales drastically declined, but the speculative pressures in the economy were by now too great to be reversed.

Specie Circular

"Van Ruin's" Depression

During Jackson's second term, his opponents had gradually come together in a new party, the Whigs. Led by Henry Clay, they charged that "King Andrew I" had dangerously concentrated power in the presidency. The Whigs also embraced Clay's "American System," designed to spur national economic development through a protective tariff, a national bank, and federal aid for internal improvements. In 1836 the Democrats nominated Martin Van Buren, who triumphed over three Whig sectional candidates.

Van Buren had less than two months in office to savor his triumph before the speculative mania collapsed, and with it the economy. After a brief recovery, the bottom fell out of the international cotton market in 1839 and the country entered a serious depression. It was not until 1843 that the economy revived.

Panic of 1837

Public opinion identified hard times with the policies of the Democratic party. Since he continued to oppose a new national bank, Van Buren instead persuaded Congress in 1840 to create an Independent Treasury to hold the government's funds. Its offices were forbidden to accept paper currency, issue any bank notes, or make any loans. The government's money would be safe, as Van Buren intended, but it would also remain unavailable to banks to make loans and stimulate the economy. Whigs, on the other hand, hoped to encourage manufacturing and revive the economy by passing a protective tariff, continuing state internal improvement projects, protecting corporations, and expanding the banking and credit system.

Independent Treasury

As the depression deepened, thousands of workers were unemployed and countless businesses failed. Nationally, wages fell 30 to 50 percent. "Business of all kinds is completely at a stand," wrote New York business and civic leader Philip Hone in 1840, "and the whole body politic sick and infirm, and calling aloud for a remedy."

The Whigs' Triumph

For the 1840 presidential campaign the Whigs turned to William Henry Harrison, who had defeated the Shawnee Indians at Tippecanoe, to oppose Van Buren. In the midst of the worst depression of the century, Whigs employed the democratic electioneering techniques that Jackson's sup-

First modern presidential campaign

This Whig cartoon blames the Democratic party for the depression that began during Van Buren's administration. Barefoot workers go unemployed, and women and children beg and sleep in the streets. Depositors clamor for their money from a bank that has suspended specie payments, while the pawnbroker and liquor store do a thriving business and the sheriff rounds up debtors.

porters had perfected. They hailed Harrison as a man of the people while painting Van Buren as a dandy and an aristocrat who wore a corset, ate off gold plates with silver spoons, and used cologne. Whig rallies featured hard cider and log cabins to reinforce Harrison's image as a man of the people. Ironically, Harrison had been born into one of Virginia's most aristocratic families and was living in a 16-room mansion in Ohio. But the Whig campaign, by casting the election as a contest between aristocracy and democracy, was perfectly attuned to the prevailing national spirit.

In the campaign of 1840, Whigs for the first time also prominently involved women, urging them to become politically informed in order to morally instruct their husbands. Women attended Whig rallies, conducted meetings, made speeches, and wrote campaign pamphlets, activities previously performed solely by men. "I never took so much interest in politics in my life," Mary Steger of Richmond confessed to a friend. Democrats were uneasy about this innovation, yet had no choice but to follow suit. Within a few years the presence of women at party rallies was commonplace.

Women take a new political role

The election produced a record turnout, with nearly four-fifths of the eligible voters going to the polls. Although the popular vote was fairly close (Harrison led by about 150,000 votes out of 2.4 million cast), in the Electoral College he won an easy victory, 234 to 60.

The "log cabin" campaign marked the final transition from the deferential politics of the Federalist era to the egalitarian politics that had emerged in the wake of the Panic of 1819. As the *Democratic Review* conceded after the Whigs' victory in 1840, "We have taught them how to conquer us."

THE JACKSONIAN PARTY SYSTEM

It is easy, given the hoopla of democratic campaigning, to be distracted from the central fact that the new political system was directly shaped by the social and economic strains of an expanding nation. Whigs and Democrats held different attitudes toward the changes brought about by the market, banks, and commerce.

Democrats, Whigs, and the Market

The Democrats tended to view society as a continuing conflict between "the people"—farmers, planters, and workers—and a set of greedy aristocrats. This "paper money aristocracy" of bankers, stock jobbers, and investors manipulated the banking system for their own profit, Democrats claimed, and sapped the nation's virtue by encouraging speculation and the desire for sudden, unearned wealth. For Democrats, the Bank War became a battle to restore the old Jeffersonian Republic with its values of simplicity, frugality, hard work, and independence. This is what Jackson meant when he said that removal of the deposits from Biddle's Bank would "preserve the morals of the people."

Democratic ideology

Jackson understood the dangers private banks posed to a democratic society. Yet Democrats, in effect, wanted the rewards and goods that the market offered without sacrificing the features of a simple agrarian republic. They wanted the wealth that the market produced without the competitive society, the complex dealings, the dominance of urban centers, and the loss of independence that came with it.

Whigs, on the other hand, were more comfortable with the market. For them, commerce and economic development were agents of civilization. Nor did they envision any conflict in society between farmers and mechanics on the one hand and businesspeople and bankers on the other. The government's responsibility was to provide a well-regulated economy that guaranteed opportunity for citizens of ability. In such an economy, banks and corporations were not only useful but necessary. A North Carolina Whig well expressed the party's vision of society: "All should be mutual friends and helpers to each other, and who ever aids and assists his fellow men from good motives, by lending money, by affording employment by precept or example, is a benefactor to his fellow men."

Whig ideology

Whigs and Democrats differed not only in their attitudes toward the market but also about how active government should be. Despite Andrew Jackson's inclination to be a strong president, Democrats as a rule believed in limited government. Government's role in the economy was to promote competition by de-

stroying monopolies and special privileges. As one New Jersey Democratic newspaper declared, "All Bank charters, all laws conferring special privileges, with all acts of incorporation, for purposes of private
gain, are monopolies, in as much as they are calculated to enhance the
power of wealth, produce inequalities among the people and to subvert liberty."

> Democrats' belief in limited government

In keeping with this philosophy of limited government, Democrats also rejected the idea that moral beliefs were the proper sphere of government action.
Religion and politics, they believed, should be kept clearly separate, and they generally opposed humanitarian legislation.

The Whigs, in contrast, viewed government power positively. They believed
that it should be used to protect individual rights and public liberty, and that it had
a special role where individual effort was ineffective. By regulating the economy
and competition, the government could ensure equal opportunity. Indeed, for Whigs the concept of government promoting the general
welfare went beyond the economy. Northern Whigs in particular also
believed that government power should be used to foster the moral

> Whigs' belief in active government

welfare of the country. They were much more likely to favor temperance or antislavery legislation and aid to education. Whigs portrayed themselves not only as
the party of prosperity, but also as the party of respectability and proper behavior.

The Social Bases of the Two Parties

In some ways the social makeup of the two parties was similar. To be competitive,
Whigs and Democrats both had to have significant support among farmers, the
largest group in society, and workers. Neither party could carry an election by appealing exclusively to the rich or the poor.

The Whigs, however, found more support among the business and commercial
classes, especially after the Bank War. Whigs appealed to planters who needed credit
to finance their cotton and rice trade in the world market, to farmers eager to sell
their surpluses, and to workers who wished to rise in society. Democrats attracted
farmers isolated from the market or uncomfortable with it, workers alienated from
the emerging industrial system, and rising entrepreneurs who wanted to break monopolies and open the economy to newcomers like themselves. The Whigs were
strongest in the towns, cities, and rural areas that were fully integrated into the market economy, whereas Democrats dominated areas of semisubsistence farming that
were more isolated and languishing economically. Attitude toward the market, rather
than economic position, was more important in determining party affiliation.

The Triumph of the Market

Jacksonian politics evolved out of the social and economic dislocation produced by
rapidly expanding economic opportunity. Yet efforts to avoid the costs of the market
while preserving its benefits were doomed to fail. In states where the Democrats eliminated all banks, so much hardship and financial chaos ensued that some system of

banking was soon restored. The expansion of the economy after 1815 had caught farmers as well as urban residents in an international network of trade and finance, tying them to the price of cotton in Liverpool or the interest rates of the Bank of England. There was no rolling back the market in a return to the ideals of Crèvecoeur.

The new national parties—like the new markets spreading across the nation—had become essential structures uniting the American nation. They advanced an ideology of equality and opportunity, which stood as a goal for the nation even though women, African Americans, and Indians were excluded. The new politics developed a system of truly national parties, competing with one another, involving large numbers of ordinary Americans, resolving differences through compromise and negotiation. Along with the market, democracy had become an integral part of American life.

chapter summary

Beginning in the 1820s, the United States experienced a democratic revolution that was identified with Andrew Jackson.

- The rise of democracy was stimulated by the Panic of 1819, which caused Americans to look toward both politicians and the government to address their needs.

- The new political culture of democracy included the use of conventions to make nominations, the celebration of the wisdom of the people, the adoption of white manhood suffrage, and the acceptance of political parties as essential for the working of the constitutional system.

- The new politics had distinct limits, however. Women were not given the vote, and racism intensified.
  - The eastern Indian tribes were forced to move to new lands west of the Mississippi River.
  - Free African Americans found themselves subject to increasingly harsh discrimination and exclusion.

- In politics, Andrew Jackson came to personify the new democratic culture. Through his forceful leadership, he significantly expanded the powers of the presidency.

- Jackson threatened to use force against South Carolina when it tried to nullify the federal tariff using John C. Calhoun's theory of nullification—that is, that a state convention could nullify a federal law.
- In response, nationalists advanced the idea of the perpetual Union. The compromise of 1833, which gradually lowered the tariff, ended the crisis.
- Jackson vetoed a bill to recharter the Second Bank of the United States and destroyed the Bank by removing its federal deposits.
- Under President Martin Van Buren, the nation entered a severe depression.

- Capitalizing on hard times and employing the democratic techniques pioneered by the Democrats, the Whigs gained national power in 1840.

- By 1840 the two parties had developed different ideologies.
  - The Whigs were more comfortable with the mechanisms of the market and linked commerce with progress.
  - The Democrats were uneasy about the market and favored limited government.

For quizzes and a variety of interactive resources, visit the book's Online Learning Center at www.mhhe.com/davidsonconcise3

SIGNIFICANT EVENTS

1819–1823	Panic and depression
1822	Denmark Vesey conspiracy
1823	Biddle becomes president of the Bank of the United States
1824	Tariff duties raised; Jackson finishes first in presidential race
1825	House elects John Quincy Adams president
1827	Cherokees adopt written constitution
1828	Tariff of Abominations passed; *South Carolina Exposition and Protest* issued; Jackson elected president
1830	Webster-Hayne debate; Indian Removal Act approved
1830–1838	Indian removal
1832	*Worcester v. Georgia*; Jackson vetoes recharter of the national bank; Jackson reelected; South Carolina nullifies tariff; Jackson issues Proclamation on Nullification
1833	Force Bill approved; tariff duties reduced; Jackson removes deposits from the Bank of the United States
1833–1834	Biddle's panic
1834	Whig party organized
1835–1842	Second Seminole war
1836	Specie Circular; Van Buren elected president
1837	Panic
1838	Trail of Tears
1839–1843	Depression
1840	Independent Treasury Act; Harrison elected president
1842	First professional minstrel troupe

CHAPTER 12

The Fires of Perfection
(1820–1850)

preview • The Second Great Awakening unleashed a cascade of reform during the 1820s and 1830s. Middle-class women were prominent in these campaigns, reflecting the profound changes in their social roles wrought by the market economy. Some reformers withdrew from everyday life to create utopian communities; others sought humanitarian reforms such as temperance, educational improvement, women's right and—most disruptive to the political system—the abolition of slavery.

In 1826 the Reverend Lyman Beecher was probably the most celebrated minister of the Republic, and the pulpit of Hanover Street Church was his to command. Beecher looked and spoke like a pious farmer, but every Sunday he was transformed when he mounted the pulpit of Boston's most imposing church. From there, he would blaze forth denunciations of dancing, drinking, dueling, or "infidelity," all the while punctuating his sermon with pump-handle strokes of the right hand.

Nor were Beecher's ambitions small. His goal was nothing less than to bring the kingdom of Christ to the nation and the world. Like many ministers, Beecher had studied the intriguing final book of the New Testament, the Revelation to John. The Revelation foretold in the latter days of the Earth a glorious millennium—a thousand years of peace and triumph—when the saints would rule and evil would be banished from the world. Beecher was convinced that the long-awaited millennium might well begin in the United States.

Prophecies of the millennium

Personal experience reinforced this optimism. Born to a sturdy line of New England blacksmiths in 1775, Beecher entered Yale College during the high tide of postwar nationalism—and, some said, the lowest ebb of religion among young people. In the revivals of the Second Great Awakening that came to many colleges in 1802, Beecher had been one of those converted.

But he was hardly a stodgy Puritan. Much of Beecher's boundless energy went into raising a family of 11 children, every one of whom he prayed would take leading roles in bringing the kingdom of God to America. He loved to wrestle on the floor with his sons or go "berrying" with his daughters. Still, the religious dimension of their lives was constant. The family attended two services on Sunday, a weekly prayer meeting, and a monthly "concert of prayer," where the devout met

Lyman Beecher (center) with his family in 1855. Five of his six sons, all of whom were ministers, stand in back. In front, daughters Catharine (holding his arm to steady it for the long exposure) and Isabella are on the left; Harriet, the author of *Uncle Tom's Cabin*, is at the far right.

to pray for the conversion of the world. Beecher's son Thomas remembered his father commanding: "Overturn and overturn till He whose right it is shall come and reign, King of nations and King of saints."

To usher in the kingdom of God entire communities and even nations would have to be swept with a divine fire. Toward that end Beecher joined other Protestant ministers in supporting a host of religious reforms and missionary organizations. Such benevolent associations distributed Bibles, promoted Sunday Schools, and ministered to the poor. Beecher also directed his righteous artillery on a host of evils that seemed to be obstructing God's kingdom. With scorn he attacked elite Unitarians, whose liberal, rational creed rejected the divinity of Jesus. But he also condemned what he viewed as sinful pastimes of the lower class: playing cards, gambling, and drinking. And he denounced Roman Catholic priests and nuns as superstitious, devious agents of "Antichrist."

Benevolent associations

Beecher's efforts at "moral reform" antagonized many immigrants and other working people who enjoyed liquor or lotteries. Thus when a blaze broke out in the basement of his church in 1830, unsympathetic local firefighters stood by while the splendid structure burned to the ground. The fires of spiritual reform had been halted, temporarily, by a blaze of a literal sort.

Any fire, real or spiritual, is unpredictable as it spreads from one scrap of tinder to the next. That proved to be the case with reform movements of the 1820s and 1830s, as they moved in diverging, sometimes contradictory ways.

Differing goals of reformers What did it mean, after all, to bring in Christ's kingdom? The goals of the early reform societies were moral rather than social. Leaders like Beecher sought to convert individuals and to church the unchurched with the help of religious revivals and benevolent associations. Their conservative aim, as he expressed it, was to restore America to "the moral government of God."

Other Christians, however, began to focus on social issues like slavery, the inequality of women, and the operation of prisons. To these problems they demanded more radical solutions. Ironically, many of Beecher's children went well beyond his more conservative strategies for hastening the millennium. They spoke out for abolition, women's rights, and education in ways that left their father distinctly uncomfortable. In their activities the Beechers reflected the diversity of the reform impulse itself.

REVIVALISM AND THE SOCIAL ORDER

Society during the Jacksonian era was undergoing deep and rapid change. The revolution in markets brought both economic expansion and periodic depressions, and in the ensuing uncertainty some reformers sought stability and moral order in the religious community. The bonds of unity created by a revival brought a sense of peace in the midst of a society in change. Revivals could reinforce strength and discipline, too, in an emerging industrial culture that demanded sobriety and regular working habits.

Other reformers, however, sought to check the excesses of Jacksonian America by radically remaking institutions or devising utopian, experimental ways of living and working together. The drive for renewal, in other words, led reformers sometimes to preserve social institutions, other times to overturn them. It led them sometimes to liberate, other times to control. And the conflicting ways in which these dynamics operated could be seen in the electric career of Charles Grandison Finney.

Finney's New Measures and New Theology

As a young man, Finney experienced a soul-shattering conversion in 1821 that led him to give up his law practice to become an itinerant minister. Between the mid-1820s and the early 1830s he conducted a series of spectacular revivals in the booming port cities along the new Erie Canal.

Like George Whitefield before him, Finney had an entrancing voice that carried great distances. His success, however, resulted as much from his use of special techniques—"the new measures." Finney held "protracted meetings" night after night to build excitement. Speaking bluntly, he prayed for sinners by name, encouraged women to testify in public gatherings, and placed those struggling with conversion on the "anxious bench" at the front of the church. Such techniques all heightened the emotions of the conversion process. The cries of agonized prayers, groans, and uncontrolled crying often resounded through the hall.

Protracted meetings and the anxious bench

Finney's new measures had actually been used during the frontier revivals of the Second Great Awakening (page 233). His contribution was to popularize the techniques and use them systematically. "A revival is not a miracle," he coolly declared, "it is a purely scientific result of the right use of constituted means."

Finney also rejected many religious doctrines of Calvinism, including predestination, which maintained that God had already determined which individuals were destined to be saved or damned, and no human effort could change this decision. But by the 1820s such a proposition seemed unreasonable to citizens of a democratic republic. Leaving the Lord little role in the drama of human deliverance, Finney embraced the doctrine of free will. All men and women who wanted to could be saved. To those anxious about their salvation, he thundered, "Do it!"

Free will and perfectionism

With salvation within reach of every individual, what might be in store for society at large? "If the church would do her duty," Finney confidently predicted, "the millennium may come in this country in three years." By the 1830s Finney had taken to preaching not merely faith in human progress but something more—human perfectibility. Embracing this new theology of "perfectionism," he boldly asserted that all Christians should "aim at being holy and not rest satisfied until they are as perfect as God." And a true Christian would not rest until society was made perfect as well.

By preaching an optimistic message of free will and salvation to all, Finney and his eager imitators transformed Protestantism. But not all clergy applauded. For Lyman Beecher, as well as many supporters of the Second Great Awakening, Finney's new measures went too far, while his theology of perfectionism verged on heresy. Undaunted by such criticism, Finney continued his revivals. As for Lyman Beecher, in 1832 he accepted the presidency of Lane Seminary in Cincinnati. By moving to the West, he planned to train the right sort of revivalists to bring about the kingdom of God in America.

Religion and the Market Economy

Revival audiences responded to the call for reform partly because they were unsettled by the era's rapid social changes. In the North, evangelical religion proved strongest not in isolated backwaters but in frontier areas just entering the market economy. Rochester, New York, a booming flour-milling center on the Erie Canal, epitomized that social environment.

When Charles Finney came to town in the winter of 1830–1831, Rochester was a community in crisis. It had grown in a decade and a half from a village of

The Slave Mortimer Describes His Conversion Experience

One day while in the field plowing I heard a voice. . . . Again the voice called, "Morte! Morte!" With this I stopped, dropped the plow, and started running, but the voice kept on speaking to me saying, "Fear not, my little one, for behold! I come to bring you a message of truth."

Everything got dark, and I was unable to stand any longer. I began to feel sick, and there was a great roaring. I tried to cry and move but I was unable to do either. I looked up and saw that I was in a new world. There were plants and animals, and all, even the water where I stopped down to drink, began to cry out, "I am blessed but you are damned! I am blessed but you are damned!" With this I began to pray, and a voice on the inside began to cry, "Mercy! Mercy! Mercy!"

. . . I again prayed, and there came a soft voice saying, "My little one, I have loved you with an everlasting love. You are this day made alive and freed from hell. You are a chosen vessel unto the Lord. Be upright before me, and I will guide you unto all truth. My grace is sufficient for you. Go, and I am with you. Preach the gospel, and I will preach with you. . . ."

About this time my master came down [to] the field. . . . I told him I had been talking with God Almighty . . . and suddenly I fell for shouting, and I shouted and began to preach. . . . When I had finished . . . my master looked at me and seemed to tremble. He told me to catch the horse and come on with him to the barn. . . .

I went on to the barn and found my master there waiting for me. Again I began to tell him of my experience. . . . My master sat . . . listening to me, and then began to cry. He turned from me and said in a broken voice, "Morte, I believe you are a preacher. From now on you can preach to the people here on my place in the old shed by the creek. But tomorrow morning, Sunday, I want you to preach to my family and neighbors. So put on your best clothes and be in front of the big house early in the morning about nine o'clock."

. . . The next morning at the time appointed I stood up on two planks in front of the porch of the big house and, without a Bible or anything, I began to preach to my master and the people. . . . My soul caught on fire, and soon I had them all in tears.

Source: Clifton H. Johnson, ed., *God Struck Me Dead* (Philadelphia: Pilgrim Press, 1962), pp. 15–18.

300 souls to a commercial city of more than 20,000. That wrenching expansion produced sharp divisions among the town's leaders, a large working class that increasingly lived apart from employers and beyond their moral control, and a rowdy saloon culture catering to canal boatmen and other transients. Finney preached almost daily in Rochester for six months, and assisted by local ministers, his revivals doubled church membership. Religion helped bring order to what had been a chaotic and fragmented city.

Although revivals like Finney's Rochester triumph drew converts from all segments of American society, they appealed especially to the middle class. Lawyers, merchants, retailers, and manufacturers all played central roles in the larger market economy and invested in factories and railroads. The market put intense pressure on these upwardly mobile citizens: they viewed success as a reflection of moral character, yet also feared that they would lose their wealth in the next economic downturn.

Revivalism's appeal to the middle class

Workers, too, were among the converted. Among other things, joining a church reflected a desire to get ahead in the new economy by accepting moral self-discipline. To a striking degree, social mobility and church membership were linked. In Rochester two-thirds of the male workers who were church members improved their occupational status in a decade. By contrast, workers who did not join a church rarely stayed in town more than a few years, and those who stayed were likely to decline in status.

Revivalists like Finney were interested in saving souls, not money, and their converts were most concerned with their spiritual state. Even so, evangelical Protestantism reinforced values needed to succeed in the new competitive economy. Churchgoers accepted the values of hard work and punctuality, self-control and sobriety. In that sense, religion was one means of fostering social order in a disordered society.

The Rise of African American Churches

Independent black churches grew in size and importance as well, as African Americans in urban areas increasingly resented being treated as second-class worshipers. In 1787, Richard Allen, a popular black preacher, was roughly ousted when he tried to pray in the area of a Philadelphia church reserved for whites. In 1794 he organized the Bethel Church, where African Americans would be free to worship without discrimination.

In the early nineteenth century, similar tensions led to the formation of black Methodist and Baptist churches in a number of northern and southern cities. The most important was the African Methodist Episcopal (AME) Church. Growing fears for the security of slavery caused southern white communities, especially in the Deep South, to suppress independent black churches after 1820. But these churches, which were strongly evangelical, continued to grow in the North. By 1860 the AME Church had about 20,000 members.

The Significance of the Second Great Awakening

As a result of the Second Great Awakening, the dominant form of Christianity in America became evangelical Protestantism. Membership in the major Protestant churches—Congregational, Presbyterian, Baptist, and Methodist—soared. By 1840 an estimated half of the adult population was nominally connected to some church, with the Methodists emerging as the largest Protestant denomination in both the North and the South.

Evangelicalism was in harmony with the basic values of early nineteenth-century Americans. Its emphasis on the ability of everyone to bring about his or her salvation upheld the American belief in individualism. By catering to a mass audience without social distinctions, the revivals reinforced the American belief in democracy and equality. And Finney's invincibly optimistic doctrine of perfectionism was exactly attuned to the spirit of the age.

Evangelicalism and American values

WOMEN'S SPHERE

Throughout the tumult of revivals, in the midst of benevolent association meetings, at "concerts of prayer," women played crucial roles. Indeed, during the Second Great Awakening, female converts outnumbered males by about three to two. Usually the first convert in a family was a woman, and many men who converted were related to women who had come forward earlier.

Women played such an important role in the Awakening partly because of changes in their own social universe. Instead of parents arranging the marriages of their children, couples were beginning to wed more often on the basis of affection. Under such conditions, a woman's prospects for marriage became less certain, and in older areas like New England, the migration of so many young men compounded this uncertainty. At the same time, marriage remained essential for a woman's economic security. The unpredictability of these social circumstances drew young women toward religion. Women between the ages of 12 and 25 were especially susceptible to conversion. Joining a church heightened a young woman's sense of purpose. By establishing respectability and widening her social circle of friends, it also enhanced her chances of marriage.

Revivalism and women's changing lives

The Ideal of Domesticity

The era's changing economic order brought other pressures to bear on wives and mothers. Most men now worked outside the home, while the rise of factories led to a decline in part-time work such as spinning, which women had once performed to supplement family income. Moreover, except on the frontier, home manufacturing was no longer essential, for the family purchased articles that women previously had made, such as cloth, soap, and candles.

This growing separation of the household from the workplace meant that the home took on a new social identity. It was idealized as a place of "domesticity," a haven away from the competitive, workaday world, with the mother firmly at its center. If men's sphere was the world of fac-

Separate spheres of influence

tories, offices, and fields, women's sphere was the home, where they were to dispense love and comfort and teach moral values to husbands and children. "Love is our life our reality, business yours," Mollie Clark told one suitor.

Women, who were considered morally stronger, were also held to a higher standard of sexual purity. A man's sexual infidelity, while hardly condoned, brought no lasting shame. But a woman who engaged in sexual relations before marriage or was unfaithful afterward was threatened with everlasting disgrace. Under this double standard, women were to be passive and submerge their identities in those of their husbands.

Most women of the era did not see this ideology as a rationale for male dominance. On the contrary, women played an important role in creating the ideal of domesticity, none more than Lyman Beecher's daughter Catharine. Like earlier advocates of "republican motherhood," Catharine Beecher argued that women exercised power as moral guardians of the nation. The proper care of a middle-class household was also a crucial responsibility, and Beecher wrote several books on efficient home management. "There is no one thing more necessary to a housekeeper in performing her varied duties, than a *habit of system and order*," she told readers. "For all the time afforded us, we must give account to God."

Catharine Beecher and women as moral guardians

Catharine Beecher also advocated giving women greater educational opportunities in order to become schoolteachers. Conceiving of the school as an extension of the home, she maintained that teachers, like mothers, should instill sound moral values in children. Women also exerted their moral authority through benevolent organizations, which fostered close friendships among women.

The ideal of domesticity was not unique to the United States. The middle class became increasingly important in Europe, so that after 1850 it was culturally dominant and formulated society's values. Employment opportunities expanded for women as industrialization accelerated in Europe, yet the social expectation among the middle class was that women would not be employed outside the home. This redefinition of women's roles was more sweeping in Europe because previously, middle-class women had left the task of childraising largely to hired nurses and governesses. By mid-century, these mothers devoted much more time to domestic duties, including rearing the children. Family size also declined, both in France and in England. The middle class was most numerous in England; indeed, the importance of the middle class in Britain during Queen Victoria's reign gave these ideals the label *Victorianism*.

Domesticity in Europe

Most American women hardly had time to make the ideal of domesticity the center of their lives. Farmers' wives had to work constantly, while lower-class families could not get by without the wages of female members. Still, most middle-class women tried to live up to the ideal, and many found the effort confining. "The great trial is that I have nothing to do," one complained. "Here I am with abundant leisure and capable, I believe, of accomplishing some good, and yet with no object on which to expend my energies."

Women's socially defined role as guardians of morality helps explain their prevalence among converts. Religious activity was one way that women could exert influence over society and one area where wives need not be subordinate to their husbands. For some males, women's prominence in revivals threatened a dangerous equality between the sexes. One unhappy man in Rochester complained about the effect of Finney's visit to his home: "He *stuffed* my wife with tracts, and alarmed her fears, and nothing short of meetings, night and day, could atone for the many fold sins my poor, simple spouse had committed." Then, getting to the heart of the matter, he added, "She made the miraculous discovery, that she had been 'unevenly yoked.' From this unhappy period, peace, quiet, and happiness have fled from my dwelling, never, I fear, to return."

The Middle-Class Family in Transition

As the middle-class family adapted to the pressures of competitive society by becoming a haven of moral virtue, it developed a new structure and new set of attitudes closer in spirit to the modern family. One basic change was the rise of privacy. The family was increasingly seen as a sheltered retreat from the outside world. In addition, the pressures to achieve success led middle-class young adults to delay marriage, since a husband was expected to support his wife.

Smaller family size was a result of delaying marriage as well, since wives began bearing children later. Especially among the urban middle class, women began to use birth control to space children further apart and minimize the risks of

As business affairs grew increasingly separate from the family in the nineteenth century, the middle-class home became a female domain. A woman's role as a wife and mother was to dispense love and moral guidance to her husband and her children. As this domestic scene makes clear, she was the center of the family, and in a world beset by flux, she was to be an unchanging symbol of morality.

pregnancy. These practices contributed to a decline in the birthrate, from slightly more than 7 children per family in 1800 to 5.4 in 1850—a 25 percent drop. Family size was directly related to the success ethic, since in the newer, market-oriented society children needed extended education and special training in order to succeed, and thus were a greater financial burden.

Smaller, more private families

Indeed, more parents showed greater concern about providing their children with advantages in the race for success. Middle-class families were increasingly willing to bear the additional expense of educating their sons longer, and they also frequently equalized inheritances rather than giving priority to the eldest son or favoring sons over daughters.

AMERICAN ROMANTICISM

The Unitarians in Boston had become accustomed to being attacked by evangelical ministers like Lyman Beecher. They were less prepared to be criticized by one of their own—and on their own home ground, no less. Yet that was what happened when a Unitarian minister named Ralph Waldo Emerson addressed the students of Harvard Divinity School one summer evening in July 1838.

Emerson warned his listeners that the true church seemed "to totter to its fall, almost all life extinct." Outside, nature's world was alive and vibrant: "The grass grows, the buds burst, the meadow is spotted with fire and gold in the tint of flowers." But from the pulpits of too many congregations came lifeless preaching. "In how many churches, by how many prophets, tell me," Emerson demanded, "is man made sensible that he is an infinite Soul?" Leaving the shocked audience to ponder his message, Emerson and his wife drove home beneath a night sky illuminated by the northern lights.

Emerson's Divinity School Address glowed much like that July aurora. The address lacked the searing fire of Finney's revivals. Yet it was bold in its own way, because it reflected a second major current of thought that shaped the reform movements of the era. That was the intellectual movement known as Romanticism.

Romanticism began in Europe as a reaction against the Enlightenment. The Enlightenment had placed reason at the center of human achievement; Romanticism instead emphasized the importance of emotion and intuition as sources of truth. It gloried in the unlimited potential of the individual, who might soar if freed from the restraints of institutions. In elevating inner feelings and heartfelt convictions, Romanticism reinforced the emotionalism of religious revivals. Philosophically, its influence was strongest among intellectuals who took part in the Transcendental movement and in the dramatic flowering of American literature. And like revivalism, Romanticism offered its own paths toward perfectionism.

European origins

The Transcendentalists

Above all, Romanticism produced individualists. Thus Transcendentalism is difficult to define, for its members resisted being lumped together. It blossomed in the mid-1830s, when a number of Unitarian clergy like George Ripley and Ralph Waldo Emerson resigned their pulpits, loudly protesting the church's smug, lifeless teachings. The new "Transcendentalist Club" attracted a small following among other discontented Boston intellectuals, including Margaret Fuller, Bronson Alcott, and Orestes Brownson.

Like European Romantics, American Transcendentalists emphasized feeling over reason, seeking a spiritual communion with nature. By transcend they meant to go beyond or to rise above—specifically above reason and beyond the material world. As part of creation, every human being contained a spark of divinity, Emerson avowed. Transcendentalists also shared in Romanticism's glorification of the individual. "Trust thyself. Every heart vibrates to that iron string," Emerson advised. Like the devout at Finney's revivals, who sought to perfect themselves and society, listeners who flocked to Emerson's lectures were infused with the spirit of optimistic reform.

As the currents of Romanticism percolated through American society, the country's literature came of age. In 1820 educated Americans still tended to ape the fashions of England and Europe. But as the population grew, education increased, and the country's literary market expanded, American writers looked with greater interest at the customs and character of their own society. Emerson's address "The American Scholar" (1837) constituted a declaration of literary independence. "Our long dependence, our long apprenticeship to the learning of other lands draws to a close," he proclaimed. "Events, actions arise, that must be sung, that will sing themselves."

The Clash between Nature and Civilization

In extolling nature, many of America's new Romantic writers betrayed a concern that the advance of civilization, with its market economy and crowded urban centers, might destroy the natural simplicity of the land. James Fenimore Cooper focused on the clash between nature and civilization in his Leatherstocking Tales, a series of five novels written between 1823 and 1841. Cooper clearly admired his hero, Natty Bumppo, a self-reliant frontiersman who represented the nobility and innocence of the wilderness. At the same time, Cooper viewed the culture of the frontier as a threat to the civilization he prized so highly.

Cooper and wilderness

Henry David Thoreau, too, used nature as a backdrop to explore the conflict between the unfettered individual and the constraints of society. In 1845 Thoreau built a cabin on the edge of Walden Pond in Concord, living by himself for 16 months to demonstrate the advantages of self-

Thoreau and individualism

reliance. His experiences became the basis for *Walden* (1854), which eloquently denounced Americans' frantic competition for material goods and wealth. Only in nature, Thoreau argued, could one find true independence, liberty, equality, and happiness. Voicing the anti-institutional impulse of Romanticism, he took individualism to its antisocial extreme.

Songs of the Self-Reliant and Darker Loomings

In contrast to Thoreau's exclusiveness, Walt Whitman was all-inclusive, embracing American society in its infinite variety. A journalist and laborer in the New York City area, Whitman was inspired by the common people, whose "manners, speech, dress, friendships . . . are unrhymed poetry." In taking their measure in *Leaves of Grass* (1855), he pioneered a new, modern form of poetry, unconcerned with meter and rhyme and filled with frank imagery and sexual references. Emerson and other critics were put off by such roughhewn methods, but Whitman, like the Transcendentalists, exalted emotions, nature, and the individual.

> Whitman and democracy

More brooding in spirit were Nathaniel Hawthorne and Herman Melville, two intellectuals who did not share the Transcendentalists' sunny optimism. Hawthorne wrote of the power of the past to shape future generations and the consequences of pride, selfishness, envy, and secret guilt. In *The Scarlet Letter* (1850), set in New England's Puritan era, Hawthorne searingly portrayed the sufferings of a woman who bore an illegitimate child as well as the Puritan neighbors who harshly condemned her.

> The skeptics: Hawthorne and Melville

Herman Melville's dark masterpiece, *Moby-Dick* (1851), drew on his youthful experiences aboard a whaling ship. The novel's Captain Ahab relentlessly drives his crew in pursuit of the great white whale Moby-Dick. In Melville's telling, Ahab becomes a powerful symbol of American character: the prototype of the ruthless businessman despoiling nature's resources in his ferocious pursuit of success.

But awash in the many opportunities opening before them, most Americans ignored such searching criticism. They preferred to celebrate, with Emerson, the glories of democracy and the individual's quest for perfection.

THE AGE OF REFORM

In the glowing fires of a fervent camp meeting, the quest for perfection often proved hard to control. At the Cane Ridge revival of 1801, the Methodist Peter Cartwright had his hands full trying to stop less orthodox preachers from gathering converts. Quite a few worshipers had joined a group known as the Shakers. Cartwright had to ride around the neighborhood "from cabin to cabin" trying to cure people of the Shaker "delusion."

The Shakers were only one group that demonstrated more radical possibilities for democratic change. While the mainline benevolent societies aimed at a more conservative reformation of individual sinners, the more radical offshoots of Romanticism and perfectionism sought to remake society at large.

Utopian Communities

One radical way of reforming the world was by withdrawing from it, to form a utopian community that would demonstrate the possibilities of perfection. Such communities looked to replace the competitive individualism of American society with a purer spiritual unity and group cooperation. During the early 1840s, for example, Emerson's friend George Ripley organized Brook Farm, a Transcendentalist community near Boston where members could live "a more wholesome and simple life than can be led amidst the pressure of our competitive institutions." Other utopian communities were more directly linked to religious movements and figures, but religious or secular, such communities shared the optimism of perfectionism and millennialism.

Brook Farm

The Shakers proved to be one of the most long-lived utopian experiments. Ann Lee, the daughter of an English blacksmith, led a small band of followers to America in 1774. Through a series of religious visions Lee became convinced that

Dancing was an integral part of the Shakers' religion, as this picture of a service at Lebanon, New York, indicates. In worshiping, men and women formed separate lines with their hands held out and moved back and forth in rhythm while singing religious songs. Note the presence of African Americans in the community.

her own life would reveal the female side of the divinity, just as Christ had come to earth exemplifying the male side. The Shaker movement's greatest growth, however, came after Lee's death, when her followers recruited converts at revivals like Cane Ridge. The new disciples founded about 20 communal settlements based on the teachings of Mother Ann, as she was known. Convinced that the end of the world was at hand and that there was no need to perpetuate the human race, Shakers practiced celibacy, separating the sexes as far as practical. Men and women normally worked apart, ate at separate tables, and had separate living quarters.

Shaker communities accorded women unusual authority and equality. Community tasks were generally assigned along gender lines, with women performing household chores and men laboring in the fields. Leadership of the church, however, was split equally between men and women. The sect's members worked hard, lived simply, and impressed outsiders with their cleanliness and order. Lacking any natural increase, membership began to decline after 1850, from a peak of about 6000 members.

The Oneida Community, founded by John Humphrey Noyes, also set out to alter the relationship between the sexes, though in a rather different way. Noyes, a convert of Charles Finney, took Finney's doctrine of perfection to extremes. While Finney argued that men and women should strive to achieve perfection, Noyes announced that he had actually reached this blessed state. Settling in Putney, Vermont, and after 1848 in Oneida, New York, Noyes set out to create a community organized on his religious ideals.

In pursuit of greater freedom, Noyes preached the doctrine of "complex marriage," by which commune members were permitted to have sexual relations with one another, but only with the approval of the community and after a searching examination of the couple's motives. Noyes eventually undertook experiments in planned reproduction by selecting "scientific" combinations of parents to produce morally perfect children.

Noyes attracted over 200 members to the Oneida Community. But in 1879 an internal dispute drove him from power and the community splintered. In 1881 its members reorganized as a business enterprise.

The Mormon Experience

The Church of Jesus Christ of Latter-Day Saints, whose members were generally known as Mormons, was founded by a young man named Joseph Smith in western New York, where the fires of revivalism flared regularly. In 1827, at the age of only 22, Smith announced that he had discovered a set of golden tablets on which was written the *Book of Mormon*. Proclaiming that he had a commission from God to reestablish the true church, Smith gathered a group of devoted followers.

Like Charles Finney's more liberal theology, Mormonism declared that salvation was available to all. Moreover, Mormon culture upheld the middle-class values of hard work, thrift, self-control, and material success. And by teaching that

Christ would return to rule the earth, it shared in the hope of a coming millennial kingdom.

Mormonism was an outgrowth less of evangelicalism, however, than of the primitive gospel movement, which sought to reestablish the ancient church. In restoring what Smith called "the ancient order of things," Mormons created a theocracy uniting church and state, reestablished biblical priesthoods and titles, and adopted temple rituals. Smith undertook to gather the saints in a "city of Zion," first in Ohio and then in Missouri, in preparation for Christ's return But his unorthodox teachings provoked bitter persecution wherever he went, and mob violence finally hounded him and his followers out of Missouri in 1839. In response, Smith established a new holy city, Nauvoo, along the Mississippi River in Illinois.

Movement to restore the ancient church

At Nauvoo, Smith introduced the most distinctive features of Mormon theology, including baptism for the dead, eternal marriage, and polygamy, or plural marriage. As a result, Mormonism increasingly diverged from traditional Christianity and became a distinct new religion. Neighboring residents, alarmed by the Mormons' growing political power and reports that church leaders were practicing polygamy, demanded that Nauvoo's charter be revoked and the Church suppressed. In 1844 Smith was murdered by an anti-Mormon mob. The Mormons abandoned Nauvoo in 1846, and the following year Brigham Young, Smith's successor, led them westward to Utah (page 382). Nauvoo ceased to be a holy city.

City of Zion: Nauvoo

Socialist Communities

The hardship and poverty that accompanied the growth of industrial factories inspired utopian communities based on science and reason rather than religion. Robert Owen, a Scottish industrialist, came to the United States in 1824 and founded the community of New Harmony in Indiana. Owen believed that the character of individuals was shaped by their surroundings, and that by changing those surroundings, one could change human character. Unfortunately, most of the 900 or so volunteers who flocked to New Harmony lacked the skills and commitment needed to make the community a success, and bitter factions soon split the settlement.

Owen's New Harmony

The experience of New Harmony and other communities demonstrated that the United States was poor soil for socialistic experiments. Wages were too high and land too cheap to interest most Americans in collectivist ventures. And individualism was too strong to create a commitment to cooperative action.

The Temperance Movement

The most significant reform movements of the period sought not to withdraw from society but to change it directly. One of the most determined of these was the temperance movement.

The origins of the campaign lay in the heavy drinking of the early nineteenth century. Alcohol consumption soared after the Revolution, so that by 1830 the average American consumed four gallons of absolute alcohol a year, the highest level in American history and nearly triple present-day levels. Anne Royale, whose travels took her cross country by stage, reported, "When I was in Virginia, it was too much whiskey—in Ohio, too much whiskey—in Tennessee, it is too, too much whiskey!" The social costs for such habits were high: broken families, abused and neglected wives and children, sickness and disability, poverty, and crime. The temperance movement undertook to eliminate these problems by curbing drinking.

Led largely by clergy, the movement at first focused on drunkenness and did not oppose moderate drinking. But in 1826 the American Temperance Society was founded, taking voluntary abstinence as its goal. During the next decade approximately 5000 local temperance societies were founded. As the movement gained momentum, annual per capita consumption of alcohol dropped sharply, so that by 1845 it had fallen below two gallons a year.

The move toward abstinence

The temperance movement was more sustained and more popular than other reforms. It appealed to young and old, to urban and rural residents, to workers and businesspeople. And it was the only reform movement with significant support in the South. Its success came partly for social reasons. Democracy necessitated sober voters; factories required sober workers. Temperance attracted the upwardly mobile—professionals and skilled artisans anxious to improve their social standing. Finally, temperance advocates stressed the suffering that men inflicted on women and children, and thus the movement appealed to women as a means to defend the home and carry out their domestic mission.

Educational Reform

In 1800 Massachusetts was the only state requiring free public schools supported by community funds. The call for tax-supported education arose first among workers, as a means to restore their deteriorating position in society. But middle-class reformers quickly took control of the movement, looking to uplift common citizens and make them responsible. Reformers appealed to business leaders by arguing that the new economic order needed educated workers.

Under Horace Mann's leadership, Massachusetts adopted a minimum-length school year, provided for training of teachers, and expanded the curriculum to include subjects such as history, geography, and various applied skills. Still, outside of Massachusetts there were only a few high schools. Moreover, compulsory attendance was rarely required, and many poor parents sent their children to work instead of school. Nevertheless, by the 1850s the number of schools, attendance figures, and school budgets had all increased sharply. School reformers enjoyed their greatest success in the Northeast and the least in the South, where planters opposed paying taxes to educate poorer white children.

Prison reformers believed that rigid discipline, extensive rules, and (in some programs) solitary confinement were necessary to rehabilitate criminals. Prisoners often had to march lockstep under strict supervision and wear uniforms such as those seen in this photograph from the 1870s.

Educational opportunities for women also expanded. Teachers like Catharine Beecher and Emma Hunt Willard established a number of private girls' schools, putting to rest the objection of many male educators that fragile female minds could not absorb large doses of mathematics, physics, or geography. In 1833 Oberlin became the nation's first coeducational college. Four years later Mary Lyon founded Mount Holyoke, the first American college for women.

Female education

The Asylum Movement

After 1820 there was also a dramatic increase in the number of asylums of every sort—orphanages, jails, and hospitals. Advocates of asylums called for isolating and separating the criminal, the insane, the ill, and the dependent from outside society. The goal of care in asylums, which earlier had focused on confinement, shifted to the reform of personal character.

Dorothea Dix, a Boston schoolteacher, took the lead in advocating state-supported asylums for the mentally ill. She attracted much attention to the movement by her report detailing the horrors to which the mentally ill were subjected, including being chained, kept in cages and closets, and beaten with rods. In response to her efforts, 28 states maintained mental institutions by 1860.

Like other reform movements, the push for new asylums and better educational facilities reflected overtones of both liberation and control. Asylums freed prisoners and the mentally ill from the harsh punishments of the past, but the new techniques of "rehabilitation" forced prisoners to march in lockstep. Education brought with it the freedom to question and to acquire knowledge, but some reformers hoped that schools would become as orderly as prisons. Louis Dwight, who advocated solitary confinement for prisoners at night and total silence by day, suggested eagerly that such methods "would greatly promote order, seriousness, and purity in large families, male and female boarding schools, and colleges."

> **Order and social control**

ABOLITIONISM

In the fall of 1834, Lyman Beecher, as president of Lane Seminary in Cincinnati, was continuing his efforts to "overturn and overturn" on behalf of the kingdom of God. The school had everything needed by an institution for training ministers to convert the West—everything, that is, except students. In October all but 8 of Lane's 100 scholars had departed after months of bitter controversy with Beecher and the trustees over the issue of abolition.

Beecher knew the source of his troubles: a scruffy yet magnetic student named Theodore Dwight Weld. Weld had been firing up his classmates over the need to immediately free the slaves. Beecher was not surprised, for Weld had been converted by that incendiary Finney. He knew, too, that Weld was a follower of William Lloyd Garrison, whose abolitionist writings had sent shock waves across the entire nation. Indeed, Beecher's troubles at Lane Seminary provided only one example of how the flames of reform, when fanned, could spread along paths not anticipated by those who first kindled them.

The Beginnings of the Abolitionist Movement

William Lloyd Garrison symbolized the transition from a moderate antislavery movement to the more militant abolitionism of the 1830s. A deeply religious young man, Garrison endorsed the colonization movement, which advocated sending blacks to Africa, and went to Baltimore in 1829 to work for Benjamin Lundy, who edited the leading antislavery newspaper in the country.

It was in Baltimore that Garrison first encountered the opinions of free African Americans, who played a major role in launching the abolitionist movement. To Garrison's surprise, most of them strongly opposed the colonization movement as proslavery and antiblack. "This is our home, and this is our country," a free black convention proclaimed in 1831. "Here we were born, and here we will die." Under their influence, Garrison soon developed views far more radical than Lundy's, and within a year of moving to Baltimore, the young firebrand was convicted of libel and imprisoned.

Upon his release Garrison hurried back to Boston, determined to publish a new kind of antislavery journal. On January 1, 1831, the first issue of *The Liberator* appeared, and abolitionism was born. In appearance, the bespectacled Garrison seemed frail, almost mousy, but in print he was abrasive, withering, and uncompromising. "On this subject, I do not wish to think, or speak, or write with moderation," he proclaimed. "I am in earnest—I will not equivocate—I will not excuse—I will not retreat a single inch—AND I WILL BE HEARD." Repudiating gradual emancipation and embracing "immediatism," Garrison insisted that slavery end at once. He denounced colonization as a racist movement and upheld the principle of racial equality. To those who suggested that slaveowners should be compensated for freeing their slaves, Garrison was firm. Southerners ought to be convinced by "moral suasion" to renounce slavery as a sin. Virtue was its own reward.

Garrison's immediatism

Garrison attracted the most attention, but other abolitionists spoke with equal conviction. Wendell Phillips, from a socially prominent Boston family, held listeners spellbound with his speeches. Lewis Tappan and his brother Arthur, two New York City silk merchants, boldly placed their wealth behind various humanitarian causes, including abolitionism. James G. Birney, an Alabama slaveholder, converted to abolitionism after wrestling with his conscience, and Angelina and Sarah Grimké, the daughters of a South Carolina planter, left their native state to speak against the institution. And there was Angelina's future husband, Theodore Weld, the restless student at Lane Seminary who had fallen so dramatically under Garrison's influence.

To abolitionists, slavery was a moral, not an economic, question. The institution seemed a contradiction of the principle of the American Revolution that all human beings had been created with natural rights. Abolitionists condemned slavery because of the breakup of marriages and families by sale, the harsh punishment of the lash, slaves' lack of access to education, and the sexual abuse of black women. But most of all, abolitionists denounced slavery as outrageously contrary to Christian teaching. As one Ohio antislavery paper declared, "We believe slavery to be a sin, always, everywhere, and only, sin—sin, in itself." Abolitionism forced the churches to face the question of slavery head-on, and in the 1840s the Methodist and Baptist churches each split into northern and southern organizations over the issue.

The Spread of Abolitionism

After helping organize the New England Anti-Slavery Society in 1832, Garrison joined with Lewis Tappan and Theodore Weld the following year to establish a national organization, the American Anti-Slavery Society. During the years before the Civil War, perhaps 200,000 northerners belonged to an abolitionist society.

Support for abolitionism

Abolitionists were concentrated in the East, especially New England, and in areas that had been settled by New Englanders, such as western New York and northern Ohio. The movement was not strong in cities or among businesspeople and workers. Most abolitionists were young, being generally in their 20s and 30s when the movement began, and had grown up in rural areas and small towns in middle-class families. Intensely religious, many had been profoundly affected by the revivals of the Second Great Awakening.

Certainly Theodore Weld was cut from this mold. After enrolling in Lane Seminary in 1833, he promoted immediate abolitionism among his fellow students. Unlike some abolitionists, who opposed slavery but disdained blacks as inferior, Lane students mingled freely with Cincinnati's free black population. In the summer of 1834, Beecher and Lane's trustees forbade any discussion of slavery on campus and ordered students to return to their studies. All but a handful left the school and enrolled at Oberlin College, where Charles Finney was professor of theology.

Free African Americans, who made up the majority of subscribers to Garrison's *Liberator*, provided important support and leadership for the movement. Frederick Douglass assumed the greatest prominence. Having escaped from slavery in Maryland, he became an eloquent critic of its evils. Initially a follower of Garrison, Douglass eventually broke with him and started his own newspaper in Rochester. Other important black abolitionists included Martin Delany, William Wells Brown, William Still, and Sojourner Truth. Most black

African American abolitionists

An escaped slave, Harriet Tubman (far left), made several forays into the South as a "conductor" on the Underground Railroad. Shown here with one group that she led to freedom, she was noted for her stealth and firm determination, qualities that helped her repeatedly to outwit her pursuers.

Americans endorsed peaceful means to end slavery, but David Walker in his *Appeal to the Colored Citizens of the World* (1829) urged slaves to use violence to end bondage.

A network of antislavery sympathizers developed in the North to convey runaway slaves to Canada and freedom. While not as extensive or as tightly organized as contemporaries claimed, the Underground Railroad hid fugitives and transported them northward from one station to the next. Free African Americans, who were more readily trusted by wary slaves, played a leading role in the Underground Railroad. One of its most famous conductors was Harriet Tubman, an escaped slave who repeatedly returned to the South and eventually escorted more than 200 slaves to freedom.

Opponents and Divisions

The drive for immediate abolition faced massive obstacles, no matter how fervent its advocates. With slavery increasingly important to the South's economic life, the abolitionist cause encountered extreme hostility there. And in the North, where racism was equally entrenched, abolitionism provoked bitter resistance. Even abolitionists like Garrison treated blacks paternalistically, contending that they should occupy a subordinate place in the antislavery movement.

Hostility toward abolitionists

On occasion, northern resistance turned violent. An antiabolitionist mob burned down the headquarters of the American Anti-Slavery Society in Philadelphia, and in 1837 in Alton, Illinois, Elijah Lovejoy was murdered when he tried to protect his printing press from an angry crowd. The leaders of these mobs were not from the bottom of society but, as one of their victims noted, were "gentlemen of property and standing." Prominent leaders in the community, they reacted vigorously to the threat that abolitionists posed to their power and prosperity and to the established order.

But abolitionists were also hindered by divisions among reformers. At Oberlin College Finney, too, ended up opposing Theodore Weld's fervent abolitionism. More conservative than Finney, Lyman Beecher saw his son Edward stand guard over Elijah Lovejoy's printing press the evening before the editor's murder. Within another decade, Beecher would see his daughter Harriet Beecher Stowe write the most successful piece of antislavery literature in the nation's history, *Uncle Tom's Cabin* (page 405). Even the abolitionists themselves splintered. More conservative reformers wanted to work within established institutions, using churches and political action to end slavery. But for Garrison and his followers, the mob violence demonstrated that slavery was only part of a deeper national disease, whose cure required the overthrow of American institutions and values.

Divisions among reformers

By the end of the decade, Garrison had worked out a program for the total reform of society. He embraced perfectionism, denounced the clergy, and urged members to leave the churches. Condemning the Constitution as proslavery—"a covenant with death and an agreement with hell"—he argued that no person of conscience could participate in the corrupt political system. This platform was radical enough on all counts, but the final straw for Garrison's opponents was his endorsement of women's rights as an inseparable part of abolitionism.

The Women's Rights Movement

Women faced many disadvantages in American society. They were kept out of most jobs, denied political rights, and given only limited access to education beyond the elementary grades. When a woman married, her husband became the legal representative of the marriage and gained complete control of her property. Any unmarried woman was made the ward of a male relative.

When abolitionists divided over the issue of female participation, women found it easy to identify with the situation of slaves, since both were victims of male tyranny. Sarah and Angelina Grimké took up the cause of women's rights after they were criticized for speaking to audiences that included men as well as women. Sarah, who had wanted to be a lawyer, responded with *Letters on the Condition of Women and the Equality of the Sexes* (1838), a pioneering feminist tract that argued that women deserved the same rights as men. Abby Kelly, another abolitionist, remarked that women "have good cause to be grateful to the slave," for in "striving to strike his irons off, we found most surely, that we were manacled *ourselves*."

Two abolitionists, Elizabeth Cady Stanton and Lucretia Mott, launched the women's rights movement after they were forced to sit behind a curtain at a world antislavery convention in London. In 1848 Stanton and Mott organized a conference in Seneca Falls, New York, that attracted about a hundred supporters. The meeting issued a Declaration of Sentiments,

Seneca Falls convention

modeled after the Declaration of Independence, that began, "All men and women are created equal." The Seneca Falls convention approved resolutions calling for educational and professional opportunities for women, control by women of their property, recognition of legal equality, and repeal of laws awarding the father custody of the children in divorce. The most controversial proposal, and the only resolution that did not pass unanimously, was one demanding the right to vote. The Seneca Falls convention established the arguments and the program for the women's rights movement for the remainder of the century.

The women's rights movement won few victories before 1860. Several states gave women greater control over their property, and a few made divorce easier or granted women the right to sue in courts. But disappointments and defeats outweighed these early victories. Still, many of the important leaders in the crusade for women's rights that emerged after the Civil War had already taken their places at the forefront of the movement. They included Stanton, Susan B. Anthony, Lucy Stone, and—as Lyman Beecher by now must have expected—one of his daughters, Isabella Beecher Hooker.

Elizabeth Cady Stanton, one of the
instigators and guiding spirits at the Seneca
Falls convention, photographed with two of her
children about that time.

The Schism of 1840

It was Garrison's position on women's rights that finally split antislavery ranks asunder. The showdown came in 1840 at the national meeting of the American Anti-Slavery Society, when delegates debated whether women could hold office in the organization. Garrison's opponents feared that this issue would drive off potential supporters, but Garrison carried the day. His opponents, led by Lewis Tappan, resigned to found the rival American and Foreign Anti-Slavery Society.

The schism of 1840 lessened the influence of abolitionism as a benevolent reform movement in American society. Although abolitionism heightened moral concern about slavery, it failed to convert the North to its program, and its supporters remained a tiny minority. For all the considerable courage they showed, their movement suffered from the lack of a realistic, long-range plan for eliminating so deeply entrenched an institution. Garrison even boasted that "the genius of the abolitionist movement is to have *no* plan." Abolitionism demonstrated the serious limitations of moral suasion and individual conversions as a solution to deeply rooted social problems.

REFORM SHAKES THE PARTY SYSTEM

"What a fog-bank we are in politically! Do you see any head-land or light—or can you get an observation—or soundings?" The words came from a puzzled Whig politician writing a friend after the Massachusetts state elections of 1853. He was in such a confused state because reformers were increasingly entering the political arena to achieve their goals.

The crusading idealism of revivalists and reformers inevitably collided with the hard reality that society could not be perfected by converting individuals. In America's democratic society, politics and government coercion promised a more effective means to impose a new moral vision on the nation.

Politicians did not particularly welcome the new interest. Because the Whig and Democratic parties both drew on evangelical and nonevangelical voters, heated moral debates over the harmful effects of drink or the evils of slavery threatened to detach regular party members from their old loyalties.

Women and the Right to Vote

As the focus of change and reform shifted toward the political arena, women in particular lost influence. As major participants in the benevolent organizations of the 1820s and 1830s, they had used their efforts on behalf of "moral suasion." But since women could not vote, they felt excluded when the temperance and abolitionist movements turned to electoral action to accomplish their goals. By the 1840s female reformers increasingly demanded the right to vote as the means to reform society.

Previously, many female reformers had accepted the right of petition as their most appropriate political activity. But *The Lily*, a women's rights paper, soon changed its tack. "Why shall [women] be left only the poor resource of petition?" it asked. "For even petitions, when they are from women, without the elective franchise to give them backbone, are of but little consequence."

The Maine Law

Although drinking had significantly declined in American society by 1840, it had hardly been eliminated. After 1845 the arrival of large numbers of German and Irish immigrants, who were accustomed to consuming alcohol, made voluntary prohibition even more remote. In response, temperance advocates proposed state laws that would outlaw the manufacture and sale of alcoholic beverages. If liquor was unavailable, reformers reasoned, the attitude of drinkers was unimportant: they would be forced to reform whether they wanted to or not.

The issue of prohibition cut across party lines, with large numbers of Whigs and Democrats on both sides of the question. When party leaders tried to dodge the issue, the temperance movement adopted the strategy of endorsing the legislative candidates who pledged to support a prohibitory law. To win additional recruits, temperance leaders took up techniques used in political campaigns, including house-to-house canvasses, parades and processions, bands and singing, banners, picnics, and mass rallies.

The temperance movement's first major triumph came in 1851 in Maine. The Maine Law, as it was known, authorized search and seizure of private property and provided stiff penalties for selling liquor. In the next few years a number of states enacted similar laws, although most were struck down by the courts or later repealed.

Even though prohibition had been temporarily defeated, the issue badly disrupted the unity of the Whig and Democratic parties. It detached a number of voters from both coalitions, greatly increased the extent of party switching, and brought to the polls a large number of new voters, including many "wets" who wanted to preserve their right to drink. By dissolving the ties between so many voters and their parties, the temperance issue played a major role in the eventual collapse of the Jacksonian party system in the 1850s.

Effect on the party system

Abolitionism and the Party System

Abolition was the most divisive issue to come out of the benevolent movement. In 1835 abolitionists distributed over a million pamphlets through the post office to southern whites. A wave of excitement swept the South when the first batches arrived. Former senator Robert Hayne led a Charleston mob that burned sacks of U.S. mail containing abolitionist literature, and postmasters in other southern cities refused to deliver the material. When the Jackson administration acquiesced in this censorship, abolitionists protested that their civil rights had been violated. In reaction, the number of antislavery societies in the North nearly tripled.

Censorship of the mails

With access to the mails impaired, abolitionists began flooding Congress with petitions against slavery. Asserting that Congress had no power over the institution, angry southern representatives persuaded the House to adopt the so-called gag rule in 1836. It tabled without consideration any petition dealing with slavery. Claiming that the right of petition was also under attack by slavery's champions, abolitionists gained new supporters. In 1844 the House finally repealed the controversial rule.

The gag rule

Many abolitionists outside Garrison's extreme circle were increasingly convinced that an antislavery third party offered a more effective means of attacking slavery. In 1840 these political abolitionists founded the Liberty party and nominated for president James Birney, a former slaveholder who had converted to abolitionism. Birney received only 7000 votes, but the Liberty party was the seed from which a stronger antislavery political movement would grow. In the next two decades, abolitionism's greatest importance would be in the political arena rather than as a voluntary reform organization.

After two decades of fiery revivals, benevolent crusades, utopian experiments, and Transcendental philosophizing, the ferment of reform had spread through urban streets, canal town churches, frontier clearings, and the halls of Congress. Abolition, potentially the most dangerous issue, seemed still under control in 1840. Birney's small vote, coupled with the disputes between the two national antislavery societies, encouraged political leaders to believe that the party system had turned back this latest threat of sectionalism.

But the growing northern concern about slavery highlighted differences between the two sections. Despite the strength of evangelicalism in the South, the reform impulse spawned by the revivals found little support there, since reform movements were discredited by their association with abolitionism. The party system confronted the difficult challenge of holding together sections that, although sharing much, were also diverging in important ways. To the residents of both sections, the South increasingly seemed to be a unique society with its own distinctive way of life.

 **chapter summary**

The Jacksonian era produced the greatest number of significant reform movements in American history.

- The movements grew out of the revivals of the Second Great Awakening, which emphasized emotion and preached the doctrines of good works and salvation available to all.
  - Evangelical Protestantism also endorsed the ideals of perfectionism and millennialism.
  - The revival theology helped people adjust to the pressures in their daily lives created by the new market economy.

- Romanticism, which emphasized the unlimited potential of each individual, also strengthened reform.

- Women's role in society was now defined by the ideal of domesticity—that women's lives should center on the home and the family.

- Middle-class women turned to religion and reform as ways to shape society.

- Utopian communities sought to establish a model society for the rest of the world to follow.

- Humanitarian movements combated a variety of social evils.
  - Crusades for temperance, educational reform, and the establishment of asylums all gained significant support.
  - Abolitionism precipitated both strong support and violent opposition, and the movement itself split in 1840.

- Temperance, abolitionism, and women's rights movements each turned to political action to accomplish their goals.

- Although it survived, the party system was seriously weakened by these reform movements.

For quizzes and a variety of interactive resources, visit the book's Online Learning Center at www.mhhe.com/davidsonconcise3

SIGNIFICANT EVENTS

1787	First Shaker commune established
1794	African American Bethel Church organized
1821	New York constructs first penitentiary
1824	New Harmony established
1824–1837	Peak of revivals
1826	James Fenimore Cooper's *The Last of the Mohicans* published; American Temperance Society founded
1829	David Walker's *Appeal to the Colored Citizens of the World* published
1830	*Book of Mormon* published
1831	*The Liberator* established
1833	American Anti-Slavery Society founded; Oberlin College admits women
1834	Lane Seminary rebellion
1835	Abolitionists' postal campaign
1836	Transcendental Club organized; gag rule passed
1837	Massachusetts establishes state board of education; Mount Holyoke Seminary commences classes; Elijah Lovejoy killed
1838	Ralph Waldo Emerson delivers Divinity School address; Sarah Grimké's *Letters on the Condition of Women and the Equality of the Sexes* published
1839–1846	Mormons at Nauvoo
1840	Schism of American Anti-Slavery Society; Liberty party organized
1841	Brook Farm established
1843	Dorothea Dix's report on treatment of the insane
1844	Joseph Smith murdered; gag rule repealed
1848	Oneida Community established; Seneca Falls convention
1850	Nathaniel Hawthorne's *The Scarlet Letter* published
1851	Maine adopts prohibition law; Herman Melville's *Moby-Dick* published
1854	Henry David Thoreau's *Walden* published
1855	Walt Whitman's *Leaves of Grass* published

CHAPTER 13

The Old South

(1820–1860)

The impeccably dressed Colonel Daniel Jordan, master of 261 slaves at Laurel Hill, strolls down his oak-lined lawn to the dock along the Waccamaw River, a day's journey north of Charleston, to board the steamship *Nina*. On Fridays, it is Colonel Jordan's custom to visit the exclusive Hot and Hot Fish Club, founded by his fellow low-country planters, to play a game of lawn bowling or billiards and be waited on by black servants in livery as he sips an iced mint julep in the refined atmosphere that for him is the South.

Several hundred miles to the west another steamboat, the *Fashion*, makes its way along the Alabama River. One of the passengers is upset by the boat's slow pace. He has been away from his plantation in the Red River country of Texas and is eager to get back. "Time's money, time's money!" he mutters. "Time's worth more'n money to me now; a hundred percent more,

preview • In the decades before the Civil War, the rural South depended on the export of staple crops like rice, tobacco, sugar, and cotton—and the slave labor used to produce them. Though most southern whites did not own slaves, those who did reaped prestige, political influence, and wealth. Excluded from white society, enslaved African Americans resisted bondage and developed their own culture, whose religion, songs, and shared experiences helped them survive a cruel and arbitrary regime.

'cause I left my niggers all alone; not a damn white man within four mile on 'em." When asked what they are doing, since the cotton crop has already been picked, he says, "I set 'em to clairin', but they ain't doin' a damn thing. . . . But I'll make it up, I'll make it up when I get thar, now you'd better believe." For this Red River planter, time is money and cotton is his world—indeed, cotton is what the South is all about. "I am a cotton man, I am, and I don't car who knows it," he proclaims. "I know cotton, I do. I'm dam' if I know anythin' but cotton."

At the other end of the South, the slave Sam Williams works in the intense heat of Buffalo Forge, an iron-making factory nine miles from Lexington, Virginia, in the Shenandoah Valley. As a refiner, Williams has the most important job at the forge, alternately heating pig iron in the white-hot coals, then slinging the ball of glowing metal on an anvil, where he pounds it with huge, water-powered hammers to remove the impurities. Ambitious and hardworking, he earns extra money (at the same rate paid to whites) for any iron he produces beyond his weekly quota.

In some years his extra income is more than $100. His wife, Nancy, who is in charge of the dairy, earns extra money as well, and their savings accounts at the local bank total more than $150. Additional income allows them to buy extra food and items for themselves and their four daughters, but more important, it helps keep their family intact in an unstable environment. They know that their owner is very unlikely to sell away slaves who work so hard. For Sam and Nancy Williams, family ties, worship at the local Baptist church, and socializing with their fellow slaves are what make life important.

In the bayous of the Deep South, only a few miles from where the Mississippi Delta meets the Gulf, Octave Johnson hears the dogs coming. For over a year now Johnson has been a runaway slave. He fled from a Louisiana plantation in St. James Parish when the overseer threatened to whip him for staying in bed. To survive, he hides in the swamps four miles behind the plantation—stealing turkeys, chickens, and pigs and trading with other slaves. As uncertain as this life is, nearly 30 other slaves have joined him over the past year.

This time when the pack of hounds bursts upon them, the slaves do not flee but kill as many dogs as possible. Then they plunge into the bayou. For Octave Johnson the real South is a matter of weighing one's prospects between

Plantation Burial, painted about 1860 by John Antrobus, portrays the black slave community from a Louisiana plantation burying a loved one. Religion played a central role in the life of slaves.

the uncertainties of alligators and the overseer's whip—and deciding when to say no.

Ferdinand Steel and his family are not forced, by the flick of the lash, to rise at five in the morning. They rise because the land demands it. Steel, in his 20s, owns 170 acres of land in Carroll County, Mississippi. His life is one of continuous hard work, caring for the animals and tending the crops. His mother, Eliza, and sister, Julia, have plenty to keep them busy: making soap, fashioning dippers out of gourds, or sewing.

The Steel family grows cotton, too, but not with the single-minded devotion of the planter aboard the *Fashion*. Self-sufficiency and family security always come first, and Steel's total crop amounts to only five or six bales. His profit is never enough for him to consider buying even one slave. In fact, he would prefer not to raise any cotton—"We are to[o] weak handed," he explains—but the cotton means cash, and cash means that he can buy things he needs in nearby Grenada. Though fiercely independent, Steel and his scattered neighbors help each other raise houses, clear fields, shuck corn, or quilt. They depend on one another and are bound together by blood, religion, obligation, and honor. For small farmers like Ferdinand Steel, these ties constitute the real South.

The portraits could go on: different people, different Souths, all of them real. Such contrasts underscore the difficulty of trying to define a regional identity. Encompassing in 1860 the 15 slave states plus the District of Columbia, the South was a land of great social and geographic diversity.

Yet despite its many differences of people and geography, the South was bonded by ties so strong, they eventually outpulled those of the nation itself. At the heart of this unity was an agricultural system that took advantage of the region's warm climate and long growing season. Most important, this rural agricultural economy was based on the institution of slavery, which had far-reaching effects on all aspects of southern society. It shaped not only the culture of the slaves themselves but the lives of their masters and mistresses, and even of farm families and herders in the hills and backwoods, who saw few slaves from day to day. To understand the Old South, then, we must understand how the southern agricultural economy and the institution of slavery affected the social class structure of both white and black southerners.

Factors unifying the South

THE SOCIAL STRUCTURE OF THE COTTON KINGDOM

We have already seen (in Chapter 10) that the spread of cotton stimulated the nation's remarkable economic growth after the War of 1812. Demand spurred by the textile industry sent the price of cotton soaring on the international market, and white southerners scrambled into the fresh lands of the Southwest to reap the profits to be made in the cotton sweepstakes.

Deep South, Upper South

As Indian lands were opened to white settlement, word spread of the "black belt" region of central Alabama (map, below), where the dark, rich soil was particularly suited to growing cotton, and of the tremendous yields from the soils along the Mississippi River's broad reaches. "The Alabama Feaver rages here with great violence and has carried off vast numbers of our Citizens," a North Carolinian wrote in 1817. "I am apprehensive if it continues to spread as it has done, it will almost depopulate the country." A generation later, in the 1830s, immigrants were still "pouring in with a ceaseless tide," an Alabama observer reported. But the boom-

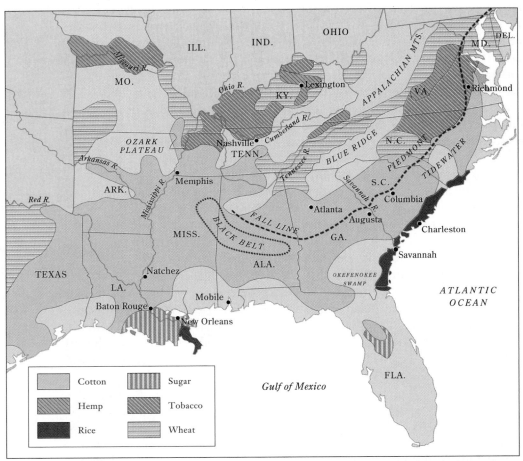

COTTON AND OTHER CROPS OF THE SOUTH   By 1860, the cotton kingdom extended across the Lower South into the Texas prairie and up the Mississippi River valley. Tobacco and hemp were the staple crops of the Upper South, where they competed with corn and wheat. Rice production was concentrated in the swampy coastal region of South Carolina and Georgia as well as the lower tip of Louisiana. The sugar district was in southern Louisiana.

ing frontier in the Deep South pushed even farther west. By the 1840s residents were leaving Alabama and Mississippi and heading for fresher cotton lands along the Red River and up into Texas. Amazingly, by the eve of the Civil War nearly a third of the total cotton crop came from west of the Mississippi River.

As Senator James Henry Hammond of South Carolina boasted in 1858, cotton was king in the Old South. True, the region devoted more acreage to corn, but cotton was the primary export and the major source of southern wealth. Indeed, by 1860 the United States produced three-fourths of the world's supply of cotton. Per capita income among southern whites actually exceeded that of the free states, though wealth was not so evenly distributed in the plantation South as in northern agricultural areas.

Cotton and southern prosperity

This prosperity, however, masked basic problems in the economy—problems that would become more apparent after the Civil War. Much of the South's new wealth resulted from migration of its population to more productive western lands. The amount of prime agricultural land was limited, and once it was settled, the South could not sustain its rate of expansion. Nor did the shift in population alter the structure of the southern economy, stimulate technological change, improve the way goods were produced and marketed, or generate internal markets.

The single-crop agriculture practiced by southern farmers (especially in tobacco and corn) rapidly wore out the soil. Planters and farmers in the Upper South increasingly shifted to wheat production to restore their soils, but because they now plowed fields rather than using the hoe, this shift accelerated soil erosion. Destruction of the forests, particularly in the Piedmont where commercial agriculture now took hold, had the same effect. In addition, reliance on a single crop increased toxins and parasites in the soil, making southern agriculture more vulnerable to destruction than diversified agriculture was.

Environmental impact of single-crop agriculture

Only the South's low population density eased such environmental damage. More remote areas remained heavily forested, wetlands were still extensive, and as late as 1860 eighty percent of the region was uncultivated. (Cattle and hogs, however, ranged over much of this acreage.)

Perhaps the most striking environmental consequence of the expansion of southern society was the increase in disease. The Lower South especially enjoyed a reputation for unhealthiness. Epidemic diseases such as malaria, yellow fever, and cholera were brought to the area by Europeans. The clearing of land—which increased runoff, precipitated floods, and produced pools of stagnant water—encouraged their spread.

As cotton transformed the boom country of the Deep South, agriculture in the Upper South also adjusted.* Scientific agricultural practices reversed the decline in tobacco, which had begun in the 1790s. More important, farmers in the Upper South

---

*The Upper South included the border states (Delaware, Maryland, Kentucky, and Missouri) and Virginia, North Carolina, Tennessee, and Arkansas. The states of the Deep South were South Carolina, Georgia, Florida, Alabama, Mississippi, Louisiana, and Texas.

The Upper South's new orientation

made wheat and corn their major crops. Because the new crops required less labor, slaveholders in the Upper South sold their surplus slaves to planters in the Deep South. The demand in the Deep South for slaves drove their price steadily up, so that by the late 1850s a prime field hand commanded $1500. Even with increased labor costs, southern agriculture flourished.

The Rural South

The Old South, then, was expanding, dynamic, and booming economically. But the region remained overwhelmingly rural, with 84 percent of its labor force engaged in agriculture in 1860, compared with 40 percent in the North. Conversely,

Lack of manufacturing

the South produced only 9 percent of the nation's manufactured goods. Efforts to diversify the South's economy made little headway in the face of the high profits from cotton.

With so little industry, few cities developed in the South. Only 1 in 10 southerners lived in cities and towns in 1860, compared with 1 out of 3 persons in the North. North Carolina, Florida, Alabama, Mississippi, Arkansas, and Texas did not contain a single city with a population of 10,000.

As a rural society, the South evidenced far less interest in education. Most wealthy planters opposed a state-supported school system, because they hired tutors or sent their children to private academies. Thus free public schools were rare,

White illiteracy

especially in rural areas that made up most of the South. Georgia in 1860 had only one county with a free school system, and Mississippi had no public schools outside its few cities. Not surprisingly, southern white children on average spent only one-fifth as much time in school as did their northern counterparts. The 1850 census showed that among native-born white citizens, 20 percent were unable to read and write. In the middle states the figure was 3 percent; in New England, only 0.4 percent.

Distribution of Slavery

Even more than agrarian ways, slavery set the South apart. Whereas in 1776 slavery had been a national institution, by 1820 it was confined to the states south of Pennsylvania and the Ohio River. The South's "peculiar institution" bound white and black southerners together in a multitude of ways.

Slaves were not evenly distributed throughout the region. More than half lived in the Deep South, where African Americans outnumbered white southerners in both South Carolina and Mississippi by the 1850s. Elsewhere in the Deep South, the black population exceeded 40 percent in all states except Texas. In the Upper South, on the other hand, whites greatly outnumbered blacks. Only in Virginia and North Carolina did the slave population top 30 percent.

The distribution of slaves showed striking geographic variations within individual states as well. In areas of fertile soil, flat or rolling countryside, and good

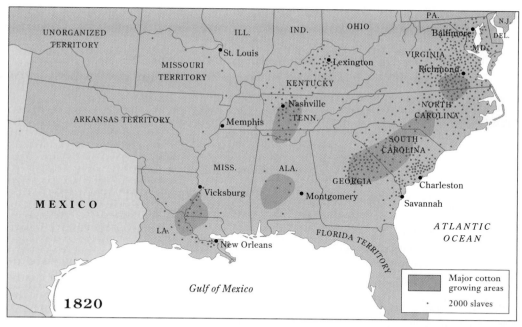

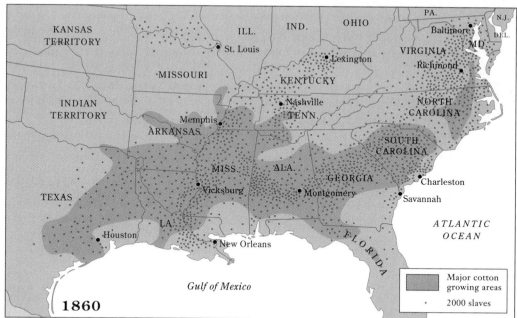

THE SPREAD OF SLAVERY, 1820–1860   Between 1820 and 1860, the slave population of
the South shifted south and westward, concentrating especially heavily in coastal
South Carolina and Georgia, in the black belt of central Alabama and Mississippi
(so named because of its rich soil), and in the Mississippi valley.

transportation, slavery and the plantation system dominated. In the pine barrens, areas isolated by lack of transportation, and hilly and mountainous regions, small family farms and few slaves were the rule.

Almost all enslaved African Americans, male and female, worked in agricultural pursuits, with only about 10 percent living in cities and towns. On large plantations, a few slaves were domestic servants, and others were skilled artisans—blacksmiths, carpenters, or bricklayers—but most toiled in the fields.

Slave occupations

Slavery as a Labor System

Slavery was, first and foremost, a system to manage and control labor. The plantation system, with its extensive estates and large labor forces, could never have developed without slavery. Slaves represented an enormous capital investment, worth more than all the land in the Old South.

Furthermore, slavery remained a highly profitable investment. The average slaveowner spent perhaps $30 to $35 a year to support an adult slave; some expended as little as half that. Even at the higher cost of support, a slaveowner took about 60 percent of the annual wealth produced by a slave's labor. For those who pinched pennies and drove slaves harder, the profits were even greater.

Profitability of slavery

By concentrating wealth and power in the hands of the planter class, slavery shaped the tone of southern society. Planters were not aristocrats in the European sense of having special legal privileges or formal titles of rank. Still, the system encouraged southern planters to think of themselves as a landed gentry upholding the aristocratic values of pride, honor, family, and hospitality.

Slavery and aristocratic values

Public opinion in Europe and in the North had grown more and more hostile to the peculiar institution, causing white southerners to feel increasingly like an isolated minority defending an embattled position. Yet they clung tenaciously to slavery, for it was the base on which the South's economic growth and way of life rested. As one Georgian observed on the eve of the Civil War, slavery was "so intimately mingled with our social conditions that it would be impossible to eradicate it."

CLASS STRUCTURE OF THE WHITE SOUTH

Once a year around Christmas time, James Henry Hammond gave a dinner for his neighbors at his South Carolina plantation, Silver Bluff. The richest man for miles around as well as an ambitious politician, the aristocratic Hammond used these dinners to put his neighbors under personal obligation to him as well as receive the honor and respect he believed his due. Indeed, Hammond's social and political ambitions caused him to carefully cultivate his neighbors, despite his low opinion of them, by hiring them to perform various tasks and by providing them a variety of services such as ginning their cotton and allowing them to use his grist mill. These services enhanced his ethic of paternalism, but his less affluent neighbors also displayed a strong personal pride. After he ungraciously complained about the inconvenience of these services, only three of his neighbors came to his Christmas dinner in 1837, a snub that enraged him. As Hammond's experience demonstrated, class relations among whites in the Old South were a complex blend of privilege, patronage, and equality.

The Slaveowners

In 1860 the region's 15 states had a population of 12 million, of which roughly two-thirds were white, one-third were black slaves, and about 2 percent were free African Americans. Because of the institution of slavery, the social structure of the antebellum South differed in important ways from that of the North. Even so, southern society was remarkably fluid, and as a result, class lines were not rigid.

Of the 8 million white southerners in 1860, only about 2 million (one-quarter) either owned slaves or were members of slaveowning families. Moreover, most slaveowners owned only a few slaves. If one uses the census definition of a planter as a person who owned 20 or more slaves, only about 1 out of every 30 white southerners belonged to families of the planter class.

A planter of consequence, however, needed to own at least 50 slaves, and there were only about 10,000 such families—less than 1 percent of the white population. This privileged group made up the aristocracy at the top of the southern class structure. Although limited in size, the planter class nevertheless owned more than half of all slaves and controlled more than 90 percent of the region's total wealth.

The typical plantation had 20 to 50 slaves and 800 to 1000 acres of land. Thus larger slaveowners usually owned several plantations, with an overseer for each one. The slaves were divided into field hands, skilled workers, and house servants, with one or more slaves serving as "drivers" to assist the overseer. While planters pioneered the application of capitalistic methods, including specialization and division of labor, to agriculture, plantations remained labor-intensive operations. Of the southern staples only the production of sugar was heavily mechanized.

Plantation administration

Tidewater and Frontier

Southern planters shared a commitment to preserve slavery as the source of their wealth and stature. Yet in other ways they were a diverse group. On the one hand, the tobacco and rice planters of the Atlantic Tidewater were part of a settled region and a culture that reached back 150 to 200 years. States such as Mississippi and Arkansas, by contrast, were at or just emerging from the frontier stage, since most residents had arrived after 1815. Consequently, the society of the Southwest was rawer and more volatile.

It was along the Tidewater, especially the bays of the Chesapeake and the South Carolina coast, that the legendary "Old South" was born. Here, masters erected substantial homes, some—especially between Charleston and Columbia—the classic white-pillared mansions in the Greek revival style. Here, more than a few planters were urbane and polished.

Tidewater society

The ideal of the Tidewater South was the country gentleman. An Irish visitor observed that in Maryland and Virginia the great planters lived in "a style which approaches nearer to that of the English country gentleman than what is to be met with anywhere else on the continent." As in England, the local gentry often served as justices of the peace, and the Episcopal church remained the socially accepted road to heaven. Here, too, family names continued to be important in politics.

While the newer regions of the South boasted of planters with cultivated manners, as a group the cotton lords were a different breed. Whatever their background, whether planters, farmers, overseers, or businessmen, these entrepreneurs had moved west for the same reason so many other white Americans had: to make their fortunes. By and large, the cotton gentry were self-made men who through hard work, aggressive business tactics, and good luck had risen from ordinary backgrounds. For them, the cotton boom and the exploitation of enslaved men and women offered the opportunity to move up in a new society that lacked an entrenched elite.

Society in the cotton kingdom

"Time's money, time's money." For men like the impatient Texan, time was indeed money, slaves were capital, and cotton by the bale signified cash in hand. This business orientation was especially apparent in the cotton kingdom, where planters sought to maximize their profits and constantly reinvested their returns in land and slaves. As one visitor said of Mississippi slaveholders: "To sell cotton in order to buy negroes—to make more cotton to buy more negroes, 'ad infinitum,' is the aim and direct tendency of all the operations of the thorough-going cotton planter: his whole soul is wrapped up in the pursuit." One shocked Virginian who visited Vicksburg claimed that its citizens ran "mad with speculation" and did business "in a kind of phrenzy." And indeed there was money to be made. The combined annual income of the richest thousand families of the cotton kingdom approached $50 million, while the wealth of the remaining 666,000 white families amounted to only about $60 million.

Slaveholders' values

Stately mansions could be found in a few areas of the South. In general, though, most planters lived humbly. Although they ranked among the richest citizens in America, their homes were often simple one- or two-story unpainted wooden frame houses, and some were log cabins. "If you wish to see people worth millions living as [if] they were not worth hundreds," advised one southwestern planter in 1839, "come to the land of cotton and negroes." Practical men, few of the new cotton lords had absorbed the culture and learning of the traditional country gentleman.

The Master at Home

Whether supervising a Tidewater plantation or creating a cotton estate on the Texas frontier, the master had to coordinate a complex agricultural operation. He gave daily instructions concerning the work to be done, settled disputes between slaves and the overseer, and generally handed out rewards and penalties. In addition, the owner made the critical decisions for planting, harvesting, and marketing of the crops as well as for investments and expenditures.

In performing his duties, the plantation owner was supposed to be the "master" of his crops, his family, and his slaves. Defenders of slavery often held up this paternalistic ideal—the care and guidance of dependent "children"—and maintained that slavery promoted a genuine bond of affection between the caring master and his loyal slaves. In real life, however, the forces of the market made this paternalistic ideal less evident. Even in the Tidewater, planters were concerned with money and profits. Indeed, some of the most brutal forms of slavery existed on rice plantations. Except for a few domestic servants, owners of large plantations generally had little contact with their slaves. Nor could paternalism mask the reality that slavery everywhere rested on violence, racism, and exploitation.

Paternalism

The Plantation Mistress

Upper-class southern white women, like those in the North, grew up with the ideal of domesticity, reinforced by the notion of a paternalistic master who was lord of the plantation. But the plantation mistress soon discovered that, given the demands placed on her, the ideal was hard to fulfill.

In her youth a genteel lady enjoyed a certain amount of leisure. But once she married and became a plantation mistress, a southern woman was often shocked by the magnitude of her responsibilities. Nursing the sick, making clothing, tending the garden, caring for the poultry, and overseeing every aspect of food preparation were all her domain. She also had to supervise and plan the work of the domestic servants and distribute clothing. After taking care of breakfast, one harried Carolina mistress recounted that she "had the [sewing] work cut out, gave orders about dinner, had the horse feed fixed in hot water, had the box filled with cork: . . . now I have to cut out the flannel jackets." Sarah Williams, the New York bride of a North Carolina planter, admitted that her mother-in-law "works harder than any Northern farmer's wife I know."

Mistress's duties

Unlike female reformers in the North, upper-class southern women did not openly challenge their role, but some certainly found their sphere confining. The greatest unhappiness stemmed from the never-ending task of managing slaves. One southern mistress confessed she was frightened at being "always among people whom I do not understand and whom I must guide, and teach and lead on like children." Yet without the labor of slaves, the lifestyle of these women was an impossibility.

Mistress's discontent

Sarah Pierce Vick, the mistress of a plantation
near Vicksburg, Mississippi, pauses to speak
to one of her slaves. A plantation mistress had
many duties and, while enjoying the comforts
brought by wealth and status, often found her
life more difficult than she had anticipated
before marriage.

Many women were deeply discontented, too, with the widespread double standard for sexual behavior and with the daily reminders of miscegenation some had to face. A man who fathered illegitimate children by slave women suffered no social or legal penalties, even in the case of rape (southern law did not recognize such a crime against slave women), whereas a white woman guilty of adultery lost all social respectability. One planter's wife spoke of "violations of the moral law that made mulattoes as common as blackberries," and another recalled, "I saw slavery . . . teemed with injustice and shame to all womankind and I hated it."

Miscegenation

Some women drew a parallel between their situation and that of the slaves. Both were subject to male dominance, and independent-minded women found the subordination of marriage difficult. Susan Dabney Smedes, in her recollection of growing up on an Alabama plantation, recalled that "it was a saying that the mistress of a plantation was the most complete slave on it."

Still, plantation mistresses were unwilling to forgo the material comforts that slavery made possible. Moreover, racism was so pervasive within American society that the few white southern women who privately criticized the institution displayed little empathy for the plight of slaves themselves, including black women. Whatever the burdens of the plantation mistress, they were hardly akin to the bondage of slavery itself.

Yeoman Farmers

In terms of numbers, yeoman farm families were the backbone of southern society, accounting for well over half the southern white population. They owned no slaves and farmed the traditional 80 to 160 acres, like northern farmers. About 80 percent owned their own land. They settled almost every-where in the South, except in the rice and sugar districts and valuable river bottomlands of the Deep South, which were monopolized by large slave-owners. Like Ferdinand Steel, most were semisubsistence farmers who raised primarily corn and hogs, along with perhaps a few bales of cotton or some tobacco, which they sold to obtain the cash needed to buy items like sugar, coffee, and salt. Yeoman farmers lacked the wealth of planters, but they had a pride and dignity that earned them the respect of their richer neighbors.

While southern farmers led more isolated lives than did their northern counterparts, their social activities were not very different. Religion played an important role at camp meetings held in late summer, after the crops were laid by and before

Lives of yeoman farmers

A majority of white southerners were members of nonslaveholding yeoman farm families. Ruggedly independent, these families depended on their own labor and often lived under primitive conditions. (Courtesy, Museum of Fine Arts, Boston)

harvest time. As in the North, neighbors also met to exchange labor and tools. The men rolled logs to clear fields of dead trees, women met for quilting bees, and adults and children alike would gather to shuck corn. Court sessions, militia musters, political rallies—these, too, were occasions that brought rural folk together.

Since yeoman farmers lacked cheap slave labor, good transportation, and access to credit, they could not compete with planters in the production of staples. And when it came to selling their corn and wheat, small farmers conducted only limited business with planters, who usually grew as much of their own food as possible. In the North urban centers became a market for small farmers, but in the South the lack of towns limited this internal market. Thus while southern yeoman farmers were not poor, they suffered from a chronic lack of money and the absence of conveniences that northern farm families enjoyed. Josiah Hinds, who hacked a farm out of the isolated woods of northern Mississippi, worried that his children were growing up "wild." He complained that "education is but little prized by my neighbours," who were satisfied "if the corn and cotton grows to perfection . . . [and] brings a fare price, and hog meat is at hand to boil with the greens."

Limits on economic opportunity

In some ways, then, the worlds of the yeoman farmers and the upper-class planters were not only different but also in conflict. Still, a hostility between the two classes did not emerge. Yeoman farmers admired planters and hoped that one day they would join the gentry themselves. Furthermore, they accepted slavery as a means of controlling African Americans as members of an inferior social caste based on race. "Now suppose they was free," one poor farmer told Frederick Law Olmsted, a northern visitor. "You see they'd all think themselves as good as we." Racism and fear of black people were sufficient to keep nonslaveholders loyal to southern institutions.

Absence of class conflict

Poor Whites

The poorest white southerners were confined to land that no one else wanted. They lived in rough, unchinked, windowless log cabins located in the remotest areas and were often squatters without title to the land they were on. The men spent their time hunting and fishing, while women did the domestic work, including what farming they could manage. Circumstances made their poverty difficult to escape. Largely illiterate, they suffered from malnutrition stemming from a monotonous diet of corn, pork, and whiskey, and they were afflicted with malaria and hookworm, diseases that sapped their energy. Other white southerners referred to them scornfully as crackers, white trash, sandhillers, and clay eaters.

The number of poor whites in the Old South is difficult to estimate. There may have been as few as 100,000 or as many as a million; probably they numbered about 500,000, or a little more than 5 percent of the white population.

Because poor whites traded with slaves, exchanging whiskey for stolen goods, contemptuous planters often bought them out simply to rid the neighborhood of them. For their part, poor whites keenly resented planters, but their hostility toward African Americans was even stronger. Poor whites refused to perform any work commonly done by slaves and vehemently opposed ending slavery. Emancipation would remove one of the few symbols of their status—that they were, at least, free.

Relations with planters

THE PECULIAR INSTITUTION

Slaves were not free. That overwhelming fact must be understood before anything is said about the kindness or the cruelty individual slaves experienced; before any consideration of healthy or unhealthy living conditions; before any discussion of how slave families coped with hardship, rejoiced in shared pleasures, or worshiped in prayer. The lives of slaves were affected day in and day out, in big ways and small, by the basic reality that slaves were not their own masters. The master determined a slave's workload, whether a slave could visit a nearby plantation, and whether a slave family remained intact. Whatever slaves wanted to do, they had always to consider the response of their masters.

When power is distributed as unequally as it was between masters and slaves, every action on the part of the enslaved involved a certain calculation, conscious or unconscious. The consequences of every act, of every expression or gesture, had to be considered. In that sense, the line between freedom and slavery penetrated every corner of a slave's life, and it was an absolute and overwhelming distinction.

One other stark fact reinforced the sharp line between freedom and slavery: slaves were distinguished on the basis of color. While the peculiar institution was an economic system of labor, it was also a caste system based on race. The color line of slavery made it easier to defend the institution and win the support of yeoman farmers and poor white southerners, even

Slavery and race

though in many ways the system held them back. Hence slavery must be understood on many levels: not only as an economic system but also as a racial and cultural one, in terms of not only its outward conditions of life and labor but also the inner demands it made on the soul.

Work and Discipline

The conditions slaves encountered varied widely, depending on the size of the farm or plantation, the crop being grown, the personality of the master, and whether he was an absentee owner. On small farms slaves worked in the fields alongside their owners and had much closer contact with whites. On plantations, in contrast, most slaves dealt primarily with the overseer, who was paid by the size of the harvest he brought in and was therefore often harsh in his approach.

House servants and the drivers, who supervised the field hands, were accorded the highest status, and skilled artisans such as carpenters and blacksmiths

Black slave driver

were also given special recognition. The hardest work was done by the field hands, both men and women, who sometimes were divided into plowhands and hoe gangs.

Some planters organized their slaves in the gang system, in which a white overseer or a black driver supervised gangs of 20 to 25 adults. Although this approach extracted long hours of reasonably hard labor, the slaves had to be constantly supervised and shirkers were difficult to detect. Other planters preferred the task system, under which each slave was given a specific daily assignment to complete, after which he or she was finished for the day. This system allowed slaves to work at their own pace, gave them an incentive to do careful work, and freed overseers from having to closely supervise the work. On the other hand, slaves resisted vigorously if masters tried to increase the workload. The task system was most common in the rice fields, whereas the gang system predominated in the cotton districts. Many planters used a combination of the two.

Gang versus task system of labor

Toil began just before sunrise and continued until dusk. During cultivation and harvest, slaves were in the field 15 to 16 hours a day, eating a noonday meal there and resting before resuming labor. Work was uncommon on Sundays, and frequently only a half day was required on Saturdays. Even so, the routine was taxing. "We . . . have everybody at work before day dawns," an Arkansas cotton planter reported. "I am never caught in bed after day light nor is any body else on the place, and we continue in the cotton fields when we can have fair weather till it is so dark we can't see to work."

Often masters gave rewards to slaves who worked diligently, but the threat of punishment was always present. Slaves could be denied passes; their food allowance could be reduced; and if all else failed, they could be sold. The most common instrument of punishment was the whip. The frequency of its use varied from plantation to plantation, but few slaves escaped the lash entirely. "We have to rely more and more on the power of fear," planter James Henry Hammond acknowledged. "We are determined to continue masters, and to do so we have to draw the reign tighter and tighter day by day to be assured that we hold them in complete check."

Rewards and punishment

Resistance and Discipline on a Cotton Plantation

August 13, 1839 . . . Ginny Jerry has not been seen since Friday morning last — has been shirkin for some time came to me Friday morning sick — suspecting him Examined him found nothing the matter complaining of pains &c. told him to go & work it off — he has concluded to woods it off. . . .

September 25 . . . G. Jerry ran off yesterday afternoon—told him at dinner I wanted to weigh his Basket. went off. Whiped him for it—Which offended his Lordship & he put out.

September 29 . . . Lewis . . . weighed cotten that had been wet & was verry much stained &c. do[d]ged off from the scaffolds not seen him since. . . .

September 30 . . . Had G. Jerry T Fill & Bts Nat up here washing all yesterday as punishment. . . .

October 3 . . . told Dennis I intended to Whip him. went up in the Gin house to empty his cotten. Went out through the receiving room & put out . . . I had rather a negro would do anything Else than runaway. Dennis & his Brother Lewis & G. Jerry the only ones that gives me any trouble to make do their part. . . .

October 4 . . . Boy Lewis came in last night—gave him the worst Whipping I ever gave any young negro. I predict he will not runaway soon. Building a Jail for him Dennis & Ginny Jerry—intend Jailing them from Saturday nights 'till Monday mornings. . . .

October 13 . . . more sickness two days yonst that Ive had this season—several pretending Put Darces in Jail last night for pretending to be sick, repeatedly. . . .

October 23 . . . Gave every cotten picker a Whipping last night for trash [i.e., picking trashy cotton]. . . .

December 6 . . . caught Capt. Howells runaway yesterday—him & my boy Dennis have been together started to their camp at Dark—. . . found every thing very comfortable. cooking utensils in abundance meat &c. . . .

December 23 . . . Turnbulls Overseer Bailey caught Dennis yesterday & brought him to me to day— he is as fat as he can be

December 24 . . . intend Exhibiting Dennis during Christmas on a scaffold in the middle of the Quarter & with a red Flannel Cap on.

December 25 . . . Dennis confined in Jail—tells me he saw & talked with several of my negros While out.

Source: Edwin Adams Davis, ed., *Plantation Life in the Florida Parishes of Louisiana 1836–1846* (New York: Columbia University Press, 1943), pp. 155–175.

Slave Maintenance

Planters generally bought rough, cheap cloth for slave clothing and each year gave adults at most only a couple of outfits and a pair of shoes. Few slaves had enough clothing or blankets to keep warm when the weather dipped below freezing. Some planters provided well-built housing, but more commonly slaves lived in cramped,

Clothing and housing

poorly built cabins that were leaky in wet weather, drafty in cold, and furnished with only a few crude chairs or benches and a table, perhaps a mattress filled with corn husks or straw, and a few pots and dishes.

Sickness among the hands was a persistent problem. In order to keep medical expenses down, slaveowners treated sick slaves themselves and called in a doctor only for serious cases. Conditions varied widely, but on average, a slaveowner spent less than a dollar a year on medical care for each slave.

Nevertheless, the United States was the only slave society in the Americas where the slave population increased naturally—indeed, at about the same rate as the white population. Even so, infant mortality among slaves was more than double that of the white population; for every 1000 live births among southern slaves, more than 200 died before the age of 5. For those who survived infancy, enslaved African Americans had a life expectancy about 8 years less than that of white Americans. As late as 1860, fewer than two-thirds of slave children survived to the age of 10.

Lower life expectancy

Resistance

Given the wide gulf between freedom and slavery, it was only natural that slaves resisted the bondage imposed on them. The most radical form of resistance was rebellion, which occurred repeatedly in slave societies in the Americas. In Latin America, slave revolts were relatively frequent, involving hundreds and even thousands of slaves and pitched battles in which large numbers were killed. The most successful slave revolt occurred in France's sugar-rich colony, Saint Dominque (the western part of the Caribbean island of Hispaniola). There, free blacks who had fought in the American Revolution because of France's alliance with the United States brought back the ideals of freedom and equality. Furthermore, the brutally overworked population of half a million slaves was ready to revolt and received further encouragement from the example of the French Revolution. Under the leadership of Toussaint-Louverture, rebellion led to the establishment of Haiti in 1804, the second independent republic in the Western Hemisphere.

Slave rebellions in the Americas

Elsewhere, Jamaica averaged one significant revolt every year from 1731 to 1823, while in 1823 thousands rose in Guiana. Jamaica also witnessed an uprising of some 20,000 slaves in 1831. These revolts, and ones in 1823 and 1824 in British-controlled Demarra, were savagely suppressed. And in Brazil, which had the largest number of slaves outside the United States, it took the government 50 years to suppress with military force a colony of some 20,000 fugitive slaves who had sought refuge in the mountains.

In contrast, slave revolts were rare in the United States. Unlike in Latin America, in the Old South whites outnumbered blacks, the government was much more powerful, a majority of slaves were native-born, and family life was much stronger. Slaves recognized the odds against them, and many potential leaders became fugitives instead. What is remarkable is that American slaves revolted at all.

Infrequency of revolts in the United States

Early in the nineteenth century several well-organized uprisings were barely thwarted. In 1800 Gabriel Prosser, a slave blacksmith, recruited perhaps a couple hundred slaves in a plan to march on Richmond and capture the governor. But a few slaves betrayed the plot, and Prosser and other leaders were eventually captured and executed. Denmark Vesey's conspiracy in Charleston in 1822 met a similar fate (page 296).

The most famous slave revolt, led by a literate slave preacher named Nat Turner, was more spontaneous. Turner, who lived on a farm in southeastern Virginia, was given unusual privileges by his master, whom he described as a kind and trusting man. A religious mystic, Turner became convinced that God had selected him to punish white people through "terror and devastation." One night in 1831 following an eclipse of the sun, he and six confederates stole out and murdered Turner's master and family. Recruiting some 70 slaves as they went, Turner's band killed 57 white men, women, and children.

Nat Turner's rebellion

The revolt lasted only 48 hours before being crushed. Turner was eventually captured, tried, and executed. Although the uprising was quickly put down, it left white southerners with a haunting uneasiness. Turner seemed a model slave, yet who could read a slave's true emotions behind the mask of obedience?

Few slaves followed Turner's violent example. But there were other, more subtle ways of resisting a master's authority. Most dramatically, slaves could do as Octave Johnson did and run away. With the odds stacked heavily against them, few runaways escaped safely to freedom except from the border states. More frequently, slaves fled to nearby woods or swamps. Some runaways stayed out only a few days; others, like Johnson, held out for months.

Day-to-day resistance

Many slaves resisted by abusing their masters' property. They mishandled animals, broke tools and machinery, misplaced items, and worked carelessly in the fields. Slaves also sought to trick the master by feigning illness or injury and by hiding rocks in the cotton they picked. Slaves complained directly to the owner about an overseer's mistreatment, thereby attempting to drive a wedge between the two.

The most common form of resistance, and a persistent annoyance to slaveowners, was theft. Slaves raided the master's smokehouse, secretly slaughtered his stock, and killed his poultry. Slaves often distinguished between "stealing" from each other and merely "taking" from white masters. "Dey allus done tell us it am wrong to lie and steal," recalled Josephine Howard, a former slave in Texas, "but why did de white folks steal my mammy and her mammy? Dey lives . . . over in Africy. . . . Dat de sinfulles' stealin' dey is."

Slaves learned to outwit their masters, one former bondsman testified, by wearing an "impenetrable mask" around whites: "How much of joy, of sorrow, of misery and anguish have they hidden from their tormentors." Frederick Douglass, the most famous fugitive slave, explained that "as the master studies to keep the slave ignorant, the slave is cunning enough to make the master think he succeeds."

Slaves' hidden feelings

SLAVE CULTURE

Trapped in bondage, slaves could at least forge a culture of their own by combining strands from their African past with customs that evolved from their life in America. This slave culture was most distinct on big plantations, where the large slave population lived farther apart from white scrutiny.

The Slave Family

Maintaining a sense of family was one of the most remarkable achievements of African Americans in bondage, given the obstacles that faced them. Southern law did not recognize slave marriages as legally binding, nor did it allow slave parents complete authority over their children. Black women faced the possibility of rape by the master or overseer without legal recourse, and husbands, wives, and children had to live with the fear of being sold and separated. From 1820 to 1860 more than two million slaves were sold in the interstate slave trade. Perhaps 600,000 husbands and wives were separated by such sales.

Breakup of families

Still, family ties remained strong, as slave culture demonstrated. The marriage ceremony among slaves varied from a formal religious service to jumping over the broomstick in front of the slave community to nothing more than the master's giving verbal approval. Whatever the ceremony, slaves viewed the ritual as a public

Slaves who have been sold are being loaded into boxcars to be transported from Richmond to plantations farther south. As they say their final sad goodbyes to family and friends, a slave trader completes his business.

affirmation of the couple's commitment to their new duties and responsibilities. Rather than adopting white norms, slaves developed
their own moral code concerning sexual relations and marriage. Although young slaves often engaged in premarital sex, they were expected to choose
a partner and become part of a stable family. It has been estimated that at least one
in five slave women had one or more children before marriage, but most of these
mothers eventually married. "The negroes had their own ideas of morality, and
they held them very strictly," the daughter of a Georgia planter recalled. "They
did not consider it wrong for a girl to have a child before she married, but after-
wards were very strict upon anything like infidelity on her part."

Family ties in slavery

The traditional nuclear family of father, mother, and children was the rule, not
the exception, among slaves. Labor in the quarters was divided according to sex.
Women did the indoor work such as cooking, washing, and sewing,
and men performed outdoor chores, such as gathering firewood, hauling water, and tending the animals and garden plots. The men also
hunted and fished to supplement the spare weekly rations. "My old daddy . . .
caught rabbits, coons an' possums," recalled Louisa Adams of North Carolina. "He
would work all day and hunt at night."

Gender roles

Songs and Stories of Protest and Celebration

In the songs they sang, slaves expressed some of their deepest feelings about life.
"The songs of the slave represent the sorrows of his heart," commented Frederick Douglass. Surely there was bitterness as well as sorrow when slaves sang:

> We raise the wheat
> They give us the corn
> We bake the bread
> They give us the crust
> We sift the meal
> They give us the husk
> We peel the meat
> They give us the skin
> And that's the way
> They take us in

Yet songs were also central to the celebrations held in the slave quarters: for
marriages, Christmas revels, and after harvest time. And a slave on the way to the
fields might sing:

> Saturday night and Sunday too
> Young gals on my mind.
> Monday morning 'way 'fore day,
> Old master's got me gwine.
> Peggy does you love me now?

Slaves expressed themselves through stories as well as song. Most often these
folk tales used animals as symbolic models for the predicaments in which slaves

Lewis Miller of York, Pennsylvania, painted this picture of Virginia slaves dancing in 1853. Dancing and music were important components of slave culture and provided a welcome respite from work under slavery.

Folk tales

found themselves. In the best known of these, the cunning Brer Rabbit was a weak fellow who defeated larger animals like Brer Fox and Brer Bear by using his wits. Other stories were less symbolic and contained more overt hostility toward white people. These stories, whether direct or symbolic, taught the young how to survive in a hostile world.

The Lord Calls Us Home

At the center of slave culture was religion. Slaveowners encouraged a carefully controlled form of religion among slaves. "Church was what they called it," one former slave protested, "but all that preacher talked about was for us slaves to obey our masters and not to lie and steal. Nothing about Jesus was ever said and the overseer stood there to see that the preacher talked as he wanted him to talk." In response, some slaves rejected all religion.

Most slaves, however, sought a Christianity firmly their own, beyond the control of the master. On many plantations they met secretly at night, when they broke into rhythmic singing and dancing, modeled on the ring shout of African religion. Even in regular services, observers noted the greater emotion of black worshippers. "The way in which we worshiped is almost indescribable," one slave preacher recalled. "The singing was accompanied

Slave religion

by a certain ecstasy of motion, clapping of hands, tossing of heads, which would continue without cessation about half an hour." In an environment where slaves, for most of the day, were prevented from expressing their deepest feelings, such meetings served as a satisfying emotional release.

Although secret religious meetings were important, the religious experience of most enslaved African Americans occurred mainly within the regular white-controlled churches of the South. It has been estimated that one million slaves were included in the southern churches before the Civil War. Black worshipers were especially numerous in the Methodist and Baptist churches; indeed, in some areas, slaves were a majority in local congregations. As a result, most slaves worshiped together with their masters rather than in separate services. At one point during the regular service ministers delivered a special message to the slaves who were present, but they also heard the same sermon as whites, with its emphasis on faith and salvation. The churches were also the one institution in the South where blacks were accorded a measure of equality. Black members were held to the same standards of conduct, were subject to same church discipline, and were allowed to testify against whites. All of these qualities helped shape the crucial significance of religion in slave culture.

Religion also provided slaves with values to guide them through their daily experiences and give them a sense of self-worth. Slaves learned that God would redeem the poor and downtrodden and raise them one day to honor and glory. Just as certainly, on the final Day of Judgment, masters would be punished for their sins. "This is one reason why I believe in hell," a former slave declared. "I don't believe a just God is going to take no such man as my former master into His Kingdom."

Again, song played a central role. Slaves sang religious "spirituals" at work and at play as well as in religious services. Seemingly meek and otherworldly, the songs often contained a hidden element of protest. Frederick Douglass disclosed that when slaves sang longingly of "Canaan, sweet Canaan," they were thinking not only of the Bible's Promised Land but of the North and freedom. While a song's lyrics might speak of an otherworldly freedom from sin in heaven, their hearts were considering a this-worldly escape from physical bondage.

Slave spirituals

Religion, then, served not only to comfort slaves after days of toil and sorrow. It also strengthened the sense of togetherness and common purpose and held out the promise of eventual freedom in this world and the next. The faith that "some ob dese days my time will come" was one of the most important ways that slaves coped with bondage and resisted its pressure to rob them of their self-esteem.

The Slave Community

While slaves managed to preserve a sense of self-worth in a culture of their own, they found it impossible to escape fully from white control. Even the social hierarchy within the slave quarters never was entirely free from the white world. The prestige of a slave driver rested ultimately on the authority of the white master, and skilled slaves and house servants often felt superior to other slaves, an attitude masters consciously promoted. Light-skinned slaves sometimes deemed their color a badge of superiority. Fanny Kemble recorded that one woman begged to be relieved of field labor, which she considered degrading, "on 'account of her color.'"

Hierarchy of color

Lucy Skipwith, who was the daughter of a driver who had been educated by her mistress, was a member of the slave elite. At Hopewell plantation in Alabama, she was in full charge of the main residence during her master's frequent absences. Eager for her master's approval, Skipwith on several occasions reported slave disobedience, which temporarily estranged her from the slave community, yet in the end she was always welcomed back. While Skipwith never rebelled or apparently considered running away, she was far from submissive. She defined white authority, protected her family, and used her influence to get rid of an overseer the slaves disliked. Like many house servants, she lived between two worlds—her master's and the slave quarters—and was never entirely comfortable in either.

Despite these divisions, the realities of slavery and white racism inevitably drove black people closer together in a common bond and forced them to depend on one another to survive. Walled in from the individualistic white society beyond, slaves out of necessity created a community of their own.

Free Black Southerners

Of the 4 million African Americans living in the South in 1860, only 260,000—about 7 percent—were free. More than 85 percent of them lived in the Upper South, with almost 200,000 in Maryland, Virginia, and North Carolina alone. Free black southerners were also much more urban than either the southern white or slave populations. In 1860 almost a third of the free African Americans in the Upper South, and more than half in the Lower South, lived in towns and cities. As a rule, free African Americans were more literate than slaves, and they were disproportionately female and much more likely to be of mixed ancestry.

Most free black southerners lived in rural areas, although usually not near plantations. A majority eked out a living farming or in low-paying unskilled jobs, but some did well enough to own slaves themselves. In 1830 about 3600 did, although commonly their "property" was their wives or children, purchased because they could not be emancipated under state laws. A few, however, were full-blown slaveowners.

Following Nat Turner's rebellion of 1831, southern legislatures increased the restrictions they placed on free African Americans. They were forbidden to enter a new state, had to carry their free papers, could not assemble when they wished, were subject to a nightly curfew, often had to post a bond and be licensed to work, and could not vote, hold office, or testify in court against white people.

Tightening control

Free African Americans occupied an uncertain position in southern society, well above black slaves but distinctly beneath even poorer white southerners. They were victims of a society that had no place for them.

SOUTHERN SOCIETY AND THE DEFENSE OF SLAVERY

While the South was a remarkably diverse region, it was united above all by the institution of slavery. As the South's economy became more and more dependent on slave-produced staples, slavery became more central to the life of the South, to its culture and its identity.

The Virginia Debate of 1832

At the time of the Revolution, the leading critics of slavery had been southerners—Jefferson, Washington, Madison, and Patrick Henry among them. But beginning in the 1820s, in the wake of the controversy over admitting Missouri as a slave state, southern leaders became less apologetic about slavery and more aggressive in defending it. The turning point occurred in the early 1830s, when the South found itself increasingly under attack. It was in 1831 that William Lloyd Garrison began publishing his abolitionist newspaper, *The Liberator.* That was also the year Nat Turner led his revolt, which frightened so many white southerners.

In response to the Turner insurrection, a number of Virginia's western counties, where there were few slaves, petitioned the legislature to adopt a program for gradual emancipation. In the end, however, the legislature refused, by a vote of 73 to 58, to consider legislation to end slavery.

The 1832 Virginia debate represented the last significant attempt of white southerners to take action against slavery. Most felt that the subject was no longer open to debate. Instead, during the 1830s and 1840s, southern leaders defended slavery as a positive good, not just for white but for black people as well. As John C. Calhoun proclaimed in 1837, "I hold that in the present state of civilization, where two races . . . distinguished by color and other physical differences, as well as intellectual, are brought together, the relation now existing in the slaveholding states between the two is, instead of an evil, a good—a positive good."

Significance of the Virginia debate

The Proslavery Argument

Politicians like Calhoun were not alone. White southern leaders justified slavery in a variety of ways. Ministers argued that under the law of Moses, Jews were authorized to enslave heathens, and emphasized that none of the Biblical prophets nor Christ himself had ever condemned slavery. Defenders of the institution also pointed out that classical Greece

Religious, racial, and social arguments

and Rome depended on slavery. They even cited John Locke, that giant of the Enlightenment, who had recognized slavery in the constitution he drafted for the colony of Carolina. African Americans belonged to an intellectually and emotionally inferior race, slavery's defenders argued, and therefore lacked the ability to care for themselves.

Proslavery writers sometimes argued that slaves in the South lived better than factory workers in the North. Masters cared for slaves for life, whereas northern workers had no claim on their employer when they were unemployed, old, or no longer able to work. In advancing this argument, white southerners exaggerated the material comforts of slavery and minimized the average worker's standard of living—to say nothing, of course, about the incalculable psychological value of freedom. Still, to many white southerners, slavery seemed a more humane system of labor relations.

Defenders of slavery did not really expect to convert Northerners. Their target was more often slaveowners themselves. As Duff Green, a southern editor, explained, "We must satisfy the consciences, we must allay the fears of our own people. We must satisfy them that slavery is of itself right—that it is not a sin against God—that it is not an evil, moral or political. In this way only," he went on, "can we prepare our own people to defend their institutions."

Closing Ranks

Not all white southerners could quell their doubts. Still, a striking change in southern opinion seems to have occurred in the three decades before the Civil War. Outside the border states, few white southerners after 1840 contended even in private that slavery was wrong. And those who continued to oppose slavery found themselves harassed, assaulted, and driven into exile. Southern mobs destroyed the presses of antislavery papers and threatened the editors into either keeping silent or leaving the state. Southern mails were forcibly closed to abolitionist propaganda, and defenders of the South's institutions carefully scrutinized textbooks and faculty members in southern schools. Southerners like James Birney and Sarah and Angelina Grimké had to leave their native region to carry on the fight against slavery from the free states.

Increasingly, too, slavery entered the national political debate. Before 1836 Andrew Jackson's popularity in the South blocked the formation of a competitive two-party system. The rise of the abolitionist movement in the 1830s, however, left many southerners uneasy, and when the Democrats nominated the northerner Martin Van Buren in 1836, southern Whigs charged that Van Buren could not be counted on to meet the abolitionist threat to slavery. The Whigs made impressive gains in the South in 1836, carrying several states and significantly narrowing the margin between the two parties.

Politics of slavery

In later presidential elections, each party in the South through its northern supporters attacked the opposing party as unreliable on slavery. This tactic was less successful in state elections, however, since both parties were led by slaveholders and were committed to protecting slavery. In addition, the depression that began in 1837 focused the attention of southern voters on economic matters. Southern Whigs appealed to the commercially oriented members of society, whereas the Democratic party's strongholds were the more isolated regions of small independent farmers. As in the North, class and occupation were less important than one's economic and moral outlook. Southern voters most comfortable with the market and the changes it brought gravitated toward the Whig party. On the other hand, those farmers who feared the loss of personal independence that banks and commercial development brought with them tended to support the Democratic party.

> **Economics and party affiliation**

During the Jacksonian era, most southern political battles did not revolve around slavery. Still, southern politicians in both parties had to be careful to avoid the stigma of antislavery, since they were under mounting pressure from John Calhoun and his followers. Frustrated in his presidential hopes by the nullification crisis, Calhoun sought to unite the South behind his leadership by agitating the slavery issue. Few southern politicians followed his lead after 1833, but they did become extremely careful about being the least bit critical of slavery or southern institutions. They knew quite well that, even if their constituents were not so fanatical as Calhoun, southern voters overwhelmingly supported slavery.

Sections and the Nation

Viewing the events of the 1830s and 1840s with the benefit of hindsight, it is natural to anticipate the Civil War looming and to focus on the major differences dividing the North and the South. Yet free white northerners and southerners had much in common as Americans.

The largest group in both sections was composed of independent farmers who cultivated their own land with their own labor and were devoted to the principles of personal independence and social egalitarianism. Although southern society was more aristocratic in tone, both sections were driven by the quest for material wealth. The Texas Red River planter for whom "time was money" did not take a back seat to the Yankee clockmaker Chauncey Jerome in the scramble for success and status. White Americans in both sections aspired to rise in society, and linking geographic mobility to opportunity, they pushed westward with astonishing frequency.

> **Forces of national unity**

Many Americans, North and South, also adhered to the teachings of evangelical Protestantism. Southern churches were less open to social reform, primarily because of its association with abolitionism, and southern churches, unlike most in the North, defended slavery as a Christian institution. Eventually both the Methodist and the Baptist churches split into separate northern and southern organizations over this issue, but their attitudes on other matters often coincided.

Finally, white northerners and southerners shared a belief in democracy and white equality. Southern as well as northern states embraced the democratic reforms of the 1820s and 1830s, and the electorate in both sections favored giving all white males the vote and making public officeholders responsible to the people. Southerners insisted that the equality proclaimed in the Declaration of Independence applied only to white Americans (and really only to white males), but the vast majority of northerners in practice took no exception to this attitude. Both sections agreed on the necessity of safeguarding equality of opportunity rather than promoting equality of wealth.

With so much in common, it was not inevitable that the two sections come to blows. Certainly, before 1840 few politicians believed that the differences between the two sections were unreconcilable. It was only in the mid-1840s, when the United States embarked on a new program of westward expansion, that the slavery issue began to loom ominously in American life and that Americans began to question whether the Union could permanently endure, half slave and half free.

chapter summary

The Old South was a complex, biracial society that increasingly diverged from the rest of the United States in the years before 1860.

- Southerners placed heavy emphasis on agriculture and upheld the superiority of the rural way of life. Few cities and towns developed.
  - Southern commercial agriculture produced staple crops for sale in northern and European markets: tobacco, sugar, rice, and above all, cotton.
  - As southern agriculture expanded into the fresh lands of the Deep South, the slave population moved steadily westward and southward, and the Upper South became more diversified agriculturally.

- Slavery played a major role in shaping the class structure of the Old South.
  - Ownership of slaves brought privilege and status, and the largest slaveowners were extraordinarily wealthy.

- Planters on the older eastern seaboard enjoyed a more refined lifestyle than did those on the new cotton frontier.
- Most slaveowners, however, owned only a few slaves, and the majority of southern whites were nonslaveowning yeoman farmers.
  - At the bottom of the white class structure were the poor whites.
  - Slavery hurt nonslaveholding whites economically, but class tensions were muted in the Old South because of racial fears.

- The institution of slavery was both a labor system and a social system, regulating relations between the races.
  - Slaves resisted bondage in many ways, ranging from the subtle to the overt. Slave revolts, however, were rare.
  - Slaves developed their own culture, in which the family, religion, and songs played key roles in helping slaves cope with the pressures of bondage.

- Slaves' shared experiences created a community based on a common identity and mutual values.

- As slavery came under mounting attack, white southerners rallied to protect their peculiar institution.
  - They developed a set of arguments defending slavery as a positive good.

- Both political parties in the South strongly defended the institution and southern rights.

- Many Americans, both North and South, shared the same values: personal independence, social egalitarianism, evangelical Protestantism. But beginning in the mid-1840s with renewed westward expansion, the slavery issue increased sectional tensions.

For quizzes and a variety of interactive resources, visit the book's Online Learning Center at www.mhhe.com/davidsonconcise3

SIGNIFICANT EVENTS

1800	Gabriel Prosser's rebellion
1815–1860	Spread of the cotton kingdom
1822	Denmark Vesey conspiracy
1830–1840	Proslavery argument developed
1830–1860	Agricultural reform movement in Upper South
1831	Nat Turner's rebellion
1832	Virginia debate on slavery
1844	Methodist church divides into northern and southern organizations
1845	Baptist church divides

CHAPTER 14

Western Expansion and the Rise of the Slavery Issue
(1820–1850)

preview • The expansion of the United States to the Pacific was a process involving many overlapping and diverse frontiers—of cultures, peoples, and even animals and disease. From the east, the ideology of Manifest Destiny brought American settlers into conflict with Mexicans in Texas, New Mexico, and California; the British in Oregon; and Native Americans west of the Mississippi. Ominously, the acquisition of new lands also reopened the debate over slavery and the Union.

At first the Crows, Arapahos, and other Indians of the Great Plains paid little attention to the new people moving out from the forests far to the east. After all, for as long as they could remember, nations like the Crow had called the plains their own. But the new arrivals were not to be taken lightly. Armed with superior weapons and bringing with them a great many women and children, their appetite for land seemed inexhaustible. They attacked the villages of the Plains Indians, massacred women and children, and forced defeated tribes to live on reservations and serve their economic interests. In little more than a century and a half—from the first days when only a handful of their hunters and trappers had come into the region—they had become the masters of the plains.

The invaders who established this political and military dominance were *not* the strange "white men," who also came from the forest. During the 1830s and early 1840s, whites were still few in number. The more dangerous people—the ones who truly worried the Plains tribes—were the Sioux.

Westward expansion is usually told as a one-dimensional tale, centering on the wagon trains pressing on toward the Pacific. But frontiers, after all, are the boundary lines between contrasting cultures or environments; and during the nineteenth century, those in the West were constantly shifting and adapting. Frontier lines moved not only east to west, as with the white and Sioux migrations, but also south to north, as Spanish culture diffused, and west to east, as Asian immigrants came to California. Furthermore, frontiers marked not only human but also animal boundaries. Horses, cattle, and pigs, all of which had been imported from Europe, moved across the continent, usually in advance of European settlers. Often they

Cultural interaction

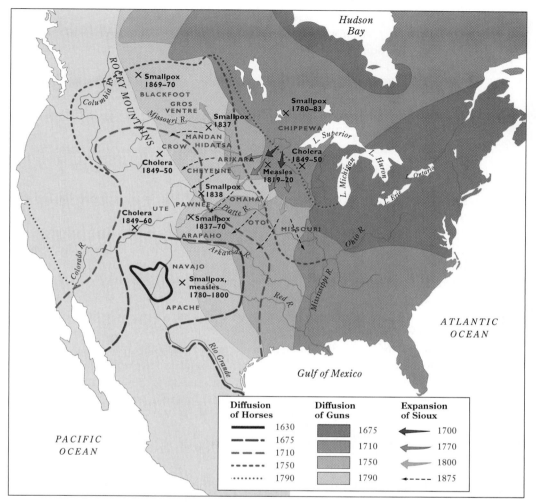

SIOUX EXPANSION AND THE HORSE AND GUN FRONTIER   In 1710 the horse and gun frontiers had not yet crossed, but by 1750 the two waves began to overlap. The Sioux pushed west during the early eighteenth century thanks to firearms; they were checked from further expansion until the 1770s, when smallpox epidemics again turned the balance of power in their favor.

transformed the way Indian peoples lived. Frontiers could also be technological, as in the case of trade goods and firearms. Moreover, as we have already seen, disease moved across the continent, with disastrous consequences for natives who had not acquired immunity to European microorganisms.

Three frontiers altered the lives of the Sioux: those of the horse, the gun, and disease. The horse frontier spread ahead of white settlement from the southwest, where horses had first been imported by the Spanish. On the other hand, the Spanish, unlike English and French

Horse, gun, and disease frontiers

traders, refused to sell firearms to Indians, so the gun frontier moved in the opposite direction, from northeast to southwest. The two waves met and crossed along the upper Missouri during the first half of the eighteenth century. For the tribes that possessed them, horses and guns conferred advantages in hunting and fighting.

The Sioux were first lured from the forest onto the Minnesota prairie during the early 1700s to hunt beaver, whose pelts could be exchanged with white traders for manufactured goods. Having obtained guns in exchange for furs, the Sioux drove the Omahas, Otos, Cheyennes, and Missouris (who had not yet acquired guns) south and west. But by the 1770s their advantage in guns had disappeared, and any farther advance was blocked by powerful tribes like the Mandans and Arikaras. These peoples were primarily horticultural, raising corn, beans, and squash and living in well-fortified towns. They also owned more horses than the Sioux, which made it easier for them to resist attacks.

But the third frontier, disease, threw the balance of power toward the Sioux after 1779. European traders brought smallpox with them onto the prairie. The horticultural tribes were hit especially hard because they lived in densely populated villages, where epidemics spread more easily. The Sioux embarked on a second wave of westward expansion in the late eighteenth century, so that by the time Lewis and Clark came through in 1804, they firmly controlled the upper Missouri as far as the Yellowstone River.

The Sioux's nomadic life enabled them to avoid the worst ravages of disease, especially the smallpox epidemic of 1837, which reduced the plains population by as much as half. Indeed, the Sioux became the largest (and most powerful) tribe on the plains. Certainly they were the only one whose high birthrate approximated that of whites. From an estimated 5000 in 1804, they grew to 25,000 by the 1850s. Their numbers increased Sioux military power as well as the need for new hunting grounds, and during the first half of the nineteenth century, they pushed even farther up the Missouri.

These shifting frontiers of animals, disease, firearms, and trade goods disrupted the political and cultural life of the Great Plains. And as white Americans moved westward, their own frontier lines produced similar disruptions, not only between white settlers and Indians but also between Anglo-American and Hispanic cultures.

Ironically, perhaps the greatest instability created by the moving frontiers occurred in established American society. As the political system of the United States struggled to incorporate western territories, North and South engaged in a fierce debate over whether the new lands should become slave or free. Just as the Sioux's cultural identity was brought into question by the moving frontier, so too was the identity of the American Republic.

DESTINIES: MANIFEST AND OTHERWISE

"Make way . . . for the young American Buffalo—he has not yet got land enough," roared one American politician in 1844. In the space of a few years, the United States acquired Texas, California, the lower half of the Oregon Territory, and the lands between the Rockies and California: nearly 1.5 million square miles in all.

John L. O'Sullivan, a prominent Democratic editor in New York, struck a responsive chord when he declared that it was the United States's "manifest destiny to overspread the continent allotted by Providence for the free development of our yearly multiplying millions." The cry of "Manifest Destiny" soon echoed in other editorial pages and in the halls of Congress.

The Roots of Manifest Destiny

Many Americans had long believed that their country had a special, even divine mission, which could be traced back to the Puritans' attempt to build a "city on a hill." Manifest Destiny also contained a political component, inherited from the ideology of the Revolution. In the mid-nineteenth century, Americans spoke of extending democracy, with widespread suffrage among white males, no king or aristocracy, and no established church, "over the whole North American continent."

Religious and political components

Americans believed that their social and economic system, too, should spread around the globe. They pointed to its broad ownership of land, individualism, and free play of economic opportunity as superior features of American life. Of course, Manifest Destiny also had its self-interested side. American business interests recognized the value of the fine harbors along the Pacific Coast, which promised a lucrative trade with Asia, and they hoped to make them American.

Finally, underlying the doctrine of Manifest Destiny was a persistent and deeply rooted racism. The United States had a duty to uplift the backward peoples of America, declared politicians and propagandists. Their reference was not so much to Indians—who refused to assimilate into American society—but to Mexicans, whose Christian nation had its roots in European culture. The Mexican race "must amalgamate and be lost, in the superior vigor of the Anglo-Saxon race," proclaimed O'Sullivan's *Democratic Review*, "or they must utterly perish."

Racist aspects

Before 1845, however, most Americans assumed that expansion would be achieved peacefully. When the time was right, neighboring provinces, like ripe fruit, would fall naturally into American hands. Texas, New Mexico, Oregon, and California—areas that were sparsely populated and weakly defended—dominated the American expansionist imagination. With time, Americans became less willing to wait patiently for the fruit to fall.

The Mexican Borderlands

The heart of Spain's American empire was Mexico City, where spacious boulevards spread out through the center of the city and where the University of Mexico, the oldest university in North America, had been accepting students since 1553, a full 85 years longer than Harvard. From the Mexican point of view, the frontier was

Although most Indians worked both in Spanish missions and on *ranchos* in conditions of near slavery, Indians were encouraged to adopt Spanish religion and customs. This Indian choir at Mission San Buenaventura sang in the mass. The Indians often made their own instruments, including flutes, drum, guitars, and triangles.

1000 miles to the north, in the provinces of Texas, New Mexico, and California. These isolated provinces developed largely free from supervision.

When Mexico won its independence from Spain in 1821, California at first was little affected. But in 1833 the Mexican Congress stripped the Catholic church of its huge tracts of California lands. These were turned over to Mexican cattle ranchers, usually in massive grants of 50,000 acres or more. The new *rancheros* ruled their estates much like great planters of the Old South. Labor was provided by Indians, who were forced to work for little more than room and board. At this time the Mexican population of California was approximately 4000. Lured by the cattle hide trade, a few Yankees settled in California as well, but in 1845 the American population amounted to only 700.

Spanish settlement of New Mexico was more dense: the province had about 44,000 inhabitants in 1827. But like California, its society was dominated by

Society in New Mexico

ranchero families who grazed large herds of sheep along the upper Rio Grande valley between El Paso and Taos. A few individuals controlled most of the wealth, while their workers eked out a meager living. Spain had long outlawed any commerce with Americans, but after Mexico declared its independence in 1821, yearly caravans from the United States began rolling into

Santa Fe. While this trade flourished over the next two decades, developments in the third Mexican borderland, neighboring Texas, worsened relations between Mexico and the United States.

The Texas Revolution

The new government of Mexico encouraged American emigration to Texas, where only about 3000 Mexicans, mostly ranchers, lived. Stephen Austin, who established a thriving colony on land granted by the government, was only the first of a new wave of American land agents, or *empresarios*. These *empresarios* obtained permission from Mexican authorities to settle families in Texas. Ninety percent of the new arrivals came from the South. Some, intending to grow cotton, brought slaves with them.

Tensions between Mexicans and American immigrants grew with the Texas economy. Most settlers from the States were Protestant, and although the Mexican government did not enforce its law that all citizens become Catholic, it barred Protestant churches. In 1829 Mexico abolished slavery, then looked the other way when Texas slaveholders evaded the law. But Texans were most disturbed because they had little say in their government, whose legislature lay about 700 miles to the south.

Cultural conflict in Texas

During the early 1830s the Mexican government made sporadic attempts to stop the influx of Americans. But immigration continued, until by mid-decade the American white population of 30,000 was nearly 10 times the number of Mexicans in the territory. Mexico also seemed determined to enforce the abolition of slavery. Even more disturbing to the American newcomers, in 1834 General Antonio Lopez de Santa Anna dissolved the Mexican Congress, proclaimed himself dictator, and led a military expedition north to enforce his new regime. When a ragtag Texas army clashed with the advance guard of Santa Anna's troops, a full-scale revolution was under way.

The Republic of Texas

As Santa Anna massed his forces for a decisive attack, a provisional government on March 2, 1836, proclaimed Texan independence. The constitution of the new Republic of Texas borrowed heavily from the U.S. Constitution, except that it explicitly prohibited the new Texas Congress from interfering with slavery. Meanwhile, Santa Anna's troops overran a Texan garrison at an old mission in San Antonio, known as the Alamo, and killed all of its 187 defenders. The Mexicans, however, paid dearly for the victory, losing more than 1500 men. The massacre of another force at Goliad after it surrendered further inflamed American resistance.

But anger was one thing; organized resistance was another. The commander of the Texas forces was Sam Houston, a former governor of Tennessee. Houston's intellectual ability and talent as a stump speaker thrust him to the forefront of the

Texas independence movement. Houston knew his army needed seasoning, so he retreated steadily eastward, buying time in order to forge a disciplined fighting force. By late April he was ready. Reinforced by eager volunteers from the United States, Houston's men surprised the Mexican army camped along the San Jacinto River. Shouting "Remember the Alamo!" they took only 15 minutes to overwhelm the Mexicans (who had been enjoying an afternoon siesta) and capture Santa Anna.

> **Houston defeats the Mexican army**

Threatened with execution, the Mexican commander signed treaties recognizing Texan independence and establishing the Rio Grande as the southern boundary of the Texas republic. The Mexican Congress (which had been reestablished in 1835) repudiated this agreement and launched several unsuccessful invasions into Texas. In the meantime, Houston assumed office in October 1836 as the first president of the new republic, determined to bring Texas into the Union as quickly as possible.

But Andrew Jackson worried that such a step would revive sectional tensions and hurt Martin Van Buren in the 1836 presidential election. Only on his last day in office did he extend formal diplomatic recognition to the Texas Republic. Van Buren was soon distracted by the economic panic that began shortly after he entered office and took no action during his term.

Rebuffed, Texans decided to go their own way. In the 10 years following independence, the "Lone Star" republic attracted more than 100,000 immigrants by offering free land to settlers. Mexico, however, refused to recognize Texan independence, and the vast majority of Texas citizens still wished to join the United States, where most of them, after all, had been born. There matters stood when the Whigs and William Henry Harrison won the presidency in 1840.

> **Texas as an independent republic**

THE TREK WEST

As thousands of Americans were moving into Texas, a much smaller trickle headed toward the Oregon country. Since 1818 the United States and Great Britain had occupied that territory jointly, as far north as latitude 54°40'. Although white settlement remained sparse, by 1836 American settlers outnumbered the British in the Willamette valley.

Pushed by the Panic of 1837 and six years of depression and pulled by tales of Oregon's lush, fertile valleys and the frost-free climate along California's Sacramento River, many American farmers struck out for the West Coast. The wife of one Missouri farmer was adamant about heading west: "Well, Dan Waldo," she announced, "if you want to stay here another summer and shake your liver out with the fever and ague, you can do it; but in the spring I am going to take the children and go to Oregon, Indians or no Indians." The wagon trains began rolling west.

The Overland Trail

Only a few hundred emigrants reached the West in 1841 and 1842, but in 1843 more than 800 followed the Overland Trail across the mountains to Oregon. From then on, they came by the thousands. The migration was primarily a family enterprise, and many couples had only recently married. Most adults were between 20 and 50, since the hard journey discouraged the elderly. Furthermore, a family of four needed about $600 to outfit their journey, an amount that excluded the poor.

Families migrate

Caravans of 20 to 30 wagons were common the first few years, but after 1845 parties traveled in smaller trains of 8 to 10 wagons. Large companies used up the grass quickly, disagreements were more likely, and breakdowns (and hence halts) were more frequent. The trip itself lasted about 6 months.

The journey west placed a special strain on women, for the rugged life along the trail disrupted their traditional sense of the home. At first, parties divided work

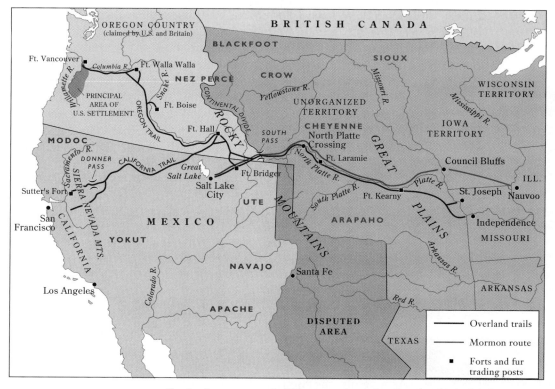

THE OVERLAND TRAIL   Beginning at several different points, the Overland Trail followed the Platte and Sweetwater rivers across the plains to South Pass, where it crossed the Continental Divide. The trail split near Fort Hall. Between 1840 and 1860 more than a quarter of a million emigrants made the trek.

Women on the Overland Trail

by gender, as had been done back home. Women cooked, washed, sewed, and took care of the children, while men drove the wagons, cared for the stock, stood guard, and did the heavy labor. Within a few weeks, however, women found themselves under the force of necessity helping to repair wagons, construct bridges, stand guard, and drive the oxen. The change in work assignments proceeded only in one direction, however, for few men did "women's work."

The extra labor did not bring women new authority or power within the family. Nor, by and large, did they seek it. Women resisted efforts to blur the division between male and female work and struggled to preserve their traditional role and image. Quarrels over work assignments often brought into the open long-simmering family tensions. One woman reported that there was "not a little fighting" in their company, which was "invariably the outcome of disputes over divisions of labor." The conflicting pressures a woman might feel were well illustrated by Mary Ellen Todd, a teenaged daughter who learned the male skill of cracking the bullwhip despite her mother's disapproval. "While I felt a secret joy," she recalled, "in being able to have a power that set things going, there was also a sense of shame over this new accomplishment."

Women's sense of loss

As women strove to maintain a semblance of home on the trail, they often experienced a profound sense of loss. Trains often traveled on the Sabbath, which had been an emblem of women's moral authority back home. Women also felt the lack of close companions to whom they could turn for comfort. One woman, whose husband separated from the train after a dispute, sadly watched the other wagons pull away: "I felt that indeed I had left all my friends to journey over the dreaded plains without one female acquaintance even for a companion—of course I wept and grieved about it but to no purpose."

Women on the trail complained, as one put it, that "we had left all civilization behind us." Civilization to women meant more than law, government, and schools; it also meant their homes and domestic mission. Once settled in the West, they strove to reestablish that order.

Indians and the Trail Experience

The nations whose lands were crossed by the wagon trains reacted in a number of ways. The Sioux were among the tribes who regularly traded with the overlanders.

Pressures on the Plains Indians

On the other hand, white migrants took a heavy toll on the Plains Indians' way of life: the emigrant parties scared off game and reduced buffalo herds, overgrazed the grass, and depleted the supply of wood. As a result, the Sioux demanded with varying success payment from the wagon trains crossing their lands. Finally in 1851 the U.S. government agreed to make an annual payment to various tribes as compensation for the damages caused by the emigrants.

Their fears aroused by sensational stories, overland parties were wary of Indians, but this menace was greatly exaggerated, especially on the plains. Few wagon trains were attacked by Indians, and emigrants killed more Indians than Indians killed emigrants. For overlanders the most aggravating problem posed by Indians was theft of stock. Many companies received valuable assistance from Indians, who acted as guides and directed them to grass and water.

THE POLITICAL ORIGINS OF EXPANSION

President William Henry Harrison made the gravest mistake of his brief presidential career when he ventured out one raw spring day, bareheaded and without an overcoat, to buy groceries at the Washington market. He caught pneumonia and died only one month after his inauguration. For the first time in the nation's history, a vice president succeeded to the nation's highest office upon the death of the president.

John Tyler of Virginia had been a states' rights Democrat who left the Democratic party because of Jackson's opposition to nullification. Tyler eventually joined the Whigs, despite his strict construction principles, and in 1840 the Whig convention nominated him as Old Tip's running mate, in order to balance the ticket sectionally.

Tyler's Texas Ploy

Tyler's courteous manner and personal warmth masked a rigid, doctrinaire mind. Repeatedly, when Henry Clay and the Whigs in Congress passed a major bill, Tyler opposed it. After Tyler twice vetoed bills to charter a new national bank, disgusted congressional Whigs formally expelled the president from their party. Most Democrats, too, avoided him as an untrustworthy "renegade." In short, Tyler became a man without a party, his support limited to federal officeholders. Still, his intense ambition led him to believe he might win another four years in the White House if only he latched onto the right popular issue. That issue, his advisers convinced him, was the annexation of Texas.

Tyler's break with the Whigs

That advice came mostly from Democrats disgruntled with Martin Van Buren, who had led the party to defeat in 1840. "They mean to throw Van overboard," reported one delighted Whig who caught wind of the plans. Meanwhile Tyler's allies circulated rumors designed to frighten southerners into pushing for annexation. Britain, they falsely claimed, was ready to offer Texas economic aid if it abolished slavery. In April 1844 Tyler sent to the Senate for ratification a treaty he had secretly negotiated to bring Texas into the Union.

Van Overboard

The front runners for the Whig and Democratic presidential nominations were Clay and Van Buren, moderates who feared the slavery issue. By prearrangement, both men issued letters opposing annexation on the grounds that it threatened the Union and would provoke war with Mexico.

As expected, the Whigs unanimously nominated Clay on a platform that ignored the expansion issue entirely. The Democrats, however, had a more difficult time. With Van Buren unable to get the two-thirds majority required

Polk's nomination

to be nominated, the delegates finally turned to James K. Polk of Tennessee, who was pro-Texas, and approved an expansion platform calling for the annexation of Texas and the occupation of Oregon all the way to its northernmost boundary at 54°40′.

Angered by the convention's outcome, Van Buren's supporters in the Senate joined the Whigs in decisively defeating Tyler's treaty of annexation by a vote of 35 to 16. Tyler eventually withdrew from the race, but the Texas issue would not go away. Seeking to shore up his support in the South, Clay finally announced he would support Texas's annexation if it would not lead to war. And in the North, a few antislavery Whigs turned to James G. Birney, running on the Liberty party ticket.

In the end, Polk squeaked through by 38,000 votes out of nearly 3 million cast. If just half of Birney's 15,000 ballots in New York had gone to Clay, he would have carried the state and been narrowly elected president. Indignant Whigs charged that by refusing to support Clay, political abolitionists had made the annexation of Texas, and hence the addition of slave territory to the Union, inevitable. And indeed, in the atmosphere following Polk's election, Congress approved a joint resolution annexing Texas. On March 3, 1845, his last day in office, Tyler invited Texas to enter the Union.

To the Pacific

Humorless, calculating, and often deceitful, President Polk pursued his objectives with dogged determination. Embracing a continental vision of the United States, he not only endorsed Tyler's offer of annexation but looked beyond, hoping to gain the three best harbors on the Pacific: San Diego, San Francisco, and Puget Sound. That meant wresting lower Oregon from Britain and California from Mexico.

Claiming that American title to all of Oregon was " clear and unquestionable," Polk induced Congress to terminate the joint occupation of Oregon. His blustering,

Compromise on Oregon

which was intended to put pressure on Great Britain, was reinforced by the knowledge that American settlers in Oregon outnumbered the British 5000 to 750. On the other hand, Polk hardly wanted war with a nation as powerful as Great Britain. So when the British offered, in June 1846, to divide the Oregon Territory along the 49th parallel, he readily agreed (see map, page 386). The arrangement gave the United States Puget Sound, which had been the president's objective all along.

The Mexican War

Disputed boundary of Texas

The Oregon settlement left Polk free to deal with Mexico. In 1845 Congress admitted Texas to the Union as a slave state, but Mexico had never formally recognized Texas's independence. It insisted, moreover, that its southern boundary was the Nueces River, not the Rio Grande, 130 miles to the south, as claimed by Texas. In reality, Texas had never controlled the disputed region, but Polk, already looking toward the Pacific, supported the Rio Grande boundary.

Knowing that the Mexican government desperately needed money, the president attempted to buy New Mexico and California. But the Mexican public overwhelmingly opposed ceding any more territory to the land-hungry Yankees. Blocked on the diplomatic front, Polk ordered General Zachary Taylor to proceed south with American troops to the Rio Grande. From the Mexican standpoint, the Americans had invaded their country and occupied their territory. On April 25 Mexican forces clashed with Taylor's troops.

THE MEXICAN WAR

Polk had already resolved to send Congress a war message citing Mexico's refusal to negotiate when word arrived of the fighting along the Rio Grande. The president quickly revised his war message, placing the entire blame for the war on Mexico. "Mexico has passed the boundary of the United States, has invaded our territory, and shed American blood upon American soil," he told Congress on May 11. "War exists, and notwithstanding all our efforts to avoid it, exists by the act of Mexico herself." The administration sent a bill to Congress calling for volunteers and requesting money to supply American troops.

The war with Mexico posed a dilemma for Whigs. They were convinced (correctly) that Polk had provoked it in order to acquire more territory from Mexico, and many northern Whigs accused the president of seeking to extend slavery. But they also feared that if they opposed the war, they would ruin their party. Therefore, they voted for military supply bills but, at the same time, strenuously attacked the conduct of "Mr. Polk's War" and, in an effort to curb sectional rivalries, opposed the acquisition of any territory from Mexico.

Opposition to the war

The Price of Victory

Even before word of hostilities arrived in California, a group of impetuous American settlers around Sacramento launched the "Bear Flag Revolt." In June 1846 they proclaimed California an independent republic. American forces in the area soon put down any Mexican resistance, and by the following January California was safely in American hands.

Meanwhile, Taylor moved south from the Rio Grande and won several decisive battles, ending the war in the northern provinces. Polk had gained the territory he sought to reach the Pacific; now he wanted only peace. But the Mexican people refused to support any government that sued for peace, so Polk ordered an invasion into the heart of the country. Only after an American army commanded by General Winfield Scott captured Mexico City on September 14, 1847, did Mexico surrender.

Conquest of Mexico

The war had cost $97 million and 13,000 American lives, mostly as a result of disease. Yet the real cost was even higher. By bringing vast new territories into the Union, the war forced the explosive slavery issue to the center of national politics and threatened to upset the balance of power between North and South. Ralph Waldo Emerson had been prophetic when he declared that the conquest of Mexico "will poison us."

The Rise of the Slavery Issue

The annexation of so much southwestern territory left not only northern Whigs but also many northern Democrats embittered. They complained that Polk, a Tennessee slaveholder, had compromised with the British on Oregon at the same time that he used military force to defend the absurd boundary claims of Texas. This discontent finally erupted in August 1846 when Polk requested $2 million from Congress. On August 8 David Wilmot, an obscure Pennsylvania congressman, startled Democratic leaders by introducing an amendment to the bill barring slavery from any territory acquired from Mexico. The Wilmot Proviso, as the amendment became known, passed the House of Representatives several times with strong northern support, only to be rejected in the Senate, where the South had greater power.

Wilmot Proviso

Wilmot was hardly an abolitionist. Indeed, he hoped to keep not only slaves but all black people out of the territories. "I would preserve for white free labor a fair country," he explained, ". . . where the sons of toil, of my own race and color, can live without the disgrace which association with negro slavery brings upon free labor." The Wilmot Proviso aimed not to destroy slavery in the South but to confine the institution to those states where it already existed.

The status of slavery in the territories became more than an abstract question when the Senate in 1848 ratified the Treaty of Guadalupe Hidalgo. Under its terms the United States acquired Mexico's provinces of New Mexico and Upper California in return for approximately $18 million. With the United States in control of the Pacific Coast from San Diego to Puget Sound, Polk's continental vision had become a reality.

Peace treaty with Mexico

NEW SOCIETIES IN THE WEST

As Hispanic, Indian, Asian, and Anglo-American cultures mixed, the patterns of settlement along the frontier varied widely. In California the new settlements were overwhelmingly shaped by the rush for gold after 1848. And in the Great Basin around Salt Lake, the Mormons established a society whose sense of religious mission was as strong as that of the Puritans.

Farming in the West

The overlanders expected to replicate the societies they had left behind. Once a wagon train arrived at its destination, members had usually exhausted their resources and thus quickly scattered in search of employment or a good farm site.

In a process repeated over and over, settlers in a new area set up the machinery of government. Churches took longer to establish, for ministers were hard to recruit and congregations were often not large enough to support a church. As the population grew, however, a more conventional society evolved. Towns and a middle class developed, the proportion of women increased, schools were established, and the residents became less mobile.

Evolution of western society

Although opportunity was greater on the frontier and early arrivals had a special advantage, more and more the agricultural frontier of the West resembled the older society of the East. With the development of markets and transportation, wealth became concentrated; some families fell to the lower rungs of society, and those who were less successful left, seeking yet another fresh start.

The Gold Rush

In January 1848, while constructing a sawmill along the American River, James Marshall noticed gold flecks in the millrace. More discoveries followed, and when the news reached the East, it spread like wildfire. The following spring the Overland Trail was jammed with eager "forty-niners." In only two years, from 1848 to the end of 1849, California's population jumped from 14,000 to 100,000. By 1860 it stood at 380,000.

Those intent on making a fortune and returning home gave no thought to putting down roots. Mining camps literally appeared and died overnight, as word of a new strike sent miners racing off to another canyon, valley, or streambed. More than 80 percent of the prospectors who poured into the gold country were Americans, including free blacks. Mexicans, Australians, Hawaiians, Chinese, French, English, and Irish also came. Whatever their nationality, the new arrivals were overwhelmingly unmarried men in their twenties and thirties.

Life in the mining camps

The constant movement, the hard labor of mining, the ready cash, and the rootlessness all made camp society unstable. "There is an excitement connected with the pursuit of gold which renders one restless and uneasy—ever hoping to do something better," explained one forty-niner. Removed from the traditional forms of social control, miners engaged in gambling, swearing, drinking, and fighting. As a Denver paper complained during that territory's gold rush a few years later, as soon as "men of decent appearance" reached a mining camp, they "sang low songs, walked openly with the painted courtesans with whom the town teems, and generally gave themselves up to what they term, 'a time!'"

Only about 5 percent of gold rush emigrants were women or children; given this scarcity, men were willing to pay top dollar to women to cook, sew, and wash.

Women in the camps

Other women ran hotels and boardinghouses. "A smart woman can do very well in this country," one woman informed a friend in the East. "It is the only country I ever was in where a woman received anything like a just compensation for work." Likewise, they suffered no shortage of suitors. "I had men come forty miles over the mountains, just to look at me," Eliza Wilson recalled, "and I never was called a handsome woman, in my best days, even by my most ardent admirers." The class of women most frequently seen in the diggings were prostitutes, who numbered perhaps 20 percent of female Californians in 1850.

Violence was common in the mining districts, so when a new camp opened, miners adopted a set of rules and regulations. Justice was dispensed promptly, either by a vote of all the miners or by an elected jury. While effective when ad-

Disappointment in the Gold Diggings

My expectations are not realized. We have been unlucky—or rather, by being inexperienced, we selected a poor spot for a location and staked all on it, and it has proved worth nothing. Had it proved as it was expected when we took it up . . . I should have today been on my way to the bosom of my family in possession of sufficient means to have made them and me comfortable through life. . . . I mostly regret the necessity of staying here longer.

I was in hopes to have sent home a good pile of money before this time, but I am not able to at present. Still, my expectations are high, and in my opinion the excitement about the gold mines was not caused by exaggeration. In fact, I believe that greater amounts of gold have been and will be taken from the mines this summer than the gold news have told. . . . But I am of the opinion that the gold will soon be gathered from these washings and then will come the hardest part of this gold fever. I therefore would advise no one to come here. . . . But were I to be unfortunate in all my business here and arrive at last at home without *one cent*, I should ever be glad that I have taken the trip to California. It has learnt me to have confidence in myself, has disciplined my impetuous disposition and has learnt me to think and act for myself and to look upon men and things in a true light. Notwithstanding all these favorable circumstances, it is a fact that no energy or industry can secure certain success in the business of mining.

Source: Excerpt from "The California Gold Rush Experience" in *The World Rushed In* by J. S. Holliday. Copyright © 1981 by J. S. Holliday. Reprinted by permission of J. S. Holliday.

ministered fairly, the system at times degenerated into lynch law. In addition, American miners frustrated by a lack of success often directed their hostility toward foreigners. The miners ruthlessly exterminated

Nativist and racial prejudices

the Indians in the area, mob violence drove Mexicans out of nearly every camp, and the Chinese were confined to claims abandoned by Americans as unprofitable. The state eventually enacted a foreign miners' tax that fell largely on the Chinese. Free African Americans felt the sting of discrimination as well. White American miners proclaimed that "colored men were not privileged to work in a country intended only for American citizens."

Before long, the most easily worked claims had been played out, and competition steadily drove down the average earnings from $20 a day in 1848 to $6 in 1852. As gold became increasingly difficult to extract, corporations using heavy equipment and employing miners working for wages came to dominate the industry. As the era of the individual miner passed, so too did mining camps and the unique society they spawned.

The damage mining did to the land endured longer. Abandoned diggings pockmarked the gold fields and created piles of debris that heavy rains washed down the valley, choking streams and rivers and ruining lands below. Excavation of hillsides, construction of dams to divert rivers, and the destruction of the forest cover to meet the heavy demand for lumber and firewood caused spring floods and serious erosion of the soil. The attitude of the individual miners differed little from the capitalists who succeeded them: both sought to exploit the environment as rapidly as possible with little thought to long-term consequences. Untempered by any sense of restraint, the quest for rapid wealth left long-lasting scars on the landscape of the gold country.

Environmental impact of mining

Instant City: San Francisco

When the United States assumed control of California, San Francisco had a population of perhaps 200. But thousands of emigrants took the water route west, passing through San Francisco's harbor on their way to the diggings. By 1856 the city's population had jumped to an astonishing 50,000. In a mere 8 years the city had attained the size New York had taken 190 years to reach.

The product of economic self-interest, San Francisco developed in helter-skelter fashion. Since the city government took virtually no role in directing

San Francisco in 1852

development, almost no land was reserved for public use. Property owners defeated a proposal to widen the streets, prompting the city's leading newspaper to complain, "To sell a few more feet of lots, the streets were compressed like a cheese, into half their width."

San Francisco's chaotic growth

The gold rush that swelled San Francisco's streets was a global phenomenon. Americans predominated in the mining population, but Latin Americans, Europeans, Australians, and the Chinese swarmed into California. An amazing assortment of languages could be heard on the city's streets: indeed, in 1860 San Francisco was 50 percent foreign-born.

The most distinctive of the ethnic groups was the Chinese. They had come to *Gum San*, the land of the golden mountain. Those who arrived in California overwhelmingly hailed from the area of southern China around Canton—and not by accident. Canton, like other provinces of China, suffered from economic distress, population pressures, social unrest, and political upheaval. But Canton had a large European presence, because it was the only port open to outsiders. That situation changed after the first Opium War (1839–1842), when Britain forced China to open other ports to trade. For Cantonese, the sudden loss of this trade monopoly produced widespread economic hardship. At the same time, a series of religious and political revolts in the region led to severe fighting that devastated the countryside. A growing number of residents concluded that emigration was the only way to survive, and the presence of western ships in the harbors of Canton and nearby Hong Kong (a British possession since 1842) made it easier for Cantonese to migrate to California rather than to southeast Asia.

Migration from China

Between 1849 and 1854, some 45,000 Chinese went to California. Among those who did was sixteen-year-old Lee Chew, who left for California after a man from his village returned with great wealth from the "country of the American wizards." Like the other gold seekers, the Chinese newcomers were overwhelmingly young and male, and they wanted only to accumulate savings and return home to their families. (Indeed, only 16 Chinese women arrived before 1854.)

When the Chinese were harassed in the mines, many opened laundries in San Francisco and elsewhere, since little capital was required. Other Chinese around San Francisco set up restaurants or worked in the fishing industry. In these early years they found Americans less hostile, so long as they stayed away from the gold fields. As immigration and the competition for jobs increased, however, anti-Chinese sentiment intensified.

Gradually, San Francisco took on the trappings of a more orderly community. The city government established a public school system, erected street lights, created a municipal water system, and halted further filling in of the bay. Fashionable neighborhoods sprouted on several hills, as high rents drove many residents from the developing commercial center. Churches and families became more common. By 1856, the city of the gold rush had been replaced by a new city whose stone and brick buildings gave it a new-found sense of permanence.

The Mormons in Utah

The makeshift, often chaotic society spawned by the gold rush was a product of largely uncontrolled economic forces. By contrast, an entirely different society evolved in the Great Basin of Utah under the control of the Church of Jesus Christ of Latter-day Saints.

After Joseph Smith's death in 1844 (page 322), the Mormon church was led by Brigham Young, who lacked Smith's religious mysticism but was a brilliant organizer. Young decided to move his followers to the Great Basin, an isolated area a thousand miles from settled regions of the United States, where they could live and worship without interference. In 1847 the first thousand settlers arrived, the vanguard of thousands more who extended Mormon settlement throughout the valley of the Great Salt Lake and the West. The Mormons' success rested on a community-oriented effort firmly controlled by church elders. Families were given only as much farmland as they could use, and church officials, headed by Young, exercised supreme power in legislative, executive, and judicial matters as well as religious affairs.

The most controversial church teaching was the doctrine of polygamy, or plural marriage, which Young finally sanctioned publicly in 1852. Visitors reported

Polygamy

with surprise that few Mormon wives seemed to rebel against the practice. If the wives lived together, the system allowed them to share domestic work. When the husband established separate households, wives enjoyed greater freedom, since he was not constantly present. Moreover, because polygamy distinguished Mormonism from other religions, plural wives saw it as an expression of their religious faith. "I want to be assured of *my position in God's estimation*," one such wife explained. "If polygamy is the Lord's order, we must carry it out."

The Mormons connected control of water to their sense of mission. The Salt Lake valley, where the Mormons established their holy community, lacked signif-

Irrigation and community

icant rivers or abundant sources of water. Thus their success depended on irrigating the region, something never before attempted. By constructing a coordinated series of dams, aqueducts, and ditches, they brought life-giving water to the valleys of the region. By 1850, there were more than 16,000 irrigated acres in what would become Utah.

Manipulation of water reinforced the Mormons' sense of hierarchy and group discipline. Centralization of authority in the hands of church officials made possible an overall plan of development, allowed for maximum exploitation of resources, and freed communities from the disputes over water rights that plagued many settlements in the arid West. In a radical departure from American ideals, church leaders insisted that water belonged to the community, not individuals, and vested this authority in the hands of the local bishop. Control of vital water resources reinforced the power of the church hierarchy over not just the faithful but dissidents as well. Thus irrigation did more than make the desert bloom. By checking the

Jeffersonian ideal of an independent, self-sufficient farmer, it also sustained a centralized, well-regulated society under the firm control of the church.

Temple City: Salt Lake City

In laying out the Mormons' "temple city" of Salt Lake, Young was also determined to avoid the commercial worldliness and competitive individualism that had plagued Joseph Smith's settlement at Nauvoo. City lots, which were distributed by lottery, could not be subdivided for sale, and real estate speculation was forbidden.

The city itself was laid out in a checkerboard grid well suited to the level terrain. Streets were 132 feet wide (compared with 60 feet in San Francisco), and a square block contained eight home lots of 1.25 acres each. Unlike in early San Francisco, in Salt Lake City the family was the basic social unit, and almost from the beginning the city had an equal balance of men and women. The planners also provided for four public squares in various parts of the city. The city was divided into 18 wards, each under the supervision of a bishop who held civil as well as religious power.

Salt Lake City's orderly growth

As the city expanded, the original plan had to be modified to accommodate the developing commercial district by dividing lots into sizes more suitable for stores. Experience and growth also eventually dictated smaller blocks and narrower streets, but the city still retained its spacious appearance and regular design. Through religious and economic discipline church leaders succeeded in preserving a sense of common purpose.

Shadows on the Moving Frontier

Transformations like Salt Lake City and San Francisco were truly remarkable. But it is important to remember that Americans were not coming into a trackless, unsettled wilderness. As frontier lines crossed, 75,000 Mexicans had to adapt to American rule.

The Treaty of Guadalupe Hidalgo guaranteed Mexicans in the ceded territory "the free enjoyment of their liberty and property." So long as Mexicans continued to be a sizable majority in a given area, such as New Mexico, their influence was strong. But wherever Anglos became more numerous, they demanded conformity to American customs. When Mexicans remained faithful to their heritage, language, and religion, these cultural differences worked to reinforce Hispanic powerlessness, social isolation, and economic exploitation.

The rush of American emigrants quickly overwhelmed Hispanic settlers in California. Even in 1848, before the discovery of gold, Americans in California outnumbered Mexicans two to one, and by 1860 Hispanics amounted to only 2 percent of the population. Changes in California land law required verification of the *rancheros*' original land grants by a federal

Hispanic-Anglo conflict

commission. Since the average claim took 17 years to complete and imposed complex procedures and hefty legal fees, many *rancheros* lost large tracts of land to Americans. Lower-class Mexicans scratched out a bare existence on ranches and farms or in the growing cities and towns.

Mexicans in Texas were also greatly outnumbered: they totaled only 6 percent of the population in 1860. Stigmatized as inferior, they were the poorest group in free society. One response to this dislocation, an option commonly taken by persecuted minorities, was social banditry. An example was the folk hero Juan Cortina. A member of a displaced landed family in southern Texas, Cortina in the 1850s began stealing from wealthy Anglos to aid poor Mexicans, proclaiming, "To me is entrusted the breaking of the chains of your slavery." He continued to raid Texas border settlements until finally imprisoned by Mexican authorities. While failing to produce any lasting change, Cortina demonstrated the depth of frustration and resentment among Hispanics over their abuse at the hands of the new Anglo majority.

ESCAPE FROM CRISIS

With the return of peace, Congress confronted the problem of whether to allow slavery in the newly won territories. David Wilmot, in his controversial proviso, had already proposed to outlaw slavery throughout the Mexican cession. John C. Calhoun, representing the extreme southern position, countered that slavery was legal in all territories. The federal government had acted as the agent of all the states in acquiring the land, he argued, and southerners had a right to take their property there, including slaves. Only when the residents of a territory drafted a state constitution could they decide the question of slavery.

Constitution and extension of slavery

Between these extremes were two moderate positions. One proposed extending the Missouri Compromise line of 36°30′ to the Pacific, which would

Senator John C. Calhoun

have continued the earlier policy of dividing the national domain between the North and the South. The other proposal, championed by Senator Lewis Cass of Michigan and Senator Stephen A. Douglas of Illinois, was to allow the people of the territory rather than Congress to decide the status of slavery. This solution, which became known as popular sovereignty, was deliberately ambiguous, since its supporters refused to specify whether the residents could make this decision at any time or only when drafting a state constitution, as Calhoun insisted.

When Congress organized the Oregon Territory in 1848, it prohibited slavery there, since even southerners admitted that the region was too far north to grow the South's staple crops. But this seemingly straightforward decision made it impossible to apply the Missouri Compromise line to the other territories. Without Oregon as a part of the package, the bulk of the remaining land would be open to slavery, something at which the North balked. Almost inadvertently, one of the two moderate solutions had been discarded by the summer of 1848.

A Two-Faced Campaign

In the election of 1848 both major parties tried to avoid the slavery issue. The Democrats nominated Lewis Cass, a supporter of popular sovereignty, while the Whigs bypassed all their prominent leaders and selected General Zachary Taylor of Louisiana, who had taken no position on any public issue.

But the slavery issue would not go away. A new antislavery coalition, the Free Soil party, brought together northern Democrats who had rallied to the Wilmot Proviso, Conscience Whigs who disavowed Taylor's nomination because he was a slaveholder, and political abolitionists in the Liberty party. To gain more votes, the Free Soil platform focused on the dangers of extending slavery rather than on the evil of slavery itself. Ironically, the party nominated Martin Van Buren—the man who for years had struggled to keep the slavery issue out of national politics.

Free Soil party

Both the Whigs and the Democrats ran different campaigns in the North and the South. To southern audiences, each party promised it would protect slavery in the territories; to northern voters, each claimed it would keep the territories free. In this two-faced, sectional campaign, the Whigs won their second national victory. Taylor held onto the core of Whig voters in both sections (Van Buren as well as Cass, after all, had long been Democrats). But in the South, where the contest pitted a southern slaveholder against two northerners, Taylor won many more votes than Clay had in 1844. As one southern Democrat complained, "We have lost hundreds of votes, solely on the ground that General Cass was a Northerner and General Taylor a Southern man." Furthermore, Van Buren polled five times as many votes as the Liberty party had four years earlier. Increasingly the two national political parties were being pulled apart along sectional lines.

The Compromise of 1850

Once he became president, Taylor could no longer remain silent. The territories gained from Mexico had to be organized; furthermore, by 1849 California had gained enough residents to be admitted as a state. In the Senate the balance of power between North and South stood at 15 states each. California's admission would break the sectional balance.

Called "Old Rough and Ready" by his troops, Taylor was a forthright man of action, but he was politically inexperienced and oversimplified complex problems.

Taylor's plan

Since even Calhoun conceded that entering states had the right to ban slavery, Taylor proposed that the way to end the sectional crisis was to skip the territorial stage by combining all the Mexican cession into two

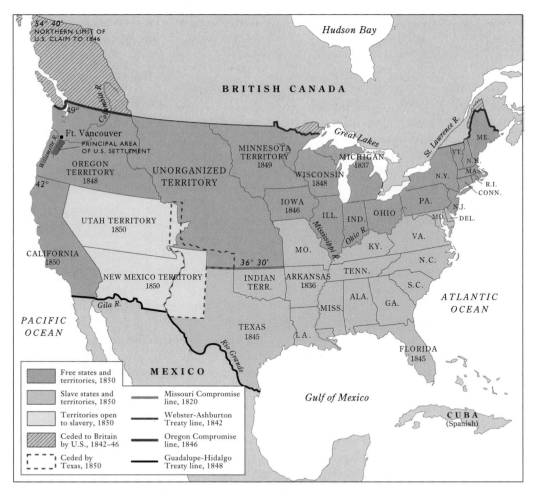

TERRITORIAL GROWTH AND THE COMPROMISE OF 1850

huge states, New Mexico and California. Even more shocking to southern Whigs, he proposed to apply the Wilmot Proviso to the entire area, since he was convinced that slavery would never flourish there. When Congress convened in December 1849, Taylor recommended that California and New Mexico be admitted as free states. The president's plan touched off the most serious sectional crisis the Union had yet confronted.

Into this turmoil stepped Henry Clay, now 73 years old and nearing the end of his career. A savvy card player all his life, Clay loved the bargaining, the wheeling and dealing, the late-night trade-offs eased along by a bottle of bourbon that were part of politics. Clay decided that a grand compromise was needed to end all disputes between the North and South and save the Union. Already, Mississippi had summoned a southern convention to meet at Nashville to discuss the crisis, and extremists were pushing for secession.

Clay's compromise, submitted in January 1850, addressed all the major controversies between the two sections. California, he proposed, should be admitted as a free state, which represented the clear wishes of most settlers there. The rest of the Mexican cession would be organized as two territories, New Mexico and Utah, under the doctrine of popular sovereignty. Thus slavery would

Clay's compromise

not be prohibited from these regions. Clay also proposed that Congress abolish the slave trade but not slavery itself in the District of Columbia and that a new, more rigorous fugitive slave law be passed to enable southerners to reclaim runaway slaves. To reinforce the idea that both North and South were yielding ground, Clay combined those provisions that dealt with the Mexican cession (and several others adjusting the Texas–New Mexico border) in a larger package known as the Omnibus Bill.

With the stakes so high, the Senate debated the bill for six months. Clay, wracked by a hacking cough, spent long hours trying to line up the needed votes. But for once, the great whist enthusiast had misplayed his hand. The Omnibus Bill required that the components of the compromise be approved as a package. Extremists in Congress from both regions, however, combined against the moderates and rejected the bill.

With Clay exhausted and his strategy in shambles, Democrat Stephen A. Douglas assumed leadership of the pro-compromise forces. The sudden death in July of President Taylor, who had threatened to veto Clay's plan, aided the compromise movement. One by one, Douglas submitted the individual measures for a vote. Northern representatives provided the neces-

Passage of the Compromise

sary votes to admit California and abolish the slave trade in the District of Columbia, while southern representatives supplied the edge needed to organize the Utah and New Mexico territories and pass the new fugitive slave law. On the face of it, everyone had compromised. But in truth, only 61 members of Congress, or 21 percent of the membership, had not voted against some part of the Compromise.

By September 17 all the separate parts of the Compromise of 1850 had passed and been signed into law by the new president, Millard Fillmore. The Union, it seemed, was safe.

Away from the Brink

The general public, both North and South, rallied to the Compromise. At the convention of southern states in Nashville, the fire-eaters—the radical proponents of

Rejection of secession

states' rights and secession—found themselves voted down by more moderate voices. Even in the Deep South, coalitions of pro-Compromise Whigs and Democrats soundly defeated secessionists in state elections. Nevertheless, most southerners felt that a firm line had been drawn. With California's admission, they were now outnumbered in the Senate, so it was critical that slaveholders be granted equal legal access to the territories. They announced that any breach of the Compromise of 1850 would justify secession.

The North, for its part, found the new fugitive slave law the hardest measure of the Compromise to swallow. The controversial law denied an accused runaway

Fugitive slave law

a trial by jury, and it required that all citizens assist federal marshals in its enforcement. Harriet Beecher Stowe's popular novel *Uncle Tom's Cabin* (1852) presented a powerful moral indictment of the law—and of slavery as an institution. Despite its crude literary techniques, the book profoundly moved its readers. Emphasizing the duty of Christians toward the downtrodden, it reached a greater audience than any previous abolitionist work. Thousands more in northern cities saw theatrical productions of the story.

In reality, however, fewer than 1000 slaves a year attempted to escape to the North, many of whom did not succeed. Despite some well-publicized cases of re-

Both sections accept the Compromise

sistance, the 1850 fugitive slave law was generally enforced in the free states. Many northerners did not like the law, but they were unwilling to tamper with the Compromise. Stephen Douglas spoke accurately enough when he boasted in 1851, "The whole country is acquiescing in the compromise measures—everywhere, North and South. Nobody proposes to repeal or disturb them."

And so calm returned. In the lackluster 1852 presidential campaign, both the Whigs and the Democrats endorsed the Compromise. Franklin Pierce, a little-known New Hampshire Democrat, soundly defeated the Whig candidate, Winfield Scott. Even more significant, the antislavery Free Soil candidate received only about half as many votes as Van Buren had four years before. With the slavery issue seemingly losing political force, it appeared that the Republic had weathered the storm unleashed by the Wilmot Proviso.

But the moving frontier still had changes to work. It had leaped from the Mississippi valley to the Pacific, but in between remained territory still unorganized. And as the North became increasingly industrialized and the South more firmly committed to an economy based on cotton and slavery, the growing conflict between the two sections would shatter the Jacksonian party system, reignite the slavery issue, and shake the Union to its foundation.

chapter summary

In the 1840s the United States expanded to the Pacific, a development that involved the cultural interaction of Americans with other groups and led to the rise of the slavery issue in national politics.

- In the 1840s Americans proclaimed that it was the United States's Manifest Destiny to expand across the North American continent.

- Americans in Texas increasingly clashed with Mexican authorities, and in 1836 Texans revolted and established an independent republic.

- Americans headed for Oregon and California on the Overland Trail.
  - The journey put special pressures on women as the traditional division of labor by gender broke down.
  - White migration also put pressure on Plains Indians' grazing lands, wood supplies, and freedom of movement.
  - The gold rush spawned a unique society that was overwhelmingly male, highly mobile, and strongly nativist and racist.

- Led by Brigham Young, the Mormons established a tightly organized, centrally controlled society in the Great Salt Lake basin.
- Throughout the Southwest the Hispanic population suffered at the hands of the new Anglo majority.

- President James K. Polk entered office with a vision of the United States as a continental nation.
  - He upheld President John Tyler's annexation of Texas and agreed to divide the Oregon country with Britain.
  - The United States eventually went to war with Mexico and acquired California and the Southwest.

- The Mexican War reinjected into national politics the issue of slavery's expansion.
  - The Wilmot Proviso sought to prohibit slavery in any territory acquired from Mexico.
  - The struggle over the Proviso eventually disrupted both major parties.
  - Congress momentarily stilled the sectional crisis with the Compromise of 1850.

For quizzes and a variety of interactive resources, visit the book's Online Learning Center at www.mhhe.com/davidsonconcise3

SIGNIFICANT EVENTS

1725–1850	Sioux expansion on the Great Plains
1821	Mexico wins independence; Santa Fe trade opens
1823	First American settlers enter Texas
1829	Mexico tries to abolish slavery in Texas
1830	Mexico attempts to halt American migration to Texas
1835	Texas Revolution
1836	Texas Republic established; Battle of the Alamo; Santa Anna defeated at San Jacinto
1841	Tyler becomes president
1843	Large-scale migration to Oregon begins
1843–1844	Tyler conducts secret negotiations with Texas
1844	Tyler's Texas treaty rejected by the Senate; Polk elected president
1845	United States annexes Texas; phrase "Manifest Destiny" coined
1846	War declared against Mexico; Bear Flag Revolt in California; Oregon Treaty ratified; Wilmot Proviso introduced
1847	Mormon migration to Utah; U.S. troops occupy Mexico City
1848	Gold discovered in California; Treaty of Guadalupe Hidalgo ratified; Free Soil party founded; Taylor elected president
1849	Gold rush; California drafts free state constitution
1850	Nashville convention; Taylor dies and Fillmore becomes president; Compromise of 1850 enacted
1850–1851	South rejects secession
1852	Harriet Beecher Stowe's *Uncle Tom's Cabin* published; Pierce elected president

Into town they rode, several hundred strong, their faces flushed with excitement. They were unshaven, rough-talking men, "armed . . . to the teeth with rifles and revolvers, cutlasses and bowie-knives." At the head of the procession flapped an American flag, and alongside it another with a crouching tiger emblazoned on black and white stripes, followed by banners proclaiming "Southern Rights" and "The Superiority of the White Race." At the rear rolled five artillery pieces, which were quickly dragged into range of the town's main street. Watching intently from a window in his office, Josiah Miller, the editor of the Lawrence *Kansas Free State*, predicted "Well, boys, we're in for it."

For residents of Lawrence, Kansas, the worst seemed at hand. The town had been founded by the New England Emigrant Aid Company, a Yankee association that recruited settlers in an effort to keep

The Union Broken
(1850–1861)

preview • During the 1850s the building of a vast railroad network and a rising tide of immigration benefited the North in terms of both economic and political power. As a result, sectional tensions grew. But the debate over slavery in the newly acquired territories—especially in Kansas—brought the crisis to a head. By 1861 the old party system had collapsed, Republican Abraham Lincoln had been elected entirely on the strength of Northern votes, and a number of southern states had seceded from the Union.

Kansas Territory from becoming a slave state. Accepting Senator Stephen Douglas's idea that the people should decide the status of slavery, the town's residents intended to see to it that under popular sovereignty Kansas entered the Union as a free state. Emigrants from the neighboring slave state of Missouri were equally determined that no "abolition tyrants" would control the territory. There had been conflict in Kansas almost immediately: land disputes, horse thievery, shootings on both sides.

In the ensuing turmoil, the federal government seemed to back the proslavery forces. A U.S. District Court indicted several of Lawrence's leading citizens for treason, and federal marshall Israel Donaldson called for a posse to help make the arrests. Donaldson's posse, swelled by eager volunteers from across the Missouri border, arrived outside Lawrence on the night of May 20, 1856.

Meanwhile, Lawrence's "committee of safety" had agreed on a policy of nonresistance. Most of those indicted had fled, but Donaldson arrested two men without incident and then dismissed his posse. But Sheriff Samuel Jones, who on his previous visit to Lawrence had been shot, had a score to settle. Falsely claiming that he had a court order, the irate sheriff took over the band and led the cheering throng into town at three o'clock in the afternoon.

The thoroughly liquored "army" quickly degenerated into a mob. Ignoring the pleas of some leaders, its members smashed the presses of two newspapers, the *Herald of Freedom* and the *Kansas Free State.* Then the horde unsuccessfully tried to blow up the now-deserted Free State Hotel, which more closely resembled a fort, before finally putting it to the torch. When the mob finally rode off, it left the residents of Lawrence unharmed but thoroughly terrified.

The "sack" of Lawrence

Retaliation by free state partisans was not long in coming. Hurrying north toward Lawrence, an older man with a grim visage and steely eyes heard the news the next morning that the town had been attacked. "Old Man Brown," as everyone called him, was on his way to provide reinforcements. A severe, God-fearing Calvinist, John Brown was also a staunch abolitionist who had once remarked that he believed "God had raised him up on purpose to break the jaws of the wicked." Brooding over the failure of the free-staters to resist the "slave hounds" from Missouri, Brown decided not to push on to Lawrence; instead, he ordered his followers to sharpen their heavy cutlasses. "Caution," he announced, "is nothing but the word of Cowardice."

Three days after the Lawrence raid, Brown headed under cover of dark toward Pottawatomie Creek with a half dozen others, including four of his sons. Announcing that they were "the Northern Army" come to serve justice, they burst into the cabin of James Doyle, a proslavery man from Tennessee, with cutlasses drawn. As Brown marched Doyle and his three sons off, Doyle's terrified wife, Mahala, begged him to spare her youngest, and the old man relented. The others were led a hundred yards down the road and hacked to death with broadswords by Owen and Salmon Brown. Old Man Brown then walked up to James Doyle's body and put a bullet through his forehead. Before the night was done, two more cabins had been visited and two more proslavery settlers brutally executed. Not one of the five murdered men owned a single slave or had any connection with the raid on Lawrence.

Pottawatomie massacre

Brown's action precipitated a new wave of fighting in Kansas, and the news of the tumult further angered residents in both sections of the nation. "Everybody here feels as if we are upon a volcano," remarked one congressman in Washington.

The country was indeed atop a smoldering volcano that would finally erupt in the spring of 1861, showering death and destruction across the land. Popular sovereignty, the last remaining moderate solution to the controversy over the expansion of slavery, had failed dismally in Kansas. The violence and disorder in the territory provided a stark reply to Stephen Douglas's proposition: What could be more peaceable, more fair than the notion of popular sovereignty?

SECTIONAL CHANGES IN AMERICAN SOCIETY

The road to war was not a straight or short one. Six years elapsed between the Compromise of 1850 and the crisis in "Bleeding Kansas." Another four would pass before the first shot was fired. And the process of separation involved more than popular fears, ineffective politicians, and an unwillingness to compromise. As we have seen, Americans were bound together by a growing transportation network, by national markets, and by a national political system. Increasingly, however, the changes occurring in American society heightened sectional tensions. As the North continued to industrialize, its society came into conflict with that of the South. The coming of Civil War, in other words, involved social and economic changes as well as political ones.

The Growth of a Railroad Economy

By the time the Compromise of 1850 produced a lull in the tensions between North and South, the American economy had left behind the depression of the early 1840s and was roaring again with speculative optimism. Its basic structure, however, was changing. Cotton remained the nation's major export, but it was no longer the driving force for American economic growth. After 1839 this role was taken over by the construction of a vast railroad network covering the eastern half of the continent. By 1850 the United States possessed more than 9000 miles of track; 10 years later it had over 30,000 miles, more than the rest of the world combined. Much of the new construction during the 1850s occurred west of the Appalachian Mountains—over 2000 miles in Ohio and Illinois alone.

Because western railroads ran through less settled areas, they were especially dependent on public aid. State and local governments made loans to rail companies and sometimes exempted them temporarily from taxes. About a quarter of the cost of railroad construction came from state and local governments, but federal land grants were crucial, too. By mortgaging or selling the land to farmers, the railroad raised construction capital and also stimulated settlement, which increased its business and profits. By 1860 Congress had allotted about 28 million acres of federal land to 40 different companies.

The effect of the new lines rippled through the economy. Nearby farmers began to specialize in cash crops and market them in distant locations. With the profits they purchased manufactured goods. Before the railroad reached Athens, Tennessee, the surrounding counties produced about 25,000 bushels of wheat, selling at less than 50 cents a bushel. Once the railroad came, farmers near Athens grew 400,000 bushels and sold their crop at a dollar a bushel. Railroads also stimulated other areas of the economy, notably the mining and iron industries. By 1860 half the domestic output of bar and sheet iron was used by railroads, and pig iron production almost tripled over the previous 20 years.

Railroads' impact on the economy

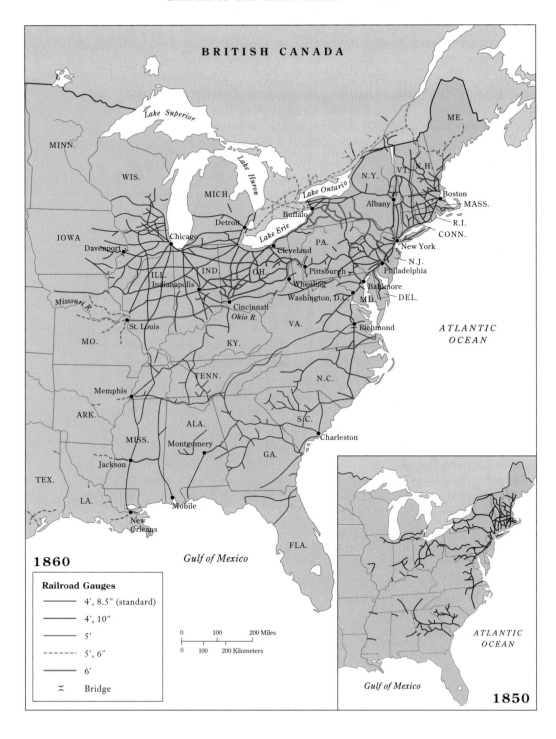

BRITISH CANADA

Lake Superior

MINN.

WIS.

MICH

Lake Huron

Lake Ontario

ME.

VT. N.H.

N.Y.

Albany

Boston

MASS.

Lake Erie

Buffalo

R.I.

CONN.

Detroit

IOWA

Chicago

Cleveland

PA.

New York

Davenport

N.J.

Pittsburgh

Philadelphia

ILL.

IND

OH.

Wheeling

Baltimore

DEL.

Indianapolis

Washington, D.C.

MD.

Missouri R.

Cincinnati
Ohio R.

VA.

Richmond

St. Louis

*ATLANTIC
OCEAN*

MO.

KY.

TENN.

N.C.

Memphis

ARK.

ALA.

S.C.

Charleston

MISS.

Montgomery

GA.

Jackson

TEX.

LA.

Mobile

New
Orleans

FLA.

1860

Gulf of Mexico

Railroad Gauges

——— 4', 8.5" (standard)

——— 4', 10"

——— 5'

- - - - 5', 6"

——— 6'

⋍ Bridge

| 0 | 100 | 200 Miles |
| 0 | 100 | 200 Kilometers |

*ATLANTIC
OCEAN*

Gulf of Mexico

1850

The new rail networks shifted the direction of western trade. In 1840 most northwestern grain was shipped down the Mississippi River to the bustling port of New Orleans. But low water made steamboat travel risky in summer, and ice shut down traffic in winter. Products such as lard, tallow, and cheese quickly spoiled if stored in New Orleans's sweltering warehouses.

With the new rail lines, traffic from the Midwest increasingly flowed west to east. Chicago became the region's hub, connecting the farms of the upper Midwest to New York and other eastern cities. Thus while the value of goods shipped by river to New Orleans continued to increase, the South's overall share of western trade dropped dramatically. The old political alliance between South and West, based on shared economic interests, was weakened by the new patterns of commerce.

Shift in flow of western trade

The growing rail network was not the only factor that led farmers in the Northeast and Midwest to become more commercially oriented. Another was the sharp rise in international demand for grain. Wheat, which in 1845 commanded $1.08 a bushel in New York City, fetched $2.46 in 1855; at the same time the price of corn nearly doubled. Farmers responded by specializing in cash crops and investing in equipment to increase productivity. "The power of cotton over the financial affairs of the Union has in the last few years rapidly diminished," the *Democratic Review* remarked in 1849, "and bread stuffs will now become the governing power."

Railroads and the Prairie Environment

As railroad lines fanned out from Chicago, farmers began to acquire open prairie land in Illinois and then Iowa, putting its deep black soil into production. Commerical agriculture transformed this remarkable treeless environment.

To settlers accustomed to woodlands, the thousands of square miles of grass taller than a person were an awesome sight. In 1838 Edmund Flagg gazed upon "the tall grasstops waving in . . . billowy beauty in the breeze; the narrow pathway winding off like a serpent over the rolling surface, disappearing and reappearing till lost in the luxuriant herbage." Tallgrass prairies had their perils too:

GROWTH OF THE RAILROAD NETWORK, 1850–1860   (See map, page 394) Although a good deal of track mileage was laid during the 1850s, total track mileage is misleading because the United States lacked a fully integrated rail network in 1860. A few trunk-line roads had combined a number of smaller lines into a single system to make shipment of goods easier. The Pennsylvania Railroad, for example, linked Philadelphia and Pittsburgh. But the existence of five major track gauges (or widths) meant that passengers and freight often had to be transferred from one line to the next. And north-south traffic was further disrupted by the lack of bridges over the Ohio River.

year round, storms sent travelers searching for the shelter of trees along river valleys, and stinging insects were thick in the summer.

Because normal plows could not penetrate the densely tangled roots of prairie grass, the earliest settlers erected farms along the boundary separating the forest from the prairie. In 1837, however, John Deere invented a sharp-cutting steel plow that sliced through the sod without soil sticking to the blade. In addition, Cyrus McCormick refined a mechanical reaper that harvested 14 times more wheat with the same amount of labor. By the 1850s McCormick was selling 1000 reapers a year and could not keep up with demand, while Deere turned out 10,000 plows annually.

Impact of technology

The new commercial farming fundamentally altered the landscape and the environment. Indians had grown corn in the region for years, but never in such large fields as those of white farmers, whose surpluses were shipped east. Prairie farmers also introduced new crops that were not part of the earlier ecological system, notably wheat, along with fruits and vegetables. Native grasses were replaced by a small number of plants cultivated as commodities. Domesticated grasses replaced native grasses in pastures for making hay.

Changes in the landscape

Western farmers altered the landscape by reducing the annual fires, often set by Indians, that had kept the prairie free from trees. In the absence of these fires, trees reappeared on land not in cultivation and, if undisturbed, eventually formed woodlots. The earlier unbroken landscape gave way to independent farms, each fenced off in the precise checkerboard pattern established by the Northwest Ordinance. It was an artificial ecosystem of animals, woodlots, and crops whose large, uniform layout made western farms more efficient than the more irregular farms in the East.

Railroads and the Urban Environment

Railroads transformed the urban environment as well. Communities soon recognized that their economic survival depended on creating adequate rail links to the countryside and to major urban markets and transshipment points. Large cities feared they would be left behind in the struggle to be the dominant city in the region, and smaller communities saw their very survival at stake in the battle for rail connections.

Location of railroads

Even communities that obtained rail links found the presence of this new technology difficult to adjust to. When a railroad began serving Jacksonville, Illinois, merchants soon complained about the noise, dirt, and billowing smoke produced by locomotives passing through the business district. "The public square was filled with teams [of horses]," one resident recalled, "and whenever the engine steamed into the square making all the noise possible, there was such a stampede." After a few years, the tracks were relocated on the outskirts of town. Increasingly communities kept railroads away from fashionable neighborhoods and shopping areas. As the tracks became a physical manifestation of social and economic divisions in the town, the notion of living "on the wrong side of the tracks" became crucial to the urban landscape.

Rising Industrialization

The expansion of commercial agriculture, along with the shift from water power to steam, also spurred the growth of industry. Out of the 10 leading American industries, 8 processed raw materials produced by agriculture, including flour milling and the manufacture of textiles, shoes, and woolens. (The only exceptions were iron and machinery.)

Most important, the factory system of organizing labor and the technology of interchangeable parts spread to other areas of the economy during the 1850s. Isaac Singer began using interchangeable parts in 1851 to mass-produce sewing machines, which made possible the ready-made clothing industry, while workers who assembled farm implements performed a single step in the process over and over again. By 1860 the United States had nearly a billion dollars invested in manufacturing, almost twice as much as in 1849. And for the first time, less than half the workers in the North were employed in agriculture.

> Expansion of industry

Immigration

The surge of industry depended on a large factory labor force. Natural increase helped swell the population to more than 30 million by 1860, but only in part, since the birthrate had begun to decline. It was the beginning of mass immigration to America during the mid-1840s that kept population growth soaring.

In the 20 years from 1820 to 1840, about 700,000 newcomers had entered the United States. That figure jumped to 1.7 million in the 1840s, then to 2.6 million in the 1850s. Though even greater numbers arrived after the Civil War, as a percentage of the nation's total population, the wave from 1845 to 1854 was the largest influx of immigrants in American history. Most of the newcomers were in the prime of life: in 1856 out of 224,000 arrivals, only 31,000 were under 10 and 20,000 were over 40. Certainly the booming economy and the lure of freedom drew immigrants, but they were also pushed by deteriorating conditions in Europe. In Ireland, a potato blight, which first struck in 1845, led to widespread famine. Out of a population of 9 million, as many as a million perished, while a million and a half more emigrated, two-thirds to the United States.

> Beginning of mass immigration

The Irish tended to be poorer than other immigrant groups of the day. Although the Protestant Scots-Irish continued to emigrate, as so many had during the eighteenth century, the decided majority of the Irish who came after 1845 were Catholic. Because they were poor and unskilled, the Irish congregated in the cities, where the women performed domestic service and took factory jobs and the men did manual labor.

> New sources of immigration

Germans and Scandinavians also had economic reasons for leaving Europe. They included small farmers whose lands had become marginal or who had been displaced by landlords, and skilled workers thrown out of work by industrialization. Some fled political and social oppression and came to live under the free institutions of the United States. Since arriving in America, wrote a Swede who settled in Iowa in 1850, "I have not been compelled to pay a penny for the privilege of living. Neither is my cap worn out from lifting it in the presence of gentlemen."

Unprecedented unrest and upheaval prevailed in Europe in 1848, the so-called year of revolutions. The famine that had driven so many Irish out of their country was part of a larger food shortage caused by a series of poor harvests. Mounting unemployment and overburdened relief programs increased suffering. In this situation, middle-class reformers, who wanted civil liberty and a more representative government, joined forces with lower-class workers to overthrow several regimes, sometimes by also appealing to nationalist feelings. France, Austria, Hungary, Italy, and Prussia all witnessed major popular uprisings. Yet though these revolts gained temporary success, they were all quashed by the forces of the old order. Liberal hopes for a more open, democratic society suffered a severe setback.

The revolutions of 1848

In the aftermath of this failure, a number of hard-pressed German workers and farmers as well as disillusioned radicals and reformers emigrated to the United States, the symbol of democratic liberalism in the world. They were joined by the first significant migration from Asia, as thousands of Chinese joined the gold rush to California and other strikes (page 381). This migration was part of a century-long phenomenon, as approximately 50 million Europeans, largely from rural areas, would migrate to the Western Hemisphere.

Although many Germans and Scandinavians arrived in modest straits, few were truly impoverished, and many could afford to buy a farm or start a business. Unlike the Irish, Germans tended to emigrate as families, and wherever they settled, they formed social, religious, and cultural organizations to maintain their language and customs. Whereas the Scandinavians, Dutch, and English immigrants were Protestant, half or more of the Germans were Catholic.

Immigrants in factories and cities

Factories came more and more to depend on immigrant labor, including children, since newcomers would work for lower wages and were less prone to protest harsh working conditions. The shift to an immigrant workforce could be seen most clearly in the textile industry, where by 1860 over half the workers in New England mills were foreign-born.

The sizable foreign-born population in many American cities severely strained urban resources. Immigrants who could barely make ends meet were forced to live in overcrowded, unheated tenement houses, damp cellars, and even shacks. Urban slums became notorious for crime and drinking, which took a heavy toll on families and the poor. In the eyes of many native-born Americans, immigrants were to blame for driving down factory wages and pushing American workers out of jobs. Overshadowing these complaints was a fear that America might not be able to assimilate the new groups, with their unfamiliar languages and customs. These fears precipitated an outburst of political nativism in the mid-1850s.

Southern Complaints

With British and northern factories buying cotton in unprecedented quantities, southern planters prospered in the 1850s. Like those of northern commercial farmers, their operations became more highly capitalized to keep up with the demand. But instead of machinery, white southerners invested in slaves. During the 1850s, the price of prime field hands reached record levels.

Nonetheless, a number of southern nationalists, who advocated that the South should be a separate nation, pressed for greater industrialization to make the region more independent. "At present, the North fattens and grows rich upon the South," one Alabama newspaper complained in 1851, noting that "we purchase all our luxuries and necessities from the North," including clothing, shoes, implements and machinery, saddles and carriages, and even books. But most southerners ignored such pleas. So long as investments in cotton and slaves absorbed most of the South's capital, efforts to promote southern industry made little headway.

Southern economic dependence

Despite southern prosperity, the section's leaders repeatedly complained that the North had used its power over banking and commerce to convert the South into a colony. Storage and shipping charges, insurance, port fees, and commissions, which added an estimated 20 percent to the cost of cotton and other commodities, went into the pockets of northern merchants, shippers, and bankers. The idea that the South was a colony of the North was inaccurate, but southern whites found it a convincing explanation of the North's growing wealth. More important, it reinforced their resistance to federal aid for economic development, which they were convinced would inevitably enrich the North at southern expense. This attitude further weakened the South's political alliance with the West, which needed federal aid for transportation.

White southerners also feared that the new tide of immigration would shift the sectional balance of power. Most immigrants shunned the South, not wanting to compete with cheap slave labor. The lack of industry and the limited demand for skilled labor also shunted immigrants northward. As a result, the North surged even further ahead of the South in population, thereby strengthening its control of the House of Representatives and heightening southern concern that the North would rapidly settle the western territories.

THE POLITICAL REALIGNMENT OF THE 1850s

When Franklin Pierce (he pronounced it "Purse") assumed the presidency in 1853, he was only 48 years old, the youngest man yet to be elected president. He was also a supporter of the "Young America" movement of the Democratic party, which enthusiastically anticipated extending democracy around the globe and annexing additional territory to the United States.

The believers in Young America felt it idle to argue about slavery when the nation could be developing new resources. In 1853 Pierce did manage to conclude

Gadsden Purchase

the Gadsden Purchase, thereby gaining control of about 45,000 square miles of Mexican desert, which contained the most practical southern route for a transcontinental railroad. He had no success accomplishing his major goal, the acquisition of Cuba, a rich sugar-producing island where slavery had once been important. In any case, he soon had his hands full with the proposals of another Democrat of the Young America stamp, Senator Stephen A. Douglas of Illinois.

The Kansas-Nebraska Act

Known as the Little Giant, Douglas was ambitious, bursting with energy, and impatient to get things done. As chairman of the Senate's Committee on Territories, he was eager to organize federal lands west of Missouri as part of his program for economic development. And as a citizen of Illinois, he wanted Chicago selected as the eastern terminus of the proposed transcontinental railroad. That necessitated the organization of the remainder of the Louisiana Purchase, since any northern rail route would have to run through that region.

Under the terms of the Missouri Compromise of 1820, slavery was prohibited in this portion of the Louisiana Purchase (page 245). But Douglas had already tried once to organize the area while keeping a ban on slavery—only to have his bill voted down by southern opposition in the Senate. In January 1854 he reintroduced the measure, and this time, in order to secure necessary Southern support, he omitted the prohibition on slavery that had been in effect for 34 years.

In its final form, the bill created two territories: Kansas, directly west of Missouri, and a much larger Nebraska Territory, located west of Iowa and the

Missouri Compromise repealed

Minnesota Territory. The Missouri Compromise was explicitly repealed. Instead, popular sovereignty was to determine the status of slavery in both territories, though it was left unclear whether residents of Kansas and Nebraska could prohibit slavery at any time or only at the time of statehood, as southerners insisted. It was widely assumed that Kansas would be a slave state and Nebraska a free state.

The Kansas-Nebraska Act outraged northern Democrats, Whigs, and Free Soilers alike. Critics rejected Douglas's contention that popular sovereignty would keep the territories free. The bill, they charged, was meant to give slaveholders—the "Slave Power"—territory previously consecrated to freedom. Most northern opponents of the bill focused on the expansion of slavery and the Slave Power rather than the moral evil of slavery. A wave of popular indignation swept across the North.

Once President Pierce endorsed the bill, Senate passage was assured. The real fight came in the House, where the North held a large majority. The president put intense pressure on his fellow northern Democrats, and finally the bill passed

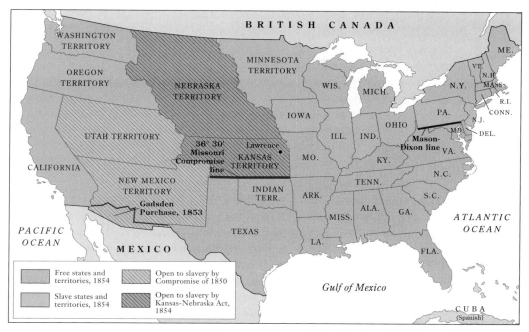

THE KANSAS-NEBRASKA ACT When the Kansas-Nebraska Act of 1854 opened the remaining portion of the Louisiana Purchase to slavery under the doctrine of popular sovereignty, conflict between the two sections focused on control of Kansas, directly west of the slave state of Missouri.

by a narrow margin, 113 to 100, largely along sectional lines. Pierce signed it on May 30, 1854, and the Missouri Compromise was repealed.

The Collapse of the Second American Party System

The furor over the Kansas-Nebraska Act laid bare the underlying social and economic tensions that had developed between the North and the South. These tensions put mounting pressure on the political parties, and in the 1850s the Jacksonian party system collapsed. Voters who had been loyal to one party for years, even decades, began switching allegiances. By the time the process of realignment was completed, a new party system had emerged, divided this time along clearly sectional lines.

Political realignment

In part, the old party system decayed because new problems had replaced the traditional economic issues of both Whigs and Democrats. The Whigs alienated many of their traditional Protestant supporters by openly seeking the support of Catholics and recent immigrants. Then, too, the growing agitation for the prohibition of alcohol divided both parties, especially the Whigs. Finally, both the Whigs and the Democrats were increasingly perceived as little more than corrupt engines of plunder and became targets of popular disillusionment.

Thus the party system was already weakened when the Kansas-Nebraska Act divided the two major parties along sectional lines. In such an unstable atmosphere, with party loyalties declining, independent parties flourished. Antislavery veterans, who had earlier sparked the Liberty and Free Soil parties, united with Whigs and anti-Nebraska Democrats in the new antislavery Republican party. Their calculations were derailed, however, when another new party capitalized on fears aroused by the recent flood of immigrants.

The Know-Nothings

In 1854 the American party, a secret nativist organization whose members were called Know-Nothings, suddenly emerged as a potent political force. (Its members, sworn to secrecy, had been instructed to answer inquiries by replying "I know nothing.") Taking as its slogan "Americans should rule America," Know-Nothings denounced illegal voting by immigrants, the rising crime and disorder in urban areas, and immigrants' heavy drinking. They were also strongly anti-Catholic and were convinced that the church's "undemocratic" hierarchy of bishops and archbishops was conspiring to undermine American democracy. Know-Nothings advocated lengthening the residency period for naturalization and ousting from office corrupt politicians who openly bid for foreign and Catholic votes.

Nativist fears

The Know-Nothings won a series of remarkable victories in the 1854 elections. Their showing spelled doom for the Whigs, already weakened by the Kansas-Nebraska Act, as the rank and file deserted in droves to the Know-Nothings. With perhaps a million voters enrolled in its lodges in every state of the Union, Know-Nothing leaders confidently predicted in 1855 that they would elect the next president.

Yet only a year later—by the end of 1856—the party had collapsed as quickly as it had risen. The collapse came in part because inexperienced leaders failed to enact the party's reform platform; but its real death knell was rising sectional tensions. In 1856 a majority of northern delegates walked out of the American party's national convention when it adopted a proslavery platform. Significantly, they deserted to the other new party, the Republicans. This party, unlike the Know-Nothings, had no base in the South. It intended to elect a president by sweeping the free states, which controlled a majority of the electoral votes.

Sudden decline

The Republicans and Bleeding Kansas

Initially, the Republican party made little headway in the North. Although it attracted a variety of Whigs, anti-Nebraska Democrats, and Free Soilers, many moderate Whigs and Democrats viewed the party as too radical. Observers predicted that it would soon go the way of all other failed antislavery parties.

Such predictions, however, did not take into account the emotions stirred up by developments in Kansas. Most early settlers migrated to Kansas for the same reason other white Americans headed west: the chance to prosper in a new land. But Douglas's idea of popular sovereignty transformed the new settlement into a referendum on slavery in the territories. A race soon developed between northerners and southerners to settle Kansas first. To the proslavery residents of neighboring Missouri, free-state communities like Lawrence seemed ominous threats. "We are playing for a mighty stake," former Senator David Rice Atchison of Missouri insisted. "If we win, we carry slavery to the Pacific Ocean; if we fail we lose Missouri, Arkansas and Texas and all the territories; the game must be played boldly."

When the first Kansas elections were held in 1854 and 1855, Missourians poured over the border, seized the polls, and stuffed the ballot boxes. A later congressional investigation concluded that more than 60 percent of the votes were cast illegally. This massive fraud tarnished popular sovereignty at the outset and greatly aroused public opinion in the North. It also provided proslavery forces with a commanding majority in the Kansas legislature, where they enacted a strict legal code designed to intimidate antislavery settlers. This Kansas Code limited such time-honored rights as freedom of speech, impartial juries, and fair elections. Mobilized into action, the free-staters in the fall of 1855 organized a separate government, drafted a state constitution prohibiting slavery, and asked Congress to admit Kansas as a free state. In such a polarized situation, violence quickly broke out between the two factions that culminated in the raid on Lawrence in May 1856.

> Turmoil in Kansas

The Caning of Charles Sumner

Only a few days before the proslavery attack on Lawrence, Republican Senator Charles Sumner of Massachusetts delivered a scathing speech, "The Crime Against Kansas." Sumner was passionate in his condemnation of slavery, and his speech included remarks that deliberately insulted the state of South Carolina and one of its senators. Preston S. Brooks, a South Carolina congressman, was outraged that Sumner had insulted his relative and mocked his state.

Several days later, on May 22, Brooks strode into the Senate after it had adjourned, went up to Sumner, who was seated at his desk, and proceeded to beat him over the head with a cane. The cane shattered into three pieces from the violence of the attack, but Brooks, swept up in the emotion of the moment, furiously continued hitting Sumner until the senator collapsed unconscious, drenched in blood.

Northerners were electrified to learn that a senator of the United States had been beaten unconscious in the Senate chamber. But what caused them even greater consternation was southern reaction to Sumner's caning— for in his own region, Preston Brooks was lionized as a hero. Instantly,

> Significance of the caning

The caning of Senator Charles Sumner of Massachusetts by Representative Preston S. Brooks of South Carolina inflamed public opinion. In this northern cartoon, the fallen Sumner, a martyr to free speech, raises his pen against Brooks's club. Rushing to capitalize on the furor, printmakers did not know what the obscure Brooks looked like and thus had to devise ingenious ways of portraying the incident. In this print, Brooks's face is hidden by his raised arm.

the Sumner caning breathed life into the fledgling Republican party. Its claims about "Bleeding Kansas" and the Slave Power now seemed credible.

The Election of 1856

In the face of the storm that had arisen over Kansas, the Democrats turned to James Buchanan of Pennsylvania as their presidential nominee. Buchanan's supreme qualification was having the good fortune to have been out of the country as minister to England when the Kansas-Nebraska Act was passed. The American party, split badly by the Kansas issue, nominated former president Millard Fillmore.

The Republicans chose John C. Frémont, a western explorer who had helped liberate California during the Mexican War. The party's platform denounced slavery as a "relic of barbarism" and demanded that Kansas be admitted as a free state. Throughout the summer the party hammered away on Bleeding Sumner and Bleeding Kansas. "A constantly increasing excitement is kept up by the intelligence coming every day from Kansas," wrote one observer. "I have never known political excitement—I ought rather to say exasperation—approach that which now rages."

In this playbill advertising a dramatic production of *Uncle Tom's Cabin*, vicious bloodhounds pursue the light-skinned Eliza, who clutches her child as she frantically leaps to safety across the ice-choked Ohio River.

A number of basic principles guided the Republican party, one of which was the ideal of free labor. Slavery degraded labor, Republicans argued, and would inevitably drive free labor out of the territories. Condemning the South as a stagnant, hierarchical, and economically backward region, Republicans praised the North as a fluid society of widespread opportunity where enterprising individuals could improve their lot. Stopping the expansion of slavery, in Republican eyes, would preserve this heritage of opportunity and economic independence for white Americans. Republicans also appealed to former Know-Nothings by criticizing the Catholic Church, particularly its political activity, and by being much more favorable to temperance.

> **Ideology of the Republican party**

Also important was the moral opposition to slavery, strengthened by works like Harriet Beecher Stowe's *Uncle Tom's Cabin*. Republican speakers and editors stressed that slavery was a moral wrong, that it was incompatible with the ideals of the Republic and Christianity. "Never forget," Republican leader Abraham Lincoln declared on one occasion, "that we have before us this whole matter of the right and wrong of slavery in this Union, though the immediate question is as to its spreading out into new Territories and States."

More negatively, Republicans gained support by shifting their attacks from slavery itself to the Slave Power, or the political influence of the planter class. Pointing to the Sumner assault and the incidents

> **Threat to white liberty**

in Kansas, Republicans contended that the Slave Power had set out to destroy the liberties of white northerners. Just as the nation's founders had battled against tyranny, aristocracy, and minority rule in the Revolution, so the North confronted the unrepublican Slave Power. "If our government, for the sake of Slavery, is to be perpetually the representative of a minority," argued the Cincinnati *Commercial*, "it may continue republican in form, but the substance of its republicanism has departed."

In the election, Buchanan all but swept the South (losing only Maryland to Fillmore) and won enough free states to push him over the top, with 174 electoral votes to Frémont's 114 and Fillmore's 8. Still, the violence in Kansas and Sumner's caning nearly carried Frémont into the presidency. He ran ahead of both Buchanan and Fillmore in the North and won 11 free states out of 16. Had he carried Pennsylvania plus one more, he would have been elected. For the first time in American history, an antislavery party based entirely in the North threatened to elect a president and snap the bonds of union.

THE WORSENING CRISIS

James Buchanan was one of the most experienced men ever elected president: he had served in Congress, in the cabinet, and in the foreign service. Moderates in both sections hoped that the new president would thwart Republicans in the North and secessionists of the Deep South, popularly known as "fire-eaters." Throughout his career, however, Buchanan had taken the southern position on sectional matters, and he proved remarkably insensitive to the concerns of northern Democrats. Moreover, on March 6, 1857, only two days after Buchanan's inauguration, the Supreme Court rendered one of the most controversial decisions in its history.

The Dred Scott *Decision*

The owner of a Missouri slave named Dred Scott had taken him to live for several years in Illinois, a free state, and in what is now Minnesota, where slavery had been banned by the Missouri Compromise. Eventually the owner returned with Scott to Missouri. Scott sued for his freedom on the grounds that his residence in a free state and a free territory had made him free, and his case ultimately went to the Supreme Court. Two northern justices joined all five southern members in ruling 7 to 2 that Scott remained a slave. The major opinion was written by Chief Justice Roger Taney of Maryland.

Wanting to strengthen the judicial protection of slavery, Taney ruled that African Americans could not be and never had been citizens of the United States. Instead, he insisted that at the time the Constitution was adopted, they were "regarded as beings of an inferior order, so far

Protection of slavery

inferior that they had no rights which the white man was bound to respect." In addition, the Court ruled that the Missouri Compromise was unconstitutional. Congress, it declared, had no power to ban slavery from *any* territory of the United States.

While southerners rejoiced at this result, Republicans denounced the Court for rejecting their party's main principle, that Congress should prohibit slavery in all territories. "We know the court . . . has often overruled its own decisions," Abraham Lincoln observed, "and we shall do what we can to have it over-rule this." For Republicans, the decision foreshadowed the spread of slavery throughout the West and even the nation.

Reaction to the decision

But the decision also was a blow to Douglas's moderate solution of popular sovereignty. If Congress had no power to prohibit slavery in a territory, how could it authorize a territorial legislature to do so? While the Court did not rule on this point, the clear implication of the *Dred Scott* decision was that popular sovereignty was also unconstitutional. The Court, in effect, had endorsed John C. Calhoun's radical view that slavery was legal in all the territories. In so doing, the Court, which had intended to settle the question of slavery in the territories, instead pushed the political debate toward new extremes.

The Panic of 1857

As the nation grappled with the *Dred Scott* decision, an economic depression aggravated sectional conflict. The Panic of 1857 was nowhere near as severe as the depression of 1839–1843. But the psychological results were far-reaching, for the South remained relatively untouched. With the price of cotton and other southern commodities still high, southern secessionists hailed the panic as proof that an independent southern nation was economically feasible. Insisting that cotton sustained the international economy, James Henry Hammond, a senator from South Carolina, boasted: "No, you dare not make war on cotton. No power on earth dares to make war on it. Cotton is king."

Uneven effects of the Panic

For their part, northerners urged federal action to bolster the economy. Southerners defeated an attempt to increase the tariff duties, which were at their lowest level since 1815, and Buchanan, under southern pressure, vetoed bills to improve navigation on the Great Lakes and to give free farms to western settlers. Many northern conservatives concluded that southern obstructionism blocked national development and now endorsed the Republican party.

The Lecompton Constitution

Although the *Dred Scott* decision and economic depression weakened the bonds of the Union, Kansas remained at the center of the political stage. In June 1857, when the territory elected delegates to draft a state constitution, free-staters boycotted the election, thereby giving proslavery forces control of the convention that met in Lecompton. The delegates promptly drafted a constitution that made slavery legal. Even more boldly, they scheduled a referendum in which voters could choose only whether to admit additional slaves into the new state. They could not vote against either the constitution or slavery. Once again, free-staters boycotted the election, and the Lecompton constitution was approved.

President Buchanan had pledged earlier there would be a free and fair vote on the Lecompton constitution. But the outcome offered the unexpected opportunity to create one additional slave state and thereby satisfy his southern supporters by pushing the Lecompton constitution through Congress. This was too much for Douglas, who broke party ranks and denounced the Lecompton constitution as a fraud. Nevertheless, the administration prevailed in the Senate. But the House, where northern representation was much stronger, rejected the constitution. In a compromise, Congress, using indirect language, returned the constitution to Kansas for another vote. This time it was decisively defeated, 11,300 to 1788. No doubt remained that as soon as Kansas had sufficient population, it would come into the Union as a free state.

Defeat of Lecompton constitution

The attempt to force slavery on the people of Kansas drove many conservative northerners into the Republican party. And Douglas now found himself assailed by the southern wing of his party. On top of that, in the summer of 1858, he faced a desperate fight in his race for reelection to the Senate against Republican Abraham Lincoln.

The Lincoln-Douglas Debates

"He is the strong man of his party . . . and the best stump speaker, with his droll ways and dry jokes, in the West," Douglas commented when he learned of Lincoln's nomination to oppose him. "He is as honest as he is shrewd, and if I beat him my victory will be hardly won." Tall (6 feet, 4 inches) and gangly, Lincoln had an awkward manner as he spoke, yet his finely honed logic and sincerity carried the audience with him. His sentences had none of the oratorical flourishes common in that day. "If we could first know *where* we are, and *whither* we are tending, we could then better judge *what* to do, and *how* to do it," Lincoln began, in accepting his party's nomination for senator in 1858. He quoted a proverb from the Bible:

"A house divided against itself cannot stand."

I believe this government cannot endure, permanently half *slave* and half *free*.

I do not expect the Union to be *dissolved*—I do not expect the house to *fall*—but I *do* expect it will cease to be divided.

It will become *all* one thing, or *all* the other.

Either the *opponents* of slavery, will arrest the further spread of it, and place it where the public mind shall rest in the belief that it is in course of ultimate extinction; or its *advocates* will push it forward, till it shall become alike lawful in *all* the States, old as well as *new*—North as well as *South*.

The message echoed through the hall and across the pages of the national press.

Superb debaters, Douglas and Lincoln nevertheless had very different speaking styles. The deep-voiced Douglas was constantly on the attack, drawing on his remarkable memory and showering points like buckshot in all directions. Lincoln, who had a high-pitched voice, developed his arguments more carefully and methodically, and he relied on his sense of humor and unmatched ability as a storyteller to drive his points home to the audience.

Born in the slave state of Kentucky, Lincoln had grown up mostly in southern Indiana and central Illinois. Yet his intense ambition lifted him above the back-woods from which he came. He compensated for a lack of schooling through disciplined self-education, and he became a shrewd courtroom lawyer of respectable social standing. Known for his sense of humor, he was nonetheless subject to fits of acute depression.

Lincoln's character

Lincoln's first love was always politics. A fervent admirer of Henry Clay and his economic program, he became a Whig and then, after the party's demise, joined the Republicans and became one of their key leaders in Illinois. Lincoln challenged Douglas to discuss the issues of slavery and the sectional controversy in a series of seven joint debates.

In the campaign, Douglas sought to portray Lincoln as a radical who preached sectional warfare. The nation *could* endure half slave and half free, Douglas declared, so long as states and territories were left alone to regulate their own affairs. Lincoln countered by insisting that the spread of slavery was a blight on the Republic. Even though Douglas had voted against the Lecompton constitution, he could not be counted on to oppose

Debate over the slavery issue

slavery's expansion, for he admitted that he didn't care whether slavery was voted "down or up."

In the debate held at Freeport, Illinois, Lincoln asked Douglas how under the *Dred Scott* decision the people of a territory could lawfully exclude slavery before statehood. Douglas answered, with what became known as the Freeport Doctrine, that slaveowners would never bring their slaves into an area where slavery was not legally protected. Therefore, Douglas explained, if the people of a territory refused to pass a slave code, slavery would never be established there.

Freeport Doctrine

In a close race, the legislature elected Douglas to another term in the Senate.* But on the national scene, southern Democrats angrily repudiated him and condemned the Freeport Doctrine. And although Lincoln lost, Republicans thought his impressive performance marked him as a possible presidential contender for 1860.

The Beleaguered South

While northerners increasingly feared that the Slave Power was conspiring to extend slavery into the free states, southerners worried that the "Black Republicans" would hem them in and undermine their political power.

The very factors that brought prosperity during the 1850s stimulated the South's sense of crisis. As the price of slaves rose sharply, the proportion of southerners who owned slaves had dropped almost a third since 1830. Land also was being consolidated into larger holdings, evidence of declining opportunity for ordinary white southerners. At the same time, California and Kansas had been closed to southern slaveholders—unfairly, in their eyes. Finally, Douglas's clever claim that a territory could effectively outlaw slavery using the Freeport Doctrine seemed to negate the *Dred Scott* decision that slavery was legal in all the territories.

Several possible solutions to the South's internal crisis had failed. Agricultural reform to restore worn-out lands had made significant headway in Virginia and Maryland, but elsewhere the rewards of a single-crop economy were too great to persuade southern farmers to adopt new methods. Another alternative—industrialization—had also failed. Indeed, the gap between the North and the South steadily widened in the 1850s. Finally, private military expeditions in Latin America, which were designed to strengthen the South by adding slave territory to the United States, came to naught.

Failed solutions

The South's growing sense of isolation made this crisis more acute. By the 1850s slavery had been abolished throughout most of the Americas, and in the

---

*State legislatures elected senators until 1913, when the Seventeenth Amendment was adopted. Although Lincoln and Douglas both campaigned for the office, Illinois voters actually voted for candidates for the legislature who were pledged to one of the senatorial candidates.

United States the South's political power was steadily shrinking. Only the expansion of slavery held out any promise of new slave states needed to preserve the South's political power and protect its way of life. "The truth is," fumed one Alabama politician, ". . . the South is excluded from the common territories of the Union. The right of expansion claimed to be a necessity of her continued existence, is practically and effectively denied the South."

THE ROAD TO WAR

In 1857 John Brown—the abolitionist firebrand—had returned to the East from Kansas, consumed with the idea of attacking slavery in the South itself. Financed by a number of prominent northern reformers, Brown gathered 21 followers, including 5 free blacks, in hope of fomenting a slave insurrection. On the night of October 16, 1859, his band seized the unguarded federal armory at Harpers Ferry in Virginia. But no slaves rallied to Brown's standard: few lived in the area to begin with. Before long the raiders found themselves surrounded and holed up in the town. Charging with bayonets fixed, federal troops commanded by Colonel Robert E. Lee soon captured Brown and his raiders. On December 2, 1859, Virginia hanged Brown for treason.

> John Brown attacks Harpers Ferry

Brown's raid at Harpers Ferry was yet another blow weakening the forces of compromise and moderation within the nation. Although the invasion itself was a dismal failure, the old man knew well how to bear himself with a martyr's dignity. Republicans made haste to denounce Brown's raid, lest they be tarred as radicals, but other northerners were less cautious. Ralph Waldo Emerson described Brown as a "saint, whose martyrdom will make the gallows as glorious as the cross." While only a minority of northerners endorsed Brown, southerners were shocked by such displays of sympathy. And they were firmly convinced that the Republican party was secretly connected to the raid. "I have always been a fervid Union man," one North Carolina resident wrote, "but I confess the endorsement of the Harpers Ferry outrage has shaken my fidelity and I am willing to take the chances of every probable evil that may arise from disunion, sooner than submit any longer to Northern insolence and Northern outrage."

A Sectional Election

When Congress convened in December, there were ominous signs everywhere of the growing sectional rift. Intent on destroying Douglas's Freeport Doctrine, southern radicals demanded a congressional slave code to protect slavery in the territories. To northern Democrats, such a platform spelled political death. As one Indiana Democrat put it, "We cannot carry a single congressional district on that doctrine in the state."

EYEWITNESS TO HISTORY

I Have Seen Nothing Like the Intensity of Feeling

You can hardly have formed an idea of the intensity of feeling and interest which has prevailed throughout the country in regard to John Brown. I have seen nothing like it. We get up excitements easily enough, but they die away usually as quickly as they rose . . . but this was different. The heart of the people was fairly reached, and an impression has been made upon it which will be permanent and produce results long hence.

. . . There was at first no word of sympathy either for Brown or his undertaking. But soon came the accounts of the panic of the Virginians, of the cruelty with which Brown's party were massacred; of his noble manliness of demeanour when, wounded, he was taken prisoner, and was questioned as to his design; of his simple declarations of his motives and aims, which were those of an enthusiast, but not of a bad man,—and a strong sympathy began to be felt for Brown personally. . . . The management of the trial, the condemnation, the speech made by Brown, the letters he wrote in prison, the visit of his wife to him,—and at last his death, wrought up the popular feeling to the highest point. . . . The mass of the people . . . have, while condemning Brown's scheme as a criminal attempt to right a great wrong by violent measures, and as equally ill-judged and rash in execution, felt for the man himself a deep sympathy and a fervent admiration. . . . They have felt that . . . he died a real martyr in the cause of freedom.

. . . What its results will be no one can tell, but they cannot be otherwise than great. One great moving fact remains that here was a man who, setting himself firm on the Gospel, was willing to sacrifice himself and his children in the cause of the oppressed. . . . The events of the last month or two . . . have done more to comfirm the opposition to Slavery at the North . . . than anything which has ever happened before, than all the anti-slavery tracts and novels that ever were written.

Source: Charles Eliot Norton to Mrs. Edward Twisleton, December 19, 1859, Sara Norton and M. A. DeWolfe Howe, eds., *Letters of Charles Eliot Norton* (Boston: Houghton Mifflin Company, 1913), v. 1, pp. 197–201.

At the Democratic convention in April, southern radicals boldly pressed their demand for a federal slave code. But instead the convention adopted the Douglas platform upholding popular sovereignty, whereupon the delegations from eight southern states walked out. The convention finally reassembled two months later and nominated Douglas. At this point most of the remaining southern Democrats departed and, together with those delegates who had seceded earlier, nominated Vice President John C. Breckinridge of Kentucky on a platform supporting a federal slave code. The last major national party had shattered.

Disruption of the Democratic party

The Republicans turned to Abraham Lincoln, a moderate on slavery who was strong in his home state of Illinois and the other doubtful states that the party had failed to carry in 1856. Republicans also sought to broaden their appeal by adding to their platform several economic planks that endorsed a moderately protective tariff, a homestead bill, and a northern transcontinental railroad.

The election that followed was really two contests in one. In the North, which had a majority of the electoral votes, only Lincoln and Douglas had any chance to carry a state. In the South, the race pitted Breckinridge against John Bell of Tennessee, the candidate of the new Constitutional Union party. Although Lincoln received less than 40 percent of the popular vote and had virtually no support in the South, he won 180 electoral votes, 27 more than needed for election. For the first time, the nation had elected a president who headed a completely sectional party and who was committed to stopping the expansion of slavery.

Lincoln's victory

Secession

Although the Republicans had not won control of either house of Congress, Lincoln's election struck many southerners as a blow of terrible finality. Lincoln had been lifted into office on the strength of the free states alone. It was not unrealistic, many fire-eaters argued, to believe that he would use federal aid to induce the border states to voluntarily free their slaves. Once slavery disappeared there, and new states were added, the necessary three-fourths majority would exist to approve a constitutional amendment abolishing slavery. Or perhaps Lincoln might send other John Browns into the South to stir up more slave insurrections. The Montgomery (Alabama) *Mail* accused Republicans of intending "to free the negroes and force amalgamation between them and the children of the poor men of the South."

Southern fears

Secession seemed the only alternative left to protect southern equality and liberty. South Carolina, which had challenged federal authority in the nullification crisis, was determined to force the other southern states to act. On December 20, 1860, a popular convention unanimously passed a resolution seceding from the Union. The rest of the Deep South followed, and on February 7, 1861, the states stretching from South Carolina to Texas organized the Confederate States of America and elected Jefferson Davis president.

Confederate States of America

But the Upper South and the border states declined to secede, hoping that once again Congress could patch together a settlement. Senator John Crittenden of Kentucky proposed extending to California the old Missouri Compromise line of 36°30'. Slavery would be prohibited north of this line and given federal protection south of it in all territories, including any acquired in the future. Furthermore, Crittenden proposed an "unamendable amendment" to the Constitution, forever safeguarding slavery in states where it already existed.

Failure of compromise in Congress

But the Crittenden Compromise was doomed for the simple reason that the two groups who were required to make concessions—Republicans and secessionists—had no interest in doing so. "The argument is exhausted," representatives from the Deep South announced, even before Crittenden had introduced his package. "We have just carried an election on principles fairly stated to the people," Lincoln wrote in opposing compromise. "Now we are told in advance, the government shall be broken up, unless we surrender to those we have beaten, before we take the offices. If we surrender, it is the end of us, and of the government."

The Outbreak of War

As his inauguration approached, Lincoln pondered what to do about secession. In his inaugural address on March 4, he sought to reassure southerners that he had no intention, "directly or indirectly, to interfere with the institution of slavery in

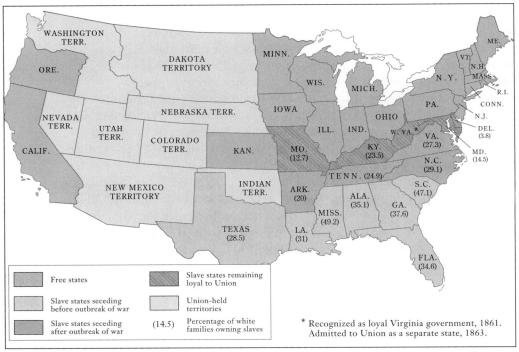

THE PATTERN OF SECESSION   Led by South Carolina, the Deep South seceded between Lincoln's election in November and his inauguration in March. The Upper South did not secede until after the firing on Fort Sumter. The four border slave states never seceded and remained in the Union throughout the war. As the map indicates, secession sentiment was strongest in states where the highest percentage of white families owned slaves.

the States where it exists." But echoing Andrew Jackson in the nullification crisis, he maintained that "the Union of these states is perpetual," and he announced that he intended to "hold, occupy and possess" federal property and collect customs duties under the tariff. He closed by calling for a restoration of the "bonds of affection" that united all Americans.

The new president hoped for time to work out a solution, but on his first day in office he was given a dispatch from Major Robert Anderson, commander of the federal garrison at Fort Sumter in Charleston harbor. Sumter was one of the few remaining federal outposts in the South. Anderson informed Fort Sumter the government that he was almost out of food and that, unless resupplied, he would have to surrender. For a month Lincoln looked for a way out, but he finally sent a relief expedition. As a conciliatory gesture, he notified the governor of South Carolina that supplies were being sent and that if the fleet were allowed to pass, only food, and not men, arms, or ammunition, would be landed.

The burden of decision now shifted to Jefferson Davis. From his point of view, secession was a constitutional right, and the Confederacy was not a bogus but a legitimate government. To allow the United States to hold property and maintain military forces within the Confederacy would destroy its claim Upper South secedes of independence. Davis therefore instructed the Confederate commander at Charleston to demand the immediate surrender of Fort Sumter and, if refused, to open fire. When Anderson declined the ultimatum, Confederate batteries began shelling the fort on April 12 at 4:30 A.M. Some 33 hours later Anderson surrendered. A wave of indignation swept across the North in response. When Lincoln subsequently called for 75,000 volunteers to put down the rebellion, four states in the Upper South, led by Virginia, also seceded. Matters had passed beyond compromise.

The Roots of a Divided Nation

And so the Union was broken. After 70 years, the forces of sectionalism and separatism had finally outpulled the ties binding "these United States." Why did affairs come to such a pass?

In some ways, as we have seen, the revolution in markets, the improving technologies of transportation, the increasingly sophisticated systems of credit and finance, all served to tie the nation together. The cotton planter who rode the steamship *Fashion* along the Alabama River ("Time's money! Time's money!") was wearing ready-made clothes manufactured in New York from southern cotton. Chauncey Jerome's clocks from Connecticut were keeping time not only for commercial planters but also for Lowell mill workers like Mary Paul, who learned to measure her lunch break in minutes. Farmers in Athens, Tennessee, and Ottumwa, Iowa, were interested in the price of wheat in New York, for it affected the profits that could be made shipping their grain by the new railroad lines. American society had become far more specialized, and therefore far more interdependent, since the days of Crèvecoeur's self-sufficient farmer of the 1780s.

But a specialized economy had not brought unity. For the North, specialization meant more factories, a higher percentage of urban workers, and a greater number of cities and towns. Industry affected midwestern farmers as well, for their steel plows and McCormick reapers allowed them to farm larger holdings and required greater capital investment in the new machinery. For its part, the South was transformed by the industrial revolution too, as textile factories made cotton the booming mainstay of its economy. But for all its growth, the region remained largely a rural society. Its prosperity stemmed from expansion westward into new areas of cotton production, not new forms of production or technology.

Diverging economies

Above all, the intensive labor required to produce cotton, rice, and sugar made slavery an inseparable part of the southern way of life—"so intimately mingled with our social conditions," as one Georgian admitted, "that it would be impossible to eradicate it." An increasing number of northerners viewed slavery as evil, not so much out of high-minded sympathy toward slaves but as a labor system that threatened the republican ideals of white American society. The new territories became the battlegrounds for two contrasting ways of life, with slavery at the center of the debate.

It fell to the political system to try to adjudicate sectional conflict, through a system of national parties that represented various interest groups and promoted democratic debate. But the political system had critical weaknesses. The American process of electing a president gave the winning candidate a state's entire electoral vote, regardless of the margin of victory. That procedure made a northern sectional party possible, since the Republicans could never have carried an election on the basis of a popular vote alone. In addition, since 1844 the Democratic party had required a two-thirds vote to nominate its presidential candidate. Unintentionally, this requirement made it difficult to pick any truly forceful leader and gave the South a veto over the party's candidate. Yet the South, by itself, could not elect a president.

Weaknesses of the political system

The nation's republican heritage also contributed to the political system's vulnerability. Ever since the Revolution, when Americans accused the king and Parliament of deliberately plotting to deprive them of their liberties, Americans were on the watch for political conspiracies. Such an outlook often stimulated exaggerated fears, unreasonable conclusions, and excessive reactions. For their part, Republicans emphasized the existence of the Slave Power bent on eradicating northern rights. Southerners, on the other hand, accused the Black Republicans of conspiring to destroy southern equality. Each side viewed itself as defending the country's republican tradition from an internal threat.

Belief in conspiracies against liberty

In 1850 southerners might have been satisfied if their section had been left alone and the agitation against slavery had ended. But a decade later, many Americans both North and South had come to accept the idea of an irrepressible conflict between two societies, one based on freedom, the other on slavery, in which only one side could ultimately prevail. At stake, it seemed, was control of the nation's future. Four years later, as a weary Abraham Lincoln looked back to the beginning of the conflict, he noted, "Both parties deprecated war, but one of them would *make* war rather than let the nation survive, and the other would *accept* war rather than let it perish, and the war came."

c h a p t e r   s u m m a r y

In the 1850s, the slavery issue reemerged in national politics and increasingly disrupted the party system, leading to the outbreak of war in 1861.

- Fundamental economic changes heightened sectional tensions in the 1850s.
  - The construction of a vast railroad network reoriented western trade from the South to the East.
  - A tide of new immigrants swelled the North's population (and hence its political power) at the expense of the South, thereby stimulating southern fears.

- The old Jacksonian party system was shattered by the nativist movement and by renewed controversy over the expansion of slavery.
  - In the Kansas-Nebraska Act, Senator Stephen A. Douglas tried to defuse the slavery debate by incorporating popular sovereignty (the idea that the people of a territory should decide the status of slavery there). This act effectively repealed the Missouri Compromise.
  - Popular sovereignty failed in the Kansas Territory, where fighting broke out between proslavery and antislavery partisans.

- Sectional violence reached a climax in May 1856 with the proslavery attack on Lawrence, Kansas, and the caning of Senator Charles Sumner of Massachusetts by Representative Preston S. Brooks of South Carolina.

- Sectional tensions sparked the formation of a new antislavery Republican party, and the party system realigned along sectional lines.
  - The Supreme Court's *Dred Scott* decision, the Panic of 1857, the congressional struggle over the proslavery Lecompton constitution, and John Brown's attack on Harpers Ferry in 1859 strengthened the two sectional extremes.

- In 1860 Abraham Lincoln became the first Republican to be elected president.
  - Following Lincoln's triumph, the seven states of the Deep South seceded.
  - When Lincoln sent supplies to the Union garrison in Fort Sumter in Charleston harbor, Confederate batteries bombarded the fort into submission.
  - The North rallied to Lincoln's decision to use force to restore the Union, and in response the four states of the Upper South seceded.

 For quizzes and a variety of interactive resources, visit the book's Online Learning Center at www.mhhe.com/davidsonconcise3

SIGNIFICANT EVENTS

1834	McCormick patents mechanical reaper
1837	John Deere patents steel plow
1840–1860	Expansion of railroad network
1846–1854	Mass immigration to United States
1849–1860	Cotton boom
1852	Pierce elected president
1853	Gadsden Purchase
1854	Kansas-Nebraska Act passed; Republican party organized; peak of immigration
1854–1855	Height of Know-Nothings' popularity
1855	Fighting begins in Kansas; Republican party organizes in key northern states
1856	Free state "government" established in Kansas; "Sack of Lawrence"; caning of Charles Sumner; Pottawatomie massacre; Buchanan elected president
1857–1861	Panic and depression
1857	*Dred Scott* decision issued; Lecompton constitution drafted
1858	Congress rejects Lecompton constitution; Lincoln-Douglas debates
1859	John Brown's raid on Harpers Ferry
1860	Democratic party ruptures; Lincoln elected president; South Carolina secedes
1861	Rest of Deep South secedes; Confederate States of America established; Crittenden Compromise defeated; war begins at Fort Sumter; Upper South secedes

The war won't last sixty days!" Of that Jim Tinkham was confident. With dreams of a hero's return, Tinkham enlisted for three months in a Massachusetts regiment. Soon he was transferred to Washington as part of the Union army being assembled under the command of General Irvin McDowell to crush the rebellion. Tinkham was elated when in mid-July the army was finally ordered to march toward the Confederates concentrated at Manassas Junction, 25 miles away.*

The battle began at dawn on July 21, with McDowell commanding 30,000 troops against General Pierre Beauregard's 22,000. Tinkham did not arrive on the field until early afternoon. As his regiment pushed toward the front, he felt faint at his first sight of the dead and wounded, some mangled horribly. But he was soon caught up in the excitement of battle as he charged up Henry Hill. Suddenly the Confederate ranks broke and exuberant Union troops shouted, "The war is over!"

Total War and the Republic (1861–1865)

preview • As the first total war in history, the Civil War was fought not just by armies but through the mobilization of each society's human and economic resources. Lincoln's leadership was key. He moved slowly at first, to keep the border slave states within the Union, but later accepted the destruction of slavery as a war aim. Indeed, the freeing of four million slaves was only the most monumental of the war's many transformations, in both the South and the North.

The timely arrival of fresh troops, however, enabled the Confederates to regroup and resume the fight. Among the reinforcements who rushed to Henry Hill was 19-year-old Randolph McKim of Baltimore. A student at the University of Virginia when the war began, McKim joined the First Maryland Infantry as a private when Abraham Lincoln imposed martial law in his home state. "The cause of the South had become identified with liberty itself," he explained. After only a week of drill, McKim boarded a train on July 21 bound for Manassas. The arrival of the First Maryland and other reinforcements in the late afternoon turned the tide of battle. The faltering Confederate line held, and Union troops began to withdraw.

---

*The Union and the Confederacy often gave different names to a battle. The Confederates called the first battle Manasses; the Union, Bull Run.

Once McDowell ordered a retreat, discipline dissolved, the army degenerated into a mob, and a stampede began. As they fled, terrified troops threw away their equipment, shoved aside officers who tried to stop them, and raced frantically past the wagons and artillery pieces that clogged the road. Joining the stampede was Jim Tinkham, who confessed he would have continued on to Boston if he had not been stopped by a guard in Washington.

All the next day in a drizzling rain, mud-spattered troops straggled into the capital in complete disorder. William Russell, an English reporter, asked one pale officer where they were coming from. "Well, sir, I guess we're all coming out of Virginny as far as we can, and pretty well whipped too," he replied. "I know I'm going home. I've had enough of fighting to last my lifetime."

The rout at Bull Run sobered the North. Gone were dreams of ending the war with one glorious battle. Gone was the illusion that 75,000 volunteers serving three months would be sufficient. As one perceptive observer noted, "We have undertaken to make war without in the least knowing how." Having cast off his earlier misconceptions, a newly determined Jim Tinkham reenlisted for a three-year hitch.

Still, it was not surprising that both sides underestimated the magnitude of the conflict. Previous warfare as it had evolved in Europe consisted largely of maneuverings that took relatively few lives, respected private property, and left civilians largely unharmed. The Civil War, on the other hand, was the first war whose major battles routinely involved more than 100,000 troops. So many combatants could be equipped only through the use of factory-produced weaponry, they could be moved and supplied only with the help of railroads, and they could be sustained only through the concerted efforts of civilian society as a whole. The morale of the population, the quality of political leadership, and the utilization of industrial and economic might were all critical to the outcome. Quite simply, the Civil War was the first total war in history.

Meaning of total war

THE DEMANDS OF TOTAL WAR

When the war began, the North had an enormous advantage in manpower and industrial capacity. The Union's population was 2.5 times larger; it contained more railroad track and rolling stock and possessed more than 10 times the industrial capacity.

From a modern perspective, the South's attempt to defend its independence against such odds seems hopeless. Yet this view indicates how much the conception of war has changed. European observers, who knew the strength and resources of the two sides, believed that the Confederacy could never be conquered. Indeed, the South enjoyed definite strategic advantages. To be victorious, it did not need to invade the North—only to defend its own land and prevent the North from destroying its armies. Southern soldiers

Southern advantages

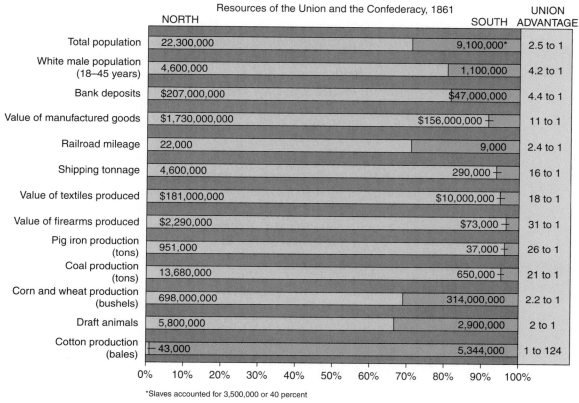

Resources of the Union and the Confederacy, 1861

	NORTH	SOUTH	UNION ADVANTAGE
Total population	22,300,000	9,100,000*	2.5 to 1
White male population (18–45 years)	4,600,000	1,100,000	4.2 to 1
Bank deposits	$207,000,000	$47,000,000	4.4 to 1
Value of manufactured goods	$1,730,000,000	$156,000,000	11 to 1
Railroad mileage	22,000	9,000	2.4 to 1
Shipping tonnage	4,600,000	290,000	16 to 1
Value of textiles produced	$181,000,000	$10,000,000	18 to 1
Value of firearms produced	$2,290,000	$73,000	31 to 1
Pig iron production (tons)	951,000	37,000	26 to 1
Coal production (tons)	13,680,000	650,000	21 to 1
Corn and wheat production (bushels)	698,000,000	314,000,000	2.2 to 1
Draft animals	5,800,000	2,900,000	2 to 1
Cotton production (bales)	43,000	5,344,000	1 to 124

0% 10% 20% 30% 40% 50% 60% 70% 80% 90% 100%

*Slaves accounted for 3,500,000 or 40 percent

Source: U.S. Census 1860 and E. B. Long, *The Civil War Day by Day* (New York: Doubleday, 1971), p. 723.

knew the topography of their home country better, and a friendly population regularly supplied them with intelligence about Union troop movements.

The North, in contrast, had to invade and conquer the Confederacy and destroy the southern will to resist. To do so, it would have to deploy thousands of soldiers to defend long supply lines in enemy territory, a situation that significantly reduced the northern advantage in manpower. Yet by 1865 Union forces had penetrated virtually every part of the 500,000 square miles of the Confederacy and were able to move almost at will. The Civil War demonstrated the capacity of a modern society to overcome the problems of distance and terrain with technology.

Political Leadership

To sustain a commitment to total war required effective political leadership. This task fell on Abraham Lincoln and Jefferson Davis, presidents of the rival governments.

Jefferson Davis grew up in Mississippi accustomed to life's advantages. Educated at West Point, he fought in the Mexican War, served as Franklin Pierce's secretary of war, and became one of the South's leading advocates in the Senate. Although he was hard-working and committed to the cause he led, his temperament was not well suited to his new post: he was quarrelsome, resented criticism, and refused to work with those he disliked. "He cannot brook opposition or criticism," one member of the Confederate Congress testified, "and those who do not bow down before him have no chance of success with him."

Davis's character

Yet for all Davis's personal handicaps, he faced an institutional one even more daunting. The Confederacy had been founded on the ideology of states' rights. Yet to meet the demands of total war, Davis would need to increase the authority of the central government beyond anything the South had ever experienced.

When Lincoln took the oath of office, his national experience consisted of one term in the House of Representatives. But Lincoln was a shrewd judge of character and a superb politician. To achieve a common goal, he willingly overlooked withering criticism and personal slights. He was not easily humbugged, overawed, or flattered and never allowed personal feelings to blind him to his larger objectives. "No man knew better how to summon and dispose of political ability to attain great political ends," commented one associate.

Lincoln's leadership

"This is essentially a People's contest," Lincoln asserted at the start of the war, and few presidents have been better able to communicate with the average citizen. He regularly visited Union troops in camp, in the field, and in army hospitals.

Jefferson Davis

"The boys liked him," wrote Joseph Twichell, from a Connecticut regiment, "in fact his popularity with the army is and has been universal." Always Lincoln reminded the public that the war was being fought for the ideals of the Revolution and the Republic. It was a test, he remarked in his famous address at Gettysburg, of whether a nation "conceived in Liberty, and dedicated to the proposition that all men are created equal" could "long endure."

He also proved the more effective military leader. Jefferson Davis took his title of commander in chief literally, constantly interfering with his generals, but he failed to formulate an effective overarching strategy. In contrast, Lincoln clearly grasped the challenge confronting the Union. He accepted General Winfield Scott's proposal to blockade the Confederacy, cut off its supplies, and slowly strangle it into submission. But unlike Scott, he realized that this plan was not enough. The South would also have to be invaded and defeated, not only on an eastern front in Virginia but in the West, where Union control of the Mississippi would divide the Confederacy. Lincoln understood that the Union's superior manpower and materiel would become decisive only when the Confederacy was simultaneously threatened along a broad front. It took time before the president found generals able to execute this novel strategy.

The Border States

When the war began, only Delaware of the border slave states was certain to remain in the Union. Lincoln's immediate political challenge was to retain the loyalty of Maryland, Kentucky, and Missouri. Maryland especially was crucial, for if it was lost, Washington itself would have to be abandoned.

Lincoln moved vigorously—even ruthlessly—to secure Maryland. He suppressed pro-Confederate newspapers and suspended the writ of habeas corpus, the right under the Constitution of an arrested person either to be charged with a specific crime or to be released. That done, he held without trial prominent Confederate sympathizers. Intervention by the army ensured that Unionists won a complete victory in the fall state election. The election ended any possibility that Maryland would join the Confederacy.

Suppression in Maryland

At the beginning of the conflict, Kentucky officially declared its neutrality. Union generals requested permission to occupy the state, but the president refused, preferring to act cautiously and wait for Unionist sentiment to assert itself. After Unionists won control of the legislature in the summer election, a Confederate army entered the state, giving Lincoln the opening he needed. He quickly sent in troops, and Kentucky stayed in the Union.

Kentucky's neutrality

In Missouri, skirmishing broke out between Union and Confederate sympathizers. Only after the Union victory at the Battle of Pea Ridge in March 1862 was Missouri secure from any Confederate threat. Even so, guerrilla warfare continued in the state throughout the remainder of the war.

In Virginia, internal divisions led to the creation of a new border state, as the hilly western counties where slavery was weak refused to support the Confederacy. After adopting a congressionally mandated program of gradual emancipation, West Virginia was formally admitted to the Union in June 1863.

The Union scored an important triumph in holding the border states. The population of all five equaled that of the four states of the Upper South that had

Importance of the border states

joined the Confederacy, and their production of military supplies—food, animals, and minerals—was greater. Furthermore, Maryland and West Virginia contained key railroad lines and were critical to the defense of Washington, while Kentucky and Missouri gave the Union army access to the major river systems of the western theater, down which it launched the first successful invasions of the Confederacy.

OPENING MOVES

As with so many Civil War battles, the Confederate victory at Bull Run achieved no decisive military results. But Congress authorized a much larger army of long-term volunteers, and Lincoln named 34-year-old George McClellan, a West Point graduate and former railroad executive, to be the new commander. Energetic and ambitious, he spent the next eight months directing the much-needed task of organizing and drilling the Army of the Potomac.

Blockade and Isolate

Although the U.S. Navy began the war with only 42 ships available to blockade 3550 miles of Confederate coastline, by the spring of 1862 it had taken control of key islands off the coasts of the Carolinas and Georgia, to use as supply bases. The navy also began building powerful gunboats to operate on the rivers. In April 1862 Flag Officer David G. Farragut ran a gauntlet of Confederate shore batteries to capture New Orleans, the Confederacy's largest port. Memphis, another important river city, fell to Union forces in June.

The blockade was hardly leakproof, and small, fast ships continued to slip through it. Still, southern trade suffered badly. In hopes of lifting the blockade, the

Ironclads

Confederacy converted the wooden U.S.S. *Merrimack*, which was rechristened the *Virginia*, into an ironclad gunboat. In March 1862 a Union ironclad, the *Monitor*, battled it to a standoff, and the Confederates scuttled the *Virginia* when they evacuated Norfolk in May. After that, the Union's naval supremacy was secure.

The Confederacy looked to diplomacy as another means to lift the blockade. With cotton so vital to European economies, especially Great Britain's, southern-

King cotton diplomacy

ers believed Europe would formally recognize the Confederacy and come to its aid. The British government favored the South, but it hesitated to act until Confederate armies demonstrated that they could win the war. Meanwhile, new supplies of cotton from Egypt and India enabled the British textile industry to recover. In the end, Britain and the rest of Europe refused to recognize the Confederacy, and the South was left to stand or fall on its own resources.

Grant in the West

In the western war theater, the first decisive Union victory was won by a short, shabbily dressed, cigar-chomping general named Ulysses S. Grant. An undistinguished student at West Point, Grant eventually had resigned his commission. He had failed at everything he tried in civilian life, and when the war broke out, he was a store clerk in Galena, Illinois. Almost 39, he promptly volunteered, and two months later became a brigadier general.

Grant's quiet, self-effacing manner gave little indication of his military ability or iron determination. He had a flair for improvising, was alert to seize any opening, and remained extraordinarily calm and clear-headed in battle. Most important, Grant grasped that hard fighting, not fancy maneuvering, would bring victory. "The art of war is simple," he once explained. "Find out where your enemy is, get at him as soon as you can and strike him as hard as you can, and keep moving on."

Grant's character

Grant realized that rivers were avenues into the interior of the Confederacy, and in February 1862, supported by Union gunboats, he captured Fort Henry on the Tennessee River and Fort Donelson on the Cumberland. These victories forced the Confederates to withdraw from Kentucky and middle Tennessee. Grant continued south with 40,000 men, but he was surprised on April 6 by General Albert Johnston at Shiloh, just north of the Tennessee-Mississippi border. Johnston was killed in the day's fierce fighting, but by nightfall his army had driven the Union troops back to the Tennessee River, where they huddled numbly as a cold rain fell. William Tecumseh Sherman, one of Grant's subordinates, found the general standing under a dripping tree, his coat collar drawn up against the damp, puffing on a cigar. Sherman was about to suggest retreat, but something in Grant's eyes, lighted by the glow of his stogey, made him hesitate. So he said only, "Well, Grant, we've had the devil's own day, haven't we." "Yes," the Union commander replied quietly. "Lick 'em tomorrow, though." And he did. With the aid of reinforcements, which he methodically ferried across the river all night, Grant counterattacked the next morning and drove the Confederates from the field.

Shiloh

But victory came at a high price, for Shiloh inflicted more than 23,000 casualties. Grant, who previously had doubted the commitment of Confederate troops, came away deeply impressed with their determination. "At Shiloh," he wrote afterward, "I gave up all idea of saving the Union except by complete conquest."

Eastern Stalemate

Grant's victories did not silence his critics, who charged he drank too much. But Lincoln was unmoved. "I can't spare this man. He fights." That was a quality in short supply in the east, where General McClellan directed operations.

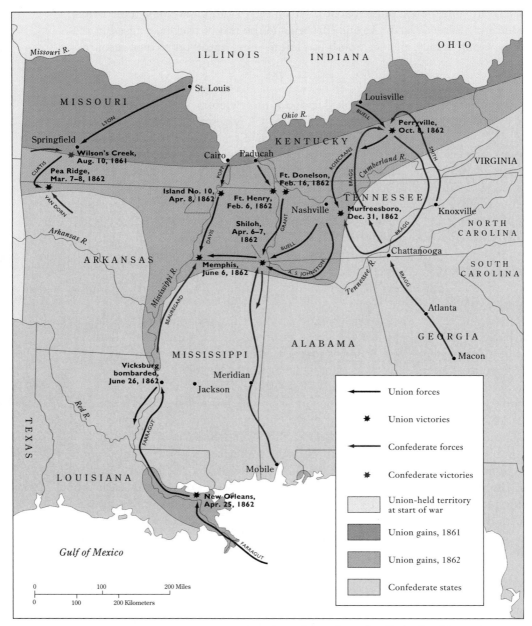

THE WAR IN THE WEST, 1861–1862   Grant's push southward stalled after his costly victory at Shiloh; nevertheless, by the end of 1862 the Union had secured Kentucky and Missouri, as well as most of Confederate Tennessee and the upper and lower stretches of the Mississippi River.

McClellan looked like a general, but beneath his arrogance and bravado lay a self-doubt that rendered him excessively cautious. As the months dragged on and McClellan did nothing but train and plan, Lincoln's frustration grew. "If General McClellan does not want to use the army I would like to *borrow* it," he remarked sarcastically. In the spring of 1862 the general finally transported his 130,000 troops to the Virginia coast and began inching toward Richmond, the Confederate capital. In May General Joseph Johnston suddenly attacked him near Fair Oaks, from which he barely escaped. Worse for McClellan, when Johnston was badly wounded, the formidable Robert E. Lee took command of the Army of Northern Virginia.

"McClellan has the slows"

Where McClellan was cautious and defensive, the aristocratic Lee was daring and ever alert to assume the offensive. His first name, one of his colleagues commented, should have been Audacity: "He will take more chances, and take them quicker than any other general in this country." In the Seven Days' battles, McClellan successfully parried the attacks of Lee and Thomas "Stonewall" Jackson but stayed on the defensive. As McClellan retreated to the protection of the Union gunboats, Lincoln ordered the Peninsula campaign abandoned and formed a new army under John Pope. After Lee badly mauled Pope at the second Battle of Bull Run in August, Lincoln restored McClellan to command.

Lee's generalship

Realizing that the Confederacy needed a decisive victory, Lee invaded the North, hoping to detach Maryland and isolate Washington. Learning that he greatly outnumbered Lee, McClellan launched a series of badly coordinated assaults near Antietam Creek on September 17 that Lee barely repulsed. The bloody exchanges horrified both sides for their sheer carnage. Nearly 5000 soldiers were killed and another 18,000 wounded, making it the bloodiest single day in American history. When McClellan allowed Lee's army to escape back into Virginia, an exasperated Lincoln permanently relieved him from command in November.

Antietam

The winter of 1862 was the North's Valley Forge, as morale sank to an all-time low. It took General Ambrose Burnside, who assumed McClellan's place, little more than a month to demonstrate his utter incompetence at the Battle of Fredericksburg. The Union's disastrous defeat there prompted Lincoln to put "Fighting Joe" Hooker in charge. In the West, Grant had emerged as the dominant figure, but the Army of the Potomac still lacked a capable commander, the deaths kept mounting, and no end to the war was in sight.

EMANCIPATION

In 1858 Abraham Lincoln had proclaimed that the United States must eventually become either all slave or all free. When the war began, however, the president refused to make emancipation a Union war aim. He perceived, accurately, that

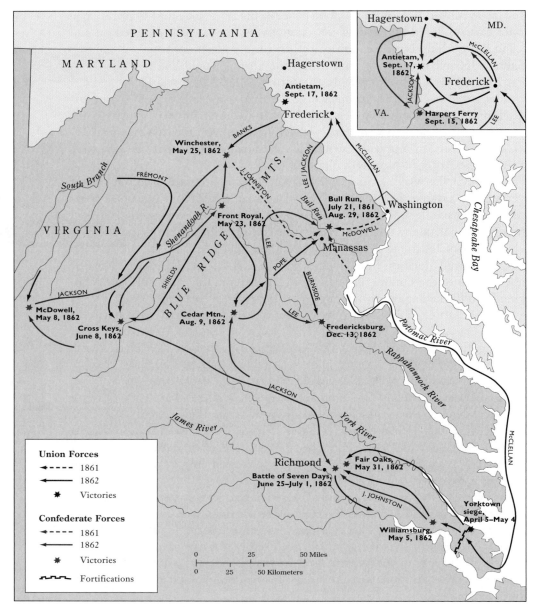

THE WAR IN THE EAST, 1861–1862 McClellan's campaign against Richmond failed when Joseph Johnston surprised him at Fair Oaks. Taking command of the Army of Northern Virginia, Lee drove back McClellan in the Seven Days' battles, then won a resounding victory over Pope in the second Battle of Bull Run. He followed this up by invading Maryland. McClellan checked his advance at Antietam. The Army of the Potomac's devastating defeat at Fredericksburg ended a year of frustration and failure for the Union in the eastern theater.

most white northerners were not deeply committed to emancipation. He feared the social upheaval that such a revolutionary step would cause, and he did not want to alarm the wavering border slave states. Thus when Congress met in special session in July 1861, Lincoln fully supported a resolution offered by John J. Crittenden of Kentucky, which declared that the war was being fought solely to save the Union. The Crittenden Resolution passed the House 117 to 2 and the Senate by 30 to 5.

Crittenden Resolution

Still, Republican radicals like Senator Charles Sumner and Horace Greeley pressed Lincoln to adopt a policy of emancipation. Slavery had caused the war, they argued; its destruction would hasten the war's end. Lincoln, however, placed first priority on saving the Union. "My paramount object in this struggle *is* to save the Union, and is *not* either to save or to destroy slavery," he wrote Greeley in 1862. "If I could save the Union without freeing *any* slave I would do it, and if I could save it by freeing *all* the slaves I would do it, and if I could save it by freeing some and leaving others alone, I would also do that." For the first year of the war, this remained Lincoln's policy.

The Logic of Events

As the Union army began to occupy Confederate territory, slaves flocked to the Union lines. In May 1861 the army adopted the policy of declaring runaway slaves "contraband of war" and refused to return them to their rebel owners. In the Confiscation Act of August 1861, Congress provided that slaves used for military purposes by the Confederacy would become free if they fell into Union hands. For a year Lincoln accepted that position but would go no further. When two of his generals, acting on their own authority, abolished slavery in their districts, he countermanded their orders.

By December 1861, opinion was beginning to shift. When the Crittenden Resolution was reintroduced in Congress, it was soundly defeated. Congress also prohibited federal troops from capturing or returning fugitive slaves and freed the 2000 slaves living in the District of Columbia with compensation to their owners. In July 1862 it passed the Second Confiscation Act, which declared that the slaves of anyone who supported the rebellion would be freed if they came into federal custody. Unlike the first act, it did not matter whether the slaves had been used for military purposes.

Growing congressional attack on slavery

Lincoln signed this bill, then proceeded to ignore it. Instead, he emphasized state action, since slavery was a domestic institution. In his first annual message to Congress, he proposed that the federal government provide grants to compensate slaveowners in any state-sponsored program of gradual emancipation. Twice the president summoned white representatives from the border states and prodded them to act before the war destroyed slavery of its own momentum. Both times they rejected his plea.

Following the failure of his second meeting with the border state leaders, Lincoln on July 22, 1862, presented to his cabinet a proposed proclamation freeing the slaves in the Confederacy. He was increasingly confident that the border states would remain in the Union, and he wanted to strike a blow that would weaken the Confederacy militarily. By making the struggle one of freedom versus slavery, such a proclamation would also undermine Confederate efforts to obtain diplomatic recognition. But Lincoln decided to wait for a Union military victory, so that his act would not seem like one of desperation.

Lincoln's decision for emancipation

The Emancipation Proclamation

On September 22, in the aftermath of the victory at Antietam, Lincoln announced that all slaves within rebel lines would be freed unless the seceded states returned to their allegiance by January 1, 1863. When that day came, the Emancipation Proclamation went into effect. Excluded from its terms were the Union slave states and areas of the Confederacy that were under Union control. In all, about 830,000 of the nation's 4 million slaves were not covered by its provisions. Since Lincoln justified his actions on strictly military grounds, he believed he had no legal right to apply it to areas not in rebellion.

After initial criticism of the Proclamation, European public opinion swung toward the Union. In the North, Republicans generally favored Lincoln's decision, while the Democrats made it a major issue in the 1862 elections. "Every white man in the North, who does not want to be swapped off for a free Nigger, should vote the Democratic ticket," urged one party orator. The results in the elections that fall, however, offered no clear verdict on the Proclamation.

Reaction to the Proclamation

Despite the mixed popular reaction, the Emancipation Proclamation had immense symbolic importance, for it redefined the nature of the war. The North was fighting, not to save the old Union, but to create a new nation. The war had become, in Lincoln's words, "remorseless revolution."

African Americans' Civil War

Under the pressure of war, slavery disintegrated. Well before federal troops entered an area, slaves took the lead in undermining the institution by openly challenging white authority and claiming greater personal freedom for themselves. One experienced overseer reported in frustration that the "slaves will do only what pleases them, go out in the morning when it suits them, come in when they please, etc."

Early in the conflict slaves concluded that emancipation would be one consequence of a Union victory. Perhaps as many as half a million—one-seventh of the total slave population of the Confederacy—fled to Union lines. The ex-slaves, called "freedmen," ended up living in

Seeking freedom

Black men, including runaway slaves, joined the Union army and navy
beginning in 1863. As soldiers, former slaves developed a new sense of
pride and confidence. At his first roll call, recruit Elijah Marrs recalled,
"I felt freedom in my bones."

refugee or contraband camps that were overcrowded and disease-ridden and provided only the most basic shelter and food.

Convinced that freed slaves would not work on their own initiative, the U.S.
government put some contrabands to work assisting the army. Their wages were
well below those paid white citizens for the same work. In the Mississippi valley,
where two-thirds of the freedpeople under Union control were located, most were
forced to work on plantations leased or owned by loyal planters. Most worked for
little more than room and board, and the conditions often approximated slavery.

Black Soldiers

In adopting the policy of emancipation, Lincoln also announced that African
Americans would be accepted into the navy and, more controversially, the army.
Resistance to accepting black volunteers in the army remained especially strong in
the Midwest. Black northerners themselves were divided over whether to enlist,
but Frederick Douglass spoke for the vast majority when he argued that once a
black man had served in the army, there was "no power on earth which can deny
that he has earned the right of citizenship in the United States."

In the end, nearly 200,000 black Americans served in the Union forces, about
10 percent of the Union's total military manpower. Some, including two of

Douglass's sons, were free, but most were former slaves who enlisted after escaping to the Union lines. As a concession to the racism of white troops, blacks served in segregated units under white officers. Not until June 1864 did Congress finally grant equal pay to African American soldiers.

Assigned at first to the most undesirable duties, black soldiers successfully lobbied for the chance to fight. They deeply impressed white troops with their courage under fire. "I have been one of those men, who never had much confidence in colored troops fighting," one Union officer admitted, "but these doubts are now all removed, for they fought as bravely as any troops in the Fort." In the end 37,000 African American servicemen gave their lives, a rate of loss about 40 percent higher than that among white soldiers. Black recruits had good reason to fight fiercely: they knew that the freedom of their race hung in the balance, they hoped to win civil rights at home by their performance on the battlefield, they resented racist sneers about their loyalty and ability, and they knew that capture might mean death.

> **Black soldiers in combat**

THE CONFEDERATE HOME FRONT

"How shall we subsist this winter?" John Jones wondered in the fall of 1862. A clerk in the War Department in Richmond, Jones found it increasingly difficult to make ends meet on his salary. Prices kept going up, essential items were in short supply, and the signs of hardship were everywhere: in the darned and patched clothing, in the absence of meat from the market, in the desperation on people's faces. Coffee was a luxury Jones could no longer afford; he sold his watch to buy fuel; and he worried incessantly about being able to feed his family. "I cannot afford to have more than an ounce of meat daily for each member of my family of six," he recorded in 1864. ". . . We see neither rats nor mice about the premises now." By the end of the year a month's supply of food and fuel was costing him $762, a sum sufficient to have supported his family for a year in peacetime. "This is war, terrible war!"

Nowhere was the effect of war more complete than within the Confederacy. These changes were especially ironic, since the southern states had seceded in order to preserve their traditional ways. The demands of war fundamentally transformed the southern economy, society, and government.

The New Economy

With the Union blockade tightening, the production of foodstuffs became crucial. More and more plantations switched from cotton to raising grain and livestock. As a result, cotton production dropped from 4.5 million bales in 1861 to 300,000 in 1864. Even so, food production declined. In the last two years of the war, the shortage was serious.

The Union blockade also made it impossible to rely on European manufactured goods. So the Confederate War Department built and ran factories, took over the region's mines, and regulated private manufacturers so as to increase the production of war goods. Although the Confederacy never became industrially self-sufficient, its accomplishments were impressive. In fact, the Confederacy sustained itself far better in industrial goods than it did in agricultural produce. It was symbolic that when Lee surrendered, his troops had sufficient guns and ammunition to continue, but they had not eaten in two days.

Attempts to industrialize

New Opportunities for Southern Women

Southern white women took an active role in the war. Some gained notoriety as spies; others smuggled military supplies into the South. Women also spent a good deal of time knitting and sewing clothes for soldiers. "We never went out to pay a visit without taking our knitting along," recalled a South Carolina woman. Perhaps most important, with so many men fighting, women took charge of agricultural production. On plantations the mistress often supervised the slaves as well as the wrenching shift from cotton to foodstuffs. "All this attention to farming is uphill work with me," one South Carolina woman confessed to her army husband.

One such woman was Emily Lyles Harris, the wife of a small slaveowner in upcountry South Carolina. When her husband joined the army in 1862, she was left to care for her seven children as well as supervise the slaves and manage the farm. She felt overwhelmed. Nevertheless, despite the disruptions of wartime, she succeeded remarkably, one year producing the largest crop of oats in the neighborhood and always making enough money for her family to live decently. She took little pride, however, in her achievements. "I shall never get used to being left as the head of affairs at home," she confessed. "The burden is very heavy, and there is no one to smile on me as I trudge wearily along in the dark with it." While she persevered in her efforts, by 1865 she openly hoped for defeat.

The war also opened up new jobs off the farm. Given the personnel shortage, "government girls" became essential to fill the growing Confederate bureaucracy. At first women were paid half the wages of male coworkers, but by the end of the war they had won equal pay. Women also staffed the new factories springing up in southern cities and towns, undertaking even dangerous work in munitions factories.

"Of all the principles developed by the late war," wrote one Alabama planter, "I think the capability of our Southern women to take care of themselves was by no means the least important."

Confederate Finance and Government

The most serious domestic problem the Confederate government faced was finance, for which officials at Richmond never developed a satisfactory program. Only in 1863 did the government begin levying a graduated income tax (from 1 to 15 percent) and a series of excise taxes. Most controversial, the government resorted to a tax-in-kind on farmers that, after exempting a certain portion, took one-tenth of their agricultural crops. Even more unpopular was the policy of impressment, which allowed the army to seize private property for its own use, often with little or no compensation.

Above all, the Confederacy financed the war effort simply by printing paper money not backed by specie, some $1.5 billion, which amounted to three times more than the federal government issued. The result was runaway inflation, so that by 1865 a Confederate dollar was worth only 1.7 cents in gold and prices had soared to 92 times their prewar base. Prices were highest in Richmond, where flour sold for $275 a barrel by early 1864 and coats for $350.

Soaring inflation

In politics even more than finance, the Confederacy exercised far greater powers than those of the federal government before 1861. Indeed, Jefferson Davis strove to meet the demands of total war by transforming the South into a centralized, national state. He sought to limit state authority over military units, and in April 1862 the Confederacy passed the first national conscription law in American history. The same year, the Congress authorized Davis to invoke martial law and suspend the writ of habeas corpus.

Centralization of power

Critics protested that Davis was destroying states' rights, the main principle of the Confederacy. Intent on preserving states' traditional powers, Confederate governors obstructed the draft and retained military supplies. When President Davis suspended the writ of habeas corpus, his own vice president, Alexander H. Stephens, accused him of aiming at a dictatorship. Davis used those powers for a limited time and only with the permission of Congress, yet in practice it made little difference whether the writ was suspended or not. With disloyalty a greater problem than in the Union, the Confederate army arrested thousands of civilians.

Opposition to Davis

But the Confederate draft, more than any other measure, produced an outcry. As one Georgia leader complained, "It's a notorious fact if a man has influential friends—or a little money to spare he will never be enrolled." Most controversially, the draft exempted from service one white man on every plantation with 20 or more slaves (later reduced to 15). This law was designed to preserve control of the slave population, but more and more nonslaveholders complained that it was a rich man's war and a poor man's fight.

Hardship and Suffering

By the last year of the conflict, food shortages had become so severe that ingenious southerners concocted various substitutes: parched corn in place of coffee, strained blackberries in place of vinegar. One scarce item for which there was no substitute was salt, which was essential for curing meat. Scarcity bred speculation, hoarding, and spiraling prices. The high prices and food shortages led to riots, most seriously in Richmond early in April 1863, when about 300 women and children chanting "Bread!" looted stores.

As always, war corroded the discipline and order of society. Speculation was rampant, gambling halls were crowded with revelers seeking relief, and many southerners spent money in frenzied haste. Even in the army, theft became common, and in Richmond, the House of Representatives was robbed and Jefferson Davis's favorite horse stolen.

Social and moral decay

The frantic effort to escape the grim reality of the war led to a forced gaiety among southern civilians. "The cities are gayer than before the war," one refugee reported, "—parties every night in Richmond, suppers costing ten and twenty thousand dollars." Walking home at night after spending several hours at the bedside of a dying soldier, Judith McGuire passed a house gay with laughter, music, and dancing. "The revulsion was sickening," she wrote in her diary. "I . . . felt shocked that our own Virginians, at such a time, should remind me of scenes which we were wont to think only belonged to . . . foreign society." The war was a cancer that ate away not only at southern society but at the southern soul itself.

THE UNION HOME FRONT

Since the war was fought mostly on southern soil, northern civilians rarely felt its effects directly. Yet to be effective, the North's economic resources had to be organized and mobilized.

Government Finances and the Economy

To begin with, the North required a comprehensive system to finance its massive campaign. Taxing the populace was one obvious means, and taxes paid for 21 percent of Union war expenses, compared with only 1 percent of the Confederacy's. In August 1861 Congress levied the first federal income tax of 3 percent on all incomes over $800 a year. When that, along with increased tariff duties, proved insufficient, Congress enacted a comprehensive tax law in 1862 that for the first time brought the tax collector into every northern household.

Economic legislation

The government also borrowed heavily, through the sale of $2.2 billion in bonds. It financed the rest of the war's cost by issuing paper money. In all, the Union printed $431 million in greenbacks (so named because of their color on one side). Congress also instituted a national banking system, allowing nationally chartered banks to issue notes backed by U.S. bonds. By taxing state bank notes out of circulation, Congress for the first time created a uniform national currency.

During the war, the Republican-controlled Congress encouraged economic development. Tariffs to protect industry from foreign competition rose to an average rate of 47 percent, compared to 19 percent in 1860. To encourage development of the West, the Homestead Act of 1862

Western development

granted 160 acres of public land—the size of the traditional American family farm—to anyone (including women) who settled and improved the land for five years. In addition, the Land Grant College Act of 1862 donated the proceeds from certain land sales to finance public colleges and universities. This aid was especially crucial in promoting higher education in the West.

A Rich Man's War

Over the course of the war the government purchased more than $1 billion worth of goods and services. In response to this heavy demand, the economy boomed and business and agriculture prospered. Since prices rose faster than wages, workers' real income dropped almost 30 percent, which meant that the working class paid a disproportionate share of financing the war.

The Republican belief that government should play a major role in the economy also fostered a cozy relationship between business and politics. In the rush to profit from government contracts, some suppliers succumbed to the temptation to sell inferior goods at inflated prices. Uniforms made of "shoddy"—bits of unused thread and recycled cloth—were fobbed off in such numbers that the word became an adjective describing inferior quality. A War Department investigation later revealed that at least 20 percent of government expenditures involved fraud.

Corruption and fraud

Stocks and dividends rose with the economy, speculation during the last two years of the war became particularly feverish, and the fortunes made went toward the purchase of ostentatious luxuries. The Chicago *Tribune* admitted: "We are clothed in purple and fine linen, wear the richest laces and jewels and fare sumptuously every day." Like Richmond, Washington became the symbol of this moral decay. Prostitution, drinking, and corruption reached epidemic proportions in the capital, and social festivities became the means to shut out the numbing horror of the casualty lists.

Women and the Workforce

Even more than in the South, the war opened new opportunities for northern women. Countless wives ran farms while their husbands were away at war. One traveler in Iowa reported, "I met more women driving teams on the road and saw more at work in the fields than men." The war also stimulated the shift to mechanization: by 1865 three times as many reapers and harvesters were in use as in 1861. Beyond the farm, women filled approximately 100,000 new jobs in industry. As in the South, they also worked as clerks in the expanding government bureaucracy. The work was tedious and the workload heavy, but the new jobs offered good wages and satisfaction in having aided the war effort.

The war also allowed women to enter and eventually dominate the profession of nursing. "Our women appear to have become almost wild on the subject of hos-

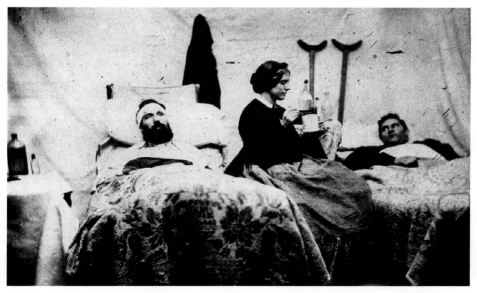

A nurse tends a wounded Union soldier in a military hospital in Nashville, Tennessee. Despite the opposition of army doctors, hundreds of female volunteers worked in army hospitals for each side.

pital nursing," protested one physician, who like many others opposed their presence. Led by Drs. Emily and Elizabeth Blackwell, Dorothea Dix, and Mary Ann Bickerdyke, women fought the bureaucratic inefficiency of the army medical corps. Their service in the hospital wards reduced the hostility to women in medicine.

Women and medicine

One nurse was Clara Barton, who later founded the Red Cross. During the battle of Fredericksburg, she worked in a battlefield hospital. She later recalled that as she rose from the side of one soldier, "I wrung the blood from the bottom of my clothing, before I could step, for the weight about my feet." She steeled herself at the sight of amputated arms and legs casually tossed in piles outside the front door as the surgeons cut away, yet she found the extent of suffering overwhelming. Sleeping in a tent nearby, she drove herself to the brink of exhaustion until the last patients were transferred to permanent hospitals.

Before 1861 teaching too had been dominated by males, but the shortage of men forced school boards in both sections to turn to women. After the war, teaching increasingly became a female profession. Women also contributed to the war effort through volunteer work. The United States Sanitary Commission was established in 1861 to provide medical supplies and care. Women raised funds for the commission, collected supplies, and worked in hospitals alongside paid nurses.

Women and teaching

Civil Liberties and Dissent

In mobilizing the northern war effort, Lincoln did not hesitate to curb dissenters. Shortly after the firing on Fort Sumter, he suspended the writ of habeas corpus in specified areas, which allowed the indefinite detention of anyone suspected of disloyalty or activity against the war. Although the Constitution permitted such suspension in time of rebellion or invasion, Lincoln did so without consulting Congress (unlike President Davis), and he used his power far more broadly, expanding it in 1862 to cover the entire North for cases involving antiwar activities. The president also decreed that those arrested under its provisions could be tried in a military court. Eventually more than 20,000 individuals were arrested, most of whom were never brought to trial.

Writ of habeas corpus suspended

Democrats attacked Lincoln as a tyrant bent on destroying the Constitution. After the war, the Supreme Court, in *Ex parte Milligan* (1866), struck down the military conviction of a civilian accused of plotting to free Confederate prisoners of war. The Court ruled that as long as the regular courts were open, civilians could not be tried by military tribunals.

Republicans labeled those who opposed the war Copperheads, conjuring up the image of a venomous snake waiting to strike the Union. Copperheads constituted the extreme peace wing of the Democratic party. They condemned the draft as an attack on individual freedom and an instrument of special privilege. According to the provisions enacted in 1863, a person would be exempt from the present draft by paying a commutation fee of $300, about a year's wages for a worker or an ordinary farmer. Or those drafted could hire a substitute, the cost of which was beyond the reach of all but the wealthy. In July 1863, largely Irish workers in New York City rose in anger against the draft. By the time order was restored four days later, at least 105 people had been killed, the worst loss of life from any riot in American history.

New York City draft riot

GONE TO BE A SOLDIER

Marcus Spiegel came to the United States after the German revolution of 1848 failed. The son of a rabbi, Spiegel married an American woman, became a naturalized citizen, and was trying to make it in the restaurant business in Ohio when the war began. He considered it his duty to preserve the Union for his children, so he enlisted in November 1861 as a lieutenant and eventually rose to the rank of colonel. Spiegel did not go to war to end slavery and flatly proclaimed that black people were not "worth fighting for." But after seeing slavery first-hand, his views changed, and by 1864 he was "in favor of doing away with the institution of Slavery." He assured his wife that "this is no hasty conclusion but a deep conviction." A few weeks later, Marcus Spiegel died while fighting in Louisiana.

By war's end about 2 million men had served the Union cause and another million the Confederate. They were mostly young, with almost 40 percent of entering soldiers 21 years of age or younger. They were not drawn disproportionately from the poor, and in both North and South, farmers and farm laborers accounted for the largest group of soldiers.

Most soldiers, like Marcus Spiegel, were volunteers who took patriotism seriously and were not ignorant of the issues of the war. Only with time, however, did the majority of Union soldiers, like Spiegel, come to endorse the destruction of slavery as a war aim.

Discipline

The near-holiday atmosphere of the war's early months soon gave way to dull routine. Men from rural areas, accustomed to the freedom of the farm, complained about the endless recurrence of reveille, roll call, and drill. "When this war is over," one Rebel promised, "I will whip the man that says 'fall in' to me." Troops in neither army cared for the spit and polish of regular army men. "They keep us very strict here," noted one Illinois soldier. "It is the most like a prison of any place I ever saw."

By modern standards training was minimal and discipline lax in both armies. Troops from rural families found it harder to adjust to army routine than did urban soldiers, especially factory workers, who were more familiar with impersonal organizations and used to greater social control. Many southerners were "not used to control of any sort," one Rebel noted, "and were not disposed to obey anyone

An infantry private from New York eats a meal in camp.

except for good and sufficient reason given." Manifesting strong feelings of equality that clashed with military hierarchy, Yanks and Rebs alike complained about officers' privileges and had no special respect for rank. "We had enlisted to put down the rebellion," an Indiana private explained, "and had no patience with the red-tape tomfoolery" of the regular army. "The boys recognized no superiors, except in the line of legitimate duty." The Union discontinued the election of lower officers, but this tradition was retained in the Confederate army, which further undermined discipline, since those known as strict disciplinarians were eventually defeated.

Camp Life

On average, soldiers spent 50 days in camp for every day in battle. Camp life was often unhealthy as well as unpleasant. Poor sanitation, miserable food, exposure, and primitive medical care contributed to widespread sickness and disease. Officers and men alike regarded army doctors as nothing more than quacks and tried to avoid them. It was a common belief that if a fellow went to the hospital, "you might as well say good bye." Conditions were even worse in the Confederate hospitals, for the Union blockade produced a shortage of medical supplies. Twice as many soldiers died from dysentery, typhoid, and other diseases as from wounds.

Disease and medical care

The boredom of camp life, the horrors of battle, and the influence of an all-male society all corrupted morals. Swearing and heavy drinking were common and gambling was pervasive, especially immediately after payday. Prostitutes flooded the camps of both armies. As in the gold fields of California, the absence of women stimulated behavior that would have been checked back home by the frowns of family and society.

Morals in camp

With death so near, some soldiers sought solace in religion, especially in Confederate camps. A wave of revivals swept their ranks during the last two winters of the war, producing between 100,000 and 200,000 conversions. Significantly, the first major revivals occurred after the South's twin defeats at Vicksburg and Gettysburg. Then, too, as battle after battle thinned Confederate ranks, the prospect of death became increasingly large.

The Changing Face of Battle

As in all modern wars, technology revolutionized the conditions under which Civil War soldiers fought. Smoothbore muskets, which at first served as the basic infantry weapon, gave way to the rifle, so named because of the grooves etched into the barrel to give a bullet spin. The percussion cap rendered a rifle serviceable in wet weather. More important, the new weapon had an effective range of 400 yards—five times greater than that of the old musket. As a result, soldiers fought each other from greater distances and battles produced many more casualties.

Impact of technology

Under such conditions, the defense became a good deal stronger than the offense. The larger artillery pieces also adopted rifled barrels, but they were too inaccurate to effectively support attacking troops. They were a deadly defensive weapon, however, that decimated advancing infantry at close range. The rising casualty lists bore down heavily on the ordinary soldier, and over 100 regiments on both sides suffered more than 50 percent casualties in a single battle.

Strength of the defense

As the haze of gunfire covered the land and the constant spray of bullets mimicked rain pattering through the treetops, soldiers discovered that their romantic notions about war had no place on the battlefield. Men witnessed horrors they had never envisioned as civilians and choked from the stench of decaying flesh. They realized that their efforts to convey to those back home the gruesome truth of combat were inadequate. "No tongue can tell, no mind can conceive, no pen portray the horrible sights I witnessed this morning," a Union soldier wrote after Antietam. And yet they tried.

An Ohio soldier at Antietam (23,000 casualties), two days after the fighting: "The smell was offul . . . there was about 5 or 6,000 dead bodes decaying over the field . . . I could have walked on the boddees all most from one end too the other." A Georgian, the day after Chancellorsville (30,000 casualties): "It looked more like a slaughter pen than anything else. . . . The shrieks and groans of the wounded . . . was heart rending beyond all description." A Maine soldier who fought at Gettysburg (50,000 casualties): "I have Seen . . . men rolling in their own blood, Some Shot in one place, Some another. . . . our dead lay in the road and the Rebels in their hast to leave dragged both their baggage wagons and artillery over them and they lay mangled and torn to pieces so that Even friends could not tell them. You can form no idea of a battle field."

Hardening Attitudes

Throughout the war, Civil War soldiers continued to speak in terms of the traditional ideals of duty, honor, and patriotism. Nevertheless, military service profoundly changed them. For the volunteers of 1861, the war was a test of courage and manhood, and thus they believed the winning side would display superior valor. Expecting a restrained war that would uphold this moral code, they admired the courage of the foe and considered it pointless to kill an isolated soldier.

But the reality of combat did not fit such expectations, and by 1864 the nature of war had been transformed. Soldiers discovered the futility of mass frontal assaults, and under the rain of fire on the battlefield sought cover wherever they could find it. As the fighting intensified, they sought to kill enemy soldiers any way they could in order to hasten the war's end. At the same time, they became indifferent to death and suffering. "The daily sight of blood and mangled bodies," observed a Rhode Island soldier, "so blunted their finer sensibilities as almost to blot out all love, all sympathy from the heart." This

Eroding moral values

hardening of attitudes produced a steady erosion of moral standards. Combatants began taking personal property from the dead and wounded and even prisoners after a battle.

As they repudiated their earlier moral assumptions, the soldiers in both armies felt increasingly alienated from civilians back home. In reaction, they developed stronger a sense of comradeship with enemy soldiers, based on their belief that only other soldiers could understand what had gone through and why they acted the way they did. They felt less an actor in the war than an impersonal object caught in a relentless process of destruction.

In the face of what Charles Francis Adams, Jr., termed "the carnival of death," soldiers braced themselves with a grim determination to see the war through to the end. Not glorious exploits but endurance became the true measure of heroism. Exclaimed one chastened Georgia soldier, "What a scourge is war."

THE UNION'S TRIUMPH

In the spring of 1863 matters still looked promising for Lee. At the battle of Chancellorsville, he won another brilliant victory. But during the fighting Stonewall Jackson was accidentally shot by his own men, and he died a few days later—a grievous setback for the Confederacy. Determined to take the offensive, Lee invaded Pennsylvania in June with an army of 75,000. Lincoln's newest general, George Gordon Meade, warily shadowed the Confederates. On the first of July, advance parties from the two armies accidentally collided at the town of Gettysburg, and the war's greatest battle ensued.

For once it was Lee who had the extended supply lines and was forced to fight on ground chosen by his opponent. After two days of assaults failed to break the Union left or right, Lee made the greatest mistake of his career, sending 14,000 men under General George Pickett in a charge up the center of the Union line. "Pickett's division just seemed to melt away in the blue musketry smoke which now covered the hill," one Confederate officer wrote. "Nothing but stragglers came back." With the loss of more than a third of his troops, Lee was never again able to assume the offensive.

Gettysburg

THE WAR IN THE EAST, 1863–1865   (See map, page 443) Lee won his most brilliant victory at Chancellorsville, then launched a second invasion of the North, which ended in defeat at Gettysburg. In 1864 Grant delivered a series of blows against Lee's outnumbered forces in Virginia. Despite staggering losses, Grant pressed on in a ruthless demonstration of total war. (Note the casualties listed from mid-May to mid-June of 1864; Grant lost nearly 60,000 men, equal to Lee's strength.) In April 1865, too weak to defend Richmond any longer, Lee surrendered at Appomattox Courthouse.

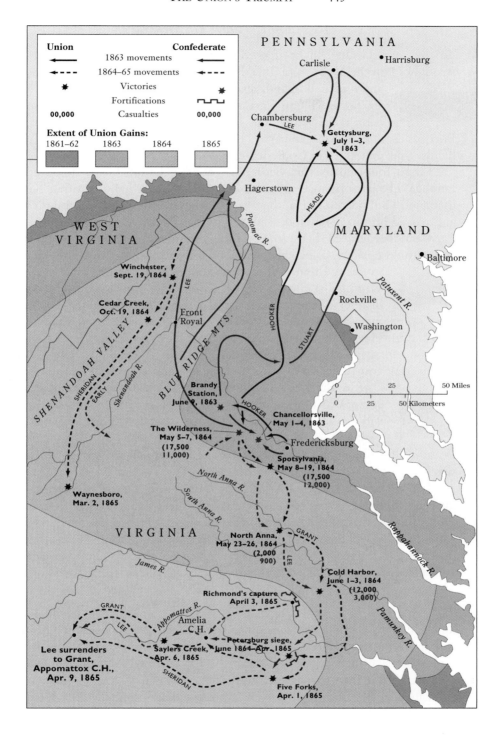

Union   **Confederate**

←   1863 movements   ←

←---   1864–65 movements   ←---

✳   Victories   ✳

Fortifications   ⊓⊔

00,000   Casualties   00,000

Extent of Union Gains:

1861–62   1863   1864   1865

PENNSYLVANIA

Harrisburg

Carlisle

Chambersburg

LEE

Gettysburg, July 1–3, 1863

Hagerstown

MARYLAND

WEST VIRGINIA

Potomac R.

MEADE

Baltimore

Winchester, Sept. 19, 1864

Cedar Creek, Oct. 19, 1864

LEE

Front Royal

HOOKER

Patuxent R.

Rockville

STUART

Washington

SHENANDOAH VALLEY

SHERIDAN

EARLY

Shenandoah R.

BLUE RIDGE MTS.

Brandy Station, June 9, 1863

HOOKER

Chancellorsville, May 1–4, 1863

The Wilderness, May 5–7, 1864 (17,500 11,000)

Fredericksburg

Spotsylvania, May 8–19, 1864 (17,500 12,000)

Waynesboro, Mar. 2, 1865

North Anna R.

South Anna R.

VIRGINIA

North Anna, May 23–26, 1864 (2,000 900)

GRANT

LEE

James R.

Cold Harbor, June 1–3, 1864 (12,000 3,000)

Richmond's capture April 3, 1865

Rappahannock R.

Pamunkey R.

GRANT

LEE

Appomattox R.

Amelia C.H.

Petersburg siege, June 1864–Apr. 1865

Lee surrenders to Grant, Appomattox C.H., Apr. 9, 1865

Saylers Creek, Apr. 6, 1865

SHERIDAN

Five Forks, Apr. 1, 1865

0   25   50 Miles

0   25   50 Kilometers

Lincoln Finds His General

To the west, Grant had been trying for months to capture Vicksburg, a Rebel stronghold on the Mississippi. In a daring maneuver, he left behind his supply lines and marched inland, feeding his army from the produce of Confederate farms. These were the tactics of total war, and seldom had they been tried before. On July 4, the city surrendered. With the fall of Port Hudson, Louisiana, four days later, the Mississippi was completely in Union hands, thus dividing the Confederacy.

Capture of Vicksburg

Grant followed up this victory by rescuing Union forces holed up in Chattanooga. His performance confirmed Lincoln's earlier judgment that "Grant is my man, and I am his the rest of the war." In March 1864 Lincoln brought Grant east and placed him in command of all the Union armies.

Grant recognized that in the past the Union's armies had "acted independently and without concert, like a balky team, no two ever pulling together." He intended to change that. While he launched a major offensive against Lee in Virginia, William Tecumseh Sherman, who replaced Grant as commander of the western army, would drive a diagonal wedge through the Confederacy from Tennessee across Georgia. Grant instructed Sherman to "get into the interior of the enemy's country so far as you can, inflicting all the damage you can against their war resources."

Grant in command

In May and June 1864 Grant tried to maneuver Lee out of the trenches and into an open battle. But Lee was too weak to win head-on, so he opted for a strategy of attrition, hoping to inflict such heavy losses that the northern will would break. It was a strategy that nearly worked, for Union casualties were staggering. In a month of fierce fighting, the Army of the Potomac lost 60,000 men. Yet at the end of the campaign Grant's reinforced army was larger than when it started, whereas Lee's was significantly weaker.

Union's summer offensive

Unable to break Lee's lines, Grant settled into a siege of Petersburg, which guarded Richmond's last remaining rail link to the south. In the west, meanwhile, the gaunt and grizzled Sherman fought his way by July to the outskirts of Atlanta, which was heavily defended and gave no sign of capitulating. "Our all depends on that army at Atlanta," wrote Mary Chesnut in August, based on her conversations with Confederate leaders in Richmond. "If that fails us, the game is up."

War in the Balance

The game was nearly up for Lincoln as the 1864 election approached. As the Union war machine swept more and more northerners south to their death, and with Grant and Sherman bogged down on the Virginia and Georgia fronts, even leaders in Lincoln's own party began to mutter he was not equal to the task.

Lincoln rejected any suggestion to postpone the presidential election, which he believed would be to lose democracy itself. Exploiting his control of the party machinery, Lincoln easily won the Republican nomination, and he made certain that the Republican platform called for adoption of a constitutional amendment abolishing slavery. To balance the ticket, Lincoln selected Andrew Johnson, the military governor of Tennessee and a prowar Democrat, as his running mate. The two men ran under the label of the "Union" party.

1864 election

The Democrats nominated George McClellan, the former Union commander. Their platform pronounced the war a failure and called for an armistice and a peace conference. Warned that a cessation of fighting would lead to disunion, McClellan partially repudiated this position, insisting that "the Union is the one condition of peace—we ask no more." In private he made it clear that if elected he intended to restore slavery. Late in August, Lincoln was still gloomy about his prospects, as well

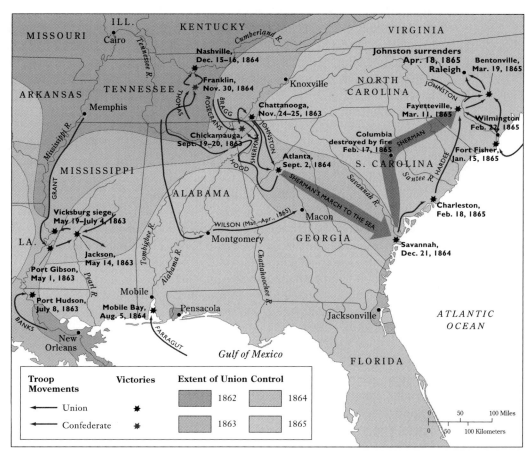

THE WAR IN THE WEST, 1863–1865   The Union continued its war of mobility in the western theater, bringing more Confederate territory under its control. After Grant captured Vicksburg, the entire Mississippi River lay in Union hands. His victories at Lookout Mountain and Missionary Ridge, near Chattanooga, ended the Confederate threat to Tennessee. In 1864 Sherman divided the Confederacy by seizing Atlanta and marching across Georgia; then he turned north. When Joseph Johnston surrendered, several weeks after Lee's capitulation at Appomattox, the war was effectively over.

as those of the Union itself. But Admiral David Farragut won a dramatic victory at Mobile Bay, and a few weeks later, in early September, Sherman finally captured Atlanta. As Secretary of State Seward gleefully noted, "Sherman and Farragut have knocked the bottom out of the Chicago [Democratic] nominations."

Polling an impressive 55 percent of the popular vote, Lincoln won 212 electoral votes to McClellan's 21. Eighteen states allowed soldiers to vote in the field, and Lincoln received nearly 80 percent of their ballots. One lifelong Democrat described the sentiment in the army: "We all want peace, but none any but an honorable one. I had rather stay out here a lifetime (much as I dislike it) than consent to a division of our country." Jefferson Davis remained defiant, but the last hope of a Confederate victory was gone.

Significance of Lincoln's reelection

Equally important, the election of 1864 ended any doubt that slavery would be abolished in the reconstructed Union. The Emancipation Proclamation had not put an end to the question, for its legal status remained unclear. Lincoln argued that as a war measure, it would have no standing once peace returned; and in any case, it had not freed slaves in the border states or those parts of the Confederacy already under Union control. Thus Lincoln and the Republicans believed that a constitutional amendment was necessary to secure emancipation.

Thirteenth Amendment

In 1864 the Senate approved an amendment that freed all slaves without compensating their owners. The measure passed the House on January 31, 1865. By December, enough states had ratified the Thirteenth Amendment to make it part of the Constitution.

Abolition as a global movement

The abolition of slavery in the United States was part of a worldwide drive against slavery. Britain spearheaded the process when Parliament abolished slavery throughout the British empire in 1833. The other colonial powers were much slower to act. Portugal did not end slavery in its New World colonies until 1836, Sweden in 1847, Denmark and France in 1848, Holland in 1863, and Spain not until 1886. Most of the Latin American republics had ended slavery when they threw off Spanish or Portuguese control, but the institution remained important in Cuba and Brazil. Spain abolished slavery in Cuba in 1886, and Brazil ended the institution in 1888. European reformers also crusaded against slavery in Africa and Asia, and indeed the antislavery movement increased European presence in Africa. At the same time, European nations ended the medieval institution of serfdom. In Russia, where serfdom most closely approximated slavery, Czar Alexander II emancipated the serfs in 1861, an act that led him to strongly favor the Union in the American Civil War.

The Twilight of the Confederacy

For the Confederacy, the outcome of the 1864 election had a terrible finality. In March 1865 the Confederate Congress authorized recruiting 300,000 slaves for military service. When he signed the bill, Davis announced that freedom would be given to those who volunteered and to their families. That same month he offered through a special envoy to abolish slavery in exchange for British diplo-

The war's greatest generals, Ulysses S. Grant (left) and Robert E. Lee (right), confronted each other in the eastern theater during the last year of the war. A member of a distinguished Virginia family, the tall, impeccably dressed Lee was every inch the aristocratic gentleman. Grant, a short, slouched figure with a stubby beard, dressed indifferently, but his determination is readily apparent in this picture, taken at his field headquarters in 1864.

matic recognition. A Mississippi paper denounced this proposal as "a total abandonment of the chief object of this war." The British rejected the offer, and the war ended before any slaves were mustered into the Confederate army, but the demands of total war had forced Confederate leaders to forsake the Old South's most important values and institutions.

Confederacy abandons slavery

In the wake of Lincoln's reelection, the Confederate will to resist rapidly disintegrated. White southerners had never fully united behind the war effort, but the large majority had endured great suffering to uphold it. As Sherman pushed deeper into the Confederacy, however, the war came home to southern civilians as never before. "We haven't got nothing in the house to eat but a little bit o meal," wrote the wife of one Alabama soldier in December 1864. ". . . Try to get off and come home and fix us all up some and then you can go back. . . . If you put off a-coming, 'twont be no use to come, for we'll all . . . [be] in the grave yard." He deserted. In the last months of the fighting, over half the Confederacy's soldiers were absent without leave.

After the fall of Atlanta, Sherman gave a frightening demonstration of the meaning of total war. Detaching a portion of his forces to engage General John Hood's army, which moved back into Tennessee, Sherman imitated Grant's strategy by abandoning his supply lines for an audacious 300-mile march to the sea. He intended to deprive Lee's army of the supplies it desperately needed to continue and to break the southern will to resist. Or as he bluntly put it, "to whip the Rebels, to humble their pride, to follow them to their recesses, and make them fear and dread us."

March to the sea

Moving in four columns, Sherman's army covered about 10 miles a day, cutting a path of destruction 50 miles wide. Sherman estimated that his men did $100 million in damage, of which $20 million was necessary to supply his army and the rest was wanton destruction. After he captured Savannah, he turned north and wreaked even greater havoc in South Carolina.

Meanwhile, General George H. Thomas defeated Hood's forces in December at Nashville, leaving the interior of the Confederacy essentially conquered. Only Lee's army remained, entrenched around Petersburg. As Grant relentlessly extended his lines, Lee's troops were forced to evacuate Richmond. Westward Grant doggedly pursued the Army of Northern Virginia, until the weary gentleman from Virginia finally asked for terms. On April 9, 1865, Lee surrendered at Appomattox Courthouse. As the vanquished foe mounted his horse, Grant saluted by raising his hat; Lee raised his respectfully and rode off at a slow trot. The guns were quiet.

Lee's surrender

Remaining resistance throughout the Confederacy collapsed within a matter of weeks. Visiting the captured city of Richmond on April 4, Lincoln was enthusiastically greeted by the black population. He looked "pale, haggard, utterly worn out," noted one observer. The lines in his face showed how much the war had aged him in only four years. Often his friends had counseled rest, but Lincoln had observed that "the tired part of me is *inside* and out of reach." The burden, he confessed, was almost too much to bear.

Back in Washington the president received news of Lee's surrender with relief. The evening of April 14, Lincoln, seeking a welcome escape, went to a comedy at Ford's Theater. In the midst of the performance John Wilkes Booth, a famous actor and Confederate sympathizer, slipped into the presidential box and shot him. Lincoln died the next morning. As he had called upon his fellow citizens to do in his Gettysburg Address, the sixteenth president had given his "last full measure of devotion" to the Republic.

Lincoln's assassination

THE IMPACT OF WAR

The assassination left a tiredness in the nation's bones—a tiredness "*inside*" and not easily within reach. In every way the conflict had produced fundamental, often devastating changes. There was, of course, the carnage. Approximately 620,000 men on both sides lost their lives, almost as many as in all the other wars the na-

A Georgia Plantation Mistress in Sherman's Path

I saw some blue-coats coming down the hill. . . . Oh God, the time of trial has come! . . . To my smoke-house, my dairy, pantry, kitchen, and cellar, like famished wolves they come, breaking locks and whatever is in their way. The thousand pounds of meat in my smoke-house is gone in a twinkling, my flour, my meat, my lard, butter, eggs, pickles of various kinds . . . —wine, jars, and jugs are all gone. My eighteen fat turkeys, my hens, chickens, and fowls, my young pigs, are shot down in my yard and hunted as if they were rebels themselves. . . .

As I stood there, from my lot I saw driven, first, old Dutch, my dear old buggy horse . . . then came old Mary, my brood mare, who for years had been too old and stiff for work, with her three-year-old colt, my two-year-old mule, and her last little baby colt. There they go! There go my mules, my sheep, and worse than all, my boys [slaves]! . . .

Their [slaves'] cabins are rifled of every valuable, the soldiers swearing that their Sunday clothes were the white people's, and that they never had money to get such things as they had. Poor Frank's chest was broken open, his money and tobacco taken. . . . All of his clothes and Rachel's clothes . . . were stolen from her. Ovens, skillets, coffee-mills . . . coffee-pots—not one have I left. Sifters all gone! . . .

Sherman himself and a greater portion of his army passed my house that day. All day, as the sad moments rolled on, were they passing not only in front of my house, but from behind; they tore down my garden palings, made a road through my back-yard and lot field, driving their stock and riding through, tearing down my fences and desolating my home—wantonly doing it when there was no necessity for it. . . .

As night drew its sable curtains around us, the heavens from every point were lit up with flames from burning buildings.

Source: Dolly Lunt, November 19, 1864, *A Woman's Wartime Journal* (Macon: J. W. Burke Co., 1927), pp. 21–31.

tion has fought from the Revolution through Vietnam combined. In material terms, the conflict cost an estimated $20 billion, more than 11 times the total amount spent by the federal government from 1789 to 1861. Even without adding the market value of freed slaves, southern wealth declined 43 percent, transforming what had been the richest section in the nation (on a white per capita basis) into the poorest.

Cost of war

The demands of total war also stimulated industrialization, especially in the heavy industries of iron and coal, machinery, and agricultural implements, while the probusiness finance and tax policies of the Republican party encouraged the formation of larger corporations in the years ahead. The war also forced manufacturers to supply the army on an unprecedented scale over great distances. One consequence was the creation of truly national industries in flour milling, meat packing, clothing and shoe manufacture, and machinery making.

Politically, the war dramatically changed the balance of power. The South lost its substantial influence, as did the Democratic party, while the Republicans emerged in a dominant position. The Union's military victory also signaled the triumph of nationalism. The war destroyed the idea that the Union was a voluntary confederacy of sovereign states, which theorists like John C. Calhoun had argued, and that the states had the right to secede.

In the short run, the price was disillusionment and bitterness. The South had to live with the humiliation of military defeat and occupation, while former slaves anxiously waited to see what their situation would be in freedom. The war's corrosive effect on morals corrupted American life and politics, destroyed idealism, and severely crippled humanitarian reform. Millennialism and perfectionism were victims of the war's appalling slaughter, forsaken for a new emphasis on practicality, order, materialism, and science. As the war unfolded, the New York *Herald* recognized the deep changes: "All sorts of old fogy ideas, manners, and customs have gone under, and all sorts of new ideas, modes, and practices have risen to the surface and become popular."

Spiritual toll of war

George Ticknor, a prominent author and critic who was sensitive to shifting intellectual and social currents, reflected on the changes that had shaken the nation in only a few short years. The war, it seemed to him, had left "a great gulf between what happened before it in our century and what has happened since. . . . It does not seem to me as if I were living in the country in which I was born."

chapter summary

As the first total war in history, the Civil War's outcome depended not just on armies but also on the mobilization of society's human, economic, and intellectual resources.

- Confederate President Jefferson Davis's policy of concentrating power in the government at Richmond, along with the resort of a draft and impressment of private property, provoked strong protests from many southerners.

- Abraham Lincoln's policies, especially his suspension of the writ of habeas corpus and his interference with civil liberties, were equally controversial.

- But Lincoln skillfully handled the delicate situation of the border states in the first year of the war, keeping them in the Union.

- Lincoln at first resisted pressure to make emancipation a Union war aim, but he eventually issued the Emancipation Proclamation, which transformed the meaning of the war.

- African Americans helped undermine slavery in the Confederacy and made a vital contribution to the Union's military victory.

- The war had a powerful impact on the home front.
  - Women confronted new responsibilities and enjoyed new occupational opportunities.
  - In the Confederacy, hardship and suffering became a fact of life.
  - The Confederate government's financial and tax policies and the tightening Union blockade increased this suffering.

- Both societies also experienced the ravages of moral decay.

- The Civil War changed the nature of warfare.
  - Technology, particularly the use of rifles and rifled artillery, revolutionized tactics and strategy.
  - The Union eventually adopted the strategy of attacking the civilian population of the South.
  - Soldiers in both armies suffered from disease and inadequate medical care, poor food, moral corruption, and the mounting death toll.

- The war altered the nation's political institutions, its economy, and its values.

For quizzes and a variety of interactive resources, visit the book's Online Learning Center at www.mhhe.com/davidsonconcise3

SIGNIFICANT EVENTS

1861 — Border states remain in the Union; Union blockade proclaimed; Lincoln suspends writ of habeas corpus in selected areas; Battle of Bull Run; Crittenden Resolution approved; First Confiscation Act passes

1862 — Forts Henry and Donelson captured; *Monitor* vs. *Virginia* (*Merrimack*); Battle of Shiloh; slavery abolished in the District of Columbia; Confederacy institutes conscription; New Orleans captured; Homestead Act; Land Grant College Act; Second Confiscation Act; Union income tax enacted; McClellan's Peninsula campaign fails; Second Battle of Bull Run; Battle of Antietam; preliminary Emancipation Proclamation issued; Lincoln suspends writ of habeas corpus throughout the Union; Battle of Fredericksburg

1863 — Emancipation Proclamation issued; National Banking Act; Union institutes conscription; Confederacy enacts general tax laws, initiates impressment; bread riots in the Confederacy; Battle of Chancellorsville; West Virginia admitted; Battle of Gettysburg; Vicksburg captured; New York City draft riots

1864 — Grant becomes Union general in chief; Grant's Virginia offensive; siege of Petersburg; Battle of Mobile Bay; fall of Atlanta; Lincoln reelected; Sherman's march to the sea

1865 — Congress passes Thirteenth Amendment; Sherman's march through the Carolinas; Lee surrenders; Lincoln assassinated; Thirteenth Amendment ratified

1866 — *Ex parte Milligan*

CHAPTER 17

Reconstructing the Union
(1865–1877)

Joseph Davis had had enough. Well on in years and financially ruined by the war, he decided to quit farming. So, on November 19, 1866, he sold his Mississippi plantations Hurricane and Brierfield to Benjamin Montgomery and his sons. The sale of southern plantations was common enough after the war, but this transaction was bound to attract attention, since Joseph Davis was the elder brother of Jefferson Davis. Indeed, before the war the ex-Confederate president had operated Brierfield as his own plantation, even though his brother retained legal title to it. But the sale was unusual for another reason— so unusual that the parties involved agreed to keep it secret. The plantation's new owners were black, and Mississippi law prohibited African Americans from owning land.

Though a slave, Benjamin Montgomery had been the business manager of the two Davis plantations before the war. He had also operated a store on Hurricane Plantation with his own line of credit in New Orleans. In 1863 Montgomery fled to the North, but when the war was over, he returned to Davis Bend, where the federal government had confiscated the Davis plantations and was leasing plots of the land to black farmers. Montgomery quickly emerged as the leader of the African American community at the Bend.

Then, in 1866, President Andrew Johnson pardoned Joseph Davis and restored his lands. Davis was now over 80 years old and lacked the will and stamina to rebuild, yet unlike many ex-slaveholders, he felt bound by obligations to his former slaves. Convinced that with proper encouragement African Americans could succeed economically in freedom, he sold his land secretly to Benjamin Montgomery. Only when the law prohibiting African Americans from owning land was overturned in 1867 did Davis publicly confirm the sale to his former slave.

preview • Reconstruction became the battleground of attempts to define the new shape of the Union. Congress rejected Andrew Johnson's lenient terms for the South's reentry and enacted a program that included the principle of black suffrage. African Americans asserted their freedom by uniting divided families, establishing churches, and seeking education and land. But when northern whites became disillusioned with reform, the ideology of white supremacy brought Reconstruction to an end.

For his part, Montgomery undertook to create a model society at Davis Bend based on mutual cooperation. He rented land to black farmers, hired others to work his own fields, sold supplies on credit, and ginned and marketed the crops. To the growing African American community, he preached the gospel of hard work, self-reliance, and education.

Various difficulties dogged these black farmers, including the destruction caused by the war, several disastrous floods, insects, droughts, and declining cotton prices. Yet before long, cotton production exceeded that of the prewar years, and in 1870 the black families at Davis Bend produced 2500 bales. The Montgomerys eventually acquired 5500 acres, which made them reputedly the third largest planters in the state, and they won national and international awards for the quality of their cotton. Their success demonstrated what African Americans, given a fair chance, might accomplish.

The experiences of Benjamin Montgomery during the years after 1865 were not those of most black southerners, who did not own land or have a powerful white benefactor. Yet Montgomery's dream of economic independence was shared by all African Americans. As one black veteran noted, "Every colored man will be a slave, and feel himself a slave until he can raise him own *bale of cotton* and put him own mark upon it and say dis is mine!" Blacks could not gain effective freedom simply through a proclamation of emancipation. They also needed economic power, including their own land that no one could unfairly take away.

For nearly two centuries the laws had prevented slaves from possessing such economic power. If such conditions were to be overturned, black Americans needed political power too. Thus the Republic would have to be reconstructed to give African Americans political power that they had been previously denied.

War, in its blunt way, had roughed out the contours of a solution, but only in broad terms. Clearly, African Americans would no longer be enslaved. The North, with its industrial might, would be the driving force in the nation's economy and retain the dominant political voice. But beyond that, the outlines of a reconstructed Republic remained vague. Would African Americans receive effective power? How would North and South readjust their economic and political relations? These questions lay at the heart of the problem of Reconstruction.

PRESIDENTIAL RECONSTRUCTION

Throughout the war Abraham Lincoln had considered Reconstruction his responsibility. Elected with less than 40 percent of the popular vote in 1860, he was acutely aware that once the states of the Confederacy were restored to the Union, the Republicans would be weakened unless they ceased to be a sectional party. By a generous peace, Lincoln hoped to attract former Whigs in the South, who supported many of the Republicans' economic policies, and build up a southern wing of the party.

Lincoln's 10 Percent Plan

Lincoln outlined his program in a Proclamation of Amnesty and Reconstruction, issued in December 1863. When a minimum of 10 percent of the qualified voters from 1860 took a loyalty oath to the Union, they could organize a state government. The new state constitution had to abolish slavery and provide for black education, but Lincoln did not insist that high-ranking Confederate leaders be barred from public life.

Lincoln indicated that he would be generous in granting pardons to prominent Confederate leaders and did not rule out compensation for slave property. Moreover, while he privately advocated limited black suffrage in the disloyal southern states, he did not demand social or political equality for black Americans, and he recognized pro-Union governments in Louisiana, Arkansas, and Tennessee that allowed only white men to vote.

The Radical Republicans found Lincoln's approach much too lenient. Strongly antislavery, Radical members of Congress had led the struggle to make emancipation a war aim. Now they led the fight to guarantee the rights of former slaves, or freedpeople. The Radicals believed that it was the duty of Congress, not the president, to set the terms under which states would regain their rights in the Union. Though the Radicals often disagreed on other matters, they were united in a determination to readmit southern states only after slavery had been ended, black rights protected, and the power of the planter class destroyed.

Radical Republicans

Under the direction of Senator Benjamin Wade of Ohio and Representative Henry Winter Davis of Maryland, Congress formulated a much stricter plan of Reconstruction. It required half the white adult males to take an oath of allegiance before drafting a new state constitution, and it restricted political power to the hard-core Unionists. When the Wade-Davis bill passed on the final day of the 1864 congressional session, Lincoln exercised his right of a pocket veto.* Still, his own program could not succeed without the assistance of Congress, which refused to recognize his governments in Louisiana and Arkansas. As the war drew to a close, Lincoln appeared ready to make concessions to the Radicals, and at his final cabinet meeting he approved placing the defeated South temporarily under military rule. But only a few days later Booth's bullet found its mark, and Lincoln's final approach to Reconstruction would never be known.

Wade-Davis bill

The Mood of the South

In the wake of defeat, the immediate reaction among white southerners was one of shock, despair, and hopelessness. Some former Confederates were openly antagonistic. A North Carolina innkeeper remarked bitterly that Yankees had stolen

---

*If a president does not sign a bill after Congress has adjourned, it has the same effect as a veto.

his slaves, burned his house, and killed all his sons, leaving him only one privilege: "To hate 'em. I git up at half-past four in the morning, and sit up till twelve at night, to hate 'em." Most Confederate soldiers were less defiant, having had their fill of war. Even among hostile civilians the feeling was widespread that the South must accept northern terms. A South Carolina paper admitted that "the conqueror has the right to make the terms, and we must submit."

This psychological moment was critical. To prevent a resurgence of resistance, the president needed to lay out in unmistakable terms what white southerners had to do to regain their old status in the Union. Perhaps even a clear and firm policy would not have been enough. But with Lincoln's death, the executive power came to rest in far less capable hands.

Johnson's Program of Reconstruction

Andrew Johnson, the new president, had been born in North Carolina and eventually moved to Tennessee, where he worked as a tailor. Barely able to read and write when he married, he rose to political power by portraying himself as the champion of the people against the wealthy planter class. "Some day I will show the stuck-up aristocrats who is running the country," he vowed as he began his political career. He had not opposed slavery before the war, and although he accepted emancipation as one consequence of the war, Johnson remained a confirmed racist with no concern for the welfare of African Americans. "Damn the negroes," he said during the war, "I am fighting these traitorous aristocrats, their masters."

Johnson's character and values

During the war he had joined the Radicals in calling for stern treatment of southern rebels. "Treason must be made odious and traitors must be punished and impoverished," he proclaimed in 1864. After serving in Congress and as military governor of Tennessee following its occupation by Union forces, Johnson, a Democrat, was tapped by Lincoln in 1864 as his running mate on the rechristened "Union" ticket.

The Radicals expected Johnson to uphold their views on Reconstruction, and upon assuming the presidency he spoke of trying Confederate leaders and breaking up planters' estates. Unlike most Republicans, however, Johnson strongly supported states' rights and opposed government aid to business. Given such differences, conflict between the president and the majority in Congress was inevitable, but Johnson's political shortcomings made the situation worse. Scarred by his humble origins, he became tactless and inflexible when challenged or criticized, and he alienated even those who sought to work with him.

Johnson moved to quickly return the southern states to their place in the Union. He prescribed a loyalty oath white southerners would have to take to regain their civil and political rights and to have their property, except for slaves, restored. Excluded were high Confederate officials and those with property worth over $20,000, who had to apply for individual pardons. Johnson announced that once a state had drafted a new constitution and elected

Johnson's program

state officers and members of Congress, he would revoke martial law and recognize the new state government. Suffrage was limited to white citizens who had taken the loyalty oath. This plan was similar to Lincoln's, though more lenient. Only informally did Johnson stipulate that the southern states were to renounce their ordinances of secession, repudiate the Confederate debt, and ratify the proposed Thirteenth Amendment abolishing slavery.

The Failure of Johnson's Program

The southern delegates who met to construct new governments soon demonstrated that they were in no frame of mind to follow Johnson's recommendations. Several states merely repealed instead of repudiating their ordinances of secession, rejected the Thirteenth Amendment, or refused to repudiate the Confederate debt.

Nor did any of the new governments allow African Americans any political rights or provide in any effective way for black education. In addition, each state passed a series of laws, often modeled on its old slave code, that applied only to African Americans. These "black codes" did give African Americans some rights that had not been granted to slaves. They legalized marriages from slavery and allowed black southerners to hold and sell property and to sue and be sued in state courts. Yet their primary intent was to keep African Americans as propertyless agricultural laborers with inferior legal rights. The new freedpeople could not serve on juries, testify against whites, or work as they pleased. Mississippi prohibited them from buying or renting farmland, and most states ominously provided that black people who were vagrants could be arrested and hired out to landowners. Many northerners were incensed by the restrictive black codes, which violated their conception of freedom.

Black codes

Southern voters under Johnson's plan also defiantly elected prominent Confederate military and political leaders to office. At this point, Johnson could have

Andrew Johnson was a staunch Unionist, but his contentious personality and inflexibility soured his relationship with Congress.

Elections in the South

called for new elections or admitted that a different program of Reconstruction was needed. Instead he caved in. For all his harsh rhetoric, he shrank from the prospect of social upheaval, and as the lines of ex-Confederates waiting to see him lengthened, he began issuing special pardons almost as fast as they could be printed. Publicly Johnson put on a bold face, announcing that Reconstruction had been successfully completed. But many members of Congress were deeply alarmed, and the stage was set for a serious confrontation.

Johnson's Break with Congress

The new Congress was by no means of one mind. A small number of Democrats and a few conservative Republicans backed the president's program of immediate and unconditional restoration. At the other end of the spectrum, a larger group of Radical Republicans, led by Thaddeus Stevens, Charles Sumner, Benjamin Wade, and others, was bent on remaking southern society in the image of the North. Reconstruction must "revolutionize Southern institutions, habits, and manners," thundered Representative Stevens, ". . . or all our blood and treasure have been spent in vain."

As a minority, the Radicals needed the aid of the moderate Republicans, the largest bloc in Congress. Led by William Pitt Fessenden and Lyman Trumbull, the moderates hoped to avoid a clash with the president, and they had no desire to foster social revolution or promote racial equality in the South. But they wanted to keep Confederate leaders from reassuming power, and they were convinced that the former slaves needed federal protection. Otherwise, Trumbull declared, the freedpeople would "be tyrannized over, abused, and virtually reenslaved."

The central issue dividing Johnson and the Radicals was the place of African Americans in American society. Johnson accused his opponents of seeking "to Africanize the southern half of our country," while the Radicals championed civil and political rights for African Americans. The only way to maintain loyal governments and develop a Republican party in the South, Radicals argued, was to give black men the ballot. Moderates agreed that the new southern governments were too harsh toward African Americans, but they feared that too great an emphasis on black civil rights would alienate northern voters.

Issue of black rights

In December 1865, when southern representatives to Congress appeared in Washington, a majority in Congress voted to exclude them. Congress also appointed a joint committee, chaired by Senator Fessenden, to look into Reconstruction.

The growing split with the president became clearer when Congress passed a bill extending the life of the Freedmen's Bureau. Created in March 1865, the Bureau provided emergency food, clothing, and medical care to war refugees (including white southerners) and took charge of settling freedpeople on abandoned lands. The new bill gave the Bureau the added responsibilities of supervising special courts to resolve disputes involving freedpeople and establishing schools for black southerners. Although this bill passed with virtually unanimous Republican support, Johnson vetoed it.

Johnson also vetoed a civil rights bill designed to overturn the more flagrant provisions of the black codes. The law made African Americans citizens of the United States and granted them the right to own property, make contracts, and have access to courts as parties and witnesses. For most Republicans Johnson's action was the last straw, and in April 1866 Congress overrode his veto. Congress then approved a slightly revised Freedmen's Bureau bill in July and promptly overrode the president's veto. Johnson's refusal to compromise drove the moderates into the arms of the Radicals.

> Johnson's vetoes

The Fourteenth Amendment

To prevent unrepentant Confederates from taking over the reconstructed state governments and denying African Americans basic freedoms, the Joint Committee on Reconstruction proposed an amendment to the Constitution, which passed both houses of Congress with the necessary two-thirds vote in June 1866.

The amendment guaranteed repayment of the national war debt and prohibited repayment of the Confederate debt. To counteract the president's wholesale pardons, it disqualified prominent Confederates from holding office and provided that only Congress by a two-thirds vote could remove this penalty. Because moderates balked at giving the vote to African Americans, the amendment merely gave Congress the right to reduce the representation of any state that did not have impartial male suffrage. The practical effect of this provision, which Radicals labeled a "swindle," was to allow northern states to retain white suffrage, since unlike southern states they had few African Americans in their populations and thus would not be penalized.

> Provisions of the amendment

The amendment's most important provision, Section 1, defined an American citizen as anyone born in the United States or naturalized, thereby automatically making African Americans citizens. Section 1 also prohibited states from abridging "the privileges or immunities" of citizens, depriving "any person of life, liberty, or property, without due process of law," or denying "any person . . . equal protection of the laws." The framers of the amendment probably intended to prohibit laws that applied to one race only, such as the black codes, or that made certain acts felonies when committed by black but not white people, or that decreed different penalties for the same crime when committed by white and black lawbreakers. The framers probably did not intend to prevent segregation (the legal separation of the races) in schools and public places.

Johnson denounced the proposed amendment and urged southern states not to ratify it. Ironically, of the seceded states only the president's own state ratified the amendment, and Congress readmitted Tennessee with no further restrictions.

The telegram sent to Congress by a longtime foe of Johnson officially announcing Tennessee's approval ended, "Give my respects to the dead dog in the White House."

The Elections of 1866

When Congress blocked his policies, Johnson undertook a speaking tour of the East and Midwest in the fall of 1866 to drum up popular support. But Johnson found it difficult to convince northern audiences that white southerners were fully repentant. Only months earlier white mobs in Memphis and New Orleans had attacked black residents and killed nearly 100 in two major race riots. "The negroes now know, to their sorrow, that it is best not to arouse the fury of the white man," boasted one Memphis newspaper. When the president encountered hostile audiences during his northern campaign, he only made matters worse by trading insults and proclaiming that the Radicals were traitors.

Not to be outdone, the Radicals vilified Johnson as a traitor aiming to turn the country over to former rebels. Resorting to the tactic of "waving the bloody shirt," they appealed to voters by reviving bitter memories of the war. In a classic example of such rhetoric, Governor Oliver Morton of Indiana proclaimed that "every bounty jumper, every deserter, every sneak who ran away from the draft" was a Democrat; every "New York rioter in 1863 who burned up little children in colored asylums called himself a Democrat. In short, the Democratic party may be described as a common sewer. . . ."

Voters soundly repudiated Johnson, as the Republicans won more than a two-thirds majority in both houses of Congress. The Radicals had reached the height

Repudiation of Johnson

of their power, propelled by genuine alarm among northerners that Johnson's policies would lose the fruits of the Union's victory. Johnson was a president virtually without a party.

CONGRESSIONAL RECONSTRUCTION

With a clear mandate in hand, congressional Republicans passed their own program of Reconstruction, beginning with the first Reconstruction Act in March 1867. Like all later pieces of Reconstruction legislation, it was repassed over Johnson's veto.

Placing the 10 unreconstructed states under military commanders, the act provided that in enrolling voters, officials were to include black adult males but not former Confederates who were barred from holding office under the Fourteenth Amendment. Delegates to the state conventions were to frame constitutions that provided for black suffrage and disqualified prominent ex-Confederates from office. The first state legislatures to meet under the new constitution were required to ratify the Fourteenth Amendment. Once these steps were completed and Congress approved the new state constitution, a state could send representatives to Congress.

White southerners found these requirements so obnoxious that officials took no steps to register voters. Congress then enacted a second Reconstruction Act, also in March, ordering the local military commanders to put the machinery of Reconstruction into motion. Johnson's efforts to limit the power of military commanders produced a third act, passed in July, that upheld their superiority in all matters. When the first election was held in Alabama to ratify the new state constitutions, whites boycotted it in sufficient numbers to prevent a majority of voters from participating. Undaunted, Congress passed the fourth Reconstruction Act (March 1868), which required ratification of the constitution by only a majority of those voting rather than those who were registered.

> Resistance of white southerners

By June 1868 Congress had readmitted the representatives of seven states. Texas, Virginia, and Mississippi did not complete the process until 1869. Georgia finally followed in 1870.

Postemancipation Societies in the Americas

With the exception of Haiti's revolution (1791–1804), the United States was the only society in the Americas in which the destruction of slavery was accomplished by violence. But the United States, uniquely among these societies, enfranchised former slaves almost immediately after the emancipation. Thus in the United States former masters and slaves battled for control of the state in ways that did not occur in other postemancipation societies. In most of the Caribbean, property requirements for voting left the planters in political control. Jamaica, for example, with a population of 500,000 in the 1860s, had only 3000 voters.

Moreover, in reaction to political efforts to mobilize disfranchised black peasants, Jamaican planters dissolved the assembly and reverted to being a Crown colony governed from London. Of the sugar islands, all but Barbados adopted the same policy, thereby blocking the potential for any future black peasant democracy. Nor did any of these societies have the counterparts of the Radical Republicans, a group of outsiders with political power that promoted the fundamental transformation of the postemancipation South. These comparisons highlight the radicalism of Reconstruction in the United States, which alone saw an effort to forge an interracial democracy.

The Land Issue

While the political process of Reconstruction proceeded, Congress debated whether land should be given to former slaves to foster economic independence. At a meeting with Secretary of War Edwin Stanton near the end of the war, African

American leaders declared, "The way we can best take care of ourselves is to have land, and till it by our own labor." The Second Confiscation Act of 1862 had authorized the government to seize and sell the property of supporters of the rebellion. In June 1866, however, President Johnson ruled that confiscation laws applied only to wartime.

For over a year Congress debated land confiscation off and on, but in the end it rejected all proposals to give land to former slaves. Even some Radicals were op-

Failure of land redistribution

posed. Given Americans' strong belief in self-reliance, little sympathy existed for the idea that government should support any group. In addition, land redistribution represented an attack on property rights, another cherished American value. "A division of rich men's lands amongst the landless," argued the *Nation*, a Radical journal, "would give a shock to our whole social and political system from which it would hardly recover without the loss of liberty." By 1867 land reform was dead.

Few freedpeople acquired land after the war, a development that severely limited African Americans' economic independence and left them vulnerable to white coercion. It is doubtful, however, that this decision was the basic cause of the failure of Reconstruction. In the face of white hostility, African Americans probably would have been no more successful in protecting their property than they were in maintaining the right to vote.

Impeachment

Throughout 1867 Congress routinely overrode Johnson's vetoes, but the president had other ways of undercutting congressional Reconstruction. He interpreted the new laws as narrowly as possible and removed military commanders who vigorously enforced them. Congress responded by restricting his power to issue orders

Tenure of Office Act

to military commanders in the South. It also passed the Tenure of Office Act, which forbade Johnson from removing any member of the cabinet without the Senate's consent. The intention of this law was to prevent him from firing Secretary of War Edwin Stanton, the only remaining Radical in the cabinet.

When Johnson tried to dismiss Stanton in February 1868, the House of Representatives angrily approved articles of impeachment. The articles focused on the violation of the Tenure of Office Act, but the charge with the most substance was that Johnson had acted to systematically obstruct Reconstruction legislation. In the trial before the Senate, his lawyers argued that a president could be impeached

Johnson's acquittal

only for an indictable crime, which Johnson clearly had not committed. The Radicals countered that impeachment applied to political offenses and not merely criminal acts. In May 1868 the Senate voted 35 to 19 to convict, one vote short of the two-thirds majority needed. The seven Republicans who joined the Democrats in voting for acquittal were uneasy about using impeachment as a political weapon.

RECONSTRUCTION IN THE SOUTH

The waning power of the Radicals in Congress, evident in the failure to remove Johnson, meant that the success or failure of Reconstruction increasingly hinged on developments in the southern states themselves. Power in these states rested with the new Republican parties, representing a coalition of black and white southerners and transplanted northerners.

Black Officeholding

Almost from the beginning of Reconstruction, African Americans had lobbied for the right to vote. After they received the franchise, black men constituted as much as 80 percent of the Republican voters in the South. They steadfastly opposed the Democratic party with its appeal to white supremacy. As one Tennessee Republican explained, "The blacks know that many conservatives [Democrats] hope to reduce them again to some form of peonage. Under the impulse of this fear they will roll up their whole strength and will go entirely for the Republican candidate whoever he may be."

Throughout Reconstruction, African Americans never held office in proportion to their voting strength. No African American was ever elected governor, and only in South Carolina, where more than 60 percent of the population was black, did they control even one house of the legislature. During Reconstruction between 15 and 20 percent of the state officers and 6 percent of members of Congress (2 senators and 15 representatives) were black. Only in South Carolina did black officeholders approach their proportion of the population.

Those who held office came from the top levels of African American society. Among state and federal officeholders, perhaps four-fifths were literate, and over a quarter had been free before the war, both marks of distinction in the black community. Their occupations also set them apart: two-fifths were professionals (mostly clergy), and of the third who were farmers, nearly all owned land. In their political and social values, African American leaders were more conservative than the rural black population, and they showed little interest in land reform.

Black political leadership

White Republicans in the South

Black citizens were a majority of the voters only in South Carolina, Mississippi, and Louisiana. Thus in most of the South the Republican party had to secure white votes to stay in power. Opponents scornfully labeled white southerners who allied with the Republican party scalawags, yet an estimated quarter of white southerners at one time voted Republican. They were primarily Unionists from the upland counties and hill areas who were largely yeoman farmers. Such voters were attracted by Republican promises to rebuild the

Scalawags

A black politician addresses former slaves at a political meeting in the South during the 1868 presidential campaign. Although only men could vote, black women are also in the audience.

South, restore prosperity, create public schools, and open isolated areas to the market with railroads.

The other group of white Republicans in the South were known as carpetbaggers. Originally from the North, they allegedly had arrived with all their worldly

Carpetbaggers

possessions stuffed in a carpetbag, ready to loot and plunder the defeated South. Some did, certainly, but northerners moved south for a variety of reasons. Though carpetbaggers made up only a small percentage of Republican voters, they controlled almost a third of the offices. More than half of all southern Republican governors and nearly half of Republican members of Congress were originally northerners.

The Republican party in the South had difficulty maintaining unity. Scalawags were especially susceptible to the race issue and social pressure. "Even my own kinspeople have turned the cold shoulder to me because I hold office under a Republican administration," testified a Mississippi white Republican. As black southerners pressed for greater recognition, white southerners increasingly defected to the Democrats. Carpetbaggers, by contrast, were less sensitive to race, although most felt that their black allies should be content with minor offices. The animosity between scalawags and carpetbaggers, which grew out of their rivalry for party honors, was particularly intense.

Reforms under the New State Governments

The new southern state constitutions enacted several significant reforms. They devised fairer systems of legislative representation and made many previously ap-

Reconstruction state constitutions

pointive offices elective. The Radical state governments also assumed some responsibility for social welfare and established the first statewide systems of public schools in the South. Although the Fourteenth Amendment prevented high Confederate officials from holding office, only Alabama and Arkansas temporarily forbade some ex-Confederates from voting.

All the new constitutions proclaimed the principle of equality and granted black adult males the right to vote. On social relations they were much more cautious. No state outlawed segregation, and South Carolina and Louisiana were the only ones that required integration in public schools (a mandate that was almost universally ignored). Sensitive to status, mulattoes pushed for prohibition of social discrimination, but white Republicans refused to adopt such a radical policy.

Race and social equality

Economic Issues and Corruption

With the southern economy in ruins at the end of the war, problems of economic reconstruction were severe. The new Republican governments sought to encourage industrial development by providing subsidies, loans, and even temporary exemptions from taxes. These governments also largely rebuilt the southern railroad system, often offering lavish aid to railroad corporations. In the two decades after 1860, the region doubled its manufacturing establishments, yet the South steadily slipped further behind the booming industrial economy of the North.

The expansion of government services offered temptations for corruption. In many southern states, officials regularly received bribes and kickbacks for their award of railroad charters, franchises, and other contracts. By 1872 the debts of the 11 states of the Confederacy had increased $132 million, largely because of railroad grants and new social services such as schools. The tax rate grew as expenditures went up, so that by the 1870s it was four times the rate of 1860.

Corruption

Corruption, however, was not only a southern problem: the decline in morality affected the entire nation. During these years, the Democratic Tweed Ring in New York City alone stole more money than all the Radical Republican governments in the South combined. Moreover, corruption in the South was hardly limited to Republicans. Many Democrats and white business leaders participated in these corrupt practices, both before and after the Radical governments were in power. Louisiana Governor Henry Warmoth, a carpetbagger, told a congressional committee, "Everybody is demoralizing down here. Corruption is the fashion."

Corruption in Radical governments undeniably existed, but southern Democrats exaggerated its extent for partisan purposes. They opposed honest Radical regimes just as bitterly as notoriously corrupt ones. In the eyes of most white southerners, the real crime of the Radical governments was that they allowed black citizens to hold some offices and tried to protect the civil rights of black Americans. Race was white conservatives' greatest weapon. And it would prove the most effective means to undermine Republican power in the South.

BLACK ASPIRATIONS

Emancipation came to slaves in different ways and at different times. Betty Jones's grandmother was told about the Emancipation Proclamation by another slave while they were hoeing corn. Mary Anderson received the news from her master near the end of the war when Sherman's army invaded North Carolina. And for Louis Napoleon, emancipation arrived after the war when Union troops occupied Tallahassee, Florida. Whatever the timing, freedom meant a host of precious blessings to people who had been in bondage all their lives.

Experiencing Freedom

The first impulse was to think of freedom as a contrast to slavery. Emancipation immediately released slaves from the most oppressive aspects of bondage—the whippings, the breakup of families, the sexual exploitation. Freedom also meant movement, the right to travel without a pass or white permission. Above all, freedom meant that African Americans' labor would be for their own benefit. One Arkansas freedman, who earned his first dollar working on a railroad, recalled that when he was paid, "I felt like the richest man in the world."

Meaning of freedom

Freedom included finding a new place to work. Changing jobs was one concrete way to break the psychological ties of slavery. Even planters with reputations for kindness sometimes found that most of their former hands had departed. The cook who left a South Carolina family, even though they offered her higher wages than her new job did, explained, "I must go. If I stays here I'll never know I'm free."

Symbolically, freedom meant having a full name. African Americans now adopted last names, most commonly the name of the first master in the family's oral history as far back as it could be recalled. Most, on the other hand, retained their first name, especially if the name had been given to them by their parents (as most often had been the case). Whatever name they took, it was important to black Americans that they made the decision themselves.

The Black Family

African Americans also sought to strengthen the family in freedom. Since slave marriages had not been recognized as legal, thousands of former slaves insisted on being married again by proper authorities, even though this was not required by law. Those who had been forcibly separated in slavery and later remarried confronted the dilemma of which spouse to take. Laura Spicer, whose husband had been sold away in slavery, wrote him after the war seeking to resume their marriage. In a series of wrenching letters, he explained that he had thought her dead, had remarried, and had a new family. "You know it never was our wishes to be separated from each other, and it never was our fault. I had rather anything to had happened to me most than ever have been parted from you and the children," he wrote. "As I am, I do not know which I love best, you or Anna." Declining to return, he closed, "Laura, truly, I have got another wife, and I am very sorry."

Upholding the family

As in white families, black husbands deemed themselves the head of the family and acted legally for their wives. They often insisted that their wives would not work in the fields as they had in slavery. "The [black] women say they never mean to do any more outdoor work," one planter reported, "that white men support their wives and they mean that their husbands shall support them." In negotiating contracts, a father also demanded the right to control his children and their labor. All these changes were designed to insulate the black family from white control.

The Schoolhouse and the Church

In freedom, the schoolhouse and the black church became essential institutions in the black community. "My Lord, Ma'am, what a great thing learning is!" a South Carolina freedman told a northern teacher. "White folks can do what they likes, for they know so much more than we." At first, northern churches and missionaries, working with the Freedmen's Bureau, set up black schools in the South. Tuition at these schools represented 10 percent or more of a laborer's monthly wages, yet these schools were full. Eventually, states established public school systems, which by 1867 enrolled 40 percent of African American children.

Black education

Black adults, who often attended night classes, had good reasons for seeking literacy. They wanted to be able to read the Bible, to defend their newly gained civil and political rights, and to protect themselves from being cheated. Both races saw that education would undermine the old servility that slavery had fostered.

The teachers in the Freedmen's Bureau schools were primarily northern middle-class white women sent south by northern missionary societies. "I feel that it is a precious privilege," Esther Douglass wrote, "to be allowed to do something for these poor people." Many saw themselves as peacetime soldiers, struggling to make emancipation a reality. Indeed, hostile white southerners sometimes destroyed black schools and threatened and even murdered white teachers. Then there were the everyday challenges: low pay, dilapidated buildings, insufficient books, classes of 100 or more children, and irregular attendance. Meanwhile, the Freedmen's Bureau undertook to train black teachers, and by 1869 a majority of the teachers in these schools were black.

Teachers in black schools

Most slaves had attended white churches or services supervised by whites. Once free, African Americans quickly established their own congregations led by black preachers. Mostly Methodist and Baptist, black churches were the only major organizations in the African American community they controlled. A white missionary reported that "the Ebony preacher who promises perfect independence from White control and direction carried the colored heart at once." Just as in slavery, religion offered African Americans a place of refuge in a hostile white world and provided them with hope, comfort, and a means of self-identification.

Independent black churches

New Working Conditions

As a largely propertyless class, blacks in the postwar South had no choice but to work for white landowners. Except for paying wages, whites wanted to retain the old system of labor, including close supervision, gang labor, and physical punishment. Determined to remove all emblems of servitude, African Americans refused to work under these conditions, and they demanded time off to devote to their own interests. Because of shorter hours and the withdrawal of children and women from the fields, blacks' output declined by an estimated 35 percent in freedom. They also refused to live in the old slave quarters located near the master's house and instead erected cabins on distant parts of the plantation. Wages initially were $5 or $6 a month plus provisions and a cabin; by 1867, they had risen to an average of $10 a month.

These changes eventually led to the rise of sharecropping. Under this arrangement African American families farmed separate plots of land and then at the end of the year divided the crop, normally on an equal basis, with the white

Sharecropping

landowner. Sharecropping had higher status and offered greater personal freedom than being a wage laborer. "I am not working for wages," one black farmer declared in defending his right to leave the plantation at will,

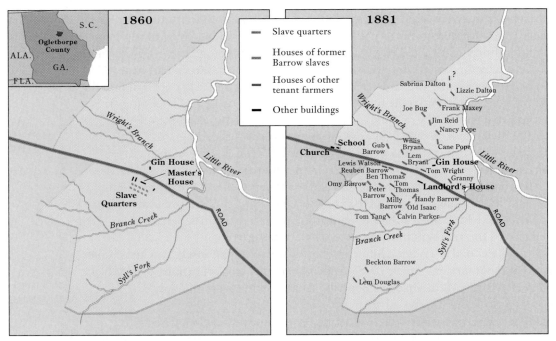

A GEORGIA PLANTATION AFTER THE WAR   After emancipation, sharecropping became the dominant form of agricultural labor in the South. Black families no longer lived in the old slave quarters but dispersed themselves to separate plots of land that they farmed themselves. At the end of the year each sharecropper turned over part of the crop to the white landowner.

"but am part owner of the crop and as [such,] I have all the rights that you or any other man has." Although black per capita agricultural income increased 40 percent in freedom, sharecropping was a harshly exploitative system in which black families often sank into perpetual debt.

The Freedmen's Bureau

The task of supervising the transition from slavery to freedom on southern plantations fell to the Freedmen's Bureau, a unique experiment in social policy supported by the federal government. Assigned the task of protecting freedpeople's economic rights, approximately 550 local agents regulated working conditions in southern agriculture after the war. The racial attitudes of Bureau agents varied widely, as did their commitment and competence. Then, too, they had to depend on the army to enforce their decisions.

Most agents required written contracts between white planters and black laborers, specifying not only wages but also the conditions of employment. Although agents sometimes intervened to protect freedpeople from unfair treatment, they also provided important help to planters. They insisted that black laborers not leave at harvest time, they arrested those who violated their contracts or refused to sign new ones at the beginning of the year, and they preached the gospel of hard work and the need to be orderly and respectful. Given such attitudes, freedpeople increasingly complained that Bureau agents were mere tools of the planter class. One observer reported, "Doing justice seems to mean seeing that the blacks don't break contracts and compelling them to submit cheerfully."

The primary means of enforcing working conditions were the Freedmen's Courts, which Congress created in 1866 in order to avoid the discrimination African Americans received in state courts. These new courts functioned as military tribunals, and often the agent was the entire court. The sympathy black laborers received varied from state to state. In 1867 one agent summarized the Bureau's experience with the labor contract system: "It has succeeded in making the freedman work and in rendering labor secure and stable—but it has failed to secure to the Freedman his just dues or compensation."

Opposed to any permanent welfare agency, Congress in 1869 decided to shut down the Bureau, and by 1872 it had gone out of business. Despite its mixed record, it was the most effective agency in protecting blacks' civil and political rights. Its disbanding signaled the beginning of the northern retreat from Reconstruction.

Planters and a New Way of Life

Planters and other white southerners faced emancipation with dread. "All the traditions and habits of both races had been suddenly overthrown," a Tennessee planter recalled, "and neither knew just what to do, or how to accommodate themselves to the new situation."

The old ideal of a paternalistic planter, which required a facade of black subservience and affection, gave way to an emphasis on strictly economic relationships. When two black laborers falsely accused her of trickery and hauled her into court, Mary Jones, a Georgia slaveholder before the war, told her assembled employees that she had previously "considered them friends and treated them as such but now they were only laborers under contract, and only the law would rule between us." Only with time did planters develop new norms to judge black behavior. What in 1865 had seemed insolence was viewed by the 1870s as the normal attitude of freedom.

Slavery had been a complex institution that welded black and white southerners together in intimate relationships. After the war, however, planters increasingly embraced the ideology of segregation. Since emancipation significantly reduced the social distance between the races, white southerners sought psychological separation and kept dealings with African Americans to a minimum. By the time Reconstruction ended, white planters had developed a new way of life based on the institutions of sharecropping and segregation and undergirded by a militant white supremacy.

Planters' new values

While most planters kept their land, they did not regain the economic prosperity of the prewar years. Cotton prices began a long decline, and southern per capita income suffered as a result. By 1880 the value of southern farms had slid 33 percent below the level of 1860.

THE ABANDONMENT OF RECONSTRUCTION

On Christmas Day 1875 a white acquaintance approached Charles Caldwell in Clinton, Mississippi, and invited him to have a drink. A former slave, Caldwell was a state senator and the leader of the Republican party in Hinds County. But the black leader's fearlessness made him a marked man. Only two months earlier, Caldwell had fled the county to escape an armed white mob. Despite threats against him, he had returned home to vote in the November state election. Now, as Caldwell and his "friend" raised their glasses in a holiday toast, a gunshot exploded through the window and Caldwell collapsed, mortally wounded. He was taken outside, where his assassins riddled his body with bullets. He died alone in the street.

Charles Caldwell shared the fate of a number of black Republican leaders in the South during Reconstruction. Resorting to violence and terror, southern whites challenged the commitment of the federal government to sustain Reconstruction. But following Johnson's acquittal, the Radical's influence waned, and the Republican party was increasingly drained of its crusading idealism. Ulysses S. Grant was hardly the cause of this change, but he certainly came to symbolize it.

The Election of Grant

In 1868 Republicans nominated Grant for president. Although he was elected, Republicans were shocked that despite his status as a great war hero, his popular margin was only 300,000 votes and that, with an estimated 450,000 black Republican votes cast in the South, a majority of whites had voted Democratic. The 1868 election helped convince Republican leaders that an amendment securing black suffrage throughout the nation was necessary.

In February 1869 Congress sent the Fifteenth Amendment to the states for ratification. It forbade any state from denying the right to vote on grounds of race, color, or previous condition of servitude. It did not forbid literacy and property requirements, as some Radicals wanted, because the moder- **Fifteenth Amendment ratified** ates feared that only a conservative version could be ratified. As a result, the final amendment left loopholes that eventually allowed southern states to disfranchise African Americans. Furthermore, advocates of women's suffrage like Lucy Stone and Susan B. Anthony were bitterly disappointed when Congress refused to prohibit voting discrimination on the basis of sex as well as race. The amendment was ratified in March 1870, aided by the votes of the four southern states that had not completed the process of Reconstruction and thus were also required to endorse this amendment before being readmitted to Congress.

The Grant Administration

Ulysses S. Grant was ill at ease with the political process: his simple, quiet manner, while superb for commanding armies, did not serve him as well in public life, and his well-known resolution withered when he was uncertain of his goal.

A series of scandals wracked Grant's presidency, so much so that "Grantism" soon became a code word in American politics for corruption, cronyism, and venality. Although Grant did not profit personally, he remained loyal to his friends and displayed little zeal to root out wrongdoing. James W. **Corruption under Grant** Grimes, one of the party's founders, denounced the Republican party under Grant as "the most corrupt and debauched political party that has ever existed."

Nor was Congress immune from the lowered tone of public life. In such a climate ruthless state machines, led by men who favored the status quo, came to dominate the party. Office and power became ends in themselves, and party leaders worked in close cooperation with northern industrial interests.

As corruption in both the North and the South worsened, reformers became more interested in cleaning up government than in protecting black rights. Congress in 1872 passed an amnesty act, removing the restrictions of the Fourteenth Amendment on officeholding, except for about 200 to 300 **Liberal Republican movement** ex-Confederate leaders. That same year liberal Republicans broke with the Republican party and nominated for president Horace Greeley, the editor of the New York *Tribune*. A one-time Radical, Greeley had become disillusioned with Reconstruction and urged a restoration of home rule in the South as well as adoption of civil service reform. Democrats decided to back the Liberal Republican ticket. The Republicans renominated Grant, who, despite the defection of a number of prominent Radicals, won an easy victory with 56 percent of the popular vote.

Grant swings from a trapeze while supporting a number of associates accused of corruption. While not personally involved in the scandals during his administration, Grant was reluctant to dismiss from office supporters accused of wrongdoing.

Growing Northern Disillusionment

During Grant's second term, Congress passed the Civil Rights Act of 1875, the last major piece of Reconstruction legislation. This law prohibited racial discrimination in public accommodations, transportation, places of amusement, and juries. At the same time, Congress rejected a ban on segregation in public schools, which was almost universally practiced in the North as well as the South. The federal government made little attempt to enforce the law, however, and in 1883 the Supreme Court struck down its provisions, except the one relating to juries.

Civil Rights Act of 1875

Despite passage of the Civil Rights Act, many northerners were growing disillusioned with Reconstruction. They were repelled by the corruption of the southern governments, they were tired of the violence and disorder that accompanied elections in the South, and they had little faith in black Americans. William Dodge, a wealthy New York capitalist and an influential Republican, wrote in 1875 that the South could never develop its resources "till confidence in her state governments can be restored, and this will never be done by federal bayonets." It had been a mistake, he went on, to make black southerners feel "that the United States government was their special friend, rather than those . . . among whom they must live and for whom they must work. We have tried this long enough," he concluded. "Now let the South alone."

As the agony of the war became more distant, the Panic of 1873, which precipitated a severe depression that lasted four years, diverted public attention from

Reconstruction to economic issues. Battered by the panic and the corruption issue, the Republicans lost a shocking 77 seats in Congress in the 1874 elections, and along with them control of the House of Representatives for the first time since 1861.

Depression and Democratic resurgence

"The truth is our people are tired out with the worn out cry of 'Southern outrages'!!" one Republican concluded. "Hard times and heavy taxes make them wish the 'ever lasting nigger' were in hell or Africa." In a bid to shore up their support in the North, Republicans took up the currency and tariff issues and clamored against tax support for parochial schools. With their gaze set northward, Republicans spoke more and more about cutting loose the unpopular southern governments.

The Triumph of White Supremacy

As northern commitment to Reconstruction waned, southern Democrats set out to overthrow the remaining Radical governments. Already white Republicans in the South felt heavy pressure to desert their party. In Mississippi one party member justified his decision to leave on the grounds that otherwise he would have "to live a life of social isolation" and his children would have no future.

To poor white southerners who lacked social standing, the Democratic appeal to racial solidarity offered great comfort. The large landowners and other wealthy groups that led southern Democrats objected less to black southerners voting, since they were confident that if outside influences were removed, they could control the black vote.

Racism

Democrats also resorted to economic pressure to undermine Republican power. In heavily black counties, newspapers published the names of black residents who cast Republican ballots and urged planters to discharge them. But terror and violence provided the most effective means to overthrow the radical regimes. A number of paramilitary organizations broke up Republican meetings, terrorized white and black Republicans, assassinated Republican leaders, and prevented black citizens from voting. The most notorious of these organizations was the Ku Klux Klan, which with similar groups functioned as an unofficial arm of the Democratic party.

Terror and violence

What became known as the Mississippi Plan was inaugurated in 1875, when Democrats decided to use as much violence as necessary to carry the state election. Local papers trumpeted, "Carry the election peaceably if we can, forcibly if we must." Recognizing that northern public opinion had grown sick of repeated federal intervention in southern elections, the Grant administration rejected the request of Republican Governor Adelbert Ames for troops to stop the violence. Bolstered by terrorism, the Democrats swept the election in Mississippi. Violence and intimidation prevented as many as 60,000 black and white Republicans from voting, converting the normal

Mississippi Plan

Two Ku Klux Klan members pose in full regalia. Violence played a major role in overthrowing the Radical governments in the South.

Republican majority into a Democratic majority of 30,000. Mississippi had been "redeemed."

The Disputed Election of 1876

With Republicans on the defensive across the nation, the 1876 presidential election was crucial to the final overthrow of Reconstruction. The Republicans nominated Ohio Governor Rutherford B. Hayes to oppose Samuel Tilden of New York. Once again, violence prevented an estimated quarter of a million Republican votes from being cast in the South. Tilden had a clear majority of 250,000 in the popular vote, but the outcome in the Electoral College was in doubt because both parties claimed South Carolina, Florida, and Louisiana, the only reconstructed states still in Republican hands.

To arbitrate the disputed returns, Congress established a 15-member electoral commission. By a straight party vote of 8 to 7, the commission awarded the disputed electoral votes—and the presidency—to Hayes.

When angry Democrats threatened a filibuster to prevent the electoral votes from being counted, key Republicans met with southern Democrats and reached an informal understanding, later known as the Compromise of 1877.

Compromise of 1877

Hayes's supporters agreed to withdraw federal troops from the South and not oppose the new Democratic state governments. For their part, southern Democrats dropped their opposition to Hayes's election and pledged to respect African Americans' rights.

Without federal support, the last Republican southern governments collapsed, and Democrats took control of the remaining states of the Confederacy. By 1877,

The Mississippi Plan in Action

Seeing that nothing but intimidation would enable them [the Democrats] to carry the election they resorted to it in every possible way, and the republicans at once found themselves in the midst of a perfect organized armed opposition that embraced the entire democratic party. . . . At Sulphur Springs they came very near precipitating a bloody riot by beating colored men over the heads with pistols. . . . The republicans . . . revoked the balance of their appointments running up to the election, and did not attempt to hold any more meetings in the Co[unty]. . . . On the night before the election armed bodies of men visited almost every neighborhood in the county, threatening death to all who voted the "radical" ticket. . . .

On the morning of the election in Aberdeen . . . the White-Liners took possession of the polls. . . . The colored men who had gathered . . . to vote were told if they did not leave the town within five minutes that the last man would be shot dead in his tracks, and that not a man could vote that day unless he voted the democratic ticket. . . . The cannon was placed in position bearing on the large crowd, . . . when the whole crowd broke & run in confusion, then the infanty & cavalry had no trouble in driving everything from town; and there are over 1,300 men in this county . . . who will swear that they were driven from the polls & could not vote.

Source: James W. Lee to Adelbert Ames, Aberdeen, Miss., February 7, 1876, 44th Cong. 1st Sess., Senate Report 527, v. 2, pp. 67–68.

the entire South was in the hands of the Redeemers, as they called themselves. Reconstruction and Republican rule had come to an end.

Racism and the Failure of Reconstruction

Reconstruction failed for a multitude of reasons. The reforming impulse that had created the Republican party in the 1850s had been battered and worn down by the war. The new materialism of industrial America inspired a jaded cynicism in many Americans. In the South, African American voters and leaders inevitably lacked a certain amount of education and experience; elsewhere, Republicans were divided over policies and options.

Yet beyond these obstacles, the sad fact remains that the ideals of Reconstruction were most clearly defeated by a deep-seated racism that permeated American life. Racism stimulated white southern resistance, undercut northern support for black rights, and eventually made northerners willing to write off Reconstruction, and with it the welfare of African Americans. While Congress might pass a constitutional amendment abolishing slavery, it could not overturn at a stroke the social habits of two centuries.

Certainly the political equations of power, in the long term, had been changed. The North had secured the power to dominate the economic and political destiny of the nation. With the overthrow of Reconstruction, the white South had won back some of the power it had lost in 1865—but not all. Even with white supremacy triumphant, African Americans did not return to the social position they had occupied before the war. They were no longer slaves, and black southerners who walked dusty roads in search of family members, sent their children to school, or worshiped in churches they controlled knew what a momentous change this was. Even under the exploitative sharecropping system, black income rose significantly in freedom. Then, too, the guarantees of "equal protection" and "due process of law" had been written into the Constitution and would be available for later generations to use in championing once again the Radicals' goal of racial equality.

But this was a struggle left to future reformers. For the time being, the clear trend was away from change or hope—especially for former slaves like Benjamin Montgomery and his sons, the owners of the old Davis plantations in Mississippi. In the 1870s bad crops, lower cotton prices, and falling land values undermined the Montgomerys' financial position, and in 1875 Jefferson Davis sued to have the sale of Brierfield invalidated.

An end to the Davis Bend experiment

A lower court ruled against Davis, since he had never received legal title to the plantation. Davis appealed to the state supreme court, which, following the overthrow of Mississippi's Radical government, had a white conservative majority. In a politically motivated decision, the court awarded Brierfield to Davis in 1878, and the Montgomerys lost Hurricane as well. The final outcome was not without bitter irony. In applying for restoration of his property after the war, Joseph Davis had convinced skeptical federal officials that he—and not his younger brother—held legal title to Brierfield. Had they decided instead that the plantation belonged to Jefferson Davis, it would have been confiscated.

But the waning days of Reconstruction were times filled with such ironies: of governments "redeemed" by violence, of Fourteenth Amendment rights designed to protect black people being used by conservative courts to protect giant corporations, of reformers taking up other causes. Disowned by its northern supporters and unmourned by public opinion, Reconstruction was over.

chapter summary

Presidents Abraham Lincoln and Andrew Johnson and the Republican-dominated Congress each developed a program of Reconstruction to quickly restore the Confederate states to the Union.

- Lincoln's 10 percent plan required that 10 percent of qualified voters from 1860 swear an oath of loyalty to begin organizing a state government.

- Following Lincoln's assassination, Andrew Johnson changed Lincoln's terms and lessened Reconstruction's requirements.

- The more radical Congress repudiated Johnson's state governments and eventually enacted its own program of Reconstruction, which included the principle of black suffrage.
  - Congress passed the Fourteenth and Fifteen Amendments and also extended the life of the Freedmen's Bureau, a unique experiment in social welfare.
  - Congress rejected land reform, however, which would have provided the freedpeople with a greater economic stake.
  - The effort to remove Johnson from office through impeachment failed.

- The Radical governments in the South, led by black and white southerners and transplanted northerners, compiled a mixed record on matters such as racial equality, education, economic issues, and corruption.

- Reconstruction was a time of both joy and frustration for former slaves.
  - Former slaves took steps to reunite their families and establish black-controlled churches.
  - They evidenced a widespread desire for land and education.
  - Black resistance to the old system of labor led to the adoption of sharecropping.
  - The Freedmen's Bureau fostered these new working arrangements and also the beginnings of black education in the South.

- Northern public opinion became disillusioned with Reconstruction during the presidency of Ulysses S. Grant.

- Southern whites used violence, economic coercion, and racism to overthrow the Republican state governments.

- In 1877 Republican leaders agreed to end Reconstruction in exchange for Rutherford B. Hayes's election as president.

- Racism played a key role in the eventual failure of Reconstruction.

 For quizzes and a variety of interactive resources, visit the book's Online Learning Center at www.mhhe.com/davidsonconcise3

SIGNIFICANT EVENTS

1863	Lincoln outlines Reconstruction program
1864	Lincoln vetoes Wade-Davis bill; Louisiana, Arkansas, and Tennessee establish governments under Lincoln's plan
1865	Freedmen's Bureau established; Johnson becomes president; presidential Reconstruction completed; Congress excludes representatives of Johnson's governments; Thirteenth Amendment ratified; Joint Committee on Reconstruction established
1865–1866	Black codes enacted
1866	Civil Rights bill passed over Johnson's veto; Memphis and New Orleans riots; Fourteenth Amendment passes Congress; Freedmen's Bureau extended; Ku Klux Klan organized; Tennessee readmitted to Congress; Republicans win decisive victory in congressional elections
1867	Congressional Reconstruction enacted; Tenure of Office Act passed
1867–1868	Constitutional conventions in the South; blacks vote in southern elections
1868	Johnson impeached but acquitted; Fourteenth Amendment ratified; Grant elected president
1869	Fifteenth Amendment passes Congress
1870	Last southern states readmitted to Congress; Fifteenth Amendment ratified
1872	General Amnesty Act; Freedmen's Bureau closes down; Liberal Republican revolt
1873–1877	Panic and depression
1874	Democrats win control of the House
1875	Civil Rights Act; Mississippi Plan
1876	Disputed Hayes-Tilden election
1877	Compromise of 1877; Hayes declared winner of electoral vote; last Republican governments in the South fall

APPENDIX

THE DECLARATION OF INDEPENDENCE

In Congress, July 4, 1776,

THE UNANIMOUS DECLARATION OF THE
THIRTEEN UNITED STATES OF AMERICA

When, in the course of human events, it becomes necessary for one people to dissolve the political bands which have connected them with another, and to assume, among the powers of the earth, the separate and equal station to which the laws of nature and of nature's God entitle them, a decent respect to the opinions of mankind requires that they should declare the causes which impel them to the separation.

We hold these truths to be self-evident, that all men are created equal; that they are endowed by their Creator with certain unalienable rights; that among these, are life, liberty, and the pursuit of happiness. That, to secure these rights, governments are instituted among men, deriving their just powers from the consent of the governed; that, whenever any form of government becomes destructive of these ends, it is the right of the people to alter or to abolish it, and to institute a new government, laying its foundation on such principles, and organizing its powers in such form, as to them shall seem most likely to effect their safety and happiness. Prudence, indeed, will dictate that governments long established, should not be changed for light and transient causes; and, accordingly, all experience hath shown, that mankind are more disposed to suffer, while evils are sufferable, than to right themselves by abolishing the forms to which they are accustomed. But, when a long train of abuses and usurpations, pursuing invariably the same object, evinces a design to reduce them under absolute despotism, it is their right, it is their duty, to throw off such government and to provide new guards for their future security. Such has been the patient sufferance of these colonies, and such is now the necessity which constrains them to alter their former systems of government. The history of the present King of Great Britain is a history of repeated injuries and usurpations, all having, in direct object, the establishment of an absolute tyranny over these States. To prove this, let facts be submitted to a candid world:

He has refused his assent to laws the most wholesome and necessary for the public good.

He has forbidden his governors to pass laws of immediate and pressing importance, unless suspended in their operation till his assent should be obtained; and, when so suspended, he has utterly neglected to attend to them.

He has refused to pass other laws for the accommodation of large districts of people, unless those people would relinquish the right of representation in the legislature; a right inestimable to them, and formidable to tyrants only.

He has called together legislative bodies at places unusual, uncomfortable, and distant from the depository of their public records, for the sole purpose of fatiguing them into compliance with his measures.

He has dissolved representative houses repeatedly for opposing, with manly firmness, his invasions on the rights of the people.

He has refused, for a long time after such dissolutions, to cause others to be elected; whereby the legislative powers, incapable of annihilation, have returned to the people at large for their exercise; the state remaining, in the meantime, exposed to all the danger of invasion from without, and convulsions within.

He has endeavored to prevent the population of these States; for that purpose, obstructing the laws for naturalization of foreigners, refusing to pass others to encourage their migration hither, and raising the conditions of new appropriations of lands.

He has obstructed the administration of justice, by refusing his assent to laws for establishing judiciary powers.

He has made judges dependent on his will alone, for the tenure of their offices, and the amount and payment of their salaries.

He has erected a multitude of new offices, and sent hither swarms of officers to harass our people, and eat out their substance.

He has kept among us, in time of peace, standing armies, without the consent of our legislatures.

He has affected to render the military independent of, and superior to, the civil power.

He has combined, with others, to subject us to a jurisdiction foreign to our Constitution, and unacknowledged by our laws; giving his assent to their acts of pretended legislation:

For quartering large bodies of armed troops among us:

For protecting them by a mock trial, from punishment, for any murders which they should commit on the inhabitants of these States:

For cutting off our trade with all parts of the world:

For imposing taxes on us without our consent:

For depriving us, in many cases, of the benefit of trial by jury:

For transporting us beyond seas to be tried for pretended offences:

For abolishing the free system of English laws in a neighboring province, establishing therein an arbitrary government, and enlarging its boundaries, so as to render it at once an example and fit instrument for introducing the same absolute rule into these colonies:

For taking away our charters, abolishing our most valuable laws, and altering, fundamentally, the powers of our governments:

For suspending our own legislatures, and declaring themselves invested with power to legislate for us in all cases whatsoever:

He has abdicated government here, by declaring us out of his protection, and waging war against us.

He has plundered our seas, ravaged our coasts, burnt our towns, and destroyed the lives of our people.

He is, at this time, transporting large armies of foreign mercenaries to complete the works of death, desolation, and tyranny, already begun, with circumstances of cruelty and perfidy scarcely paralleled in the most barbarous ages, and totally unworthy the head of a civilized nation.

He has constrained our fellow citizens, taken captive on the high seas, to bear arms against their country, to become the executioners of their friends, and brethren, or to fall themselves by their hands.

He has excited domestic insurrections amongst us, and has endeavored to bring on the inhabitants of our frontiers, the merciless Indian savages, whose known rule of warfare is an undistinguished destruction of all ages, sexes, and conditions.

In every stage of these oppressions, we have petitioned for redress, in the most humble terms; our repeated petitions have been answered only by repeated injury. A prince, whose character is thus marked by every act which may define a tyrant, is unfit to be the ruler of a free people.

Nor have we been wanting in attention to our British brethren. We have warned them from time to time, of attempts made by their legislature to extend an unwarrantable jurisdiction over us. We have reminded them of the circumstances of our emigration and settlement here. We have appealed to their native justice and magnanimity, and we have conjured them, by the ties of our common kindred, to disavow these usurpations, which would inevitably interrupt our connections and correspondence. They, too, have been deaf to the voice of justice and consanguinity. We must, therefore, acquiesce in the necessity which denounces our separation, and hold them as we hold the rest of mankind, enemies in war, in peace, friends.

We, therefore, the representatives of the United States of America, in general Congress assembled, appealing to the Supreme Judge of the world for the rectitude of our intentions, do, in the name, and by the authority of the good people of these colonies, solemnly publish and declare, that these united colonies are, and of right ought to be, free and independent states: that they are absolved from all allegiance to the British Crown, and that all political connection between them and the state of Great Britain is and ought to be, totally dissolved; and that, as free and independent states, they have full power to levy war, conclude peace, contract alliances, establish commerce, and to do all other acts and things which independent states may of right do. And, for the support of this declaration, with a firm reliance on the protection of Divine Providence, we mutually pledge to each other our lives, our fortunes, and our sacred honor.

The foregoing Declaration was, by order of Congress, engrossed, and signed by the following members:

JOHN HANCOCK

New Hampshire	New York	Delaware	North Carolina
Josiah Bartlett	William Floyd	Caesar Rodney	William Hooper
William Whipple	Philip Livingston	George Reed	Joseph Hewes
Matthew Thornton	Francis Lewis	Thomas M'Kean	John Penn
	Lewis Morris		

Massachusetts Bay	New Jersey	Maryland	South Carolina
Samuel Adams	Richard Stockton	Samuel Chase	Edward Rutledge
John Adams	John Witherspoon	William Paca	Thomas Heyward, Jr.
Robert Treat Paine	Francis Hopkinson	Thomas Stone	Thomas Lynch, Jr.
Elbridge Gerry	John Hart	Charles Carroll,	Arthur Middleton
	Abraham Clark	of Carrollton	

Rhode Island	Pennsylvania	Virginia	Georgia
Stephen Hopkins	Robert Morris	George Wythe	Button Gwinnett
William Ellery	Benjamin Rush	Richard Henry Lee	Lyman Hall
	Benjamin Franklin	Thomas Jefferson	George Walton
Connecticut	John Morton	Benjamin Harrison	
Roger Sherman	George Clymer	Thomas Nelson, Jr.	
Samuel Huntington	James Smith	Francis Lightfoot Lee	
William Williams	George Taylor	Carter Braxton	
Oliver Wolcott	James Wilson		
	George Ross		

Resolved, That copies of the Declaration be sent to the several assemblies, conventions, and committees, or councils of safety, and to the several commanding officers of the continental troops; that it be proclaimed in each of the United States, at the head of the army.

THE CONSTITUTION OF THE UNITED STATES OF AMERICA[1]

We the People of the United States, in Order to form a more perfect Union, establish Justice, insure domestic Tranquility, provide for the common defence, promote the general Welfare, and secure the Blessings of Liberty to ourselves and our Posterity, do ordain and establish this CONSTITUTION for the United States of America.

ARTICLE I

Section 1.   All legislative Powers herein granted shall be vested in a Congress of the United States, which shall consist of a Senate and House of Representatives.

Section 2.   The House of Representatives shall be composed of Members chosen every second Year by the People of the several States, and the Electors in each State shall have the Qualifications requisite for Electors of the most numerous Branch of the State Legislature.

No Person shall be a Representative who shall not have attained to the Age of twenty-five Years, and been seven Years a Citizen of the United States, and who shall not, when elected, be an Inhabitant of that State in which he shall be chosen.

[Representatives and direct Taxes[2] shall be apportioned among the several States which may be included within this Union, according to their respective Numbers, which shall be determined by adding to the whole Number of free Persons, including those bound to Service for a Term of Years, and excluding Indians not taxed, three fifths of all other Persons.][3] The actual Enumeration shall be made within three Years after the first Meeting of the Congress of the United States, and within every subsequent Term of ten Years, in such Manner as they shall by Law direct. The Number of Representatives shall not exceed one for every thirty Thousand, but each State shall have at Least one Representative; and until such enumeration shall be made, the State of New Hampshire shall be entitled to chuse three, Massachusetts eight, Rhode-Island and Providence Plantations one, Connecticut five, New York six, New Jersey four, Pennsylvania eight, Delaware one, Maryland six, Virginia ten, North Carolina five, South Carolina five, and Georgia three.

When vacancies happen in the Representation from any State, the Executive Authority thereof shall issue Writs of Election to fill such Vacancies.

The House of Representatives shall chuse their Speaker and other Officers; and shall have the sole Power of Impeachment.

Section 3.   The Senate of the United States shall be composed of two Senators from each State, chosen by the Legislature thereof, for six Years; and each Senator shall have one Vote.

Immediately after they shall be assembled in Consequence of the first Election, they shall be divided as equally as may be into three Classes. The Seats of the Senators of the first Class shall be vacated at the Expiration of the second Year, of the second Class at the Expiration of the fourth Year, and of the third Class at the Expiration of the sixth Year, so that one-third may be chosen every second Year; and if Vacancies happen by Resignation, or otherwise, during the

---

[1]This version follows the original Constitution in capitalization and spelling. It is adapted from the text published by the United States Department of the Interior, Office of Education.

[2]Altered by the Sixteenth Amendment.

[3]Negated by the Fourteenth Amendment.

Recess of the Legislature of any State, the Executive thereof may make temporary Appointments until the next Meeting of the Legislature, which shall then fill such Vacancies.

No Person shall be a Senator who shall not have attained to the Age of thirty Years, and been nine Years a Citizen of the United States, and who shall not, when elected, be an Inhabitant of that State for which he shall be chosen.

The Vice President of the United States shall be President of the Senate, but shall have no vote, unless they be equally divided.

The Senate shall chuse their other Officers and also a President pro tempore, in the absence of the Vice President, or when he shall exercise the Office of President of the United States.

The Senate shall have the sole Power to try all Impeachments. When sitting for that purpose they shall be on Oath or Affirmation. When the President of the United States is tried, the Chief Justice shall preside: And no person shall be convicted without the Concurrence of two thirds of the Members present.

Judgment in Cases of Impeachment shall not extend further than to removal from Office, and disqualification to hold and enjoy any Office of honor, Trust, or Profit under the United States: but the Party convicted shall nevertheless be liable and subject to Indictment, Trial, Judgment, and Punishment, according to Law:

Section 4. The Times, Places and Manner of holding Elections for Senators and Representatives, shall be prescribed in each State by the Legislature thereof; but the Congress may at any time by Law make or alter such Regulations, except as to the Places of Chusing Senators.

The Congress shall assemble at least once in every Year, and such Meeting shall be on the first Monday in December, unless they shall by Law appoint a different Day.

Section 5. Each House shall be the Judge of the Elections, Returns and Qualifications of its own Members, and a Majority of each shall constitute a Quorum to do Business; but a smaller number may adjourn from day to day, and may be authorized to compel the Attendance of absent Members, in such Manner, and under such Penalties, as each House may provide.

Each House may determine the Rules of its Proceedings, punish its Members for disorderly Behaviour, and, with the Concurrence of two thirds, expel a Member.

Each House shall keep a Journal of its Proceedings, and from time to time publish the same, excepting such Parts as may in their Judgment require Secrecy; and the Yeas and Nays of the Members of either House on any question shall, at the Desire of one fifth of those Present, be entered on the Journal.

Neither House, during the Session of Congress, shall, without the Consent of the other, adjourn for more than three days, nor to any other Place than that in which the two Houses shall be sitting.

Section 6. The Senators and Representatives shall receive a Compensation for their Services, to be ascertained by Law, and paid out of the Treasury of the United States. They shall in all Cases, except Treason, Felony, and Breach of the Peace, be privileged from Arrest during their Attendance at the Session of their respective Houses, and in going to and returning from the same; and for any Speech or Debate in either House, they shall not be questioned in any other Place.

No Senator or Representative shall, during the Time for which he was elected, be appointed to any civil Office under the Authority of the United States, which shall have been created, or the Emoluments whereof shall have been increased, during such time; and no Person holding any Office under the United States shall be a Member of either House during his continuance in Office.

Section 7. All Bills for raising Revenue shall originate in the House of Representatives; but the Senate may propose or concur with Amendments as on other bills.

Every Bill which shall have passed the House of Representatives and the Senate, shall, before it become a Law, be presented to the President of the United States; If he approve he shall sign it, but if not he shall return it, with his Objections, to that House in which it shall have originated, who shall enter the Objections at large on their Journal, and proceed to reconsider it. If after such Reconsideration two thirds of that House shall agree to pass the bill, it shall be sent, together with the objections, to the other House, by which it shall likewise be reconsidered, and if approved by two thirds of that House, it shall become a Law. But in all such Cases the Votes of both Houses shall be determined by Yeas and Nays, and the Names of the Persons voting for and against the Bill shall be entered on the Journal of each House respectively. If any Bill shall not be returned by the President within ten Days (Sundays excepted) after it shall have been presented to him, the Same shall be a Law, in like Manner as if he had signed it, unless the Congress by their Adjournment prevent its Return, in which Case it shall not be a Law.

Every Order, Resolution, or Vote to which the Concurrence of the Senate and House of Representatives may be necessary (except on a question of Adjournment) shall be presented to the President of the United States; and before the Same shall take Effect, shall be approved by him, or being disapproved by him, shall be repassed by two thirds of the Senate and House of Representatives, according to the Rules and Limitations prescribed in the Case of a Bill.

Section 8. The Congress shall have Power To lay and collect Taxes, Duties, Imposts and Excises, to pay the Debts and provide for the common Defence and general Welfare of the United States; but all Duties, Imposts and Excises shall be uniform throughout the United States;

To borrow money on the credit of the United States;

To regulate Commerce with foreign Nations, and among the several States, and with the Indian Tribes;

To establish an uniform rule of Naturalization, and uniform Laws on the subject of Bankruptcies throughout the United States;

To coin Money, regulate the Value thereof, and of foreign Coin, and fix the Standard of Weights and Measures;

To provide for the Punishment of counterfeiting the Securities and current Coin of the United States;

To establish Post Offices and post Roads;

To promote the Progress of Science and useful Arts, by securing for limited Times to Authors and Inventors the exclusive Right to their respective Writings and Discoveries;

To constitute Tribunals inferior to the Supreme Court;

To define and punish Piracies and Felonies committed on the high Seas, and Offenses against the Law of Nations;

To declare War, grant Letters of Marque and Reprisal, and make Rules concerning Captures on Land and Water;

To raise and support Armies, but no Appropriation of Money to that Use shall be for a longer Term than two Years;

To provide and maintain a Navy;

To make Rules for the Government and Regulation of the land and naval forces;

To provide for calling forth the Militia to execute the Laws of the Union, suppress Insurrections and repel Invasions;

To provide for organizing, arming, and disciplining the Militia, and for governing such Part of them as may be employed in the Service of the United States, reserving to the States respectively, the Appointment of the Officers, and the Authority of training the Militia according to the discipline prescribed by Congress;

To exercise exclusive Legislation in all Cases whatsoever, over such District (not exceeding ten Miles square) as may, by Cession of particular States, and the acceptance of Congress, become the Seat of the Government of the United States, and to exercise like Authority over all Places purchased by the Consent of the Legislature of the State in which the Same shall be, for the Erection of Forts, Magazines, Arsenals, Dock-yards, and other needful Buildings;—And

To make all Laws which shall be necessary and proper for carrying into Execution the foregoing Powers, and all other Powers vested by this Constitution in the Government of the United States, or in any Department or Officer thereof.

Section 9. The Migration or Importation of such Persons as any of the States now existing shall think proper to admit, shall not be prohibited by the Congress prior to the Year one thousand eight hundred and eight, but a tax or duty may be imposed on such Importation, not exceeding ten dollars for each Person.

The privilege of the Writ of Habeas Corpus shall not be suspended, unless when in Cases of Rebellion or Invasion the public Safety may require it.

No bill of Attainder or ex post facto Law shall be passed.

No capitation, or other direct, Tax shall be laid unless in Proportion to the Census or Enumeration herein before directed to be taken.

No Tax or Duty shall be laid on Articles exported from any State.

No Preference shall be given by any Regulation of Commerce or Revenue to the Ports of one State over those of another: nor shall Vessels bound to, or from, one State, be obliged to enter, clear, or pay Duties in another.

No Money shall be drawn from the Treasury, but in Consequence of Appropriations made by Law; and a regular Statement and Account of the Receipts and Expenditures of all public Money shall be published from time to time.

No Title of Nobility shall be granted by the United States: And no Person holding any Office of Profit or Trust under them, shall, without the Consent of the Congress, accept of any present, Emolument, Office, or Title, of any kind whatever, from any King, Prince, or foreign State.

Section 10. No State shall enter into any Treaty, Alliance, or Confederation; grant Letters of Marque and Reprisal; coin Money; emit Bills of Credit; make any Thing but gold and silver Coin a Tender in Payment of Debts; pass any Bill of Attainder, ex post facto Law, or Law impairing the Obligation of Contracts, or grant any Title of Nobility.

No State shall, without the Consent of the Congress, lay any Imposts or Duties on Imports or Exports, except what may be absolutely necessary for executing its inspection Laws; and the net Produce of all Duties and Imposts, laid by any State on Imports or Exports, shall be for the use of the Treasury of the United States; and all such Laws shall be subject to the Revision and Control of the Congress.

No state shall, without the Consent of Congress, lay any duty of Tonnage, keep Troops, or Ships of War in time of Peace, enter into any Agreement or Compact with another State, or with a foreign Power, or engage in War, unless actually invaded, or in such imminent Danger as will not admit of delay.

ARTICLE II

Section 1. The executive Power shall be vested in a President of the United States of America. He shall hold his Office during the Term of four years, and, together with the Vice President, chosen for the same Term, be elected, as follows:

Each State shall appoint, in such Manner as the Legislature thereof may direct, a Number of Electors, equal to the whole Number of Senators and Representatives to which the State may be entitled in the Congress: but no Senator or Representative, or Person holding an Office of Trust or Profit under the United States, shall be appointed an Elector.

[The Electors shall meet in their respective States, and vote by Ballot for two persons, of whom one at least shall not be an Inhabitant of the same State with themselves. And they shall make a List of all the Persons voted for, and of the Number of Votes for each; which List they shall sign and certify, and transmit sealed to the Seat of the Government of the United States, directed to the President of the Senate. The President of the Senate shall, in the Presence of the Senate and House of Representatives, open all the Certificates, and the Votes shall then be counted. The Person having the greatest Number of Votes shall be the President, if such Number be a Majority of the whole Number of Electors appointed; and if there be more than one who have such Majority, and have an equal Number of Votes, then the House of Representatives shall immediately chuse by Ballot one of them for President; and if no Person have a Majority, then from the five highest on the List the said House shall in like Manner chuse the President. But in chusing the President, the Votes shall be taken by States, the Representation from each State having one Vote; a quorum for this Purpose shall consist of a Member or Members from two-thirds of the States, and a Majority of all the States shall be necessary to a Choice. In every Case, after the Choice of the President, the Person having the greatest Number of Votes of the Electors shall be the Vice President. But if there should remain two or more who have equal votes, the Senate shall chuse from them by Ballot the Vice President.][4]

The Congress may determine the Time of chusing the Electors, and the Day on which they shall give their Votes; which Day shall be the same throughout the United States.

No person except a natural-born Citizen, or a Citizen of the United States, at the time of the Adoption of this Constitution, shall be eligible to the Office of President; neither shall any Person be eligible to that Office who shall not have attained to the Age of thirty-five years, and been fourteen Years a Resident within the United States.

In Case of the Removal of the President from Office, or of his Death, Resignation, or Inability to discharge the Powers and Duties of the said Office, the same shall devolve on the Vice President, and the Congress may by Law provide for the Case of Removal, Death, Resignation, or Inability, both of the President and Vice President, declaring what Officer shall then act as President, and such Officer shall act accordingly, until the disability be removed, or a President shall be elected.

The President shall, at stated Times, receive for his Services a Compensation, which shall neither be increased nor diminished during the Period for which he shall have been elected, and he shall not receive within that Period any other Emolument from the United States, or any of them.

Before he enter on the execution of his Office, he shall take the following Oath or Affirmation:—"I do solemnly swear (or affirm) that I will faithfully execute the Office of President of the United States, and will, to the best of my Ability, preserve, protect, and defend the Constitution of the United States."

Section 2.   The President shall be Commander in Chief of the Army and Navy of the United States, and of the Militia of the several States, when called into the actual Service of the United States; he may require the Opinion, in writing, of the principal Officer in each of the executive Departments, upon any subject relating to the Duties of their respective Offices, and he shall have Power to Grant Reprieves and Pardons for Offenses against the United States, except in Cases of Impeachment.

---

[4]Revised by the Twelfth Amendment.

He shall have Power, by and with the Advice and Consent of the Senate, to make Treaties, provided two-thirds of the Senators present concur; and he shall nominate, and by and with the Advice and Consent of the Senate, shall appoint Ambassadors, other public Ministers and Consuls, Judges of the Supreme Court, and all other Officers of the United States, whose Appointments are not herein otherwise provided for, and which shall be established by Law: but the Congress may by Law vest the Appointment of such inferior Officers, as they think proper, in the President alone, in the Courts of Law, or in the Heads of Departments.

The President shall have Power to fill up all Vacancies that may happen during the Recess of the Senate, by granting Commissions which shall expire at the End of their next Session.

Section 3. He shall from time to time give to the Congress Information of the State of the Union, and recommend to their Consideration such Measures as he shall judge necessary and expedient; he may, on extraordinary occasions, convene both Houses, or either of them, and in Case of Disagreement between them, with respect to the Time of Adjournment, he may adjourn them to such Time as he shall think proper; he shall receive Ambassadors and other public Ministers; he shall take care that the Laws be faithfully executed, and shall Commission all the Officers of the United States.

Section 4. The President, Vice President and all civil Officers of the United States, shall be removed from Office on Impeachment for, and Conviction of, Treason, Bribery, or other high Crimes and Misdemeanors.

ARTICLE III

Section 1. The judicial Power of the United States, shall be vested in one supreme Court, and in such inferior Courts as the Congress may from time to time ordain and establish. The Judges, both of the supreme and inferior Courts, shall hold their Offices during good Behaviour, and shall, at stated Times, receive for their Services, a Compensation, which shall not be diminished during their Continuance in Office.

Section 2. The judicial Power shall extend to all Cases, in Law and Equity, arising under this Constitution, the Laws of the United States, and Treaties made, or which shall be made, under their Authority;—to all Cases affecting ambassadors, other public ministers and consuls;—to all cases of admiralty and maritime Jurisdiction;—to Controversies to which the United States shall be a Party;—to Controversies between two or more States;—between a State and Citizens of another State;[5]—between Citizens of different States—between Citizens of the same State claiming Lands under Grants of different States, and between a State, or the Citizens thereof, and foreign States, Citizens, or Subjects.

In all Cases affecting Ambassadors, other public Ministers and Consuls, and those in which a State shall be Party, the supreme Court shall have original Jurisdiction. In all the other Cases before mentioned, the supreme Court shall have appellate Jurisdiction, both as to Law and Fact, with such Exceptions, and under such Regulations as the Congress shall make.

The trial of all Crimes, except in Cases of Impeachment, shall be by Jury; and such Trial shall be held in the State where the said Crimes shall have been committed; but when not committed within any State, the Trial shall be at such Place or Places as the Congress may by Law have directed.

---

[5]Qualified by the Eleventh Amendment.

Section 3. Treason against the United States, shall consist only in levying War against them, or in adhering to their Enemies, giving them Aid and Comfort. No Person shall be convicted of Treason unless on the Testimony of two Witnesses to the same overt Act, or on Confession in open Court.

The Congress shall have power to declare the Punishment of Treason, but no Attainder of Treason shall work Corruption of Blood, or Forfeiture except during the Life of the Person attainted.

ARTICLE IV

Section 1. Full Faith and Credit shall be given in each State to the public Acts, Records, and judicial Proceedings of every other State. And the Congress may by general Laws prescribe the Manner in which such Acts, Records and Proceedings shall be proved, and the Effect thereof.

Section 2. The Citizens of each State shall be entitled to all Privileges and Immunities of Citizens in the several States.

A Person charged in any State with Treason, Felony, or other Crime, who shall flee from Justice, and be found in another State, shall on demand of the executive Authority of the State from which he fled, be delivered up, to be removed to the State having Jurisdiction of the crime.

No Person held to Service or Labour in one State, under the Laws thereof, escaping into another, shall, in Consequence of any Law or Regulation therein, be discharged from such Service or Labour, but shall be delivered up on Claim of the Party to whom such Service or Labour may be due.

Section 3. New States may be admitted by the Congress into this Union; but no new State shall be formed or erected within the Jurisdiction of any other State; nor any State be formed by the Junction of two or more States, or parts of States, without the Consent of the Legislatures of the States concerned as well as of the Congress.

The Congress shall have Power to dispose of and make all needful Rules and Regulations respecting the Territory or other Property belonging to the United States; and nothing in this Constitution shall be so construed as to Prejudice any Claims of the United States, or of any particular State.

Section 4. The United States shall guarantee to every State in this Union a Republican Form of Government, and shall protect each of them against Invasion; and on Application of the Legislature, or of the Executive (when the Legislature cannot be convened) against domestic Violence.

ARTICLE V

The Congress, whenever two-thirds of both Houses shall deem it necessary, shall propose Amendments to this Constitution, or, on the Application of the Legislatures of two-thirds of the several States, shall call a Convention for proposing Amendments, which, in either Case, shall be valid to all Intents and Purposes, as part of this Constitution, when ratified by the Legislatures of three-fourths of the several States, or by Conventions in three-fourths thereof, as the one or the other Mode of Ratification may be proposed by the Congress; Provided that no Amendment which may be made prior to the Year One thousand eight hundred and eight shall in any Manner affect the first and fourth Clauses in the Ninth Section of the first Article; and that no State, without its Consent, shall be deprived of its equal Suffrage in the Senate.

ARTICLE VI

All Debts contracted and Engagements entered into, before the Adoption of this Constitution, shall be as valid against the United States under this Constitution, as under the Confederation.

This Constitution, and the Laws of the United States which shall be made in Pursuance thereof; and all Treaties made, or which shall be made, under the Authority of the United States, shall be the supreme Law of the Land; and the Judges in every State shall be bound thereby, any Thing in the Constitution or Laws of any State to the Contrary notwithstanding.

The Senators and Representatives before mentioned, and the Members of the several State Legislatures, and all executive and judicial Officers, both of the United States and of the several States, shall be bound by Oath or Affirmation to support this Constitution; but no religious Tests shall ever be required as a qualification to any Office or public Trust under the United States.

ARTICLE VII

The Ratification of the Conventions of nine States shall be sufficient for the Establishment of this Constitution between the States so ratifying the same.

Done in Convention by the Unanimous Consent of the States present the Seventeenth Day of September in the Year of our Lord one thousand seven hundred and Eighty seven, and of the Independence of the United States of America the Twelfth. In Witness whereof We have hereunto subscribed our Names.[6]

GEORGE WASHINGTON

PRESIDENT AND DEPUTY FROM VIRGINIA

New Hampshire
John Langdon
Nicholas Gilman

Massachusetts
Nathaniel Gorham
Rufus King

Connecticut
William Samuel
    Johnson
Roger Sherman

New York
Alexander Hamilton

New Jersey
William Livingston
David Brearley
William Paterson
Jonathan Dayton

Pennsylvania
Benjamin Franklin
Thomas Mifflin
Robert Morris
George Clymer
Thomas FitzSimons
Jared Ingersoll
James Wilson
Gouverneur Morris

Delaware
George Read
Gunning Bedford, Jr.
John Dickinson
Richard Bassett
Jacob Broom

Maryland
James McHenry
Daniel of
    St. Thomas Jenifer
Daniel Carroll

Virginia
John Blair
James Madison, Jr.

North Carolina
William Blount
Richard Dobbs
    Spaight
Hugh Williamson

South Carolina
John Rutledge
Charles Cotesworth
    Pinckney
Charles Pinckney
Pierce Butler

Georgia
William Few
Abraham Baldwin

---

[6]These are the full names of the signers, which in some cases are not the signatures on the document.

Articles in Addition to, and Amendment of, the Constitution of the United States of America, Proposed by Congress, and Ratified by the Legislatures of the Several States, Pursuant to the Fifth Article of the Original Constitution[7]

[AMENDMENT I]

Congress shall make no law respecting an establishment of religion, or prohibiting the free exercise thereof; or abridging the freedom of speech, or of the press; or the right of the people peaceably to assemble, and to petition the Government for a redress of grievances.

[AMENDMENT II]

A well regulated Militia, being necessary to the security of a free State, the right of the people to keep and bear Arms shall not be infringed.

[AMENDMENT III]

No Soldier shall, in time of peace, be quartered in any house, without the consent of the Owner, nor in time of war, but in a manner to be prescribed by law.

[AMENDMENT IV]

The right of the people to be secure in their persons, houses, papers, and effects, against unreasonable searches and seizures, shall not be violated, and no Warrants shall issue, but upon probable cause, supported by Oath or affirmation, and particularly describing the place to be searched, and the persons or things to be seized.

[AMENDMENT V]

No person shall be held to answer for a capital or otherwise infamous crime, unless on a presentment or indictment of a Grand Jury, except in cases arising in the land or naval forces, or in the Militia, when in actual service in time of War or public danger; nor shall any person be subject for the same offence to be twice put in jeopardy of life or limb; nor shall be compelled in any criminal case to be a witness against himself, nor be deprived of life, liberty, or property, without due process of law; nor shall private property be taken for public use, without just compensation.

[AMENDMENT VI]

In all criminal prosecutions, the accused shall enjoy the right to a speedy and public trial, by an impartial jury of the State and district wherein the crime shall have been committed, which dis-

---

[7]This heading appears only in the joint resolution submitting the first ten amendments, known as the Bill of Rights.

trict shall have been previously ascertained by law, and to be informed of the nature and cause of the accusation; to be confronted with the witnesses against him; to have compulsory process for obtaining witnesses in his favour, and to have the Assistance of Counsel for his defence.

[AMENDMENT VII]

In suits at common law, where the value in controversy shall exceed twenty dollars, the right of trial by jury shall be preserved, and no fact tried by a jury, shall be otherwise reexamined in any Court of the United States, than according to the rules of the common law.

[AMENDMENT VIII]

Excessive bail shall not be required, nor excessive fines imposed, nor cruel and unusual punishments inflicted.

[AMENDMENT IX]

The enumeration of the Constitution, of certain rights, shall not be construed to deny or disparage others retained by the people.

[AMENDMENT X]

The powers not delegated to the United States by the Constitution, nor prohibited by it to the States, are reserved to the States respectively, or to the people.
[Amendments I–X, in force 1791.]

[AMENDMENT XI][8]

The Judicial power of the United States shall not be construed to extend to any suit in law or equity, commenced or prosecuted against one of the United States by Citizens of another State, or by Citizens or Subjects of any Foreign State.

[AMENDMENT XII][9]

The Electors shall meet in their respective States and vote by ballot for President and Vice-President, one of whom, at least, shall not be an inhabitant of the same State with themselves; they shall name in their ballots the person voted for as President, and in distinct ballots the person voted for as Vice-President, and they shall make distinct lists of all persons voted for as

---

[8]Adopted in 1798.
[9]Adopted in 1804.

President, and of all persons voted for as Vice-President, and of the number of votes for each, which lists they shall sign and certify, and transmit sealed to the seat of the government of the United States, directed to the President of the Senate;—The President of the Senate shall, in the presence of the Senate and House of Representatives, open all the certificates and the votes shall then be counted;—The person having the greatest number of votes for President, shall be the President, if such number be a majority of the whole number of Electros appointed; and if no person have such majority, then from the persons having the highest numbers not exceeding three on the list of those voted for as President, the House of Representatives shall choose immediately, by ballot, the President. But in choosing the President, the votes shall be taken by states, the representation from each state having one vote; a quorum for this purpose shall consist of a member or members from two-thirds of the states, and a majority of all the states shall be necessary to a choice. And if the House of Representatives shall not choose a President whenever the right of choice shall devolve upon them, before the fourth day of March next following, then the Vice-President shall act as President, as in the case of the death or other constitutional disability of the President.—The person having the greatest number of votes as Vice-President, shall be the Vice-President, if such number be a majority of the whole number of Electors appointed, and if no person have a majority, then from the two highest numbers on the list, the Senate shall choose the Vice-President; a quorum for the purpose shall consist of two-thirds of the whole number of Senators, and a majority of the whole number shall be necessary to a choice. But no person constitutionally ineligible to the office of President shall be eligible to that of Vice-President of the United States.

[AMENDMENT XIII][10]

Section 1.   Neither slavery nor involuntary servitude, except as a punishment for crime whereof the party shall have been duly convicted, shall exist within the United States, or any place subject to their jurisdiction.

Section 2.   Congress shall have power to enforce this article by appropriate legislation.

[AMENDMENT XIV][11]

Section 1.   All persons born or naturalized in the United States, and subject to the jurisdiction thereof, are citizens of the United States and of the State wherein they reside. No State shall abridge the privileges or immunities of citizens of the United States; nor shall any State deprive any person of life, liberty, or property, without due process of law; nor deny to any person within its jurisdiction the equal protection of the laws.

Section 2.   Representatives shall be apportioned among the several States according to their respective numbers, counting the whole number of persons in each State, excluding Indians not taxed. But when the right to vote at any election for the choice of electors for President and Vice-President of the United States, Representatives in Congress, the Executive and Judicial officers of a State, or the members of the Legislature thereof, is denied to any of the male inhabitants of such State, being twenty-one years of age, and citizens of the United States, or in any

---

[10]Adopted in 1865.
[11]Adopted in 1868.

way abridged, except for participation in rebellion, or other crime, the basis of representation therein shall be reduced in the proportion which the number of such male citizens shall bear to the whole number of male citizens twenty-one years of age in such State.

Section 3. No person shall be a Senator or Representative in Congress, or elector of President and Vice-President, or hold any office, civil or military, under the United States, or under any State, who, having previously taken an oath, as a member of Congress, or as an officer of the United States, or as a member of any State legislature, or as an executive or judicial officer of any State, to support the Constitution of the United States, shall have engaged in insurrection or rebellion against the same, or given aid or comfort to the enemies thereof. But Congress may by a vote of two-thirds of each House, remove such disability.

Section 4. The validity of the public debt of the United States, authorized by law, including debts incurred for payment of pensions and bounties for services in suppressing insurrection or rebellion, shall not be questioned. But neither the United States nor any State shall assume or pay any debts or obligation incurred in aid of insurrection or rebellion against the United States, or any claim for the loss or emancipation of any slave; but all such debts, obligations, and claims shall be held illegal and void.

Section 5. The Congress shall have the power to enforce, by appropriate legislation, the provisions of this article.

[AMENDMENT XV][12]

Section 1. The right of citizens of the United States to vote shall not be denied or abridged by the United States or by any State on account of race, color, or previous condition of servitude—

Section 2. The Congress shall have power to enforce this article by appropriate legislation.

[AMENDMENT XVI][13]

The Congress shall have power to lay and collect taxes on incomes, from whatever source derived, without apportionment among the several States, and without regard to any census or enumeration.

[AMENDMENT XVII][14]

The Senate of the United States shall be composed of two Senators from each State, elected by the people thereof, for six years; and each Senator shall have one vote. The electors in each State shall have the qualifications requisite for electors of the most numerous branch of the State legislatures.

---

[12]Adopted in 1870.
[13]Adopted in 1913.
[14]Adopted in 1913.

When vacancies happen in the representation of any State in the Senate, the executive authority of such State shall issue writs of election to fill such vacancies: *Provided*, That the legislature of any State may empower the executive thereof to make temporary appointments until the people fill the vacancies by election as the legislature may direct.

This amendment shall not be so construed as to affect the election or term of any Senator chosen before it becomes valid as part of the Constitution.

[AMENDMENT XVIII][15]

Section 1.   After one year from the ratification of this article the manufacture, sale, or transportation of intoxicating liquors within, the importation thereof into, or the exportation thereof from the United States and all territory subject to the jurisdiction thereof for beverage purposes is hereby prohibited.

Section 2.   The Congress and the several States shall have concurrent power to enforce this article by appropriate legislation.

Section 3.   This article shall be inoperative unless it shall have been ratified as an amendment to the Constitution by the legislatures of the several States, as provided in the Constitution, within seven years from the date of the submission hereof to the States by the Congress.

[AMENDMENT XIX][16]

The right of citizens of the United States to vote shall not be denied or abridged by the United States or by any State on account of sex.

Congress shall have power to enforce this article by appropriate legislation.

[AMENDMENT XX][17]

Section 1.   The terms of the President and Vice-President shall end at noon on the 20th day of January, and the terms of Senators and Representatives at noon on the 3d day of January, of the years in which such terms would have ended if this article had not been ratified; and the terms of their successors shall then begin.

Section 2.   The Congress shall assemble at least once in every year, and such meeting shall begin at noon on the 3d day of January, unless they shall by law appoint a different day.

Section 3.   If, at the time fixed for the beginning of the term of the President, the President elect shall have died, the Vice-President elect shall become President. If a President shall not have been chosen before the time fixed for the beginning of his term or if the President elect shall have failed to qualify, then the Vice-President elect shall act as President until a President

---

[15]Adopted in 1918.
[16]Adopted in 1920.
[17]Adopted in 1933.

shall have qualified; and the Congress may by law provide for the case wherein neither a President elect nor a Vice-President elect shall have qualified, declaring who shall then act as President, or the manner in which one who is to act shall be selected, and such person shall act accordingly until a President or Vice-President shall have qualified.

Section 4. The Congress may by law provide for the case of the death of any of the persons from whom the House of Representatives may choose a President whenever the right of choice shall have devolved upon them, and for the case of the death of any of the persons from whom the Senate may choose a Vice-President whenever the right of choice shall have devolved upon them.

Section 5. Section 1 and 2 shall take effect on the 15th day of October following the ratification of this article.

Section 6. This article shall be inoperative unless it shall have been ratified as an amendment to the Constitution by the legislatures of three-fourths of the several States within seven years from the date of its submission.

[AMENDMENT XXI][18]

Section 1. The eighteenth article of amendment to the Constitution of the United States is hereby repealed.

Section 2. The transportation or importation into any State, Territory, or possession of the United States for delivery or use therein of intoxicating liquors, in violation of the laws thereof, is hereby prohibited.

Section 3. This article shall be inoperative unless it shall have been ratified as an amendment to the Constitution by conventions in the several States, as provided in the Constitution, within seven years from the date of the submission hereof to the States by the Congress.

[AMENDMENT XXII][19]

No person shall be elected to the office of the President more than twice, and no person who has held the office of President, or acted as President, for more than two years of a term to which some other person was elected President shall be elected to the office of the President more than once.

But this Article shall not apply to any person holding the office of President when this Article was proposed by the Congress, and shall not prevent any person who may be holding the office of President, or acting as President, during the term within which this Article becomes operative from holding the office of President or acting as President during the remainder of such term.

This article shall be inoperative unless it shall have been ratified as an amendment to the Constitution by the legislatures of three-fourths of the several states within seven years from the date of its submission to the states by the Congress.

---

[18]Adopted in 1933.
[19]Adopted in 1961.

[AMENDMENT XXIII][20]

Section 1. The District constituting the seat of Government of the United States shall appoint in such manner as the Congress may direct:

A number of electors of President and Vice-President equal to the whole number of Senators and Representatives in Congress to which the District would be entitled if it were a State, but in no event more than the least populous State; they shall be in addition to those appointed by the States, but they shall be considered, for the purpose of the election of President and Vice-President, to be electors appointed by a State; and they shall meet in the District and perform such duties as provided by the twelfth article of amendment.

Section 2. The Congress shall have power to enforce this article by appropriate legislation.

[AMENDMENT XXIV][21]

Section 1. The right of citizens of the United States to vote in any primary or other election for President or Vice-President, for electors for President or Vice-President, or for Senator or Representative in Congress, shall not be denied or abridged by the United States or any state by reason of failure to pay any poll tax or other tax.

Section 2. The Congress shall have the power to enforce this article by appropriate legislation.

[AMENDMENT XXV][22]

Section 1. In case of the removal of the President from office or of his death or resignation, the Vice-President shall become President.

Section 2. Whenever there is a vacancy in the office of the Vice-President, the President shall nominate a Vice-President who shall take office upon confirmation by a majority vote of both Houses of Congress.

Section 3. Whenever the President transmits to the President Pro Tempore of the Senate and the Speaker of the House of Representatives his written declaration that he is unable to discharge the powers and duties of his office, and until he transmits to them a written declaration to the contrary, such powers and duties shall be discharged by the Vice-President as Acting President.

Section 4. Whenever the Vice-President and a majority of either the principal officers of the executive departments or of such other body as Congress may by law provide, transmit to the President Pro Tempore of the Senate and the Speaker of the House of Representatives their written declaration that the President is unable to discharge the powers and duties of his office,

---

[20]Adopted in 1961.
[21]Adopted in 1964.
[22]Adopted in 1967.

the Vice-President shall immediately assume the powers and duties of the office as Acting President.

Thereafter, when the President transmits to the President Pro Tempore of the Senate and the Speaker of the House of Representatives his written declaration that no inability exists, he shall resume the powers and duties of his office unless the Vice-President and a majority of either the principal officers of the executive departments or of such other boby as Congress may by law provide, transmit within four days to the President Pro Tempore of the Senate and the Speaker of the House of Representatives their written declaration that the President is unable to discharge the powers and duties of his office. Thereupon Congress shall decide the issue, assembling within forty-eight hours for that purpose if not in session. If the Congress, within twenty-one days after reciept of the latter written declaration, or, if Congress is not in session, within twenty-one days after Congress is required to assemble, determines by two-thirds vote of both Houses that the President is unable to discharge the powers and duties of his office, the Vice-President shall continue to discharge the same as Acting President; otherwise, the President shall resume the powers and duties of his office.

[AMENDMENT XXVI][23]

Section 1.   The right of citizens of the United States, who are eighteen years of age or older, to vote shall not be denied or abridged by the United States or by any State on account of age.

Section 2.   The Congress shall have power to enforce this article by appropriate legislation.

[AMENDMENT XXVII][24]

No law, varying the compensation for the services of the Senators and Representatives, shall take effect, until an election of Representatives shall have intervened.

---

[23]Adopted in 1971.
[24]Adopted in 1992.

JUSTICES OF THE SUPREME COURT

	Term of Service	Years of Service	Life Span		Term of Service	Years of Service	Life Span
John Jay	1789–1795	5	1745–1829	Ward Hunt	1873–1882	9	1810–1886
John Rutledge	1789–1791	1	1739–1800	*Morrison R. Waite*	1874–1888	14	1816–1888
William Cushing	1789–1810	20	1732–1810	John M. Harlan	1877–1911	34	1833–1911
James Wilson	1789–1798	8	1742–1798	William B. Woods	1880–1887	7	1824–1887
John Blair	1789–1796	6	1732–1800	Stanley Matthews	1881–1889	7	1824–1889
Robert H. Harrison	1789–1790	–	1745–1790	Horace Gray	1882–1902	20	1828–1902
James Iredell	1790–1799	9	1751–1799	Samuel Blatchford	1882–1893	11	1820–1893
Thomas Johnson	1791–1793	1	1732–1819	Lucius Q. C. Lamar	1888–1893	5	1825–1893
William Paterson	1793–1806	13	1745–1806	*Melville W. Fuller*	1888–1910	21	1833–1910
*John Rutledge**	1795	–	1739–1800	David J. Brewer	1890–1910	20	1837–1910
Samuel Chase	1796–1811	15	1741–1811	Henry B. Brown	1890–1906	16	1836–1913
Oliver Ellsworth	1796–1800	4	1745–1807	George Shiras Jr.	1892–1903	10	1832–1924
Bushrod Washington	1798–1829	31	1762–1829	Howell E. Jackson	1893–1895	2	1832–1895
Alfred Moore	1799–1804	4	1755–1810	Edward D. White	1894–1910	16	1845–1921
John Marshall	1801–1835	34	1755–1835	Rufus W. Peckham	1895–1909	14	1838–1909
William Johnson	1804–1834	30	1771–1834	Joseph McKenna	1898–1925	26	1843–1926
H. Brockholst				Oliver W. Holmes	1902–1932	30	1841–1935
Livingston	1806–1823	16	1757–1823	William R. Day	1903–1922	19	1849–1923
Thomas Todd	1807–1826	18	1765–1826	William H. Moody	1906–1910	3	1853–1917
Joseph Story	1811–1845	33	1779–1845	Horace H. Lurton	1909–1914	4	1844–1914
Gabriel Duval	1811–1835	24	1752–1844	Charles E. Hughes	1910–1916	5	1862–1948
Smith Thompson	1823–1843	20	1768–1843	*Edward D. White*	1910–1921	11	1845–1921
Robert Trimble	1826–1828	2	1777–1828	Willis Van Devanter	1911–1937	26	1859–1941
John McLean	1829–1861	32	1785–1861	Joseph R. Lamar	1911–1916	5	1857–1916
Henry Baldwin	1830–1844	14	1780–1844	Mahlon Pitney	1912–1922	10	1858–1924
James M. Wayne	1835–1867	32	1790–1867	James C. McReynolds	1914–1941	26	1862–1946
Roger B. Taney	1836–1864	28	1777–1864	Louis D. Brandeis	1916–1939	22	1856–1941
Philip P. Barbour	1836–1841	4	1783–1841	John H. Clarke	1916–1922	6	1857–1945
John Catron	1837–1865	28	1786–1865	William H. Taft	1921–1930	8	1857–1930
John McKinley	1837–1852	15	1780–1852	George Sutherland	1922–1938	15	1862–1942
Peter V. Daniel	1841–1860	19	1784–1860	Pierce Butler	1922–1939	16	1866–1939
Samuel Nelson	1845–1872	27	1792–1873	Edward T. Sanford	1923–1930	7	1865–1930
Levi Woodbury	1845–1851	5	1789–1851	Harlan F. Stone	1925–1941	16	1872–1946
Robert C. Grier	1846–1870	23	1794–1870	*Charles E. Hughes*	1930–1941	11	1862–1948
Benjamin R. Curtis	1851–1857	6	1809–1874	Owen J. Roberts	1930–1945	15	1875–1955
John A. Campbell	1853–1861	8	1811–1889	Benjamin N. Cardozo	1932–1938	6	1870–1938
Nathan Clifford	1858–1881	23	1803–1881	Hugo L. Black	1937–1971	34	1886–1971
Noah H. Swayne	1862–1881	18	1804–1884	Stanley F. Reed	1938–1957	19	1884–1980
Samuel F. Miller	1862–1890	28	1816–1890	Felix Frankfurter	1939–1962	23	1882–1965
David Davis	1862–1877	14	1815–1886	William O. Douglas	1939–1975	36	1898–1980
Stephen J. Field	1863–1897	34	1816–1899	Frank Murphy	1940–1949	9	1890–1949
Salmon P. Chase	1864–1873	8	1808–1873	Harlan F. Stone	1941–1946	5	1872–1946
William Strong	1870–1880	10	1808–1895	James F. Byrnes	1941–1942	1	1879–1972
Joseph P. Bradley	1870–1892	22	1813–1892	Robert H. Jackson	1941–1954	13	1892–1954

	Term of Service	Years of Service	Life Span		Term of Service	Years of Service	Life Span
Wiley B. Rutledge	1943–1949	6	1894–1949	*Warren C. Burger*	1969–1986	17	1907–1995
Harold H. Burton	1945–1958	13	1888–1964	Harry A. Blackmun	1970–1994	24	1908–1999
Fred M. Vinson	1946–1953	7	1890–1953	Lewis F. Powell Jr.	1972–1987	15	1907–
Tom C. Clark	1949–1967	18	1899–1977	William H. Rehnquist	1972–1986	14	1924–
Sherman Minton	1949–1956	7	1890–1965	John P. Stevens III	1975–	–	1920–
Earl Warren	1953–1969	16	1891–1974	Sandra Day O'Connor	1981–	–	1930–
John Marshall Harlan	1955–1971	16	1899–1971	*William H. Rehnquist*	1986–	–	1924–
William J. Brennan Jr.	1956–1990	33	1906–1997	Antonin Scalia	1986–	–	1936–
Charles E. Whittaker	1957–1962	5	1901–1973	Anthony M. Kennedy	1987–	–	1936–
Potter Stewart	1958–1981	23	1915–1985	David H. Souter	1990–	–	1939–
Byron R. White	1962–1993	31	1917–	Clarence Thomas	1991–	–	1948–
Arthur J. Goldberg	1962–1965	3	1908–1990	Ruth Bader Ginsburg	1993–	–	1933–
Abe Fortas	1965–1969	4	1910–1982	Stephen G. Breyer	1994–	–	1938–
Thurgood Marshall	1967–1991	24	1908–1993				

Appointed and served one term, but not confirmed by the Senate.
Note: Chief justices are in italics.

PRESIDENTIAL ELECTIONS

Year	Candidates	Parties	Popular Vote	% of Popular Vote	Electoral Vote	% Voter Partici- pation
1789	**George Washington**				69	
	John Adams				34	
	Other candidates				35	
1792	**George Washington**				132	
	John Adams				77	
	George Clinton				50	
	Other candidates				5	
1796	**John Adams**	Federalist			71	
	Thomas Jefferson	Dem.-Rep.			68	
	Thomas Pinckney	Federalist			59	
	Aaron Burr	Dem.-Rep.			30	
	Other candidates				48	
1800	**Thomas Jefferson**	Dem.-Rep.			73	
	Aaron Burr	Dem.-Rep.			73	
	John Adams	Federalist			65	
	Charles C. Pinckney	Federalist			64	
	John Jay	Federalist			1	
1804	**Thomas Jefferson**	Dem.-Rep.			162	
	Charles C. Pinckney	Federalist			14	
1808	**James Madison**	Dem.-Rep.			122	
	Charles C. Pinckney	Federalist			47	
	George Clinton	Dem.-Rep.			6	
1812	**James Madison**	Dem.-Rep.			128	
	DeWitt Clinton	Federalist			89	
1816	**James Monroe**	Dem.-Rep.			183	
	Rufus King	Federalist			34	
1820	**James Monroe**	Dem.-Rep.			231	
	John Quincy Adams	Indep.-Rep.			1	
1824	**John Quincy Adams**	Dem.-Rep.	108,740	31.0	84	26.9
	Andrew Jackson	Dem.-Rep.	153,544	43.0	99	
	Henry Clay	Dem.-Rep.	47,136	13.0	37	
	William H. Crawford	Dem.-Rep.	46,618	13.0	41	
1828	**Andrew Jackson**	Democratic	647,286	56.0	178	57.6
	John Quincy Adams	National Republican	508,064	44.0	83	
1832	**Andrew Jackson**	Democratic	688,242	54.5	219	55.4
	Henry Clay	National Republican	473,462	37.5	49	
	William Wirt	Anti-Masonic ⎫	101,051	8.0	7	
	John Floyd	Democratic ⎭			11	
1836	**Martin Van Buren**	Democratic	765,483	50.9	170	57.8
	William H. Harrison	Whig ⎫		49.1	73	
	Hugh L. White	Whig ⎪	739,795		26	
	Daniel Webster	Whig ⎬			14	
	W. P. Mangum	Whig ⎭			11	

Year	Candidates	Parties	Popular Vote	% of Popular Vote	Electoral Vote	% Voter Partici- pation
1840	**William H. Harrison**	Whig	1,275,016	53.0	234	80.2
	Martin Van Buren	Democratic	1,129,102	47.0	60	
1844	**James K. Polk**	Democratic	1,338,464	49.6	170	78.9
	Henry Clay	Whig	1,300,097	48.1	105	
	James G. Birney	Liberty	62,300	2.3		
1848	**Zachary Taylor**	Whig	1,360,967	47.4	163	72.7
	Lewis Cass	Democratic	1,222,342	42.5	127	
	Martin Van Buren	Free Soil	291,263	10.1		
1852	**Franklin Pierce**	Democratic	1,601,117	50.9	254	69.6
	Winfield Scott	Whig	1,385,453	44.1	42	
	John P. Hale	Free Soil	155,825	5.0		
1856	**James Buchanan**	Democratic	1,832,955	45.3	174	78.9
	John C. Fremont	Republican	1,339,932	33.1	114	
	Millard Fillmore	American	871,731	21.6	8	
1860	**Abraham Lincoln**	Republican	1,866,452	39.8	180	81.2
	Stephen A. Douglas	Democratic	1,375,157	29.5	12	
	John C. Breckinridge	Democratic	847,953	18.1	72	
	John Bell	Constitutional Union	590,631	12.6	39	
1864	**Abraham Lincoln**	Republican	2,206,938	55.0	212	73.8
	George B. McClellan	Democratic	1,803,787	45.0	21	
1868	**Ulysses S. Grant**	Republican	3,013,421	52.7	214	78.1
	Horatio Seymour	Democratic	2,706,829	47.3	80	
1872	**Ulysses S. Grant**	Republican	3,596,745	55.6	286	71.3
	Horace Greeley	Democratic	2,843,446	43.9	66	
1876	**Rutherford B. Hayes**	Republican	4,036,298	48.0	185	81.8
	Samuel J. Tilden	Democratic	4,300,590	51.0	184	
1880	**James A. Garfield**	Republican	4,453,295	48.5	214	79.4
	Winfield S. Hancock	Democratic	4,414,082	48.1	155	
	James B. Weaver	Greenback-Labor	308,578	3.4		
1884	**Grover Cleveland**	Democratic	4,879,507	48.5	219	77.5
	James G. Blaine	Republican	4,850,293	48.2	182	
	Benjamin F. Butler	Greenback-Labor	175,370	1.8		
	John P. St. John	Prohibition	150,369	1.5		
1888	**Benjamin Harrison**	Republican	5,477,129	47.9	233	79.3
	Grover Cleveland	Democratic	5,537,857	48.6	168	
	Clinton B. Fisk	Prohibition	249,506	2.2		
	Anson J. Streeter	Union Labor	146,935	1.3		
1892	**Grover Cleveland**	Democratic	5,555,426	46.1	277	74.7
	Benjamin Harrison	Republican	5,182,690	43.0	145	
	James B. Weaver	People's	1,029,846	8.5	22	
	John Bidwell	Prohibition	264,133	2.2		
1896	**William McKinley**	Republican	7,104,779	52.0	271	79.3
	William J. Bryan	Democratic	6,502,925	48.0	176	
1900	**William McKinley**	Republican	7,218,491	51.7	292	73.2
	William J. Bryan	Democratic; Populist	6,356,734	45.5	155	
	John C. Wooley	Prohibition	208,914	1.5		

Year	Candidates	Parties	Popular Vote	% of Popular Vote	Electoral Vote	% Voter Partici- pation
1904	**Theodore Roosevelt**	Republican	7,628,461	57.4	336	65.2
	Alton B. Parker	Democratic	5,084,223	37.6	140	
	Eugene V. Debs	Socialist	402,283	3.0		
	Silas C. Swallow	Prohibition	258,536	1.9		
1908	**William H. Taft**	Republican	7,675,320	51.6	321	65.4
	William J. Bryan	Democratic	6,412,294	43.1	162	
	Eugene V. Debs	Socialist	420,793	2.8		
	Eugene W. Chafin	Prohibition	253,840	1.7		
1912	**Woodrow Wilson**	Democratic	6,293,454	42.0	435	58.8
	Theodore Roosevelt	Progressive	4,119,538	28.0	88	
	William H. Taft	Republican	3,484,980	24.0	8	
	Eugene V. Debs	Socialist	900,672	6.0		
	Eugene W. Chafin	Prohibition	206,275	1.4		
1916	**Woodrow Wilson**	Democratic	9,129,606	49.4	277	61.6
	Charles E. Hughes	Republican	8,538,221	46.2	254	
	A. L. Benson	Socialist	585,113	3.2		
	J. Frank Hanly	Prohibition	220,506	1.2		
1920	**Warren G. Harding**	Republican	16,143,407	60.4	404	49.2
	James M. Cox	Democratic	9,130,328	34.2	127	
	Eugene V. Debs	Socialist	919,799	3.4		
	P. P. Christensen	Farmer-Labor	265,411	1.0		
1924	**Calvin Coolidge**	Republican	15,718,211	54.0	382	48.9
	John W. Davis	Democratic	8,385,283	28.8	136	
	Robert M. La Follette	Progressive	4,831,289	16.6	13	
1928	**Herbert C. Hoover**	Republican	21,391,381	58.2	444	56.9
	Alfred E. Smith	Democratic	15,016,443	40.9	87	
1932	**Franklin D. Roosevelt**	Democratic	22,821,857	57.4	472	56.9
	Herbert C. Hoover	Republican	15,761,841	39.7	59	
	Norman Thomas	Socialist	881,951	2.2		
1936	**Franklin D. Roosevelt**	Democratic	27,751,597	60.8	523	61.0
	Alfred M. Landon	Republican	16,679,583	36.5	8	
	William Lemke	Union	882,479	1.9		
1940	**Franklin D. Roosevelt**	Democratic	27,307,819	54.8	449	62.5
	Wendell L. Wilkie	Republican	22,321,018	44.8	82	
1944	**Franklin D. Roosevelt**	Democratic	25,606,585	53.5	432	55.9
	Thomas E. Dewey	Republican	22,014,745	46.0	99	
1948	**Harry S Truman**	Democratic	24,105,812	50.0	303	53.0
	Thomas E. Dewey	Republican	21,970,065	46.0	189	
	J. Strom Thurmond	States' Rights	1,169,021	2.0	39	
	Henry A. Wallace	Progressive	1,157,172	2.0		
1952	**Dwight D. Eisenhower**	Republican	33,936,234	55.1	442	63.3
	Adlai E. Stevenson	Democratic	27,314,992	44.4	89	
1956	**Dwight D. Eisenhower**	Republican	35,590,472	57.6	457	60.6
	Adlai E. Stevenson	Democratic	26,022,752	42.1	73	
1960	**John F. Kennedy**	Democratic	34,227,096	49.7	303	62.8
	Richard M. Nixon	Republican	34,107,646	49.6	219	
	Harry F. Byrd	Independent	501,643		15	

Year	Candidates	Parties	Popular Vote	% of Popular Vote	Electoral Vote	% Voter Partici- pation
1964	**Lyndon B. Johnson**	Democratic	43,129,566	61.1	486	61.7
	Barry M. Goldwater	Republican	27,178,188	38.5	52	
1968	**Richard M. Nixon**	Republican	31,785,480	44.0	301	60.6
	Hubert H. Humphrey	Democratic	31,275,166	42.7	191	
	George C. Wallace	American Independent	9,906,473	13.5	46	
1972	**Richard M. Nixon**	Republican	47,169,911	60.7	520	55.2
	George S. McGovern	Democratic	29,170,383	37.5	17	
	John G. Schmitz	American	1,099,482	1.4		
1976	**Jimmy Carter**	Democratic	40,830,763	50.1	297	53.5
	Gerald R. Ford	Republican	39,147,793	48.0	240	
1980	**Ronald Reagan**	Republican	43,899,248	51.0	489	52.6
	Jimmy Carter	Democratic	35,481,432	41.0	49	
	John B. Anderson	Independent	5,719,437	7.0		
	Ed Clark	Libertarian	920,859	1.0		
1984	**Ronald Reagan**	Republican	54,451,521	58.8	525	53.3
	Walter Mondale	Democratic	37,565,334	40.5	13	
1988	**George H. Bush**	Republican	48,881,221	53.9	426	48.6
	Michael Dukakis	Democratic	41,805,422	46.1	111	
1992	**William J. Clinton**	Democratic	44,908,254	43.0	370	55.9
	George H. Bush	Republican	39,102,343	37.4	168	
	H. Ross Perot	Independent	19,741,065	18.9		
1996	**William J. Clinton**	Democratic	47,401,185	49.3	379	49
	Robert Dole	Republican	39,197,469	40.7	159	
	H. Ross Perot	Reform	8,085,294	8.4		
2000*	**George W. Bush**	Republican	49,820,094	48	271	50.7
	Albert A. Gore Jr.	Democratic	50,158,094	48	267	
	Ralph Nader	Green	2,703,722	3		
	Patrick J. Buchanan	Reform	438,407			

Preliminary figures

A SOCIAL PROFILE OF THE AMERICAN REPUBLIC

			POPULATION					
Year	Population	Percent Increase	Population Per Square Mile	Percent Urban/ Rural	Percent Male/ Female	Percent White/ Nonwhite	Persons Per Household	Media Age
1790	3,929,214		4.5	5.1/94.9	NA	80.7/19.3	5.79	NA
1800	5,308,483	35.1	6.1	6.1/93.9	NA	81.1/18.9	NA	NA
1810	7,239,881	36.4	4.3	7.3/92.7	NA	81.0/19.0	NA	NA
1820	9,638,453	33.1	5.5	7.2/92.8	50.8/49.2	81.6/18.4	NA	16.7
1830	12,866,020	33.5	7.4	8.8/91.2	50.8/49.2	81.9/18.1	NA	17.2
1840	17,069,453	32.7	9.8	10.8/89.2	50.9/49.1	83.2/16.8	NA	17.8
1850	23,191,876	35.9	7.9	15.3/84.7	51.0/49.0	84.3/15.7	5.55	18.9
1860	31,443,321	35.6	10.6	19.8/80.2	51.2/48.8	85.6/14.4	5.28	19.4
1870	39,818,449	26.6	13.4	25.7/74.3	50.6/49.4	86.2/13.8	5.09	20.2
1880	50,155,783	26.0	16.9	28.2/71.8	50.9/49.1	86.5/13.5	5.04	20.9
1890	62,947,714	25.5	21.2	35.1/64.9	51.2/48.8	87.5/12.5	4.93	22.0
1900	75,994,575	20.7	25.6	39.6/60.4	51.1/48.9	87.9/12.1	4.76	22.9
1910	91,972,266	21.0	31.0	45.6/54.4	51.5/48.5	88.9/11.1	4.54	24.1
1920	105,710,620	14.9	35.6	51.2/48.8	51.0/49.0	89.7/10.3	4.34	25.3
1930	122,775,046	16.1	41.2	56.1/43.9	50.6/49.4	89.8/10.2	4.11	26.4
1940	131,669,275	7.2	44.2	56.5/43.5	50.2/49.8	89.8/10.2	3.67	29.0
1950	150,697,361	14.5	50.7	64.0/36.0	49.7/50.3	89.5/10.5	3.37	30.2
1960	179,323,175	18.5	50.6	69.9/30.1	49.3/50.7	88.6/11.4	3.33	29.5
1970	203,302,031	13.4	57.4	73.5/26.5	48.7/51.3	87.6/12.4	3.14	28.0
1980	226,545,805	11.4	64.0	73.7/26.3	48.6/51.4	86.0/14.0	2.76	30.0
1990	248,709,873	9.8	70.3	NA	48.7/51.3	80.3/19.7	2.63	32.9
2000*	276,382,000	7.1	75.8	NA	48.9/51.1	82.6/17.4	NA	NA

NA = Not available.
*Projections.

		VITAL STATISTICS (rates per thousand)				
Year	Births	Year	Births	Deaths*	Marriages*	Divorces
1800	55.0	1900	32.3	17.2	NA	NA
1810	54.3	1910	30.1	14.7	NA	NA
1820	55.2	1920	27.7	13.0	12.0	1.6
1830	51.4	1930	21.3	11.3	9.2	1.6
1840	51.8	1940	19.4	10.8	12.1	2.0
1850	43.3	1950	24.1	9.6	11.1	2.6
1860	44.3	1960	23.7	9.5	8.5	2.2
1870	38.3	1970	18.4	9.5	10.6	3.5
1880	39.8	1980	15.9	8.8	10.6	5.2
1890	31.5	1990	16.7	8.6	9.8	4.6

NA = Not available.
*Data not available before 1900.

LIFE EXPECTANCY (in years)

Year	Total Population	White Females	Nonwhite Females	White Males	Nonwhite Males
1900	47.3	48.7	33.5	46.6	32.5
1910	50.1	52.0	37.5	48.6	33.8
1920	54.1	55.6	45.2	54.4	45.5
1930	59.7	63.5	49.2	59.7	47.3
1940	62.9	66.6	54.9	62.1	51.5
1950	68.2	72.2	62.9	66.5	59.1
1960	69.7	74.1	66.3	67.4	61.1
1970	70.9	75.6	69.4	68.0	61.3
1980	73.7	78.1	73.6	70.7	65.3
1990	75.4	79.3	76.3	72.6	68.4

REGIONAL ORIGIN OF IMMIGRANTS (percent)

Year	Total Number of Immigrants	EUROPE				Western Hemisphere	Asia
		Total Europe	North and West	East and Central	South and Other		
1821–1830	143,389	69.2	67.1	—	2.1	8.4	—
1831–1840	599,125	82.8	81.8	—	1.0	5.5	—
1841–1850	1,713,251	93.8	92.9	0.1	0.3	3.6	—
1851–1860	2,598,214	94.4	93.6	0.1	0.8	2.9	1.6
1861–1870	2,314,824	89.2	87.8	0.5	0.9	7.2	2.8
1871–1880	2,812,191	80.8	73.6	4.5	2.7	14.4	4.4
1881–1890	5,246,613	90.3	72.0	11.9	6.3	8.1	1.3
1891–1900	3,687,546	96.5	44.5	32.8	19.1	1.1	1.9
1901–1910	8,795,386	92.5	21.7	44.5	6.3	4.1	2.8
1911–1920	5,735,811	76.3	17.4	33.4	25.5	19.9	3.4
1921–1930	4,107,209	60.3	31.7	14.4	14.3	36.9	2.4
1931–1940	528,431	65.9	38.8	11.0	16.1	30.3	2.8
1941–1950	1,035,039	60.1	47.5	4.6	7.9	34.3	3.1
1951–1960	2,515,479	52.8	17.7	24.3	10.8	39.6	6.0
1961–1970	3,321,677	33.8	11.7	9.4	12.9	51.7	12.9
1971–1980	4,493,300	17.8	4.3	5.6	8.4	44.3	35.2
1981–1990	7,338,000	10.4	5.9	4.8	1.1	49.3	37.3

Dash indicates less than 0.1 percent.

RECENT TRENDS IN IMMIGRATION (in thousands)

	1961–1970	1971–1980	1981–1990	1991	PERCENT 1961–1970	1971–1980	1981–1990
All countries	3,321.7	4,493.3	7,338.0	1,827.2	100.0	100.0	100.0
Europe	1,123.5	800.4	761.5	146.7	33.8	17.8	10.4
Austria	20.6	9.5	18.9	3.5	0.6	0.2	0.3
Hungry	5.4	6.6	5.9	0.9	0.2	0.1	0.1
Belgium	9.2	5.3	6.6	0.7	0.3	0.1	0.1
Czechoslovakia	3.3	6.0	5.4	0.6	0.1	0.1	0.1
Denmark	9.2	4.4	2.8	0.6	0.3	0.1	0.1
France	45.2	25.1	92.1	4.0	1.4	0.6	1.3
Germany	190.8	74.4	159.0	10.9	5.7	1.7	2.2
Greece	86.0	92.4	31.9	2.9	2.6	2.1	0.4
Ireland	33.0	11.5	67.2	4.6	1.0	0.3	0.9
Italy	214.1	129.4	12.3	30.3	6.4	2.9	0.2
Netherlands	30.6	10.5	4.2	1.3	0.9	0.2	0.1
Norway	15.5	3.9	83.2	0.6	0.5	0.1	1.1
Poland	53.5	37.2	40.3	17.1	1.6	0.8	0.5
Portugal	76.1	101.7	20.5	4.6	2.3	2.3	0.3
Spain	44.7	39.1	11.1	2.7	1.3	0.9	0.2
Sweden	17.1	6.5	8.0	1.2	0.5	0.1	0.1
Switzerland	18.5	8.2	57.6	1.0	0.6	0.2	0.8
USSR	2.5	39.0	18.7	31.6	0.1	0.9	0.3
United Kingdom	213.8	137.4	159.4	16.8	6.4	3.1	2.2
Yugoslavia	20.4	30.5	37.3	2.8	0.6	0.7	0.5
Other Europe	9.1	18.9	7.7	1.2	0.2	0.2	0.0
Asia	427.6	1,588.2	2,738.1	342.2	12.9	35.2	37.3
China	34.8	124.3	298.9	24.0	1.0	2.8	4.1
HongKong	75.0	113.5	98.2	15.9	2.3	2.5	1.3
India	27.2	164.1	250.7	42.7	0.8	3.7	3.4
Iran	10.3	45.1	116.0	9.9	0.3	1.0	1.6
Israel	29.6	37.7	44.2	5.1	0.9	0.8	0.6
Japan	40.0	49.8	47.0	5.6	1.2	1.1	0.6
Korea	34.5	267.6	333.8	25.4	1.0	6.0	4.5
Philippines	98.4	355.0	548.7	68.8	3.0	7.9	7.5
Turkey	10.1	13.4	23.4	3.5	0.3	0.3	0.3
Vietnam	4.3	172.8	281.0	14.8	1.1	3.8	3.8
Other Asia	36.5	176.1	631.4	126.4	1.1	3.8	8.6
America	1,716.4	1,982.5	3,615.6	1,297.6	51.7	44.3	49.3
Argentina	49.7	29.9	27.3	4.2	1.5	0.7	0.4
Canada	413.3	169.9	158.0	19.9	12.4	3.8	2.2
Colombia	72.0	77.3	122.9	19.3	2.2	1.7	1.7
Cuba	208.5	264.9	144.6	9.5	6.3	5.9	2.0
Dominican Rep.	93.3	148.1	252.0	42.4	2.8	3.3	3.4
Ecuador	36.8	50.1	56.2	10.0	1.1	1.1	0.8
El Salvador	15.0	34.4	213.5	46.9	0.5	0.8	2.9
Haiti	34.5	56.3	138.4	47.0	1.0	1.3	1.9
Jamaica	74.9	137.6	208.1	23.0	2.3	3.1	2.8
Mexico	453.9	640.3	1,655.7	947.9	13.7	14.3	22.6
Other America	264.4	373.8	639.3	128.4	7.9	8.3	8.7
Africa	29.0	80.8	176.8	33.5	0.9	1.8	2.4
Oceania	25.1	41.2	45.2	7.1	0.8	0.9	0.6

Figures may not add to total due to rounding.

AMERICAN WORKERS AND FARMERS

Year	Total Number of Workers (thousands)	Percent of Worker Male/Female	Percent of Female Workers Married	Percent of Workers in Female Population	Percent of Workers in Labor Unions	Farm Population (thousands)	Farm Population as Percent of Total Population
1870	12,506	85/15	NA	NA	NA	NA	NA
1880	17,392	85/15	NA	NA	NA	21,973	43.8
1890	23,318	83/17	13.9	18.9	NA	24,771	42.3
1900	29,073	82/18	15.4	20.6	3	29,875	41.9
1910	38,167	79/21	24.7	25.4	6	32,077	34.9
1920	41,614	79/21	23.0	23.7	12	31,974	30.1
1930	48,830	78/22	28.9	24.8	7	30,529	24.9
1940	53,011	76/24	36.4	27.4	27	30,547	23.2
1950	59,643	72/28	52.1	31.4	25	23,048	15.3
1960	69,877	68/32	59.9	37.7	26	15,635	8.7
1970	82,049	63/37	63.4	43.4	25	9,712	4.8
1980	108,544	58/42	59.7	51.5	23	6,051	2.7
1990	117,914	55/45	58.4	44.3	16	4,591	1.8

THE ECONOMY AND FEDERAL SPENDING

Year	Gross National Product (GNP) (in billion)	FOREIGN TRADE (in millions)			Federal Budget (in billions)	Federal Surplus/Deficit (in billions)	Federal Debt (in billions)
		Exports	Imports	Balance of Trade			
1790	NA	$ 20	$ 23	$ −3	$ 0.004	$ +0.00015	$ 0.076
1800	NA	71	91	−20	0.011	+0.0006	0.083
1810	NA	67	85	−18	0.008	+0.0012	0.053
1820	NA	70	74	−4	0.018	−0.0004	0.091
1830	NA	74	71	+3	0.015	+0.100	0.049
1840	NA	132	107	+25	0.024	−0.005	0.004
1850	NA	152	178	−26	0.040	+0.004	0.064
1860	NA	400	362	−38	0.063	−0.01	0.065
1870	$ 7.4	451	462	−11	0.310	+0.10	2.4
1880	11.2	853	761	+92	0.268	+0.07	2.1
1890	13.1	910	823	+87	0.318	+0.09	1.2
1900	18.7	1,499	930	+569	0.521	+0.05	1.2
1910	35.3	1,919	1,646	+273	0.694	−0.02	1.1
1920	91.5	8,664	5,784	+2,880	6.357	+0.3	24.3
1930	90.7	4,013	3,500	+513	3.320	+0.7	16.3
1940	100.0	4,030	7,433	−3,403	9.6	−2.7	43.0
1950	286.5	10,816	9,125	+1,691	43.1	−2.2	257.4
1960	506.5	19,600	15,046	+4,556	92.2	+0.3	286.3
1970	992.7	42,700	40,189	+2,511	195.6	−2.8	371.0
1980	2,631.7	220,783	244,871	+24,088	590.9	−73.8	907.7
1990	5,524.5	421,730	487,129	−65,399	1,251.8	−220.5	3,233.3

AMERICAN WARS				
	U.S. Military Personnel (thousands)	**Personnel as % of Population**	**U.S. Deaths**	**U.S. Wounds**	**Direct Cost 1990 Dollars (millions)**
American Revolution					
Apr. 1775–Sept. 1783	184–250	9–12	4,004	6,004	$100–140
War of 1812					
June 1812–Feb. 1815	286	3	1,950	4,000	87
Mexican War					
May 1846–Feb.1848	116	0.5	13,271	4,102	82
Civil War: Union	3,393	14	360,222	275,175	2,302
Civil War: Confederacy					
Apr. 1861–Apr. 1865	1,034	11	258,000	NA	1,032
Spanish–American War					
Apr. 1898–Aug. 1898	307	0.4	2,446	1,662	270
World WarI					
Apr. 1917–Nov. 1918	4,714	5	116,516	204,002	32,740
World War II					
Dec.1941–Aug. 1945	16,354	12	405,399	670,846	360,000
Korean War					
June 1950–June 1953	5,764	4	54,246	103,284	50,000
Vietnam War					
Aug. 1964–June 1973	8,400	4	47,704	219,573	140,644
Persian Gulf War					
Jan.1991–Feb. 1991	467	0.1	293	467	NA

Bibliography

CHAPTER 1: OLD WORLD, NEW WORLDS

Discovery and Exploration in the Sixteenth Century

Kenneth R. Andrews, *Trade, Plunder, and Settlement: Maritime Enterprise and the Genesis of the British Empire, 1480–1630* (1985); K. R. Andrews, N. P. Canny, and P. E. H. Hair, eds., *The Westward Enterprise: English Activities in Ireland, the Atlantic, and America, 1480–1650* (1979); Ralph Davis, *The Rise of Atlantic Economies* (1973); J. H. Elliott, *The Old World and the New, 1492–1650* (1970); Paul E. Hoffman, *A New Andalucia and a Way to the Orient: The American Southeast during the Sixteenth Century* (1990); James Lang, *Conquest and Commerce: Spain and England in the Americas* (1975); W. H. McNeil, *The Rise of the West* (1963); Samuel Eliot Morison, *The European Discovery of America: The Northern Voyages, 500–1600* (1971) and *The European Discovery of America: The Southern Voyages, 1492–1616* (1974); J. H. Parry, *The Age of Reconnaissance* (1963); David Beers Quinn, *England and the Discovery of America, 1481–1620* (1974), *North America from Earliest Discovery to First Settlements* (1977), and *Set Fair for Roanoke* (1985).

Indian Civilizations

Inga Clendinnen, *The Aztecs: An Interpretation* (1991); Alfred W. Crosby Jr., *The Columbian Exchange: Biological and Cultural Consequences of 1492* (1972); Nigel Davies, *The Aztecs* (1973); Harold Driver, *Indians of North America*, 2d ed. (1970); Brian Fagan, *Kingdoms of God, Kingdoms of Jade: The Americans before Columbus* (1991); Peter Farb, *Man's Rise to Civilization* (1968); Francis Jennings, *The Founders of America* (1993); Jesse D. Jennings, ed., *Ancient North America* (1983); Alfred M. Josephy, ed., *America in 1492* (1992); Alice B. Kehoe, *North American Indians* (1992); Roger Kennedy, *Hidden Cities: The Discovery and Loss of Ancient North American Civilization* (1994); R. C. Padden, *The Hummingbird and the Hawk* (1962); Miguel Leon-Portilla, *The Broken Spears: The Aztec Account of the Conquest of Mexico* (1962); William C. Sturtevant, general editor, *Handbook of North American Indians*, 20 volumes projected (1978–); Carl Waldman, *Atlas of the North American Indian* (1985); Wilcomb E. Washburn, *The Indian in America* (1975).

The Spanish Empire in the Sixteenth Century

Fernand Braudel, *The Mediterranean and the Mediterranean World in the Age of Philip the Second*, vols. 1 and 2 (1976); Bernal Diaz, *The Conquest of New Spain*, trans. J. M. Cohen (1963); J. H. Elliott, *Imperial Spain, 1469–1716* (1963); Charles Gibson, *The Aztecs under Spanish Rule* (1964); James Lockhart, *The Nahuas after Conquest: A Social and Cultural history of the Indians of Central Mexico, Sixteenth through Eighteenth Centuries* (1992) and *Spanish Peru, 1532–1560* (1968); James Lockhart and Stuart B. Schwartz, *Early Latin America: A History of Colonial Spanish America and Brazil* (1983); Hugh Thomas, *Conquest: Montezuma, Cortes, and the Fall of Old Mexico* (1993).

The Protestant Reformation

Owen Chadwick, *The Reformation* (1964); Patrick Collinson, *The Elizabethan Puritan Movement* (1967) and *The Religion of Protestants* (1982); A. G. Dickens, *The English Reformation* (1974); Richard Dunn, *The Age of Religious Wars, 1159–1689* (1979); Erik Erikson, *Young Man Luther* (1962); Charles George and Katherine George, *The Protestant Mind of the English Reformation* (1961); De Lamaar Jensen, *Reformation Europe, Age of Reform and Revolution* (1981); Steven Ozment, *The Age of Reform, 1250–1550* (1980) and *The Reformation in the Cities* (1975); Keith Thomas, *Religion and the Decline of Magic* (1971); H. R. Trevor-Roper, *Religion, Reformation, Social Change, and Other Essays* (1967).

Elizabethan and Stuart England

Trevor Ashton, ed., *Crisis in Europe, 1560–1660* (1965); Carl Bridenbaugh, *Vexed and Troubled Englishmen, 1590–1642* (1968); Peter Laslett, *The World We Have Lost* (1965); Lawrence Stone, *The Crisis of the Aristocracy, 1558–1641* (1965); Keith Wrightson, *English Society, 1580–1680* (1982).

Ireland in the Sixteenth Century

Nicholas Canny, *The Elizabethan Conquest of Ireland* (1976) and *Kingdom and Colony: Ireland in the Atlantic*

World, 1560–1800 (1988); David Beers Quinn, The Elizabethans and the Irish (1976).

CHAPTER 2: THE FIRST CENTURY OF SETTLEMENT IN THE COLONIAL SOUTH

General Histories
Charles M. Andrews, The Colonial Period in American History (1934–1938); Wesley Frank Craven, The Southern Colonies in the Seventeenth Century, 1607–1689 (1949); David Galenson, White Servitude in Colonial America (1981); Sidney Mintz, Sweetness and Power: The Place of Sugar in Modern History (1985); Gary Nash, Red, White, and Black: The Peoples of Early America (1974); John E. Pomfret, Founding the American Colonies, 1583–1660 (1970); R. C. Simmons, The American Colonies (1976).

Indians in the Early South
Karen Kupperman, Settling with the Indians (1980) and Indians and English (2000); Nancy Lurie, "Indian Cultural Adjustment to European Civilization," in James M. Smith, ed., Seventeenth-Century America, (1959); James Merrell, The Indians' New World (1989); Gary Nash, Red, White, and Black: The Peoples of Early America (1974).

Race and Slavery
Ira Berlin, Many Thousands Gone (1999); Wesley Frank Craven, White, Red, and Black: The Seventeenth-Century Virginian (1971); Philip Curtin, The Atlantic Slave Trade (1969); Basil Davidson, The African Genius (1970); David B. Davis, The Problem of Slavery in Western Culture (1966); Carl N. Degler, Neither White nor Black: Slavery and Race Relations in Brazil and the United States (1971); Winthrop Jordan, White over Black (1968); Herbert Klein, The Middle Passage (1978) and Slavery in the Americas: A Comparative Study of Virginia and Cuba (1967); Richard Olaniyan, African History and Culture (1982); Roland Oliver, ed., The Cambridge History of Africa, vol. 3: c. 1050–c. 1600 (1977); Orlando Patterson, Slavery and Social Death: A Comparative Study (1982); John Thornton, Africa and Africans in the Making of the Atlantic World, 1400–1680 (1992); Peter Wood, Black Majority (1974) and "'I Did the Best I Could for My Day': The Study of Early Black History during the Second Reconstruction, 1960 to 1976," William and Mary Quarterly (1978).

The Early Chesapeake Colonies
Lois Green Carr, Russell R. Menard, and Lorena S. Walsh, Robert Cole's World: Agriculture and Society in Early Maryland (1991); Lois Green Carr, Philip D. Morgan, and Jean B. Russo, Colonial Chesapeake Society (1989); Lois Green Carr and Lorena Walsh, "The Planter's Wife: The Experience of White Women in Seventeenth-Century Maryland," William and Mary Quarterly (1977); Ivor Noel Hume, Martin's Hundred: The Discovery of a Lost Virginia Settlement (1979); Gloria Main, Tobacco Colony: Life in Early Maryland, 1650–1720 (1982); Edmund S. Morgan, American Slavery, American Freedom (1976); James Russell Perry, The Formation of a Society on Virginia's Eastern Shore, 1615–1655 (1990); Darrett and Anita Rutman, A Place in Time (1984); Thad Tate and David Ammerman, eds., The Chesapeake in the Seventeenth Century (1979).

The English Revolution
Christopher Hill, The Century of Revolution, 1603–1714 (1961), Puritanism and Revolution (1964), and The World Turned Upside Down (1972); R. C. Richardson, The Debate on the English Revolution (1977); Lawrence Stone, The Causes of the English Revolution, 1529–1642 (1972); Michael Walzer, The Revolution of the Saints (1965).

The Carolinas
Peter Coclanis, The Shadow of a Dream (1989); Verner Crane, The Southern Frontier, 1670–1732 (1929); Daniel Littlefield, Rice and Slaves (1981); H. T. Merrens, Colonial North Carolina (1964); Timothy Silver, A New Face on the Countryside (1990); M. Eugene Sirmans, Colonial South Carolina (1966); Robert Weir, Colonial South Carolina (1982).

Georgia
Harold E. Davis, The Fledgling Province: Social and Cultural Life in Colonial Georgia, 1733–1776 (1976); Hardy Jackson and Phinizy Spalding, eds., Forty Years of Diversity; Essays on Colonial Georgia (1984); Phinizy Spalding, Oglethorpe in America (1977).

The British Caribbean
Hilary McD. Beckles, White Servitude and Black Slavery in Barbados, 1627–1715 (1989); Richard Dunn, Sugar and Slaves (1972); Sidney Mintz, Sweetness and Power: The Place of Sugar in Modern History (1985); Gary Puckrein, Little England: Plantation Society and Anglo-Barbadian Politics, 1627–1700 (1984).

The Spanish Empire in the Southwest
Sherbune F. Cook, The Conflict between the California Indian and White Civilization (1943); Charles Gibson, Spain in America (1966); Ramón A. Gutiérrez, When Jesus Came, the Corn Mothers Went Away: Marriage, Sexuality, and Power in New Mexico, 1500–1846 (1991);

Edward H. Spicer, *Cycles of Conquest: The Impact of Spain, Mexico, and the United States on the Indians of the Southwest, 1533–1960* (1962); David J. Weber, *The Spanish Frontier in North America* (1992).

CHAPTER 3: THE FIRST CENTURY OF SETTLEMENT IN THE COLONIAL NORTH

Indians and Northern Colonials
James Axtell, *The European and the Indian* (1981) and *The Invasion Within* (1985); William Cronon, *Changes in the Land: Indians, Colonists, and the Ecology of New England* (1983); Francis Jennings, *The Ambiguous Iroquois Empire* (1984) and *The Invasion of America* (1975); Jill Lepore, *The Name of War* (1999); Daniel K. Richter and James H. Merrell, *Beyond the Covenant Chain: The Iroquois and Their Neighbors in Indian North America, 1600–1800* (1987); Neal Salisbury, *Manitou and Providence: Indians, Europeans, and the Making of New England* (1982); Bruce G. Trigger, *The Children of Aataentsic: A History of the Huron People to 1660* (1976); Alden Vaughan, *The New England Frontier* (1965); Anthony F. C. Wallace, *The Death and Rebirth of the Seneca* (1972).

The French in North America
W. J. Eccles, *The Canadian Frontier, 1534–1760* (1969) and *France in America* (1972); Allan Greer, *Peasant, Lord, and Merchant: Rural Society in the Three Quebec Parishes, 1740–1840* (1985); Richard Colebrook Harris, *The Seigneurial System in Early Canada* (1966); C. E. O'Neill, *Church and State in French Colonial Louisiana* (1966).

New England Puritanism
Francis Bremer, *The Puritan Experiment* (1976); Charles L. Cohen, *God's Caress: The Psychology of Puritan Religious Experience* (1986); Stephen Foster, *The Long Argument: English Puritanism and the Shaping of New England Culture, 1570–1700* (1991) and *Their Solitary Way: The Puritan Social Ethic in the First Century of Settlement in New England* (1971); Richard Godbeer, *The Devil's Dominion: Magic and Religion in Early New England* (1992); David Hall, *Worlds of Wonder, Days of Judgment* (1989); Charles Hambrick-Stowe, *The Practice of Piety: Puritan Devotional Literature in Seventeenth-Century New England* (1982); Robert Middlekauff, *The Mathers* (1971); Perry Miller, *The New England Mind: From Colony to Province* (1953); Edmund S. Morgan, *The Puritan Dilemma* (1958) and *Visible Saints* (1963); Amanda Porterfield, *Female Piety in Puritan New England: The Emergence of Religious Humanism* (1992); Harry Stout, *The New England Soul* (1986).

The New England Colonies
Virginia DeJohn Anderson, *New England's Generation: The Great Migration and the Formation of Society and Culture in the Seventeenth Century* (1991); Paul Boyer and Stephen Nissenbaum, *Salem Possessed: The Social Origins of Witchcraft* (1974); John P. Demos, *Entertaining Satan: Witchcraft and the Culture of Early New England* (1982) and *A Little Commonwealth: Family Life in Plymouth Colony* (1970); Philip Greven, *Four Generations: Land, Population, and Family in Colonial Andover, Massachusetts* (1970); Stephen Innes, *To Labor in a New Land: Economy and Society in Seventeenth-Century Springfield* (1983); Carol Karlsen, *The Devil in the Shape of a Woman: Witchcraft in Colonial New England* (1987); George Langdon, *Pilgrim Colony* (1960); Kenneth Lockridge, *A New England Town* (1970); John Frederick Martin, *Profits in the Wilderness: Entrepreneurship and the Founding of New England Towns in the Seventeenth Century* (1991); Edmund S. Morgan, *The Puritan Family*, rev. ed. (1966); Darrett Rutman, *Winthrop's Boston* (1965); Laurel Thatcher Ulrich, *Good Wives* (1982).

The Middle Colonies
Randall H. Balmer, *A Perfect Babel of Confusion: Dutch Religion and English Culture in the Middle Colonies* (1989); Patricia Bonomi, *A Factious People: Politics and Society in Colonial New York* (1971); Mary Maples Dunn, *William Penn* (1967); Richard and Mary Maples Dunn, eds., *The World of William Penn* (1986); Melvin B. Endy, *William Penn and Early Quakerism* (1973); Joyce Goodfriend, *Before the Melting Pot* (1991); Joseph Illick, *Colonial Pennsylvania* (1976); Michael Kammen, *Colonial New York* (1975); Barry Levy, *Quakers and the American Family* (1988); Donna Merwick, *Possessing Albany, 1630–1710* (1990); Gary B. Nash, *Quakers and Politics: Pennsylvania, 1681–1726* (1968); J. E. Pomfret, *Colonial New Jersey* (1973); Oliver A. Rink, *Holland on the Hudson: An Economic and Social History of Dutch New York* (1986); Robert C. Ritchie, *The Duke's Province: A Study of Politics and Society in Colonial New York, 1660–1691* (1977); Alan Tully, *William Penn's Legacy* (1977).

The Imperial Connection
Michael Hall, *Edward Randolph and the American Colonies, 1676–1703* (1960); David Lovejoy, *The Glorious Revolution in America* (1972); Richard R. Johnson, *Adjustment to Empire* (1981); Ian K. Steele, *Politics of Colonial Policy: The Board of Trade in Colonial*

Administration (1968); Stephen Saunders Webb, *The Governors-General: The English Army and the Definition of Empire, 1569–1681* (1979).

CHAPTER 4: THE MOSAIC OF EIGHTEENTH-CENTURY AMERICA

General Histories

Michael Bellesiles, *Arming America* (2000); Patricia Bonomi, *Under the Cope of Heaven* (1986); Jon Butler, *Awash in a Sea of Faith: Christianizing the American People* (1990) and *Becoming America* (2000); Jack P. Greene, *Pursuits of Happiness: The Social Development of Early Modern British Colonies and the Formation of American Culture* (1988); Philip Greven, *The Protestant Temperament: Patterns of Childrearing, Religious Experience, and Self in Early America* (1977); James Henretta, *The Evolution of American Society, 1700–1815* (1973); Stephen Innes, ed., *Work and Labor in Early America* (1988); Alice Hanson Jones, *Wealth of a Nation to Be: The American Colonies on the Eve of the Revolution* (1980); Jackson Turner Main, *The Social Structure of Revolutionary America* (1965); John McCusker and Russell Menard, *The Economy of British America, 1607–1787* (1985); D. W. Meinig, *The Shaping of America: A Geographical Perspective on 500 Years of History*, vol. 1, *Atlantic America, 1492–1800* (1986); Mary Beth Norton, *Liberty's Daughters: The Revolutionary Experience of American Women, 1750–1800* (1980); Carole Shammas, *The Pre-Industrial Consumer in England and America* (1990); Gary M. Walton and James F. Shepherd, *The Economic Rise of Early America* (1979); Robert V. Wells, *The Population of the British Colonies in America before 1776* (1975).

Immigration

Bernard Bailyn, *Voyagers to the West* (1986); Bernard Bailyn and Philip Morgan, eds., *Strangers within the Realm* (1991); Jon Butler, *The Huguenots in America* (1983); R. J. Dickson, *Ulster Immigration to Colonial America, 1718–1775* (1966); Ned Landsman, *Scotland and Its First American Colony, 1683–1765* (1985).

Rural Society in Eighteenth-Century America

Charles Grant, *Democracy in the Frontier Town of Kent* (1961); James Henretta, "Farms and Families: Mentalité in Pre-Industrial America," *William and Mary Quarterly* (1978); Christopher M. Jedrey, *The World of John Cleaveland* (1979); Sung Bok Kim, *Landlord and Tenant in Colonial New York* (1978); James T. Lemon, *The Best Poor Man's Country: A Geographical Study of Early Southeastern Pennsylvania* (1972); Gregory Stiverson, *Poverty in the Land of Plenty: Tenancy in Eighteenth-Century Mary-land* (1978); Michael Zuckerman, *Peaceable Kingdoms: New England Towns in the Eighteenth Century* (1970).

The Frontier

Richard Beeman, *The Evolution of the Southern Backcountry* (1984); Michael Bellesiles, *Revolutionary Outlaws: Ethan Allen and the Struggle for Independence in the Early American Frontier* (1994); Richard M. Brown, *The South Carolina Regulators* (1963); Andrew Cayton and Fredrika Teute, eds., *Contact Points* (1998); David H. Corkran, *The Cherokee Frontier: Conflict and Survival, 1740–1762* (1962) and *The Creek Frontier, 1540–1783* (1967); John Mack Faragher, *Daniel Boone: The Life and Legend of an American Pioneer* (1992); Eric Hinderaker, *Elusive Empires* (1997); Rachel Klein, *The Unification of a Slave State* (1990); Peter Mancall, *Valley of Opportunity: Economic Culture along the Upper Susquehanna, 1700–1800* (1991); Michael N. McConnell, *A Country Between: The Upper Ohio Valley and Its Peoples, 1724–1774* (1992); James Merrell, *Into the Pennsylvania Woods* (1999); Robert D. Mitchell, *Commercialism and Frontier: Perspectives on the Early Shenandoah Valley* (1977); Gregory H. Nobles, "Breaking into the Back-Country: New Approaches to the Early American Frontier," *William and Mary Quarterly* (1989); Daniel K. Richter, *The Ordeal of the Longhouse: The Peoples of the Iroquois League in the Era of European Colonization* (1992); Malcolm J. Rohrbough, *The Trans-Appalachian Frontier* (1978); Alan Taylor, *Liberty Men and Great Proprietors: The Revolutionary Settlement on the Maine Frontier, 1760–1820* (1990); Albert H. Tillson Jr., *Gentry and Common Folk: Political Culture on a Virginia Frontier, 1740–1789* (1991); Daniel H. Usner Jr., *Indians, Settlers, and Slaves in a Frontier Exchange Economy: The Lower Mississippi Valley before 1783* (1992); Richard White, *The Middle Ground: Indians, Empires, and Republics in the Great Lakes Region, 1650–1815* (1991).

Provincial Seaports

Carl Bridenbaugh, *Cities in the Wilderness* (1938) and *Cities in Revolt* (1955); Elaine Forman Crane, *A Dependent People: Newport, Rhode Island in the Revolutionary Era* (1985); Thomas Doerflinger, *A Vigorous Spirit of Enterprise: Merchants and Economic Development in Revolutionary Philadelphia* (1986); Christine Leigh Heyrman, *Commerce and Culture: The Maritime Communities of Colonial Massachusetts, 1690–1750* (1984); Gary B. Nash, *The Urban Crucible* (1979); Jacob M. Price, "Economic Function and the Growth of American Port Towns in the Eighteenth Century," *Perspectives in American History* (1974); Marcus Rediker, *Between the Devil and the Deep Blue Sea: Merchant Seamen,*

Pirates, and the Anglo-American Maritime Works, 1700–1750 (1987); Frederick B. Tolles, *Meetinghouse and Countinghouse: The Quaker Merchants of Colonial Philadelphia* (1948); Gerald B. Warden, *Boston, 1687–1776* (1970); Stephanie Grauman Wolf, *Urban Village: Population, Community, and Family Structure in Germantown, Pennsylvania, 1683–1800* (1976).

Blacks in Eighteenth-Century America
Thomas J. Davis, *A Rumor of Revolt: The "Great Negro Plot" in Colonial New York* (1985); Herbert Gutman, *The Black Family in Slavery and Freedom, 1750–1925* (1976); Jean Butenhoff Lee, "The Problem of the Slave Community in the Eighteenth-Century Chesapeake," *William and Mary Quarterly* (1986); Gerald W. Mullin, *Flight and Rebellion: Slave Resistance in Eighteenth-Century Virginia* (1972); Jean R. Soderlund, *Quakers and Slavery* (1985); Betty Wood, *Slavery in Colonial Georgia, 1730–1775* (1984).

The Eighteenth-Century South
Carl Bridenbaugh, *Myths and Realities: Societies of the Colonial South* (1952); A. Roger Ekirch, *"Poor Carolina": Politics and Society in Colonial North Carolina, 1729–1776* (1981); Rhys Isaac, *The Transformation of Virginia, 1740–1790* (1982); Allan Kulikoff, *Tobacco and Slaves* (1987); Jan Lewis, *The Pursuit of Happiness: Family and Values in Jefferson's Virginia* (1983); Philip Morgan, *Slave Counterpoint* (1999); Daniel Blake Smith, *Inside the Great House: Planter Family Life in Eighteenth-Century Chesapeake Society* (1980); Mechal Sobel, *The World They Made Together* (1987); Julia Cherry Spruill, *Women's Life and Work in the Southern Colonies* (1938); Charles Sydnor, *Gentlemen Freeholders: Political Practices in Washington's Virginia* (1956).

The Enlightenment
Henry May, *The Enlightenment in America* (1976); Esmond Wright, *Franklin of Philadelphia* (1986); Louis B. Wright, *The Cultural Life of the American Colonies* (1957).

The Great Awakening
Edwin Scott Gaustad, *The Great Awakening in New England* (1957); Patricia Tracy, *Jonathan Edwards, Pastor* (1979); Marilyn Westerkamp, *The Triumph of the Laity: Scots-Irish Piety and the Great Awakening, 1625–1760* (1988).

Colonial Political Development in the Eighteenth Century
Edward M. Cook, *The Fathers of the Towns: Leadership and Community Structure in Eighteenth-Century New England* (1976); Jack P. Greene, *The Quest for Power: The Lower Houses of Assembly in the Southern Royal Colonies, 1689–1776* (1963); Robert Zemsky, *Merchants, Farmers, and River Gods: An Eassy on Eighteenth Century American Politics* (1971).

CHAPTER 5: TOWARD THE WAR FOR AMERICAN INDEPENDENCE

General Histories
Charles M. Andrews, *The Colonial Background of the American Revolution*, rev. ed. (1931); Ian Christie and Benjamin Labaree, *Empire or Independence, 1760–1776* (1976); Edward Countryman, *The American Revolution* (1985); Lawrence Henry Gipson, *The Coming of the Revolution, 1763–1775* (1954); Edmund S. Morgan, *The Birth of the Republic* (1956); Alfred Young, ed., *The American Revolution: Explorations in the History of American Radicalism* (1976).

The Seven Years' War
Fred Anderson, *Crucible of War* (2000) and *A People's Army* (1984); Francis Jennings, *Empire of Fortune: Crown, Colonies, and Tribes in the Seven Years War in America* (1989); Howard H. Peckham, *The Colonial Wars, 1689–1762* (1963).

British Society and Politics
John Brewer, *Party Ideology and Popular Politics at the Accession of George III* (1976); John Brooke, *King George III* (1972); J. C. D. Clark, *English Society, 1688–1832* (1985); M. Dorothy George, *London Life in the Eighteenth Century* (1965); Lawrence Henry Gipson, *The British Empire before the American Revolution* (1936–1970); Derek Jarrett, *England in the Age of Hogarth* (1985); Lewis B. Namier, *England in the Age of the American Revolution*, 2d ed. (1961); Richard Pares, *King George III and the Politicians* (1953); J. H. Plumb, *The First Four Georges* (1956); W. A. Speck, *Stability and Strife: England, 1714–1760* (1979).

The Intellectual Sources of Resistance and Revolution
Bernard Bailyn, *The Ideological Origins of the American Revolution* (1967); Nathan O. Hatch, *The Sacred Cause of Liberty: Republican Thought and the Millennium in Revolutionary New England* (1977); Isaac Kramnick, *Bolingbroke and His Circle: The Politics of Nostalgia in the Age of Walpole* (1968) and *Republicanism and Bourgeois Radicalism: Political Ideology in Late Eighteenth-Century England and America* (1990); Edmund S. Morgan, *The Challenge of the American Revolution* (1976) and

Inventing the People: The Rise of Popular Sovereignty in England and America (1988); J. G. A. Pocock, *The Machiavellian Moment: Florentine Political Thought and the Atlantic Republican Tradition* (1975); Caroline Robbins, *The Eighteenth-Century Commonwealthman: Studies in the Transmission, Development, and Circumstances of English Liberal Thought from the Restoration of Charles II until the War with the Thirteen Colonies* (1959).

A Decade of Resistance

David Ammerman, *In the Common Cause: The American Response to the Coercive Acts of 1774* (1974); Timothy Breen, *Tobacco Culture* (1985); Richard D. Brown, *Revolutionary Politics in Massachusetts: The Boston Committee of Correspondence and the Towns, 1772–1774* (1970); Joseph Ernst, *Money and Politics in America, 1755–1775* (1973); Paul A. Gilje, *The Road to Mobocracy: Popular Disorder in New York City, 1763–1834* (1987); Robert Gross, *The Minutemen and Their World* (1976); Benjamin Labaree, *The Boston Tea Party* (1964); Pauline Maier, *From Resistance to Revolution* (1972); Edmund S. and Helen M. Morgan, *The Stamp Act Crisis* (1953); Gregory H. Nobles, *Divisions throughout the Whole: Politics and Society in Hampshire County, Massachusetts, 1740–1775* (1983); William Penack, *War, Politics, and Revolution in Provincial Massachusetts* (1981); Peter Shaw, *American Patriots and the Rituals of Revolution* (1981); John Shy, *Toward Lexington: The Role of the British Army in the Coming of the American Revolution* (1965); Richard Walsh, *Charleston's Sons of Liberty: A Study of the Artisans, 1763–1789* (1959); Hiller B. Zobel, *The Boston Massacre* (1970).

Leaders of the American Resistance

Bernard Bailyn, *The Ordeal of Thomas Hutchinson* (1974); Richard R. Beeman, *Patrick Henry* (1974); Joseph Ellis, *American Sphinx* (1998) and *Founding Brothers* (2000); Eric Foner, *Tom Paine and Revolutionary America* (1976); David Hawke, *Paine* (1974); Pauline Maier, *The Old Revolutionaries* (1980); Peter Shaw, *The Character of John Adams* (1976); John J. Waters, *The Otis Family in Provincial and Revolutionary Massachusetts* (1968).

CHAPTER 6: THE AMERICAN PEOPLE AND THE AMERICAN REVOLUTION

General Histories

John R. Alden, *The American Revolution* (1964); Ira Gruber, *The Howe Brothers and the American Revolution* (1972); Don Higginbotham, *The American War for In-*dependence (1971); Piers Makesy, *The War for America* (1964); Robert Middlekauff, *The Glorious Cause, 1763–1789* (1982); Mary Beth Norton, *Liberty's Daughters* (1980).

Thomas Jefferson and the Declaration of Independence

Carl Becker, *The Declaration of Independence* (1922); Jay Fliegelman, *Declaring Independence: Jefferson, Natural Language, and the Culture of Performance* (1993); Pauline Maier, *American Scripture* (1998); Garry Wills, *Inventing America* (1978).

The Loyalists

Wallace Brown, *The King's Friends* (1966); Robert M. Calhoon, *The Loyalists in Revolutionary America* (1973); Mary Beth Norton, *The British-Americans* (1972).

George Washington and the Continental Army

E. Wayne Carp, *To Starve the Army at Pleasure: Continental Army Administration and American Political Culture, 1775–1783* (1984); James T. Flexner, *George Washington in the American Revolution* (1968); Douglas Southall Freeman, *George Washington* (1948–1957); Ronald Hoffman and Peter J. Albert, eds., *Arms and Independence: The Military Character of the American Revolution* (1984); James Kirby Martin and Mark Lender, *A Respectable Army: The Military Origins of the Republic, 1763–1789* (1982); Charles Royster, *A Revolutionary People at War* (1979); John Shy, *A People Numerous and Armed* (1976).

Diplomacy

Samuel F. Bemis, *The Diplomacy of the American Revolution* (1935); Jonathan R. Dull, *A Diplomatic History of the American Revolution* (1985); Ronald Hoffman and Peter J. Albert, eds., *Peace and the Peacemakers: The Treaty of 1783* (1986); Richard B. Morris, *The Peacemakers: The Great Powers and American Independence* (1965); Gerald Stourzh, *Benjamin Franklin and American Foreign Policy*, rev. ed. (1969).

The North and the American Revolution

John Brooke, *The Heart of the Commonwealth: Society and Political Culture in Worcester County, Massachusetts, 1713–1861* (1991); Joy Day Buel and Richard Buel Jr., *The Way of Duty* (1984); Edward Countryman, *A People in Revolution: The American Revolution and Political Society in New York, 1760–1790* (1981); Robert J. Taylor, *Western Massachusetts in the Revolution* (1954); Donald Wallace White, *A Village at War: Chatham, New Jersey and the American Revolution* (1979); Alfred F. Young,

"George Robert Twelves Hewes (1742–1840): A Boston Shoemaker and the Memory of the American Revolution," *William and Mary Quarterly* (1981).

Indians and the Revolutionary Frontier

Barbara Graymont, *The Iroquois in the American Revolution* (1972); Isabel Thomson Kelsey, *Joseph Brant, 1743–1807: Man of Two Worlds* (1984); James H. O'Donnell III, *Southern Indians in the American Revolution* (1973); J. M. Sosin, *The Revolutionary Frontier, 1763–1783* (1967).

The South and the American Revolution

John R. Alden, *The South in the Revolution, 1763–1789* (1957); Jeffrey J. Crow and Larry E. Tise, eds., *The Southern Experience in the American Revolution* (1978); Ronald Hoffman, Thad W. Tate, and Peter J. Albert, eds., *An Uncivil War: The Southern Backcountry during the American Revolution* (1985); Jerome J. Nadelhaft, *The Disorders of War: The Revolution in South Carolina* (1981).

The Black Experience and the American Revolution

Ira Berlin and Ronald Hoffman, eds., *Slavery and Freedom in the Age of the American Revolution* (1983); David Brion Davis, *The Problem of Slavery in the Age of Revolution* (1975); Sylvia Frey, *Water from the Rock* (1991); Duncan MacLeod, *Slavery, Race, and the American Revolution* (1974); Gary B. Nash, *Race and Revolution* (1990); Benjamin Quarles, *The Negro in the American Revolution* (1961).

CHAPTER 7: CRISIS AND CONSTITUTION

General Histories

Linda Kerber, *Women of the Republic* (1980); Forrest MacDonald, *E Pluribus Unum* (1965) and *Novus Ordo Seclorum* (1985); Curtis P. Nettels, *The Emergence of a National Economy, 1775–1815* (1962); Robert R. Palmer, *The Age of Democratic Revolution: A Political History of Europe and America, 1760–1800* (1959, 1964); Gordon Wood, *The Creation of the American Republic* (1969) and *The Radicalism of the American Revolution* (1992).

State Politics and State Constitutions

Willi Paul Adams, *The First American Constitutions* (1980); Ronald Hoffman and Peter Albert, eds., *Sovereign States in an Age of Uncertainty* (1981); Jackson Turner Main, *The Sovereign States, 1775–1783* (1973) and *Political Parties before the Constitution* (1973);

Stephen E. Patterson, *Political Parties in Revolutionary Massachusetts* (1973); David Szatmary, *Shays' Rebellion: The Making of an Agrarian Insurrection* (1980).

The Articles of Confederation

Joseph L. Davis, *Sectionalism in American Politics, 1774–1787* (1977); E. James Ferguson, *The Power of the Purse: A History of American Public Finance, 1776–1790* (1961); H. James Henderson, *Party Politics in the Continental Congress* (1974); Merrill D. Jensen, *The Articles of Confederation*, rev. ed. (1959) and *The New Nation* (1950); Peter S. Onuf, *The Origins of the Federal Republic: Jurisdictional Controversies in the United States, 1775–1787* (1983); Jack N. Rakove, *The Beginnings of National Politics* (1979).

Society in the New Republic

John Brooke, *The Heart of the Commonwealth* (1991); Christopher Clark, *The Roots of Rural Capitalism: Western Massachusetts, 1780–1860* (1990); Nancy Cott, "Divorce and the Changing Status of Women in Massachusetts," *William and Mary Quarterly* (1976); Joseph J. Ellis, *After the Revolution: Profiles of Early American Culture* (1979); Jay Fliegelman, *Prodigals and Pilgrims: The American Revolution against Patriarchal Authority, 1750–1800* (1982); Sylvia Frey and Betty Wood, *Come Shouting to Zion* (1998); J. Franklin Jameson, *The American Revolution Considered as a Social Movement* (1962); Benjamin W. Labaree, *The Merchants of Newburyport, 1764–1815* (1962); Jan Lewis, "The Republican Wife: Virtue and Seduction in the Early Republic," *William and Mary Quarterly* (1987); Forrest McDonald and Ellen Shapiro McDonald, "The Ethnic Origins of the American People, 1790," *William and Mary Quarterly* (1980); Gary Nash, *Forging Freedom: The Formation of Philadelphia's Black Community, 1720–1840* (1988); Donald L. Robinson, *Slavery in the Structure of American Politics, 1765–1820* (1971); Howard Rock, *Artisans of the New Republic: Tradesmen of New York City in the Age of Jefferson* (1979); Charles G. Steffen, *The Mechanics of Baltimore: Workers and Politics in the Age of Revolution, 1763–1812* (1984); Alan Taylor, *William Cooper's Town* (1995); Shane White, *Somewhat More Independent* (1991); Lynne Withey, *Dearest Friend: A Life of Abigail Adams* (1981); Arthur Zilversmit, *The First Emancipation: The Abolition of Slavery in the North* (1967).

The Federal Constitution

Douglass Adair, *Fame and the Founding Fathers* (1974); Lance Banning, "James Madison and the Nationalists, 1780–1783," *William and Mary Quarterly* (1983);

Charles Beard, *An Economic Interpretation of the Constitution of the United States* (1913); Richard Beeman, Stephen Botein, and Edward C. Carter II, eds., *Beyond Confederation: Origins of the Constitution and American National Identity* (1987); Irving Brant, *James Madison: The Nationalist, 1780–1787* (1948); Robert E. Brown, *Charles Beard and the Constitution*, (1956); Linda Grant DePauw, *The Eleventh Pillar: New York State and the Federal Constitution* (1966); John P. Diggins, *The Lost Soul of American Politics: Virtue, Self-Interest, and the Foundations of Liberalism* (1984); Max Farrand, *The Framing of the Constitution* (1913); Cecilia Kenyon, "Men of Little Faith: The Anti-Federalists and the Nature of Representative Government," *William and Mary Quarterly*, 12 (1955); Ralph Ketcham, *James Madison* (1971); Leonard Levy, ed., *Essays on the Making of the Constitution* (1969); Forrest MacDonald, *We the People: The Economic Origins of the Constitution* (1958); Jack Rakove, *Original Meanings* (1997); Clinton Rossiter, *1787: The Grand Convention* (1973); Gerald Stourzh, *Alexander Hamilton and the Idea of Republican Government* (1970); Garry Wills, *Explaining America: The Federalist* (1981).

CHAPTER 8: THE REPUBLIC LAUNCHED

Society

Jeanne Boydston, *Home and Work: Housework, Wages, and the Ideology of Labor in the Early Republic* (1990); Nancy F. Cott, *The Bonds of Womanhood: "Woman's Sphere" in New England, 1780–1835* (1977); Joseph J. Ellis, *After the Revolution: Profiles of Early American Culture* (1979); Reginald Horsman, *The Frontier in the Formative Years, 1783–1815* (1970); Jack Larkin, *The Reshaping of Everyday Life, 1790–1840* (1988); Howard Rock, *Artisans of The New Republic* (1979); Malcolm J. Rohrbough, *The Trans-Appalachian Frontier: Peoples, Societies, and Institutions, 1775–1850* (1978); Thomas P. Slaughter, *The Whiskey Rebellion: Frontier Epilogue to the American Revolution* (1986); Billy G. Smith, *The "Lower Sort": Philadelphia's Laboring People, 1759–1800* (1990); Charles G. Steffen, *The Mechanics of Baltimore: Workers and Politics in the Age of Revolution, 1763–1812* (1984); Laurel Thatcher Ulrich, *A Midwife's Tale* (1990).

National Government

Ralph Adams Brown, *The Presidency of John Adams* (1975); Stanley Elkins and Eric McKitrick, *The Age of Federalism* (1993); Ralph Ketcham, *Presidents over Party: The First American Presidency, 1789–1829* (1984); Richard H. Kohn, *Eagle and Sword: The Federalists and the Creation of a Military Establishment in America, 1783–1802* (1975); Forrest McDonald, *The Presidency of George Washington* (1974); John C. Miller, *The Federalist Era, 1789–1801* (1960); Wiley Sword, *President Washington's Indian War: The Struggle for the Old Northwest, 1790–1795* (1985).

Party Politics

Noble Cunningham, *The Jeffersonian Republican's* (1963); Paul Goodman, *The Democratic Republicans of Massachusetts* (1964); John F. Hoadley, *Origins of American Political Parties, 1789–1803* (1986); Richard Hofstadter, *The Idea of a Party System: The Rise of Legitimate Opposition in the United States, 1780–1840* (1969); Stephen G. Kurtz, *The Presidency of John Adams* (1957); Norman Risjord, *Chesapeake Politics, 1781–1800* (1978); James Roger Sharp, *American Politics in the Early Republic* (1993); Alfred Young, *The Democratic Republicans of New York: The Origins, 1763–1797* (1967).

Party Ideology

Joyce Appleby, *Capitalism and a New Social Order: The Republican Vision of the 1970s* (1984); Lance Banning, *The Jeffersonian Persuasion* (1978); Richard W. Buel Jr., *Securing the Republic: Ideology in American Politics, 1789–1815* (1972); John R. Howe Jr., *The Changing Political Thought of John Adams* (1966); Drew R. McCoy, *The Elusive Republic* (1980); Gerald Stourzh, *Alexander Hamilton and the Idea of Republican Government* (1970); John Zvesper, *Political Philosophy and Rhetoric: A Study of the Origins of Party Politics* (1977).

Constitutional Developments

Leonard Levy, *Legacy of Suppression: Freedom of Speech and Press in Early American History* (1960); Bernard Schwartz, *The Great Rights of Mankind: A History of the American Bill of Rights* (1977); James M. Smith, *Freedom's Fetters: The Alien and Sedition Laws and American Civil Liberties* (1956).

Foreign Policy

Harry Ammon, *The Genet Mission* (1973); Jerald Combs, *The Jay Treaty: Political Battleground of the Founding Fathers* (1970); Alexander DeConde, *Entangling Alliance: Politics and Diplomacy under George Washington* (1958) and *The Quasi-War: The Politics and Diplomacy of the Undeclared War with France, 1797–1801* (1966); Felix Gilbert, *To the Farewell Address: Ideas of Early American Foreign Policy* (1961); Paul A. Varg, *Foreign Policies of the Founding Fathers* (1963).

Biographies

Charles W. Aikers, *Abigail Adams* (1980); Irving Brant, *James Madison: Father of the Constitution, 1787–1800*

(1950); Jacob E. Cooke, *Alexander Hamilton* (1982); Merrill Peterson, *Thomas Jefferson and the New Nation* (1970); Page Smith, *John Adams* (1962); Garry Wills, *Cincinnatus: George Washington and the Enlightenment* (1984).

CHAPTER 9: THE JEFFERSONIAN REPUBLIC

General Histories
Richard Hofstadter, *The Idea of a Party System: The Rise of Legitimate Opposition in the United States, 1780–1840* (1969); Marshall Smelser, *The Democratic Republic* (1968).

Jeffersonians in Power
Alexander Balinky, *Albert Gallatin: Fiscal Theories and Policy* (1958); James Banner, *To the Hartford Convention: The Federalists and the Origins of Party Politics in the Early Republic, 1789–1815* (1970); Theodore J. Crackel, *Mr. Jefferson's Army: Political and Social Reform of the Military Establishment, 1801–1809* (1987); Noble Cunningham, *The Jeffersonian Republicans in Power: Party Operations, 1801–1809* (1963); Paul Goodman, *The Democratic Republicans of Massachusetts* (1964); David Hackett Fischer, *The Revolution of American Conservatism* (1965); Robert M. Johnstone Jr., *Jefferson and the Presidency: Leadership in the Young Republic* (1978); Linda K. Kerber, *Federalists in Dissent: Imagery and Ideology in Jeffersonian America* (1970); Drew R. McCoy, *The Elusive Republic* (1980); Norman K. Risjord, *The Old Republicans: Southern Conservatism in the Age of Jefferson* (1965); Robert A. Rutland, *The Presidency of James Madison* (1990); Robert W. Tucker and David C. Hendrickson, *Empire of Liberty: The Statecraft of Thomas Jefferson* (1990).

Indian Affairs and Western Expansion
John Boles, *The Great Revival in the South* (1972); Paul K. Conklin, *Cane Ridge: America's Pentecost* (1990); R. David Edmunds, *Tecumseh and the Quest for Indian Leadership* (1984); Christine Heyrman, *Southern Cross: The Beginnings of the Bible Belt* (1998); Reginald Horsman, *Expansion and American Indian Policy, 1783–1812* (1967) and *The Frontier in the Formative Years, 1783–1815* (1970); R. Douglas Hurt, *The Ohio Frontier* (1996); Donald Jackson, *Thomas Jefferson and the Stony Mountains: Exploring the West from Monticello* (1979); T. Scott Miyakawa, *Protestants and Pioneers: Individualism and Conformity on the American Frontier* (1964); Malcolm J. Rohrbough, *The Trans-Appalachian Frontier* (1978); Bernard W. Sheehan, *Seeds of Extinction:*

Jeffersonian Philanthropy and the American Indians (1973); Michael Williams, *Americans and Their Forests: A Historical Geography* (1989).

The Judiciary
Richard E. Ellis, *The Jeffersonian Crisis: Courts and Politics in the Early Republic* (1971); Robert K. Faulkner, *The Jurisprudence of John Marshall* (1968); R. K. Newmyer, *The Supreme Court under Marshall and Taney* (1968).

Foreign Affairs and the War of 1812
Roger H. Brown, *The Republic in Peril* (1964); Alexander DeConde, *This Affair of Louisiana* (1976); Donald C. Hickey, *The War of 1812: A Forgotten Conflict* (1989); Bradford Perkins, *Prologue to War: England and the United States, 1805–1812* (1961); Robert A. Rutland, *Madison's Alternatives: The Jeffersonian Republicans and the Coming of War, 1805–1812* (1975); Burton Spivak, *Jefferson's English Crisis: Commerce, Embargo and the Republican Revolution* (1978); J. C. A. Stagg, *Mr. Madison's War: Politics, Diplomacy, and Warfare in the Early American Republic, 1783–1830* (1983).

The Era of Good Feelings
Samuel F. Bemis, *John Quincy Adams and the Foundations of American Foreign Policy* (1949); Noble Cunningham, *The Presidency of James Monroe* (1996); George Dangerfield, *The Awakening of American Nationalism* (1965); Ernest R. May, *The Making of the Monroe Doctrine* (1976); Glover Moore, *The Missouri Controversy, 1819–1821* (1953).

Biographies
Harry Ammon, *James Monroe: The Quest for National Identity* (1979); Leonard Baker, *John Marshall: A Life in Law* (1974); R. David Edmunds, *The Shawnee Prophet* (1983); Ralph Ketcham, *James Madison: A Biography* (1971); Dumas Malone, *Jefferson the President: First Term, 1801–1805* (1970) and *Jefferson the President: Second Term, 1805–1809* (1974); Drew R. McCoy, *The Last of the Fathers: James Madison and the Republican Legacy* (1989); Merrill Peterson, *Thomas Jefferson and the New Nation: A Biography* (1970); Robert Remini, *Andrew Jackson and the Course of American Empire, 1767–1821* (1977).

CHAPTER 10: THE OPENING OF AMERICA

General Histories
Stuart Bruchey, *The Roots of American Economic Growth, 1607–1861* (1965); Mary Kupiec Cayton et al., eds., *Encyclopedia of American Social History*, 3 vols. (1993);

Douglass C. North, *The Economic Growth of the United States 1790–1860* (1961); Charles Sellers, *The Market Revolution* (1991); Melvin Stokes and Stephen Conway, eds., *The Market Revolution in America* (1996); Peter Temin, *Causal Factors in American Economic Growth in the Nineteenth Century* (1975).

Transportation

Carter Goodrich, *Government Promotion of American Canals and Railroads, 1800–1860* (1974); Erik F. Haites et al., *Western River Transportation: The Era of Early Internal Development, 1810–1860* (1975); Ronald Shaw, *Canals for a Nation: The Canal Era in the United States, 1790–1860* (1990); Carol Sheriff, *The Artificial River: The Erie Canal and the Paradox of Progress, 1817–1862* (1996); George R. Taylor, *The Transportation Revolution, 1815–1860* (1951); Peter Way, *Common Labour: Workers and the Digging of North American Canals, 1780–1860* (1993).

Industrialization and the Economy

Jeremy Atack and Peter Passell, *A New Economic View of American History* (1994); Thomas C. Cochran, *Frontiers of Change: Early Industrialism in America* (1981); Gary Cross and Rick Szostak, *Technology and American Society* (1995); Robert F. Dalzell Jr., *Enterprising Elite: The Boston Associates and the World They Made* (1987); David J. Jeremy, *Transatlantic Industrial Revolution: The Diffusion of Textile Technology between Britain and America, 1790–1830* (1981); Diane Lindstrom, *Economic Development in the Philadelphia Region, 1810–1850* (1978); Nathan Rosenberg, *Technology and American Economic Growth* (1972); Darwin H. Stapleton, *The Transfer of Early Industrial Technologies to America* (1987); Barbara M. Tucker, *Samuel Slater and the Origins of the American Textile Industry, 1790–1860* (1984).

Agriculture

Jeremy Atack and Fred Bateman, *To Their Own Soil: Agriculture in the Antebellum North* (1987); Clarence Danhof, *Changes in Agriculture: The Northern United States, 1820–1870* (1969); Paul W. Gates, *The Farmer's Age: Agriculture, 1815–1860* (1960); Winifred Barr Rothenberg, *From Market-Places to a Market Economy: The Transformation of Rural Massachusetts, 1750–1850* (1992).

Workers and Community Studies

Stuart M. Blumin, *The Urban Threshold* (1976); Christopher Clark, *The Roots of Rural Capitalism* (1990); Don H. Doyle, *The Social Order of a Frontier Community: Jacksonville, Illinois, 1825–70* (1983); Thomas Dublin, *Transforming Women's Work: New England Lives in the Industrial Revolution* (1994) and *Women at Work* (1979); Daniel S. Dupre, *Transforming the Cotton Frontier: Madison County, Alabama, 1800–1840* (1997); Paul G. Faler, *Mechanics and Manufacturers in the Early Industrial Revolution* (1981); John Mack Faragher, *Sugar Creek* (1986); Paul A. Gilje, *The Road to Mobocracy: Popular Disorder in New York City, 1763–1834* (1987); Bruce Laurie, *Working People of Philadelphia, 1800–1850* (1980); Jonathan Prude, *The Coming of Industrial Order: Town and Factory Life in Rural Massachusetts, 1810–1860* (1983); Steven J. Ross, *Workers on the Edge: Work, Leisure, and Politics in Industrializing Cincinnati, 1788–1890* (1985); Christine Stansell, *City of Women: Sex and Class in New York, 1789–1860* (1986); Richard B. Stott, *Workers in the Metropolis: Class, Ethnicity, and Youth in Antebellum New York City* (1990); Sean Wilentz, *Chants Democratic: New York City and the Rise of the American Working Class, 1788–1850* (1984); David A. Zonderman, *Aspirations and Anxieties: New England Workers and the Mechanized Factory System, 1815–1850* (1992).

Society and Values

Stuart Blumin, *The Emergence of the Middle Class* (1989); Daniel J. Boorstin, *The Americans: The National Experience* (1965); Richard D. Brown, *Knowledge Is Power: The Diffusion of Information in Early America, 1700–1865* (1989); Richard L. Bushman, *The Refinement of America: Persons, Houses, Cities* (1992); Clyde and Sally Griffen, *Natives and Newcomers: The Ordering of Opportunity in Mid-Nineteenth Poughkeepsie* (1978); David Grimsted, *American Mobbing, 1828–1861* (1998); James L. Huston, *Securing the Fruits of Labor: The American Concept of Wealth Distribution, 1765–1900* (1998); Richard R. John, *Spreading the News: The American Postal System from Franklin to Morse* (1996); Jack Larkin, *The Reshaping of Everyday Life, 1790–1840* (1988); Lawrence W. Levine, *High Brow/Low Brow: The Emergence of Cultural Hierarchy in America* (1988); Russel B. Nye, *Society and Culture in America, 1830–1860* (1974); Michael O'Malley, *Keeping Watch: A History of American Time* (1990); William H. and Jane H. Pease, *The Web of Progress: Private Values and Public Styles in Boston and Charleston, 1828–1843* (1985); Edward Pessen, *Riches, Class, and Power before the Civil War* (1973); Alexander Saxton, *The Rise and Fall of the White Republic: Class Politics and Mass Culture in Nineteenth-Century America* (1990); Stephan Thernstrom, *Poverty and Progress: Social Mobility in a Nineteenth-Century City* (1964); Robert H. Wiebe, *The Opening of American Society: From the Adoption of the Constitution to the Eve of Disunion* (1984).

Land and the West

Daniel Feller, *The Public Lands in Jacksonian Politics* (1984); Malcolm J. Rohrbough, *The Land Office Business: The Settlement and Administration of American Public Lands, 1789–1837* (1968); David J. Wishart, *The Fur Trade of the American West, 1817–1840* (1979).

Environment

Carolyn Merchant, *Ecological Revolutions: Nature, Gender, and Science in New England* (1989); Theodore Steinberg, *Nature Incorporated: Industrialization and the Waters of New England* (1991); Michael Williams, *Americans and Their Forests: A Historical Geography* (1989).

Politics and Law

George Dangerfield, *The Awakening of American Nationalism, 1815–1828* (1965); Robert K. Faulkner, *The Jurisprudence of John Marshall* (1968); Morton J. Horwitz, *The Transformation of American Law, 1780–1860* (1977); R. Kent Newmyer, *The Supreme Court under Marshall and Taney* (1968); M. N. Rothbard, *The Panic of 1819: Reactions and Policies* (1962).

CHAPTER 11: THE RISE OF DEMOCRACY

General Histories

George Dangerfield, *The Awakening of American Nationalism, 1815–1828* (1965); Edward Pessen, *Jacksonian America: Society, Personality, and Politics*, rev. ed. (1978); Arthur M. Schlesinger Jr., *The Age of Jackson* (1945); Charles Sellers, *The Market Revolution* (1991); Glyndon G. Van Deusen, *The Jacksonian Era, 1828–1845* (1959); Harry Watson, *Liberty and Power* (1990).

Society and Values

James O. and Lois E. Horton, *In Hope of Liberty: Community and Protest among Northern Free Blacks, 1700–1860* (1997); Douglas T. Miller, *Jacksonian Aristocracy: Class and Democracy in New York, 1830–1860* (1967); Russel B. Nye, *Society and Culture in America, 1830–1860* (1960); Edward Pessen, *Riches, Class, and Power before the Civil War* (1973); Alexis de Tocqueville, *Democracy in America* (1945); John William Ward, *Andrew Jackson: Symbol for an Age* (1955); Julie Winch, *Philadelphia's Black Elite: Activism, Accommodation, and the Struggle for Autonomy, 1787–1848* (1988).

The Emergence of Democracy

James S. Chase, *Emergence of the Presidential Nominating Convention, 1789–1832* (1973); Richard Hofstadter, *The Idea of a Party System: The Rise of Legitimate Opposition in the United States, 1780–1840* (1969); Richard

P. McCormick, *The Presidential Game: The Origins of American Presidential Politics* (1982); Robert Remini, *The Election of Andrew Jackson* (1963) and *The Legacy of Andrew Jackson* (1988); Chilton Williamson, *American Suffrage from Property to Democracy, 1760–1860* (1960).

The Jacksonian Party System

Glenn C. Altschuler and Stuart M. Blumin, *Rude Republic: Americans and Their Politics in the Nineteenth Century* (2000); Lee Benson, *The Concept of Jacksonian Democracy: New York as a Test Case* (1961); Paul Goodman, *Towards a Christian Republic* (1988); Mary W. M. Hargreaves, *The Presidency of John Quincy Adams* (1985); Richard Hofstadter, *The American Political Tradition* (1948); Michael F. Holt, *The Rise and Fall of the American Whig Party* (1999); Daniel Walker Howe, *The Political Culture of the American Whigs* (1979); Lawrence Frederick Kohl, *The Politics of Individualism* (1988); Richard B. Latner, *The Presidency of Andrew Jackson: White House Politics, 1829–1837* (1979); Marvin Meyers, *The Jacksonian Persuasion* (1957); Mary P. Ryan, *Women in Public: Between Banners and Ballots, 1825–1880* (1990); William G. Shade, *Democratizing the Old Dominion: Virginia and the Second Party System, 1824–1861* (1997); Joel H. Silbey, *The American Political Nation, 1838–1893* (1991); Elizabeth R. Varon, *We Mean to Be Counted: White Women and Politics in Antebellum Virginia* (1998).

Banking and the Economy

John M. McFaul, *The Politics of Jacksonian Finance* (1972); Robert Remini, *Andrew Jackson and the Bank War* (1967); James Roger Sharp, *The Jacksonians versus the Banks: Politics in the States after the Panic of 1837* (1970); Peter Temin, *The Jacksonian Economy* (1969).

Nullification

Richard Ellis, *The Union at Risk: Jacksonian Democracy, States' Rights and the Nullification Crisis* (1987); William W. Freehling, *Prelude to Civil War* (1966); Merrill D. Peterson, *Olive Branch and Sword: The Compromise of 1833* (1982).

Indian Removal

Arthur H. DeRosier Jr., *The Removal of the Choctaw Indians* (1970); Michael D. Green, *The Politics of Indian Removal* (1982); John K. Mahon, *History of the Second Seminole War, 1835–1842* (1967); William G. McLoughlin, *Cherakee Renascence in the New Republic* (1986); Francis P. Prucha, *American Indian Policy in the Formative Years* (1962); Ronald N. Satz, *American Indian Policy in the Jacksonian Era* (1975).

Biographies

Donald Cole, *Martin Van Buren and the American Political System* (1984); Thomas P. Govan, *Nicholas Biddle: Nationalist and Public Banker* (1959); John Niven, *John C. Calhoun and the Price of Union: A Biography* (1988) and *Martin Van Buren: The Romantic Age of American Politics* (1983); Merrill D. Peterson, *The Great Triumvirate: Webster, Clay, and Calhoun* (1987); Robert V. Remini, *Daniel Webster: The Man and His Time* (1997), *Henry Clay: Statesman for the Union* (1991), and *The Life of Andrew Jackson* (1988); Charles W. Wiltse, *John C. Calhoun, Nullifier, 1829–1839* (1949).

CHAPTER 12: THE FIRES OF PERFECTION

General Histories

John D'Emilio and Estelle B. Freedman, *Intimate Matters: A History of Sexuality in America* (1988); John F. Kasson, *Rudeness and Civility: Manners in Nineteenth Century America* (1990); Russel B. Nye, *Society and Culture in America, 1830–1860* (1974); Lewis Perry, *Boats against the Current: American Culture between Revolution and Modernity, 1820–1860* (1993).

Religion and Revivalism

Whitney Cross, *The Burned Over District* (1950); Nathan O. Hatch, *The Democratization of American Christianity* (1989); Christine Heyrman, *Southern Cross: The Beginnings of the Bible Belt* (1998); Paul Johnson, *A Shopkeeper's Millennium* (1978); Paul E. Johnson and Sean Wilentz, *The Kingdom of Matthias* (1994); William G. McLoughlin, *Modern Revivalism: Charles Grandison Finney to Billy Graham* (1959); Jan Shipps, *Mormonism: The Story of a New Religious Tradition* (1985); George H. Thomas, *Revivalism and Cultural Change* (1989).

Women's Sphere and Feminism

Norma Balsch, *In the Eyes of the Law: Women, Marriage, and Property in Nineteenth-Century New York* (1982); Patricia Cohen, *The Murder of Helen Jewett* (1999); Nancy Cott, *The Bonds of Womanhood* (1977); Carl Degler, *At Odds* (1977); Ann Douglas, *The Feminization of American Culture* (1977); Ellen C. DuBois, *Feminism and Suffrage* (1978); Barbara Epstein, *The Politics of Domesticity* (1981); Timothy J. Gilfoyle, *City of Eros: New York City, Prostitution, and the Commercialization of Sex, 1790–1920* (1992); Lori D. Ginzberg, *Women and the Work of Benevolence* (1990); Nancy Hewitt, *Women's Activism and Social Change: Rochester, New York, 1822–1872* (1984); Sylvia D. Hoffert, *Private Matters: American Attitudes toward Childbearing and Infant Nurture in the Urban North, 1800–1860* (1989); Jean V. Matthews, *Women's Struggle for Equality* (1997); Keith E. Melder, *Beginnings of Sisterhood: The American Women's Rights Movement, 1800–1850* (1977); James Reed, *From Private Vice to Public Virtue: The Birth Control Movement in America* (1978); Mary P. Ryan, *The Cradle of the Middle Class* (1981); Jean Fagan Yellin, *Women and Sisters: The Antislavery Feminists in American Culture* (1989).

Family

Clifford E. Clark Jr., *The American Family Home, 1800–1860* (1986); Thomas R. Cole, *The Journey of Life: A Cultural History of Aging in America* (1992); Stephen M. Frank, *Life with Father: Parenthood and Masculinity in the Nineteenth-Century American North* (1998); Steven Mintz and Susan Kellogg, *Domestic Revolutions: A Social History of American Family Life* (1988); Walter T. K. Nugent, *Structures of American Social History* (1981); Robert V. Wells, *Revolutions in Americans' Lives: A Demographic Perspective on the History of Americans, Their Families, and Their Society* (1982).

American Romanticism

Paul F. Boller Jr., *American Transcendentalism, 1830–1860: An Intellectual Inquiry* (1974); Mary Kupiec Cayton, *Emerson's Emergence: Self and Society in the Transformation of New England, 1800–1845* (1989); Susan P. Conrad, *Perish the Thought: Intellectual Women in Romantic America, 1830–1860* (1976); F. O. Matthiessen, *American Renaissance: Art and Expression in the Age of Emerson and Whitman* (1941); Anne C. Rose, *Transcendentalism as a Social Movement, 1830–1850* (1981); Lazar Ziff, *Literary Democracy: The Declaration of Cultural Independence in America* (1982).

Utopian Communities

Lawrence Foster, *Religion and Sexuality: Three American Communal Experiments of the Nineteenth Century* (1981); Carl J. Guarneri, *The Utopian Alternative: Fourierism in Nineteenth-Century America* (1991); J. F. C. Harrison, *Quest for the New Moral World: Robert Owen and the Owenites in Britain and America* (1969); Louis Kern, *An Ordered Love: Sex Roles and Sexuality in Victorian Utopias* (1981); Carol A. Kolmerten, *Women in Utopia: The Ideology of Gender in the American Owenite Communities* (1990); Stephen Stein, *The Shaker Experience in America* (1992).

Reform Movements

Robert H. Abzug, *Cosmos Crumbling: American Reform and the Religious Imagination* (1994); Charles Leslie

Glenn Jr., *The Myth of the Common School* (1988); Clifford S. Griffin, *Their Brothers' Keepers: Moral Stewardship in the United States, 1800–1865* (1960); Carl F. Kaestle, *Pillars of the Republic* (1983); Steven Mintz, *Moralists and Modernizers: American's Pre-Civil War Reformers* (1995); W. J. Rorabaugh, *The Alcoholic Republic: An American Tradition* (1979); David Rothman, *The Discovery of the Asylum: Social Order and Disorder in the New Republic* (1971); Alice Felt Tyler, *Freedom's Ferment* (1944); Ian R. Tyrrell, *Sobering Up: From Temperance to Prohibition in Antebellum America, 1800–1860* (1979); Ronald G. Walters, *American Reformers, 1815–1860* (1978).

Abolitionism

Paul Goodman, *Of One Blood: Abolitionism and the Origins of Racial Equality* (1998); Julie Jeffrey, *The Great Silent Army of Abolitionism: Ordinary Women in the Antislavery Movement* (1998); John R. McKivigan, *The War against Proslavery Religion: Abolitionism and the Northern Churches* (1984); William Lee Miller, *Arguing about Slavery: The Great Battle in the United States Congress* (1996); William H. and Jane H. Pease, *They Who Would Be Free: Blacks' Search for Freedom, 1830–1861* (1974); Lewis Perry, *Radical Abolitionism: Anarchy and the Government of God in Antislavery Thought* (1973); Leonard Richards, *"Gentlemen of Property and Standing": Anti-Abolition Mobs in Jacksonian America* (1970); James B. Stewart, *Holy Warriors* (1976).

Biographies

Robert H. Abzug, *Passionate Liberator: Theodore Dwight Weld and the Dilemma of Reform* (1980); Lois Banner, *Elizabeth Cady Stanton: A Radical for Woman's Rights* (1980); Fawn Brodie, *No Man Knows My History: The Life of Joseph Smith, the Mormon Prophet*, 2d ed. (1971); Thomas J. Brown, *Dorothea Dix: New England Reformer* (1998); Richard L. Bushman, *Joseph Smith and the Beginnings of Mormonism* (1984); Charles Capper, *Margaret Fuller: An American Romantic Life, the Private Years* (1992); Keith J. Hardman, *Charles Grandison Finney, 1792–1875: Revivalist and Reformer* (1987); Gerda Lerner, *The Grimké Sisters of South Carolina: Rebels against Slavery* (1967); William S. McFeely, *Frederick Douglass* (1991); Nell Painter, *Sojourner Truth: A Life, a Symbol* (1996); Katherine Kish Sklar, *Catharine Beecher: A Study in American Domesticity* (1973); John L. Thomas, *The Liberator: William Lloyd Garrison* (1963); Robert D. Thomas, *The Man Who Would Be Perfect: John Humphrey Noyes and the Utopian Impulse* (1977); Bertram Wyatt-Brown, *Lewis Tappan and the Evangelical War against Slavery* (1969).

CHAPTER 13: THE OLD SOUTH

General Histories

John B. Boles, *The South through Time: A History of an American Region* (1995); William J. Cooper and Thomas Terrill, *The American South*, 2d ed. (1996); Albert Cowdrey, *This Land, This South: An Environmental History*, rev. ed. (1996); William W. Freehling, *The Road to Disunion* (1990); Charles S. Sydnor, *The Development of Southern Sectionalism, 1819–1848* (1948).

Southern Economy

Fred Bateman and Thomas Weiss, *A Deplorable Scarcity: The Failure of Industrialization in the Slave Economy* (1981); Lewis C. Gray, *History of Agriculture in the Southern United States to 1860*, 2 vols. (1933); Gavin Wright, *The Political Economy of the Cotton South: Households, Markets, and Wealth in the Nineteenth Century* (1978).

Southern Society

Ira Berlin, *Slaves without Masters* (1974); John B. Boles, ed., *Masters and Slaves in the House of the Lord: Race and Religion in the American South, 1740–1870* (1988); Orville Vernon Burton, *In My Father's House Are Many Mansions: Family and Community in Edgefield, South Carolina* (1985); Dickson D. Bruce Jr., *Violence and Culture in the Antebellum South* (1979); Joan E. Cashin, *A Family Venture* (1991); Bill Cecil-Fronsman, *Common Whites: Class and Culture in Antebellum North Carolina* (1992); J. William Harris, *Plain Folk and Gentry in a Slave Society: White Liberty and Black Slavery in Augusta's Hinterlands* (1985); Christine Heyrman, *Southern Cross: The Beginnings of the Bible Belt* (1998); Donald G. Mathews, *Religion in the Old South* (1977); Stephanie McCurry, *Masters of Small Worlds: Yeoman Households, Gender Relations, and the Political Culture of the Antebellum South Carolina Low Country* (1995); Robert Tracy McKenzie, *One South or Many? Plantation Belt and Upcountry in Civil War–Era Tennessee* (1994); John Hebron Moore, *The Emergence of the Cotton Kingdom in the Old Southwest: Mississippi, 1770–1860* (1988); Thomas D. Morris, *Slavery and the Law, 1619–1860* (1996); James Oakes, *Slavery and Freedom* (1990); Frederick Law Olmsted, *The Cotton Kingdom* (1860, reprinted 1984); Frank Owsley, *Plain Folk of the Old South* (1949); William H. and Jane H. Pease, *The Web of Progress: Private Values and Public Styles in Boston and Charleston, 1828–1843* (1985); Mark M. Smith, *Mastered by the Clock: Time, Slavery, and Freedom in the American South* (1997); Bertram Wyatt-Brown, *Honor and Violence in the Old South* (1986).

Southern Women

Victoria E. Bynum, *Unruly Women: The Politics of Social and Sexual Control in the Old South* (1992); Jane Turner Censer, *North Carolina Planters and Their Children, 1800–1860* (1984); Catherine Clinton, *The Plantation Mistress: Woman's World in the Old South* (1983); Elizabeth Fox-Genovese, *Within the Plantation Household* (1988); Martha Hodes, *White Women, Black Men: Illicit Sex in the Nineteenth-Century South* (1997); Suzanne Lebsock, *Free Women of Petersburg: Status and Culture in a Southern Town, 1784–1860* (1984); Brenda E. Stevenson, *Life in Black and White: Family and Community in the Slave South* (1996); Marli F. Weiner, *Mistresses and Slaves: Plantation Women in South Carolina, 1830–1880* (1998).

Slavery and Slaveowners

Peter A. Coclanis, *The Shadow of a Dream: Economic Life and Death in the South Carolina Low Country, 1670–1920* (1989); Paul A. David et al., *Reckoning with Slavery: A Critical Study in the Quantitative History of American Negro Slavery* (1976); James Oakes, *The Ruling Race* (1982); Todd L. Savitt, *Medicine and Slavery: The Diseases and Health Care of Blacks in Antebellum Virginia* (1978); Kenneth M. Stampp, *The Peculiar Institution* (1956); Richard H. Steckel, *The Economics of U.S. Slave and Southern White Fertility* (1985); Michael Tadman, *Speculators and Slaves: Masters, Traders, and Slaves in the Old South* (1989); William L. Van Deburg, *The Slave Drivers: Black Agricultural Labor Supervisors in the Antebellum South* (1988).

Slave Culture

John W. Blassingame, *The Slave Community: Plantation Life in the Ante-Bellum South*, rev. ed. (1979); John B. Boles, *Black Southerners, 1619–1869* (1984); Eugene D. Genovese, *Roll, Jordon, Roll* (1974); Herbert G. Gutman, *The Black Family in Slavery and Freedom, 1750–1925* (1976); Charles Joyner, *Down by the Riverside* (1984); Wilma King, *Stolen Childhood: Slave Youth in Nineteenth Century America* (1995); Lawrence Levine, *Black Culture and Black Consciousness: Afro-American Folk Thought from Slavery to Freedom* (1977); Ann Patton Malone, *Sweet Chariot: Slave Family and Household Structure in Nineteenth-Century Louisiana* (1993); Christopher Morris, *Becoming Southern: The Evolution of a Way of Life, Warren County and Vicksburg, Mississippi. 1770–1860* (1995); Albert J. Raboteau, *Slave Religion: The "Invisible Institution" in the Antebellum South* (1978); Mechal Sobel, *Trabelin' On: The Slave Journey to an Afro-Baptist Faith* (1979); Sterling Stuckey, *Slave Culture: Nationalist Theory and the Foundations of Black America* (1987).

Slave Resistance

Norrece T. Jones, *Born a Child of Freedom, Yet a Slave: Mechanisms of Control and Strategies of Resistance in Antebellum South* (1990); Winthrop Jordan, *Tumult and Silence at Second Creek* (1993); John Lofton, *Denmark Vesey's Revolt* (1983); Stephen B. Oates, *The Fires of Jubilee: Nat Turner's Fierce Rebellion* (1975).

The Defense of Slavery

Clement Eaton, *Freedom of Thought in the Old South* (1940); William J. Cooper Jr., *The Politics of Slavery* (1978); Drew Faust, *A Sacred Circle* (1977); George M. Fredrickson, *The Black Image in the White Mind: The Debate on Afro-American Character and Destiny, 1817–1914* (1971); Alison Goodyear Freehling, *Drift toward Dissolution: The Virginia Slavery Debate of 1831–1832* (1982).

CHAPTER 14: WESTERN EXPANSION AND THE RISE OF THE SLAVERY ISSUE

General Histories

Ray A. Billington and Martin Ridge, *Westward Expansion*, 5th ed. (1982); William H. Goetzmann, *Exploration and Empire: The Explorer and the Scientist in the Winning of the American West* (1978); Henry Nash Smith, *Virgin Land: The American West as Symbol and Myth* (1950); Elliott West, *The Way to the West* (1995); Richard White, *It's Your Misfortune and None of My Own* (1991).

American Expansionism

John Mack Faragher, *Women and Men on the Overland Trail* (1979); Thomas R. Hietala, *Manifest Design* (1985); Reginald Horsman, *Race and Manifest Destiny: The Origins of American Racial Anglo-Saxonism* (1981); Frederick Merk, *Manifest Destiny and Mission in American History* (1963), *The Monroe Doctrine and American Expansionism, 1843–1849* (1966), and *The Oregon Question: Essays in Anglo-American Diplomacy and Politics* (1967); John D. Unruh Jr., *The Plains Across* (1979).

Societies in the West

Leonard J. Arrington and Davis Bitton, *The Mormon Experience*, 2d ed. (1992); Gunther Barth, *Instant Cities: Urbanization and the Rise of San Francisco and Denver* (1975); William C. Binkley, *The Texas Revolution* (1952); Malcolm Clark Jr., *Eden Seekers: The Settlement of Oregon, 1812–1862* (1981); Thomas D. Hall, *Social Change in the Southwest, 1350–1880* (1989); Robert F. Heizer and Alan J. Almquist, *The Other Californians: Prejudice and Discrimination under Spain, Mexico, and* the *United States to 1920* (1971); Donald D. Jackson, *Gold Dust* (1980); Julie R. Jeffrey, *Frontier Women* (1979); Dorothy O. Johansen and Charles M. Gates, *Empire on the Columbia: A History of the Pacific Northwest*, 2d ed. (1967); Susan Lee Johnson, *Roaring Camp: The Social World of the California Gold Rush* (2000); Sandra L. Myres, *Westering Women and the Frontier Experience, 1800–1915* (1982); Leonard Pitt, *The Decline of the Californios: A Social History of the Spanish-Speaking Californians, 1846–1890* (1966); David J. Weber, *The Mexican Frontier, 1821–1846* (1982); Elliott West, *Growing Up with the Country: Childhood on the Far Western Frontier* (1989); Donald Worster, *Rivers of Empire: Water, Aridity, and the Growth of the American West* (1985).

Expansion and the Party System
Paul B. Bergeron, *The Presidency of James K. Polk* (1987); William R. Brock, *Parties and Political Conscience* (1970); Michael F. Holt, *The Rise and Fall of the American Whig Party* (1999); Frederick Merk, *Slavery and the Annexation of Texas* (1972); James C. N. Paul, *Rift in the Democracy* (1961); Norma L. Peterson, *The Presidencies of William Henry Harrison and John Tyler* (1989); Charles G. Sellers Jr., *James K. Polk, Continentalist, 1843–1846* (1966).

The War with Mexico
K. Jack Bauer, *The Mexican War, 1846–1848* (1974); Neal Harlow, *California Conquered: The Annexation of a Mexican Province, 1846–1850* (1982); Robert W. Johannsen, *To the Halls of the Montezumas: The Mexican War in the American Imagination* (1985); David M. Pletcher, *The Diplomacy of Annexation: Texas, Oregon, and the Mexican War* (1973); John H. Schroeder, *Mr. Polk's War: American Opposition and Dissent, 1846–1848* (1973).

The Sectional Crisis and the Expansion of Slavery
Frederick J. Blue, *The Free Soilers: Third Party Politics, 1848–1854* (1973); William J. Cooper Jr., *The South and the Politics of Slavery, 1828–1856* (1978); William W. Freehling, *The Road to Disunion* (1990); Holman Hamilton, *Prologue to Conflict* (1964); Michael A. Morrison, *Slavery and the American West* (1997); David M. Potter, *The Impending Crisis, 1848–1861* (1976); Richard H. Sewell, *Ballots for Freedom: Antislavery Politics in the United States, 1837–1860* (1976); Elbert B. Smith, *The Presidencies of Zachary Taylor and Millard Fillmore* (1988); Mark J. Stegmaier, *Texas, New Mexico, and the Compromise of 1859* (1996).

Biographies
Leonard J. Arrington, *Brigham Young: American Moses* (1985); K. Jack Bauer, *Zachary Taylor: Soldier, Planter, Statesman of the Old Southwest* (1985); Robert F. Dalzell, *Daniel Webster and the Trial of American Nationalism, 1843–1852* (1972); Robert W. Johannsen, *Stephen A. Douglas* (1973); Robert Remini, *Henry Clay: Statesman for the Union* (1991).

CHAPTER 15: THE UNION BROKEN

General Histories
Avery Craven, *The Coming of the Civil War*, 2d ed. rev. (1975); James M. McPherson, *Battle Cry of Freedom* (1988); Allan Nevins, *Ordeal of the Union*, 2 vols. (1947) and *The Emergence of Lincoln*, 2 vols. (1950); David M. Potter, *The Impending Crisis, 1848–1861* (1976).

Economic Development and the Environment
William Cronon, *Nature's Metropolis: Chicago and the Great West* (1991); Albert Fishlow, *American Railroads and the Transformation of the Antebellum Economy* (1965); Robert William Fogel, *Without Consent or Contract: The Rise and Fall of American Slavery* (1989); Paul W. Gates, *The Farmer's Age: Agriculture, 1815–1860* (1960); James Huston, *The Panic of 1857 and the Coming of the Civil War* (1987); John F. Stover, *Iron Road to the West: American Railroads in the 1850s* (1978).

Immigration and Nativism
Tyler Anbinder, *Nativism and Slavery: The Northern Know Nothings and the Politics of the 1850s* (1992); John P. Dolan, *The Immigrant Church: New York's Irish and German Catholics, 1815–1865* (1975); Oscar Handlin, *Boston's Immigrants: A Study of Acculturation*, rev. ed. (1959); Michael F. Holt, "The Antimasonic and Know Nothing Parties," in Arthur M. Schlesinger Jr., ed., *History of U.S. Political Parties*, vol. 1, pp. 575–737 (1973); Bruce Levine, *The Spirit of 1848: German Immigrants, Labor Conflict, and the Coming of the Civil War* (1992); Stanley Nadel, *Little Germany: Ethnicity, Religion, and Class in New York City, 1845–80* (1990); Philip D. Taylor, *The Distant Magnet* (1971).

Southern Sectionalism and Nationalism
Charles H. Brown, *Agents for Manifest Destiny: The Lives and Times of the Filibusterers* (1979); Robert E. May, *The Southern Dream of a Caribbean Empire, 1854–1861* (1973); John McCardell, *The Idea of a Southern Nation* (1979); Mitchell Snay, *Gospel of Disunion: Religion and Separatism in the Antebellum South* (1993); Eric H. Walther, *The Fire-Eaters* (1992).

Sectionalism and National Politics
Jean H. Baker, *Affairs of Party: The Political Culture of Northern Democrats in the Mid-Nineteenth Century* (1983); Eugene H. Berwanger, *The Frontier against Slavery: Western Anti-Negro Prejudice and the Slavery Extension Controversy* (1967); Don E. Fehrenbacher, *Slavery, Law, and Politics: The Dred Scott Case in Historical Perspective* (1981); Eric Foner, *Free Soil, Free Labor, Free Men* (1970); Larry Gara, *The Presidency of Franklin Pierce* (1991); William E. Gienapp, *The Origins of the Republican Party, 1852–1856* (1987); Michael F. Holt, *The Political Crisis of the 1850s* (1978); Michael A. Morrison, *Slavery and the American West* (1997); Roy F. Nichols, *The Disruption of American Democracy* (1948); James A. Rawley, *Race and Politics: "Bleeding Kansas" and the Coming of the Civil War* (1969); Richard H. Sewell, *Ballots for Freedom: Antislavery Politics in the United States, 1837–1860* (1976); Kenneth M. Stampp, *America in 1857* (1990).

Secession and the Outbreak of War
William L. Barney, *The Secessionist Impulse: Alabama and Mississippi in 1860* (1974); Stephen A. Channing, *Crisis of Fear* (1974); Daniel W. Crofts, *Reluctant Confederates: Upper South Unionists in the Secession Crisis* (1989); Lacy K. Ford Jr., *Origins of Southern Radicalism: The South Carolina Upcountry, 1800–1860* (1988); David M. Potter, *Lincoln and His Party in the Secession Crisis* (1942); Kenneth M. Stampp, *And the War Came* (1950); J. Mills Thornton, *Politics and Power in a Slave Society: Alabama, 1800–1860* (1978).

The Causes of the Civil War
Gabor Boritt, ed., *Why the War Came* (1996); David M. Potter, *The South and the Sectional Conflict* (1969); Brian H. Reid, *The Origins of the American Civil War* (1996).

Biographies
Don E. Fehrenbacher, *Prelude to Greatness: Lincoln in the 1850s* (1962); Robert W. Johannsen, *Stephen A. Douglas* (1973); Philip Shriver Klein, *President James Buchanan* (1962); Roy F. Nichols, *Franklin Pierce: Young Hickory of the Granite Hills*, 2d ed. rev. (1958); Stephen B. Oates, *To Purge This Land with Blood: A Biography of John Brown* (1970).

CHAPTER 16: TOTAL WAR AND THE REPUBLIC

General Histories
Richard F. Bensel, *Yankee Leviathan: The Origins of Central State Authority in America, 1859–1877* (1990);

Richard E. Beringer et al., *The Elements of Confederate Defeat: Nationalism, War Aims, and Religion* (1989); Gabor S. Boritt, ed., *Why the Confederacy Lost* (1992); David H. Donald, ed., *Why the North Won the Civil War* (1961); Randall Jimerson, *The Private Civil War: Popular Thought during the Sectional Conflict* (1988); James M. McPherson, *Battle Cry of Freedom* (1988); Allan Nevins, *The War for the Union*, 4 vols. (1959–1971).

Military History
Bern Anderson, *By Sea and by River: The Naval History of the Civil War* (1962); Bruce Catton, *The Centennial History of the Civil War*, 3 vols. (1961–1965); Thomas L. Connelly, *Army of the Heartland: The Army of Tennessee, 1861–1862* (1967) and *Autumn of Glory: The Army of Tennessee, 1862–1865* (1971); Thomas L. Connelly and Archer Jones, *The Politics of Command: Factions and Ideas in Confederate Strategy* (1973); Mark Grimsley, *The Hard Hand of War* (1995); Herman Hattaway and Archer Jones, *How the North Won: A Military History of the Civil War* (1983); Charles Royster, *The Destructive War: William Tecumseh Sherman, Stonewall Jackson, and the Americans* (1991); Russell F. Weigley, *A Great Civil War* (2000); T. Harry Williams, *Lincoln and His Generals* (1952); Steven E. Woodworth, *Jefferson Davis and His Generals: The Failure of Confederate Command in the West* (1990) and *Davis and Lee at War* (1995).

Common Soldiers
Joseph A. Frank, *With Ballot and Bayonet: The Political Socialization of American Civil War Soldiers* (1998); Joseph T. Glatthaar, *Forged in Battle: The Civil War Alliance of Black Soldiers and White Officers* (1990) and *The March to the Sea and Beyond: Sherman's Troops in the Savannah and Carolinas Campaigns* (1985); Gerald F. Linderman, *Embattled Courage* (1987); James M. McPherson, *For Cause and Comrades* (1997); Reid Mitchell, *Civil War Soldiers: Their Expectations and Their Experiences* (1988) and *The Vacant Chair: The Northern Soldier Leaves Home* (1993); J. Tracy Power, *Lee's Miserables: Life in the Army of Northern Virginia from the Wilderness to Appomattox* (1998); Bell I. Wiley, *The Life of Johnny Reb* (1943) and *The Life of Billy Yank* (1952).

Union Politics
Leonard P. Curry, *Blueprint for Modern America: Non-Military Legislation of the First Civil War Congress* (1968); William B. Hesseltine, *Lincoln and the War Governors* (1948); Harold M. Hyman, *A More Perfect Union: The Impact of the Civil War and Reconstruction on the Constitution* (1973); Mark E. Neely, *The Fate of Liberty* (1991);

Philip S. Paludan, *The Presidency of Abraham Lincoln* (1994); James A. Rawley, *The Politics of Union: Northern Politics during the Civil War* (1974); Joel H. Silbey, *A Respectable Minority: The Democratic Party in the Civil War Era* (1977); Bruce Tap, *Over Lincoln's Shoulder: The Committee on the Conduct of the War* (1998).

Union Home Front
Ralph Andreano, ed., *The Economic Impact of the American Civil War* (1962); Iver Bernstein, *The New York City Draft Riots: Their Significance for American Society and Politics in the Age of the Civil War* (1990); George Fredrickson, *The Inner Civil War: Northern Intellectuals and the Crisis of the Union* (1965); J. Matthew Gallman, *The North Fights the Civil War* (1994); Paul W. Gates, *Agriculture and the Civil War* (1965); James W. Geary, *We Need Men: The Union Draft in the Civil War* (1991); Earl J. Hess, *Liberty, Virtue, and Progress: Northerners and Their War for the Union* (1988); Frank L. Klement, *The Copperheads in the Middle West* (1960); James Marten, *The Children's Civil War* (1998); James H. Moorhead, *American Apocalypse: Yankee Protestants and the Civil War, 1860–1869* (1978); Philip S. Paludan, *"A People's Contest": The Union and Civil War, 1861–1865* (1988).

Confederate Politics
Douglas C. Ball, *Financial Failure and Confederate Defeat* (1991); William C. Davis, *"A Government of Our Own": The Making of the Confederacy* (1994); Paul Escott, *After Secession: Jefferson Davis and the Failure of Confederate Nationalism* (1978); Mark E. Neely Jr., *Southern Rights: Political Prisoners and the Myth of Confederate Constitutionalism* (1999); Frank Owsley, *State Rights in the Confederacy* (1925); George C. Rable, *The Confederate Republic* (1994); Emory M. Thomas, *The Confederate Nation, 1861–1865* (1979); Wilfred B. Yearns, *The Confederate Congress* (1960).

Confederate Home Front
Stephen V. Ash, *When the Yankees Came* (1995); William Blair, *Virginia's Private War: Feeding Body and Soul in the Confederacy, 1861–1865* (1998); Mary A. DeCredico, *Patriotism for Profit: Georgia's Urban Entrepreneurs and the Confederate War Effort* (1990); Thomas G. Dyer, *Secret Yankees: The Union Circle in Confederate Atlanta* (1999); Drew Faust, *Mothers of Invention* (1996); Gary W. Gallagher, *The Confederate War* (1997); Mary Elizabeth Massey, *Refugee Life in the Confederacy* (1964); Charles W. Ramsdell, *Behind the Lines in the Southern Confederacy* (1944); Daniel Sutherland, *Seasons of War* (1995); Bell Wiley, *The Plain People of the Confederacy* (1943) and *The Road to Appomattox* (1956).

Women and the Civil War
Catherine Clinton and Nina Silber, eds., *Divided Houses: Gender and the Civil War* (1992); Elizabeth D. Leonard, *All the Daring of the Soldier: Women of the Civil War Armies* (1999) and *Yankee Women: Gender Battles in the Civil War* (1994); Mary Elizabeth Massey, *Bonnet Brigades: American Women and the Civil War* (1966); George C. Rable, *Civil Wars: Women and the Crisis of Southern Nationalism* (1989); Agatha Young, *Women and the Crisis: Women of the North in the Civil War* (1959).

Emancipation and the Black Experience
Dudley T. Cornish, *The Sable Arm: Negro Troops in the Union Army, 1861–1865* (1956); LaWanda Cox, *Lincoln and Black Freedom: A Study in Presidential Leadership* (1981); Barbara Jeanne Fields, *Slavery and Freedom on the Middle Ground: Maryland during the Nineteenth Century* (1985); John Hope Franklin, *The Emancipation Proclamation* (1963); Louis Gerteis, *From Contraband to Freedman: Federal Policy toward Southern Blacks, 1861–1865* (1973); Leon Litwack, *Been in the Storm So Long* (1979); James M. McPherson, *The Struggle for Equality: Abolitionists and the Negro in the Civil War and Reconstruction* (1964); Clarence L. Mohr, *On the Threshold of Freedom: Masters and Slaves in Civil War Georgia* (1986); James L. Roark, *Masters without Slaves* (1977); Willie Lee Rose, *Rehearsal for Reconstruction: The Port Royal Experiment* (1964); V. Jacque Voegli, *Free but Not Equal: The Midwest and the Negro during the Civil War* (1967).

Diplomacy
David P. Crook, *Diplomacy during the American Civil War* (1975); Norman Ferris, *The Trent Affair: A Diplomatic Crisis* (1977); Charles Hubbard, *The Burden of Confederate Diplomacy* (1998); Howard Jones, *Abraham Lincoln and a New Birth of Freedom: The Union and Slavery in the Diplomacy of the Civil War* (1999); Frank L. Owsley, *King Cotton Diplomacy*, rev. ed. (1959).

Biographies
David W. Blight, *Frederick Douglass' Civil War: Keeping Faith in Jubilee* (1989); Bruce Catton, *Grant Moves South* (1960) and *Grant Takes Command* (1969); William J. Cooper Jr., *Jefferson Davis, American* (2000); David Donald, *Lincoln* (1995); Mark E. Neely Jr., *The Last Best Hope of Earth: Abraham Lincoln and the Promise of America* (1993); Stephen B. Oates, *A Woman of Valor: Clara Barton and the Civil War* (1994); James G. Randall and Richard N. Current, *Lincoln the President*, 4 vols. (1945–1955); Emory M. Thomas, *Robert E. Lee* (1995).

CHAPTER 17: RECONSTRUCTING THE UNION

General Histories
Eric Foner, *Reconstruction* (1988); James McPherson, *Ordeal by Fire: The Civil War and Reconstruction* (1982); Kenneth M. Stampp, *The Era of Reconstruction, 1865–1877* (1965).

National Politics
Herman Belz, *Emancipation and Equal Rights: Politics and Constitutionalism in the Civil War Era* (1978); Michael Les Benedict, *A Compromise of Principle: Congressional Republicans and Reconstruction* (1974) and *The Impeachment and Trial of Andrew Johnson* (1973); W. R. Brock, *An American Crisis: Congress and Reconstruction, 1865–1867* (1963); John and LaWanda Cox, *Politics, Principles, and Prejudice, 1865–1866* (1963); William C. Harris, *With Charity for All: Lincoln and the Restoration of the Union* (1997); Eric McKitrick, *Andrew Johnson and Reconstruction* (1966); James M. McPherson, *The Struggle for Equality: Abolitionists and the Negro in the Civil War and Reconstruction* (1964); Hans L. Trefousse, *The Radical Republicans: Lincoln's Vanguard for Racial Justice* (1969); Xi Wang, *The Trial of Democracy: Black Suffrage and Northern Republicans, 1866–1910* (1997).

Reconstruction and the Constitution
William Gillette, *The Right to Vote: Politics and the Passage of the Fifteenth Amendment* (1965); Harold M. Hyman, *A More Perfect Union: The Impact of the Civil War and Reconstruction on the Constitution* (1973); William E. Nelson, *The Fourteenth Amendment: From Political Principle to Judicial Doctrine* (1988).

The Black Experience in Reconstruction
James D. Anderson, *The Education of Blacks in the South, 1860–1935* (1988); Herbert G. Gutman, *The Black Family in Slavery and Freedom, 1750–1925* (1976); Janet Sharp Hermann, *The Pursuit of a Dream* (1981); Thomas Holt, *Black over White* (1977); Leon Litwack, *Been in the Storm So Long* (1979); Howard Rabinowitz, ed., *Southern Black Leaders in Reconstruction* (1982); Vernon L. Wharton, *The Negro in Mississippi, 1865–1890* (1947); Joel Williamson, *After Slavery: The Negro in South Carolina during Reconstruction* (1966).

Reconstruction in the South
Dan T. Carter, *When the War Was Over* (1985); Richard N. Current, *Those Terrible Carpetbaggers: A Reinterpretation* (1988); William C. Harris, *Day of the Carpetbagger: Republican Reconstruction in Mississippi* (1979); George C. Rable, *But There Was No Peace: The Role of Violence in the Politics of Reconstruction* (1984); Allen Trelease, *White Terror: The Ku Klux Klan Conspiracy and Southern Reconstruction* (1967); Ted Tunnell, *Crucible of Reconstruction: War, Radicalism, and Race in Louisiana, 1862–1877* (1974); Sarah Woolfolk Wiggins, *The Scalawag in Alabama Politics, 1865–1881* (1977).

Social and Economic Reconstruction
Paul A. Cimbala, *Under the Guardianship of the Nation: The Freedmen's Bureau and the Reconstruction of Georgia, 1865–1870* (1997); Laura F. Edwards, *Gendered Strife and Confusion: The Political Culture of Reconstruction* (1997); Steven Hahn, *The Roots of Southern Populism: Yeoman Farmers and the Transformation of the Georgia Upcountry, 1850–1890* (1983); Jacqueline Jones, *Soldiers of Light and Love: Northern Teachers and Georgia Blacks, 1865–1873* (1980); Donald Nieman, *To Set the Law in Motion: The Freedmen's Bureau and the Legal Rights of Blacks, 1865–1868* (1979); Lawrence N. Powell, *New Masters: Northern Planters during the Civil War and Reconstruction* (1984); Roger L. Ransom and Richard Sutch, *One Kind of Freedom: The Economic Consequences of Emancipation* (1977); James L. Roark, *Masters without Slaves* (1977); Willie Lee Rose, *Rehearsal for Reconstruction* (1964); Julie Saville, *The Work of Reconstruction* (1995); Mark W. Summers, *Railroads, Reconstruction, and the Gospel of Prosperity* (1984).

The End of Reconstruction
William Gillette, *Retreat from Reconstruction, 1869–1879* (1980); Michael Perman, *The Road to Redemption* (1984); Keith Ian Polakoff, *The Politics of Inertia: The Election of 1876 and the End of Reconstruction* (1973); C. Vann Woodward, *Reunion and Reaction: The Compromise of 1877 and the End of Reconstruction* (1951).

Biographies
David Donald, *Charles Sumner and the Rights of Man* (1970); William S. McFeely, *Yankee Stepfather: General O. Howard and the Freedmen* (1968) and *Grant: A Biography* (1981); Brooks D. Simpson, *Let Us Have Peace: Ulysses S. Grant and the Politics of War and Reconstruction, 1861–1868* (1991); Hans L. Trefousse, *Andrew Johnson: A Biography* (1989).

CREDITS

PHOTO CREDITS

Chapter 1 © The British Museum, 7; Museo de America, Madrid, Spain, 18; Culver Pictures, Inc., 24; Corbis/Bettmann, 28.

Chapter 2 Ashmolean Museum, Oxford, UK, 34; Courtesy of the A. H. Robins Company. Photo by Don Eiler's Custom Photography, 37; Colonial Williamsburg Foundation, 49; Arizona State Museum, University of Arizona, 58.

Chapter 3 Centre Marguerite-Bourgeoys, Montreal, 65; Courtesy of the Archives Departmentales de la Gironde, Bordeaux, France, 65; Corbis/Bettmann, 76; George Heriot, *Calumet Dance, 1799.* Art Gallery of Windsor, 80; Corbis/Bettmann, 82.

Chapter 4 Abby Aldrich Rockefeller Folk Art Center, Williamsburg, VA, 101; © The British Museum, 108 and 110.

Chapter 5 Victoria and Albert Museum, London, 133; Library of Congress, 138; *"British Grenadier,"* Artist Unknown. The Historical Society of Pennsylvania. (HSP), [931.5], 141; Engraving by Wm. Sharp, after Romney. Prints Division. The New York Public Library. Astor, Lenox and Tilden Foundations, 144.

Chapter 6 Yale University Art Gallery, Trumbull Collection, 147; Yale University Art Gallery, Trumbull Collection, 150; Library of Congress, 152; By permission of the Houghton Library, Harvard University, 160; Virginia Historical Society, 168.

Chapter 7 Print Collection Miriam & Ira D. Wallach Division of Arts, Prints and Photographs. The New York Public Library. Astor, Lenox and Tilden Foundations, 174; Corbis/Bettmann, 177; The Metropolitan Museum of Art, Rogers Fun, 1942. (42.95.19), 184; James Peale, *"Mrs. John McAllister."* Reproduced by permission of Gloria Manney [159]. Photo © 2000 The Metropolitan Museum of Art, New York, 188; Bowdoin College Museum of Art, 193.

Chapter 8 Culver Pictures, Inc., 201; Courtesy John and Lillian Harney, 207; *John Trumbull, Alexander Hamilton.* Oil on canvas. 30¼ × 24 inches. Yale Univer-

sity Art Gallery, 209; © Collection of The New York Historical Society #2737, 216; Courtesy, Winterthur Museum, (detail), 221.

Chapter 9 © Collection of The New York Historical Society #6003, 226; Library of Congress. Illustration by A. Rider, 234; © The Field Museum, Neg# A93851c, 236.

Chapter 10 American Clock & Watch Museum, Bristol, CT, 253; Beinecke Rare Book and Manuscript Library, Yale University, 262; Missouri Historical Society (Neg. #CT SS831), 264; Corbis Bettmann, 268; Lowell Historical Society, 269.

Chapter 11 Nicolino Calyo, *"The Butcher,"* c. 1840–44. Museum of the City of New York, Gift of Mars. Francis P. Garvan in memory of Francis P. Garvan, 282; The St. Louis Art Museum, 287; © Collection of The New York Historical Society #6165, 290; Collection of Jay P. Altmayer, 295; The New York Public Library, 298; Museum of the City of New York, The J. Clarence Davies Collection, 303.

Chapter 12 Harriet Beecher Stowe Center, Hartford CT, 309; Stock Montage, 316; Print Collection Miriam & Ira D. Wallach Division of Arts, Prints and Photographs. The New York Public Library. Astor, Lenox and Tilden Foundations, 320; Corbis/Bettmann, 324; Courtesy of Rhoda Barney Jenkins, 327.

Chapter 13 Historic New Orleans Collection, 336; Historic New Orleans Collection, 346; Bequest of Henry Lee Shattuck, in memory of the late Ralph W. Gray. Courtesy, Museum of Fine Arts, Boston, 347; Chicago Historical Society ICHi08428, 354; Print Collection Miriam & Ira D. Wallach Division of Arts, Prints and Photographs. The New York Public Library. Astor, Lenox and Tilden Foundations, 356.

Chapter 14 Seaver Center for Western History Research, Los Angeles County Museum of Natural History, 368; © Collection of The New-York Historical Society #26280, 380; Library of Congress, 384.

Index

Note: Page numbers in *italics* indicate illustrations; page numbers followed by *m* indicate maps; page numbers followed by *n* indicate footnotes.